How to
SETTLE
YOUR LIVING
TRUST

P9-BYT-887

CAN I BE OF MORE ASSISTANCE?

As a result of the overwhelming response to my best-selling books, I receive thousands of requests for additional information on estate planning. To learn more about a Henry W. Abts III Living Trust and my company, *The Estate Plan*™, please call 1-800-350-1234, or, if you prefer, you may E-mail us at info@theestateplan.com or visit our web site at www.theestateplan.com. I have developed a free estate planning Internet newsletter, *The Living Trust E-Times*, to keep you abreast of significant changes and methods to preserve your estate. If you would like to receive this newsletter, please contact us, as indicated above.

BECOME A CERTIFIED ESTATE PLANNING PROFESSIONAL (CEPP)

I have spent over a quarter of a century developing the finest wealth preservation programs for my clients. At the same time, I have developed a nationwide network of independent Certified Estate Planning Professionals to assist those in need of quality estate planning. If you would be interested in joining me in this work, please call us at 1-800-292-0223. I offer to teach you my estate planning techniques, share my programs, and include you in our network.

ABOUT THE AUTHOR

Henry W. Abts III has spent more than a quarter of a century as a financial advisor and estate planning specialist to businesses, corporations, and individuals. He recently retired as a licensed Registered Investment Advisor from H. W. Abts & Associates, a company he founded and chaired. He is founder and chairman of *The Estate Plan*™, the exclusive producers of the Henry W. Abts III Living Trust, and the oldest, most comprehensive, and trusted estate planning firm of its kind. This company is the result of his extensive experience and the input of a nationwide network of independent advisors and attorneys.

Mr. Abts is a nationally recognized authority on the Living Trust and has given more than three thousand seminars on wealth preservation. He has dedicated the better part of his life to educating people about one of the most crucial and beneficial concepts to family wealth planning—the Living Trust. *The Living Trust*, his first book, now in its third edition, is the national best-selling book on this subject and is considered to be the industry "bible."

Mr. Abts, a tireless advocate for consumers' interests, founded the Abts Institute for Estate Preservation, a nonprofit organization dedicated to raising consumer awareness of the need for good estate planning. This institute provides professional training in estate preservation techniques. Graduates are awarded the title of Certified Estate Planning Professional (CEPP).

Mr. Abts is a charter member of the Certified Estate Planners Association (CEPA) and is recognized as a member of *Who's Who in Executives and Business*.

Mr. Abts is a graduate of the University of Southern California and the Stanford Graduate School of Business. He and his wife, Bonnie Jean, are the parents of four grown children and six grandchildren.

NEW SOFTWARE—TO SIMPLIFY THE ESTATE SETTLEMENT PROCESS

Settling your Living Trust may seem to be complex, but it is really quite simple. Having read this book, you should be able to settle an estate in a Living Trust with little difficulty. However, I'm going to make the settlement process even simpler. I am in the process of developing a software program that will present much of the material in this book (such as check-lists, ledger forms, and IRS forms) in a format that you can actually answer just a simple "yes" or "no." The program will then produce the appropriate forms.

If you are interested in learning more about this software program and how it will easily help you to settle your estate, simply return the appropriate Reply Card (found in the middle of the book), visit our web site at www.theestateplan.com, call us at 1-800-350-1234, or send me an E-mail at info@theestateplan.com.

HOW TO
SETTLE
YOUR LIVING
TRUST

HOW YOU CAN SETTLE A LIVING TRUST SWIFTLY, EASILY, AND SAFELY

HENRY W. ABTS III

CB
CONTEMPORARY BOOKS

MATAWAN-ABERDEEN PUBLIC LIBRARY
165 MAIN STREET
MATAWAN, NJ 07747

Quality
3/00
21.96
c.1

Library of Congress Cataloging-in-Publication Data

Abts, Henry W.
    How to settle your living trust : how you can settle your living trust swiftly,
easily, and safely / Henry W. Abts III.
        p.   cm.
    Includes index.
    ISBN 0-8092-2844-0
    1. Living trusts—United States—Popular works.   I. Title.
KF734.Z9A25   1999
346.7305 9—dc21   98-39669
                                                              CIP

Many examples are used throughout the book to illustrate various points in explaining how to settle a Living Trust. All of the examples in the book are actual situations encountered by my clients. However, even though real-life situations are used, the names in the examples are fictitious to preserve the privacy of the individuals involved. In particular, to provide some continuity in the various sample documents used throughout the text, I have created two fictitious characters, John Howard Jones and Mary R. Jones, husband and wife. John and Mary created their Living Trust in 1979, known as "The Jones Family Trust."

The material contained in *How to Settle Your Living Trust* is intended to present a comprehensive overview of what you must do to settle an estate in a Living Trust. This book is not intended to be a substitute for qualified estate-planning specialists, competent accounting professionals, or knowledgeable legal counsel; rather, it is designed to help the reader work with qualified professionals to properly settle a Living Trust. *How to Settle Your Living Trust* is sold with the understanding that the publisher is not engaged in rendering legal, accounting, estate-planning, or other professional services.

The information supplied has been reviewed and approved by estate planners. However, as no published work can be totally current, all information and statements should be checked against the most recent developments by a qualified estate-planning specialist.

While every attempt has been made to provide accurate information, neither the author nor the publisher can be held accountable for any error or omission.

Roth Legacy Trust℠ is a licensed service mark of The Estate Plan.
Unless indicated otherwise, all Figures and Tables © 1998 by The Estate Plan

Cover design by Scott Rattray

Published by Contemporary Books
A division of NTC/Contemporary Publishing Group, Inc.
4255 West Touhy Avenue, Lincolnwood (Chicago), Illinois 60646-1975 U.S.A.
Copyright © 1999 by Henry W. Abts III
All rights reserved. No part of this book may be reproduced, stored in a retrieval
system, or transmitted in any form or by any means, electronic, mechanical,
photocopying, recording, or otherwise, without the prior permission of
NTC/Contemporary Publishing Group, Inc.
Printed in the United States of America
International Standard Book Number: 0-8092-2844-0

99 00 01 02 03 04 CU 19 18 17 16 15 14 13 12 11 10 9 8 7 6 5 4 3 2 1

To my bride of thirty-four years who has provided unrelenting love, support, and patience. To my son Chris, who has managed our business so well, and in doing so has permitted me the freedom to write. To my son Skip, who enhanced our company's Trust production process with his special computer program. And to our other children, Laurel Ashley Abts and Jeremy Stephen Abts, who have given me the incentive to strive to do my very best in every facet of life. I must also add that life can't get much better when we count our six (so far) lovely grandchildren.

In Memory of Martha Bunce Desch, December 29, 1940–September 2, 1998

Contents

Appendixes

Preface

I have awakened the sleeping giant, and now it must be tamed.

My first book, *The Living Trust*, was published in 1989 and was an instant success throughout the United States. This book was the first that described, in layperson's terms that almost anyone could understand, the many advantages of a *good* Living Trust, as well as the pitfalls that could be avoided by having a Living Trust instead of a Will. The book quickly became a bestseller and the de facto standard for what should be contained in a good Living Trust. *The Living Trust* is now in its third edition, with updated versions published in 1993 and 1997 to keep abreast of changes in tax law.

From the many letters, telephone calls, and personal comments that I have received from all over the country, I know that I have been able to help a great number of people—which was my original intent. However, I now realize that I have unfortunately, and inadvertently, left many people in the lurch—they have Living Trusts, but they really don't know what to do when a spouse or other loved one dies and how their Trusts should be used to drastically simplify the process of settling their estates.

The primary purpose of this book, *How to Settle Your Living Trust*, is to fill the void and to guide you, in simple step-by-step fashion, in the matters required to settle your estate. Don't be alarmed! Having a good Living Trust, instead of a Will, greatly simplifies the settling of an estate, keeps your financial matters private, and costs almost nothing—compared to the agony, lengthy delays, and high cost of going through the probate process.

PROLOGUE

Let me briefly digress and relate to you the events that led me, through frustration and a sense of duty, to establish a new company, The Estate Plan, to make a good Living Trust available to the general public throughout the United States, and to write *The Living Trust*.

The Final Straw

The straw that broke the camel's back was an experience I had in 1978, when, within a three-month period, three different corporate presidents independently agreed with me that they should have Living Trusts but felt obligated to consult with their corporate attorneys, with whom they had worked closely for some ten to twenty years, to draw up their Living Trusts. Six months passed, and then, within a period of weeks, each corporate president asked me to review his new Living Trust. Each Trust had been drawn by a separate attorney, each unknown to the other. In 1978, the Trusts had cost from $2,500 to $3,500.

I naively agreed and reviewed the three Trusts. I was stunned when I realized that none of the Trusts was worth the paper on which it was written. I suddenly had a serious dilemma on my hands. How could I tell these men that they had wasted substantial dollars on their Trusts—at my recommendation? I didn't care so much about the current impact of the Trusts, but I was deeply concerned about the impact on these families when one of the spouses died and part of the Trust became irrevocable.

To confirm my conclusion, I took the Trusts to one of the leading Trust attorneys and asked for his opinion. This attorney also concluded that the documents were "almost worthless." He wrote to each of my clients and stated his findings, but he felt a professional responsibility to put things right, and he went even further. He said there was nothing he could do to fix their existing documents, so he offered to provide them with his own Living Trust (which at that time was selling for $450) for only $225—half the cost. Each of my clients was embarrassed and ended up doing nothing. To my knowledge, they have done nothing to this day.

I realized that I had unintentionally done these gentlemen a great disservice. I had assumed that any attorney who claimed to be capable of drawing a Living Trust was capable of doing so. Instead, these attorneys, who were undoubtedly good at their corporate work, charged their clients for their learning experience and yet wrote documents of minimal value to their clients.

The Company
Following this sad experience and many similar ones, I approached a very knowledgeable

attorney in the field of Living Trusts and asked him to help me create a company to produce Living Trust documents for my investment clients. I decided that the adage "If you want it done right, do it yourself" was apropos, and my conscience said, "Do it now!"

In 1982, I formed a company called The Estate Plan, solely to produce Living Trusts for my investment clients. As we continued to create, and then eventually settle, many Trusts, we learned valuable lessons that we incorporated in all of our future documents. This process of continued improvement based on actual experience and client feedback has never stopped. Our Living Trust documents continue to evolve—ensuring that a good Living Trust is available to everyone.

Seeds of the First Book
The book *The Living Trust* did not just materialize overnight. Instead, the seeds germinated for many years and were influenced by personal experiences and a whole host of different situations that happened to my clients.

After my father's death in 1966, I went through an agonizing and frustrating probate of his estate. I knew that there just had to be a better way, and shortly thereafter, I discovered the Living Trust and its many advantages. At that time, I was a financial advisor, and once I became fully aware of the dangers of probate, I began to advise my clients that the best way to preserve their estates and to save their family unnecessary heartache was to get a Living Trust.

Several years later, I was stunned to discover that I had done my clients a great disservice by casting them to the mercy of the legal fraternity. I eventually learned that many of my clients were not benefiting from the many advantages of a good Living Trust for several different reasons:

- They were talked out of a Living Trust and into a Will, especially by probate attorneys.
- They purchased Living Trusts that were not worth the paper on which they were written.
- They didn't understand their Living Trusts and, therefore, did not sign them.
- They did sign their Living Trusts but didn't

understand the necessity to fund their Trusts by placing their assets inside the Trusts.

As the years passed, many of my clients and eventually a book publishing agent asked me to write a book about the Living Trust in layperson's terms. They felt I had a way of taking complex concepts and explaining them simply and understandably. After four years of writing and a year of editing, *The Living Trust* was first published in June 1989. The book immediately became a nationwide success.

My company was soon inundated with requests for our Living Trust documents from almost every state in the country. Our challenge over the next several years was to find and train competent advisors and attorneys throughout the United States and to work out a legal and ethical method to serve our potential clients.

The Seminars

After *The Living Trust* was published, I began a nationwide seminar tour to further spread the good word that probate was unnecessary. These seminars were simply an extension of the seminars that I had been giving in southern California since 1978. However, as I traveled throughout the nation, I was continually confronted by seminar attendees who said, "Henry, I read your book and went to an attorney for my Living Trust, but my Trust turned out to be nothing like what you have talked about here today." The more frequently I gave seminars, the more often I heard these same words.

When I first wrote *The Living Trust*, I sincerely felt that I had done something good by educating hundreds of thousands of people about Living Trusts. However, during my nationwide seminar tour, I began to realize, sadly and with some alarm, that I was somehow letting my readers down. My elation quickly turned to concern.

The Aftermath

As time went on, I began to hear terrible tales of wasted time, frustration, and the cost of settling an estate in a Living Trust. Initially, it seemed that the Will and Probate attorneys were doing everything possible to turn people away from the Living Trust; however, eventually many of these attorneys decided to stop their fight and simply offer the Living Trust themselves. Unfortunately, the content of *good* Living Trusts is not taught in law school, so the attorneys were, to a great degree, on their own and simply creating documents as best they could.

Most of the documents were terribly inadequate, which meant that, upon the death of one or both trustors, the successor trustees of their Living Trust would have to appeal to the courts to rectify the areas of inadequacy in the Trust. However, such situations didn't bother these attorneys, because they would be the ones taking the Trust to court—and earning hefty fees in the process. If a person's Living Trust wasn't properly funded, that was all right, too, because the attorneys would be the ones taking the client through probate. If everything in the estate happened to be in order, so much the better, because there was less work for the attorneys to do, but their fees always seemed to parallel what a probate fee would have been. Therefore, many Will and Probate attorneys decided not to fight the Living Trust, but to join our march—with the objective that they would inevitably get their fees in the end, when one or both parties died.

My Personal Experience

Then came my own sad experience, when my mother died several years ago. Unfortunately, she and I had parted ways following my father's death in 1966. For years, I had urged her to create a Living Trust, and, following her wishes, I created three separate Living Trusts over a number of years, none of which she adopted. Instead, two years before she died, she asked her cousin to refer her to a La Jolla attorney, who created her Living Trust and named her cousin as trustee. Following her death, our chief legal counsel offered the attorney who drew the Trust his services to help settle the estate. This offer seemed appropriate, since our four children were partial beneficiaries. Our services were flatly turned down, with the response that "he [the attorney] was an expert in Living Trusts."

I then watched in agony as the attorney treated the estate settlement in the same manner as he would probate a Will. Most of his legal actions were unnecessary, and many were ill advised—as I watched his legal fees mount higher and higher. I decided then and there that this new book, *How to Settle Your Living Trust*, must be written to inform the public, in simple and understandable terms, how to settle an estate in a Living Trust, so that the surviving spouse and/or successor trustees and beneficiaries need not go through the cost and frustrations my children had experienced. In somewhat of a strange way, I am almost grateful to the La Jolla attorney who is an "expert in Living Trusts" for motivating me to finally write this much-needed book.

TAXPAYER RELIEF ACT OF 1997

As this book was being written, President Clinton signed into law the Taxpayer Relief Act of 1997. Although President Clinton and congressional leaders claim to have given the taxpayers great relief, the provisions (other than changes in the capital gains tax rate) offer very little relief—and that relief is spread out over many years to come. In reality, the Taxpayer Relief Act is almost a hoax—perpetrated on the hardworking American taxpayers by our "leaders" in Washington.

The Taxpayer Relief Act of 1997 will *eventually* change some of the taxation limits that affect the settling of an estate:

- The amount of the individual federal estate tax exemption is slowly increasing from $625,000 in 1998 to $1 million some ten years down the road.
- The one-time $125,000 exclusion for selling your home is eliminated. It is replaced with an enhanced $250,000 homeowner's exemption when selling your home, which is no longer limited to once in a lifetime.
- The law provides a much-needed Small Business and Farm Exclusion (which is of minimal benefit to many—and almost disappears in just a few short years).
- The law lowers the capital gains tax rate when you sell real estate (other than your primary residence) and when you sell stocks

and mutual funds that have been held for more than eighteen months. (Prior to publication of this book, the time period was reduced by the Republican-led Congress to twelve months.)

The Taxpayer Relief Act of 1997 contains many new and, sometimes, very confusing and complex tax issues. Each of the issues just listed has many restrictions, limitations, and exclusions—much too detailed for discussion in this book. However, Appendix A contains some of my thoughts on this new tax bill for those of you who might be interested. In a nutshell, much of this new tax law is little more than smoke and mirrors. However, some features will affect people who are settling an estate, so Appendix A also includes a brief discussion of the law's salient points.

During the writing of this book, Congress has continued to change some of the provisions of the Taxpayer Relief Act of 1997, and the IRS repeatedly issues new and revised interpretations of the tax implications relating to this legislation. As these changes have occurred, I have repeatedly changed the content of this book, trying to keep current with the latest interpretation. Ultimately, however, the publishing process must go on, and we reach a cutoff point beyond which last-minute changes cannot be included. This book includes IRS tax interpretations as of September 1, 1998. Subsequent updates to this book in later years will include revisions that reflect the then-current congressional changes and ever-present IRS interpretations.

BRIEF OVERVIEW

Although this book focuses on how to settle your Living Trust, it also provides you with a review of the horrors and agony of probate, describes the onerous federal estate tax on large estates, and explains why everyone needs a *good* Living Trust.

This book is organized into two sections:

- Part I (Chapters 1–20) provides you with all of the information needed to settle an average estate. (Everyone should read Part I.)
- Part II (Chapters 21–24) contains informa-

tion that pertains only to those fortunate people who have amassed substantial estates and who, therefore, can benefit from specialized estate-preservation vehicles.

Surviving family members themselves can easily settle the estates of most average Americans (about 90 percent of the population) by reading Part I and following its advice.

The first few chapters acquaint you with the federal government's consumptive estate tax, the danger estate taxes pose to your estate, the consequences you face in trying to protect your estate assets from a catastrophic illness, the adverse consequences of not having a Living Trust, and the ancillary documents that should accompany a good Living Trust. Later chapters introduce you to the rules of the Living Trust game, as well as how to play the game to minimize unnecessary estate taxation. A brief review is then provided to remind you about what must be done once you have created a Living Trust. Most of the chapters are devoted to explaining what to do when the first spouse dies and when the second spouse dies. The chapters explain the differences between separate property states and community property states. Subsequent chapters provide you with a reminder on how to manage a Trust, especially after the death of the first spouse.

Since Individual Retirement Accounts (IRAs) are becoming a larger part of people's estates, two chapters are devoted exclusively to IRAs (including the new Roth IRA). These chapters address the severe tax consequences you incur if you die without having used up (i.e., spent) *all* of your traditional IRA.

Several chapters are devoted to providing you with information about the issues and procedures of settling Married A-B Trusts and Married A-B-C Trusts in separate property states and community property states. (Yes, there are some significant differences.)

If you are among the fortunate few who have amassed a sizable estate, I recommend that you seek professional assistance in minimizing the tax bite of Uncle Sam and, thus, be better able to pass on as much of your estate as possible to your heirs. By reading the chapters in Part II, you will be better able to understand some of the more complex estate settlement options that are available to you. Working with competent financial and legal professionals, the surviving family members should be able to settle even complex estates without undue delays or unnecessary expenses.

UNFULFILLED NEED

Since the publication of my first book, *The Living Trust*, many people across the United States have created Living Trusts to preserve their estates for their heirs, but few people really know how to settle an estate when a loved one dies. Unfortunately, many Will and Probate attorneys are now taking unfair advantage of far too many people by settling Living Trusts in the same way as they would probate estates—and charging nearly the same (*and totally unnecessary*) fees. This book, *How to Settle Your Living Trust*, is intended to solve that problem and to show you that most estates can be easily settled with complete privacy and with little or no delay.

As you read through this book, I hope you will come to understand the many benefits of having a good Living Trust, as well as how easily most estates can be settled without going through the agony of probate, incurring unnecessary legal fees, and enduring long delays associated with the probate process.

The American public no longer need be the unwilling (and often unknowing) victims of unscrupulous attorneys when the inevitable time comes to settle the estate of a loved one. By understanding the basic principles presented in this book, you will at least be familiar with the concepts of settling an estate in a Living Trust and, thus, better able to chart your own course.

As you will see as you read through this book, settling an estate in a good Living Trust can be fast, easy, private, and done at almost no cost to the surviving family members themselves!

Acknowledgments

This book was made possible by the help of many. First and foremost was the editing by Michael and Martha Desch. Michael and Martha became clients with the creation of their Living Trust in 1983. As the years passed, I had the opportunity to read many of Martha's articles. I enjoyed what I read, so in 1988 I asked Martha to edit my first book, *The Living Trust*, published in June 1989. At the time, I did not realize that I was getting her husband, Michael, as well. As a team, they worked for a year editing *The Living Trust* and did an outstanding job. They also edited the subsequent revisions to *The Living Trust*. It was only natural that I would again turn to their combined editing expertise to edit this book. They were responsible for the ultimate organization and very extensive editorial presentation. Martha's contribution can be seen in both style and content. She made this book come alive. She worked to the end and then passed the baton to Michael for final completion. Martha died of breast cancer on September 2, 1998.

John F. Mulligan, Esq., LLM, of Avansino, Melarkey, Knobel, McMullen & Mulligan provided his expertise in the areas of estate planning and taxation. Robert S. Keebler, CPA, MST, of Schumaker, Romensko & Associates, S.C., graciously shared his IRA expertise to enable me to write the chapters on the traditional IRA and the Roth IRA. Natalie B. Choate, Esq., of Bingham, Dana, LLP, also contributed her expertise in IRAs. She is the author of *Life and Death Planning for Retirement Benefits*. She has also permitted us to use her IRA Beneficiary forms. John F. McKenna, CPA, of Freeman Williams, LLP, shared the most current input on changing tax rules and provided the various illustrations of tax forms. I also wish to credit Nanda Kunde for coordinating the numerous illustrations and for transcribing my original dictation.

Five skilled attorneys reviewed the final manuscript and made excellent suggestions: Charles Matthews, Byron Countryman, John Mulligan, Jeff Blankstein, and Ben Jablow. The wonderful reality of a project like this book is that you can't work in a fish bowl. I want to personally thank the sixty-five Estate Plan advisors who attended my special institute on

"How to Settle Your Living Trust." As experts in their own related fields, they offered many constructive suggestions before the final manuscript was completed. As you can see, many generous individuals have had a hand in producing this book, and my deep gratitude goes to all of them.

My sincere thanks to Eugene Carragee, MD, at Stanford University Hospital, who used his surgical skills to return me to full health and enable me to write this book.

Introduction

Henry W. Abts III brought the Living Trust to the attention of the American public with his first book, *The Living Trust*, which is considered the industry standard with more than 500,000 copies sold. Now, in clear, direct language stripped of legal jargon and with carefully constructed illustrations, estate planning specialist Henry W. Abts III takes you through the important steps of how to settle your Living Trust. This is a how-to book written for every surviving spouse, child, or friend, as well as attorneys and accountants who may be called upon to settle Living Trusts. The author's intent is to guide the individual through a process that is all too arcane and, hopefully, to also establish a standard reference for those professionals engaged in settling Living Trusts. Few people truly understand that the settlement process for a Living Trust can be simple and can usually be done by the surviving family members themselves, without requiring the services of expensive attorneys and accountants.

This book is divided into two basic sections: settlement steps for everyone to follow (applicable to most average-sized estates) and advanced estate settlement options (applicable to highly valued estates). The book devotes separate chapters to the estate settlement differences between separate property states and community property states. This book shows you how to easily settle your Living Trust— without lawyers, courts, or the probate system. If you choose to engage a professional to help settle your estate, this book becomes a reference and a guide to direct their efforts in the proper direction. If you are a client of The Estate Plan, your advisor will take you through the estate settlement steps appropriate for your estate at a very nominal fee.

This book discusses the most important current tax changes affecting your estate, including the most recent changes to the traditional IRA and the new Roth IRA:

- Federal estate tax exemption
- Small business and farm exclusion
- Capital gains
- Traditional IRA
- Roth IRA

This book covers important estate settlement steps in detail:

- Important steps to take following the death of a loved one
- When and how to value assets (and the significant differences between separate property states and community property states)
- When and how to allocate assets to the A, B, and/or C sub-trusts
- How to title assets following the death of a loved one (and how to avoid retitling assets)
- When to use the survivor's social security number and when to use the Trust identification number
- How to use the Ledger Method, with appropriate worksheets specifically designed for separate property states and community property states

This book also lays out the "Rules of the Game" to preserve the decedent's federal estate tax exemption:

- Establish a separate bank account (for decedent's affairs)
- When to use Form SS-4 to request a Trust Identification Number
- Use the Ledger Method instead of changing title to assets
- Use worksheets for valuation and allocation to Ledger Sheets
- Proper use of Form 1041 and Schedule K-1
- Importance of timely filing of Form 706, Schedule R, to make the QTIP election and the GST exemption

This book discusses important areas of estate settlement in a Living Trust:

- Importance of the Remainder Beneficiary (and what to do as a trustee)

- Why the surviving spouse does not want to resign as surviving trustee
- Notice to Creditors (how to take advantage of creditor protection)
- When and how to distribute assets
- What to do with a business interest
- Avoid the administrative nightmare of dual Trusts (separate Trusts for husband and wife)
- What to do if you are ill, tired, or incompetent (make certain that you have the appropriate ancillary "Living Documents")
- Importance of the Memorandum

Since IRAs and/or 401(k) plans are now a significant part of most people's estates, this book devotes separate chapters to the traditional IRA and the Roth IRA. These chapters also address the most current IRA tax changes that can drastically impact the value of your estate. These chapters also discuss:

- The mysterious IRAs and the importance of the Roth IRA
- Advantages of the Roth IRA (how it uses the magic of tax-free compound growth to benefit your children and grandchildren)
- The problem with revocable Living Trusts as a beneficiary of an IRA (and the solution)

This book devotes a separate section to advanced settlement options for estates of substantial value, including special estate preservation techniques such as:

- General Power of Appointment
- Disclaiming assets
- IRA-QTIP Trust
- Roth Legacy Trust℠

Part I

What You Need to Know
to Settle Your Living Trust

More than 90 percent of all Living Trusts can be settled swiftly, easily, and at minimal cost by surviving family members (without the unnecessary expense of attorneys and accountants). To find out how, read Chapters 1 through 20 of Part I. Then use the techniques that are appropriate for your particular estate.

1

The Danger to Our Economy

The present federal estate tax presents an inherent danger to our small businesses and farms, making it a pernicious tax that can ultimately destroy our economy. The concept of "redistributing the wealth" is no longer valid. The United States has shifted from an industrial-oriented economy to a service-oriented economy. Instead of a number of large industrial giants, the economy is now based on hundreds of thousands of small businesses.

THE DANGER TO SMALL BUSINESSES

Let me relate to you a not-uncommon disaster that is faced by surviving spouses, sons, and daughters all over the United States when a business owner dies—and the Internal Revenue Service (IRS) greedily steps in to claim "its due amount."

Akren Industrial Pressure Valve Company had been a staid business in its community for twenty years. Originally a supplier of air-pressure valves, the company expanded into all areas of pressure fittings and associated products.

Thomas Russell joined Akren, his father's business, in 1988. During the next five years, the company enjoyed a substantial increase in sales as a result of introducing computers and a software program designed to efficiently manage its inventory. During that same period, Akren's employees grew in number from twenty-five to seventy-five.

In recent years several salespersons were equipped with laptop computers, which gave them the ability to identify their company's inventory and to place orders directly from their client's place of business, while also reducing delivery time by up to five days—a substantial service to the customer.

Thomas took over management of the company when his father started battling prostate cancer. (His mother, who had also been active in the business, had died of a heart attack three years earlier.) The future of the company looked extremely promising until Thomas's father died a year later.

Akren Contributes to the Community. Thomas's father had not really been active in his community, since he spent most of his time involved in his business, but he took great pride in the character and growth of his employees. Whenever possible, he hired disabled individuals and unskilled single mothers. Once the new employees had completed training in their particular areas of responsibility, they were paid well above the minimum wage scale.

Some people considered Mr. Russell wealthy, since he owned a business worth $3 million. However, Mr. Russell strongly disagreed. He and his wife took home a combined annual salary of only $65,000. They lived modestly, and Mr. Russell spent what little free time he had worrying about his competition and, particularly, how to protect his business from the inroads of foreign interests who were trying to invade the market. In addition, Mr. Russell was always concerned about meeting next month's payroll.

The Beginning of the End. Upon his father's death, Thomas was suddenly confronted with a seemingly insurmountable obstacle to the continued future of the company. The company had annual revenues of $3 million and, therefore, was valued by the IRS at $3 million. (The IRS has consistently stated that it values a small business at one year's annual revenue.) The $3 million evaluation for Akren yielded an estate tax rate of 50 percent, or $1.5 million. Thomas's accountant and attorney therefore advised him that he faced a federal estate tax bill of $1.5 million.

However, Akren made a net profit of only $200,000 annually, which was reinvested in the business in the form of new equipment and computer software. This reinvestment was essential to advance technologically in order to keep ahead of or at least abreast of the competition—a vitally important step, since foreign interests were anxiously seeking to take over Akren's segment of the market.

Uncle Sam Gets His Due. The accountant and attorney recommended that the company elect to pay the $1.5 million federal estate taxes due over a ten-year period. When the principal and interest were computed, the tax bill was $267,000 a year for the next ten years! Thomas immediately recognized that such a heavy tax burden would force him to eliminate the $200,000 annual investment in new technology. The heavy tax bite also necessitated the dismissal of three employees—a most unfortunate and sad event, since all of the employees were dedicated and hardworking, and each employee contributed his or her fair share to a very efficient organization.

After agonizing over his dilemma, Thomas finally bit the bullet and committed to annual IRS payments of $267,000, the elimination of investment in new technology, and the termination of three good employees. Then, almost immediately, Thomas was confronted with another unexpected blow to the financial well-being of his company. Since federal estate taxes were owed and outstanding, the IRS placed a lien on the business for the entire balance of the taxes due. The IRS lien took first priority over any loans, so the local bank withdrew its line of credit that the company had used for years to meet its payroll in slow periods. As a result, Thomas had to terminate even more employees.

The Competitive Dilemma. Thomas went through the next few years feeling as if he were slowly being strangled to death, with no way out of his ever-worsening dilemma. Competition, particularly foreign interests, got a foothold in his market. Having no money to invest in the newest technology, Akren began to lose market share, and sales declined. Due to the declining sales, Akren again had to reduce the number of employees. Thomas continued his desperate struggle to keep his company alive and prosperous, but he no longer had the bank to rely on for help to meet his payroll during slow times. Thomas was forced to again lay off more employees—and so the downward spiral continued.

After three years of blood, sweat, tears, and much heartache, Thomas sadly realized that he couldn't maintain the business and pay the federal estate taxes that it still owed. He acknowledged defeat, declared bankruptcy, and turned the business over to the IRS—which immediately closed the business and eventually sold it for pennies on the dollar to satisfy some of the federal estate taxes owed.

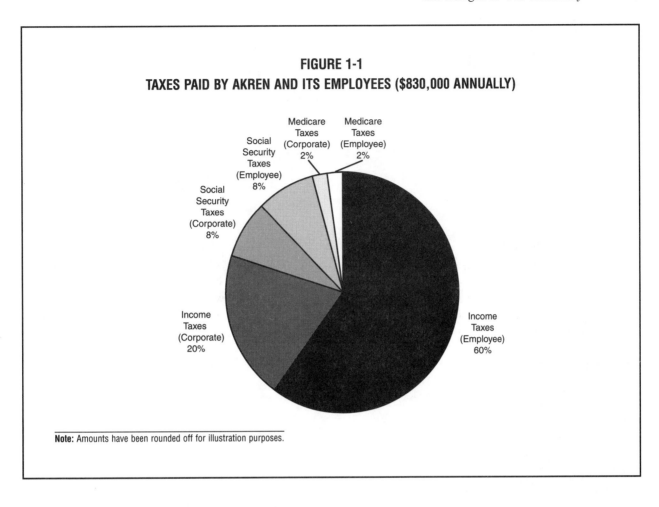

FIGURE 1-1
TAXES PAID BY AKREN AND ITS EMPLOYEES ($830,000 ANNUALLY)

Medicare Taxes (Employee) 2%

Medicare Taxes (Corporate) 2%

Social Security Taxes (Employee) 8%

Social Security Taxes (Corporate) 8%

Income Taxes (Corporate) 20%

Income Taxes (Employee) 60%

Note: Amounts have been rounded off for illustration purposes.

What a shame that the outcome ended so sadly—and for many more people than just the surviving heirs. Examples such as this one happen all the time and in ever-increasing numbers—ultimately destroying the American dream and the futures of thousands of people.

"Redistribution" of Wealth

Some people would call the just-described example a "redistribution of wealth"—taking from the rich (a business valued at $3 million) and giving it to low-income Americans through government benefits. In reality, however, the question is, Did the wealth really get redistributed? And, of course, the answer is a resounding No!

Let's take a closer look at both the direct and indirect contributions that Akren was making to the economy. At the national level, Akren was responsible for contributing $830,000 annually to the federal government in various forms of taxes, as shown in Figure 1-1 (above).

If the company had remained in business for ten years (and remained static, neither growing nor shrinking), it would have contributed ten times the $830,000 paid in yearly taxes—more than $8 million!

Everyone Loses

Another way to view the demise of Akren is in terms of the often-forgotten contribution that it made to the local community and surrounding areas. Akren paid out $3 million annually. Of that amount, almost $250,000 went to the federal government in the form of direct payments from the company (see Table 1-1 on page 6). (An additional amount of approximately $580,000 was paid by the employees in the form of income taxes, social security taxes, and Medicare taxes.) The balance of more than $2.7 million flowed into the community in various forms:

TABLE 1-1
FEDERAL TAXES PAID BY AKREN AND ITS EMPLOYEES

Federal Taxes Paid by Akren Directly

Social security taxes	$ 66,000
Medicare taxes	$ 17,000
Income taxes	$ 166,000
Total	$ 249,000

Federal Taxes Paid by Akren Employees

Social security taxes	$ 66,000
Medicare taxes	$ 17,000
Income taxes	$ 497,000
Total	$ 580,000

Note: Amounts are rounded off for illustration purposes.

- Wages and salaries—$2 million
- Operating expenses—$500,000 for rent, utilities, supplies, equipment, and services
- Reinvestment in the business—$250,000 for technological equipment and supplies

The biggest losers of all, and the most tragic, were the seventy-five hardworking employees, some disabled and many of them single mothers, now without work. Consequently, when Akren ceased to be a thriving business, the entire community lost, not just the owners or the former employees—and the IRS lost far more in total dollars received than if the business had continued to prosper.

The end result is appalling. Akren is no longer in business as a thriving, vibrant contributor to the community, more than seventy-five people are without a means of gainful support, and the product void is now filled by

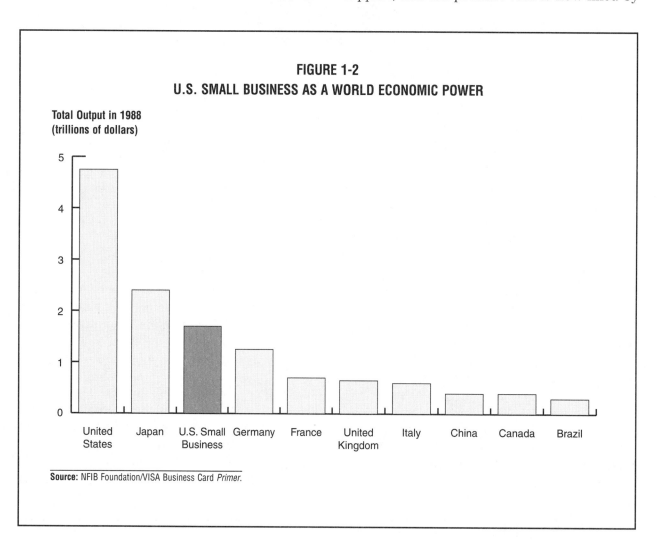

FIGURE 1-2
U.S. SMALL BUSINESS AS A WORLD ECONOMIC POWER

Total Output in 1988 (trillions of dollars)

Source: NFIB Foundation/VISA Business Card *Primer*.

foreign interests—while the IRS took in only part of the tax money it could have.

The Real Danger to the Economy

The real danger to the economy is that this scenario is being repeated time and again. Historically, the United States has been an industrial nation. In the past three decades, however, our nation has been rapidly moving toward a service economy comprising thousands of small businesses just like the Akren Company. Sometime around 1970, an entrepreneurial explosion occurred, and no matter how the phenomenon is measured, something fundamental seemed to change about that time. The number of businesses suddenly rose dramatically, as did the number of people owning and operating them. The number of business tax returns grew from 13 million in 1980 to an estimated 21 million by 1992.

Individually, small businesses produce relatively few goods and services, but added together, American small businesses become a world economic power all by themselves. Only the United States (including American small business) and Japan produce more, as illustrated in Figure 1-2.

What is most significant is that almost all small businesses are *very* small. More than half of the U.S. small businesses employ fewer than five people, and almost 90 percent of the small businesses employ fewer than twenty people. Figure 1-3 below gives you a glimpse of just how important small businesses are to the American economy, especially in creating jobs for hardworking people. A most important fact that goes almost unnoticed, but is very significant to the healthy American economy, is that these small businesses employ over half of our non-government workforce!

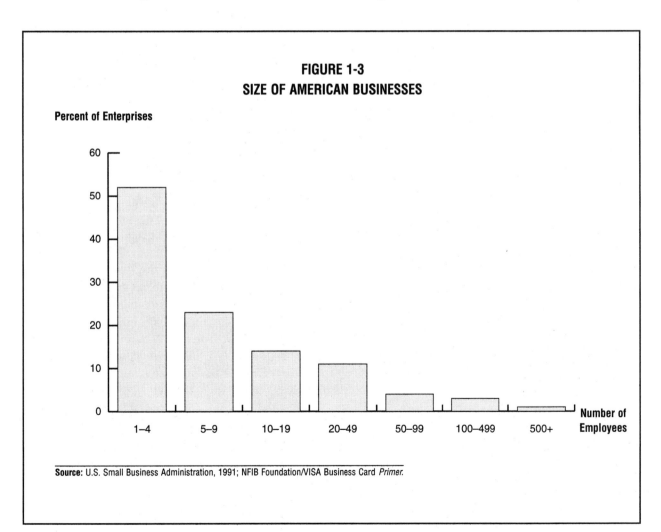

FIGURE 1-3
SIZE OF AMERICAN BUSINESSES

Percent of Enterprises

Number of Employees

Source: U.S. Small Business Administration, 1991; NFIB Foundation/VISA Business Card *Primer.*

Sadly, it is these small businesses that today are in greatest jeopardy of being destroyed by the federal estate tax when their founders die. According to a recent Gallup Poll, one-third of all small businesses face the same dilemma as Thomas Russell did. Admittedly, the founders of these businesses can do much to protect their businesses through very sophisticated estate planning, but this course of action can be costly, requires experts in many fields, and is foreign to most business people who have worked hard to master their particular industry. As a result, some businesses will continue, but far too many will fail when the founders die (or be forced into an early demise by the IRS). Will your company be one of them? Experience says that you have a very good possibility of getting caught in this catastrophe, either by the failure of your own company or by the ripple effect of the many business losses occurring throughout the nation as a whole.

And for all the heartache, loss of jobs, and reduced contributions (both tangible and intangible) to our communities, the shocking part of the story is that the federal estate tax contributes only 1 percent of total federal revenue! The ultimate loss in business and jobs results in a far greater loss of overall federal revenue.

THE DANGER TO OUR FARMERS

While the demise of thousands of small businesses, due to onerous federal estate taxes when the founders die, is a sad commentary on the freedoms that we have come to expect by living in the United States, small family farms also are rapidly becoming extinct. This trend is partly due to increasing expenses and competition from "big business" agricultural interests, but also is due to the federal government's unfair estate taxation system, which in essence prevents small family-owned farms from being passed down to the next generation.

The same scenario—losing a thriving business due to estate taxation when the owner dies—also applies to the typical American farmer, whose small farm is equally in jeopardy. Farming is a high-investment, low-profit-margin business. It is not uncommon to meet farmers who are "paper millionaires"—asset rich but cash poor. Let me relate to you an excellent example of this common phenomenon among today's dwindling number of small farmers.

A client of mine brought his parents to me back in 1978, when the federal estate tax was incredibly unfair and consumptive. Both aging parents wondered why they were in my office, since they sincerely believed that they were poor and had no reason to consider estate planning.

The father said they were retired and received only $17,000 a year—from a small pension, from social security, and the balance from renting their farm. I asked the couple how many acres they owned. The husband said that they had 600 acres. The couple had acquired one-third of the farm in 1929 for very little money, acquired another third of the farm when the husband's father died, and received the balance of the farm when his mother died. I asked him how much the farm was worth per acre. The husband responded that their acreage was worth about $1,000 per acre. When I told the husband that their estate was therefore worth $600,000, he looked at me aghast and in disbelief. He blurted out, "But we only earn $17,000 a year!"

Back in 1978, there was a federal estate tax on the first spouse to die, and the tax code did not yet allow stepped-up valuation. (We will discuss "stepped-up valuation" in a later chapter.) Both parents were in ill health, and I had estimated that, on the death of the first spouse, the federal estate tax due on $300,000 (half of the estate) would be $90,000. Now, how would the surviving family members get $90,000 cash from a 600-acre farm to satisfy the IRS? Could the family just sell the "back forty acres"? Unfortunately, life—and the tax code—don't work that way. The survivor must sell the *entire* farm to pay off the federal estate taxes. Since there was basically zero cost basis (and no stepped-up valuation back in 1978), the sale of the entire farm at $600,000 would create a capital gains tax of $120,000. (Back in 1978, the capital gains tax was only 20 percent.) Therefore, upon the death of the first spouse, the entire farm would have to be sold to satisfy the federal tax bill—the original estate tax due of $90,000 and the additional capital gains tax of $120,000, for a total combined federal tax of $210,000! A sad ending, indeed, for a once hardworking family.

As a result of this kind of confiscatory taxation, farmers were turning to offshore Trusts to protect their farms from onerous estate taxes. From my perspective and years of financial planning experience, I have learned that you can push the American people only so far, and then they throw the tea into the harbor. President Ronald Reagan met this crisis head-on with the Tax Reform Act of 1981, which dramatically reformed the method of estate taxation. Today, the United States is once again approaching that same type of crisis.

It is not my intent to address in this book the areas of very complicated and sophisticated estate planning that some estates require, but, rather, to inform you of the potential dangers ahead for all of us. Americans all depend upon a healthy and growing economy. My purpose in writing my previous book, *The Living Trust*, was to alert the American populace to the agony of probate and to make them aware of the economic havoc being perpetrated by Will and Probate attorneys on millions of unsuspecting people. My purpose in writing this book, *How to Settle Your Living Trust*, is to help people who have created Living Trusts to avoid a new (and entirely unnecessary) tactic of the Will and Probate attorneys—settling an estate in a Living Trust in almost the same manner as if the estate were going through probate. My goal is to show you how to preserve and protect your own estate for your heirs, as well as how simply an estate can be settled without agony, unnecessary cost, and years of wasted time.

THE TAXPAYER RELIEF ACT OF 1997

The inequities of the present federal estate tax imposed on hardworking American families, as shown by the two previous examples, is a most sad commentary. The Small Business and Farm Exclusion, enacted as part of the Taxpayer Relief Act of 1997, attempts, although very lamely, to soften the inequity of onerous estate taxation.

Small Business and Farm Exclusion

Congress, in its own floundering way, has now provided a $1.3 million exemption from estate taxation for farms and small businesses, but you must be aware that this exemption is effectively *in lieu of* the $600,000 individual exemption already available from the 1981 Tax Reform Act. What is hailed as a $1.3 million protective gift to small businesses and farms is really worth only $675,000 for 1998 and steadily reduces to only $300,000 by 2006.

The Small Business and Farm Exclusion is too little, too late, and it all but vanishes with time.

Be very aware that the Small Business and Farm Exclusion includes your individual federal estate tax exemption. Table 1-2 on page 10 shows you how the individual federal estate tax exemption increases over the next several years and how that increase effectively reduces the Small Business and Farm Exclusion.

For example, for 1998, your individual federal estate tax exemption is $625,000. However, this amount is first deducted from the $1.3 million Small Business and Farm Exclusion. Therefore, if you have utilized your individual federal estate tax exemption on assets other than your business, you have only $675,000 remaining to apply against your business for 1998. The built-in inequity in this so-called taxpayer relief is that as the individual federal estate tax exemption rises, the Small Business and Farm Exclusion decreases. Figure 1-4 on page 10 graphically illustrates this "declining benefit."

Beware: As the individual federal estate tax exemption increases, the Small Business and Farm Exclusion decreases.

Even seemingly simple tax relief usually has strings attached—conditions that must be met before you even qualify for the exemption or exclusion. As you might have already guessed, the Small Business and Farm Exclusion is no exception. For your estate to qualify for the Small Business and Farm Exclusion, the following conditions must be satisfied:

TABLE 1-2
SMALL BUSINESS AND FARM EXCLUSION REMAINING AFTER INDIVIDUAL EXEMPTION

Year	Individual Estate Tax Exemption	Small Business and Farm Exclusion	Remaining Small Business and Farm Exclusion
1998	$625,000	$1,300,000	$675,000
1999	$650,000	$1,300,000	$650,000
2000	$675,000	$1,300,000	$625,000
2001	$675,000	$1,300,000	$625,000
2002	$700,000	$1,300,000	$600,000
2003	$700,000	$1,300,000	$600,000
2004	$850,000	$1,300,000	$450,000
2005	$950,000	$1,300,000	$350,000
2006	$1,000,000	$1,300,000	$300,000

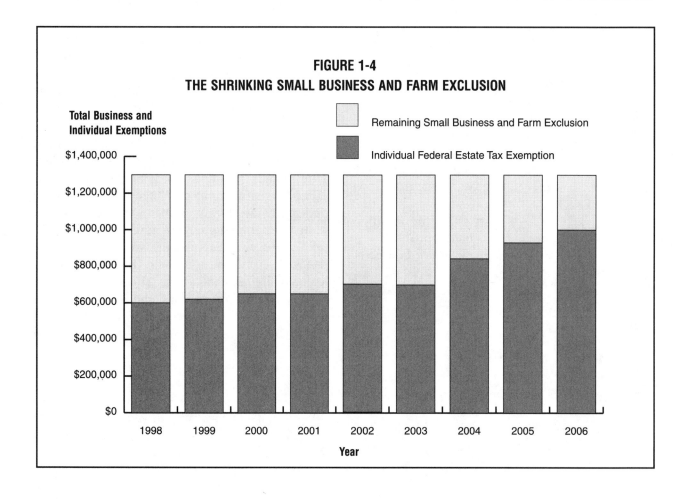

FIGURE 1-4
THE SHRINKING SMALL BUSINESS AND FARM EXCLUSION

- The business or farm must constitute more than 50 percent of your estate.
- You or a member of your family must have owned and materially participated in the business or farm for at least five of the last eight years preceding your death.
- Your heirs must maintain an ownership and an active participation in the business or farm for the next ten years.

The Small Business and Farm Exclusion became effective January 1, 1998. The purported tax relief offers far too little, and the consequences (the loss of family-owned farms and businesses and the related loss of jobs for productive people) are far too great.

Redistribution-of-Wealth Concept Is Antiquated

At the turn of the century, the United States had large businesses and wealthy families, such as the Rockefellers, Astors, DuPonts, Hancocks, Stanfords, Huntingtons, Vanderbilts, and numerous other famous families. Back then, many of the less fortunate people throughout the country hailed the concept of redistributing the wealth. However, in the 1990s, America's economy is made up of thousands of entrepreneurs who have built their businesses by the sweat of their brow and by the toil of their loyal employees. If the United States doesn't quickly alter its present taxation structure, the entire country will find itself to be in a house of cards that will quickly come tumbling down. Not just the Akren Company will be lost, but also a myriad of similarly once-thriving companies—and then it will be too late for Congress to reverse its onerous course of ever-increasing taxation of estates. Karen Kerrigan, president of the Small Business Survival Committee, says, "Estate taxes are nothing less than a hostile government takeover of family business."

Federal Estate Tax Exemption

Congressional leaders, along with President Clinton, hailed the 1997 tax bill as a wonderful reduction of some $90 billion over the coming years. One of the great gifts to the American public was to raise the individual federal estate tax exemption from $600,000 to $1 million, but that gift will take nine years to reach the maximum amount. There are two significant shortcomings of this tax exemption:

- Significant increases are delayed seven more years.
- The rise in the exemption amount does not keep pace with inflation.

The amount of the slowly increasing exemption is illustrated in Figure 1-5 on page 12.

Significant Increases Delayed Seven Years

A closer look at the actual wording of the exemption reveals that the sizable increases do not come until the last three years (2004 to 2006). To utilize this "boon" to your estate, you need to live at least seven years—at least until the year 2004—to take real advantage of the benefit, as illustrated in Figure 1-6 on page 12.

When President Reagan first took office back in 1981, one of his first significant actions was to present a major set of tax changes, which Congress ultimately enacted into law. The primary benefit to individuals and their estates was increasing the individual federal estate tax exemption from $125,000 in 1982 up to $600,000 in 1987—where it stayed for the next ten years.

The American public was offered another increase in the individual federal estate tax equivalent exemption, rising from $625,000 (in 1998) to a maximum of $1 million over nine years—a $400,000 increase in the exemption over a twenty-year period (from $600,000 in 1987 to $1 million in 2006).

Increase in Exemption Does Not Keep Up with Inflation

Unfortunately, although the increase may seem at first glance to be sizable, it does not, in reality, even keep up with inflation. According to the Bureau of Labor Statistics, the average inflation rate since 1987 has been 3.5 percent. However, the increase in the individual federal estate tax exemption amount falls substantially short of a 3.5 percent inflation rate, as illustrated in Figure 1-7 on page 13. Congress has "given" the American taxpayer a federal estate

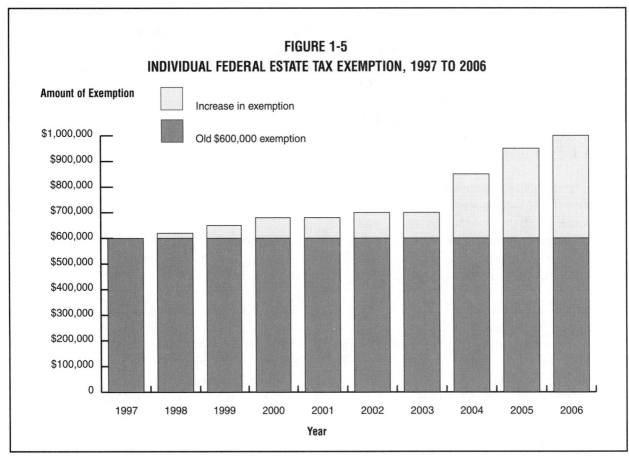

FIGURE 1-5
INDIVIDUAL FEDERAL ESTATE TAX EXEMPTION, 1997 TO 2006

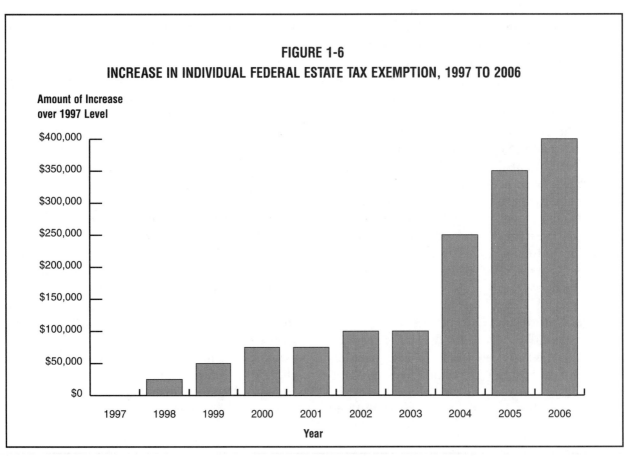

FIGURE 1-6
INCREASE IN INDIVIDUAL FEDERAL ESTATE TAX EXEMPTION, 1997 TO 2006

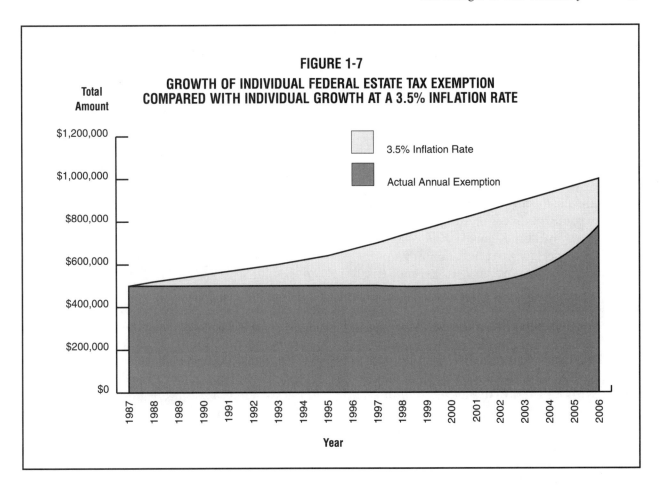

FIGURE 1-7

GROWTH OF INDIVIDUAL FEDERAL ESTATE TAX EXEMPTION COMPARED WITH INDIVIDUAL GROWTH AT A 3.5% INFLATION RATE

tax exemption that doesn't even keep up with the rate of inflation—that's not a gift, that's a crime!

I can vividly remember giving Living Trust seminars in the early 1980s. Back then, my audience had little concern about federal estate taxes, because their individual exemptions would exceed the value of their estates. Taxpayers had been given true estate tax relief—with individual federal estate tax exemptions starting at $125,000 and rising to $600,000. Starting in 1985, however, my audiences began to register concern about the federal estate tax exemption, when they realized that it wasn't going to be sufficient to protect their estates. What had happened in just a few short years? Inflation and dramatic growth in the value of real estate were rapidly eroding the benefits of the individual federal estate tax exemption. Thereafter, the seminar attendees would frequently ask, "When is Congress going to adjust the federal estate exemption to compensate for inflation?" I had to respond, "Congress doesn't act, it reacts." Now we have been presented

with a highly touted $1 million federal estate tax exemption—that still falls far short of the annual average rate of inflation.

CATASTROPHIC ILLNESS

In the latter part of 1996, Congress passed the Kennedy-Kassebaum Bill, also referred to as the welfare bill. The night before that bill came to the Senate floor, an amendment was quietly added to it that made it a felony for anyone to take any steps to protect his or her estate in the event of, or anticipation of, a catastrophic illness. To this date, no one in Congress has admitted to authoring this amendment; in fact, all members of Congress have denied any part of this grossly unfair bill, but the fact remains that it is still the law. Specifically, this law says, if you gift any part of your estate to any of your family, to a Trust, or to any friend (or anyone for that matter) and then eventually suffer a catastrophic illness, exhaust your hard-earned life savings, and are forced to turn to Medicaid for assistance, you have just committed a criminal felony!

With the aging of Americans, with older people living longer, and with the increase in serious maladies such as cancer and Alzheimer's disease, such a law is unconscionable and does a serious injustice to all of our senior citizens who have toiled for so many years to make the United States such a great and prosperous country. This law is unjust and should be abolished immediately.

It Became a Felony to Protect Your Estate

Because some members of Congress slipped an amendment into the Kennedy-Kassebaum Bill, which became law effective January 1, 1997, anyone who does anything to protect his or her assets in the event of a catastrophic illness now is considered to have committed a felony. (Please note, however, that the Catastrophic Illness Trust is still applicable for individuals who placed their assets into such a Trust by December 31, 1996.) Let's take a brief look at how you could, without even realizing it, commit what is considered to be an illegal act.

In 1997, Will Thomas, who was in excellent health, gifted $100,000 to his children. However, three years later, Mr. Thomas suffers a stroke and eventually is forced to go on Medicaid for continual medical treatment. According to the Kennedy-Kassebaum Bill, Will Thomas and his children have committed a felony, even though it was totally unintentional. Beware, my friends, of an insidious trap!

Alzheimer's Disease

There are innumerable causes of catastrophic illness, only one of which is cancer. My most numerous and saddest experiences with clients have been with Alzheimer's disease. I have worked with hundreds of couples who have come into my office with one spouse having been diagnosed with Alzheimer's disease. Alzheimer's is such an incredibly costly disease because eventually the afflicted person must be placed in a nursing home, at great expense, to receive specialized medical and nursing care. Many of these people live a long time and will eventually use up whatever nest egg the husband and wife have spent their lifetimes

creating. In the end, the Alzheimer's victim dies, and the surviving spouse is then essentially penniless.

Today, over four million people have Alzheimer's disease. The chance of being diagnosed with Alzheimer's disease increases as a person's age increases. Alzheimer's disease strikes 5 percent of those who are age 65, and the percentage rises to 10 percent for those people who are age 85. This disease is considered to be the third most expensive disease to treat, and it typically costs $18,000 to $25,000 per year for each patient who must be confined to an Alzheimer's care facility.

A Nation with a Social Conscience

Many citizens of the United States consider it a nation with a social conscience. When there is poverty in Africa, we rush to send food. When there is strife in Bosnia, we rush to send our young soldiers to make peace. Therefore, it makes absolutely no sense whatever that, here in America, Congress (thanks to the Kennedy-Kassebaum Bill) would prefer that the surviving spouses of victims of a catastrophic illness be deprived of everything they have worked so hard for and end up paupers in this nation of plenty! And, heaven forbid that they might try to protect some of their estates, because, if they do, they could be put in prison as felons.

Our older population is rapidly increasing in size, people are living longer, and their illnesses and infirmities are becoming more costly. I am not proposing that we become a welfare nation, but I do believe that individuals' or couples' efforts to protect their estates from consumption by catastrophic illness should in no way be met by criminal punishment. With more than 50 percent of the population of this country now age 50 and older, this problem is simply going to get worse. We must all realize—and I implore Congress to wake up to the fact—that, the surviving spouse of a catastrophic illness victim, can, in the long run, only drag the economic health of this nation down to new lows of depression and increase the number of people unwillingly reduced to accepting welfare as their only means of survival. I can only conclude that, whatever your belief, you must agree that God will not look favorably upon a nation that legislates surviving spouses into poverty.

Unconscionable Congressional Action
I find this act on the part of Congress to be utterly unconscionable and thus felt compelled to write the following letter to our congressional leaders.

June 25, 1997
The Honorable _____
Washington, DC

Dear Sir/Madam:

I am the author of the bestselling book *The Living Trust*, as well as chairman of The Estate Plan, a national estate-planning corporation. I am in the process of writing a new book, which is a sequel to *The Living Trust*. Before concluding this book, I would like to know what Congress plans to do about modifying the Kennedy-Kassebaum Bill—specifically, regarding the provision that any gift of funds from an estate of an individual who eventually qualifies for Medicaid will be considered a felony.

For years, I have worked with couples who have come to me with estates of around $400,000, where one of the members is facing the horrendous medical expense that accompanies Alzheimer's disease. They fear the surviving spouse will end up being a penniless pauper. Under such circumstances, I have always felt justified in transferring their estate to a Catastrophic Illness Trust, in order to provide for the future financial support of the surviving spouse. The victim of Alzheimer's disease eventually qualifies for Medicaid. However, under the Kennedy-Kassebaum Bill, the above scenario would be considered a felony! It also means the surviving spouse must accept the fate of being penniless—and often dependent on welfare to live out his or her remaining years. Such a fate seems totally unfair!

Years ago, my church asked me to do a Living Trust for a widow, and I did so at no cost.

The widow and her husband had worked hard to save their golden nest egg. The husband worked for a large aerospace company in southern California for more than twenty years. However, when he was age 54, the company terminated him so that his pension would not vest, and so he would not qualify for lifetime medical benefits at age 55. Instead, this hardworking professional received only one year of medical benefits. Three months after his medical benefits ceased, the couple discovered that the husband had cancer. Over the next eight years, the husband and wife used up their golden nest egg and every other source of funds in their estate, in a futile attempt to control the cancer. When the husband finally died, he left a widow with only the roof over her head—and nothing else. The church now puts the food on her table and the clothes on her back, and pays for her utilities.

This true story is a sad commentary in our nation of plenty. In times past, the widow's estate could have been preserved with proper estate planning. Today, however, such planning is now considered a felony! I consider this action to be a national disgrace.

The issue is not to pursue welfare, but rather to allow individuals to protect what assets they have already duly earned, against the costly consequences of a catastrophic illness.

My question to you is this: Is Congress going to take any action during this term to modify this disastrous and unjust penalty?

Thank you for your consideration.

Yours truly,

Henry W. Abts III
Chairman

Admittedly, our welfare system has been plagued by tremendous fraud, waste, and abuse. However, in the example cited above, there was no fraud. Here were two people, solid citizens who contributed their best talents and paid their debts—and then paid the ultimate price of poverty due to the husband's unexpected catastrophic illness. Such a fate is a fear that must touch the heart of every one of us. You might ask, "Could this situation happen to me? And if it did, would I leave my wife or husband penniless because of it?"

The situation I referred to in the letter is very real and still quite vivid in my memory.

> After working for more than twenty years, the two people had every reason to believe that within a year the husband's pension plan would be vested, and they would receive lifetime medical benefits. Now, however, the widow is totally reliant on the church to provide her with food, clothing, and payment of her utilities. What a sad commentary in our nation of plenty.

If I had only known this couple in the early days of the husband's illness, together we could have taken the appropriate estate-planning steps to protect the estate for the surviving widow. Unfortunately, I didn't know them then.

Since then, I have had the opportunity to help similar couples protect their estates for the surviving spouse with a Catastrophic Illness Trust, which was designed specifically for that purpose. In 1993, Congress attempted to eliminate this type of Trust vehicle. Why Congress made the attempt to eliminate the Catastrophic Illness Trust, I will never know. It is beyond my comprehension that Congress can be so terribly heartless and unmoved by this absolute need. I believe that Congress's attempt in 1993 was really only halfhearted, since our company was able to redesign the Catastrophic Illness Trust to satisfy the 1993 tax restrictions.

Congress Finally Answers

What is most significant about my letter to congressional leaders is that it went *unanswered* by most of its recipients in Congress! Eventually, however, two congressional leaders responded: Republican Senator Orrin G. Hatch of Utah, chairman of the Senate Judiciary Committee, and Democratic Senator Richard H. Bryan of Nevada, a member of the Finance Committee. I appreciated their responses, particularly in view of the silence of so many others. Both of these gentlemen advised me that Section 4734

of the Balanced Budget Agreement (P.L. 105-33 of 1997) amended this section of the Social Security Act to clarify that sanctions will be imposed *only against individuals who, for a fee, assist another individual to dispose of assets in order to qualify for Medicaid.*

Thus, you as an individual may take the necessary steps to protect your estate. However, you must not seek professional advice, since such advice is considered to be a criminal act on the part of the "advisor." Even this less-strict wording still poses a serious problem, and the American Bar Association (ABA) is vigorously encouraging Congress to further amend this act. The ABA rightfully argues that if an individual goes to an attorney for advice, the attorney is morally bound to provide the client with appropriate and correct information that would entitle the individual to preserve the estate for his or her spouse in the event of a catastrophic illness. It is my fervent hope that Congress will see the light and rectify this serious inequity.

On March 11, 1998, Attorney General Janet Reno wrote to the Honorable Newt Gingrich, then Speaker of the House, to advise Congress that her office found that to prohibit attorneys and other professionals from assisting individuals to dispose of their assets in order to become eligible for medical assistance was *unconstitutional* and that her office would not bring any criminal prosecutions.

For example, in instances such as those just described, an attorney would (or should) advise individuals facing the consumption of their estate as the result of a catastrophic illness to utilize their individual federal estate tax exemptions and to gift their assets to their children. The children would be advised to place these gifted assets in a separate revocable Living Trust, with the children named as the trustees and beneficiaries. The funds would (or should) then be used, *at the sole discretion of the trustees*, to provide for the future medical or institutional needs of the afflicted parent(s).

I wish to personally thank Senators Hatch and Bryan for their courtesy in responding to my letter, as well as for their support in passing this amendment. Hopefully, the senators will be equally successful in further amending this act to eliminate the serious discrepancies that still exist within it.

Long-Term Health Care

In discussing the horrors of catastrophic illnesses, I would be remiss if I did not recommend that everyone who can afford it should have long-term health care insurance—to provide for their needs when they eventually become infirm. Sadly, as the population ages, more and more families watch their hard-earned assets be eaten totally away by the high cost of one or both spouses being placed in a long-term care facility for many years. Unfortunately, most elderly people, the ones who need it the most, cannot afford this rather expensive insurance—and Medicare essentially does *not* cover the horrendous costs of long-term care.

If you have aging or elderly parents who have accumulated a modest estate, consider paying for their long-term care insurance yourself—as a means of ultimately preserving their estate (and what could be considered *your* future inheritance).

2

The Danger to Your Estate

The newspaper *USA Today* recently reported that $20 trillion will pass from parents to their baby boomer children over the next twenty years. This article is only one of many that have been appearing in the news lately.

This tremendously large sum of money was produced by the generation that, in one form or another, made great sacrifices in World War II or the Korean War. These people paid a dear price to support their nation and ensure its continued freedom. They demonstrated their undying loyalty, and then they turned from war to rebuild this nation in peace. These people became educated, got married, had children, and raised their families. They made incredible contributions to this nation, which all Americans are able to enjoy today. It is these same individuals who come to the end of their life span, having spent their lives building their estates, which, in the next ten to twenty years, will pass on to their children—to those we refer to as the baby boomers.

When this huge sum of money—$20 trillion—is transferred from one generation to another, the unfortunate fact is that a large percentage of this potential windfall to the baby boomer generation will be needlessly siphoned

off by other institutions and individuals. Major dangers are lying in wait to snare part of this large sum of money:

- The IRS—for federal estate taxes and gift taxes
- Will and Probate Attorneys—for unnecessary and sometimes multiple probates
- Misguided (or uninformed) individuals—holding property in joint tenancy
- Unfortunate individuals—having dual Trusts or a poorly written Living Trust

If properly informed and adequately prepared, most individuals can pass on their entire estates to their heirs without part of their hard-earned nest eggs being forever lost to their loved ones due to poor planning.

THE DREADED FEDERAL ESTATE TAX

In today's inflated economic times, many older individuals will suddenly be faced with an unexpected dilemma. The good news is they will discover that their estates, especially their homes, are worth much more than they might have at first imagined. The bad news, for many people, is that much of their estate is ripe for the picking by the IRS in the form of federal estate taxes. For the average couple with an average estate (i.e., less than $1.25 million for a couple), proper estate planning can shield their hard-earned assets from federal estate taxes. For the more well-to-do couples, however, the payment of *some* estate tax is inevitable, but the amount can be minimized with proper planning.

The IRS Smells Money

Not only is the print media publishing more articles about this large sum of money that will ultimately pass to the baby boomers, but the IRS also has suddenly awakened to this wonderful potential source of new revenue. The IRS is now very aggressively pursuing the opportunity of capturing its fair share of this windfall and is beseeching Congress not to alter the estate tax. In fact, the IRS would actually like Congress to *increase* the estate tax. What irony—that this nation owes such a tremendous debt to the elder generation who gave so much of themselves to provide all of us with what we have today, only to find that, in the end, the IRS stands, like a vulture, waiting for death so that it can swoop in to cleanse the carcass of hard-earned assets that should rightfully be passed to the heirs!

It's Your Exemption—Use It or Lose It

The United States Congress and the President gave the elder generation a great boon by raising the individual federal estate tax exemption from $600,000 to $1 million over the next ten years. This growth in the exemption amounts to an average of only 3 percent yearly (from 1987), which doesn't even keep pace with inflation. However, I do commend Congress for not caving in to those loud voices a couple of years ago that had advocated reducing the individual federal estate tax exemption from $600,000 to $200,000. Instead, I am grateful to say, Congress held its own and even increased the exemption.

What you must understand, however, is that *each* person has a right to one federal estate tax exemption. If you don't take the necessary steps to protect your exemption, then someday you will lose it. Congress gives us benefits, such

as the federal estate tax exemption, but Congress has never mandated that we take advantage of the benefits by using them.

The massive wealth of $20 trillion, passing to the baby boomers over the next twenty years, will pass mostly in small amounts—from couples who have spent their lifetimes working to build estates of whatever size and who would like to pass their estates on to their children. You need to know how to accomplish this transfer of wealth from one generation to the next without unnecessary taxation or expense.

Be Wise: Learn how to transfer your hard-earned estate to your children without unnecessary taxation or expense.

THE AGONY OF PROBATE

An even bigger threat to maximizing the amount of your estate that is passed down to your heirs is the totally unnecessary, time-consuming, and costly process of probate. This subject, and the agony that accompanies it, has already been addressed in great detail in my first book, *The Living Trust*, but you need to be reminded to avoid it—and to be aware of the hordes of Will and Probate attorneys just salivating at the thought of the probate fees they stand to rake in, as much of the $20 trillion is passed down to the next generation. With proper planning, you can easily avoid the entire probate process. You are urged to take the necessary steps to ensure that your estate avoids probate.

Another Hand in Your Pocket

Besides the federal government, another entity very much wants to grab a share of your estate—the Will and Probate attorneys. Taking the most conservative position and estimating that only *half* of the $20 trillion will pass to the baby boomer generation over the next twenty years, that an estate will only go through probate on the death of the second spouse (but not on the death of the first spouse), and that the cost of probate will be only 5 percent of the gross estate (a highly unlikely possibility), simple arithmetic shows us that the Will and Probate attorneys will extract more than *$25 billion annually* for the probate process! This huge waste is what I call "the $25 billion scam."

Not only is the staggering yearly sum of $25 billion an unnecessary cost, but the time of the probate process, usually eighteen months to two years, is also a costly waste. Even more important, however, is the often-forgotten or never-imagined agony of probate. Not only are time and money wasted, but this agony also is absolutely unnecessary.

I must emphasize, again, that if you have a Will, you *will* go through the probate process. I extensively addressed this subject in my previous book, *The Living Trust*, but I know that I must reemphasize the point over and over again. And, please, don't fall for the typical attorney ruse that "If you have a Will, you *avoid* probate!" Nothing could be farther from the truth!

Remember: If you have a Will, you will *go through probate!*

You should be equally aware that if you own property in more than one state, you must go through a separate probate in *each* state. Probate is difficult enough in your state of residence, but it is an absolute nightmare in "non-resident" states. In some states, the agony of probate can be multiplied unmercifully. For example, in Nevada, you must go through a separate probate in each *county* where you own assets!

The Probate Process Can Be Destructive
The probate process can be more than costly; it can be destructive. An attorney with whom I worked in southern California when we presented Living Trust seminars frequently recounts this classic and very sad, but true, example of how ruinous the probate process can be.

A young woman had come to my attorney friend for help in an effort to resolve the probate dilemma in which she was unhappily involved. The woman explained that her boyfriend had died and left her an apartment building in his Will. The probate process had been going on for some *eight years* and was still not settled!

During this time the attorney who was acting as executor of the estate and probating the estate refused to bring in new tenants to the apartment building when the old tenants vacated, and the vacancy rate had risen to alarming levels. The attorney explained that he did not want to take on the possibility of any liability that could result from a tenant injuring himself or herself on the property and then suing the estate.

The problem with this overly conservative approach was that the mortgage still had to be paid, and the occupancy level had fallen so low that the income was not sufficient to meet the mortgage payments. The result was that the woman stood a very good chance of losing the apartment building entirely (to foreclosure) once the probate was concluded.

My attorney associate had to advise this distraught woman that, unfortunately, there was nothing he could do, and that his entry into the case would simply add more probate expense. The unfortunate woman had no alternative but to wait until the probate process was completed and then hope she could salvage what had once been a good source of income.

This example illustrates the dilemma of probate: once you are caught up in that process, you are absolutely helpless. What comes from the probate process may be disastrous and usually is *not* in your best interest.

Invasion of Privacy
Some people have sufficient money to hire the best attorneys, and they have done so to advise them in estate-planning matters. Certainly, one of the objectives is privacy, yet, unwittingly, at the advice of their very expensive attorneys, these people select (or are steered by the attorneys into selecting) the probate process.

An excellent example of such a course of action is the very private person Jacqueline

Kennedy Onassis. Of all the people who valued privacy, she probably valued it the most. Yet, if you would like to read her Will, you don't even have to go to New York; you need only turn to the Internet and look up this Web address: www.caprobate.com/wills.htm.

Mrs. Onassis's Will clearly illustrates why one would want to keep private the decisions in such matters. Due to her nature, it is most certain that she did not want her remarks about her sister, Lee Radziwill, put on the Internet for everyone to see.

You may recall all of the television hoopla that accompanied the much-publicized auction of many of Mrs. Onassis's precious assets. It is still amazing to me that, of all the famous people of wealth, Jacqueline Kennedy Onassis did not have a Living Trust—a document that would have retained her privacy and possibly have avoided the degrading process of having her personal assets publicly auctioned to the highest bidder, all to satisfy the insatiable hunger of the IRS.

Another example is Jack Kent Cooke, who was the former owner of the Los Angeles Lakers and was responsible for building the Los Angeles Forum. To settle a painful divorce, Mr. Cooke was forced to sell his interest in these entities. He later became the owner of the Redskins.

Mr. Cooke died in 1997. Shortly after his Will was filed, with nine codicils, the *Washington Post* put up a special Web site on the Internet. This Web site not only showed Mr. Cooke's Will and his nine codicils (which inherited and disinherited various wives and children), but also linked the *Washington Post*'s past news stories with those codicils. If anyone ever wanted to retain privacy, I'm sure it would have been Jack Kent Cooke.

Shortly before he died, Mr. Cooke set up a foundation as part of his estate in an effort to provide his son with a vehicle to raise sufficient funds to meet the soon-to-be-crushing estate tax burden. Mr. Cooke took such action in an attempt to avoid the fate of the former owner of the Miami Dolphins, Joe Robbie. The overwhelming estate tax burden after the death of Joe Robbie forced his heirs to quickly sell the Dolphins team to a wealthy individual (a person whom Robbie just didn't like).

As a side note, it was interesting to read that six weeks after his father's death, John Kent Cooke said that he would be managing the Redskins and would manage the team in a less flamboyant style than his father. It is my prediction that John Kent Cooke will be forced to sell the Redskins in order to settle the estate taxes.

THE FALLACY OF JOINT TENANCY

For decades, people have thought, and even been told, that the best way for a husband and wife to hold title to their assets was in joint tenancy. However, nothing could be farther from the truth! Yes, joint tenancy might be beneficial in a few isolated cases, which were discussed in my first book, *The Living Trust*, but for most people joint tenancy is an unwise and costly choice.

Don't Be Seduced by Joint Tenancy

All of us have heard people say, "We will avoid probate by putting our assets in joint tenancy." That philosophy may work on the death of the first spouse, but it does not work on the death of the second spouse. On the death of the second spouse, with all of the assets now in the name of the survivor, all of the assets in the estate must go through probate. Also, the first spouse's federal estate tax exemption will have been wasted (i.e., not used to offset half the value of the estate). Depending on the year in which the person dies, this unused exemption could have been worth from $600,000 up to $1 million.

Some people say, "Well, when the first spouse dies, we will give half the property to our children, and when the surviving parent dies, we will pass the rest of the property to our children through joint tenancy and thereby avoid probate." Why not? Such ill-advised actions are taken almost every day. Unfortunately, and much too often, I become aware of a case where one of the children has an automobile accident, a lawsuit is filed against the child (exceeding the coverage of the child's automobile insurance), and then, sadly, the home and property of the *still-surviving spouse* are lost to the *child's* creditors.

The other frequent type of case occurs when the child is married, the child and his or her spouse get divorced, and the divorced individual makes a claim for a one-fourth interest in all of the surviving spouse's assets. Such a claim is a rightful claim.

Far more important, however, is the position that the IRS takes on such matters, because the IRS is all too aware of the joint-tenancy-with-children method of trying to avoid estate taxes. The first thing the IRS looks at upon the death of the surviving spouse is the child's cost basis of the assets held in joint tenancy. In other words, how did the child acquire that part of the estate? If the child did not pay for his or her share of the asset, the IRS will include the child's share of the assets back into the surviving spouse's estate, not only to impose the proper estate tax, but to impose penalties and interest as well. In one case, the IRS went back *seventeen years* to audit an estate and then imposed penalties and interest!

Beware of the Unintentional Gift
Uninformed couples can very easily and unintentionally add insult to injury. If you gift part of your estate to your heirs to establish them as joint tenants (and thus try to avoid that part of your estate having to go through probate), and years later you are forced to go on Medicaid, you and your children will have committed a felony, according to the Kennedy-Kassebaum Bill. This situation is just one more reason to avoid the approach of gifting part of your estate and creating a joint tenancy.

It is appropriate here to include the comment of Margaret Milner Richardson, who was the head of the IRS from May 1993 to May 1997. She openly stated, "Unfortunately, many tax penalties have been enacted to produce revenue, not necessarily to affect behavior." Ms. Richardson also said that penalties and interest "frequently are greater than the tax originally owed, leading to the collection problems that raise the most concern." Although creating more penalties has become an easy way for the government to raise revenue, "it is a very

poor way to administer the tax system," she added. Congress should correct the penalties imposed by the IRS because they are designed not for the purpose of penalizing the person for wrongdoing, but for the purpose of raising more money; in effect, the penalties are way out of line.

"Unfortunately, many tax penalties have been enacted to produce revenue, not necessarily to affect behavior."
—Margaret Milner Richardson

Joint Tenancy Can Generate Multiple Probates
Another, and sometimes significant, disadvantage to holding assets in joint tenancy is that you may become entangled in multiple probates being conducted in more than one state. For example, let me relate to you how joint tenancy can potentially end up in a nightmare of multiple probates and the unnecessary extra probate expenses that are siphoned from the estate.

The head of the probation department in Alaska called me one day and said that his sister's ex-husband had died in Kansas City, Kansas, leaving his estate to his sister, Barbara. At the time, Barbara lived in Omaha, Nebraska, in a home that she owned in joint tenancy with her ex-husband. Barbara also owned a home in Iowa in joint tenancy with her ex-husband. The ex-husband's Will also bequeathed a third home in Kansas City, owned solely in his name, to Barbara.

The probate attorney in Kansas City who was handling the ex-husband's probate had called Barbara and asked that she provide a list of all the assets owned by her ex-husband (which would include the half interest in her home in Omaha and the half interest in the home in Iowa, as well as the home in Kansas City).

The head of the probation department was calling me to find out why the probate attorney wanted to know the value of all of the ex-husband's assets. He had an intuitive feeling that the probate attorney's request was unreasonable. I checked my records and was able to clarify for him that Kansas state law, like the law in more than 30 percent of the states, allows the probate attorney to base his probate fee on the total assets held by the individual whose estate is being probated.

To circumvent this unreasonable probate fee, I suggested that Barbara should be advised to have her Omaha, Nebraska, home (currently held in joint tenancy) transferred to her sole ownership using a death certificate of her ex-husband. I also recommended that Barbara do the same thing with the home in Iowa (also held in joint tenancy). Once these joint tenancy assets had been transferred solely into Barbara's name, she could then advise the probate attorney in Kansas City that the only asset held by her ex-husband was the home in Kansas City. The attorney's probate fee would then be restricted to only the value of the Kansas City home.

This example is just one of many unpleasant, and often costly, situations that can arise from owning assets in joint tenancy. This story, in principle, had a happy ending, but if Barbara's brother had not called me, the probate of her ex-husband's estate could have been very costly for her.

LIVING TRUSTS

As you are well aware, having a *good* Living Trust can protect your hard-earned estate from unnecessary federal estate taxes, avoids the agony and high cost of probate, maintains the privacy of your personal matters, and helps ensure that your assets are distributed to the beneficiaries in the manner that you desire.

However, now that more and more people are learning about Living Trusts, more and more attorneys are very happy to take your money—but most of them do not know how to write a *good* Living Trust that protects your estate in the future. You must be aware that having the wrong or a poorly written Living Trust can be almost as disastrous to the financial health of your estate as having to go through probate.

To ensure the financial well-being of your estate, you need to be aware of the following three facts:

- A poor Living Trust can be your worst nightmare.
- Dual Trusts are unnecessary and difficult to administer.
- You must have a *good* Living Trust.

Your Worst Nightmare— A Poor Living Trust

Although a good Living Trust will resolve most of the problems of settling an estate mentioned so far in this book, please be aware that if the Trust is not properly drawn (i.e., if it is a poorly written Trust that does not contain all of the necessary provisions or is poorly worded), it can be a nightmare to the survivor. After publishing *The Living Trust*, I received a very powerful letter (sent to me by the publisher of my book) from a widow in Florida. After reading that letter, I was very moved by her plight and felt obliged to call her.

The woman, a most pleasant person, told me that her husband had owned a business in New York. In their later years, they bought a condominium in Florida and spent the winter months there. After her husband developed throat cancer, they sold the business in New York and moved to Florida as permanent residents. Two years before her husband's death, the couple attended a Living Trust seminar in Florida put on by an attorney who was just two years out of law school. As a result of that seminar, the couple recognized the importance of the Living Trust, and her husband commissioned this same young attorney to write a Living Trust for them. The attorney wrote their Trust and charged them $1,500.

Two years later, the husband's throat cancer had progressed to the stage where he had to enter the hospital. The woman told me that her husband wanted to make an amendment to their Living Trust, and he called the attorney who had drawn their original Trust to come to the hospital. He asked the attorney to draw the amendment. The attorney agreed to do so, but she said that the cost for the amendment would be $2,500. In spite of the unexpected high charge, the husband told the attorney to proceed with the amendment. It was two months later before the attorney finally returned with the amendment. By this time, the husband's physical and mental condition had degraded substantially, and the wife was certain that her husband did not really read the amendment—or at least did not do so very carefully.

The wife explained to me that her husband had always handled all of the couple's financial affairs. She did not think to review the new amendment but left it up to her husband. The husband died only a few weeks later. Shortly thereafter, the widow was shocked when she discovered that the young attorney, in drawing up the amendment, had changed the surviving trustee to be the attorney instead of the widow! (I can't imagine a more flagrant breach of professional ethics.) The wife (now a widow) found herself in the dilemma of trying to survive the trauma of being forced from her home and losing her entire estate.

After a year of struggle, the widow's octogenarian neighbor in Florida recommended that she obtain a copy of *The Living Trust* and explained that by following this book, the widow might be able to extract herself from her dilemma. When I talked to her on the telephone, she said that she had finally extracted herself from that problem, but that it had taken an entire year. The woman said that she had been able to solve her dilemma because of my book, and she was extremely grateful to me.

The woman also said that she had received a bill from the attorney for the amendment (not for the originally stated $2,500, but for an astounding $6,000). The woman wrote the attorney and stated that she refused to pay such an exorbitant amount. The young attorney promptly filed suit against the woman in the amount of $15,000! For another $4,000, the nearly distraught woman hired a local attorney, who advised her to "just pay the $15,000."

I asked the woman if I could use her story as a warning to others, and she was wonderfully obliging.

About nine months later, I was giving a Living Trust seminar in Palm Beach, Florida, to an overflowing house. As I always do, I greeted each person as he or she came in. The first couple who came in was an elderly woman and her octogenarian friend. The woman immediately introduced herself and said, "I am the wife who went through such a dilemma with the young attorney." She smiled and added, "If I can be of any help in this seminar, I would be more than happy to share my testimony of what your book has done for me." I was flattered and thanked her, and then we conducted the seminar.

At the conclusion of the seminar, I opened the floor for questions and answers. I noticed, as I stood in front of the large audience, that the woman was in the front row, sitting on the aisle. Another woman in the very back raised her hand and asked why she couldn't have her own attorney draw up her Living Trust. I answered her question in the most tactful, but direct, way possible, but I realized that I had not convinced her and there was little I could say to convince her otherwise.

At that moment, I happened to look down at the woman whom I had previously helped. She raised her hand and asked if she could respond to the woman in the back, and I agreed. This woman then stood up, turned around to face the audience, and said, "My husband and I had a Living Trust that we got from an attorney here in Florida, and I want you to know that it cost me $100,000 to extract my estate from the grips of that attorney! That should be reason enough to make sure that you have a good Living Trust from a reputable organization. I cannot speak more highly of the help that Mr. Abts has given me."

What a shame that an unethical attorney had taken advantage of this woman and that she was forced to spend $100,000 to get out of her dilemma—a sad story that upset me no end.

Dual Trusts—
An Administrative Nightmare

The concept of dual Trusts is simply a separate single Trust for the husband and a separate single Trust for the wife. I first ran into this concept shortly after the publication of my first book, *The Living Trust*, in 1989. I was asked to fly up to Steamboat Springs, Colorado, to counter two attorneys who were selling the concept of dual Trusts to the local wealthy farmers at $15,000 apiece—that is, $15,000 for *each spouse!* My first reaction was that dual Trusts were created by some smart attorney in order to generate more money by selling two Trusts instead of only one Trust for both husband and wife. Now, years later, I'm more convinced than ever that greed was the primary reason for instigating dual Trusts, although part of the reason might have been the fact that most attorneys have little or no idea of how to settle an estate wherein a husband and wife have only one Trust.

The marketing of dual Trusts is incredibly prevalent in Florida and seems to extend on up into the Middle West. At every seminar that I have ever given in Florida, someone invariably raises his or her hand and says, "My attorney told me that we must have separate Trusts for husband and wife." I explain why separate Trusts are unnecessary and why it is an administrative nightmare. I usually then see the same hand raised again almost immediately, and the next question is, "What do we do with our home? Which Trust or Trusts do we put it in?" I tell the people that they need to go back to the attorney who got them into that nightmare. This scenario is repeated all too often and is a typical example of the administrative nightmare of dual Trusts. A husband and wife bought the Trusts, but they still haven't figured out what to do with their home (and, in most cases, the attorney doesn't really know either).

In my most recent revision of *The Living Trust*, published in 1997, I addressed the issue of dual Trusts at length. Let me say, here and now, that there is absolutely no legal justification for dual Trusts. On the contrary, dual Trusts create an absolute administrative nightmare for both the husband and wife. With dual Trusts, the husband and wife must decide which assets go into which Trust, place the assets therein, and then maintain that asset placement! As I prepared to write this book, I did exhaustive research to ensure the accuracy of its contents. I am now convinced that, besides greed, attorneys inflict dual Trusts on the public because the attorneys do not know how to settle a joint Trust (i.e., a Married A-B Trust or a Married A-B-C Trust) for a husband and wife.

The Living Trust is not taught in law school. My first book, *The Living Trust*, brought the Living Trust to the attention of the general public when it was first published. Prior to that time, for some twelve years, I had been giving "estate-planning seminars" about Living Trusts. Back then, we couldn't really call them "Living Trust seminars," because few people knew what a Living Trust was. Since the publication of *The Living Trust*, however, attorneys and financial organizations all over the country have been selling Living Trusts to the American public. Some of the attorneys and organizations are reputable, but far too many are disreputable.

I am sorry to say that there are now innumerable very poor Living Trusts in the hands of the unsuspecting American public. People have Trusts that may not be suitable for their particular estates; even more important is that neither the public nor the attorneys really know how to settle estates that are in Living Trusts. This situation is what motivated me to write this book on how to settle an estate in a *good* Living Trust. I hope I have eliminated, once and for all, the ill-conceived demand for the dual Living Trust.

You Must Have a *Good* Living Trust

I cannot express strongly enough the need for everyone to have a *good* Living Trust. A good Living Trust incorporates every possible contingency imaginable. In *The Living Trust*, I originally identified 100 provisions that you *must* have in a good Living Trust. In the 1997 edition, this list had grown to over 150 of these "must-have" provisions. You need to understand that Living Trusts are governed by the statutes of each particular state. If the Trust is drawn up properly, the provisions of the Living Trust override the statutes—the provisions govern the Trust. On the other hand, if the provisions are not written in the Trust, then the statutes of each state govern the Trust.

The objective in writing a good Living Trust is to anticipate any possible event that might arise—in effect, to solve the problem before it arises and, therefore, to prevent any delay in handling the problem—and, particularly, to prevent any necessity for court intervention. Allow me to relate two examples where the proper language in the Trust solves a problem.

Every Trust names a successor trustee, but what happens upon the death of both spouses if the named successor trustee has preceded them in death? You now have a Trust with no successor trustee. What do you do? You must now go into the court and ask the court to put itself "into the shoes of the deceased" and to determine what they would have wanted. This process is costly and time-consuming. However, there is a most simple solution. A good Living Trust includes a provision that says, if a successor trustee is not named, the primary beneficiaries have the right to elect a successor trustee. I have seen this election of successor trustees done countless times by a simple agreement of the beneficiaries and a written statement placed with the Trust document to the effect that the beneficiaries have named all, or one, as the successor trustees. After each beneficiary signs the statement, the problem is resolved.

Every good Living Trust also contains precise wording that explicitly states that if there is more than one named successor trustee, they must all "act in concert" (they must all agree). I strongly suggest that you name several, if not all, of your children as successor trustees, since they must all "act in concert"—and the key word is *all*. All trustees must agree on decisions that affect the Trust. This requirement has a very stabilizing effect. One child may be extreme in one direction, another child may be extreme in the opposite direction, and the third child may walk the middle line; however, the end result is that, in order to accomplish what

is best, *all* successor trustees must agree (they must "act in concert"), which results in actions that are in the best interest of the parents' desires.

This Trust language eliminates obvious potential contention among siblings. However, what if a beneficiary is dissatisfied with the outcome of his or her share of the assets and decides to sue the Trust? A good Living Trust clearly states that if the beneficiary were to file suit against the Trust, that beneficiary's interest would cease (i.e., he or she would be effectively disinherited).

I could go on indefinitely talking about many different "essential" provisions. Time and again my own clients have asked me whether the numerous provisions will directly affect them. Most estates are easily settled, and the myriad of provisions need not be used. However, of 1,000 clients I meet with annually, I can assure you that at least one of them will be confronted with the need for one or more of these special provisions.

Quite often when I begin the process of settling an estate, I will see the necessity of having a particular provision in the Trust—and the consequences if you don't. By citing just a few examples, I hope that you can see how having provisions in your Trust to cover any contingency makes your estate easy to settle. If you have an incomplete or poorly written Living Trust, please take the necessary steps to get a well-written and thorough one. In the long run, a good Living Trust is a boon to the surviving spouse and/or his or her heirs.

Your Personal Needs Are a Vital Part of Your Trust

Each good Living Trust should be specifically written to include the unique desires and circumstances for each individual or couple. There is no such thing as "one Trust fits all"! A good Living Trust protects your estate and ensures that your wishes are ultimately carried out as you desired. You play a very important role in ensuring that the Trust meets your particular needs, both now and later on when you may be infirm or incompetent. This fact brings to mind a marvelous Living Trust seminar given by the University of Southern California Law School, several years ago.

The Living Trust seminar was an all-day session with over 1,000 attorneys in attendance, and I was privileged to be included in this group. The seminar presented numerous panels of attorneys who were experts in the Living Trust. I was awed at their tremendous knowledge of the tax code and their ability to spew out specific tax codes that applied to each area.

However, as I was driving home that evening (and feeling somewhat overwhelmed by the attorneys' knowledge of the tax code), it suddenly dawned on me that, although these individuals knew the tax code to a T, they were totally oblivious to the needs of the people for whom they were writing the Trusts. The attorneys could draw up Trusts that satisfied all of the Internal Revenue Service requirements, but, at the same time, they did not understand the personal needs of their clients and, particularly, the potential conflicts and unexpected difficulties that could eventually arise in their estates.

Unfortunately, I realized, such would always be the case, because the attorneys would sit across the desk from clients, and they would only think in terms of the IRS tax code. The attorneys could not put themselves in the shoes of their clients. The attorneys were able to tell the clients what they thought they needed, but the attorneys were not able to listen to their clients' needs.

Our Living Trust has always satisfied the tax codes and has never been questioned. I have been listening to my individual clients' needs for more than twenty-five years. I have gone into hospitals with individuals as they watched their spouses pass away. I have time and again gone into hospitals to have an individual execute a Living Trust before he or she passed away. I have worked with individuals who have eventually become incompetent or have had a spouse who has become incompetent. I have settled innumerable estates. I have seen every type of successor trustee and every type of heir—both good and bad.

As a result of my personal experience with my clients, over the years I have created and continue to expand what I consider to be the must-have provisions in every good Living Trust. As you will see as I progress into describing the process of settling an estate, it is our intent to avoid the courts, to avoid any administrative process, to avoid attorneys wherever possible—and, in effect, to make the settlement process not only simple, but painless and almost cost free.

Without a Living Trust, oftentimes your estate is not handled in the manner that you desired, especially when it involves the distribution of your assets or the gifting of assets or money. The following true story illustrates that your wishes are not always carried out and that you should stay away from a professional institution as the trustee for your estate. I discussed at length in *The Living Trust* why Testamentary Trusts are to be avoided. (A Testamentary Trust becomes effective only *after* the first spouse has died and the assets have gone through probate.)

Most of you remember, or have at least heard of, the great comedian Groucho Marx, who brought joy to so many people. However, in his last years of life, he suffered greatly. Actress Erin Fleming was a very dear friend of Groucho Marx, and, in his last months of life, she was Groucho's great support. Three months before his death, as a means of appreciation, Groucho Marx gave Erin Fleming $150,000.

Following Groucho's death, Bank of America, which had been named the trustee of his Testamentary Trust, went into court and declared that Groucho Marx's gift had been invalid because, the bank claimed, Groucho Marx was incompetent when he made the gift. (The intent of Bank of America was, of course, to retain as much money as possible in trust, which the bank would control as trustee—thus, retaining higher fees.)

The intent of Groucho Marx was to repay a dear friend for her kindness. Unfortunately, the bank won its case, and Erin Fleming was forced to return the $150,000 to the estate under the control of Bank of America.

I wonder how Groucho Marx felt about this unfortunate change to his well-intentioned gift as he stood in his next life and looked down at those events, which were contrary to his *Will*. Such a flagrant redirection of Groucho's true desires could have been easily resolved if he had created a Living Trust instead of a Testamentary Trust. If Groucho had had a Living Trust, he could have gifted the $150,000 to Erin Fleming and had his successor trustees agree to the gift. Such an action would have resolved any question of competency and stopped Bank of America from invalidating the generous gift.

A Living Trust Is a Must for Second Marriages

Individuals often ask me what they should do when they are in a second marriage. This situation is particularly true for older couples who have established their own estates and then, as a result of the death of a spouse or divorce, have found the opportunity to start a second life in a new marriage. The answer is that these couples need a Married A-B Living Trust and Separate Property Agreements.

Everyone in a second marriage needs a Married A-B Living Trust and Separate Property Agreements.

The Separate Property Agreements clearly identify the separate property of each spouse and become critically important when each spouse has children from his or her former marriage. Let's examine the situation where a man has two children from his first marriage and a woman has two children from her former marriage. The man and woman fall in love and decide to get married. They want to combine their assets for the benefit of each other and to retain those assets in trust for the benefit of the surviving member of this second marriage. When the surviving spouse dies, however, the man and the woman each want their separate property, as well as their share of marital assets, to flow to their children. The husband's separate property and his share of the joint estate would go to his children, and

the wife's separate property and her share of the joint estate would go to her children. The couple can easily accomplish such an arrangement by creating an A-B Living Trust with Separate Property Agreements. (This subject is treated in more detail in *The Living Trust*. Here, it is significant simply to point out the appropriateness and the need for an A-B Living Trust with Separate Property Agreements for second marriages.)

All too often, I encounter the situation where a couple in a second marriage comes into my office with serious problems that are tearing the marriage apart, yet the husband and wife are unable to identify the real problem. Typically, they have been married for about five years. Most often, the husband sold his home and moved into his wife's home and used some of his money to improve his wife's home—maybe to add a room or to put a new roof on the home. Five years have passed. The husband has worked around the house, has maintained the house, and feels—rightly so—that it is his home as well.

One morning, the husband awakens and realizes that if, God forbid, his wife were to die, he would be without a home. The problem is that his wife has a Will, and it says that, upon her death, everything goes to her children. Neither spouse had thought about these consequences, and suddenly the husband recognizes the reality of what could happen. However, the husband doesn't know how to approach his wife or how to discuss this subject with her, and he begins to internalize this conflict, and a strain begins to come into the marriage.

This real, but often unforeseen, problem is easily and readily identifiable—and it is so easy to solve. An A-B Living Trust is created for the husband and wife, and the home is identified as the separate property of the wife. The wording of the Living Trust specifies that, if the wife predeceases the husband, the husband has the right to remain in the home as long as he desires. If desired, this right could be restricted; for example, if the husband were to remarry again, he could no longer stay in the home. (An important note: If your Trust contains this restriction or comparable restrictions on the home, the home does not qualify for being included in the decedent's C sub-trust or QTIP Trust. For the home to qualify for inclusion in the C sub-trust, the surviving spouse must have an unrestricted right to live in the home for the remainder of his or her life. Any such restrictions, however, still qualify the house to be included in the decedent's B Trust.)

One of my most dramatic experiences in handling the problems that might develop in second marriages was a meeting I had with a regional head of personnel of Exxon Corporation.

The gentleman came into my office to discuss his potential problem. He said that his wife had been previously married to a doctor, who had died at a young age and left her with a young son and the proceeds from his $100,000 life insurance policy. The gentleman's own wife had died and left him with three young children. These two people, the widow and widower, had married some time ago. He loved his present wife dearly, and she assured him that she loved him as well.

However, the present husband said his wife had recently become almost paranoid with the fear of what would happen to the $100,000 that she had received from her deceased husband's insurance policy. The woman desired that the entire $100,000 eventually go to her son.

The woman's fear was caused by the fact that both the new husband and wife had Wills, like almost everyone. Their Wills were what I call "Loving Wills," which say, if the husband dies first, all of his assets go to his wife, and,

if the wife dies first, all of her assets go to her husband. The wife feared that, if she were the first to die, all of her assets (including the $100,000) would go to her husband, leaving it up to her husband to eventually see that those funds went to her son. For some unknown reason, the woman seemed to fear that her son might not get the $100,000, and this concern was creating great tension in their marriage—to the extent that their marriage was about to be destroyed.

I listened to their plight and then offered an incredibly simple solution. I suggested to the husband and wife that they create an A-B Living Trust and identify the $100,000 life insurance proceeds as the woman's separate property. I further explained to them that, in the woman's section of their Living Trust specifying her allocation and distribution desires, she should specify that the $100,000 be used for the education of her son, and that the residual balance (the amount of money remaining after the son's education was completed) would eventually pass on to her son when he attained the age of 25. The Living Trust provided such a simple solution to such a devastating problem.

Once again, a well-written Living Trust was a simple solution to a couple's devastating problem. This example is just one of many sad marital problems perceived by couples in a second marriage that can be so easily resolved—by a good Living Trust containing the proper provisions that reflect the desires of the settlors.

3

The Living Documents

Too often, most people tend to think of their Living Trust only as a form of their last Will and Testament. However, a good Living Trust does much more than that. The Living Trust and its accompanying ancillary documents are designed to work for you even while you are alive and to care for you and your estate if you should become ill, incompetent, or simply too tired to manage your affairs.

A good Living Trust contains many vital ancillary documents that serve you well, even while you are alive but unable to manage your own estate. A good Living Trust contains the following ancillary documents:

- Durable Power of Attorney for Health Care
- Durable Power of Attorney for General Assets
- Competency Clause
- Nomination of Conservator
- Guardianship for Minor or Handicapped Children
- Living Will (Right-to-Die Clause)

Each of these documents serves a unique need, and all are vital to ensure that your estate is handled properly—even if you are unable to do so yourself.

ACT NOW—BEFORE THE NEED

The documents briefly mentioned in this chapter are designed to protect you, your estate, and your heirs if something should unexpectedly make you unable to manage the affairs of your estate or to care for yourself. However, it is most important that these documents be prepared, signed, and often notarized long *before* you need them.

In 1990, I had completed a series of seminars in Minneapolis, when I suddenly found myself in Abbot Northwestern Hospital about to undergo double-bypass heart surgery. As the nurse was about to roll me into surgery, she asked, "Henry, do you have a Durable Power of Attorney for Health Care?" I said, "Yes." Then she asked, "Do you have a Living Will?" I again said, "Yes."

I don't know about you, but when I go into a hospital for life-saving surgery, I have far too many important things on my mind, and the last thing I want to hear is, Do I have the Durable Power of Attorney for Health Care and do I have the Living Will?

When you are being wheeled into the hospital is *not* the time to make these types of decisions. Such decisions should be made *now*, while you are mentally competent and not burdened with a prospective crisis. The documents mentioned in the example are so important that, by law, hospitals are required to tell you about them (and ask if you have them) before you are admitted.

Necessary and Vital Ancillary Documents

A good Living Trust contains much more than just the explicit legal language that creates the Trust. Several ancillary documents *must* be included with your Trust to properly protect your estate.

Durable Power of Attorney for Health Care

The Durable Power of Attorney for Health Care document identifies whom you would want to make medical decisions for you if you were unable to do so yourself. I remember, years ago, when an emergency trauma center doctor was in my office to create his Living Trust. The doctor said, "Henry, please convey to your clients how important it is that they have the Durable Power of Attorney for Health Care. They need to understand that, although they can act for their minor children, once their children reach the age of 18, the age of maturity, the parents no longer have the right to act for their children! Every child who reaches the age of 18 should have his or her own Durable Power of Attorney for Health Care."

Hospitals will automatically accept the other spouse's signature for attention to his or her spouse. However, what happens if his or her spouse is unconscious or has died because of a mutual accident? Emergency care cannot be administered until authorized by someone who has that power. The Durable Power of Attorney for Health Care is essential in such a case—authorizing someone you have previously designated to make medical decisions on your behalf. And, although it is true that one spouse can act for the other spouse in times of medical need, what happens when one spouse passes away? Does the surviving spouse suddenly remember to get a Durable Power of Attorney for Health Care? I think not.

Even though you and your spouse are currently living and may be fortunate to be young and in good health, I beseech you to get separate Durable Powers of Attorney for Health Care—and be sure that each of you selects a different individual to make medical decisions for you.

Durable Power of Attorney for General Assets

The Durable Power of Attorney for General Assets document has two primary functions. First, if you become incompetent and if you have left one or more assets outside your Trust, this document authorizes that individual whom you have named as the Durable Power of Attorney for General Assets to transfer those assets into the Trust. Financial institutions have become more familiar with this document than the Living Trust. Therefore, it is helpful to name one of your Living Trust's successor trustees as the individual for your Durable Power of Attorney for General Assets and to then have the Durable Power of Attorney for General Assets accompany your Living Trust document when administering those assets for an individual who is incompetent. Together, the two documents make it very clear to the financial institutions that the individual has the power to transact whatever financial actions are required.

Every child who reaches the age of 18 should have his or her own Durable Power of Attorney for Health Care.

A second, and highly important, use for this document is to create a Living Trust. For example, if a parent or loved one became incompetent and, for some reason, did not have a Living Trust but did have a Durable Power of Attorney for General Assets wherein you have been named as the "attorney-in-fact," you can utilize this document as your authorization to create a Living Trust for the incompetent individual. By creating a Living Trust for the incompetent person, you can save the heirs the cost, time, and agony of probate. By ensuring that the Living Trust language reflects the desires stated in the now-incompetent person's Will, you preserve the desired allocation and distribution of assets, and the Living Trust avoids the pernicious probate process.

Competency Clause

The Competency Clause authorizes the surviving trustee (usually the spouse) and/or successor trustees to assume the management of the assets that are in the Living Trust. In a well-written Trust, the surviving spouse and/or successor trustees are directed to use the Trust assets for the benefit of the individual who has become incompetent. Remember that if assets have inadvertently been left outside the Trust, the individual named in the Durable Power of Attorney for General Assets can transfer those assets into the Living Trust when an individual is incompetent.

The Competency Clause typically requires that two doctors each write a letter stating that the individual is no longer competent. These letters, along with the Competency Clause, authorize the surviving trustee or the successor trustee to manage the assets for the incompetent individual. If the individual were later to recover competency, the same doctors can write letters attesting to the individual's regained competency, and the individual then regains control over his or her estate. If an individual feels that he or she is competent, even though two doctors write a letter with a contrary opinion, the individual has recourse in the courts to preserve the right to continue managing his or her own affairs. However, in my more than twenty-five years of experience with the Living Trust, I have yet to see this action occur.

Nomination of Conservator

The Nomination of Conservator document designates the individual whom you would want to be responsible for your person (i.e., your physical body) in the event of your incompetence. The conservator is typically someone whom you believe is empathetic to your needs and whom you feel you want to be responsible for your person in the event you become incompetent. The function of the conservator has nothing to do with your assets, only your physical person. For example, if you became incompetent and had to be placed in a home or in some type of special care, the conservator would have the power to take such actions on your behalf.

With more than 50 percent of the population now over the age of 50, and with people living much longer, we are unfortunately going to see, more and more, the difficulty of parents eventually becoming incompetent and their children having to care for them. A good Living Trust, along with a Nomination of Conservator document, easily allows the children to take the steps needed to assume proper care of their parents.

Alzheimer's disease is currently plaguing more than four million people, and this number is increasing year by year. The cost of care continues to mount, and, unfortunately, it is inevitable that a victim of Alzheimer's disease is eventually going to have to be placed in a home that specializes in the care of people with that disease. Here, again, the Nomination of Conservator document provides the surviving children with the ability to make the best decisions in placing the afflicted parent in the best care possible.

The Nomination of Conservator document, along with a good Living Trust, also readily applies to a disabled parent. The parent may or may not be able to continue living in his or her home with the disability. If the parent is able to live at home, the children would be able to see that he or she received proper care at home. However, it is becoming more and more necessary for children to bring an aging parent into their own home for care, and it may be necessary to eventually put the parent in an institution to receive professional care. With a good Living Trust and the proper ancillary documents, the children can readily ensure that aging parents are properly cared for and that all of their physical and medical needs are met.

Guardianship for Minor or Handicapped Children

The Guardianship for Minor or Handicapped Children document is essential. In the case of minor children, it is becoming more and more common in our society that minor children are being raised in a second marriage, usually one in which the mother has been previously married and the children now have a stepfather. The children are being raised by a blood parent (the biological mother or father) and a stepparent. It is quite common in such a marriage that the blood parent name the stepparent as the guardian of the minor children, to take effect upon the demise or incompetency of the blood parent.

Let's say, for example, that a married couple has two young children, but the parents get divorced when the oldest child is 3 and the youngest child is only a year old, and the children remain with their mother. The mother remarries when the oldest child is 5 years old. Over the next ten years, the woman's new husband is like a father to the two young children, who are now ages 15 and 13.

Unexpectedly, the mother contracts breast cancer and dies. She had desired that her current husband, who has raised these children as his own, would continue to be able to raise them. Although the surviving blood parent (the biological father of the children) does have a claim to the children, the court will usually award custody of the minor child or children of a deceased or incompetent parent to the individual nominated by the deceased or incompetent parent who had parental custody. However, the key to such a dilemma is that the guardianship desires be stated legally in guardianship papers. The same issues of guardianship would also be true for a handicapped child.

Please be aware, however, that to legally retain custody of the children, the named guardian of the minor children must engage the services of an attorney to obtain court approval of the guardianship papers. This process is fairly simple and should take less than six weeks. The key point to remember is that to legally enforce the guardianship papers, you do need the services of an attorney. What you are concerned about is the best interest of the minor children or the handicapped children, and the guardianship papers can accomplish this task when they have been solidified by court approval.

Living Will

The Living Will is also known, and frequently referred to, as the Right-to-Die Clause. This document simply says that you do not want extraordinary means taken to keep you alive. My mother-in-law used this document very effectively during the last months of her life.

Edna was a lovely woman who had contracted emphysema. She spent the last seven years of her life struggling for breath, each year getting worse. Edna had a Living Will, and when she was finally moved into a nursing home, she taped her Living Will on her door and had another copy of the document placed as the top papers on her medical chart. She took this action so that if there were any emergency services necessary, everyone would know she did not want any extraordinary measures taken, nor did she want to be placed on life support.

One day, when visiting Edna, we noticed that the Living Will was missing from her door. We checked her medical chart and discovered that her Living Will was also missing from there. We then contacted the head of the nursing home, who told us that the principals of the nursing home didn't believe in the Living Will. We explained our position and tactfully pointed out that, if necessary, we would take the required legal steps to enforce that document. Thereafter, the head of the nursing home became quite cooperative, and we were most grateful for her change of attitude.

About three months later, our sons came to me as I was concluding a seminar one evening and told me that the nursing home had called for the family. We immediately went to the nursing home, where we learned that Edna now had pneumonia. Typically, under these circumstances, the nursing home would send the individual to the hospital to cure the pneumonia, and then the hospital would send the individual back to the nursing home. Fortunately, the nursing home was following our request and had ensured that Edna was made comfortable. When we learned that the doctor had prescribed antibiotics for her that afternoon, we called the doctor and asked him to stop the antibiotics, and he did so.

Within the next few hours, Edna fell into a deep sleep, and I believe this was the first real sleep that she had gotten in almost three years. Edna never awakened from that sleep. She peacefully passed away and was at last free from her suffering. To have put Edna on life support would have simply prolonged the agony that she had come to dread so much.

Several years after Edna's passing, I had the opportunity to talk to a woman who had been in charge of a hospice in Ireland. The woman said it was her experience that when artificial means were introduced to prolong a life, thereafter the person's life was usually one of agony. The woman went on to say it had been her experience that if life were simply allowed to take its normal course, the individual typically passed away in peace. From such testimony, as well as my own personal experience, I am therefore a very strong advocate of the Living Will (the Right-to-Die Clause), and I implore everyone to be sure that he or she has such an important document.

What *Not* to Do
It is all well and good to create a good Living Trust and to have all of the necessary ancillary documents that go along with the Trust, but don't make the mistake of locking up these important documents where the survivors cannot get to them without your competence or well-being. The following example clearly illustrates what can happen if you don't think ahead.

A client who had a Living Will (the Right-to-Die Clause) was placed on life support against his desire. His Living Will was in his safe-deposit box, and, most unfortunately, the safe-deposit box was *not* in the name of his Living Trust. As a result, the bank would not let the family members or his attorney into the safe-deposit box to get his Living Will. The client also did not have a Durable Power of Attorney for General Assets. Since the safe-deposit box was not in the name of the Living Trust, the bank refused to grant access to it.

If the client had executed a Durable Power of Attorney for General Assets, the named Attorney-in-Fact could then have been granted access to the safe-deposit box to retrieve the Living Will. Because the client lacked the appropriate documents to provide access to his safe-deposit box, he was placed on life support against his will. The only solution left was for the family to hire an attorney to go into court in order to request a guardianship for the client who was now on life support. Sadly, such an action would take about six weeks and would cost $3,500 in legal fees.

This example is a sad commentary about getting only half of the job done—when the client created the initial documents. Don't let this happen to you.

RESIGNING AS SURVIVING TRUSTEE
As a surviving spouse continues to age, there may come a time when the spouse is too aged, too infirm, or simply too tired to continue managing the estate. A well-written Living Trust provides for this eventuality and allows the surviving trustee to resign—and thus allows the successor trustees to take over the administration of the Trust.

Too Tired to Manage Your Affairs
The documents that provide for those who are ill or incompetent work just as effectively for someone who is just plain tired out. For example, following the death of my father-in-law, I watched my mother-in-law manage her estate very nicely for many years, and then she was stricken with emphysema. She continued to manage her estate for the next three or four years, but as her breathing got more and more difficult, she just did not have the energy to manage her estate any longer. At that point, she simply resigned as trustee. In so doing, she let her son, as successor trustee, manage the estate and provide for her needs. The son managed his mother's estate well, and the mother received all necessary care. (As we discuss later, the more prudent course of action is for the individual to resign as *sole trustee* in favor of acting jointly as a *co-trustee*, if at all possible, to prevent the survivor's A Trust from becoming irrevocable.)

Consequences of Resigning as Surviving Trustee

You need to be aware of a possible significant impact to the Trust when a surviving spouse resigns as the surviving trustee. When the surviving spouse resigns, the survivor's A Trust is then treated as irrevocable. Therefore, you must file Form SS-4 to obtain a Trust identification number. Then you must file Form 1041 U.S. Income Tax Return for Estates and Trusts (with the appropriate Schedule K-1s) annually. Use the Trust identification number (not the surviving spouse's social security number) on Form 1041 and Schedule K-1. (Use of these Trust tax forms is described more fully in Chapter 8.) Also, be very aware that the IRS will challenge any gifts made within three years of the "death" of the second spouse, which is presumed to occur when this person resigns as trustee.

A better solution than the surviving trustee resigning is to have the surviving spouse relinquish the position as *sole trustee* and then to appoint one or more successor trustees to act as *co-trustees* with the surviving spouse. The Trust administration continues as before, and the survivor's A Trust continues to be revocable (until the death of the surviving spouse). Therefore, the trustees do not have to file the Form 1041 Trust Income Tax Return and its accompanying Schedule K-1s. (The trustees continue to use the Form 1040 Individual Income Tax Return with the surviving spouse's social security number.)

Recently a client came to me and said that he was most grateful for the Living Trust, because he found it incredibly easy to administer his parents' estate when they became incompetent. He was able to provide for their every need without any problem. The Trust and the ancillary documents had made life simple for him and were certainly a boon for his mother and father.

The Living Trust with its accompanying ancillary documents resolves many incredible problems that could be very serious but, with these documents, can be made so simple. The most important blessing that the Living Trust and its accompanying ancillary documents provide is peace of mind, not only to the individuals who have the Trust, but to their children and beneficiaries as well.

---— 4 ———

How to Play the Living Trust Game

Creating, using, and settling a Living Trust are much like playing a game. If you know the rules and follow them, a game can be most enjoyable, and you probably have a good chance of winning. If you don't follow the rules, you encounter chaos, and you usually lose. However, the one difference between playing a game and having a good Living Trust is that if you follow the rules you *will* win, but if you don't follow the rules, you can lose, and the IRS and probate attorneys will gladly pluck your estate like an unfortunate chicken.

More and more people are becoming aware of the Living Trust and the many advantages that a good Trust has to offer. More and more attorneys and financial institutions are offering Living Trusts to their clients. And, as you might expect, more and more people are purchasing Living Trusts, thinking that they have just solved their estate-planning chore. Unfortunately, such is not always the case. All too often, well-intentioned couples buy a Living Trust, but then they don't know what to do next—and the sad fact is that the people from whom they bought the Trust often don't know what to do either.

The following two questions are the most common:

- What do I need to do after I get a Living Trust?
- What do I need to do to settle my estate?

This chapter will begin to answer these questions, as well as to acquaint (or reacquaint) you with the basics of Trust terminology.

FOLLOW THE RULES—AND YOU WIN
Most of us have played tennis at one time in our lives. As you recall, when you play singles (one player on each side of the net), you use the inside set of lines. However, when you play doubles (two players on each side of the net), you use the outside set of lines. If you hit the ball to the other side of the net and the ball bounces inside the appropriate set of lines, great, but if the ball bounces outside the appropriate set of lines, it doesn't count. It is really that simple.

Having a Living Trust and gaining the benefits therefrom are in some ways very much like a tennis game. You need to follow the rules.

Unlike professional tennis, which requires great skill and stamina (and even then a win is not assured), with a Living Trust, you simply need to follow the rules in order to win every time. The rules that you must follow are really quite simple, but they are also fairly specific. And, unlike in a game, there aren't really winners and losers per se, but those who don't follow the rules will definitely lose—and their estates will suffer the loss.

Most of us can remember the great comedy skit in which Bill Cosby tries to describe the game of baseball to someone who has never seen it. The commentary is hysterically funny and impossible to understand if you know nothing about the game. Like baseball or tennis, the Living Trust has some very basic and simple rules that you must know and follow. Once you are familiar with the rules (you don't need to be an expert), then you—and especially your estate—will win. If you don't follow the rules, you can lose, and the loss is usually extremely costly—both to your estate and to your heirs.

The most important thing to understand is that *you* can successfully create, administer, and settle your estate with a Living Trust. You can easily do so within your own family, without outside help (in most cases), and do so quite simply, without almost any cost. You need not be afraid of settling an estate—you need only be familiar with the rules and follow them.

Option to Do Nothing

If you are faint of heart, you always have the option of doing nothing. However, this course of action (and, yes, doing nothing *is* a course of action) will eventually lead your estate into the time-consuming and costly probate process, which dates back to antiquity. Imagine how you would feel if you were confronted with the necessity of inventorying all of the assets of James Shields's estate in Williamsburg, Virginia, upon Shields's death in 1779. Figure 4-1 shows only part of the inventory included in the Will of James Shields.

The Will

Until just a few short years ago, most people thought they had to have a Will to protect their estates. The Will is a very formal document and is structured with very specific requirements because of its abuse throughout history. Originally, people on their deathbeds orally gave their Wills to their religious leaders. However, as time went on, people began to realize that the church was getting most of the assets. It was time to establish some protection! Thereafter, it was required that a witness be present when the dying individual orally made his or her Will to the religious leader. Interestingly, however, the church still continued to get an unusually large share of the assets.

As a result of such abuses, the Will further evolved into a very formal document that must be witnessed by two persons in the presence of each other and the person whose Will is being witnessed. Once witnessed, the document may not be changed except in a similar (formal and witnessed) manner. This very formal procedure is intended to prevent the past abuses of the Will. In the United States, many of the states also require that a Will be notarized to "prove the Will."

Unfortunately, most of us still have a preconceived notion that probate is required. People seem to be convinced that in order to settle their estates, they must somehow go through some long legal process that requires attorneys. Fortunately, for you *and* your estate, such a philosophy is totally erroneous.

Interestingly, few people know that the primary purpose of probate is to pay the creditors. In 1990, the American Association of Retired Persons (AARP) published a study, *A Report on Probate: Consumer Prospectives and Concerns*, which pointed out that 95 percent of all debts owed by a deceased person are readily paid by the person administering the estate. Therefore, there is really no longer any purpose for the probate process. Probate is incredibly costly, time-consuming, and agonizing.

There *Is* a Better Way: A Living Trust

The Living Trust—this "new" vehicle created to save us from the agony and economic disaster of probate—was adopted by the English from the Romans in 1200 A.D.! The United States later automatically adopted the Living Trust when the nation's founders incorporated English law as the basis for U.S. law. The first known Living Trust in the United States was

FIGURE 4-1
PARTIAL INVENTORY OF JAMES SHIELDS'S WILL

A Partial Inventory of the Estate of James Shields
Excerpts from the Inventory of the Estate of James Shields, Deceased.

In the Parlour.

2 Oval Tables   1 Square Do.   8 Leather Chairs   1 Chest of Draws   1 Looking Glass
1 Corner Cupboard & 5 old Pictures

In the Hall.

2 Looking Glasses   20 Pictures   1 Corner Cupboard   4 China Chocolate Cups   6 earthen Tea
Cups   1 Glass Bowl   3 China Do.   1 Pottle Decanter   1 Desk and Book Case   15 Leather
Chairs   3 Oval Tables   2 Square Do.   2 Backgammon Tables   1 Tea Chest   1 Dozen Silver
handle Knives &c.   9 Silver Table Spoons & Case   11 Silver handle Knives & 12 forks   1 Case for
Do.   1 dozen Ivory handle Knives & 3½ dozen China Plates   1 Basket for Do.   2 French Servers
1 Clock   3 Pint Silver cans   1 Pottle Silver Tankard   4 Silver Salts   2 Silver Butter Boats
1 Silver Soop Spoon   1 Silver Punch Ladle   1 French Sugar Castor   4 Brass Candlesticks
3 Waiters   2 Chaifing Dishes   1 Pottle Stone Mugg   28 Wine Glasses   1 Plate Basket
22 Books   8 pair Scissors   1 Load Stone   1 flesh Brush   1 pair Money Scales &c.   1 pair Dogs
1 pair Tongs and Shovel . . .

In the Barr.

4 Empty Carboys   1 Case and Bottles   1 Square Table   1 old Fiddle   1 old Hautboy   1 Tin
funnel   1 old Gun Lock   1 old Quart Pot   1 Copper Cann   2 large Butter pots   1 Bird Cage
1 pair large Money Scales . . .

In the Chamber & Kitchen.

2 Beds and furniture   2 Tables   1 Brass Candlestick   1 old Trunk   1 pair Dogs   2 Quart
Decanters   7 pair Snuffers   5 Glass Salts   1 Wine Glass   1 pair old Money Scales   1 pair large
brass Scales   One Chafing Dish   4 Chairs   3 Earthen Bowles   2 Coffee Pots   1 Chocolate Pot
1 Pewter Bason   1 Turene   1 Tin dish Cover   24 Pewter Dishes   1 dozen Deep Plates
4½ dozen flatt Do.   3 Earthen Dishes   1 Tea Kettle   1 Trivet   2 Box Irons &c.   1 Grater
1 Silver Punch Strainer   1 Silver Punch Spoon   2 Sugar Boxes   1 Tea Board   a Parcel China
5 Silver tea spoons   1 Marble Morter &c.   1 Bell Metal Morter &c.   Dutch Oven   2 Dozen
Candle Moulds   2 Stewpans and Stoppers   3 Iron Pots   1 Bell Metal Skillett   1 large Copper
1 Brass Kettle   1 Jack   1 Coffee Mill   1 Silver Watch   2 Iron Spits   1 pair Dogs   4 Pails
4 Tubs   2 large Butter Pots   2 frying Pans   1 fish Kettle   3 Potracks   1 Grid Iron
1 Dripping Pan   2 old Pewter Dishes   7 old Ivory handle Knives &c.   1 Warming Pan
2 old Square Tables   3 Butter pots . . .

ANN SHIELDS Exx.

Returned into York County Court the 21st of January 1750/51 and ordered to be recorded.

Teste
Thomas Everard Cl. Cur.

written by Patrick Henry for the governor of Virginia.

A Living Trust Is a Contract

The Living Trust is really much simpler than a Will, although it may look much more complex. The Living Trust is a contract between husband and wife or, if an individual is single, it is an implied contract between the individual (the creator of the Trust) and the beneficiaries. Since a Living Trust follows contractual law rather than the abused law of Wills, far more can be done with it. For example, unlike a Will, the Living Trust, as a contract, can legally specify (and this can be successfully enforced in court) that a beneficiary is to be eliminated from receiving any part of the estate if he or she sues the Trust.

Trustee Powers Are Crucial

The trustee powers are the most critically important legal language in your Living Trust.

The trustee powers, spelled out in detail in the Living Trust, explicitly define what powers are given to the trustee or are allowed by state law under the probate code. The trustee only has the authority to take actions that are specifically stated in the language of the Trust.

It is critical for you to understand that the more extensive the powers your Living Trust spells out, the greater the freedom the surviving trustee or successor trustees have in administering the Trust. Be very aware of the danger of failing to adequately provide complete trustee powers, thus requiring the trustee to formally petition the probate court for the additional trustee powers that are needed. The necessity to petition the court for trustee powers incurs attorney fees and other additional costs, consumes unnecessary time, and generates frustration. The solution to avoiding this danger is to make certain that you have a well-drawn Living Trust (i.e., one that I call a *good* Living Trust) that provides extensive trustee powers.

The trustee only has the authority to take actions that are specifically stated in the language of the Trust.

Far too many poorly written Trusts do not provide the trustees with all the powers they need to properly administer a Living Trust. A good Living Trust, on the other hand, provides extensive trustee powers to assure proper administration of the Trust, regardless of the unusual situations that may arise.

A Living Trust Continues After Your Death

If you have placed all of your assets in the name of your Living Trust, you avoid the probate process entirely. In simple terms, for example, my personal Living Trust is simply a contract stating that upon my incompetence or death, I have named my wife to step into my shoes and to carry on as I would have done. And, upon my wife's death, the contract further states that our four children are to step in and carry on—acting together to make decisions regarding our estate and to carry out the distribution of our estate as we have specified

in our Trust. It couldn't be more simple or private. No attorneys, no legal fees, and no court appearances are needed; the estate is settled quickly, privately, and entirely by the surviving children.

Quite often, many people initially do not truly understand the many benefits (both emotional and financial) of having a good Living Trust. Most people quickly grasp the financial benefits of having a Trust—particularly to avoid the onerous probate fees charged by probate attorneys. However, many people do not understand the issue of privacy—and the stark difference between an estate being probated and an estate being settled in a Living Trust. The following story is an example of a reluctant prospect who finally saw the light.

Joseph Walsh recently called one of our advisors and asked that we create one of our Living Trusts for his wife and himself. Joseph said that he had attended one of my seminars about four years earlier and heard my estimate that the cost of probate could be as much as 8 percent of his total estate. At that time, Joseph said that he didn't believe that figure, so when he left the seminar, he took no action to create a Living Trust. Now, some four years later, Mr. Walsh had become very concerned about the privacy of his estate, and he wanted to create a Living Trust to protect his privacy.

Mr. Walsh is typical of many potential clients, who don't immediately grasp the significant advantages of a Living Trust, but who eventually realize the benefits to their estates.

Settling a Living Trust Is Simple

I must reiterate the simplicity of settling an estate in a good Living Trust. I have personally given over 3,000 seminars, my company has produced over 40,000 Living Trusts, and we have settled over 4,000 estates—all of them swiftly, simply, and without incident. I have personally settled over 200 estates, and I can testify to just how simple it really is—if you follow the rules.

SUB-TRUSTS

Many people are confused by Trust designations such as "Married A-B Trust" or "Married

A-B-C Trust." Oftentimes, people erroneously believe that more than one Trust is involved. However, *only one* Living Trust is involved—even though one, two, or three subparts make up the Trust (a Married A Trust, a Married A-B Trust, or a Married A-B-C Trust).

The A Trust, B Trust, and C Trust "parts" of the Living Trust are called sub-trusts. Until the death of a spouse, none of the sub-trusts has any application. However, when a spouse dies, each of these sub-trusts becomes *extremely important*.

The significance and primary advantage of a joint A-B Trust or A-B-C Trust for a married couple is that the assets are not allocated to the sub-trusts until the death of the first spouse. This procedure avoids the administrative nightmare experienced by those who needlessly have two separate Trusts (one for the husband and one for the wife).

To help dispel the confusion about the various "parts" of a Living Trust, future references in this book will refer to the A sub-trust, the B sub-trust, and the C sub-trust. Remember, however, that these sub-trusts are all part of one Living Trust.

The A Sub-Trust

Sub-trust A—commonly referred to as the survivor's A Trust (or the survivor's A sub-trust)—becomes the sub-trust for holding the survivor's assets. This sub-trust remains revocable (changeable) as long as the surviving spouse is alive *and* competent.

The B Sub-Trust and C Sub-Trust

Sub-trust B (for a Married A-B or A-B-C Trust) and sub-trust C (for a Married A-B-C Trust) are commonly referred to as the decedent's B Trust or decedent's B sub-trust and the decedent's C Trust or decedent's C sub-trust. These sub-trusts become the "buckets" for holding the decedent's assets; the sub-trusts become *irrevocable* (unchangeable) when the first spouse dies. Sub-trust B becomes the Credit Shelter Trust, retaining the decedent's assets to qualify for the individual federal estate tax exemption.

The QTIP and QDOT Trusts

If the decedent's spouse is a resident citizen, sub-trust C is also known, and often referred to, as the QTIP (Qualified Terminal Interest Property) Trust. If the decedent's spouse is a non-citizen resident, the C sub-trust must conform to the requirements of a QDOT Trust (otherwise known as a Qualified Domestic Trust) in which a surviving trustee or co-trustee must be a U.S. citizen.

EVERY GAME HAS PLAYERS— AS DOES A LIVING TRUST

One of the first steps in learning a new game—even before we learn the rules of the game—is to learn who the players are and what each player (in his or her assigned position) is supposed to do. The same can be said for a Living Trust. In the games of baseball and football, for example, a set of players perform individual functions—but it is their teamwork, their working together, that produces a winning team. And so it is with a Living Trust.

Since a Living Trust is a legal entity, much like a corporation, several "players" have a role in the Trust; each has designated functions, and some must take a more active role in creating and managing the Trust.

Most sports fanatics can name the different positions (players) on baseball, football, or hockey teams. However, few people can readily name the key "players" in a Living Trust. The Living Trust players are the following:

- Trustor
- Settlor
- Trustee
- Beneficiary
- Contingent beneficiary
- Remainder beneficiary

Trustor

The trustor is the creator of the Trust. A husband and wife are typically the trustors (i.e., the creators) of their own Trust. A single individual, likewise, would be the trustor of his or her Trust.

The trustors have the right to alter the Trust at any time. However, when the trustor(s) die, the ability to alter or change that Trust ceases, and the terms of the Trust become irrevocable and permanent. For a married couple, when the first spouse dies, the decedent's B sub-trust becomes irrevocable, but the survivor's A sub-trust continues to be revocable (changeable) as long as the surviving spouse is living and competent. When the surviving spouse dies, the survivor's A sub-trust then becomes irrevocable. When a single person dies, his or her entire Trust becomes irrevocable.

Settlor

The settlor is the individual or couple (if married) who transfers the assets into the Living Trust. Typically, the settlors of a Trust are the husband and wife. For a single individual, he or she is usually the sole settlor of the Trust.

As with the trustor's rights, the ability to transfer assets into the Trust ceases when the settlor(s) die. The ability to transfer assets into the B sub-trust and/or C sub-trust of the decedent (the first spouse to die) ceases upon the death of the first spouse. The ability to transfer assets into the survivor's A sub-trust ceases upon the death of the surviving spouse. Likewise, when a single individual dies, he or she obviously no longer may transfer assets into the Trust. (Any assets not already in the Trust upon the death of a settlor must go through the probate process!) The IRS refers to the settlor as a *grantor*. Because of this designation, the IRS refers to a Living Trust as a Grantor Trust.

Trustee

The trustee is the administrator of the Trust (i.e., manages the assets therein). For a married couple, typically the husband and wife jointly serve as the trustees for their Trust. Since an individual can create a Trust, he or she also is usually the trustee of the Living Trust and has all the rights needed to manage the Trust assets (in almost the same manner as if the assets were not held in the name of the Trust). A single individual is usually the sole trustee of his or her Trust. However, there are circumstances wherein a single individual may have a co-trustee to help in administering the estate.

Upon the incompetence or demise of an original trustee, the trustee is simply replaced. For example, if the husband or wife becomes incompetent, the surviving spouse typically is then known as the surviving trustee and continues to manage the Trust affairs.

Since a Living Trust is a legal document that outlives the trustors and settlors, a good Living Trust specifies a line of succession for the trustees to ensure that the Trust always has someone to manage its assets. When the surviving trustee dies or becomes incompetent, a good Living Trust specifies the individual or individuals who replace the original trustees and continue to manage the Trust assets. These individuals are known as successor trustees. Usually, the children are named to become the successor trustees for their parents' Living Trust upon the death or incompetence of the original trustees. It is particularly important for a single individual to name one or more successor trustees, who can take over the Trust administration responsibilities upon the death or incompetence of the original trustee.

Beneficiaries

The beneficiary—or beneficiaries, since there is often more than one—receives the benefits (i.e., the assets) of the Trust. Because of our Will mentality, we tend to think of the beneficiaries as being our children, because that's whom we have named in our Will. However, it is important to realize the difference between a Will and a Living Trust. A Will does not become effective until someone dies, whereas a Living Trust becomes effective the moment it is created (when it is signed by the creators, the document is notarized, and the assets are placed inside the Trust).

The term *beneficiary* is used in different ways and at different times and even refers to different types of beneficiaries. When dealing with a Living Trust, you may often see three beneficiary designations:

- Beneficiary
- Contingent beneficiary
- Remainder beneficiary

During the life of a Trust, it is common for particular individuals to be considered contingent beneficiaries and remainder beneficiaries at different times, and sometimes even both types of beneficiary at the same time. Let me explain the differences among the three types of beneficiary listed.

Beneficiary

Many people overlook the fact that, typically, the husband and wife are the initial beneficiaries of their own Trust. When a Living Trust is first created, a husband and wife (if married) or an individual (if single) are designated as the Trust "beneficiaries." These individuals have a beneficial interest in the Trust assets and enjoy the income and principal from assets in the Trust.

Upon the demise of a spouse, the surviving spouse usually becomes the remaining beneficiary of the Trust. Remember, though, that the creators have the ability to alter the beneficiary designations for their share of the assets in whatever way they may so desire. In a good Living Trust, each of the settlors has the power to separately designate the beneficiaries of his or her share of the Trust assets, as well as to specify *when* the beneficiaries are to receive the assets.

For example, assume that a husband and wife who created a Living Trust are both in their second marriage and that the husband brought separate property into this marriage. The husband desires that upon his death, the joint marital assets remain in trust for the benefit of his surviving spouse but his separate property be given to his children. This arrangement can be easily specified in the Living Trust.

For couples who have not been remarried, in most cases, all of the assets are retained in trust, and the surviving spouse becomes the surviving beneficiary. It is important to remember that it is only *after* a settlor dies that the named heirs become beneficiaries of the Living Trust—not before then.

Contingent Beneficiary

Any future beneficiary designations, usually the children, made by the individual (if single) or the husband and wife (if married) are considered to be "contingent beneficiaries." As long as the individual or the husband and wife are still living and competent, they can change the beneficiary designations at any time.

It is quite common, when a couple is involved in a second marriage, for the husband and wife to name different contingent beneficiaries (usually each spouse's own children from a previous marriage). While both spouses are still living, the spouses are the beneficiaries of their Living Trust, and the children of both spouses are considered to be contingent beneficiaries of the Trust, since the beneficiary designations can be changed at any time, as long as the husband and wife remain alive and competent.

Remainder Beneficiary

To play the game properly, you need to understand the importance of remainder beneficiaries, but the concern for remainder beneficiaries only comes into play when the husband and wife name different beneficiaries. While the husband and wife are living, they are the beneficiaries of their Living Trust, and they can change the contingent beneficiaries of their Trust at any time they desire. A similar scenario is also true for the single individual who has a Living Trust; he or she need not be concerned about any contingent beneficiaries, because the beneficiary designations can be changed at any time while the original trustee is still alive and competent.

A remainder beneficiary is an individual who is *irrevocably* named as the beneficiary of a Trust. A beneficiary designation becomes irrevocable when the person making such designation dies; the named beneficiary then becomes a remainder beneficiary. A surviving spouse cannot change the beneficiary designations of the decedent spouse.

Recall, if you will, that when the first spouse dies, the B sub-trust (and C sub-trust, if it exists) becomes irrevocable; it cannot be changed by the surviving spouse. Therefore, when the first spouse dies, any beneficiary designations made by that spouse are no longer "contingent"; instead, contingent beneficiaries become irrevocable remainder beneficiaries of the B sub-trust (and/or C sub-trust). However, even after the first spouse has died, the beneficiaries named by the surviving spouse are still contingent beneficiaries for the second spouse's A sub-trust, since the surviving spouse may still change the beneficiary designations as long as he or she is alive and competent.

Let's assume for a moment that a husband and wife (still in their first marriage) have two children, and that each spouse has named both children as beneficiaries. As long as both spouses are still living, the children are considered to be contingent beneficiaries. However, when the first spouse dies, the beneficiaries named by the first spouse now become remainder beneficiaries (an irrevocable designation) of the decedent's B sub-trust (and/or C sub-trust), but these same children continue to be contingent beneficiaries of the survivor's A sub-trust. Thus, at the same time, the children are both remainder beneficiaries and contingent beneficiaries. When the second spouse dies, the children become remainder beneficiaries of the second spouse's A sub-trust as well.

The significance of the remainder beneficiary comes into play when one spouse dies (where there is a Married A-B Living Trust or A-B-C Living Trust), leaving the surviving spouse as sole trustee and primary beneficiary. In this instance, the surviving spouse is the beneficiary of the survivor's A sub-trust (his or her own Trust) and need not be concerned with the contingent beneficiaries of the A sub-trust, because the surviving spouse can change the beneficiaries of the A sub-trust at any time. The situation is very different, however, for the decedent's B sub-trust and/or C sub-trust, since the Trust provisions (and beneficiary designations) became irrevocable upon the death of the first spouse—and the contingent beneficiaries became the remainder beneficiaries. The remainder beneficiaries of the decedent's B sub-trust now become very important. The surviving spouse, acting as trustee, must recognize that these remainder beneficiaries will ultimately be the recipients of the residual (the assets remaining in the B sub-trust and/or C sub-trust)—and their rights *cannot be altered*.

Since the rights of the remainder beneficiaries cannot be altered, they must be protected. If the remainder beneficiaries are the joint children of both spouses, there should be no concern. However, in the case of a second marriage with children from each spouse, the surviving spouse (acting as surviving trustee) needs to follow the rules very carefully.

As an example, let's briefly explore the case where a husband has two children from his former marriage and his wife also has two children from her former marriage. The husband dies, leaving his share of the assets in trust for the benefit of his surviving spouse.

Under these circumstances, the surviving spouse needs to judiciously recognize the ultimate rights of the husband's children. The surviving spouse must clearly understand and govern her actions according to the knowledge that if she abuses her rights as trustee and abridges the rights of the husband's children, she could ultimately end up in grave legal difficulty with the husband's children.

This brief example is only a caution. I will address the subject in more detail as we move further into the rules of the game.

WHAT TO DO AFTER GETTING A LIVING TRUST

One of the greatest mysteries for people who have just created a Living Trust is what to do next. The question they most often ask is, What do I need to do now that I have a Living Trust? The first and most important action to take immediately is to make sure that *all* of your titled assets are transferred into the name of your Living Trust. By "titled assets," I am referring to assets such as your house (and other real estate), all your securities (such as stocks, bonds, and mutual funds), and any retirement or pension plans in which you have a vested interest.

Once your assets have been placed in your Trust, you should place one copy of your Trust in your safe-deposit box (for future safekeeping) and keep a second copy of your Trust at home, so that it is readily at hand for any changes that you wish to make and available to your heirs if something should happen to you. I strongly urge you to tell your successor trustees where a copy of your Living Trust is located. They don't necessarily have to see it, but please let them know where you put it. (For our clients, I recommend that they place one original set of documents in their Estate Plan Binder, which they should keep at home with them.)

Keeping one copy of your Trust at home gives you the opportunity to change your Trust whenever you desire. You simply make the desired change in pen and initial it, and such a change will be upheld in any court. However, I always recommend to my clients that if they make such a change, they should come into our office when convenient and allow us to formalize the change as an amendment to the Trust. It is our experience that this procedure allows us to assure that the desired change is made correctly and that it is consistent with the rest of the Trust documents.

This ability to make any change to the Living Trust at any time insulates the Trust from the most common attack made against Wills. Let's take a moment and look at a very real situation that frequently occurs with Wills.

A husband and wife, who have four grown children, have Wills that were drawn many years before their deaths. In their Wills, the husband and wife specify different amounts of inheritance to their children, based on how well each child has prospered as an adult. The husband and wife wanted to try to equalize the worth of the children by bequeathing more of their estate to the children who were not as financially well off as their siblings, who were bequeathed proportionately less.

Eventually, after both the husband and wife pass away, the two children who received lesser amounts of their parents' estate feel cheated and believe that all of them should be treated equally. Since the parents' Wills explicitly called out the amount to be given to each child, the children go into court and fight over the issue, claiming that the parents wrote the Will ten or fifteen years before, placed it in a safe-deposit box, and never looked at it again. The children further claim that in the interim, specific different circumstances took place in their parents' lives, and if the parents could be brought back to the court today, they would make changes to their Will. Sadly, in situations like this, courts often overturn the wishes of the parents.

The problem presented in this example cannot apply to a good Living Trust. Time after time, disgruntled beneficiaries have attempted the same tactic of going to court to have the distribution of Trust assets changed—but to no avail. I am not yet aware of any such case where the court has overturned the desires explicitly set forth in a *good* Living Trust.

Transfer Your Assets into Your Living Trust

The subject of transferring assets into your Living Trust is covered in detail in my first book, *The Living Trust*, but I would like to address five areas that could be of possible concern to many people. Often it is not a question of *what* should be transferred, but of *how* the asset should be transferred. Let me cover the five most important assets that make up the greatest percentage of most people's estates: real estate, credit union accounts, securities, dividend reinvestment accounts, and bearer bonds.

Home or Other Real Estate

To transfer your home, or any real estate, into your Living Trust, you need to have the deed for each parcel redrawn in the name of your Trust and then recorded with the county recorder's office. The actual "transfer" takes place when you sign the deed and notarize it. Recording the deed with the county recorder's office has nothing to do with placing the deed inside your Living Trust, but it does protect you in the future with a clear title.

Most home mortgages (or mortgages on other real estate) are governed by the Federal Home Loan Insurance Board. Under its rules, transferring your home into a Living Trust has no effect on your mortgage's due-on-sale clause (a paragraph in your mortgage stating that the entire outstanding balance is due and payable if the house is sold). Therefore, the due-on-sale clause should not be triggered for transferring your own property into your own Living Trust. However, as a precautionary measure, I do recommend that you notify your mortgage lender that the retitling of the deed is simply a "paper transfer."

Credit Union Accounts

Typically, credit unions have been slow to recognize the Living Trust as a viable entity for titling your accounts. There is no basis, other than its own ignorance, for a credit union not allowing you to place your account in the name of your Living Trust. If a credit union refuses to allow you to transfer your account into your

Living Trust, a simple alternative solution is to fill out a Payable-on-Death Form for your checking and savings accounts. On this form, you simply name your Living Trust as the named beneficiary. Then, upon your death, your credit union assets would automatically be moved into your Living Trust.

Securities

I recommend that all of your securities be transferred into the name of your Living Trust. As Living Trusts are becoming more common, most financial institutions and securities dealers now provide special forms that easily allow you to title your securities in the name of your Living Trust. However, for those institutions that don't understand the Living Trust or refuse to allow your securities to be held in the name of your Living Trust, you can use the Uniform Transfer-on-Death Provision for your securities. This provision acts just like the Payable-on-Death Form for your credit union accounts. If you have difficulty with your transfer agent or brokerage firm, the alternative to filling out the Uniform Transfer-on-Death Provision is to name your Living Trust as the beneficiary—an elegantly simple solution.

Dividend Reinvestment Accounts

People who invest in stocks and/or mutual funds often overlook their dividend reinvestment accounts. Many people invest in stocks— and particularly in mutual funds—that have dividend reinvestment provisions. Particularly for investments in stocks, the brokerage firm typically sets up a dividend reinvestment account to temporarily hold the stock dividends that are paid. These dividend reinvestment accounts can very nicely increase in value. Although most people put the basic instrument (the stocks and/or mutual funds) into their Living Trusts, all too often they forget to also put the dividend reinvestment accounts into the name of their Living Trusts as well. Please recognize that the dividend rein-

vestment account is a separate account, and it needs to be transferred specifically into the name of your Living Trust.

Bearer Bonds

A bearer bond is an unsigned bond that may be cashed by whoever presents it for payment— very much like cash. Most people place their bearer bonds in their safe-deposit box. In addition, I recommend that you write up a Bill of Sale/Letter of Transfer that, in effect, transfers these bearer bonds into the name of your Living Trust. Then, simply place the Bill of Sale/Letter of Transfer in your safe-deposit box with the bearer bonds. That way, there is no question of the legal owner of the bonds.

What Must I Do to Settle My Living Trust?
When clients first create Living Trusts, for some reason they often are immediately concerned about how to settle their estates. Many clients ask, "What do we need to do to settle our estate in our Living Trust?" I usually smile and simply tell them, "You really began settling your estate when you created your Living Trust and put your assets inside the Trust." As you continue reading this book, you will see the simple truth in that statement.

ORGANIZE YOUR ESTATE

I conclude this chapter with a reminder of my recommendation that you tell your successor trustee where you keep your Trust. I further recommend that, not only should you have a specific place for your Trust, but you should organize your estate in an Estate Plan Binder. We provide an Estate Plan Binder for every one of our clients.

As you progress further through this book, you will see that the rules of the Living Trust "game" are relatively simple and that if you simply follow them, you *will* win—by preserving your estate from unnecessary federal estate taxes and providing your heirs with a pleasant legacy.

5

The First Step
Make Arrangements and Notify Institutions

The most difficult part of settling the estate of a beloved spouse, parent, or friend is overcoming our grief and immediately attending to the important matters, particularly to find out and follow the wishes of the deceased person. If you are the spouse of the newly deceased, your emotional state is understandably shaky—and you most likely are so overcome with grief that you cannot think clearly or rationally.

THE MOST DIFFICULT PART
In spite of the loss of a beloved spouse or parent, some important steps must be taken. First, you must make the appropriate arrangements for the deceased; then you have to notify various agencies, institutions, and employers that the person has died. The steps that need to be taken are really quite simple—but they often overwhelm us, since we are still grief-stricken and many times are in deep emotional shock.

The simple steps detailed in this chapter are those that you must take first. The actual settling of the estate can wait until later on.

Locate the Individual's Living Trust
We provide our clients with two copies of their executed Trusts. We recommend that they place one copy of their Trust in a safe place,

such as a safe-deposit box, and the second copy in their Estate Plan Binder. Again, remember to tell your successor trustees where your Trust documents are located. Your successor trustees will need to see your Living Trust, and they *must* know where it is kept, so that when you or your spouse die or become incompetent, your successor trustees can find your Trust.

During the past twenty years or so, I have encountered innumerable times that having a second *fully executed* copy of a Living Trust has been most important. All of us have the best of intentions about putting things away, but sometimes we don't get around to it. The following example points out what can happen to your own copy of your Living Trust.

A wonderful woman, Mary Hawthorne, was seriously afflicted with arthritis. Her pain was so great that she was almost incapacitated. She had a little crane in the trunk of her car that lifted her wheelchair in and out of her car, so that when she was traveling any distance from her car, she could do so in her wheelchair. One day, Ms. Hawthorne came to my office to make some changes to her Trust. After the changes were made, she signed the papers and put them in her Estate Plan Binder, and she left our office. Sadly, I later discovered that Mary Hawthorne died that night.

Mary's daughter and son-in-law, who were also clients of mine, came into my office quite upset because they could not find Mary's Estate Plan Binder, which had her Trust in it. Fortunately, a second fully executed copy of Mary's Trust was on file in our office, and we were able to locate the second copy for Mary's daughter.

Three months later, when Mary's daughter was cleaning out her mother's home to prepare it for sale, the daughter came upon a cardboard box in the garage. The box looked as if it contained only some recently purchased items; however, underneath lay the long-lost Estate Plan Binder with Mary's Trust in it. Apparently, upon returning home, Mary had set the carton aside, taken out her wheelchair, and gone into the house. Whether she became too ill to come back for the carton or simply forgot it, we will never know.

This example concerning Mary Hawthorne clearly shows the reason for executing *two* copies of your Living Trust and then placing them in separate locations.

Review Personal Data Sheet

If the deceased person has a good Living Trust, you should be able to find a personal data sheet among the Trust and its accompanying documents. The personal data sheet contains all the necessary historical information about the deceased that is needed by the mortuary to complete the death certificate.

A personal data sheet should contain the following items:

- Person's full name (including original middle name)
- Date of birth
- Place of birth (city and state/country)
- Full name of the father
- Father's place of birth
- Full name of the mother (including her maiden name)
- Mother's place of birth

- Date of person's marriage
- Place of person's marriage

Although this information seems quite elementary, few of us can recite from memory all of the above information for our spouse or especially for our parents. However, the information is required for the death certificate, so be sure to have this data available.

Let me relate to you a personal incident when my mother-in-law passed away.

I can well remember the passing of my mother-in-law. She had specifically requested that she be cremated and that there be no services for her.

One Sunday, following my mother-in-law's death, I asked my wife if she would like me to go to the funeral home to pick up her mother's ashes in order to save her from making an emotionally difficult trip, and she readily assented.

As I entered the funeral home, I was invited into the office, where they told me very nicely, "Before we turn the ashes over to you, we need some specific information. When and where was your mother-in-law born? What was the name of your mother-in-law's father, and where was he born? And what was the name of your mother-in-law's mother, including her maiden name, and where was she born?" At that point, I could only laugh, for I hadn't the slightest idea of the answers to those questions. I then said, "Excuse me, I don't have the answers in my head, but I'll return shortly with the answers."

I returned home, retrieved my mother-in-law's Estate Plan Binder that contained her personal data sheet and returned to the funeral home somewhat abashed. If anyone should have known better, I should have.

This personal experience is an excellent example of what all of us will be confronted with eventually. Where do we get such personal information, unless we make sure that it is recorded *now* and put in a known place, so that it is available when eventually needed?

If you haven't already created a personal data sheet of your own, you should do so now.

Your personal data sheet should include all of the information shown in the previous list. A personal data sheet is automatically provided with each of our Living Trusts.

Keep Accurate Records

I encourage you to keep accurate records of costs for the last illness and funeral for the deceased person. These expenses can be deducted on the deceased person's Form 1040 Individual Income Tax Return (or on the Form 706 Federal Estate Tax Return, if one must be filed). Expenses for the last illness and the funeral may be included on either tax form; the choice is yours.

Check Safe-Deposit Box

Immediately after the person's death, and *before* you make any funeral arrangements, I urge you to check the deceased person's safe-deposit box for special instructions or messages. Hopefully, the deceased person had the foresight to ensure that the surviving trustee or the successor trustees were authorized access to the safe-deposit box!

It is vitally important for you to make certain that your surviving spouse or successor trustees know where your safe-deposit box *key* (as well as your safe-deposit *box*) is located and, most important of all, that the appropriate individuals are authorized to enter the box. As well as placing your safe-deposit box in the name of your Living Trust, you should include at least one successor trustee on the signature card that grants access to your safe-deposit box.

Locate Veteran's Papers

If the individual who passed away was a veteran, locate the person's military discharge papers and take them with you to the funeral home. Each veteran is entitled to a $150 cemetery allowance, a burial flag, and a grave marker. The grave marker is usually a bronze plaque with the name, date of death, and the branch of service in which the individual served, as well as the dates of service. If the veteran was married, the spouse is entitled to be buried in the same plot, and the grave marker may also include the spouse's name.

If you wish to get further information about veteran's benefits, you can may call the Veterans' Administration at (800) 827-1000.

Cremation or Burial

Out of respect for the deceased person, you should attempt to determine the person's desires regarding burial or cremation. In a good Living Trust, you will find this desire listed in the section titled "Trustor's Last Request." In some states, the title to cemetery plots is transferable and may be put in the name of your Trust. If this situation applies to your state, I would suggest that you put your cemetery plot in the name of your Trust and also include a provision in your Trust that authorizes your surviving or successor trustee to transfer your cemetery plot. Of course, such a provision is meaningless in states that do not allow cemetery plots to be transferred. Many people may want these instructions to include additional information about where they want to be buried and even identify the plot if they have acquired one.

Unfortunately, not all people respect the last wishes of the deceased, and I must therefore offer a word of caution. The following story relates what can sometimes happen.

Many years ago, I had a client, Herbert Marsh, who was a world-renowned orthopedic surgeon. His wife, to whom he had been married for some fifty years, became afflicted with Alzheimer's disease and passed away some ten years later.

Six months following his wife's death, Herbert remarried. I have to assume that this lovely man, who had been married to a wife whom he loved so dearly, naturally assumed that all women were just as fine as his wife of 50-plus years. However, in the ensuing months, I could tell that this once very happy man was now quite unhappy. One day, Herbert came into my office to make some changes to his Trust. Shortly thereafter, I was shocked to learn that Herbert had been taken to the hospital because his prostate cancer had reoccurred. I also learned that his new wife had moved into the adjacent bed in his hospital room.

Herbert's new wife called me one day to tell me that, although she was aware that Herbert had specified in his Pour-Over Will that he was to be cremated and his ashes placed next to his former wife's ashes, she was not going to abide by that directive. She explained that she was Jewish, did not believe in cremation, and, therefore, was going to make certain that he would be buried in the same Jewish cemetery where the remains of Al Jolsen and Marilyn Monroe were interred.

The next day, Herbert died, and his children came to see me, quite upset over the recent turn of events. I had to advise them that, although they had the law on their side (the directive in the Pour-Over Will), the wheels of justice turn very slowly. I explained that they could go into court and have a court order immediately issued directing the funeral home to withhold any action on the body. However, I also had to explain to Herbert's children that they would then have to wait for about six weeks for the judge to uphold the directive. Unfortunately, when a loved one dies, the loss of the loved one creates an open wound that is not healed until closure is attained by either burial or cremation. Sadly, I had to ask Herbert's children if they really wanted to wait those six long weeks for closure, and their answer was obviously in the negative.

This sad case has been my only experience with this type of situation, where a surviving spouse refused to go along with the desires of the person who had passed away. Unfortunately, I know that such an experience won't be my last one. Every person should be allowed to make his or her own selection regarding the handling of and final resting place for his or her remains, but you must also be aware that your desires can be overridden and ignored.

Order Sufficient Death Certificates

Typically, most funeral homes will order about six death certificates. However, I recommend that you initially order at least one or two dozen copies of the death certificate. You will need one death certificate for each asset in the Trust.

Invariably, clients ask me, "Do I need a death certificate for every stock certificate?" The answer depends on how your stock certificates are held. If each stock certificate is registered in the name of the Trust, then the answer is yes, you will need a death certificate for each separate stock. On the other hand, if the stock certificates are held by your broker in a street account (that is, in the name of the brokerage firm), then you need only one death certificate for each brokerage firm. Additionally, you will need one death certificate for each insurance policy and each annuity, as well as each IRA, retirement plan, or pension.

It has been my experience that you can never have too many death certificates. If you wait and order these death certificates later, it may take you as long as four to six weeks to get the additional copies. Waiting for these extra death certificates simply delays the process of settlement.

NOTIFY INSTITUTIONS AND AGENCIES

Once you have completed the emotionally difficult actions of making the necessary funeral arrangements, you must be sure to notify a number of different agencies and institutions to inform them of the death. It is important to notify various agencies and companies so that they can stop monthly payments for such benefits as social security, company pensions, and annuity payouts. It is equally important, however, to notify the insurance companies where the deceased had insurance policies, to ensure that the estate is paid any amounts due from the insurance proceeds.

Social Security Administration

If the individual was receiving social security benefits, you need to notify the Social Security Administration that the individual has passed away. Be sure that you retain, in the deceased individual's bank account, any future social security checks that may continue to arrive on behalf of the deceased individual. The Social Security Administration will eventually contact the heirs or surviving spouse of the deceased person and ask for a refund of all excess payments made after the date of death.

You must also be aware that the surviving

spouse is eligible for social security survivor benefits. These benefits begin in the month of the date of death of the decedent spouse. The surviving spouse will need to provide a marriage certificate in order to establish his or her eligibility for the spousal social security benefits. If the surviving spouse is eligible for Medicare, such medical benefits will continue.

The Social Security Administration also provides a burial benefit for the deceased in the amount of $255.

Medicaid

If the deceased individual had been receiving Medicaid, you should notify Medicaid that the individual has passed away.

Former Employer(s)

Quite often, many of our elderly people were receiving some type of pension from their former employers. I suggest that you contact the company's human resources department to determine what employee benefits the company was providing and to inform them that one of their ex-employees has passed away. Many individuals have benefits such as insurance policies, stock options, and pension or retirement programs.

Military Retirement

If the deceased person served as a member of the armed forces, the bureau of personnel for the particular branch of service should be notified of the individual's death. Also notify the bureau of any surviving spouse who would be eligible for survivor's benefits and medical benefits.

Annuities and Insurance Policies

The next task that you need to do is to look for any annuities and insurance policies that may have been in force for the deceased person. You will need to notify the life insurance companies of the person's death and provide them with a *certified* copy of the death certificate for each policy and annuity. A certified copy of a death certificate is simply the copy that you received from the county recorder's office and that has been stamped with its seal indicating that the certificate is a "certified copy." Please be aware that most financial institutions do *not* accept photocopies of death certificates.

DON'T OVERLOOK IMPORTANT OBLIGATIONS

Once you have taken care of the deceased and notified the various agencies of the death, a few steps still remain to be completed—steps that are often overlooked by the grieving family members but that are nonetheless important.

Locate Credit Cards

You must locate the deceased individual's credit cards and then determine which credit cards should be changed into the name of the surviving spouse and which should be canceled. If you have an Estate Plan Binder, I suggest that you refer to the list of credit cards identified under the section entitled "Final Instructions."

Maintain Homeowner's Policies

A final word of caution is in order at this point. In the early stages of settling an estate, people are often distraught over the loss of a loved one. Being upset is a normal reaction, but please don't let your pain interrupt the necessities of life. Make sure, for example, that you don't let the fire and theft insurance policies lapse on the home and personal effects in the interim.

Pay Monthly Bills

During this time of such emotional distress, don't forget the monthly obligations of the deceased. Be sure that the ongoing monthly bills—especially the mortgage payment—continue to be paid!

Pay Real Estate Taxes

Don't forget to pay the real estate property taxes for assets in the Trust. If the surviving spouse is the trustee, it makes no difference whether the real estate taxes are paid from the income of the decedent's B sub-trust and/or C sub-trust or from the survivor's income. By year-end, the tax payments will be properly accounted for on the survivor's Form 1040 Individual Income Tax Return.

6

The Second Step
Settle Financial Matters

Now it is time for you to take the second step: settling the financial matters of the deceased person and his or her estate. Once you have taken care of the immediate needs of the deceased individual and his or her estate, many "administrative" tasks remain to be accomplished. Though the tasks mentioned in this chapter seem elementary, many of them are often overlooked due to the mental paralysis that most people experience as the result of losing a beloved spouse or parent.

DETERMINE THE NEED FOR PROBATE

Whoa! Why am I even mentioning the need for probate if the deceased individual had a Living Trust? Although I constantly espouse the theme of avoiding probate, there are rare instances where probating *only that part of an estate that is being challenged* can be the best solution to resolving a problem—without wasting time and expending exorbitant amounts of money on legal fees.

In two rare situations that may arise in settling an estate, probate provides a fairly rapid solution to often "questionable" claims. First, if any creditor claims have questionable validity or if any lawsuits are pending against the

deceased person, then the surviving trustee or successor trustees should seriously consider seeking a swift and favorable judgment from the probate court on those claims. Of course, for this step to be taken, the Living Trust must authorize the trustee to run Trust assets through probate. Second, if any assets of the deceased person have not been placed inside his or her Living Trust, those assets must go through the probate process.

If you must go through the probate process, I suggest that you go to a number of attorneys and ask them to give you *written* quotations on what they will charge to probate those specific assets. Take the lowest bid, since all probate filings are essentially the same. Do *not* let an unscrupulous attorney convince you that the assets need to be placed in a Testamentary Trust!

Lawsuits

Although the situation is highly unlikely, you need to determine whether any lawsuits are pending against the deceased person. In the unlikely event that such a suit is pending (i.e., has not been brought to trial and settled), the suit should be transferred and disposed of through the probate court rather than the regular judicial process. Invariably, lawsuits involve attorneys and juries, the process drags on interminably, the suit ends up being very costly, and the outcome is not necessarily just. The probate court, on the other hand, is responsible for preserving the deceased person's estate and settles any lawsuits swiftly and at the greatest benefit to the estate.

The Pour-Over Will

Do you really need to file a Pour-Over Will? Proper procedure would normally dictate that you always file the Pour-Over Will with the county recorder's office. If all assets are already in the Living Trust, such an act is redundant. However, if any assets have been inadvertently left outside the Trust, then the Pour-Over Will must be filed—and probated—for the assets outside the Living Trust.

Although filing the Pour-Over Will automatically invalidates all prior Wills and codicils, if everything is in the Living Trust, I consider the filing of the Pour-Over Will to be an unnecessary step. If all of the deceased person's assets are in the Living Trust, then there is nothing that a previously written Will could ever challenge. In fact, a well-written Pour-Over Will states in its first paragraph that all prior Wills are revoked automatically. Therefore, filing the Pour-Over Will would be meaningless and would simply clutter up the court's files. I believe that, similar to so many other issues, as people file more and more meaningless Pour-Over Wills, the courts will eventually take the necessary steps to see that such unnecessary filings cease. The courts don't want to be inundated by unnecessary paperwork any more than you do.

If any assets are inadvertently left outside the Trust and do need to go through probate, these assets will do so under the jurisdiction of the Pour-Over Will. Once the probate process is complete, these assets will automatically "pour over" into the decedent's B sub-trust and/or C sub-trust.

SETTLE FINANCIAL MATTERS

Most of us realize that the financial matters pertaining to the estate of the deceased must be finalized before we can fully determine the value of the estate. Most people remember that bills (such as the mortgage, utilities, and credit cards) must be paid, but almost no one remembers to check to see whether any money (such as loans or notes) is owed *to* the deceased person.

Collect Debts Owed

Determine whether any outstanding debts are owed to the estate. Collect any such debts before distributing any of the estate assets. The successor trustees seldom think about this step. The surviving spouse may be aware of such debts but often does not think about this subject during a time of such emotional distress. Be sure that you don't forget this important step.

Pay Debts Due

If the estate owes debts, you should pay off these debts. For notes and mortgages that have been paid on a monthly schedule, you need only continue the same scheduled payments. With a Living Trust, this type of debt does not become due and payable upon death (as it does in the probate process).

If any assets are left outside the Trust, you must determine who should make the payments to the creditors—the executor or the trustee. This situation, although rare, is an example of why it is appropriate to name one of the successor trustees as the executor.

TAKE INVENTORY OF ASSETS

Once you have settled the necessary legal and financial tasks, it is time to take inventory of all the estate assets. I am not talking about personal effects here, but rather the "real" assets (titled assets), such as real estate, stocks, bonds, mutual funds, checking accounts, and savings accounts. The first and most important concern is to determine the title in which each of these assets is held. You must ensure that all of these assets are already within the Trust. If the Trust documents and asset titles can be easily located, your job is much simplified.

In case you are uncertain about whether an asset is in the Trust, let me try to explain it with the simple examples in Table 6-1. The important thing to look for is how the document is addressed or how the "owner" is stated.

TABLE 6-1
DETERMINATION OF WHETHER ASSETS ARE IN TRUST BY WORDING OF OWNERSHIP

Items in the Trust	Items Not in the Trust
The Jones Family Trust	Mr. and Mrs. John Jones
John Jones and Mary Jones, Trustees	John and Mary Jones, Joint Tenants
John Jones, FBO* The Jones Trust	John and Mary Jones, JTWROS**

*FBO means "for the benefit of."

**JTWROS means "joint tenants with right of survivorship."

If you have an Estate Plan Binder, turn to the sections titled "Savings and Investment Documents," "Real Estate Documents," "Insurance Policies," and "Business Agreements and Documents." In these sections, you should be able to easily determine the title for all of the estate assets. Remember, however, that if any assets are left outside the Trust, those assets need to be probated. You must acknowledge the fact, find a good attorney, and start the probate process.

The reason for taking an inventory of all the assets is to get a complete list of what is in the deceased person's estate. The next chapter discusses how to determine the value of each asset, which is required for determining whether any inheritance taxes are due, as well as ensuring an equitable distribution of the assets to the heirs.

FILE NOTICE TO CREDITORS
For estates going through probate, it is standard procedure to file a Notice to Creditors. This filing puts the creditors on notice that, if they have claims against the estate, they must bring the claims forward or else lose their right to make such claims in the future. Typically, such notice will cut off creditors' claims in four months (i.e., if creditors do not file a claim within four months, they cannot collect on unpaid amounts that may be due to them).

About five years ago, California changed its statute to allow the surviving trustee or successor trustees of Living Trusts to also file a Notice to Creditors. This change was quickly picked up by the state of Washington and is beginning to be adopted by other states. As this book is being written, four states have adopted the Notice to Creditors: California, Idaho, Nevada, and Washington. Hopefully, many other states will adopt this progressive statute in the near future. Regardless of your particular state of residence, however, I recommend that you file a Notice to Creditors, even if the deceased has a Living Trust. Although the filing may lack statutory substance in your particular state, it establishes a legal precedent of its own (i.e., you legitimately attempted to notify any potential creditors).

The Notice to Creditors should be filed with the county clerk within three to six weeks following the date of death. Each state has its own form. To obtain the necessary form, you need only call the clerk of the county probate court and ask for a copy. An example of California's Notice to Creditors form appears in Figure 6-1 on page 56. The California form is typical of the form used by most states. Such a form may be used in those states that have not adopted the Notice to Creditors process.

Once you have filed the notice with the county clerk, you also need to have it published in the local newspapers. The notice must be published three times within fifteen days, with no more than five days between each notice.

Correctly performing this procedure for notice filing and publishing cuts off all spurious creditor claims after a period of four months has elapsed. By creditors, I refer to businesses and institutions that were not "normally" known and were not paid on a regularly scheduled plan. Such cases would consist primarily of unknown claims that might arise in the future. Filing the Notice to Creditors will force any unknown claims to be stated and made known to the survivors.

If the claims are valid, you can readily pay them. If the validity of a claim is questionable, a good Living Trust authorizes the surviving trustee or successor trustees to take the appropriate asset or assets outside the Trust and have

FIGURE 6-1
SAMPLE NOTICE TO CREDITORS

NOTICE TO CREDITORS

OF JOHN HOWARD JONES
#732854 [Case #]
SUPERIOR COURT OF CALIFORNIA
COUNTY OF LOS ANGELES

Notice is hereby given to the creditors and contingent creditors of the above-named decedent, that all persons having claims against the decedent are required to file them with the Superior Court, at 1547 Hill St., Los Angeles, CA, and mail a copy to Mary R. Jones, as trustee of the trust dated September 17, 1979, wherein the decedent was the settlor at 7832 Willow Lane, Los Angeles, CA 92101, within the later of four months after February 11, 1981 (the date of the first publication of notice to creditors) or, if notice is mailed or personally delivered to you, 30 days after the date this notice is mailed or personally delivered to you. A claim form may be obtained from the court clerk. For your protection, you are encouraged to file your claim by certified mail, with return receipt requested.

Mary R. Jones, Trustee
7832 Willow Lane
Los Angeles, CA 92101

the claim settled through probate in order to discharge it. The probate court is responsible for preserving the assets of an estate and therefore does not look favorably upon questionable claims. The court will uphold valid claims but will immediately dismiss questionable claims. When the deceased has a Living Trust, disposing of questionable or invalid claims against the estate of the deceased is one of the few instances where using the probate process can be beneficial. During my more than twenty-five years of experience with Living Trusts, I have found that less than 1 percent of the claims that arise need to be dealt with in probate court.

Please be aware, however, that when a Notice to Creditors has been filed, the trustees should delay any distribution of assets from the estate until the four-month time period has elapsed and all claims have been settled.

INHERITANCE TAXES
In addition to paying Uncle Sam for federal estate taxes, in many states you also must pay inheritance taxes (see Table E in Appendix E). Two states, Delaware and Louisiana, even require an income tax to be paid on death of the first spouse! However, more and more states are now following California's lead and have gone to a "pickup tax"—which is simply a percentage of the federal estate tax. Unfortunately, numerous states still follow the antiquated system of requiring the separate payment of inheritance taxes.

The more progressive states that have switched from requiring the separate payment of inheritance taxes and now employ the more realistic pickup tax are listed in Table 6-2, along with states that charge no tax at all.

Although payment of inheritance taxes is not one of the immediate tasks that you must do after the death of a loved one, you need to be aware that if inheritance taxes are owed, payment is due *in cold, hard cash* within nine months of the date of death. If inheritance taxes are due, don't wait until the last minute to try to come up with the necessary cash. Such a procrastinator's approach is most often very detrimental to the survivors and beneficiaries of the estate. Later in the book, this subject is described in much greater detail. To determine whether inheritance taxes are owed, you need to "value the assets" in the estate, which you will learn how to do in the next chapter.

Few people truly recognize the extent to which their hard-earned estates—their children's inheritance—can be consumed by the voracious bite of federal estate taxes and, often, state inheritance taxes. Proper estate planning can often eliminate or at least significantly reduce the impact of such estate taxes, as well as provide a means of paying any estate taxes due without requiring the forced sale of estate assets.

TABLE 6-2

STATES WITH NO INHERITANCE TAX

(OR ONLY A PICKUP TAX)

Alabama	Missouri
Alaska	Nevada
Arizona	New Mexico
Arkansas	New York
California	North Dakota
Colorado	Oregon
District of Columbia	Rhode Island
Florida	South Carolina
Georgia	Texas
Hawaii	Utah
Idaho	Vermont
Illinois	Virginia
Maine	Washington
Massachusetts	West Virginia
Michigan	Wisconsin
Minnesota	Wyoming

7

The Third Step

Determine the Value of the Estate

Now that you have taken care of the most time-critical tasks, you must take the next step in settling the estate: determining the value of the estate assets. This step involves a bit of work but can usually be done by the surviving spouse or by the successor trustees. I will point out the few situations that call for competent professional assistance.

Most people are unaware that the death of a loved one triggers an accounting practice, known as *stepped-up valuation*, that often can drastically reduce the potential capital gains taxes that must be paid on the estate assets of the deceased that have appreciated (grown in value). This chapter explains stepped-up valuation in greater detail.

There is a plethora of information in this chapter, and much of it does not apply to each individual estate. My advice to you, therefore, is to not read the entire chapter. Make your life simple, and read only those sections that apply to your estate.

ASSET VALUATION—
A MOST IMPORTANT STEP

Establishing the proper valuation for the estate assets is a vitally important step. You need this valuation to determine whether federal estate taxes are due (upon the death of the surviving spouse), to equitably apportion the assets into the appropriate survivor's A sub-trust and the decedent's B sub-trust and/or C sub-trust (upon the death of the first spouse), and to make equitable distribution of assets to the beneficiaries, as specified in the Living Trust.

Before you can proceed further, you need to value the assets. It is important that you determine the value of each asset as of the deceased person's date of death. You need to make a timely valuation and one that can be substantiated. Asset valuation is a very critical element in determining two factors: the ultimate value of the estate for estate tax purposes and the stepped-up valuation. Estate taxation is discussed in greater detail in the next chapter. All you really need to know at this point is that if the estate exceeds $625,000 (for a single person) or $1.25 million (for a married couple), federal estate taxes will ultimately be due and payable. (Remember that the individual exemption will rise to $1 million by the year 2006, an increase that will provide little benefit to most estates because it doesn't keep pace with inflation.) Stepped-up valuation is quite critical, affects any capital gains tax on the future sale of an asset, and is usually very beneficial to the estate and potential heirs.

Don't Delay Valuing and Allocating Assets

The IRS gets very irritated if a substantial period of time passes before the estate assets are valued and then allocated to the appropriate A sub-trust, B sub-trust, and/or C sub-trust. A delay in valuing the assets can cause two problems:

- If the asset appreciates (rises in value) during the time between the date of death and the time of valuation, the IRS will take the position that your valuation was biased and will probably challenge it.
- If you delay in allocating the assets (six to nine months from the date of death), you need to apply for a separate federal tax identification number for the Trust for this "administrative period." You also then need to file a final Form 1041 U.S. Income Tax Return for Estates and Trusts for the administrative period—and you incur much *unnecessary* confusion associated with a temporary taxpayer.

I cannot emphasize enough the importance of valuing the estate assets as soon as possible. Please do not get caught in the IRS quagmire that could result from a lengthy delay.

Later on, this chapter will cover in greater detail the subject of how to value the various assets of an estate.

Obtain Written Valuation of Real Assets

It is absolutely essential that you obtain written valuation of the estate's real assets, but it is equally important that the written valuation be realistic and substantiated. By the term *real asset*, I mean an asset that is titled (such as a home or other real estate), as well as an asset that has named owners associated with it (such as stocks, bonds, and mutual funds). Obtaining written valuations of an asset (which help substantiate its value if the IRS ever challenges it) is really quite simple, as is explained later in this chapter.

A classic example of what *not* to do when determining the value of an asset and not sub-

stantiating the valuation can be best illustrated with the case of Harry and Ida Hamilton.

Harry Hamilton died, leaving an estate of $3 million. Harry and Ida had a Married A-B Living Trust. Ida asked the family attorney to settle the estate. However, the family attorney, although a good friend, had never settled a Living Trust before. The attorney valued the home at $600,000 and placed it in the decedent's B sub-trust. The attorney then proceeded to file his first Form 706 U.S. Estate (and Generation-Skipping Transfer) Tax Return, having almost no idea what he was really doing. Form 706 was entirely *unnecessary* for Harry's estate, since no federal estate tax was due on the first spouse to die and there was no decedent's C sub-trust, or QTIP Trust, to elect. Furthermore, the Form 706 filed by the attorney was fraught with errors!

Two and a half years after the attorney had filed Form 706 for Harry's estate, the IRS came back and challenged the valuation of the home. The IRS estimated the home to be worth $1 million! Unfortunately, the attorney had no documentation for his off-the-cuff valuation of the home, and therefore, there was nothing in writing that could be used to support the original valuation of $600,000.

Since there was no *substantiated* documentation, the IRS valued the home at $1 million and then assessed penalties and interest for the difference between the original $600,000 valuation and the IRS value of $1 million. Besides assessing $160,000 in federal estate taxes, the IRS further assessed penalties and interest for the preceding two and a half years!

Ida then found it necessary to engage the services of an experienced estate-planning attorney to help resolve this disaster. To add insult to injury, the legal fees from the new attorney amounted to another $25,000.

The sad part of this story is that the entire incident never should have happened. The filing of the error-laden Form 706 was totally unnecessary, and the filing is what triggered the IRS audit. The point to remember is that the home should have been valued realistically, and the valuation should have been substantiated in writing—otherwise, it is incredibly difficult to battle against the IRS. Later in this chapter, I will tell you just how easy it is to get written and substantiated valuations on real estate.

Valuation Date

Surprisingly, you have two choices of time periods for valuing the estate assets. You may value the assets as of the date of death or six months later. (Using the latter date is basically meaningless, upon the death of the first spouse, since no estate taxes are due.) If you use the alternate valuation date (six months following date of death), you must include the *entire estate* in the revaluation. For example, maybe the home has lost value, but the stocks have increased in value; however, the latest value of *all* assets must be taken into consideration for the revaluation. In practicality, there is little merit to using the alternate valuation date unless there has been a drastic change in the estate valuation. Also, be aware that using the alternate valuation date of six months after the death of a decedent usually raises a red flag to the IRS and often triggers an audit of the estate.

Stepped-Up Valuation

One of the important benefits to a married couple with an A-B Living Trust is that stepped-up valuation can be achieved (for the benefit of the estate) when *each* of the pair dies. Stepped-up valuation can significantly reduce the amount of capital gains tax that your estate may have to pay upon the death of the second (surviving) spouse.

Few people understand the concept of stepped-up valuation. Allow me to digress and explain to you how this important concept works. Recall from the first chapter of this book the story of a family who owned a farm consisting of 600 acres, estimated to be worth $1,000 an acre. The couple was stunned when the realization struck home that the farm was worth $600,000, since their income was only about $17,000 a year! This husband and wife were "paper wealthy"—asset rich but cash poor. Back in 1978, if one spouse died, a federal estate tax of $90,000 would be due on half of the farm. The only way to pay that federal estate tax was to sell the farm, but since the

husband had acquired the farm at basically zero cost basis, the sale would trigger a capital gains tax of $120,000. The survivor would have to sell the farm and pay $120,000 in capital gains tax in order to pay the original $90,000 of federal estate tax! In effect, the family would be forced to pay a "tax upon a tax."

President Reagan's Tax Reform Act of 1981 recognized the unfairness of imposing a tax upon a tax. The revised tax code allowed the surviving spouse or heirs to use the appreciated value of the asset as its new cost basis. For the farm couple, following the 1981 tax change, the farm's new cost basis (after a spouse died) would become $600,000 instead of almost zero. Thus, if the farm were later sold, the sale would not incur a capital gains tax (saving the surviving spouse an additional $120,000). This stepped-up valuation made more sense and was certainly fairer. Simply stated, "stepped-up valuation" means that, upon the death of a spouse, the survivor gets the decedent's share of assets at their then-current market value, which is used as the new cost basis for the asset.

Let me illustrate the concept of stepped-up valuation with a more lengthy example that will lead you step by step through the process.

Let's assume that you originally bought your home for $50,000; that amount would be considered your cost basis. Let's further assume that you have lived in that home for fifteen years, and the house is now worth $200,000. Finally, assume that you and your spouse own the home in joint tenancy as husband and wife.

	Husband and Wife	
Market value	$200,000	
Cost basis	$ 50,000	OURS

If you own the home in joint tenancy with your spouse, for tax purposes the IRS effectively cuts the home in half, with the husband owning one-half of the house and the wife owning the other half of the house. This IRS interpretation means that each spouse owns half a home worth $100,000 and with a cost basis of $25,000.

	Husband			Wife
Market value	$100,000	HIS	HERS	$100,000
Cost basis	$ 25,000			$ 25,000

Now, let's further assume that the husband is the first to die. The cost basis for the husband's half of the house would receive a special tax benefit called stepped-up valuation—whereby his former cost basis of $25,000 jumps up to be the same as the current market value (for his half) at the date of his death. The new cost basis for the husband's half of the home would now be $100,000, but not so for the wife's half of the house. Her cost basis stays at the original $25,000. Since the home is owned in joint tenancy, however, the wife would inherit a home worth $200,000 (its current market value), along with her husband's new cost basis of $100,000, and she would retain her original cost basis of $25,000.

The surviving spouse now ends up with a home that is worth $200,000 and has a combined cost basis of $125,000. If the surviving spouse decided to sell the home, she would recognize a taxable gain of only $75,000—substantially better than the taxable gain of $150,000 that the couple would have to recognize if they had sold their home while they both were living.

	HIS	HERS	
	Husband	Wife	Survivor
Market value	$100,000	$100,000	$200,000
Cost basis		$ 25,000	($ 25,000)
Stepped-up valuation	$100,000		($100,000)
Taxable gain			$ 75,000

Let's continue this same example and assume that the surviving wife lives in the home for another ten years. During that time, the home continues to increase in value and is now worth $300,000. If the surviving spouse dies, the cost basis for her half of the house now receives stepped-up valuation. The new cost basis for the entire house now becomes the market value ($300,000) at the date of her death. Her children, as her beneficiaries, inherit a home that is worth $300,000 and has a cost basis of $300,000. If the children decide to sell the home, they would have no capital gain (and no taxes to pay)!

BENEFICIARIES		
Market value	OURS	$300,000
Cost basis		($300,000)
Taxable gain		$ 0

I caution you, however, to be aware of the "gotcha" in the Taxpayer Relief Act of 1997. Although Congress has provided a $250,000 homeowner's exemption for real estate (i.e., the first $250,000 is exempt from capital gains tax), in order to qualify for the enhanced exemption, you must have lived in the home for two of the past five years. This requirement means that, following the death of the surviving spouse (or an individual if single), in most instances of estate settlements, the $250,000 exemption will have little meaning for the beneficiaries. This exemption will only be beneficial if the surviving spouse decides to sell the home. Now, here is the catch. Most parents think of passing their home to their children after the death of one or both parents. However, in almost all cases, the children will not qualify for the homeowner's exemption, since they have not lived in the house for two of the past five years. For most people's estates, the beneficiaries will not qualify for the enhanced exemption—and stepped-up valuation continues to retain its importance.

In July 1998, Congress approved a modification to the Taxpayer Relief Act of 1997 (retroactive to January 1, 1998) that sets the capital gains tax rate at 20 percent for assets held for at least twelve months, and at 18 percent for assets held for at least five years. (The 18 percent capital gains tax rate becomes effective in 2001.) Remember, however, that by using stepped-up valuation, you can avoid, or at least minimize, any capital gains tax.

Although I have illustrated the concept of stepped-up valuation on a home, this concept applies to almost *every* asset—be it real estate, stocks, bonds, mutual funds, or other appreciating assets. Stepped-up valuation is a crucial reason to value the estate—and then to document that valuation.

Series EE Bonds

From a tax standpoint, you need to be aware of the fact that Series EE bonds do not receive stepped-up valuation because all income from a Series EE bond is taxable. However, you may show all income from the Series EE bonds on the decedent's final Form 1040 Individual Income Tax Return and may deduct final medical and funeral expenses from such income.

Asset Valuation for Estate Taxation

The federal estate tax is based on the *net* value of your estate, meaning the stepped-up value of the asset, less any liabilities such as a mortgage. The top of Table 7-1 shows the net value of a home that is retained in a Trust. When an asset is sold, you can also reduce the asset value by the amount of the brokerage fee or commission you paid, as shown on the bottom in Table 7-1.

TABLE 7-1
VALUATION OF A HOME FOR ESTATE TAXATION

Home Retained in Trust

Market value	$300,000
Less: Mortgage	($100,000)
Part of taxable estate	$200,000

Home Sold

Market value	$300,000
Less: Mortgage	($100,000)
Less: Real estate fee	($ 18,000)
Part of taxable estate	$182,000

When getting assets valued (after the death of a spouse, for example) or selling an asset, there is an important aspect that almost everyone overlooks, since we are all conditioned to "get the most from it." In some situations, however, it may *not* be in the best interest of your estate to sell (or value) an asset at its highest worth. As a general rule, if you won't have to pay estate taxes, you want the highest fair market value; but if your estate is large enough to owe estate tax, then, typically, you want the lowest fair market value (because the lower the value, the lower the estate tax).

Although stepped-up valuation is important, its value is only relative. Stepped-up valuation can eliminate capital gains taxes, allowing you to avoid the 20 percent capital gains tax (if the asset has been held for at least twelve months). On the other hand, you must be aware that the federal estate tax ranges from 37 percent up to 55 percent (37 to 55% if you are single, 40 to 55% if you are married). I don't know about you, but I am always willing to *pay* a 20 percent capital gains tax in order to *avoid* a 37 percent to 55 percent federal estate tax! To qualify for the lower 20 percent tax rate, however, the individual must have held the asset for at least twelve months.

You also need to be aware of an unexpected boon to the taxpayer. The IRS grants stepped-up valuation on the death of an individual, but the time clock for capital gains computation continues from the original date of acquisition by the deceased person and continues on to the Trust and to the beneficiaries. For example, let's assume that an individual bought a parcel of real estate for $100,000 two years ago. When the individual dies, the real estate is worth $200,000, so the cost basis receives stepped-up valuation to the current market value of $200,000, yielding a new cost basis of $200,000. A year later, the real estate appreciates to $300,000 and is distributed to a beneficiary, who decides to sell it. The beneficiary inherits a $300,000 parcel of real estate with a cost basis of $200,000, yielding a taxable capital gain of $100,000. The beneficiary is able to use the decedent's purchase date; therefore, the capital gain would be taxed at the 20 percent rate, since the asset has been held (from the time of its initial purchase) for more than twelve months.

SPECIFIC ASSET VALUATION

It is important to understand that *each* asset must be specifically valued and the valuation clearly documented for possible later substantiation by the IRS. When you begin this process of asset evaluation, I suggest that you review the Living Trust documents and determine which assets, if any, have been identified as separate property in the Separate Property Agreements. Separate assets of the surviving spouse are not included when determining the value of the deceased person's estate. All other assets in the estate will be treated as shared marital assets.

Bank and Credit Union Accounts

Quite often, one of the most frustrating tasks in settling a person's estate is trying to determine all of the financial institutions where the deceased person has checking accounts, savings accounts, money market accounts, CDs, and a safe-deposit box. If you are lucky and the deceased person had organized his or her estate assets, your task should be simplified by finding his or her Estate Plan Binder and turning to the tab entitled "Savings and Investment Documents." There you should find a complete list providing you with the name, address, and account number of each account of the deceased person. Otherwise, you will need to set out on a treasure hunt by digging through old mail or finding where past account statements have been stored. Good luck!

It is important that you identify the various accounts and then obtain a statement from each institution to determine the value at the date of death. Quite often, the simplest way to do this task is to find the most recent account statement or to wait until the next monthly statement arrives in the mail.

Securities

To value stocks, bonds, and mutual funds, use the stock market's closing value on the date of death or six months later. Since most people with a portfolio of stocks and bonds have a brokerage account, the easiest way to accomplish the valuation of the deceased person's account is to simply ask the brokerage firm to provide you with a valuation of the stocks and bonds on the date of death.

Another alternative is to purchase a copy of the *Wall Street Journal* on the date of death and then save it for future substantiation of the portfolio valuation. If you are one of the ever-increasing number of individuals who is computer literate, you can usually obtain the necessary portfolio price quite easily by using your computer and Web browser. Remember to save your printouts for later substantiation if you are ever challenged by the IRS.

Identification Number

Although some attorneys insist on changing the taxpayer identification number for the stocks and bonds to the decedent's B sub-trust and/or C sub-trust identification number, I strongly oppose this unnecessary step. Once you identify which stocks, bonds, and mutual funds are to be placed into the B sub-trust and/or C sub-trust, the easiest and most flexible approach is to simply ask the brokerage firm and mutual fund companies to list those accounts under the surviving spouse's social security number and to differentiate those accounts by recording them as Account B. Once the securities are titled in this way, the brokerage firm automatically does the accounting for you. However, you still have the flexibility of being able to transfer these assets if desired. The subject of asset transfers is treated thoroughly later in this book.

Upon the death of the surviving spouse (or an individual if single), if any securities (stocks, bonds, and mutual funds) are retained in the Trust, then the taxpayer identification number for those assets should be changed to the Trust identification number (from the social security number of the deceased person). For a Married A-B Trust or a Married A-B-C Trust, the new number would be the Employer Identification Number (EIN) assigned to the Trust by the IRS upon the death of the first spouse. For an individual, the new number would be the Trust identification number assigned by the IRS for the individual's Trust. You would retain assets in the Trust, for future distribution, if the Trust specified that certain beneficiaries were not to receive assets until some future date (e.g., until a beneficiary reached a certain age).

Remember: Use only one Trust identification number for the sub-trusts—first for the decedent's B sub-trust and C sub-trust, and then for the survivor's A sub-trust.

If the assets are to be distributed, then they should be transferred to the beneficiary and should utilize the social security number of that beneficiary. To accomplish this change in taxpayer identification number, you obtain Form W-9 from the IRS or the brokerage firm and submit it to the IRS.

Naming the Accounts

Upon the death of the first spouse, the surviving spouse should rename the securities accounts in the following manner. Let's assume that, before the death of the first spouse, the couple's Living Trust read, "The Doe Family Trust, dated November 7, 1992, John Doe and Mary Doe, Trustors and Trustees." Let's also assume that John and Mary moved their assets into their Living Trust, and therefore, their brokerage account would be in the name of their Trust, and John's social security number would be used as the taxpayer identification number. If John were to pass on, Mary would have each of the accounts' taxpayer identification numbers changed over to her social security number, but the accounts would still be in the name of the Trust—the name on the accounts remains the same.

However, to make future accounting simple, the account names for each security would be amended (by the addition of "Account A," and/or "Account B") to designate into which of the sub-trusts each asset had been placed. The suffix "Account A" would be used for the assets in the survivor's A sub-trust, the suffix "Account B" for the assets retained in the decedent's B and/or C sub-trusts. For example, the title for the assets in the B and/or C sub-trusts would read, "The Doe Family Trust, dated November 7, 1992, John Doe and Mary Doe, Trustors, and Mary Doe, Trustee, Account B." Simply adding the proper suffix to the account registration for each asset should require no extra effort from the surviving spouse, other than to give specific instructions to the brokerage firm on how to title each asset.

Upon Mary's death, all of the assets would retain the original Trust name, but the Trust name would be amended to include the change of trustees, specifying the names of the successor trustees. Assume that there are two children, Robert and Sarah, who become the successor trustees. The registration of the assets would now read, "The Doe Family Trust, dated November 7, 1992, Robert Doe and Sarah Doe, Successor Trustees." Thereafter, the name of the accounts need not be changed until the assets are finally transferred from the Trust to the beneficiaries.

Guaranteed Signature

Upon Mary's death, the stock brokerage accounts would presumably pass on to the beneficiaries. However, if the Trust so specified, the accounts might be retained in trust until such time as the Trust specifies that the assets are to be distributed to the beneficiaries. The latter would apply if the Trust language specifies that the trustee is to distribute the assets to the children, for example, at ages 25, 30, and 35, and the children have not yet attained those ages. Regardless of whether the assets are to be distributed to the beneficiaries or to be retained in trust, the brokerage account will need a guaranteed signature from the trustee directing the transfer of the assets. This guaranteed signature is required by the transfer agent for all securities; it is a standard requirement for brokerage transactions and need not cause concern.

Unlike having a document notarized, you can have your signature guaranteed only through a bank or a major stock brokerage firm. The transfer agent will usually require a certified copy of the death certificate, as well as a copy of the Living Trust Abstract for the financial institution. The abstract is simply a legal summary of the Trust. Sometimes, in lieu of the abstract, the transfer agent may require a complete copy of the Living Trust or only a Trust Certification form. Certification of Trusts is discussed in the next chapter.)

Annuities

If the estate includes any annuities, ask the insurance company or an experienced financial advisor to determine the accumulated value of the annuity or of the death benefit if the deceased was named as the annuitant. If the deceased was the annuitant, you will need to submit a certified copy of the death certificate to the insurance company in order to collect the death benefit proceeds of the annuity.

Insurance Policies

The next items to look for are any insurance policies, especially those where the deceased person was named as an insured. Identify all insurance policies in the estate assets. If the deceased person was named as the insured on any of the policies, then you need to notify the insurance company that a death has occurred and that an insurance benefit is due. As with annuities, the insurance company will require a certified copy of the death certificate for each insurance policy paying a death benefit.

If there are any insurance policies on the life of the surviving spouse, you need to determine the cash value of each such insurance policy, since the cash value of each policy must be included in the value of the estate. To do that you need to contact the insurance company and request that it provide you with the cash value in the survivor's policy as of the date requested (the date of death of the first spouse). Use IRS Form 712.

Please keep in mind, however, that if the insurance policies have previously been placed in an Insurance Trust, and if the Insurance Trust and the insurance policies have been properly drawn, then these policies will be excluded from the estate. In that case, they are not included when calculating the value of the estate for estate or inheritance tax purposes.

Real Estate

When a person who has a Living Trust dies, it is very important that you obtain realistic (and able to be substantiated) evaluations of the worth of each piece of real estate in the estate. This step is especially important if the value of the real estate has increased sizably since it was purchased, since the surviving spouse or heirs can benefit greatly by taking advantage of stepped-up valuation to reduce or eliminate any future capital gains taxes when the real estate is eventually sold.

For a very valuable piece of real estate, I suggest that you spend $150 to $300 for a professional real estate appraiser to appraise the current value of your real estate. For most other pieces of real estate, ranging from $100,000 to $500,000, it is my opinion that you only need to call two different real estate brokers from two different companies. Tell them that you have always been interested in the possibility of selling that particular piece of real estate and would like to get a written estimate of its market value. Be sure to request the real estate brokers to back up their estimates by including "comparables" (sales of similar pieces of real estate in the near vicinity in the recent past). If you so desire, you may also request that the real estate broker value your real estate on either the high or the low side of the current market. Such a request is very appropriate, as long as the resultant valuation is not out of line. If the valuations from the two brokerage firms are reasonably close, you need only to calculate the average between the two valuations and use the average as the current value for that particular piece of real estate. However, if the valuations are far apart, as sometimes happens, I suggest that you ask a third real estate brokerage firm to give you its valuation for the same property. Then, looking at all three valuations, simply take the two closest valuations and calculate the average between those two.

As I have said before, once you have established a valuation for each piece of real estate in the Trust, make sure that you substantiate the valuation by putting all the written documentation (the written letters of valuation and comparables) in a safe place, so that you can use the documentation in the future to justify the valuation.

I cannot stress strongly enough the necessity of obtaining real estate valuations in a timely manner—within the first month after death, *not* months or years later! Let me share with you yet another example of what can occur when attorneys who are unskilled in settling estates in a Living Trust procrastinate and fail to appropriately value assets and allocate them within the Trust.

In 1987, Martha Howard came to me with a dilemma. Her husband Jim had died six years earlier. The couple had a Living Trust, but unfortunately the couple's assets had been left outside the Trust. As a result, the assets had to go through probate. Eventually, the firm that drew up the couple's Living Trust took the assets through probate. Immediately following her husband's death, Martha realized that the estate assets had to be allocated to the survivor's A sub-trust and the decedent's B sub-trust. She hounded the legal firm in an effort to get this simple task accomplished, but all she received in response were costly bills for her telephone calls—and no action. After a full six years of this frustration, Martha had become so uncomfortable with the lack of proper Trust asset allocation and documentation that she came to me for help.

My challenge was to determine the valuation of her assets—some six years earlier! I can assure you that with the rapid rise of real estate prices during that period in southern California, my task was almost impossible. I eventually solved the dilemma by taking the valuations as set forth by Martha's law firm for the probate court. Based on those asset valuations, I made the appropriate allocations to the A sub-trust and the B sub-trust.

However, I did make a very careful footnote that the valuations were based on the law firm's probate documents as submitted to the court. The purpose of the footnote was to make it very clear, if there were ever a challenge to Martha's estate, where the liability for the original valuations existed.

The point of this story is to show you that it is very simple to make the valuation of real estate near the date of death. However, when you go much beyond this period of time, it becomes difficult, and almost impossible, to successfully defend your valuation—a difficulty that can be very costly to the estate.

Retitling Real Estate

Many attorneys will go through the time and expense to "retitle" real estate placed in the decedent's B sub-trust and/or C sub-trust. However, I oppose this unnecessary approach and prefer to resolve this issue by using the ledger method, which is discussed in the next chapter. You need to be very aware that if you retitle part or all of the estate's real estate in the name of the decedent's B sub-trust and/or C sub-trust, the property may be subject to property tax reappraisal. In addition, you also lose the $250,000 capital gains exemption on that part of the property identified as being in the Trust, because the exemption applies to an individual only, and not to a Trust. In Chapter 8, you will learn how to place part or all of the real estate in the decedent's B sub-trust and/or C sub-trust by using the ledger method and then later on make a transfer back to the survivor's A sub-trust on a dollar-for-dollar transfer—thus avoiding tax reappraisal and yet still being able to claim the $250,000 exemption.

Upon the death of the surviving spouse, the real estate should be retitled. If the real estate is to be distributed outright, I recommend that you delay retitling the real estate until the asset is actually distributed. At that time, the asset should be retitled in the name of the beneficiary(s).

When you retitle a real estate deed, I recommend that you use a Trust Warranty Deed instead of a Quitclaim Deed or a Grant Deed. By using a Trust Warranty Deed, you will retain the original warranties, whereas a Grant Deed only passes title to the property. You can easily make such a transfer yourself by going to the transfer company and asking it to retitle the deed. Most companies will readily do so and will usually only charge you the recording fee, which is typically about $10.

When you retitle a deed, I suggest that you include a Preliminary Change of Ownership form, if appropriate. Using this form helps to establish that no tax is due as a result of this transfer.

The Preliminary Change of Ownership form is absolutely essential if you are going to transfer title of all or part of the real estate into the decedent's B sub-trust and/or C sub-trust, or if you retain only part of the real estate in the survivor's A sub-trust. Using a Preliminary Change of Ownership form can eliminate, or at least reduce, the potential for the title transfer to trigger a property tax reappraisal.

As mentioned earlier, a simpler approach is not to retitle the deed at all, but to use the ledger method, more fully described in the next chapter.

Again, I urge you to make sure that you keep copies (not the originals) of all real estate deeds with your Living Trust. The Estate Plan Binder provides a convenient place under the tab titled "Real Estate." If you are missing a deed, you can request a duplicate copy of it, for a very reasonable fee, from the county recorder's office in the state and county where the real estate is located. As with all important documents, I strongly recommend that you keep all the original deeds in your safe-deposit box.

Outright Distribution of Real Estate

Following the death of a single individual or the death of the surviving spouse, if the assets are to be distributed outright, I recommend that real estate be directly transferred (by change of title) to the beneficiaries, rather than being sold and the resultant cash proceeds then being distributed. Taking this course of action is beneficial in two ways:

- You eliminate unnecessary real estate fees and commissions.
- You are able to pass on to the beneficiary any tax loss on the real estate.

Remember that a Trust cannot use a loss on real estate to offset other Trust income. If the beneficiaries do not want the home and there is no loss to consider, then it could be advantageous to sell the real estate while in the Trust, in order to use the real estate sales fee as a deduction from the cost basis of the real estate, thus reducing any potential capital gains tax.

Here is a short example to illustrate the points just mentioned.

In 1992, Bob Stokes told me that his father had died. Bob further related to me that his father had a Testamentary Trust and had named his bank as the executor and trustee. The estate had been tied up in probate for almost three years and was now about to be closed. The bank had placed the home in the Testamentary Trust and was about to sell it.

Bob's concern was that during the past two years, the home had lost substantial value, and he was not sure that selling the home was the best thing to do. I informed Bob that a Trust cannot distribute a loss. Therefore, if the bank sold the home and realized a loss on the sale (i.e., received less cash for the home than the original appraisal price), the loss could not be passed on to the beneficiary. A tax loss is retained, unused, within the Trust.

I recommended to Bob that he have the bank distribute the home outright to him by transferring title to him. Thereafter, Bob could sell the home and realize the loss himself, using it as a write-off on his income tax. Bob did as I recommended and reported the loss against his income on his Form 1040 Individual Income Tax Return for that year.

BUSINESS INTEREST

Following the death of a business owner, the business often deteriorates substantially and quickly. When there is a business interest in the Trust, it is, therefore, most significant for you to consider both the initial business valuation (at date of death) and also the alternate valuation date (six months after date of death).

If there is any question as to whether or not there is a business interest in an estate, you can usually find out by looking at the deceased individual's income tax returns for the past five years. Look specifically for a Schedule C form. Schedule C identifies any business-related deductions. Finding a Schedule C could be the start of your trail to finding that business interest. If you find that there is, indeed, a business interest in the Trust, you need to then attempt to locate any business agreements and determine what action, disposition, and benefits there might be.

Buy/Sell Agreement

You need to find out if there is a Buy/Sell Agreement, and whether or not it is funded with life insurance. Every business should have a Buy/Sell Agreement, because such an agreement substantiates the value of the business—since the joint owners have, in effect, agreed on the value of their individual shares. Historically, the IRS will value the business at the highest value possible. In contrast, if there is a Buy/Sell Agreement in effect for the business, the tax courts have upheld that the value stated in the Buy/Sell Agreement, even if seriously understated, is the value to be used for estate tax purposes.

To a great extent, a Buy/Sell Agreement is only as good as the funding behind it. Every Buy/Sell Agreement should have current life insurance in place to fund the agreement. If there is a funded Buy/Sell Agreement, you immediately know the value of the business. Most Buy/Sell Agreements stipulate that, when one of the joint business owners dies, the surviving business owners buy out the business interest of the deceased person. The business interest of the deceased person must be transferred to the surviving business owners in exchange for the estate receiving the stipulated buyout dollars, which are provided by the life insurance.

Competent Appraisal

If there is no Buy/Sell Agreement for a business interest of the deceased person, you must find a *competent* business appraiser to value the business. Be aware that there are at least fourteen different methods that the IRS could use to value the deceased person's business—and the IRS will use the method that yields the highest value! Therefore, without a Buy/Sell Agreement, your next line of defense is a good appraiser. I recommend that you have the business's attorney hire the appraiser, because attorney/client privilege prevents the IRS from hiring that same appraiser.

The business valuation is an essential step,

even when there is no estate tax to pay on the death of the first spouse. Such a valuation determines the new cost basis for the decedent's share of the business and will then permit all or part of the business interest to be placed in the decedent's B sub-trust and/or C sub-trust.

Different Business Types

As you are no doubt well aware, there are different types of business entities, ranging from sole proprietorships to large multinational corporations. However, when there is a business interest involving a deceased individual, the type of business usually falls into one of the following categories:

- Sole proprietorship
- Partnership
- Corporation
- Professional corporation
- Qualified sub-chapter S corporation
- Limited-liability corporation
- Family limited partnership
- Limited partnership

Sole Proprietorship

A sole proprietorship is a business typically owned and operated by an individual or a married couple. There is no formal "title" for such an entity. The most common way to place a sole proprietorship into a Living Trust is with a Bill of Sale/Letter of Transfer.

Since the business depends upon a single individual or a married couple, the loss of the key individual can be devastating. Usually, sole proprietorships deteriorate rapidly following the death of an individual owner. If the sole proprietorship is to be sold, it should be done soon after the person's death and while the business is still functioning. The principal business assets to be sold are the equipment, the inventory, and the goodwill.

Partnership

A partnership is a business typically owned and operated by two or more persons. Most partnerships fail to have a formal written partnership agreement. In this case, a Bill of

Sale/Letter of Transfer is used to place the partnership into a Living Trust.

The statutes specify that a partnership entity ceases upon the death of a partner, and if the surviving partner or partners continue the business, they are fully responsible for any new liabilities incurred. If it is desirable to continue the partnership, the remaining partners should enter into a new partnership agreement, for the protection of all parties.

Ideally, each of the partners in a partnership should have Buy-Sell Agreements, funded with life insurance, so that the deceased partner can quickly be bought out and the surviving partner(s) can re-form as a new partnership. Please be aware that, if the new partnership is to be included in the decedent's B sub-trust and/or C sub-trust, the trustee of the Living Trust *must* be named as a partner of the partnership.

Corporation

What most people think of as a corporation is known as a C Corporation. Ownership is formalized in the form of stock certificates, which may be privately held or openly traded on the public stock exchanges. Stock certificates should be retitled in the name of the individual's Living Trust.

Upon the death of the individual, whether the sole owner and president or one of the key officers of the corporation, the corporation lives on as an entity, without burdensome piles of bureaucratic red tape. Any corporate income is chargeable to the corporate entity for income tax purposes. If the income is passed on to the shareholders, the income is considered dividends and taxed again to the individual recipient as ordinary income.

Professional Corporation

A professional corporation is a corporation for a professional, such as an attorney or a doctor. The tax code says that only a professional may participate in a professional corporation; unless the surviving spouse is also such a professional, the professional corporation must be sold or liquidated within sixty to ninety days following the death of the professional. If the professional corporation consists of a group of professionals, they should have all entered into

Buy/Sell Agreements covering the death of each member and funded each agreement with life insurance. If so, the value of the decedent's interest in the professional corporation is readily established, and the funds available from the insurance company will pay for (buy out) the deceased person's interest in the professional corporation.

Neither a Trust nor a non-professional may hold an interest in a professional corporation. If the professional corporation is a singular enterprise (e.g., a doctor), then the corporation must be liquidated. When the corporation has only one professional, the assets are typically the receivables (i.e., money due to the corporation) and the equipment. There also may be some goodwill. Under these circumstances, not only is it legally necessary to liquidate the business interest, but it is to the advantage of the estate to liquidate the assets as quickly as possible, since they depreciate very rapidly.

Qualified Sub-Chapter S Corporation

The primary advantage of a Sub-Chapter S Corporation (often referred to as a Sub S Corporation) is to pass the corporate income and losses directly to the stockholders—thus eliminating double taxation. A standard corporation (a C Corporation) must pay tax on its profits and then distribute the remaining profits as dividends to the shareholders. However, when the shareholders receive those dividends, they must declare those dividends as income for personal income tax purposes. The end result is that the corporate profits are taxed twice.

The Sub S Corporation can be particularly advantageous to real estate developers. Typically, real estate, in the early stages of development, has substantial tax losses that would be locked up in a standard corporation. In a Sub S Corporation, these losses are passed through to the shareholders, who may use the losses as deductions on their Form 1040 Individual Income Tax Returns.

If a spouse dies while holding an interest in a Sub S Corporation and leaves a surviving spouse with the Sub S Corporation stock, the Trust may continue to hold the Sub S stock if the trustee powers in the Trust provide for doing so. Additionally, the decedent's share of the stock can be placed in the decedent's B sub-trust if the surviving spouse is the sole income beneficiary. The decedent's share can also be placed in the QTIP or QDOT Trust (C sub-trust; see Chapter 21) if it qualifies (the surviving spouse must have the right to all income from the B sub-trust and the C sub-trust) and if the Trust language allows the holding of Sub S Corporation stock—but only if the surviving spouse is the sole income beneficiary of the QTIP Trust or QDOT Trust. The surviving spouse may hold the survivor's share in the survivor's A sub-trust, because that Trust is revocable as long as the survivor is alive.

Upon the death of the surviving spouse, or an individual if single, the Trust can continue to hold the Sub S stock *if* the Trust is authorized to do so—*and* if the beneficiaries are all named as holding a beneficial interest in the shares of stock. To maintain the Sub S election after the death of the trustor, the beneficiaries must consent to the Sub S election. Such an election is made on IRS Form 2553, Election by a Small Business Corporation.

Following the death of the surviving spouse, or an individual if single, and the election to retain the Sub S Corporation status within the Trust, the Sub S Corporation must thereafter issue a separate Form 1120 with Schedule K-1 to each shareholder (beneficiary) of the Trust. If the Sub S Corporation is included in both the A sub-trust and the B sub-trust, then a separate schedule will have to be issued for each sub-trust.

When Sub S status is elected, all the corporate income will be distributed to the income beneficiaries and is taxable to them on their Form 1040 Individual Income Tax Returns. For a surviving spouse, the income (or loss) that flows from the Sub S Corporation to the decedent's B sub-trust and/or C sub-trust will, in effect, flow to the surviving spouse and must be reported on the surviving spouse's Form 1040 Individual Income Tax Return. The beneficiaries need to recognize that the income is taxable to them regardless of the corporate cash flow.

Although the Sub S Corporation has been advantageous for certain tax benefits, Congress has made it an administrative nightmare following the death of an individual. However, I believe that there is a very simple solution to this problem. I would recommend that the trustee(s) simply elect to change the type of corporation to a standard C Corporation—a regular corporation that retains its own income and losses and is taxed accordingly. Possibly an even better approach is the use of a newer concept known as the *limited-liability corporation* (LLC). The limited-liability corporation provides the same tax benefits as a Sub S Corporation does, but without the bureaucratic restrictions.

Limited-Liability Corporation

The limited-liability corporation is a new form of corporation that has recently received considerable attention. As with a Sub S Corporation, all of the income and losses of the corporation flow through to the stockholders, but a limited-liability corporation is not ensnared in all the red tape of a Sub S Corporation.

One of the greatest advantages of a limited-liability corporation is that its liability is substantially protected—an especially important factor in this day of ever-increasing (and often unwarranted) litigation. Although most states now allow the creation of limited-liability corporations, the liability protection afforded these corporations varies widely among the states, from very strong to very weak.

If you are interested in forming a limited-liability corporation, I would recommend a limited-liability corporation formed in Nevada, which, to my knowledge, has the best protection against frivolous lawsuits. Nevada, in its thinking, is still part of the new frontier; it does not like people infringing on its businesses. The knowledge that your business is a limited-liability corporation formed in Nevada can act as a powerful deterrent against someone who wishes to bring a lawsuit against your corporation. For any knowledgeable attorney, the fact that your corporation is a limited-liability corporation formed in Nevada should cause reconsideration of continuing any further legal action.

For the unwitting attorney, however, the

suing party could go to all of the expense of a court suit and could even conceivably win, but his or her win could be very costly. By winning the suit, the winning party does not get an interest in the corporation, but only receives a charging order against the corporation. A charging order simply means that the winning party has the right to all, or part, of the income of that corporation. What few people realize, however, is that a limited-liability corporation is not *required* to make *any* cash distribution. Thus, the individual with the charging order could end up with a very high taxable "income" (from the corporation), but with no cash to pay the taxes. I suspect that not too long thereafter, the "winning party" would return to his or her attorney and demand to know what kind of legal and financial mess the attorney has created.

I strongly recommend consideration of the limited-liability corporation, if only to protect the corporation against frivolous lawsuits. I also highly favor a limited-liability corporation to avoid the bureaucratic red tape associated with a Sub-Chapter S Corporation.

Family Limited Partnership

A family limited partnership is an excellent vehicle to reduce estate taxes and also acts as a deterrent against frivolous lawsuits. The subject of family limited partnerships is discussed at length in my 1997 revision of *The Living Trust*. As a rule, the family limited partnership dissolves upon the death of a general partner. In practicality, however, the surviving partners can swiftly reinstate the partnership. However, such reinstatement must be done in a timely manner—usually within thirty to sixty days following the date of death. If the decedent's B sub-trust or C sub-trust is to hold any part of the family limited partnership, the surviving trustee must be a partner in the family limited partnership.

In creating a family limited partnership and placing the assets therein, a family can attain as high as a 50 percent reduction in the value of its estate. This reduction in value in the assets placed in a family limited partnership occurs because each of the partners now has only a "minority interest." A minority interest means that a partner lacks control of the assets. No one partner, including husband or wife, would have more than a 50 percent interest, thus lacking control. Because of the minority interest, the assets experience a marketability discount, reflecting the restricted ability to market or sell the assets, owing to the lack of control.

If a family limited partnership is created for the purpose of estate planning, it is essential that you have the assets carefully appraised by a good appraiser and be certain that the appraisal is carefully documented. I recommend that the family attorney hire the appraiser, in order to retain the attorney/client privilege. Upon the death of an individual, whether it be the first or the second spouse or a single person, the family limited partnership should then be reappraised, preferably by the original appraiser.

Limited Partnership

Limited partnerships have historically been a good investment vehicle, particularly for real estate. Unfortunately, the 1986 Tax Act decimated most of these successful limited partnerships, but a number of very successful limited partnerships still exist. The value of many limited partnerships can be obtained directly from the New York Stock Exchange, where they are traded as limited partnerships. However, since many limited partnerships are not openly traded, the simplest way of attaining the valuation of a limited partnership interest usually is to write to the general partner and specifically request a valuation for the deceased person's share of the partnership as of the date of death.

As in any partnership, upon the death of a general partner (usually a person who is actively involved in managing or running the partnership), the partnership terminates. Typically, the partners will reinstate the partnership upon agreement of all of the remaining partners. Reinstatement of the limited partnership should be done in a timely manner, preferably not exceeding thirty to sixty days following the death of a partner.

The partnership need not be terminated upon the death of a limited partner, since limited partners are not actively involved in running the business. If the limited partnership is eventually placed in the decedent's B sub-trust and/or C sub-trust, the surviving trustee must be named as a limited partner.

BANKRUPTCY

A Trust, per se, cannot file bankruptcy. Although the trustees cannot be held accountable for the estate's deficiency, it is prudent for the trustees to err on the side of caution. If there are insufficient assets in the Trust to pay creditors, the trustees should be aware that there is a priority arrangement for payments:

- Employee income
- Employee withholding taxes
- Federal and state taxes
- Creditors

I recommend that the trustees allocate the remaining estate assets to the creditors on a percentage basis and then submit the itemized allocation to the probate court for approval. Once the court approves the allocation, the trustees are released from any further responsibility.

PERSONAL EFFECTS

Personal effects in an estate include furniture, fixtures, antiques, artwork, clothing, furs, jewelry, and personal mementos and trinkets. More specifically, *personal effects* describes any asset that does not have a specific title associated with it (i.e., items other than real estate, securities, motor vehicles, and the like).

Don't Overvalue Personal Effects

No estate-planning specialist worth his or her salt would value personal effects at more than $5,000 to $10,000. I know this statement must come as a shock to many people. We sit in our homes and look at the costly furniture, fixtures, and accessories, thinking about the cost of all our trappings and how much it would cost to replace them. Unfortunately, however, we have filled our homes with personal effects that satisfy *our* tastes—but not everyone has the same tastes. Particular furnishings, artwork, or china and dinnerware that we adore, quite naturally,

may not be appreciated or wanted by someone else. My mother was an excellent example of this paradox.

My mother's home was filled with very expensive furnishings, fixtures, paintings, and accessories. She knew that some day, when she died, the valuation of her personal effects would be horrendous. Whatever I had to say to her, however, always fell on deaf ears.

As time marched on and my mother's health declined, she was forced to leave her very expensive home and to sell all of her furniture, fixtures, and accessories. The resultant sale of her cherished possessions—for ten cents on the dollar—was a devastating shock to her. Unfortunately, what happened to my mother is the reality of life.

Because everyone's personal taste differs, it can be a very costly mistake to your estate to value your personal effects based on what you paid for them or what you "think" they are worth. A remarkable example of what *not* to do when valuing personal effects can be illustrated by the estate of Clara Tucker.

When Clara died, she left an estate of about $2 million, which included an abundance of jewelry. Clara left her estate to her grandchildren, which only compounded the problem. Clara had a Living Trust and had all of her assets inside the Trust.

The attorney who drew up her Living Trust later acted as legal counsel to the trustee. As a result of the attorney's advice, the trustee administered the estate as if it were going through probate.

An appraiser was hired, at a cost of $1,500, to appraise Clara's jewelry. The appraiser valued the jewelry at "market value" of $60,000. Few people buy good jewelry at market prices; they usually buy jewelry at wholesale prices. Furthermore, most people today prefer modern or contemporary settings, as opposed to Clara's antique taste in jewelry (which was the norm during her younger years).

The estate tax on the $60,000 appraised value of the jewelry amounted to $24,000. Since the estate was passing directly to the grandchildren, there was an additional generation-skipping tax on the jewelry, amounting to another $12,000. The $60,000 worth of jewelry cost the heirs $36,000 in taxes plus $1,500 in appraisal fees—a total of $37,500!

Eventually, the jewelry was sold on consignment for approximately $7,500. The end result was a net *loss* to the beneficiaries in the amount of $30,000—stemming from the over-payment of estate taxes and generation-skipping taxes.

The example of Clara Tucker's jewelry should serve as a reminder to all of us to not let our sentiments get in the way of realistically valuing personal effects. For estate tax purposes, value the personal effects between $5,000 and $10,000.

8

Settling a Living Trust
Know and Follow the Rules

Now that you have become acquainted (or, hopefully, reacquainted) with the Living Trust and had a brief overview of how to put your assets inside your Trust, we now arrive at the main purpose of this book: explaining how to settle your estate in a good Living Trust. The importance of "following the rules" cannot be emphasized too much. Failing to play by the rules may cause the IRS to heavily penalize your estate with what should have been unnecessary taxes and penalties.

As you learned, albeit in simple terms, in Chapter 4, certain rules must be followed by those who wish to successfully win the game by easily settling an estate in a Living Trust. The tax court has established many precedents that require you to follow certain aspects of the IRS regulations (as well as simple, but sound, accounting practices). When you follow these rules, you clearly satisfy the IRS that you are playing the game by the rules—and you win.

KNOW THE RULES
If you expect to win a game, you must be familiar with the rules of the game. As everyone knows, in order to follow the rules, you've got to know the rules. The rules are really quite simple, and if you follow them, you *will* win. If you don't follow them, you can lose, and the loss can be very costly—to your estate and your heirs. The tax court has established that these elements clearly ensure that the sub-trusts are created and the assets appropriately assigned. (Sub-trusts are simply the survivor's A Trust, the decedent's B Trust, and the decedent's C Trust.)

Here is a brief synopsis of the rules of the game:

- **Create a separate bank account**—and use this account only for the assets in the decedent's B sub-trust and/or C sub-trust.
- **Don't bother to file Form 56**—it is only an "information form," and it is redundant and unnecessary.
- **File Form SS-4** when the first spouse dies, in order to get a Trust identification number for the decedent's B sub-trust and/or C sub-trust. (The same tax number will be used for both the B sub-trust and the C sub-trust.)

- **Use the ledger method** to properly allocate estate assets among the A sub-trust, B sub-trust, and/or C sub-trust.
- **File Form 1041** U.S. Income Tax Return for Estates and Trusts for the irrevocable decedent's B sub-trust and/or C sub-trust. Use the new Trust identification number provided by the IRS. (The surviving spouse or remainder beneficiaries will file Form 1040 Individual Income Tax Returns as they always have in the past, showing any income received from the Trusts.)
- **Attach any required Schedule K-1s** to Form 1041. The Schedule K-1 forms identify to whom any Trust income (from the B sub-trust and/or C sub-trust) was distributed.
- **File Form 706** U.S. Estate (and Generation-Skipping Transfer) Tax Return *only* if necessary. File Form 706, Schedule R, *as an information return*, to elect the QTIP Trust (when the first spouse has died and the surviving spouse, who is a resident citizen, wishes to elect the C sub-trust, also known as the QTIP Trust). Such filing of this form also fully utilizes your generation-skipping tax exemption. Also file Form 706 when the value of the estate exceeds the federal estate tax exemption and the person who died was single or the surviving spouse. (Any taxes due must be paid within nine months after the date of death.) Each of the rules will be explained in much greater detail in the rest of the chapter.

Create a Separate Bank Account

To keep the IRS happy, be sure that you create a separate bank account for the decedent's B sub-trust and/or C sub-trust when the first spouse dies. Use this bank account only for transactions that are related to the decedent's affairs. The same checking account can be used for both the B sub-trust and/or the C sub-trust.

"But, why do I need to create another bank account?" you may ask. Remember that the decedent's B sub-trust and/or C sub-trust became irrevocable when the first spouse died. If the surviving spouse were to use the decedent's B sub-trust (and/or C sub-trust)

assets as his or her own assets, then the IRS will consider that the decedent's Trust assets are, in fact, the survivor's assets—and as such, the value of the assets in the B sub-trust will lose their right of insulation. The loss of insulation means that you lose the decedent's federal estate tax exemption! None of us wants to lose that valuable exemption, since it insulates $625,000 of the estate from federal estate taxation (rising to $1 million by the year 2006).

Simply set up a separate bank account for transactions exclusively relating to assets in the B sub-trust and/or C sub-trust, and the IRS will (usually) leave you alone. As an added precaution, however, have the new checks imprinted with the name of the Trust. For example, let's assume that John Jones has passed away. The new checks for the B sub-trust and/or C sub-trust should read "The Jones Family Trust, dated November 7, 1992, John Jones and Mary Jones, Trustors, and Mary Jones, Trustee." Imprinting the checks in this manner is just one more method of showing the IRS that you are fully playing the game by the rules. Typically, any checks written on this account are going to go to institutions expecting such expenditures—typically, the funeral home (for funeral costs) and the hospital (for final medical expenses).

When the second spouse (or a single person) dies, the A sub-trust becomes irrevocable. I suggest that you open a separate bank account for the A sub-trust to pay the final expenses, even if you are going to distribute the estate assets shortly thereafter. Once you have distributed the assets, you can close the bank account. If estate assets are going to remain in the Trust for some period of time, keep this checking account open, since you should use it to handle the receipt of Trust income and the disbursement of income to the Trust beneficiaries.

Don't File Form 56

Even though filing Form 56 is identified as one of the rules of the game, we strongly urge our clients to *avoid* filing Form 56. This form simply identifies the name of the Trust and requests that you send a copy of your Trust along with Form 56. The IRS would love to look at your Trust, but this step is unnecessary and therefore should be avoided. You accomplish the same thing by filing the other forms listed below, and you don't need to send a copy of your Trust to the IRS, unless you are filing Form 706, Schedule R, as mentioned in a following section. (Form SS-4 requests a Trust identification number, and filing Form 1041 Trust Income Tax Return establishes that a Trust does exist.) I never want to give the IRS anything more than what is actually required. Only if you were to go through an extended settlement period (six, seven, or eight months, which is entirely unnecessary) would you want to utilize Form 56. Since there is no IRS *requirement* to file this form, do not file it!

File Form SS-4

You must fill out Form SS-4 and send it to the IRS in order to request your Trust identification number. The IRS refers to this number as an Employer Identification Number (EIN), but the number is also valid for Trusts. This Trust identification number is used for the B sub-trust and/or C sub-trust upon the death of the first spouse, and for the A sub-trust, B sub-trust, and/or C sub-trust upon the death of the second spouse. This indentification number is also used for the A sub-trust upon the death of a single person.

Once you have filled out your Form SS-4, you can fax it to the IRS or simply call the IRS, and its representative will take the required data over the telephone. However, I suggest that you fill out the form first, because the IRS representative will ask you for specific information contained on the form. You may obtain the appropriate IRS fax number (the numbers differ by region) or simply apply by telephone by calling 1-800-829-1040. The regional office telephone numbers are listed in the Form SS-4 instructions. (I attempted to obtain the IRS regional fax numbers to include them here as a reference for you, but the IRS—true to form—chose to be uncooperative.)

Form SS-4 is really quite simple to complete. An example of the form is shown in Figure 8-1 on page 78. Instructions for completing Form SS-4 are presented in Appendix F.

Use the Ledger Method

The ledger method consists of allocating your assets to the decedent's B sub-trust and/or C sub-trust and to the survivor's A sub-trust and then transferring the assets to the appropriate sub-trust. The ledger method is very easy to use, but it is one of the most important rules of the game. Failure to follow this rule could result in you losing the game—with disastrous consequences to your estate.

The ledger method of asset allocation applies only after the death of the *first spouse* and only in allocating assets to the decedent's B sub-trust and/or C sub-trust and to the survivor's A sub-trust. Upon the death of the second spouse (or a person who is single), you need not use the ledger method. However, the assets still must be valued and any liabilities deducted, in order to determine the net value of the estate for federal estate tax purposes.

The ledger method uses a *ledger worksheet* to help you allocate estate assets to the A sub-trust, B sub-trust, and C sub-trust, as well as *ledger sheets* to transfer assets into the sub-trusts.

Before you can use the ledger method to allocate or transfer assets to and from the A sub-trust, the B sub-trust, and/or the C sub-trust, you must first complete the step of valuing the assets, as previously described in Chapter 7.

However, there are differences in asset allocation in separate property states and in community property states. Each kind of state has different rules and regulations about how assets can be handled for a married couple. Different ledger worksheets are used in separate property states and in community property states since the survivor's share of the assets does not receive stepped-up valuation in separate property states.

When filling out the appropriate ledger worksheet (depending on whether your estate is in a separate property state or a community property state), be sure to use the net value of the assets. The net value is the current market

FIGURE 8-1

SAMPLE IRS FORM SS-4

Form **SS-4** (Rev. December 1995) Department of the Treasury Internal Revenue Service	**Application for Employer Identification Number** (For use by employers, corporations, partnerships, trusts, estates, churches, government agencies, certain individuals, and others. See instructions.) ▶ Keep a copy for your records.	EIN OMB No. 1545-0003

Please type or print clearly.

1 Name of applicant (Legal name) (See instructions.)
The Jones Family Trust, dated September 17, 1979

2 Trade name of business (if different from name on line 1)

3 Executor, trustee, "care of" name
Mary R. Jones, Trustee

4a Mailing address (street address) (room, apt., or suite no.)
450 N. Rossmore Ave.

5a Business address (if different from address in lines 4a and 4b)

4b City, state, and ZIP code
Los Angeles, CA 90004

5b City, state, and ZIP code

6 County and state where principal business is located
Los Angeles, CA

7 Name of principal officer, general partner, grantor, owner, or trustor — SSN required (See instructions.) ▶ 545-32-3940
John Howard Jones

8a Type of entity (Check only one box.) (See instructions.)

- [ ] Sole proprietor (SSN) _____
- [ ] Partnership
- [ ] REMIC
- [ ] State/local government
- [ ] Other nonprofit organization (specify) ▶ _____
- [ ] Other (specify) ▶
- [ ] Personal service corp.
- [ ] Limited liability co.
- [ ] National Guard
- [ ] Estate (SSN of decedent) _____
- [ ] Plan administrator - SSN _____
- [ ] Other corporation (specify) ▶ _____
- [X] Trust
- [ ] Federal Government/military
- [ ] Farmers' cooperative
- [ ] Church or church-controlled organization

(enter GEN if applicable) _____

8b If a corporation, name the state or foreign country (if applicable) where incorporated | State | Foreign country |

9 Reason for applying (Check only one box.)

- [ ] Started new business (specify) ▶ _____
- [ ] Hired employees
- [ ] Created a pension plan (specify type) ▶
- [ ] Banking purpose (specify) ▶ _____
- [ ] Changed type of organization (specify) ▶ _____
- [ ] Purchased going business
- [X] Created a trust (specify) ▶ Irrevocable
- [ ] Other (specify) ▶

10 Date business started or acquired (Mo., day, year) (See instructions.)
February 4, 1981

11 Closing month of accounting year (See instructions.)
December 31

12 First date wages or annuities were paid or will be paid (Mo., day, year). Note: If applicant is a withholding agent, enter date income will first be paid to nonresident alien. (Mo., day, year) .... ▶

13 Highest number of employees expected in the next 12 months. Note: If the applicant does not expect to have any employees during the period, enter -0- (See instructions.) .... ▶ | Nonagricultural | Agricultural | Household |

14 Principal activity (See instructions.) ▶ Trust Administration

15 Is the principal business activity manufacturing? .... [ ] Yes [X] No
If "Yes," principal product and raw material used ▶

16 To whom are most of the products or services sold? Please check the appropriate box.
[ ] Public (retail)   [ ] Other (specify) ▶   [ ] Business (wholesale)   [X] N/A

17a Has the applicant ever applied for an identification number for this or any other business? .... [ ] Yes [X] No
Note: If "Yes," please complete lines 17b and 17c.

17b If you checked "Yes" on line 17a, give applicant's legal name and trade name shown on prior application, if different than name shown on line 1 or 2 above.
Legal name ▶   Trade name ▶

17c Approximate date when and city and state where the application was filed. Enter previous employer identification number if known.

Approximate date when filed (Mo., day, year)	City and state where filed	Previous EIN

Under penalties of perjury, I declare that I have examined this application, and to the best of my knowledge and belief, it is true, correct, and complete. | Business telephone number (include area code) 213-469-8732

Fax telephone number (include area code)

Name and title (Please type or print clearly.) ▶ Mary R. Jones, Trustee

Signature ▶ *Mary R. Jones*   Date ▶ February 12, 1981

Note: Do not write below this line. For official use only.

Please leave blank ▶	Geo.	Ind.	Class	Size	Reason for applying

For Paperwork Reduction Act Notice, see page 4.
ISA

Form **SS-4** (Rev. 12-95)

value of the asset minus any outstanding liabilities against that asset, such as a mortgage. An example of a ledger worksheet for a community property state is shown in Figure 8-2 on page 80.

Once appropriate asset allocations have been made to the sub-trusts, ledger sheets are used to transfer the assets into the sub-trusts *without physically retitling the assets*. Figure 8-3 on page 81 shows how the assets are transferred to the appropriate sub-trusts.

The ledger method is described in greater detail and illustrated in Chapter 14 and shows you examples of how the *ledger worksheet* is used to *allocate assets* to the sub-trusts and how the *ledger sheets* are used to *transfer assets* into the sub-trusts. Chapter 14A provides examples for separate property states, and Chapter 14B provides examples for community property states.

Distribution or Retention of Assets

Once you have allocated the estate assets to the appropriate Trusts, your next task is to identify which assets are to be retained in the Trust for the surviving spouse, which assets are to be distributed directly to the heirs, and which assets are to be retained in trust for later distribution to the heirs. You need to determine which estate assets should be distributed directly to the beneficiaries or heirs, which assets should be sold outright, and which assets (such as stocks or mutual funds) should be sold and converted into income. While you are assessing what to do with the estate assets, it is most appropriate for you to consider whether you need to convert certain growth assets to income-producing assets for the surviving spouse. In some situations, you may also want to retain some of the growth assets in the Trust for later distribution to the beneficiaries.

Distribution of Personal Effects

Once the personal effects have been valued, those designated to be distributed outright should be given to the beneficiaries, as specified in the Memorandum. The Memorandum is considered a legal document.

If the trustors have followed the recommendations in their Living Trust, a Memorandum should be included with the Living Trust. A Memorandum page is included in our Estate Plan Binder (see my previous book, *The Living Trust*) in the section titled "Memorandum." The upper part of the Memorandum is typically for the wife (or for an individual), and the lower part for the husband. The illustration in Figure 8-4 on page 82 shows you an example of a typical Memorandum. If the trustors have used the Memorandum properly, the important personal effects will already be identified and allocated to specific individuals.

After you locate the Memorandum, ascertain whether any particular personal effects are to go to one or more named individuals, then distribute those personal effects accordingly. Distribute the remaining personal effects according to the same allocations identified in the Trust. For example, my wife and I have four children, and we have specified that our assets are to go to our four children "equally." Though this verbiage applies to all of our assets, it also includes personal effects. Therefore, after the specific Memorandum items are distributed to the named individuals, the balance of our personal effects will be distributed to each of the children equally.

You may wonder, "But how do you accomplish equal distribution when you don't really know the value of the items?" The solution is really quite simple. Gather the beneficiaries around a table; give them the opportunity to draw straws to see who goes first, second, third, and fourth. Each beneficiary chooses one item when it is his or her turn to pick, going around the table to each beneficiary in turn. Repeat the process and continue until all of the personal assets of interest have been allocated. Such a simple approach usually eliminates any contention.

If no Memorandum is found in the Living Trust, then the easiest and least contentious way to distribute personal effects to the heirs is to use the "go 'round the table" method just described.

Importance of the Memorandum

As the years pass, the children and grandchildren grow older, and quite often the grandparents, their children, and the grandchildren reach "understandings" as to which person gets which item from the estate when the grandparents pass away. However, as often happens,

FIGURE 8-2

LEDGER WORKSHEET FOR A COMMUNITY PROPERTY STATE

Description of Property	SEPARATE PROPERTY		MARITAL SHARE OF ASSETS		TRUSTS		
	Deceased	Survivor	Deceased	Survivor	C	B	A
	Net Stepped-Up Valuation	Net Cost Basis	Net Stepped-Up Valuation	Net Stepped-Up Valuation	Net Stepped-Up Valuation	Net Stepped-Up Valuation	Net Stepped-Up Valuation
Checking	$	$	$	$	$	$	$
Money Market							
Securities			$100,000	$ 100,000		$100,000	$ 100,000
Bonds							
Home			$200,000	$ 200,000		$200,000	$ 200,000
Other Real Estate			$400,000	$ 400,000	$100,000	$300,000	$ 400,000
Personal Effects							
IRA				$1,000,000			$1,000,000
Separate Property of Decedent Spouse	$100,000				$100,000		
Separate Property of Surviving Spouse		$50,000*					$ 50,000

*Separate property of surviving spouse does not receive stepped-up valuation.

© Copyright The Estate Plan® 1996. All rights reserved.

FIGURE 8-3
ASSET DISTRIBUTION BY SUB-TRUST

TRUST A

Asset Description	Valuation		
	Amount	Date	Source*
Home located at 1538 Spruce Drive	$ 200,000	2/16/81	Comparables
Canoga Park, CA			
Securities	$ 100,000	2/20/81	Statement
Other Real Estate	$ 400,000	2/27/81	Comparables
Survivor's Separate Property	$ 100,000	2/12/81	Statement
IRA	$1,000,000	2/14/81	Statement

Date: 2/27/81   Signature of Trustee: *Mary R. Jones*
                                                    Mary R. Jones

*Source of Valuation

TRUST B

Asset Description	Valuation		
	Amount	Date	Source*
Home (listed above)	$200,000	2/16/81	Comparables
Securities	$100,000	2/20/81	Statement
Other Real Estate	$300,000	2/27/81	Comparables

Date: 2/27/81   Signature of Trustee: *Mary R. Jones*
                                                    Mary R. Jones

*Source of Valuation

TRUST C

Asset Description	Valuation		
	Amount	Date	Source*
Other Real Estate	$100,000	2/27/81	Comparables
Decedent's Separate Property	$100,000	2/12/81	Statement

Date: 2/27/81   Signature of Trustee: *Mary R. Jones*
                                                    Mary R. Jones

*Source of Valuation

FIGURE 8-4
SAMPLE MEMORANDUM

DESIRED DISTRIBUTION OF PERSONAL PROPERTY

My personal effects have special meaning and I desire that upon my death these items be given to those herein indicated.

Description of Personal Property	Desired Recipient and Relationship	Date	Initial
Piano of Mary Jones	Theresa Lawrence (daughter)	10/9/80	MRJ

Mary R. Jones
Signed: Mary R. Jones

Description of Personal Property	Desired Recipient and Relationship	Date	Initial
Tools of John Jones	James Jones (son)	10/9/80	JHJ

John H. Jones
Signed: John H. Jones

---

these understandings are not communicated to all the heirs—which can result in family discord.

The Memorandum usually goes a long way toward minimizing jealousy among the heirs over coveted personal effects, since it has been filled out by the original trustees of the Trust and clearly states which items are to go to which heir. The heirs may not always agree, but the Memorandum leaves no doubt as to the desires of the deceased for passing on their personal effects. For example, it may be appropriate to pass your tools on to a son who has shown an inclination to use them appropriately, a painting to another son who has always indicated an interest in it, and possibly the piano to a daughter.

The Memorandum is absolutely vital to couples who are in a second marriage—particularly if both husband and wife have children from their former marriages. The Memorandum is where the father would specify which of his children are to get specific items of his personal effects, and the mother would likewise for her children and her personal effects.

The following story is a classic example of the misunderstandings that can often cause hard feelings among siblings, especially when the children have come from a previous marriage of their mother or father.

Joe and Sally Purdy had been previously married, and each had a daughter from their previous marriages. I had created a Living Trust for Joe and Sally, and I had strongly urged them to complete the Memorandum form. Unfortunately, the couple never filled it out.

Several years later, Joe died, and since he had been a widower, he had retained the china and silver from his previous marriage. Upon his death, the china and silver remained in the home. Two years later, Sally died, and *all* the personal effects passed to *her* daughter.

Shortly thereafter, I got a call at my office from a very upset young lady, Joe's daughter, who said she always had understood that she was to eventually get her mother's china and silver that were now in the hands of her stepmother's daughter. Joe's daughter went on to say that her stepmother's daughter had married well and did not need "her" china and silver. Apparently, there was some bad blood between the two girls, so I was the middleman left to do the negotiating.

In this case, there was a happy ending. I was able to call Sally's daughter and explain the situation to her. Sally's daughter quickly agreed to return her stepdad's china and silver—but she did not want to see Joe's daughter. Sally's daughter asked me if she could bring the china and silver to my office, where it could eventually be picked up by Joe's daughter. I agreed to act as the go-between, and soon the exchange was completed. In the end, everyone was happy.

The point of this story is to emphasize that Joe had an obligation to specify in his part of the Memorandum that the china and silver from his former marriage were to go to his daughter. Joe had failed to do that. In the absence of any such Memorandum, the only recourse is to appeal to the kindhearted nature of the other person. In this case, such an appeal worked. However, in many cases, the appeal goes for naught.

Let this example be a warning and admonition to all who are in a second marriage. You have an *obligation* to fill out the Memorandum and identify your specific family assets that should go to certain individuals. Children of a former marriage often desire those treasured possessions from their parents' first marriage, and these treasures should eventually pass to those children. Your failure to "do your part"—to complete the Memorandum section—could potentially leave *your* children without any mementos or treasured keepsakes that remind them of their past. Please—don't forget this simple task of filling out the Memorandum.

Keep an Accurate Record of the Last Illness and Funeral Expenses

You have the option of deducting the last illness expenses and the funeral expenses of a deceased person on the individual's Form 1040 Individual Income Tax Return or on Form 706 Federal Estate Tax Return (if one needs to be filed)—the choice is yours. Upon the death of the surviving spouse or a single person, you must file a Form 1040 tax return for the decedent.

The person who should file the Form 1040 tax return for the decedent is the executor, because the estate usually receives income from outside the Trust. Of course, the trustee and executor may be the same person.

Form 1040

The surviving spouse is entitled to file a joint Form 1040 Individual Income Tax Return for the tax year in which the other spouse died, regardless of when the death occurred during the year. Filing a joint return (as opposed to a single return) usually results in tax advantages. The joint tax return would be no different than if the deceased spouse were still alive. The surviving spouse would continue to report all income using the same individual social security number that had been used previously.

When filling out the decedent's final Form 1040 Individual Income Tax Return, you should review the deceased person's income tax returns for the past five years. In particular, look for any tax loss carryforwards or any particular expense deductions that could be used on the final Form 1040 tax return. A good example of such a deduction would be depreciation on rental property.

Form 1041

Form 1041 U.S. Income Tax Return for Estates and Trusts is really an income tax information return for the decedent's B sub-trust and/or C sub-trust. Typically, all of the income from the decedent's B sub-trust and/or C sub-trust is passed to the surviving spouse and is reported on the surviving spouse's Form 1040 Individual Income Tax Return. If the surviving spouse is no longer living, the income is typically paid out to the heirs of the decedent's A sub-trust, B sub-trust, and C sub-trust and is reported on each heir's Form 1040 Individual Income Tax Return. (Appendix G illustrates a Form 1041 tax return that specifies all Trust income being distributed to the surviving spouse. Appendix H illustrates a Form 1040 wherein the surviving spouse declares the income received from the Trust on his or her own individual tax return.)

A Form 1041 must be filed for the decedent's share of the assets that are retained in trust. The form simply identifies the income generated inside the irrevocable Trust. Form 1041 should also be filed for the remaining months of the year in which the decedent died (since assets are usually retained in trust for the surviving spouse). Continue to file Form 1041 each year, as long as income is generated within the Trust.

Usually, however, Form 1041 (accompanied by a Schedule K-1 for each person who received Trust income) is only an "information return," since all of the Trust income usually flows to the surviving spouse (or if there is no surviving spouse, the income then flows to the beneficiaries). The information-only return shows that all Trust income was paid out and, thus, that there is no Trust income tax to pay. When all Trust income is paid out to the surviving spouse (or beneficiaries), Form 1041 becomes very simple and is often filled out by the trustee. You need to recognize that any income retained inside the Trust is taxed at a 39.6 percent tax rate, whereas most individuals' tax rates are lower (except for those who pay taxes at the highest individual income tax rate).

File a Form 1041 Trust Income Tax Return for the first year after the death of the first spouse, just to establish with the IRS that you have an irrevocable Trust. However, if the annual Trust income is less than $700, you need not file Form 1041.

Be aware, however, that an irrevocable Trust does not have the right to carry forward a loss. I recommend that any asset with a loss being carried forward be placed in the survivor's A sub-trust (or, if appropriate, distributed to the heirs), in order to let the spouse and/or heirs take advantage of the tax loss carryforward on their own individual income tax returns.

A Word of Advice: If you can possibly avoid it, do not take a loss inside your Trust. Instead, first distribute the assets (with losses), then let the beneficiaries recognize the loss on their personal Form 1040 Individual Income Tax Returns.

Schedule K-1

A Schedule K-1 accompanies the Form 1041 tax return and simply identifies who was the recipient of the income of the irrevocable Trust, typically the surviving spouse. If the surviving spouse—or an individual, if single—has passed away, then the Trust income usually passes to the heirs. Schedule K-1 forms must also include the surviving spouse's and/or the heirs' individual social security number(s).

Form 706

One of the most unpleasant aspects of settling an estate is to determine whether any federal estate taxes are due. You need to file Form 706 U.S. Estate (and Generation-Skipping Transfer) Tax Return only if estate taxes are due or if you need to make a QTIP election.

If the value of the estate of an individual is less than $625,000 or the estate of a married couple (with a Married A-B Trust) is less than $1.25 million (in 1998), then no federal estate tax is due—and *no Form 706 should be filed.* On the other hand, if the value of your estate exceeds the exemption levels, then, unfortunately, someone (usually a tax accountant) must fill out the horrendous Form 706—all eighteen pages of it—and someone must pay the estate taxes within nine months. Form 706 has Schedules A through S—a lot of schedules—but most of us will use very few of them.

In years past, most people of "ordinary means" who had a Living Trust seldom had to be worried about paying federal estate taxes. A Form 706 did not have to be filed for a single person's estate valued at $600,000 or less or for a married couple with an estate valued at $1.2 million or less. (In 1998, these exemption limits began increasing gradually and will continue to do so until the year 2006, when the exemption limits will be $1 million for a single person and $2 million for a married couple.) However, as more and more families now consist of two working spouses who reside in a large house that is rapidly appreciating in value or couples who are able to invest a significant amount of their income, it is becoming more and more commonplace for couples to unexpectedly find themselves with an estate that is valued at more than the exemption limit—thus raising the unpleasant specter of having to pay federal estate taxes upon their deaths.

Remember, however, for a married couple, there is one exception to this rule. Upon the death of the first spouse, if the estate exceeds the exemption limit, no estate tax is due, because the estate tax does not need to be paid until the death of the second spouse. However, if there is a C sub-trust (QTIP Trust), in order to elect this Trust, the surviving spouse must file a Form 706 "information return" within nine months of the date of death of the first spouse. You will probably also want to elect the generation-skipping exemption for the decedent. (I will explain this exemption later on in Chapter 21).

I again caution you to file a Form 706 *only* when the value of an estate exceeds the allowable federal estate tax exemptions, thus necessitating the payment of estate taxes. I must warn you that many attorneys operate in a "cautionary mode" and file a Form 706 upon the death of the first spouse, even when no federal estate tax is due! The attorneys file a Form 706 to supposedly "lock in" the stepped-up valuation of the assets. Remember, however, that you have the option of filing using either of two asset valuations: the value of the assets as of the date of death or the asset value six months following the date of death. You need to be very aware of the problem with such a cautionary approach. The IRS is now taking the position that, upon the death of the second spouse, it can take a look back and reevaluate the assets upon the death of the first spouse. If the IRS deems that those assets were valued too low, it will revalue them. Therefore, filing the Form 706 upon the death of the first spouse does not necessarily lock in the value of the assets—and thus becomes an entirely unnecessary administrative process!

Single Person with an A Trust

If a single individual dies and his or her net estate exceeds one federal estate tax exemption ($625,000 in 1998, rising to $1 million in 2006), you must file Form 706 and pay the appropriate federal estate taxes within nine months of the date of death. If there are no federal estate taxes to pay, do not file this form. Remember that the net value of an estate is the current market value of all the assets minus any liabilities.

Married Couple with an A Trust

If a married couple has a Married A Trust and the first spouse dies, do not file a Form 706, since there are no estate taxes to pay upon the death of the first spouse. There is also no QTIP or QDOT election to be made (since such election applies only to a Married A-B-C Trust).

Upon the death of the surviving spouse, if the net value of the estate (total assets minus any liabilities) in the survivor's A sub-trust exceeds one federal estate tax exemption ($625,000 in 1998, rising to $1 million in 2006), you must file Form 706 and pay the appropriate federal estate taxes within nine months of the date of death of the second spouse. If no federal estate taxes are due, do not file Form 706.

Married Couple with an A-B Trust

If a married couple has a Married A-B Trust and the first spouse dies, do not file a Form 706, since there are no estate taxes to pay on the first spouse to die. There is also no QTIP or QDOT election to be made because there is no C sub-trust.

Upon the death of the surviving spouse, if the net value of the estate in the survivor's A sub-trust exceeds one federal estate tax exemption ($625,000 in 1998, rising to $1 million in 2006), you must file Form 706 and pay the appropriate federal estate taxes within nine months of the date of death of the second spouse. If no federal estate taxes are due, do not file Form 706. Remember that the net value of an estate is the current market value of all the assets minus any liabilities.

Married Couple with an A-B-C Trust

If a married couple has a Married A-B-C Trust, the first spouse dies, and the net estate approaches or exceeds two federal estate tax exemptions ($1.25 million in 1998, rising to $2 million in 2006), you should file Form 706, with a Schedule R, even though no federal estate taxes are due upon the death of the first spouse. The reasons for filing Form 706 after the death of the first spouse are to elect the QTIP or QDOT Trust and to preserve the decedent's generation-skipping exemption. The QTIP and QDOT Trusts, as well as generation-skipping exemptions and Generation-Skipping Trusts, are covered more fully in Chapter 21, which presents advanced estate settlement options.

An example of a Schedule R for a Form 706 tax return, showing the QTIP election and the generation-skipping exemption, appears in Figure 8-5. Appendix I illustrates a complete Form 706, including a Schedule R where the QTIP election is specified. Appendix J illustrates a complete Form 706, including a Schedule R where the generation-skipping exemption is specified.

Upon the death of the surviving spouse, if the net value of the estate in the survivor's A sub-trust and the decedent's C sub-trust exceeds one federal estate tax exemption ($625,000 in 1998, rising to $1 million in 2006), you must file Form 706 and pay the appropriate federal estate taxes within nine months of the date of death of the second spouse. Remember, if no federal estate taxes are due, do not file Form 706.

Who Should Prepare Form 706

I implore you to *not* use your family attorney to fill out Form 706 for any estate taxes that may be owed or to specify either the QTIP election or the generation-skipping exemption, and don't use your family attorney to file your Form 1041 tax return. Instead, I urge you to use your accountant or find an accountant who has filled out numerous Form 706s for Living Trusts and numerous Form 1041s for Living Trusts. Now is not the time for an accountant to learn—at your expense, which could be very costly if he or she makes significant mistakes.

If you need to file Form 706—because the value of the estate exceeds the federal estate tax exemption limits or the surviving spouse desires to elect the QTIP Trust and/or to preserve the decedent's generation-skipping exemption—I urge you to find a competent accountant (one who has had wide experience in filing many Form 706s, particularly for Living Trusts). An attorney will usually charge you a small fortune (after first hiring an accountant to complete Form 706).

Another alternative, which is often more palatable and satisfactory, is for you to find several accountants who are familiar with the Form 706 and have regularly filed many of them. Request quotations from each accountant, and then select the most reasonable one. However, if you are dealing with a very substantial estate (in excess of $2 million), you are probably better served to find an attorney with an LLM degree (which is a masters degree in taxation). Although many attorneys profess great experience in the area of estate taxes, few rarely have the requisite experience. An experienced attorney can save you many thousands of dollars in the long run. Allow the attorney to select an accountant and especially an appraiser, if needed. Remember, as I mentioned earlier, if the appraiser works for the attorney, the IRS is forestalled from hiring that same appraiser to audit your estate because of the attorney/client privilege. It has been my experience that a well-planned and well-documented approach to valuation of estate assets can survive most IRS challenges.

Be proactive! Don't just hire an attorney and then sit back and wait for the double whammy: the attorney's bill for services rendered and the

FIGURE 8-5

SAMPLE SCHEDULE R WITH QTIP ELECTION AND GST EXEMPTION

Form 706 (Rev. 7-98)

JOHN H. JONES **Schedule R—Generation-Skipping Transfer Tax**   123-45-6789

Note: To avoid application of the deemed allocation rules, Form 706 and Schedule R should be filed to allocate the GST exemption to trusts that may later have taxable terminations or distributions under section 2612 even if the form is not required to be filed to report estate or GST tax.

The GST tax is imposed on taxable transfers of interests in property located **outside the United States** as well as property located inside the United States.

See instructions beginning on page 17.

Part 1.—GST Exemption Reconciliation (Section 2631) and Section 2652(a)(3) (Special QTIP) Election

You no longer need to check a box to make a section 2652(a)(3) (special QTIP) election. If you list qualifying property in Part 1, line 9, below, you will be considered to have made this election. See page 19 of the separate instructions for details.

1 Maximum allowable GST exemption	1	$1,000,000
2 Total GST exemption allocated by the decedent against decedent's lifetime transfers	2	
3 Total GST exemption allocated by the executor, using Form 709, against decedent's lifetime transfers	3	
4 GST exemption allocated on line 6 of Schedule R, Part 2	4	
5 GST exemption allocated on line 6 of Schedule R, Part 3	5	
6 Total GST exemption allocated on line 4 of Schedule(s) R-1	6	1,000,000
7 Total GST exemption allocated to intervivos transfers and direct skips (add lines 2-6)	7	1,000,000
8 GST exemption available to allocate to trusts and section 2032A interests (subtract line 7 from line 1).	8	

9 Allocation of GST exemption to trusts (as defined for GST tax purposes):

A Name of trust	B Trust's EIN (if any)	C GST exemption allocated on lines 2-6, above (see instructions)	D Additional GST exemption allocated (see instructions)	E Trust's inclusion ratio (optional-see instructions)
The Jones Family Trust, dated September 19, 1979 John Jones & Mary Jones, trustors and trustees	95-2693713			

9D Total. May not exceed line 8, above	9D	0	

10 GST exemption available to allocate to section 2032A interests received by individual beneficiaries (subtract line 9D from line 8). You must attach special use allocation schedule (see instructions)   **10**   0

(The instructions to Schedule R are in the separate instructions.)   **Schedule R—Page 33**

Form 706 with the amount of taxes due and payable. You *must* be knowledgeable, and you need to assure yourself that your attorney is pursuing the right approach. Be cautioned that anyone can take the conservative approach and simply concede the highest tax rate—at your expense! If you have a large estate, you need a very competent and knowledgeable team that will be aggressive on your behalf.

Lastly, you should be knowledgeable enough to forestall asking the many often unnecessary questions that can end up costing you an arm and a leg. Sadly, I know a very prominent and competent Living Trust attorney who feels that it is his responsibility to hold the hands of the surviving spouse or children when they are settling an estate—and then charges them a fortune to do so. Use common sense. Use your attorney for the essential task of protecting your estate against onerous taxes, not as a companion, hand-holder, or healer.

IRS Audit of Form 706
If the IRS is going to audit your Form 706 tax return, it must do so within three years of the date of your submission, unless there has been fraud. If you owe estate taxes, you are required to file Form 706 within nine months following the date of death. Typically, if the IRS is going to audit your estate, it will do so twenty-two months later, or approximately thirty-one months following the date of death.

INHERITANCE TAXES
You also need to determine whether your state requires the payment of an inheritance tax. Most states now simply impose a pickup tax. Typically, the pickup tax is calculated as a percentage of the federal estate tax; if no estate tax is due, then no pickup tax is due.

A state inheritance tax is not usually imposed upon the death of the first spouse, but only after the surviving spouse has passed away. However, not all states play by the same set of rules. Some states impose an inheritance tax on the estate after the death of the first spouse, some states only impose an inheritance tax on the estate after the death of the second spouse, and some states even impose a separate *additional* tax on the estate of a deceased single person.

The states that impose separate inheritance taxes (instead of using the pickup tax) are identified in Appendix E. However, I recommend that you check with your own state tax collection department to verify the requirements in your own state, since each state alters its tax requirements from time to time. If you find that you owe inheritance taxes, follow my previous advice to find yourself a good accountant who is familiar with your state's specific requirements. If your state requires an inheritance tax, you will have to file an inventory of estate assets, along with an affidavit certifying that the inventory is a true accounting of the estate assets.

ADMINISTRATIVE TRUST PROCEDURE
Most law schools teach attorneys how to probate a Will—a fundamental task of most attorneys. However, course work familiarizing the students with how to create and administer Living Trusts is sadly lacking in law school curricula. The same lack of familiarization is equally true for how to settle a Living Trust—which is an absolutely foreign concept to most attorneys. This alarming oversight can be readily substantiated by simply noting the lack of books on the subject of settling an estate in a Living Trust (one of several reasons that I felt compelled to write this book).

Because of this lack of knowledge about Living Trusts, attorneys often opt for the cautious approach and turn to the area of familiarity—Wills and probate. There is a legal procedure known as the Administrative Trust Procedure, which parallels the probate procedure (akin to taking a Trust through probate). The process, used by an attorney who is not familiar with settling Living Trusts, is long, frustrating, costly, and absolutely unnecessary. You should avoid this procedure at all cost.

SIMULTANEOUS DEATH OF BOTH SPOUSES
The simultaneous death of both spouses—or their deaths within nine months of each other—poses an interesting problem. The dece-

dent's C sub-trust (QTIP Trust) is not applicable in such an unfortunate circumstance, since the surviving spouse did not survive to receive income before Form 706 needed to be filed.

Let's take a brief look at a scenario that unfortunately occurs much too easily.

A husband and wife have a Married A-B Trust, and the Trust specifies that the assets are to be distributed outright upon the death of the surviving spouse. However, both husband and wife die in an airplane crash. The estate is not large enough to require payment of federal estate taxes, so no Form 706 is filed (since it is unnecessary). In fact, no special forms or paperwork really need to be filed, per se. There is no need to file Form SS-4 to obtain a Trust identification number, since all of the assets are going to be swiftly distributed to the beneficiaries. There is no need to file a Form 1041 Trust Income Tax Return or any Schedule K-1s, since all of the income is being distributed to the beneficiaries and then reported on their own Form 1040 Individual Income Tax Returns.

Such an approach seems logical and reasonable, but by following this "logical" approach, the successor trustees (the beneficiaries, in most cases) have created an interesting dilemma that could be very costly to the estate. The successor trustees failed to establish with the IRS that there was a qualified A-B Trust that preserved both spouse's federal estate tax exemptions.

Remember the rules of the game, and play within the rules. Especially in the case of simultaneous (or near simultaneous) death, you must remember to play by the rules—in order to protect both exemptions. First, and most important, establish and document the asset valuations, in order to provide substantiated stepped-up valuation for the heirs. Once the asset valuations are completed, use the valuations in the following steps:

- Establish a separate bank account.
- Obtain the irrevocable Trust identification number by filing Form SS-4.
- Allocate the assets to the A sub-trust and B sub-trust using the ledger method.
- File a Form 1041 U.S. Income Tax Return for Estates and Trusts and its associated Schedule K-1s (showing that all Trust income was passed to the beneficiaries).

Although these steps are easy to overlook, such an oversight could be extremely costly; without these steps, the heirs could forfeit the value of one federal estate tax exemption— $625,000 to $1 million! Even though it is true that these steps are only "paper transactions," they are essential to ensuring the preservation of both federal estate tax exemptions.

DO NOT PROBATE A LIVING TRUST

Although I have mentioned before that you should not probate a Living Trust and the reasons why such action is totally unnecessary, cases of this nature still come to my attention. One of our associate attorneys recently told me of a case that his local county probate clerk brought to his attention. An attorney in this county had probated a Living Trust where all the assets were already inside the Trust. The county clerk commented, correctly so, that such action by the attorney was criminal. Unfortunately, such unnecessary probates of Living Trusts happen all too frequently. Don't let it happen to you!

ASSET TRANSFER OR SALE

After the first three steps of settling an estate have been completed following the death of an individual, the next major task facing most surviving trustees, or the successor trustees, is transferring estate assets to the beneficiaries or selling the assets. Though the surviving spouse or other family members can easily accomplish the process of settling an estate in a good Living Trust, selling or transferring estate assets often presents challenges that, although easy to handle if you have the right "tools," can be exasperating unless you know what to expect.

Be very aware that all financial institutions are going to be very cautious. They must be satisfied that you have the proper authoriza-

FIGURE 8-6
SAMPLE AFFIDAVIT OF SURVIVING TRUSTEE

AFFIDAVIT OF SURVIVING TRUSTEE

I, Mary R. Jones, the undersigned, affirm under penalty of perjury under the laws of the State of California that the following is true and correct:

(1)   By instrument dated September 17, 1979, John H. Jones and I executed "The Jones Family Trust, dated September 17, 1979, John H. Jones and Mary R. Jones, Trustors and/or Trustees."

(2)   Said Trust appointed me to serve as sole Surviving Trustee upon the death or incapacity of John H. Jones.

(3)   John H. Jones died on February 4, 1981, at Los Angeles, California, a resident of Los Angeles County, California. Attached hereto is a certified copy of the death certificate of John H. Jones.

(4)   Pursuant to the terms of the Trust, I have assumed the responsibilities of sole Surviving Trustee.

(5)   I am authorized under the terms of the Trust and the provisions of the California Probate Code to act as the Surviving Trustee with respect to the Trust's interest in property.

(6)   No other person has a right to the interest of the Trust in the described property.

(7)   The described property shall be transferred to me as Surviving Trustee.

Executed on ___February 14, 1981___ , at Los Angeles, California.

Mary R. Jones
Mary R. Jones, Trustee

Note: Notary Certificate of Acknowledgment omitted from illustration.

tion to have legal access to the assets. Therefore, to transfer or sell estate assets, the surviving trustee or successor trustees will have to show proof that they are duly authorized to have access to the estate assets. Depending on the procedures used by different financial institutions, they may require you to provide them with one or more of the following authorizations (as applicable) before they grant you access to the estate assets:

- An Affidavit of Surviving Trustee (or Affidavit of Death of Trustee) form
- The Living Trust document and a certified copy of the death certificate
- Letters from two doctors stating that the trustee is incompetent
- A Trust Certification form

The financial institution will also want to look at the section of the Trust titled "Trustee Powers," in order to ensure that the trustee is authorized to act in the particular capacity to buy, sell, or transfer the specific type of asset. The financial institution also will want to see the last page of the Trust, to verify that the Trust was signed and appropriately notarized.

Affidavit of Surviving Trustee
The Affidavit of Surviving Trustee can be a helpful instrument. This form, though not essential, can help you establish your right, as the surviving trustee (or successor trustee), to have access to the estate assets. (This form is also often referred to as Affidavit of Death of Trustee.) This form need not be complex; it must be notarized but can be as simple as the example shown in Figure 8-6.

In lieu of the Affidavit of Death of Trustee form, you will need to provide a copy of your Living Trust along with a *certified* copy of the death certificate. All death certificates provided by the county recorder's office will be certified. Photocopies or other reproductions of a certified copy of the death certificate are *not* acceptable.

Living Trust with Certified Copy of Death Certificate
Most financial institutions act with utmost caution when handling titled assets, and most of

these institutions still want to see a copy of the Living Trust and a certified copy of the death certificate. The institutions will enforce this requirement for the surviving spouse as the surviving trustee and, following the death of the surviving spouse, particularly for the successor trustee(s). Typically, the financial institution wants to see two basic areas of the Living Trust: the first page, to see who are the original trustors and trustees, and the section titled "Successor Trustees," to see who are the named successor trustees.

Also, the financial institution will require the successor trustee(s) to provide proper identification, usually including a photo ID, to ensure that the individuals truly are the designated successor trustees. In most cases, a valid driver's license or current United States passport should suffice for the identification.

Let me show you three typical instances of how the documents are used to satisfy financial institutions, upon the death of an original trustee, that you are duly authorized in the Trust document to have access to the Trust assets.

Upon Death of the First Spouse
After John died, Mary took their Living Trust and John's death certificate to their financial institution, as shown in Figure 8-7 on page 92. The first page showed that John Jones and Mary Jones were the trustors and trustees of their Trust. Mary also presented a certified death certificate for her husband, John Jones, to show that John was no longer living and, therefore, was no longer a trustee. Mary then turned to the section in her Trust titled "Successor Trustees" to identify that Mary, as the surviving spouse, was the named surviving trustee.

Upon Death of the Second Spouse
When Mary died, her children took their parents' Living Trust and death certificates for both John and Mary to the financial institution that held most of the estate assets. The children presented the documents to the financial institution, as shown in Figure 8-8 on page 93. The first page of the Trust showed that John and Mary Jones were the trustors and trustees. The children presented the two certified death

FIGURE 8-7
LIVING TRUST WITH CERTIFIED COPY OF DEATH CERTIFICATE FOR JOHN JONES

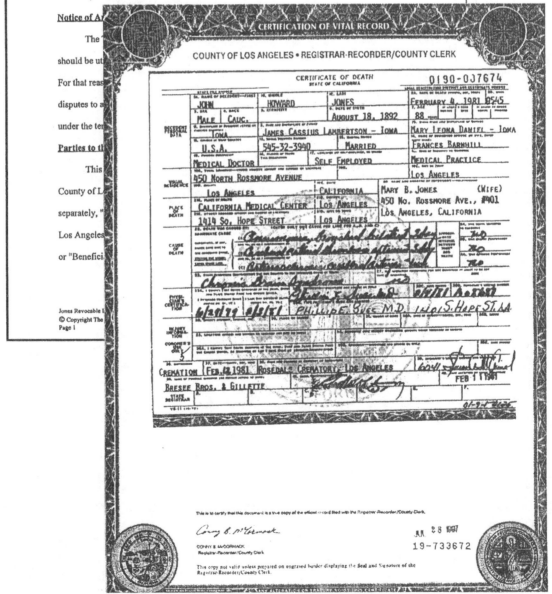

THE JONES FAMILY TRUST

(Married A-B Living Trust)

CREATION OF THE TRUST

This revocable Living Trust is formed to hold title to real and personal property for the

benefit of the creators of this Trust and to provide for the orderly use and/or transfer of such

assets during the existence of this Trust and upon the demise of the creators of this Trust.

<u>Name of Trust</u>

This Trust shall be known as:

"The Jones Family Trust, dated September 19, 1979, John Howard Jones and Mary

B. Jones, Trustors and/or Trustees."

FIGURE 8-8
LIVING TRUST WITH CERTIFIED COPIES OF DEATH CERTIFICATES FOR JOHN AND MARY JONES

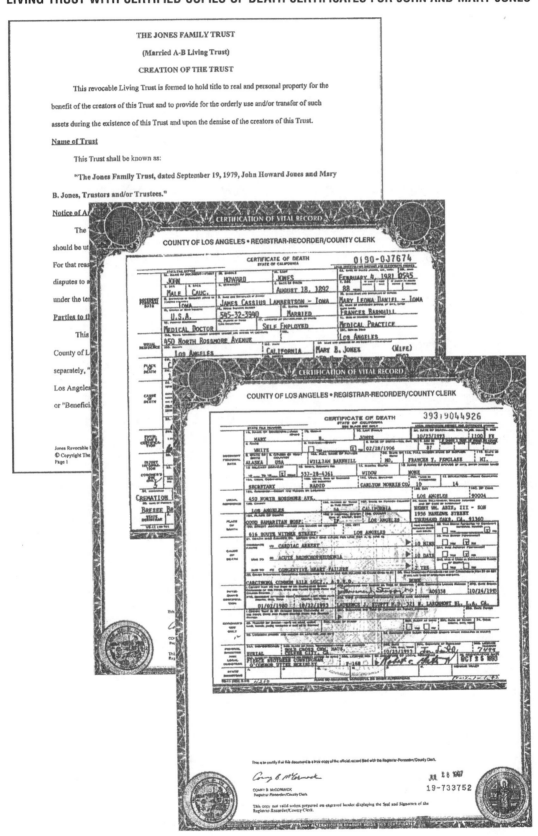

certificates to show that John and Mary were no longer living and therefore were no longer trustees. The children then turned to the section in the Living Trust titled "Successor Trustees" to show that they, the children, were now the successor trustees.

Upon Death of a Single Individual

When a single individual dies, the person(s) named as successor trustee(s) would go to the financial institution with a copy of the deceased individual's Living Trust and a certified copy of the death certificate for the individual. The Living Trust would show that the individual was the original trustee, and the death certificate would prove that the individual is no longer living and, therefore, is no longer the trustee. The successor trustee(s) would turn to the section of the Trust titled "Successor Trustees," which would clearly name the individual(s) who were to be the successor trustee(s).

Incompetence of a Trustee

As more and more of our population ages, there is an unfortunate increase in the number of individuals afflicted with Alzheimer's disease—who, eventually, become incompetent to manage the administration of their estates and their Living Trusts. A well-written Living Trust provides for such an eventuality by allowing two different doctors to write letters attesting to the individual's incompetency. The Trust language specifies that the named successor trustee(s) are then authorized to take over the administration of the estate.

A Spouse Becomes Incompetent

If a spouse becomes incompetent, the Living Trust documents, along with the two letters from the doctors verifying the spouse's incompetency, would enable the competent spouse to gain access to the estate assets. The competent spouse then is clearly shown to be the surviving spouse and surviving trustee.

A Surviving Spouse Becomes Incompetent

If a surviving spouse (usually also a parent) should become incompetent, the Living Trust document, along with the two letters from the doctors verifying the surviving spouse's incompetency, would enable the named successor trustee(s) to gain access to the estate assets in the same manner as if the surviving spouse had died.

A Single Individual Becomes Incompetent

If a single individual becomes incompetent, then the Living Trust document, along with the two letters from the doctors verifying such incompetency, enables the named successor trustee(s) to gain access to the estate assets.

Trust Certification

Trust certification assures a financial institution that the Trust and any amendments, as presented, are complete. More and more financial institutions are now requesting a Trust certification before they allow successor trustees access to estate assets.

A recent newspaper article published in the *Arizona Daily Star* raised an ugly specter of doubt about the ease of settling a Living Trust. The article, written by Kathy M. Kristof, the personal finance columnist for the *Los Angeles Times*, profiled a son's struggles with a financial investment broker in attempting to close his deceased mother's mutual fund account. The broker refused to release the funds without a certified copy of the Trust. The broker maintained (mistakenly so, I might add) that an "authorized" person at a bank or brokerage firm must write on the Trust document: "This is a true and complete copy of the original and is in full force and effect"; the "authorized" person must then sign and date the "certification" and write in the name of the certifying institution.

This newspaper article is just one more illustration of why it is essential that people with Living Trusts have a solid organization behind them—a place they can turn to in times of need. I can only imagine that this son was petrified when he ran afoul of this overly cautious investment broker, who really didn't know what he was talking about and probably used this opportunity to delay transferring the funds. Unfortunately, the author of the newspaper article was equally ill informed. However, the saddest aspect of this illustration is that I suspect the article caused a furor in the mind of many a reader, who either had a Living Trust or had thought about getting one.

What's the real answer? Let me give you some background on Trust certification. The words *Trust certification* probably sound ominous to many people, but in reality the process is not really as bad as it sounds. Occasionally, ten to twenty years ago, a financial institution would ask a client to have his or her Trust certified. In response to many queries from my own clients, I would ask an individual at the financial institution what he or she wanted as certification. None of them seemed to know. As president of The Estate Plan, I wrote a letter to the financial institution, stating that the Trust was appropriate, was duly executed, and therefore was in full force. Usually, my letters were accepted without further question. Occasionally, however, the financial institution would request that my letter be notarized and, on occasion, even [my signature] guaranteed. All of my letters were accepted by the financial institutions because none of the institutions really understood what they meant by "Trust certification."

Eventually, the financial institutions determined that to "certify a Trust" meant that the trustee had to affirm that the Trust and any amendments, as presented, were complete. As a result, in our Estate Plan Binder, we now provide a "Trust Certification" form to be signed by the trustee(s), with space to enter the dates of any amendments. Originally, Trust certification was requested of the trustors, the creators of the Trust, so our Trust Certification forms had the name(s) of the trustor(s) as also being the trustees already entered on the forms.

Now, however, as time marches on, more and more of our clients are passing on to a better life, and their successor trustees are stepping in as the trustees to administer the estate assets. It is now the successor trustees who are being asked by the financial institutions to certify the Trust, but the same principle applies. The successor trustees, as the duly named trustees of the Living Trust, are asked to identify themselves as the current trustees and to affirm that the Trust and any amendments, as presented, are complete and in force.

The Trust Certification form should identify the individuals who are the current trustee(s) and should also indicate whether there have been any Trust amendments and, if so, the date of any such amendment(s). The trustee(s) should then sign and date the Trust Certification form. It's really that simple. Figure 8-9 on page 96 shows an example of a typical Trust Certification form now accepted by most financial institutions.

Most Trusts are originals and not complete amendments (replacements). However, as many people realize that the value of their estates has increased to be near the exemption limit, they have "replaced" their Married A-B Trusts with Married A-B-C Trusts. If your Trust is a complete amendment, it should say so in the first paragraph. If the current Living Trust document is a complete amendment (a new Trust document completely replacing a previously existing Trust), a statement to that effect should also be included on the Trust Certification form (e.g., "This is a complete amendment to the Doe Family Trust, dated July 22, 1996").

The Trust Certification form usually need not be witnessed or notarized. I suggest that you partially fill out the form and then photocopy it as needed for future requests. The forms should be completed and dated only at the time of certification—that is, whenever the financial institution asks for a Trust certification.

ADVANCED ESTATE SETTLEMENT OPTIONS

This chapter has discussed the estate settlement options that affect the vast majority of estates in a Living Trust. However, for a married couple who has amassed a sizable estate that substantially exceeds the value of two federal estate tax exemptions, even a Married A-B-C Trust leaves a significant part of the estate subject to onerous federal estate taxation. If one of the partners happens to be a non-citizen, even more disastrous estate tax consequences could decimate the value of the estate.

Chapter 21 addresses some of the advanced estate settlement options that can be of value

FIGURE 8-9
SAMPLE TRUST CERTIFICATION FORM

TRUST CERTIFICATION

TO WHOM IT MAY CONCERN: Date: _____

Re: The Jones Family Trust, dated September 17, 1979, John H. Jones and
Mary R. Jones, Trustors and/or Trustees, made under the laws of the State
of California, by John H. Jones and Mary R. Jones.

The undersigned Trustees for the Trustors certify to you that:

1. The above Trust Agreement is in full force and effect.

2. The names of the Trustee(s) [Co-Trustee(s)] now acting under the Trust
Agreement (and who are the only Trustee(s) qualified to act) are:

John H. Jones and Mary R. Jones.

3. The attached is a full copy of the above referenced Trust Agreement
together with all amendments and/or supplements thereto.

4. The above-referenced Trust Agreement has not been amended, modified,
supplemented, or revoked, except as follows:

[List amendments, supplements, etc.]

_____

_____

_____

_____   _____
John H. Jones, Trustee   Mary R. Jones, Trustee

© Copyright The Estate Plan® 1996. All rights reserved.

TABLE 8-1
RESPONSIBILITIES TO ASSIGN

1. Destroy or replace applicable credit cards.
2. Check safe-deposit box.
3. If appropriate:
    a. Locate veteran's papers.
    b. Notify Social Security Administration of recipient's death.
    c. Apply to Social Security Administration for widow's benefits. (Locate marriage certificate.)
    d. Notify Medicaid of recipient's death.
4. Contact employer's human resources department for employee benefits.
5. Collect insurance policies and annuities.
6. Establish separate bank account.
7. Review Trust document.
    a. Who is surviving or successor trustee(s)?
    b. What are the specified powers of the trustee(s)?
    c. What assets should be distributed, and how?
8. Establish certification of Trust.
9. Establish Affidavit of Surviving Trustee or Affidavit of Death of Trustee.
10. Review Memorandum for special allocation and distribution of personal effects.
11. Make sure that homeowner's, personal property, and casualty insurance policies are paid up.
12. Keep an accurate record of last illness expenses and burial costs.
13. Review income tax returns for past five years for tax loss carryforward and any business interests.
14. File Notice to Creditors.
15. Collect debts owed.
16. Pay debts due.
17. Determine whether all assets are in the Living Trust. If some assets are not in the Trust, file Pour-Over Will with county clerk and begin probate process.
18. Determine whether any lawsuits are pending; if so, resolve by the probate process.
19. File Form SS-4.
20. Value assets.
21. Establish ledger (required on death of first spouse only).
22. File Form 1041 U.S. Income Tax Return for Estates and Trusts for balance of year of death.
23. File Schedule K-1s (attached to Form 1041) for balance of year of death.
24. File Form 1040 Individual Income Tax Return for balance of year. (File joint return upon death of first spouse.)
25. Determine whether Form 706 U.S. Estate (and Generation-Skipping Transfer) Tax Return needs to be filed on the death of the first spouse.
    a. If applicable, elect the QTIP Trust and preserve the decedent's generation-skipping exemption.
    b. Upon the death of a single person or the surviving spouse, determine whether any federal estate tax is due.
26. Determine whether state inheritance taxes need to be paid.
27. Roll over the IRA.
28. If appropriate, transfer title of assets to the heirs.

SPECIAL INSTRUCTIONS

If the decedent was living alone:
1. Remove important documents and valuables to a safe location.
2. Notify utility companies and landlord.
3. Advise post office where to send mail.

in minimizing the federal estate tax liability on estates of substantial worth. The topics covered in Chapter 21 include the following areas of advanced estate settlement options:

- QDOT Trust (where one spouse is not a citizen)
- Generation skip
- Generation-skipping exemption
- Reverse QTIP Provision
- Generation-Skipping Trust

If you have an estate of substantial worth (i.e., valued at more than $2 million), I urge you to read Part II and, thus, become acquainted with the estate settlement options that may help to minimize the onerous impact of federal estate taxes on your children's inheritance.

ASSIGN RESPONSIBILITIES

Numerous things must be done in settling an estate. The most efficient approach is to assign someone to accomplish each required step and *to do so in writing*, along with a specified date of completion. By taking this approach, you can ease the burden on the trustee(s) and be assured that nothing important falls through the cracks. The list of tasks in Table 8-1, shown on the preceding page, is meant only as a general reminder of those tasks that must be accomplished. The table is not intended to be complete; you will want to add to it yourself. However, the list at least covers the essential requirements needed in settling an estate.

9

Trust Management

Once you have created a Living Trust and have placed all your assets inside the Trust, you have taken a major financial-planning step—ensuring that your hard-earned assets are appropriately passed to your desired beneficiaries. You have ensured that the value of your estate will not be gobbled up by unnecessary attorney fees and administrative costs and that you have minimized any estate liability. Congratulations!

However, too many people mistakenly believe that managing their estates (once they are in Living Trusts) requires a lot of paperwork and administrative tasks. In fact, nothing could be farther from the truth! Managing a Living Trust is really quite simple and is almost always done by the trustors themselves, or their children.

Creating a Living Trust and putting your assets inside the Trust does not change the way that you manage your affairs. While you are alive, nothing changes when you have a Trust. There is no additional paperwork to do, there is no additional accounting to do, and you continue to file your Form 1040 Individual Income Tax Return as you have always done. The Internal Revenue Service looks at your income and expenses as being totally transparent (i.e., your Living Trust makes no difference). In effect, as the original trustee(s), you have no restrictions on your actions. You may do with your assets whatever you desire—I caution you, however, to make sure to retain your assets in your Living Trust.

TRUSTEES

If you are a single person, you typically (and logically) act as the trustee of your own Trust. If you are married, both you and your spouse are typically the trustees of your Trust. The trustees administer the Trust. Presuming that you have managed your assets reasonably well before you created your Trust, there is no reason to think that you would somehow not continue in the same manner now that you are the trustee.

For a married couple, the surviving spouse typically becomes the surviving trustee upon the death of the first spouse. Then, upon the death of the surviving spouse (or an individual if you are single), one or more of your adult children, a close family member, or close friends are typically selected as successor trustees.

Surviving Spouse as Trustee

The surviving spouse, as the surviving trustee, basically has the right to use all of the Trust assets without restriction. However, the surviving trustee must not abridge the rights of the remainder beneficiaries. The remainder beneficiaries are the individuals who become the direct beneficiaries of the Trust assets after the death of the surviving spouse.

In the usual case, the remainder beneficiaries are the children of both the husband and wife, and there are usually no problems with the asset distribution to the beneficiaries. However, if the surviving spouse is the surviving trustee and the remainder beneficiaries come from different marriages (some children from the husband's previous marriage and some children from the wife's previous marriage), the chance of potential difficulty arising is always of concern. For example, let's assume that the husband and the wife each had two children from a former marriage. If the father dies first, his children, who will ultimately become beneficiaries, could be concerned that their father's assets might not be properly protected. As the trustee, the surviving spouse must act prudently to protect the rights of *all* beneficiaries.

Act Like a Trustee

Regardless of who the remainder beneficiaries are, the surviving spouse, as surviving trustee, must act like a trustee. As I mentioned in the last chapter, the trustee must follow the rules:

- Using the ledger method, the estate assets have been allocated to the survivor's A sub-trust and the decedent's B sub-trust and/or C sub-trust.
- A separate checking account has been opened for the decedent's B sub-trust and/or C sub-trust and is used for income and expenses related to these assets.

Even though all of the income from assets in the decedent's B sub-trust and/or C sub-trust

passes to the surviving spouse, such income must first be collected in the appropriate checking account. Remember that the IRS has clearly established that if the surviving spouse uses the assets in the decedent's B sub-trust and/or C sub-trust as if the assets were those of the surviving spouse, then the decedent's assets will lose their protection under the Trust and, therefore, lose their federal estate tax exemption—a very costly loss.

Right to Decedent's Income

In most Living Trusts, the surviving spouse is given three rights to the income/assets in the decedent's B sub-trust and/or C sub-trust:

- The right to all of the income
- The right to use the principal to maintain his or her same standard of living
- The "frivolous" right to spend $5,000 (or 5 percent of the asset value in the decedent's B sub-trust and/or C sub-trust) for any purpose whatsoever

Thus, besides the right to use all of the income of the decedent's B sub-trust and/or C sub-trust, the surviving spouse has the right to use the principal for his or her health, education, maintenance, and support (referred to as HEMS). Also, many Living Trusts customarily give the surviving spouse an additional right to $5,000 or 5 percent (whichever is greater) of all of the assets in the decedent's B sub-trust and/or C sub-trust. For example, if the assets in the decedent's B sub-trust have a value of $600,000, the surviving spouse has the right to $5,000 or 5 percent of $600,000 (which would be $30,000). This right is granted annually, but the right is *not* cumulative, so the spouse must use it or lose it. The surviving spouse has the right to use this 5 percent or $5,000 annually, but if the right is not used for that year, the right expires for that year. There are no restrictions on how the spouse may use the funds granted under the "frivolous" right. The surviving spouse could take a trip to Europe or purchase a Cadillac.

These three rights—the right to all of the income, the right to the principal to maintain the same standard of living (HEMS), and the frivolous right to $5,000 or 5 percent of the asset value—truly give the surviving spouse the right to prudently use the assets in the decedent's B sub-trust and C sub-trust basically without restriction.

Discretionary Distributions

With the three rights—to income, HEMS, and the frivolous use of $5,000 or 5 percent of the assets—the surviving spouse has all the rights necessary to use the assets in the decedent's B sub-trust and/or C sub-trust as needed. However, be aware that if the Living Trust is also written in a manner that gives the surviving spouse *discretionary access* to the assets in the decedent's B sub-trust and/or C sub-trust, then the Internal Revenue Service claims that the surviving spouse may not also serve as the trustee! In retrospect, the IRS says that such discretionary powers of the trustee provide the surviving spouse with too much freedom over the assets in the decedent's B sub-trust and/or C sub-trust. If the language of your Living Trust provides such discretionary powers to the trustee, you must name a trustee *other than the surviving spouse*. However, any such trustee can then use his or her discretion in determining what is appropriate for the surviving spouse.

Surviving Spouse Not Sole Income Beneficiary

If the surviving spouse is not the sole income beneficiary of the decedent's B sub-trust and/or C sub-trust, then an annual financial report must be provided to the surviving spouse. Also, the C sub-trust would not qualify as a QTIP Trust since the surviving spouse must have the right to *all* of the income of that Trust.

Surviving Spouse Not a Trustee of Survivor's A Trust

If the surviving spouse is not a trustee of the survivor's A sub-trust, then the IRS insists that certain requirements must be met. The surviving spouse could be ill, incompetent, or tired and, therefore, have no desire or ability to competently act as the trustee of the survivor's A sub-trust. In such a case, the survivor's A sub-trust must then be treated as if it were an *irrevocable* Trust, even though the trustor is still alive.

In this situation, you need to file a Form SS-4 with the IRS to acquire a Trust identification number for the survivor's A sub-trust. You must also annually file a Form 1041 tax return along with the accompanying Schedule K-1. You also need to be aware that when you file a Form 1041 tax return for the survivor's A sub-trust, the IRS will challenge any gifts (excluding $10,000 gifts, which may be made annually to as many different individuals as desired) made within three years of the death of the second spouse.

A simple solution is to retain the surviving spouse as the co-trustee whenever possible.

Successor Trustees

Upon the death of the surviving spouse (or an individual, if single), one or more successor trustee(s) administer the Trust. I recommend that you designate as successor trustees one or more of your adult children, a close family member, or a close friend. My clients frequently ask, "Should we name our most mature child as the sole successor trustee, or should we name all of our children, so that no one feels neglected?" In reality, usually it doesn't really make any difference. However, over the years, I have discovered that, where appropriate, naming two or more (and preferably all if there are four or fewer) of your children as successor trustees eliminates much sibling discord. There is always greater security in numbers.

When a Trust names more than one successor trustee, a well-written Living Trust will require that all trustees must act in concert. In other words, all trustees must agree before any action can be taken that affects the assets in the Trust. (Sadly, I find that this provision is of utmost importance. I am amazed at the rancor that sometimes arises among close siblings when they are faced with settling the estate of their parents and distributing its assets.)

As an example of successor trustees working together, let's assume that you have three children. Let's further assume that upon the death of the second spouse, your three children step in as successor trustees. One child is extremely conservative and recommends that all the assets be converted to cash and the cash placed under the mattress. The second child disagrees, because the child knows of a high-flier investment that will "double the money overnight." The third child disagrees with both of the others and recommends that the assets be placed in certificates of deposit. Since the successor trustees must act in concert or else nothing happens, obviously, the cash is not going to be stashed under the mattress, and the assets are also not going to be used in a get-rich-quick scheme. For all three of these successor trustees, each with totally differing opinions, to agree, they are going to compromise and end up with a sensible solution somewhere in the middle. And that is where the trustees really belong—in the middle, where the decisions are most likely to be in the best interest of the Trust (and its beneficiaries). It is my experience that two or more successor trustees acting in concert do a very effective job of Trust management (see my previous book, *The Living Trust*).

TRUSTEE FEES

The trustee(s) of a Living Trust are authorized to charge a fee for administering the Trust, but they rarely do so, because they are usually direct beneficiaries of the Trust—it would be like paying yourself your own money. If you are the original trustee and you charge yourself trustee fees, you are simply taking money that is already your own and paying it to yourself (and creating taxable income) which really doesn't make much sense.

Several years ago, while in Memphis, Tennessee, for a seminar, I had the opportunity to be interviewed by the financial editor of the major Memphis newspaper. After we had exchanged pleasantries, I spent several minutes explaining why probate is so incredibly costly, time consuming, and agonizing.

Immediately thereafter, the financial editor verbally attacked me, saying, "Why would I ever want a Living Trust when I am only 45 years of age? I would have to pay a trustee fee

to manage the Trust, and considering my life expectancy, I would end up paying far more than my estate would ever cost to go through probate." I explained to the editor that most people manage their own Trusts *without* using an outside management firm as trustee. I then asked him why in the world he would want to pay himself a trustee fee, thus generating additional taxable income for himself. His response was only a smug look.

I assumed that the gentleman had managed his assets reasonably well to this point in time and would therefore continue to manage his assets as the trustee of his Living Trust. As such, if he wished, he *could* pay himself 1 percent to 1½ percent of his assets under his management.

A month before our interview, an attorney had written an article in this same newspaper, in which he stated that the Living Trust could be a good estate-planning tool for some but not for most people, because "if you have a Living Trust, you *must* have a trustee to manage your assets and you would have to pay a substantial annual management fee." Although my statement provided logic, the attorney's article appealed to emotion. Unfortunately, this financial editor came into our interview with a mind-set that was not about to be altered by logic.

I am certain that, to this day, this individual is still convinced that a Living Trust would be far too costly to consider for his estate because of the "trustee fees."

The tactic of talking about trustee fees or Trust management fees is a powerful argument frequently made by the Will and Probate attorneys to turn unknowing individuals away from the Living Trust and eventually force them into the agonizing and costly probate process. Unless your Living Trust is being managed by a financial institution or a professional Trust management firm, there is no need whatsoever for you to pay trustee fees! Most Living Trusts are managed quite successfully by the original trustees, the surviving trustee, or the successor trustees—without spending unnecessary Trust funds for "management." If you are the trustee of your own Trust, trustee fees or Trust management fees should be a non-issue.

Surviving Spouse

For the same reasons just given, the surviving spouse typically does not collect any trustee fees. In effect, you would be charging yourself for your own services. The surviving spouse has the right to all of the assets in the survivor's A sub-trust, as well as the right to use the assets in the decedent's B sub-trust and/or C sub-trust.

Successor Trustee(s)

The successor trustees might deem it appropriate to charge a trustee fee, but they usually forgo assessing or collecting such fees. Typically, the successor trustees are also the beneficiaries, and they will eventually receive their parts of the estate. The estate assets that are distributed to the beneficiaries—as an inheritance—are disbursed *tax free*. On the other hand, any trustee fees paid out must be declared as taxable income to the trustee—just one more reason why it makes more economic sense for successor trustees (who are also beneficiaries) to forgo receiving trustee fees. The trustees eventually receive their shares of the assets tax free.

However, in certain situations, it may be appropriate for a successor trustee to charge trustee fees to cover expenses.

For example, let's assume that the mother, the surviving spouse, is ill and is housed in a nursing home in San Francisco. Let's further assume that the mother has four children, all of whom are successor trustees, and each child lives in a different city—one in Los Angeles, one in Chicago, one in New York City, and one in Miami.

The four successor trustees concur that their mother needs to be cared for. Recognizing the distance of three of the successor trustees, they designate the child living in Los Angeles as the successor trustee to provide for their mother's care.

The successor trustee in Los Angeles will need to periodically fly to San Francisco to see and care for the ill mother. In so doing, this trustee will incur expenses for air transportation, automobile rental, and overnight accommodation, as well as food. The four successor trustees agree to set up a separate checking account and to allow the child in Los Angeles, as a successor trustee, access to the checking account in order to care for their mother, as well as to cover the costs of his or her expenses. Such an arrangement would be most appropriate.

An alternative approach would be to designate the trustee living in Los Angeles as the "managing trustee." This designation does *not* relieve the other trustees of their full responsibilities as trustees, but it does satisfy some financial institutions.

If the successor trustee is not a beneficiary, it is appropriate and proper for the successor trustee to be compensated for his or her services. An example would be an uncle of the children or a dear friend of the family who has been named as successor trustee. Trustee fees can be readily determined by calling the local banks and asking about the current rate for trustee fees. Generally, the yearly rate has been in the range of 1 percent to 1½ percent of the total value of the assets under management. For an estate valued at $800,000, the appropriate yearly trustee fee would thus be $8,000 to $12,000.

If the trustee charges a fee, it should be paid half from principal and half from income of the Trust. The trustee must treat the trustee fee as income received (i.e., it is taxable). Remember, however, that trustee fees need be paid only when an "outside" individual or firm manages the Trust assets.

In addition to the trustee fee, a successor trustee may charge an extra fee for his or her expertise in preparing the Form 1041 Trust Income Tax Return (and any accompanying Schedule K-1s) and/or the Form 1040 Individual Income Tax Return, as well as the Form 706 Federal Estate Tax Return. A typical fee for such tax preparation would be about $150 per hour. Again, however, many successor trustees perform these tasks for no charge.

PRUDENT PERSON RULE

The trustees of a Living Trust are required to operate under what is called the "Prudent Person Rule," which specifies that a trustee must pursue a strategy that looks for overall return, rather than just investing for a "reasonable income and preservation of capital." Translated into simple English, the words mean that a "prudent person" should invest the assets in a conservative manner, in order to protect both income and principal, as well as to protect the estate from inflation.

Some years ago, as I was about to give a seminar in Pennsylvania, a gentleman came up to me and asked if he could tell me his tale of woe. The gentleman said his father had died in 1933, leaving him (the son) $28,000 in trust, managed by the bank. Fifty-three years later, the bank finally distributed the Trust assets to the son—and he received only $28,000!

What an appalling tale. In fifty-three years, under the bank's administration, that $28,000 estate had not grown one penny! Obviously, the bank did not pay any attention whatsoever to the "Prudent Person Rule."

Even though a person may not have the personal capability or desire to manage an estate's securities (such as stocks, bonds, and mutual funds), usually that same person is quite able to hire an individual with the necessary qualifications to do so, as described in the following story.

Several years ago, John Dunlap asked me to redo his Living Trust. John was the president of a large insurance company, and he had established a substantial portfolio of stocks and bonds. Recognizing that his wife did not understand stocks and bonds, John had named his bank as the surviving trustee in his original Trust. I strongly urged John to change his designation of trustee and to name his spouse as the surviving trustee.

I realized that John's wife knew nothing about stocks and bonds, but I also recognized that she was very capable of hiring someone who did understand securities. If John's wife ever became dissatisfied with the performance of whomever she selected to manage the portfolio, she could fire the individual or firm and replace either of them with another choice. Such reasoning made sense to John, and we then set up his Living Trust accordingly.

Here is another, more personal example of why large financial institutions are seldom a good choice as trustee for managing the assets of a Trust.

My father-in-law was a vice president of the Bank of America. At my urging, my in-laws finally created a Living Trust and logically (or so it seemed to them at the time) named the Bank of America as the surviving trustee. In those days, the bank did a marvelous job of caring for the widows of their executives.

As you might suspect, I then stepped in where angels fear to tread. I urged my in-laws to change their Living Trust and to name my mother-in-law as the surviving trustee. It took some six months of persuasion, but I was eventually successful, and my in-laws finally amended their Trust to make my mother-in-law the surviving trustee.

Ten years later, my father-in-law died, and my mother-in-law took over as the surviving trustee. She immediately appointed the Bank of America to manage the Trust assets. However, this arrangement lasted for only about six months. In total disgust at the bank's mismanagement of the Trust assets and many incredible errors, my mother-in-law assumed the management of the Trust herself.

For the next several years, my mother-in-law continued to manage the Trust assets and did so extremely well. Eventually, due to her worsening emphysema, my mother-in-law resigned in favor of her son, who assumed management as successor trustee.

The main point of these examples is that you don't need to be knowledgeable in the investment field in order to successfully manage an estate as a trustee. You can hire an investment advisor; if you don't feel comfortable with the investment advisor's performance, you can fire and then replace the individual or firm. I strongly urge you to leave the management of your Living Trust in the hands of your surviving spouse or your named successor trustees, such as your adult children.

REVIEW THE INVESTMENTS

Following the death of the first spouse, it is most appropriate to review the investments in the Trust to see if they meet the objectives of income, growth, and security. Determine whether it is appropriate to reinvest some assets in order to provide adequate income as well as appropriate growth for a hedge against inflation. You should review the investments at least annually to determine whether any of them should be changed (e.g., sell income stocks and buy growth stocks, or vice versa) to more closely match changing financial conditions. Needless to say, tax credits would *not* be considered a wise investment for the trustee to make on behalf of the Trust.

Upon the death of the first spouse, it may well be appropriate to convert growth assets to income-producing assets, in order to provide adequate income for the surviving spouse. Usually, it is advisable to fund the B sub-trust (place assets therein) with growth assets (assets that are appreciating in value), because all future growth will be insulated from any federal estate taxation. It is usually advantageous to put income-producing assets in the decedent's C sub-trust.

Although the concept may seem "backward" to the surviving spouse, it is preferable to *consume* the assets in the survivor's A sub-trust and to *preserve* the assets in the decedent's B sub-trust. This concept is particularly apropos if you have an estate that will ultimately be subject to federal estate taxes. The assets in the B sub-trust will never be subject to federal estate taxes, whereas upon the death of the surviving spouse, the assets in the A sub-trust and the C sub-trust will be added together, and any amount that exceeds one federal estate tax exemption ($625,000 in 1998, rising to $1 million in 2006) will be subject to federal estate

taxes beginning at 40 percent and rising to 55 percent. Thus, consuming the assets in the survivor's A sub-trust and preserving the assets in the decedent's B sub-trust minimizes estate taxes. However, taking a particular action strictly on the basis of future tax reduction is not always the proper concept to adopt for a particular Trust.

Beneficiaries Must Be Considered

When acting as the trustee for a Living Trust, you must consider many variables, and you cannot overlook or forget the interests of the beneficiaries. Rather, you must be mindful of the remainder beneficiaries. If the remainder beneficiaries are the children of the marriage of both creators of the Trust (husband and wife), then consuming the assets in the A sub-trust and preserving the assets in the B sub-trust is a logical approach.

On the other hand, if the trustors have each been previously married and each has children from the former marriage, and if the husband and wife each desire that their share of the combined estate eventually pass to their own children, then the "tax-wise" approach previously discussed would not be the most prudent approach for the surviving spouse to use. For example, let's assume that the husband had two children from a former marriage. Let's further assume that he died and left his share of the estate in the decedent's B sub-trust to provide for the surviving spouse while she is alive. The husband had desired that, upon the death of the surviving spouse, the assets in the decedent's B sub-trust were to pass to his own children. Similarly, his wife desires that the assets in the survivor's A sub-trust pass to her own children upon her death. In this instance—which is almost universal among those in second marriages—it is more appropriate (i.e., prudent) for the surviving spouse to withdraw funds *equally* from the assets in the A sub-trust and the B sub-trust, so that the children of both spouses are treated equally.

Upon the death of a single person or the surviving spouse, if the assets are to be distributed outright, then presumably little change needs to be made in the investments, since, in most cases, they will be distributed shortly to the beneficiaries. On the other hand, if the assets are to remain in trust for a period of time to provide future benefits for the beneficiaries, then you need to review the assets to see if they currently meet the desired objectives (i.e., income, growth, or a combination of the two), or whether the assets should be repositioned so that they provide the appropriate benefits for the beneficiaries.

As a future protection (for both you, as trustee, and the estate assets), I suggest that you take the prudent precaution of documenting your actions whenever you change the investment of Trust assets. As the trustee, whenever you alter the investment portfolio, you should document your reasons for making these particular investment decisions. It is advisable for you to also document the alternative options that you considered. Although such documentation may seem unnecessary, it protects you from future challenges. Hindsight can turn out to be your worst enemy. When considering investments, people look at the present and try to anticipate the future. Unfortunately, none of us has a crystal ball and not all of our decisions may prove advantageous to the estate. Therefore, it can protect you to document your reasons for making particular investments and to note any alternatives you considered.

Use an Investment Advisor
It is also very appropriate for the trustee to hire an investment advisor, and such an action is referred to as an implied right of the trustee. If you use the services of an investment advisor to change the investment mix of estate assets, you can place the burden of justification and documentation on the investment advisor. However, be sure to ask him or her to give you the recommendations and justifications in writing. Retain these written recommendations in your Trust records.

Let me offer a fatherly bit of advice to the surviving and/or successor trustee. Whenever appropriate, you should provide information to the remainder beneficiaries of the Trust when you make significant changes to the asset mix. In so doing, you establish a good relationship with the beneficiaries, engender good feelings, and usually forestall any potential future criticism or conflict.

REMAINDER BENEFICIARIES
The remainder beneficiaries are those individuals named in the Trust to become the primary beneficiaries upon the death of the surviving spouse. Prior to the death of the first spouse, the named beneficiaries have no rights, since the trustors are still living and can change the beneficiaries—or their allocation and/or distribution—at any point in time. However, upon the death of the first spouse, the B sub-trust

and sub-trust become *irrevocable*—at which time the remainder beneficiaries' interest in the estate also becomes locked in.

The remainder beneficiaries have a right to have their prospective assets protected. Remember that the surviving spouse is given three rights to the decedent's irrevocable Trust assets: all of the income, the right to adequately provide for health, education, maintenance, and support (HEMS), and the annual frivolous right to use $5,000 or 5 percent of the assets in trust (whichever is greater) in whatever manner the surviving spouse desires. These rights give the surviving spouse all of the necessary and appropriate powers to sustain himself or herself. However, the surviving spouse may not take assets from the decedent's B subtrust and move them into the survivor's A subtrust in order to provide a greater inheritance for the beneficiaries of the surviving spouse. The surviving spouse also cannot gift the assets in the decedent's B sub-trust to any of the remainder beneficiaries. (The subject of gifting is covered later in this chapter.)

Right to Trust Information
By common law, the remainder beneficiaries have a right to know the provisions of the Trust that relate directly to *their particular interest* in the Trust. If the surviving spouse were to refuse to provide any information about the Trust to the remainder beneficiaries, the remainder beneficiaries could go to court and sue for discovery and, as a result, obtain a right to look at the Trust. However, in my more than twenty-five years of experience with Living Trusts, I have never known of a case where such an action was ever carried out. It is very easy for the surviving trustee to retain harmony with all of the remainder beneficiaries simply by providing them with the appropriate information that applies to each individual's part of the Trust.

Annual Financial Statement
You, as trustee, need to be aware that the remainder beneficiaries have the right to receive an annual financial statement relating to their parts of the Trust assets. You can easily provide this annual statement by giving each beneficiary a copy of the Form 1041 Trust

Income Tax Return with its accompanying Schedule K-1s.

Upon the death of the surviving spouse, the remainder beneficiaries become the primary beneficiaries. Primary beneficiaries have the same rights as are granted by common law to remainder beneficiaries. Primary beneficiaries have the right to know information in the Trust that applies directly to them, and they also have the right to an annual financial statement.

As you might expect, conflicts can arise when children from different marriages are named as beneficiaries. As I have already mentioned, the easiest solution to this kind of problem is to provide all appropriate Trust information to the remainder beneficiaries. A flood of information ahead of time can usually prevent or solve a myriad of prospective problems later on.

If the surviving trustee abuses the right as the trustee, the remainder beneficiaries can go to court and have the surviving trustee replaced. However, in all my years of experience, I have yet to see such an action happen. The same recourse is obviously available against successor trustees. The beneficiaries have the same right to go to court and force an abusive successor trustee to resign. Such resignation would require a court order, and I have yet to see such an action take place.

INCOME PAID OUT TO SPOUSE AND BENEFICIARIES
Most Trusts specify that all income must be distributed to the surviving spouse, as the income beneficiary. If you fail to distribute all the income, you create "phantom income" for the surviving spouse. If the income, or any part of it, is retained in the decedent's B sub-trust and/or C sub-trust and those sub-trusts specify that the income is to be paid out to the income beneficiary, then phantom income has been created. Phantom income means that all of the income of the B sub-trust and/or C subtrust must be reported on the income beneficiary's Form 1040 Individual Income Tax Return! Even if no cash is paid out, the income beneficiaries must still pay the income tax! Such a situation of retaining income in the Trust is certainly not advisable—unless you have some obscure reason to build up the value

of the decedent's B sub-trust. Beware of the IRS; it can ultimately rule that such funds retained in the B sub-trust are those of the surviving spouse!

You must also be aware of what happens with the survivor's A sub-trust. Any income retained in the survivor's A sub-trust tends to accumulate and ultimately increases the value of the estate when the surviving spouse dies. Remember, any value in the survivor's A sub-trust that exceeds one federal estate tax exemption will be subject to federal estate taxes beginning at 37 percent.

Even more disconcerting, however, is the startling fact that some states (such as Ohio) tax even the *first dollar of income* retained in a decedent's Trust. Remember that the IRS taxes any income retained in an irrevocable Trust at the 39.6 percent rate. Therefore, it is far more appropriate, in most cases, to distribute the income to the income beneficiary (who is usually in a lower tax bracket).

Income is typically paid quarterly, although it may be paid more frequently. The IRS requires that Trust income must be paid within sixty-five days following the calendar year end.

Occasionally, a surviving spouse asks me if he or she may disclaim part of the income (from the decedent's B sub-trust and/or C sub-trust) and pass it on to the remainder beneficiaries of the decedent's Trust. Unfortunately, the answer, in most cases, is no. The surviving spouse may pass income directly to the remainder beneficiaries *only* if the Trust language authorizes the trustee to pay income to the surviving spouse *and/or* the remainder beneficiaries. This particular situation is just one more example of why the many special provisions contained in a well-written Living Trust can be so important. With the properly worded provision, the surviving spouse would have the option to pass some or all of the income from the decedent's Trust to the remainder beneficiaries.

If the surviving spouse, as the surviving trustee, chooses to pass income to the remainder beneficiaries, it is essential to be absolutely certain of the particular state's inheritance tax laws. You must be very aware that some states

tax *any of the decedent's assets* passing directly to someone other than the surviving spouse. In these states, the income passing to the remainder beneficiaries would be subject to a state inheritance tax. You may wish to review the state inheritance tax chart in Appendix E, but do not rely upon the chart entirely as guidance in the special situation of remainder beneficiaries directly receiving income from the decedent's Trust(s). Seek out a competent accountant for verification.

Capital Gains

Capital gains are considered increases in the Trust principal and are usually retained in the decedent's B sub-trust. If the Trust language permits (as is the case with a well-written Living Trust), capital gains on *mutual funds* may be paid out to the surviving spouse and then declared on the surviving spouse's Form 1040 Individual Income Tax Return. Often, yearly capital gains received from mutual funds and reported to you on a Form 1099 are not going to meet the twelve-month holding test (per the 1997 Taxpayer Relief Act), so they are going to be taxed at 28 percent—whether retained in the Trust or declared by the income beneficiary. All other assets in the decedent's B sub-trust that are sold and that create a capital gain will be taxed at the 28 percent rate, unless the assets are held for at least twelve months, in which case the capital gains tax rate will be 20 percent.

Income of Decedent's C Trust

Although the surviving spouse may pass the income from the decedent's B sub-trust to the remainder beneficiaries (if the Trust documents so authorize), the same is *not* true of the decedent's C sub-trust (QTIP Trust). All income of the C sub-trust *must pass to the surviving spouse* for the QTIP Trust to qualify (i.e., for assets in the C sub-trust not to be subject to federal estate tax liability until the death of the second spouse).

GIFTING

The IRS recognizes the right of an individual to make gifts of up to $10,000 per year per recipient and to exclude this amount from the estate when valuing the estate for future estate taxation. This right to give excluded gifts is restricted to *individuals*; such gifts may not be given by an irrevocable Trust (i.e., the decedent's B sub-trust and/or C sub-trust).

It is most appropriate for the surviving spouse to use the "excluded gift" privilege to make gifts from the surviving spouse's A sub-trust, and the surviving spouse can do so without restriction. However, the surviving spouse may not make "excluded gifts" from the decedent's B sub-trust and/or C sub-trust. However, the surviving spouse *may* withdraw funds from the decedent's B sub-trust—in the form of income, HEMS, or the $5,000 or 5 percent frivolous right—and then, as an individual, make excluded gifts of $10,000 to the remainder beneficiaries. The surviving spouse, as surviving trustee, should not use any of the *decedent's assets* to make gifts to anyone other than the decedent's remainder beneficiaries.

TRUSTEE RESIGNATION

The surviving spouse, or any successor trustee, may resign as a trustee at any time by simply attesting to such desire in writing. A copy of any such letter should be given to each of the beneficiaries. An example of a trustee resignation letter is shown in Figure 9-1 on page 110.

As the following story so aptly illustrates, the mental competence to act as a trustee is not always easy to ascertain.

Years ago, a husband and wife came into my office and created a Living Trust. The husband named his wife and his oldest daughter as co-trustees, since the husband knew that he was dying of cancer. However, the husband was extremely concerned for the welfare of his wife, who was rapidly deteriorating mentally.

Months later, the younger daughter complained bitterly to her father that she felt her older sister was trying to grab the estate. In frustration, the father brought the younger daughter to my office, and I explained the Trust to the daughter and what would happen upon the father's demise—and why. Our

discussion seemed to satisfy the younger daughter.

A year passed, and the father died. Within the ensuing months, the mother continued to deteriorate mentally. One day, when the mother and the older daughter were in the bank, the mother offered to resign as co-trustee. The bank officer called me and asked what should be done. I suggested that he type a letter indicating that the mother had agreed to resign as trustee and have the woman sign it. The letter was typed, and the woman signed it.

Within the month, the younger daughter, along with her mother, was back in my office. In anger and frustration, the younger daughter charged that her mother had been forced out as a co-trustee by the older daughter's intimidation. I turned to the mother, and we had an interesting conversation for the next half hour. For the first twenty minutes, the mother was coherent; her talk made absolute sense, and she sounded as able and capable as anyone. However, during the last ten minutes, the woman's coherency and apparent mental competency seemed to literally deteriorate in front of our eyes—and her talk ended up being little more than an incoherent babble.

I didn't have to say anything further. It was now obvious to the younger daughter, as well as myself, that the mother's mental capacity did not allow her to prudently function as a trustee. Mother and daughter rose and left my office without any further comment, and that was the end of that issue.

I must remind you, however, that if the surviving spouse is not the trustee of the survivor's A sub-trust, then an annual Form 1041 Trust Income Tax Return with the accompanying Schedule K-1 must be filed for the survivor's A sub-trust, using a Trust identification number (just as if the surviving spouse were deceased).

FINANCIAL INSTITUTION

Only as a last resort should you name a financial institution as the successor trustee for your Trust. However, there are two situations where it may be prudent for a financial institution to

---

FIGURE 9-1
SAMPLE TRUSTEE RESIGNATION LETTER

September 7, 1992

Martha Albright
James Jones
Theresa Lawrence
Helen Martin
Jane Willows

Re: Resignation of Surviving Trustee

Notice is hereby given of my resignation as Surviving Trustee of "The Jones Family Trust, dated September 17, 1979, John H. Jones and Mary R. Jones, Trustors and/or Trustees" (hereinafter "Trust"). I will continue as acting Trustee until such time as a Successor Trustee or Trustees named under the Trust accepts the position of Trustee. I will be contacting the named Successor Trustee(s) of the Trust to determine his/her/their willingness to accept this office. Upon acceptance, the Successor Trustee(s) will contact you and provide you with his/her/their address and phone number for future inquiries.

If you have any questions or concerns, feel free to contact me at 213-546-4830.

Yours truly,

Mary R. Jones

Mary R. Jones

Note: This letter should be sent by certified mail, return receipt requested.

---

be named as successor trustee. The first situation is where both a husband and wife have immigrated to the United States, have minor children, and have neither relatives nor friends in this country who would be able to provide for their minor children if something were to happen to the parents. The second situation is one in which an only child is handicapped and there are no other family members who would be responsible for the care of the child. In these situations, naming a financial institution as a successor trustee is prudent. However, unless there are special circumstances that necessitate your naming a financial institution as the successor trustee for your Trust, I strongly advise you not to name a financial institution as successor trustee!

In most cases, I only have very strong negative comments about financial institutions acting as trustees of a Trust. The horror stories that I have heard from beneficiaries whose assets were managed by financial institutions are endless. In the early 1920s, the financial institutions discovered that the Living Trust was an ideal vehicle with which to ultimately take control of your assets. Most such institutions are not interested in the welfare of the heirs, but instead they are motivated by controlling your assets—and raking in hefty trustee fees for the privilege! You can walk into almost any bank lobby and find brochures about why you ought to have a Living Trust. It is interesting to note that the first advantage cited in the brochures is that, with a Living Trust, the financial institution can manage your assets. The attitude of financial institutions hasn't changed in seventy years!

Caution: Unless there are extenuating circumstances, I strongly advise you not *to name a financial institution as successor trustee of your Trust.*

Remember my earlier story of the individual whose father died in 1933, leaving him an estate of $28,000 in trust, with the bank as trustee. Fifty-three years later, the estate assets were finally distributed to the son—all $28,000 of them! Obviously, the bank did not pay any attention whatsoever to the "Prudent Person Rule." Who benefited from the long period of trusteeship, the beneficiary or the bank? Take heed, and don't let this happen to your estate.

Let me share with you another tale of mismanagement of an estate by a financial institution.

A widow came to me some years ago with the complaint that her husband, a doctor, had passed away and left her a $1 million estate in a Testamentary Trust managed by Security Pacific Bank. The widow was receiving only $1,500 every three months! The widow complained that she really wasn't able to live on such a paltry amount, and she was dipping into her personal funds to stay afloat. The widow said that her small stipend from the Trust was not what her husband had intended.

I asked the woman to call the trustee at the bank and to ask him if he had invested the Trust assets for income or for growth. I knew the answer, even before the woman asked the question. The trustee at the bank told the woman that the assets were invested for growth. Now, how can anyone truly conceive of growth securities as an appropriate investment for an 81-year-old widow! I then suggested to the woman that I would be glad to have our attorney contact the trustee at the bank to see if some much-needed changes could be made. The woman concurred with my suggestion, and on Monday afternoon, our attorney talked to the bank trustee, who immediately agreed to meet with our attorney on Wednesday afternoon.

However, following this conversation, the bank's Trust attorney immediately called the widow and invited her to lunch on Tuesday. The bank sent a chauffeured limousine to pick up the woman and drove her to its headquarters in Los Angeles, where she dined at the boardroom table. Following lunch, the widow was chauffeured back to her apartment.

Sadly, such royal treatment by the bank caused the widow to do exactly as the bank had hoped. The woman called me and said, "These people are so nice that I don't want to do anything to upset them, so please cancel your Wednesday meeting." I honored the woman's request.

The widow lived for another six years and continued to receive only $1,500 every three months—from an estate valued at $1 million! What a travesty. Again, I must ask you—who was better served, the beneficiary or the bank?

Try as I may, in my many years of experience, I have found only one financial institution that I can, in good conscience, recommend for consideration as a successor trustee. The company is Northern Trust Corporation, whose address is 50 S. LaSalle Street, Chicago, IL 60675 (telephone 312-630-6000). This company is one of the oldest Trust services companies in the country, and it has a highly respected tradition of service. Occasionally, people from other parts of the country call me in frustration because this company is based in the Midwest. However, Northern Trust Corporation has offices in Arizona, California, Colorado, Florida, Illinois, and Texas. This company is the only financial institution I have found that I feel comfortable in recommending to you for consideration as a successor trustee.

MANAGING A TRUST IS SIMPLE

Managing an estate in a Living Trust is not very difficult and is usually a do-it-yourself task. For most estates, you seldom need to go to the expense of using high-priced accountants, attorneys, or financial specialists. To do a good job of managing a Trust, you just need to "follow the rules." Typically, the surviving spouse has full and appropriate rights to access the assets in the decedent's B sub-trust and/or C sub-trust—and is the recipient of all income, HEMS, and an annual frivolous right to $5,000 or 5 percent of the principal (whichever is greater). The surviving spouse or successor trustees are only required to manage the Trust assets as would a "prudent person."

If you don't feel comfortable managing Trust assets such as stocks, bonds, or mutual funds, the easiest solution is to hire an investment advisor to do the investing for you. And, then, I would advise any trustee(s) to provide a wealth of information to the remainder beneficiaries and/or the primary beneficiaries, so that they are kept informed as to what is happening to the Trust assets.

In all but the rarest of situations, the management of your estate is handled in a more beneficial manner by the surviving spouse or the successor trustees. The adage "keep it in the family" is very apropos when it comes to managing estate assets—and is the preferred method.

10

Less Common
Estate Settlement Procedures

Settling an estate in a revocable Living Trust is really not difficult. The most difficult part of settling an estate is for the surviving family members to put their grief aside and to devote their energy to accomplishing a few simple, but very important, steps to ensure that the estate is properly handled. For all but very highly valued estates or estates with complex allocation or distribution situations, the settlement process does *not* require the services of attorneys or accountants. Most estates can be easily settled by the surviving family members themselves.

This chapter addresses the settlement procedures that pertain to three of the less common types of estates:

- Estate with a Single A Trust
- Estate with a Married A Trust
- Estate of a gay or lesbian couple

The vast majority of estates have Married A-B Trusts or Married A-B-C Trusts. The settlement of these common estates is discussed in greater detail in subsequent chapters of this book.

ESTATE WITH A SINGLE A TRUST

The Single A Trust is the simplest form of Living Trust and, therefore, one of the easiest estates to settle. There is only one trustor (the decedent) and no surviving spouse. Assuming that all of the estate assets are in the Trust, you only need to follow the settlement procedures presented in Chapter 8.

As a precautionary measure, remember to file the Notice to Creditors. If the assets are to be distributed outright, you need not file a Form SS-4 to obtain a Trust identification number, nor do you need to file a Form 1041 Trust Income Tax Return (or any associated Schedule K-1s). However, you should open a separate checking account for the estate and keep close track of final medical expenses and burial costs.

Lastly, it is essential that you establish asset valuation for all the estate assets—both to determine whether there are any estate taxes to pay and to establish a new stepped-up valuation for the heirs. If the estate is valued in excess of $625,000 (rising to $1 million in 2006), then, of course, you must fill out the lengthy Form 706 Federal Estate Tax Return and pay the taxes due.

Retention or Distribution of Assets

Upon the death of the trustor, the successor trustees have only two choices regarding the assets of the estate:

- Retain the assets in trust (to be distributed to the beneficiaries at a later time)
- Distribute the assets to the beneficiaries

Assets to Be Retained

If the estate assets are to remain in trust for a specified period of time for the benefit of the beneficiaries, then the successor trustee(s) must remember to manage the assets according to the "Prudent Person Rule." If there are substantial asset holdings in stocks and bonds, an investment advisor should counsel the successor trustee(s).

If assets are retained in the Trust, you need to file Form SS-4 to request a Trust identification number from the IRS, and you must then file a Form 1041 tax return and any associated Schedule K-1s *each* year that assets remain in the Trust. If any estate tax is due, remember that you must fill out and file a Form 706 tax return within nine months following the date of death and also pay any appropriate estate taxes due. The same would be true if there was any state inheritance tax to be paid.

Trust income should be paid quarterly to the beneficiaries. Remember that you don't want to retain income in the Trust, where it will be taxed at 39.6 percent. Instead, it is far better for the income to be paid out to the beneficiaries and taxed in their individual income tax brackets (usually lower).

Presumably, the assets remain in trust for the future benefit of the heirs. At some future time (i.e., when the heirs reach the age at which distribution is specified in the Trust), the assets would be distributed to the heirs.

Assets to Be Distributed

If the assets are to be distributed outright to the beneficiaries, you should wait until the

Notice to Creditors period of four months has elapsed before making any distributions. If there are beneficiaries who are not trustees, each beneficiary must receive an accounting of the estate and should sign a Receipt and Release form before any assets are distributed. If any estate or inheritance taxes are due, you should ensure that the necessary funds are set aside in the bank, since the taxes are due nine months following the date of death.

Once all of the liabilities have been paid, all of the other estate assets can be distributed outright to the beneficiaries. You should make such distributions *in kind* rather than selling the assets and distributing the cash proceeds to the beneficiaries. Let me show you why, using stocks as an example. If you were to sell the stock, you would have to pay a commission to a stockbroker for selling the stock, and the net proceeds (selling price of the stock minus the broker's commission) distributed to the beneficiaries would be less. When you then distribute the resultant cash to the beneficiaries, presumably many of them might turn right around and reinvest the money back into stocks—and pay a second stock brokerage commission in the process. You can readily avoid such a situation by distributing the assets in kind (i.e., distributing the stock directly to the beneficiaries by simply having the stock certificates reissued in the names of the beneficiaries).

Real estate can also be transferred in kind by simply rewriting and recording the deed in the name of the beneficiary. If there is more than one beneficiary, then each beneficiary would receive an undivided interest in the real estate, meaning each beneficiary would receive an equal share of the assets but would be unable to sell that share independently. For example, if there are four beneficiaries, each person would receive a one-fourth undivided interest in, let's say, a house. However, since an undivided interest cannot be sold separately from the other undivided interests, all of the beneficiaries would have to agree to sell the house before the undivided interests could be converted into cash. Having received title to the real estate, the beneficiaries can decide what they want to do with the real estate thereafter. On the other hand, if the beneficiaries are only going to sell the real estate anyway and if estate taxes are payable, it might be appropriate to sell the real estate while it is still in the Trust, because you can deduct the real estate brokerage commission from the estate, reducing the amount of estate taxes due.

The Single A Trust is by far the simplest Trust to settle and administer after the demise of the trustor.

ESTATE WITH A MARRIED A TRUST

A Married A Trust is an enigma to me. Although a Married A Trust is a valid Trust, in today's economic times it makes *no sense whatsoever* for a married couple to have only an A Trust! Every married couple—regardless of the size of their estate—should have an A-B Trust or an A-B-C Trust. I will not write a Married A Trust. Regardless of the size of the estate, I always write a Married A-B Trust or Married A-B-C Trust for a couple. Writing a Married A Trust for a couple can ultimately be to their detriment.

In 1981, I settled three different estates where a married couple had only a Married A Trust. When the first spouse died, these three estates were valued at $100,000, $125,000, and $150,000, respectively. Some twelve years later, because of inflation and the appreciation of California real estate, each of these estates had grown in value until they exceeded the surviving spouse's federal estate tax exemption of $600,000. However, since one of the trustors had died, there was nothing that could be done to change the situation by creating a Married A-B Trust; therefore, upon the death of the surviving spouse, the part of the estate that exceeded the surviving spouse's federal estate tax exemption would be subject to federal estate taxes, beginning at a rate of 37 percent. Such miscalculations on the part of both husband and wife were very costly to their estates. The miscalculations are not surprising, however, because people seldom fully realize (and, therefore, do not plan to account for) the impact of inflation and appreciation on their estates over a five- or ten-year period of time.

Let me relate to you what can happen, especially unexpectedly, to the value of an estate.

About two years ago, a client's son who lived in New York called our legal counsel and said he was going to sue me. The son told our legal counsel that I had created a Married A Trust for his parents in 1984, when they had an estate valued at $748,000. The son's mother had died some years before, and his father had just recently died—and the estate was now worth $1.5 million! Since the parents had only a Married A Trust, they had forfeited one federal estate tax exemption, which would cost the estate an unnecessary $235,000 in federal estate taxes. The son blamed me for not creating a Married A-B Trust for his parents.

In reviewing my detailed client file, it was evident that, when I created the parents' Living Trust, their estate was worth only $433,000 and that I had strongly urged them to accept a Married A-B Trust. I was unsuccessful in convincing the couple and, therefore, requested that they document in writing (as a disclaimer) their decision to decline the Married A-B Trust. I conveyed this finding to the son.

Our chief legal counsel recognized that this decision of the son's parents would cost the estate an additional $235,000 in federal estate taxes. The son asked our counsel what the additional cost would have been for a Married A-B Trust back in 1984, as opposed to a Married A Trust. When our counsel told him that the extra cost to his parents would have been only $85, the son broke down in tears—and he had very good reason to cry.

Such stories were too often repeated in years past. Experience teaches us all a lesson—and I now will not write a Trust other than a Married A-B Trust or a Married A-B-C Trust for a married couple.

If you are a married person with only a Married A Trust, I implore you to immediately rectify your situation and create a Married A-B

Trust as a complete amendment to your Married A Trust. Don't wait! Do it now while you are both still living and of sound mind.

If you are a widow or widower with only a Married A Trust, don't despair—for all is not yet lost. A recent tax court decision now allows the surviving spouse to disclaim (renounce interest in) his or her interest in an amount of the decedent's estate up to the federal estate tax exemption ($600,000 prior to 1998) and, in so doing, create a Bypass Trust (equivalent to the decedent's B sub-trust). However, any such disclaimer must be done *within nine months from the date of death*, or the right to disclaim is lost. The downside is that the disclaimer process is costly. To make such a disclaimer and to create a decedent's B sub-trust would cost in the range of $3,500 to $5,000. The important thing to remember, however, is that the disclaimer *can* be done—and can save up to $235,000 and more in unnecessary federal estate taxes. Disclaiming an interest in assets is discussed more fully in Chapters 23 and 24 where advanced settlement options are presented. However, it is so much easier, and so much less costly, to create a Married A-B Trust from the very beginning.

Settling a Married A Trust

Settling a Married A Trust is almost as simple as settling a Single A Trust. The settlement steps are almost the same. However, you need to remember that you have only *one* federal estate tax exemption to use in offsetting the value of the estate for estate tax purposes. Unfortunately, any excess estate value beyond the amount of one exemption will require that you fill out the horrendous Form 706 tax return and pay any federal estate taxes due. Remember that the onerous estate tax rate *starts* at 40 percent and quickly goes higher!

In a separate property state, the decedent's share of the assets receives stepped-up valuation to the current market value, whereas the survivor's share of the assets retains its original cost basis. Upon the death of the surviving spouse, the second spouse's assets finally receive stepped-up valuation to current market value.

In a community property state, all of the marital assets as well as the decedent's separate property receive full stepped-up valuation to the current market value. Only the survivor's separate property retains its original cost basis. Upon the death of the surviving spouse, all of the second spouse's assets receive stepped-up valuation to the current market value.

If you are married, I urge you to make your life (and the lives of your children) simple—by creating a Married A-B Trust, regardless of the present size of your estate.

ESTATE OF A GAY OR LESBIAN COUPLE

Although I have never personally created a Living Trust for a gay or lesbian couple, our company, The Estate Plan, has created innumerable Trusts for such people, primarily through attorneys who specialize in this type of service. In fact, years ago, our company created the Partner A-A Trust, specifically designed for gay and lesbian partners.

Although some states are seriously considering legalizing marriages between members of the same sex, you must recognize that, with the exception of state inheritance taxes (which can be incredibly high in some states for gay and lesbian partners), you are dealing primarily with federal law. In fact, the greatest adverse financial impact on estates of deceased gay and lesbian couples may come from the IRS. Regardless of what tax laws a state may enact, the IRS tenaciously clings to any means, no matter how regressive or antiquated, to accomplish its end—to collect the maximum amount of tax dollars from whomever it can. (However, the federal income tax is more favorable to a gay or lesbian couple than it is to a married couple.) Most of the following discussion therefore falls into categories that are of particular interest to the IRS.

Estate-Planning Concerns for Gay or Lesbian Couples

The primary estate-planning concerns for a gay or lesbian couple are the type of Living Trust that has been created to shelter its assets and whether the couple has attained the best utilization of the available federal estate tax exemptions.

Appropriate Type of Living Trust

Gay or lesbian couples typically use two types of Living Trusts:

- Separate Single A Trusts (one Trust for each partner)
- A joint A-B Trust, where the assets in trust are shared, except for those assets explicitly specified as the separate property of either partner

Either type of Living Trust is appropriate for a gay or lesbian couple.

Even with a Living Trust, upon the death of a partner, the Trust assets will be subject to federal estate taxation and, in some states, to high state inheritance taxes. (See Appendix E for a list of states that still impose an inheritance tax.) However, the primary benefit of a Living Trust is that it can retain those assets in trust for the benefit of the surviving partner, where the assets will not be subjected again to federal estate taxation upon the death of the surviving partner. These shared Trust assets are treated as if they were owned by tenants in common, which means that each partner has the right to identify his or her own beneficiary(s), as well as eventually how and when to allocate and distribute the assets. In contrast, any other method of estate planning (or forfeiture, without estate planning) typically passes the decedent's assets to the surviving partner, where the assets will eventually be subject again, upon the death of the surviving partner, to consumptive federal estate taxation.

Utilization of Both
Federal Estate Tax Exemptions

If one partner has a larger estate than the other partner, and if the partners are not fully utilizing both federal estate tax exemptions, it may be desirable for one partner to gift assets to the other partner. If one partner has an estate that exceeds the value of one federal estate tax exemption and the other partner has an estate valued at substantially less than one federal estate tax exemption, then it may be desirable for the partner with the larger estate to gift a portion of his or her estate to the partner with the smaller estate—to *fully utilize* both federal estate tax exemptions. For example, if one partner has an estate worth $800,000 and the other partner has an estate worth $400,000, then gifting $200,000 from the larger estate to the smaller estate (e.g., $10,000 per year for twenty years) would fully utilize both partners' federal estate tax exemptions. The $200,000 could be gifted in a lump sum, but the gift would reduce the $625,000 federal estate tax exemption by $200,000—which defeats the purpose of gifting.

Unequal Tax Treatment

Let me relate to you an excellent example of the difference in the federal tax code for a heterosexual married couple, as opposed to a same-sex couple. The IRS allows an individual in a heterosexual marriage to gift his or her entire estate to the other spouse, without any tax consequences whatsoever. In contrast, however, an individual in a same-sex union is limited to only an excluded gift of $10,000 per year! However, even a $10,000 gift can be quite effective, particularly if you are gifting a highly appreciating asset.

Be aware that any gift from one partner to another that exceeds the $10,000 annual exclusion will be considered a part of the lifetime federal estate tax exemption, which essentially defeats the purpose of gifting. Remember, also, that you may gift only during the partner's lifetime—you may *not* gift to a deceased partner.

If a deceased partner has made a bequest to a surviving partner, such a bequest eventually will be included in the surviving partner's estate for estate taxation purposes. A better approach is for the decedent partner to specify that his or her assets are to be retained in trust for the use of the surviving partner.

Settlement of Separate Single A Trusts

If gay or lesbian partners have separate Living Trusts, you should follow the settlement procedures described for the Single A Trust. The surviving partner may be both the successor trustee and the beneficiary of the decedent's Trust.

Settlement of a Joint A-B Trust

If gay or lesbian partners have a joint A-B Living Trust, you should follow the settlement procedures described for the Single A Trust, but with the following conditions:

- The surviving partner may be both the successor trustee and the beneficiary of the decedent's now irrevocable part of the joint A-B Trust.
- The shared assets will be divided equally and will be treated, legally, as being held by tenants in common.
- Regardless of whether the partners live in a separate property state or a community property state, only the decedent's assets receive stepped-up valuation. The survivor's assets retain their original cost basis for purposes of the capital gains tax.
- Upon the death of the first partner, you should file a Form SS-4 to obtain a Trust identification number for the decedent's now irrevocable share of the joint A-B Trust.
- File the decedent's Form 1040 Individual Income Tax Return for the year of the decedent's death.
- File a Form 1041 Trust Income Tax Return and the accompanying Schedule K-1 each year thereafter for the decedent's share of the Trust income. If income from the decedent's assets passes to the surviving partner, the survivor will simply identify that income on the Schedule K-1 and will then report that income on the survivor's Form 1040 Individual Income Tax Return.
- Do not file a Form 56.

- If the value of the decedent's estate exceeds one federal estate tax exemption, file a Form 706 Federal Estate Tax Return and pay the resultant tax liability within nine months of the decedent's date of death. (For a gay or lesbian couple, neither the maximum marital deduction nor the QTIP Trust have any applicability.)
- If applicable, be sure to elect the generation-skipping transfer tax exemption.
- If the partners' state of residence imposes an inheritance tax, pay this tax within nine months of the decedent's date of death.
- Make appropriate allocations and distributions to the designated beneficiaries.

If an IRA is involved in the estate of the deceased partner, typically the surviving partner would be the beneficiary of the decedent's IRA—and *not* the partner's Living Trust. A Roth IRA would be far more appropriate, especially for a gay or lesbian couple, since the Roth IRA has far fewer restrictions and tax consequences when passed to a beneficiary.

Upon the Death of the Second Partner

Upon the death of the surviving partner, the Trust settlement procedure for a gay or lesbian couple would be the same as specified for a Single A Trust.

A Living Trust Is Still the Best Solution

Even though numerous federal estate tax laws available to a heterosexual married couple do not apply to a gay or lesbian couple, there is an obvious advantage for gay or lesbian partners to use a Living Trust, as opposed to any other method of estate planning. A Living Trust preserves the federal estate tax exemptions of *both* partners.

11

Community Property States vs. Separate Property States

Before you can settle a Married A-B Living Trust or a Married A-B-C Living Trust, you need to understand some basic principles:

- You need to know the difference between community property states and separate property states.
- You need to understand the difference between marital property and separate property.
- You must understand the difference between the theories of itemization allocation and aggregate allocation.

Most of the states in the United States are separate property states, except the following states, which are established as community property states: Arizona, California, Idaho, Louisiana, Nevada, New Mexico, Texas, Washington, and Wisconsin.

SEPARATE PROPERTY STATES

The concept of owning property in separate property states comes from English common law. Basically, the concept of separate property presupposes that the husband owns *all* of the marital assets and the wife owns *none* of the marital assets. Most people living in separate

property states are not aware of this distinction, and they usually inadvertently circumvent the ownership distinction of separate property by titling their assets in joint tenancy—in effect, specifying that each spouse has one-half ownership of the marital assets. (Marital assets are those assets generated by and as a result of the marriage.) Although joint tenancy appears to rectify the separate property problem, the solution is only temporary at best, since, upon the death of a spouse, all of the assets flow to the surviving spouse—which results in "throwing away" one federal estate tax exemption.

When people create a Living Trust, most people are holding their assets in joint tenancy. However, due to the many pitfalls of joint tenancy, the people need to transfer their assets from joint tenancy and into their Living Trust. To ensure that the clients' desires are met (and at the same time satisfying the law), we ask our clients to sign a Letter of Intent/Declaration of Gift. Figure 11-1 on page 120 shows you an example of a form used for the Letter of Intent/Declaration of Gift for a separate property state. This document should be notarized.

The Letter of Intent/Declaration of Gift states that all of the assets are owned fifty-fifty, share and share alike between husband and wife,

119

FIGURE 11-1
SAMPLE LETTER OF INTENT/DECLARATION OF GIFT

Mr. and Mrs. John H. Jones
125 East 5th Avenue
Salt Lake City, Utah 84103

LETTER OF INTENT and DECLARATION OF GIFT

As part of our estate plan, we have established a Revocable Living Trust. We have transferred property into the Trust and in the future we will take property out and put it into the Trust as we desire. It is our intent that all property held in the Trust be our commonly owned or community property, subject to the laws governing joint ownership. In confirmation of this intent, we make the following declaration:

1. All property held by the undersigned in the Trust known as: **The Jones Family Trust, dated September 19, 1979, John H. Jones and Mary R. Jones, Trustors and/or Trustees** is the commonly owned or community property of the said Trustors unless otherwise designated by writing in the Trust documents, or in the manner in which title is held in the Trust.

2. All property which is the separate property of either Trustor has been and will be so designated in writing and signed by the Trustors.

3. Any property in the said Trust which had its origin as separate property, or which cannot be traced as to its origin, is the commonly owned or marital property of the Trustors. If any question should arise, it is the intent of each of the Trustors to gift, in consideration of their mutual love and affection, so much of any disputed property to the other as is necessary to create joint ownership in both Trustors. This gift is intended and made as and when any asset is placed into the Trust.

IN WITNESS WHEREOF, the parties have hereto executed this Letter of Intent and Declaration of Gift this 19th day of September, 1979.

_____   _____
John H. Jones   Mary R. Jones

_____
Note: Notary Certificate of Acknowledgment omitted from illustration.

© Copyright The Estate Plan® 1997. All rights reserved.

unless certain assets are *specifically* designated as separate property. This type of separate property is discussed in greater detail later on in this chapter.

Remember the discussion about stepped-up valuation in Chapter 7? You need to be very aware of the potential adverse economic impact on your estate if you live in a separate property state. One very significant difference in a separate property state is that the Internal Revenue Service affirms that it can clearly distinguish the assets owned by the husband from the assets owned by the wife. Therefore, in a separate property state, only those assets owned by the decedent spouse get full stepped-up valuation. The assets owned by the surviving spouse do not receive any stepped-up valuation benefit!

COMMUNITY PROPERTY STATES

Most community property states are in areas that were once Spanish territory. In the process of acquiring these areas that later became states, the federal government ultimately realized that it had "acquired" the Spanish concept of property division. It was typical of the Spanish to provide the husband with a dowry from the wife. Therefore, it also made sense that if there was later a divorce, the wife, having brought a dowry into the marriage, would have a right to half of the marital assets. Marital assets are defined as those assets generated by, during, and as a result of the marriage. The equal right to half of the marital assets prevails today in all community property states.

Although Louisiana and Wisconsin were not associated with Spanish territorial acquisitions, they are nevertheless community property states. Louisiana is a community property state stemming from its French origins, and Wisconsin is a community property state by statute of its state legislature.

Stepped-Up Valuation

Unlike in separate property states, all marital assets in community property states receive full stepped-up valuation upon the death of the first spouse. For some unknown reason, the IRS concedes that it somehow cannot "equally divide" the marital assets in community property states. Therefore, upon the death of the first spouse, all marital assets receive full stepped-up valuation. The decedent's assets (marital share and separate property) receive full stepped-up valuation, and the survivor's share of the marital assets also receives full stepped-up valuation. However, the survivor's separate property (in contrast to marital assets) does *not* receive stepped-up valuation.

A Letter of Intent/Declaration of Gift form is also used in community property states. An example of this form is shown in Figure 11-2 on page 122.

Moving to and from a Community Property State

It is very important to understand that when a married couple from a separate property state moves to a community property state, the marital assets are immediately considered to be community property. The legal term for the property after this change is *quasi-community property*. For couples domiciled in a community property state, the marital assets will be recognized as community property, even though those marital assets were acquired in a separate property state.

The converse is also true. If the couple moves from a community property state to a separate property state, the marital assets become separate property.

However, if your assets are inside a Living Trust, the rules change. With a Living Trust, all marital assets (except excluded individual separate property) are considered to be community property. Community property assets in a Living Trust *retain their characteristics as community property assets*, even if you move to a separate property state. The assets may even change form without affecting their status as community property. For example, you may sell a home in a community property state, changing the proceeds of the home into cash. Then, you use that "community property cash" to buy a new home in a separate property state. However, since you bought the new home with community property money, the home is still considered to be community property.

FIGURE 11-2
SAMPLE LETTER OF INTENT/DECLARATION OF GIFT

Mr. and Mrs. John H. Jones
12345 Anywhere Street
Los Angeles, California 91361

LETTER OF INTENT and DECLARATION OF GIFT

As part of our estate plan, we have established a Revocable Living Trust. We have transferred property into the Trust and in the future we will take property out and put it into the Trust as we desire. It is our intent that all property held in the Trust be our commonly owned or community property, subject to the laws governing joint ownership. In confirmation of this intent, we make the following declaration:

1. All property held by the undersigned in the Trust known as: **The Jones Family Trust, dated September 19, 1979, John H. Jones and Mary R. Jones, Trustors and/or Trustees** is the commonly owned or community property of the said Trustors unless otherwise designated by writing in the Trust documents, or in the manner in which title is held in the Trust.

2. All property which is the separate property of either Trustor has been and will be so designated in writing and signed by the Trustors.

3. Any property in the said Trust which had its origin as separate property, or which cannot be traced as to its origin, is the commonly owned or community property of the Trustors. If any question should arise, it is the intent of each of the Trustors to gift, in consideration of their mutual love and affection, so much of any disputed property to the other as is necessary to create joint ownership in both Trustors. This gift is intended and made as and when any asset is placed into the Trust.

4. Any previous community property agreement entered into between the undersigned shall no longer be applicable to, and is thereby revoked with respect to, all property held by the undersigned in the Trust known as: **The Jones Family Trust, dated September 19, 1979, John H. Jones and Mary R. Jones, Trustors and/or Trustees.**

IN WITNESS WHEREOF, the parties have hereto executed this Letter of Intent and Declaration of Gift this 19th day of September, 1979.

_____
John H. Jones

_____
Mary R. Jones

Note: Notary Certificate of Acknowledgment omitted from illustration.

© Copyright The Estate Plan® 1997. All rights reserved.

SEPARATE PROPERTY
(OF INDIVIDUALS)

Although I have discussed separate property states and community property states, you need to understand that separate property (of an individual) is an entirely different concept—and is very important, especially for couples in a second marriage. Individual separate property (usually referred to as simply "separate property") consists of assets acquired prior to the marriage, assets received by gift, or assets received by inheritance. These assets are considered to be the separate property of the individual—and are recognized as such in both separate property states and community property states.

To retain or to initially establish an asset's characteristic as individual separate property, you must enter into a Separate Property Agreement between husband and wife. Figure 11-3 on page 124 shows you a very abbreviated sample of a typical Separate Property Agreement. Appendix C contains an example of a complete Separate Property Agreement, which is intended to be used as an addendum to a Living Trust. This document should be notarized.

Separate Property Agreements become part of the couple's Living Trust. Even after years of commingling separate property assets in a marriage, the separate property of each spouse can once again be separated—by mutual agreement and by using Separate Property Agreements. The key, however, is the use of the Separate Property Agreement. If you do not have a Separate Property Agreement, the commingled assets are considered marital property assets.

An important part of a Separate Property Agreement are the exhibits that specifically designate which property items are the separate property of each spouse. It is important to designate the source of the separate property, as well as to indicate that both spouses agree that such property is indeed separate property of the specified spouse. If both spouses have separate property (e.g., from previous marriages or inheritances), each spouse should execute a specific Separate Property Exhibit that explicitly lists his or her separate property. An example of a separate property exhibit designating the specific separate property of a spouse is shown in Table 11-1 on page 125.

ITEMIZATION ALLOCATION VS. AGGREGATE ALLOCATION

Many people worry, "When will Congress take away the Living Trust?" This question comes from the reasoning that the Living Trust just seems to be too good for Congress not to tamper with it. The answer, however, is quite simple. Congress lacks the right to tamper with the Living Trust because the Trust is part of the fabric and common law of the United States. As I have mentioned numerous times, one very important advantage of the Living Trust is that it enables a married couple to preserve both federal estate tax exemptions—and such is our right.

You must be aware, though, that the Internal Revenue Service is also becoming more and more aware of the Living Trust and is now carefully scrutinizing the Living Trust and its provisions. If you play the game by the rules, as I have identified so far, you will win the game—and need not worry. However, if you don't play by the rules, in the end, the IRS will win, depriving you and your spouse of one of your federal estate tax exemptions, which could be extremely costly to your estate. Remember: Understand and follow the rules—they really aren't difficult.

Some of the most important rules specify how to allocate property between the spouses. The methods available are itemization allocation and aggregate (valuation) allocation.

Itemization Method of Allocation

Typically, separate property states require the use of the itemization method of allocation. The itemization method of allocation simply means that each marital asset is divided in half; one-half is placed in the decedent's part of the estate, and the other one-half is placed in the survivor's side of the estate.

To see how this works, let's look at the estate of a married couple who owns securities worth $200,000 and a home worth $400,000. Table 11-2 on page 126 shows how these assets would be allocated with the itemization method.

FIGURE 11-3
ABBREVIATED SAMPLE OF A SEPARATE PROPERTY AGREEMENT

SEPARATE PROPERTY AGREEMENT
(Addendum to Living Trust)

This Agreement is entered into by and between John Jones and Mary Jones, who were married October 15, 1970, at Lake Charles, Louisiana, and who intend by this Agreement to acknowledge their respective rights in the property of the other, and to avoid such interests which, except for the operation of this Agreement, they might acquire in the property of the other as incidents of their marriage relationship.

Separate Property
The parties desire that all property. . . .

Consideration
This Agreement is entered into in consideration. . . .

Mutual Release of Property
Mary Jones covenants and agrees that all of the separate property. . . .
John Jones covenants and agrees that all of the separate property. . . .

Mutual Release of Rights
It is mutually agreed that each party waives, discharges, and releases . . . but not limited to:
    Exhibits
The parties have attached Exhibits hereto, listing their separate property. . . .

After-Acquired Separate Property
This Agreement is not intended to prohibit other property acquired by a spouse. . . .

Living Trust
The parties are executing this Separate Property Agreement coincidentally with the execution of a revocable Living Trust, to which this Agreement is attached as an addendum. . . .

Other Documents
Both parties covenant that they will willingly, at the request of the other. . . .

Revocation
This Agreement is not intended to revoke a Pre-Marital Agreement executed by the parties. . . .

Resolution of Conflict
The parties agree that should any dispute arise between them regarding properties. . . .

Representations and Release
Each party represents that he or she has made a full and complete disclosure of all property. . . .

Governing Law
This Agreement shall be governed by the laws of the State of California.

Binding on Heirs
This Agreement is binding upon the heirs, beneficiaries, Trustees. . . .

Modifications
This Agreement may be modified only by an Agreement in writing signed. . . .

Execution
IN WITNESS WHEREOF, the parties have executed this Agreement this. . . .

TABLE 11-1
SAMPLE EXHIBIT TO SEPARATE PROPERTY AGREEMENTS

Separate Property of John H. Jones

Item	Source*	Net Value	Description	Both Spouses Initial**
1.	P	$200,000	Merrill Lynch stock brokerage Account No. 1987765	*JHJ MRJ*
2.				
3.				
4.				
5.				
6.				
7.				
8.				
9.				
10.				
11.				
12.				
13.				
14.				
15.				

*Source Code: P = Prior to current marriage; G = Gift; I = Inheritance.

**Both spouses initial new items written in.

© Copyright The Estate Plan® 1998. All rights reserved.

TABLE 11-2
ALLOCATION OF ESTATE ASSETS
(ITEMIZATION METHOD FOR A SMALL ESTATE)

	Basic Estate Assets	Decedent's Share	Survivor's Share
Home	$400,000	$200,000	$200,000
Securities	$200,000	$100,000	$100,000
Total	$600,000	$300,000	$300,000

However, such an approach can have serious consequences to the estate. The consequences can be especially severe when you recognize that retirement programs such as IRAs, Keogh plans, simplified employee pension (SEP) plans, pension plans, profit-sharing plans, employee stock ownership plans (ESOPs), and deferred-compensation plans all pass *outside the Trust* to the surviving spouse. Therefore, the retirement programs of a decedent spouse end up in the surviving spouse's share of the estate—which can thoroughly throw your estate allocations out of kilter, particularly if your estate includes a large retirement plan, such as an IRA.

Remember: In a separate property state, when the first spouse dies, only the decedent's share of the marital assets receives full stepped-up valuation. The decedent's separate property also receives full stepped-up valuation, but the survivor's separate property does not receive stepped-up valuation.

Let's now look at a larger estate of a married couple who owns securities worth $200,000, a home worth $400,000, and also an IRA worth $1 million. Table 11-3 shows the result of using the itemization method of allocation. Since the securities and home are in the couple's Trust, one-half of the securities and one-half of the home's value are placed in the decedent's estate, and one-half of the securities and one-half of the home's value are placed in the

survivor's estate. Since the $1 million IRA flows to the surviving spouse as the beneficiary, the surviving spouse ends up with the entire $1 million IRA.

TABLE 11-3
ALLOCATION OF ESTATE ASSETS
(ITEMIZATION METHOD FOR A LARGE ESTATE)

	Basic Estate Assets	Decedent's Share	Survivor's Share
Home	$ 400,000	$200,000	$ 200,000
Securities	$ 200,000	$100,000	$ 100,000
IRA	$1,000,000		$1,000,000
Total	$1,600,000	$300,000	$1,300,000

As you can see, there is now a large imbalance in the two halves of the estate. The result will be that about half of the decedent's $625,000 federal estate tax exemption (rising to $1 million in 2006) will be wasted (i.e., go unused), whereas the surviving spouse's share of the estate will eventually be subject to significant estate taxes. This scenario can be financially hazardous to the size of your estate and the eventual inheritance of the beneficiaries!

There is a solution to this problem, however—the use of a Married IRA–QTIP Trust (which is discussed in Chapter 22, where advanced estate settlement options are presented).

Aggregate (Valuation) Method of Allocation

All community property states allow the aggregate (valuation) method of allocation to be used. "Aggregate method" is the legal term for the more commonly used "valuation method." For simplicity, we will use the term "valuation method" for all allocations in community property states. Under the aggregate (valuation) method, you may allocate your assets by value (i.e., dollar amount). With the aggregate (valuation) method of allocation, you are allowed to allocate varying percentages of an asset's value to either the decedent's B sub-trust or the survivor's A sub-trust, to make best use of both federal estate tax exemptions. You may also include IRAs in the value allocation.

Let's return to the example of the estate of a married couple who owns securities worth $200,000, a home worth $400,000, and an IRA worth $1 million. The total value of the marital estate is $1.6 million.

In Table 11-4, the dollar value of the estate is equally divided between the decedent and the survivor, allocating $800,000 to each. This approach uses the full amount of the decedent's estate tax exemption, thus minimizing potential estate taxes. This method of allocation, obviously, can be most advantageous to retaining the maximum amount of your estate for your eventual beneficiaries.

TABLE 11-4
ALLOCATION OF ESTATE ASSETS
(VALUATION METHOD FOR A LARGE ESTATE)

	Basic Estate Assets	Decedent's Share	Survivor's Share
Home	$ 400,000	$200,000	$200,000
Securities	$ 200,000	$100,000	$100,000
IRA	$1,000,000	$500,000	$500,000
Total	$1,600,000	$800,000	$800,000

Aggregate Community Property Agreement

Don't be lulled into a false sense of security if you happen to be one of those fortunate enough to live in a community property state. Even in a community property state, asset allocation will be done by the itemization method of allocation—unless you have executed an Aggregate Community Property Agreement. An Aggregate Community Property Agreement allows you to split the ownership of an IRA, for example, and this split ownership can be very important in taking maximum advantage of the federal estate tax exemption of the first spouse to die. An Aggregate Community Property Agreement allows you to divide the estate assets by dollar value, rather than item by item.

An abbreviated example of an Aggregate

Community Property Agreement appears in Figure 11-4 on page 128. Appendix D provides a complete version.

Anyone considering an Aggregate Community Property Agreement, however, must proceed with caution. If there is a Separate Property Agreement in effect that identifies certain assets as being nonmarital assets in the estate, then an Aggregate Community Property Agreement will cause the surviving spouse's separate property to be brought into the decedent's Trust, *unless* the separate property has been properly identified as such. This trap can be easily avoided by drawing the Aggregate Community Property Agreement in such a manner that it specifies that the separate property is exempt from being considered for inclusion in the Aggregate Community Property Agreement. With the proper wording in the agreement, the survivor's separate property will remain in the survivor's estate.

Remember: *In a community property state, when the first spouse dies, all of the marital assets receive full stepped-up valuation—for both the decedent and the surviving spouse. The decedent's separate property also receives full stepped-up valuation, but the survivor's separate property does not receive stepped-up valuation.*

Insurance

Like retirement assets, insurance is not included as an asset of the Trust. Insurance benefits flow to the named beneficiary without going through the Trust. Thus, insurance on a decedent, with the spouse as the primary beneficiary, would flow to the surviving spouse and be included in the surviving spouse's A sub-trust. You may circumvent the insurance benefit flowing into the survivor's A sub-trust by creating an Insurance Preservation Trust and then placing the insurance inside the Insurance Preservation Trust. The Insurance Preservation Trust is an irrevocable Trust; therefore, if the Insurance Trust is named as the owner/beneficiary of the insurance, the insurance value is

FIGURE 11-4
ABBREVIATED EXAMPLE OF AN AGGREGATE COMMUNITY PROPERTY AGREEMENT

COMMUNITY PROPERTY RECOGNITION AGREEMENT

THIS AGREEMENT entered into by and between John Jones (Husband) and Mary Jones (Wife) and shall be effective as of the 19th day of September, 1979.

Recitals and Terms

JOINT TENANCY PROPERTY. The parties may have acquired certain real property. . . .

SEPARATE PROPERTY. The parties may have acquired certain real property, personal property. . . .

FAMILY TRUST AGREEMENT. The parties have entered into a revocable inter vivos (living) trust agreement for estate-planning purposes. . . .

COMMUNITY PROPERTY ESTATE. The term Community Property Estate refers to any and all. . . .

RETIREMENT PROCEEDS. John Jones may own and participate in a qualified retirement plan known. . . .

ESTATE-PLANNING OBJECTIVES. The parties desire to enter into an agreement that achieves. . . .

Agreement

To give effect to their intent, the parties agree as follows:

1. ALL PROPERTY IS COMMUNITY PROPERTY. John Jones and Mary Jones mutually agree. . . .

2. EXCEPTION FOR CERTAIN JOINT TENANCY ASSETS. Notwithstanding the provisions of Paragraph 1 above, the parties agree that the following assets held by them as joint tenants. . . .

3. COMMUNITY PROPERTY AGREEMENT. The parties agree that each of them owns an undivided one-half (½) interest in the total aggregate value of their Community Property Estate. . . .

4. DIVISION OF COMMUNITY PROPERTY ESTATE. Following the death of the first to die, John Jones and Mary Jones intend to effect a division of their Community Property Estate . . . :

    A. JOHN JONES DIES FIRST. Mary Jones shall be designated as the primary death beneficiary of John Jones's Retirement Plan. . . .

    B. MARY JONES DIES FIRST. John Jones shall be designated as the primary death beneficiary of Mary Jones's Retirement Plan. . . .

    C. DISCRETION TO DIVIDE COMMUNITY PROPERTY ESTATE. The parties further agree that the division of the Community Property Estate. . . .

    D. SURVIVING SPOUSE'S RIGHT TO CHANGE BENEFICIARY OF RETIREMENT PROCEEDS. The parties expressly agree that the surviving spouse shall have the unrestricted right to. . . .

5. BINDING AGREEMENT. This Agreement shall be binding on the administrators, executors, successors, and assigns of the parties hereto.

6. WRITTEN MODIFICATIONS. Agreement between them. Any modifications or changes to this Agreement must be in writing, making specific reference to this Agreement and. . . .

7. SEVERABILITY. If any provision or part of a provision of this Agreement shall be determined. . . .

8. APPLICABLE LAW. Except where otherwise provided for herein, all matters pertaining to. . . .

9. WAIVER OF NONMARITAL AND OTHER RIGHTS AND REPRESENTATION BY ATTORNEY. Each party acknowledges that he or she has had the opportunity to discuss with an independent. . . .

IN WITNESS WHEREOF, the parties have executed this agreement as of the 19th day of September, 1979. [Followed by signatures and notarization] *not included* in the surviving spouse's estate. The Insurance Preservation Trust is described in more detail in my previous book, *The Living Trust*, and to some extent in Chapter 18 of this book.

GENERAL POWER OF APPOINTMENT (GPOA)

Another tool that can provide important benefits under certain circumstances is the General Power of Appointment (GPOA). The GPOA applies to the trustors only, usually a husband and wife who have created a Living Trust. The GPOA document gives *absolute power* to each spouse over the other spouse's assets. However, this power ceases upon the death of the first spouse.

The primary purpose of the GPOA is that, upon the death of the first spouse, *all assets* flow to the decedent's B sub-trust and/or C sub-trust and attain full stepped-up valuation, regardless of whether you reside in a separate property state or a community property state. (By "all assets," I mean all assets within the Trust. Retirement assets, such as IRAs, are outside the Trust and therefore do not flow to the decedent spouse. Instead, the assets flow to the surviving spouse's A sub-trust.) Even though all the Trust assets flow to the decedent's B sub-trust and/or C sub-trust, the surviving spouse, as the *trustee/beneficiary*, basically has the right to use those assets (income, HEMS, $5,000 or 5 percent) without restriction.

Before you consider using a General Power of Appointment, you must be aware of the consequences; use of a GPOA is not recommended in certain situations. You should not consider using a GPOA if the surviving spouse is not the trustee/beneficiary of the decedent's B sub-trust and/or C sub-trust or if the surviving spouse is "restricted" as a beneficiary. Such restrictions could be the deletion of the frivolous right (the spending of $5,000 or 5 percent of the assets, whichever is greater); the right to use the principal, as necessary, to provide for health, education, maintenance, and support (HEMS); or the right to use all of the income. You should also seriously consider the potentially adverse consequences of using the GPOA if one or more

of the beneficiaries would be disinherited. For example, if a couple is in a second marriage and each spouse has separate children from former marriages, a GPOA is not recommended. The reason is that the effect of the GPOA would be to pass all of the assets to the decedent's side of the Trust (B sub-trust and/or C sub-trust), leaving only retirement assets in the survivor's A sub-trust—which could ultimately be a disservice to the survivor's beneficiaries.

Caution: Upon the death of the first spouse, a GPOA causes all Trust assets to be placed in the decedent's B sub-trust and/or C sub-trust.

Let's take a look at a married couple who has $200,000 in securities, $400,000 in a home, and an IRA worth $100,000. Table 11-5 shows how the assets would be allocated with a General Power of Appointment.

TABLE 11-5
ALLOCATION OF ESTATE ASSETS
(WITH GENERAL POWER OF APPOINTMENT)

	Basic Estate Assets	Decedent's Share	Survivor's Share
Home	$400,000	$400,000	
Securities	$200,000	$200,000	
IRA	$100,000		$100,000
Total	$700,000	$600,000	$100,000

Also, you need to be very aware that the GPOA will effectively put all of the *survivor's separate property* into the decedent's B sub-trust—which could be a serious disadvantage to the survivor's heirs. The GPOA transfers all of the Trust assets to the decedent's B sub-trust and/or C sub-trust. Remember, however, that the retirement assets pass to the surviving spouse, as beneficiary, because the retirement assets are outside the Trust. All of the Trust assets then receive full stepped-up valuation.

However, doing this essentially throws away the survivor's federal estate tax exemption—which could turn out to be a poor trade-off. The GPOA can be drawn up to exclude the individual's separate property. (Part II of this book, which discusses advanced estate settlement options, will show you how to utilize the GPOA to accomplish the best of both worlds.)

The GPOA provides very powerful benefits *if* it is used properly. Besides providing full stepped-up valuation on all assets (which is particularly significant in separate property states), the use of the GPOA provides full asset protection from creditors by placing all of the estate assets in the decedent's B sub-trust and/or C sub-trust, which become irrevocable and impenetrable upon the death of the first spouse.

The flip side to these protections is that none of these estate assets will receive stepped-up valuation upon the death of the second spouse. However, in many cases, the loss of stepped-up valuation is relatively insignificant, when you consider that you have used the decedent's federal estate tax exemption to offset any potential estate taxes.

Remember: The GPOA causes all *Trust assets to flow into the decedent's B sub-trust and C sub-trust upon the death of the first spouse. It provides very powerful benefits* if *it is used properly.*

DEBT PAYMENT POWER OF APPOINTMENT (DPPA)

In lieu of the General Power of Appointment (GPOA), I recommend that you use a Debt Payment Power of Appointment (DPPA). With the Debt Payment Power of Appointment, the surviving spouse has access to all of the assets in the decedent's B sub-trust and/or C sub-trust but is limited in the use of those assets. The surviving spouse may use the assets only to pay the creditors of the decedent's estate, not the creditors of the survivor's estate. The DPPA is a more restrictive provision, and it prevents the surviving spouse from passing the decedent's assets to anyone desired by the surviv-

ing spouse. The DPPA can be drawn up to exclude the survivor's separate property.

LIMITATIONS ON GPOA AND DPPA

For a couple to adopt a General Power of Appointment or a Debt Payment Power of Appointment, both individuals must be competent, and the document must be executed at least one year prior to the death of either individual. The Internal Revenue Service has challenged a GPOA that was executed when one of the parties was on his deathbed, but the ruling has yet to be handed down. However, if a GPOA or a DPPA is executed at least one year prior to the death of either of the individuals, any of these documents should successfully withstand IRS scrutiny.

Once again, if there is separate property in the estate, I strongly recommend that you refrain from using a General Power of Appointment or a Debt Payment Power of Appointment. Remember that these documents cause the survivor's separate property to be placed in the decedent's side of the Trust, which could be a disservice to the beneficiaries of the survivor's A sub-trust. However, you can exclude the survivor's separate property by properly wording the GPOA or DPPA.

Also, if you are in a second marriage and there are children from the former marriages, you should seriously consider refraining from utilizing a GPOA or a DPPA. On the other hand, remember that, if the GPOA or DPPA is properly drawn, the separate property of the surviving spouse can be specifically exempted from being affected by the GPOA or the DPPA.

Appropriate Use

Before authorizing a General Power of Appointment or a Debt Payment Power of Appointment, I use a questionnaire, shown in Figure 11-5, to measure the appropriateness of this provision for each couple. Before I will incorporate the GPOA into one of our Living Trust documents, the clients must satisfactorily answer these questions to ascertain the appropriateness of the GPOA for their case. Also, the GPOA is only useful for a married couple with a Married A-B Trust or a Married A-B-C Trust.

FIGURE 11-5
SURVEY TO MEASURE APPROPRIATENESS OF THE GENERAL POWER OF APPOINTMENT (GPOA)

USE OF THE GENERAL POWER OF APPOINTMENT (GPOA)
[Also applies to use of the Limited Power of Appointment (LPOA) and
to the Debt Payment Power of Appointment (DPPA)]

The effect of a GPOA is to pull all of the assets (*separate property* of each spouse may be exempted) into the estate of the first spouse to die. This will result in full stepped-up valuation for *all* of the assets that end up in the decedent's estate and will provide creditor protection for those assets for the surviving spouse.

Please circle your appropriate response, as it relates to your specific circumstances. (With the exceptions of questions 3, 6, and 7, if any of the answers to the other questions are "No," then the GPOA, DPPA, or LPOA should not be incorporated into your Living Trust.)

1. Are you married, and do you have a Married A-B or Married A-B-C Living Trust?

   Yes   **No**

2. Are you aware that by using the GPOA you may give up part or all of one federal estate tax exemption? (The federal estate tax exemption would apply to the survivor's separate property if retained in the survivor's estate.)

   Yes   **No**

3. Does each spouse have different heirs?

   Yes   **No**

4. Do you recognize that by using the GPOA you will fully, or partially (if you elect to exclude separate property from the GPOA), disinherit the heirs of the surviving spouse?

   Yes   **No**

5. Are you aware that the result of the GPOA is to pull all assets into the decedent's estate? (*Separate property* of each spouse may be excluded from the GPOA.)

   Yes   **No**

6. Do you have separate property—personal property that is separate from your spouse—and identified as such in Separate Property Agreements?

   Yes   **No**

7. Do you desire that the separate property be included in the GPOA (pulled over to the decedent's estate) or excluded from the GPOA (survivor's separate property to be retained in the survivor's estate)?

   Yes (*Include* separate   **No** (*Exclude* separate
       property in GPOA)   property from GPOA)

8. Are you aware that to be effective, the GPOA must be put into effect at least one year before the death of the first spouse?

   Yes   **No**

BENEFIT OF THE GPOA AND DPPA

Although use of the GPOA and DPPA has limitations, some people choose them because of the powerful benefit they provide for creditor protection.

By using either the GPOA or the DPPA (and I favor using the DPPA), you establish that all of the estate assets will pass to the decedent's B sub-trust and/or C sub-trust upon the death of the first spouse, thus leaving only the retirement assets in the survivor's A sub-trust. The assets in the decedent's irrevocable B sub-trust and/or C sub-trust are thereafter protected from attack by creditors. This protection can be used to very effective advantage—particularly against frivolous lawsuits.

If an estate is fortunate enough to have substantial retirement assets—a very large IRA or 401(k) plan—these assets also can be passed to the decedent's estate through a special Married IRA–QTIP Trust (which is discussed in Chapter 22).

USING THE PROPER STRATEGY

To adequately protect the assets of your hard-earned estate from being unnecessarily consumed by federal estate taxes, you need to employ the proper strategy—and the strategy can differ between separate property states and community property states. If one or both spouses has a significant amount of separate property, this situation will also affect the proper strategy.

Determining the proper strategy—and whether to use the rather sophisticated techniques of a General Power of Appointment or a Debt Payment Power of Appointment—requires careful consideration of many factors. You should consult with an experienced financial planner who is knowledgeable about these specialized documents.

Subsequent chapters in this book will explain how these documents can be used to minimize federal estate tax consequences for large estates.

—12—

The Mysterious IRAs

Almost everyone today knows the term "IRA," and some people even know that the initials stand for Individual Retirement Account. Most people believe that an IRA is a good way to save money for their retirement; few people know of the complex tax implications involved with IRAs; and even fewer people—including some financial planners, lawyers, and CPAs—have the slightest hint of just how complex IRAs can be when it comes to settling an estate. This chapter is intended to shed some badly needed light upon this poorly understood area that can significantly affect the ultimate value of a person's after-tax estate.

Before proceeding further into the intricacies of settling an estate in a Living Trust, you need to understand the impact of both income taxes and estate taxes on your IRA and to identify the potential steps appropriate for your particular situation.

As I began to grapple with the subject of IRAs, I realized how incredibly important—and overwhelming—the subject really is to almost everyone. Most people have no inkling that the IRA choice they make today can have a drastic impact on their future estates.

The content of this chapter represents the collaboration and combined knowledge of many professionals. I extend my thanks to the efforts of all those individuals—particularly to Robert Keebler, CPA, MST, who gave so freely of his time and expertise. Hopefully, the extensive treatment of an almost impossible-to-understand subject, the IRA, will clear up many hazy areas, shed needed light on many heretofore unknown or misunderstood areas, and do so in a clear and reasonably understandable manner.

This chapter is written for those who have traditional IRAs (which until recently included just about everyone). I have done my best to make this chapter as understandable as possible, even though the subject is much more complex than most people could ever imagine. Please realize that the IRS has created a maze of traps for the unknowing and unwary.

Most people can see the advantage of tax-deferred savings, but few people can even begin to fathom the "tax hell" that awaits the beneficiaries of those people who have accumulated fairly large IRAs but die before the funds in those IRAs have been consumed.

Beware, my friends, the IRS can, and does, ravage such hard-earned savings—and often grabs more than half of the funds in the form of income taxes and estate taxes!

However, the new Roth IRA provides many benefits above and beyond the traditional IRA—and is a tremendous boon to all Americans. The details of the Roth IRA are covered in the next chapter, which shows you just how simple this new "dream IRA" can be. After comparing the traditional IRAs to the Roth IRAs, I now see great reason for most individuals to opt out of the cumbersome traditional IRA and to move into a far simpler and often more beneficial Roth IRA.

RETIREMENT VEHICLE WITH PITFALLS
The traditional Individual Retirement Account, known to most people as simply an IRA, is probably one of the most misunderstood savings vehicles available to all of us. The basic principle of a traditional IRA, as established by Congress, is to provide you a means to save money for your retirement, and nothing else. The traditional IRA was never designed to enable you to pass those hard-earned and saved assets to your heirs. If you understand this basic premise, you will be better prepared for the hard truth—that it is entirely possible for your traditional IRA to ultimately "disappear" in the form of taxes, upon the death of the second spouse! If that revelation comes as a complete shock to you, don't blame me; I didn't design the IRA.

There are some steps that you can take to help preserve the value of your traditional IRA when you die, but upon the death of the second spouse, your traditional IRA is subject to federal estate taxation and is then also taxable as income to the beneficiaries. Thus, literally up to 75 percent of your traditional IRA can be consumed by taxes! Once you understand the basic principle that the traditional IRA is meant *for retirement only*, then you will be better able to understand and appreciate the content of this chapter.

The traditional IRA is a paradox. People are urged to invest in an IRA to protect themselves in their old age, since social security supposedly will be insufficient to cover their retirement needs. The key to properly handling the traditional IRA is to know the unknowable: when you are going to die. If you could determine your life span, then you would know how much money to spend in the intervening years. The ideal, but almost impossible, goal is to spend your IRA funds at a rate so that when you (as an individual) die or you and your spouse (if married) die, you have exhausted the funds in your IRA.

Unfortunately, most people are not blessed with such prophetic knowledge. Furthermore, it is human nature that the older people get, the more conservative they become in spending their retirement assets. Aging people naturally tend to spend less, to make sure that there will be enough money left for their later years. Unfortunately, as is often the case, when these people die, they leave a substantial sum of money in their traditional IRAs. Please recognize that, under most circumstances, whatever funds are left in the IRA will be decimated by Uncle Sam in the guise of income taxes and estate taxes. I heartily concur with you if you are thinking, "But that just isn't fair!" However, whether anyone likes it or not, that's the way the tax law is written.

IRS Intervention
Adding to the ever-growing IRA dilemma of onerous taxation is the specter of constantly changing rules and regulations governing your IRA. Congress first creates the law, then the Treasury Department transforms that law into what are called Treasury Regulations; thereafter, the IRS interprets the Treasury Regulations into Internal Revenue notices and publications—three separate organizations detailing the law. And what eventually comes down to you and me is often grossly unfair, as well as not always being what Congress intended. Unfortunately, however, the process doesn't even stop there. The IRS routinely re-interprets its own rules in what are called IRS Letter Rulings, or simply IRS Letters of Interpretation. This meddling occurs all too frequently and often varies widely from what Congress originally intended. What has happened to the traditional IRA is a perfect example of IRS meddling.

About five years ago, the IRS issued a Letter Ruling on the IRA that was *the exact opposite* of what was spelled out in the Treasury Regulations! Such action was patently illegal. Many highly qualified tax experts and financial planners called the IRS on the interpretation. Amazingly, the IRS simply answered, "So what!" The IRS has seemingly become an entity unto itself, independent of Congress and beholden to no one. As a result, the IRS continues to define and redefine the rules for the IRA, and therefore keeping up with the constantly changing interpretations has become incredibly difficult.

Today's Intricacies of the IRA Can Affect All of Us

Following the death of an individual, the disposition of an IRA is rather complex, and the tax laws continue to change frequently. I know of no other asset that is so blessed with advantages and yet so fraught with pitfalls as the IRA. The end result to you and your estate can be either beneficial or disastrous, depending upon the decisions that you make while living.

Many people have been fortunate to accumulate sizable IRAs, but few people realize the devastating impact that such fortune may ultimately have on their estates—and the extent to which their hard-earned nest eggs are likely to be gobbled up by Uncle Sam.

> John Drew retired with a qualified retirement plan—a 401(k) plan—invested in his company's stock and rolled over his retirement plan into an IRA. Today, because of the appreciation in his former company's stock, John's IRA is now worth $7 million. John has a serious problem.

Unfortunately, John's case is not unique. Many Americans are caught in the same trap. We tend to think of such people as rich and very fortunate, but most of us are unaware of the disastrous tax consequences that will befall such estates when the person dies.

> Harvey Anderson owns a home worth $200,000 and an IRA worth $1 million. Harvey also has a problem.

Unfortunately, Harvey's case also is not unique. In fact, there are a lot more Harveys out there with similar problems. This chapter is dedicated to the millions of hardworking Americans who have invested in an IRA to enhance their future retirement—and who need to preserve as much of their estates as possible.

THE QUALIFIED PLAN

I strongly urge you to engage good financial counsel before making any decisions about your IRA; you need to know some basic principles. As a general rule, the same basic principles apply to all other retirement programs, such as Keogh plans, simplified employee pension (SEP) plans, pension plans, profit-sharing plans, and employee stock ownership plans (ESOPs). The laws are even more complex for these latter plans.

There is one significant difference between qualified retirement plans and IRAs. Qualified retirement plans are governed by the Employee Retirement Income Security Act (ERISA), and qualified withdrawals are permitted beginning at age 55 (assuming the individual has left the company), whereas IRA withdrawals are not permitted until age 59½. Since the Taxpayer Relief Act of 1997 finally eliminated the 15 percent excise tax on "excessive accumulations and distributions," it is now extremely important to closely examine the economics of distributing highly appreciated stock in a qualified retirement plan, rather than rolling it over into an IRA. According to the latest IRS ruling, the capital gains tax rate of 20 percent now applies to all distributions from retirement plans, regardless of how long the company may have held stock in the plan. (Whether the 18 percent tax rate—for assets held for at least five years—will apply when it becomes effective in the year 2001 is yet to be revealed, but, personally, I doubt that it will.) From a tax standpoint, the lower capital gains tax rate can be far more attractive than rolling over your qualified retirement plan into an IRA and then eventually withdrawing those rolled-over funds from an IRA at your then-current individual income tax rate (most often 28 percent to as high as 39.6 percent, plus any state income taxes).

Be very aware that if you withdraw your retirement funds and pay the capital gains tax, you *may not* invest these funds in a Roth IRA!

To invest your retirement funds in a Roth IRA, you must first roll over the funds into a traditional IRA, convert the traditional IRA to a Roth IRA, and then pay the income tax liability due from the conversion—not a very wise tax approach.

FOUR TYPES OF IRAS

With the advent of the Taxpayer Relief Act of 1997, there are four different types of IRAs:

- The traditional (tax-deductible) IRA
- The traditional non-tax-deductible IRA
- The Roth IRA (commonly referred to as the "dream IRA")
- The education IRA

Each individual needs to be aware of the impact of each type of IRA upon his or her estate.

Traditional (Tax-Deductible) IRA

The latest tax rules allow an individual to make a $2,000 *tax-deductible* contribution to an IRA, as long as the individual's annual adjusted gross income does not exceed $30,000 for a person filing an individual single return (rising to $50,000 by the year 2005). An individual filing jointly can make a $2,000 tax-deductible contribution to an IRA as long as the couple's annual adjusted gross income does not exceed $50,000 (rising to $80,000 by the year 2007). The Taxpayer Relief Act of 1997 also allows a working spouse to contribute $2,000 to an IRA, even if the other spouse is enrolled in a qualified company pension plan. In addition, a nonworking spouse may contribute $2,000 annually to a traditional IRA.

Traditional Non-Deductible IRA

People who don't qualify for the traditional tax-deductible IRA or the Roth IRA because their adjusted gross income is higher than the qualification limits can still take advantage of the traditional non-deductible IRA. If an individual's adjusted gross income does not exceed $95,000 (for a single person) or $150,000 (for a married couple), that person may contribute $2,000 annually, in after-tax dollars, to a tra-

ditional IRA, but any such contribution is *not* tax deductible. Each spouse is allowed to make a non-deductible contribution, and all other IRA advantages (and disadvantages) still apply. All contributions grow on a tax-deferred basis, but all *growth* is taxable upon withdrawal, which *must begin* no later than age 70½. It is important to remember that, following your demise, any residual "growth money" in your IRA will be taxable as income to your children as beneficiaries.

Roth (or "Dream") IRA

The Roth IRA, or "dream IRA," is an entirely new IRA that allows an individual to make a $2,000 *non-deductible* (after-tax) contribution to an IRA, depending on the person's annual adjusted gross income. Eligibility quickly phases out as adjusted gross income increases. A single person's eligibility, based on adjusted gross income, ranges from $95,000 (full eligibility) to $110,000 (no eligibility). Married individuals filing a joint return can also make a $2,000 *non-deductible* contribution to a Roth IRA, with their eligibility also related to their annual adjusted gross income. Eligibility for a married couple ranges from $150,000 (full eligibility) to $160,000 (no eligibility). The next chapter is devoted entirely to explaining this amazing retirement vehicle and the many advantages that it has to offer.

Education IRA

The Taxpayer Relief Act of 1997 also introduced an entirely new IRA that enables a parent or grandparent to make a yearly $500 *non-tax-deductible* contribution to an education IRA for each of his or her children or grandchildren. The moneys may be withdrawn tax free but *must* be used for college or other post-secondary school education expenses. While the paltry amount of $500 is but a drop in the bucket for college expenses, it was anticipated that the Technical Corrections Bill would increase the allowable contribution amount to $2,500 per child or grandchild and extend the tax-free withdrawals to include use for elementary school or high school education expenses. Unfortunately, this increase in the allowable contribution did not happen. The education IRA is available to those individuals whose adjusted gross income does not exceed $95,000 (for a single person) or $150,000 (for a married couple filing jointly).

COST BASIS OF AN IRA

Throughout this text, I refer to the cost basis of an IRA being zero, meaning that all withdrawals from the IRA are fully taxable as ordinary income (at the taxpayer's then-current income tax rate). For the sharp-eyed tax accountants, however, I must acknowledge that *not all* IRAs have a cost basis of zero. For those people who are contributing to a qualified retirement plan at their place of employment (and thus do not qualify for a tax-deductible IRA contribution), the original contribution to an IRA (that was not tax deductible) can be recovered before any taxes are owed. However, for the vast majority of the population who receive a tax deduction for their IRA contributions, my basic premise is still accurate— that the cost basis of an IRA is zero. To continually make distinctions throughout this book about the different cost bases of IRAs would unnecessarily complicate the text and make the reading of this book confusing to the majority of people for whom this book is intended. Therefore, the text and examples throughout the rest of the book state that the cost basis of an IRA is zero.

REQUIRED MINIMUM IRA WITHDRAWALS

Most people are now fairly familiar with the traditional tax-deductible IRA. However, very few people realize that the IRA has some very serious tax consequences that the IRS has imposed over the years. Most people have heard that IRA withdrawals may start at age 59½ and that withdrawals *must* begin no later than at age 70½. However, few people realize that the IRS mandates the minimum amount that must be withdrawn each year!

If you have not done so at an earlier age, when you reach the age of 70½, you *must* make an election as to how your IRA funds will be withdrawn (i.e., how much and how fre-

quently). You may choose from among three different types of withdrawal methods:

- The recalculation method
- The life expectancy method
- The hybrid method (a combination of the first two methods)

Each of these withdrawal methods uses the IRS life expectancy tables to determine the amounts that may be withdrawn. These tables are shown in Appendix B.

Recalculation Method

The recalculation method gives you the longest period of withdrawal by allowing you to effectively recalculate your life expectancy each year based on IRS life expectancy tables. However, this method can have significant adverse tax consequences. For example, for a married couple, if the wife dies first, the husband must change his election to life expectancy, which could potentially require him to increase his withdrawals and therefore his income tax consequences. If both spouses elect the recalculation method and both spouses later die simultaneously, the entire IRA becomes taxable to the beneficiaries by December 31 of the following year!

Life Expectancy Method

The life expectancy method allows you to calculate your withdrawals based on your life expectancy. For example, at age 70, your life expectancy is sixteen more years. Therefore, the first year you would withdraw one-sixteenth of your IRA, and each year thereafter the denominator of your withdrawal fraction would be one less (i.e., one-fifteenth of your remaining IRA in the second year, then one-fourteenth, and so on). The problem with electing this method is that if you are still alive at age 85, your IRA is completely exhausted of funds.

Hybrid Method

For a married couple, the most efficient approach, with the least tax consequences, is to elect the hybrid method. With this method, the IRA owner (usually the husband) elects the recalculation method, and the other spouse (usually the wife) elects the life expectancy method. If the wife dies first, there is no impact on the husband's recalculation method since the husband continues to take distributions based on his own life expectancy. If the husband dies first and the wife is the named beneficiary of the IRA, the wife can roll over the IRA into her own IRA and then elect to withdraw the funds based on her own life expectancy. Alternatively, the wife could decide to split the rollover IRA into separate IRAs, with each child named as beneficiary of a separate IRA. Then, when the wife dies, each child can ultimately take the IRA distributions over his or her own life expectancy.

WITHDRAWAL ELECTION AND ULTIMATE DISTRIBUTION

Few people realize that by age 70½, they are required to elect a withdrawal method and select the IRA beneficiary. It is of utmost importance that people understand that their selection of a beneficiary for their IRA (in case they die before their IRA funds have been completely withdrawn) can also have a major impact on the ultimate financial health of their estate. The consequences of how you elect to make your IRA withdrawals and whom or what you designate as beneficiaries of your IRA can either be most beneficial or incredibly disastrous. The intent of this section is to provide you with a basic understanding of your choices—and the consequences of each.

Spouse as Beneficiary (and Loss of That Spouse)

Once you reach the age of 70½ and name your spouse as your IRA beneficiary, the *time period* for required withdrawal of your IRA funds is now locked in. If the spouse named as beneficiary then passed away and the surviving IRA owner were to later remarry, the IRA owner could change the IRA beneficiary to his or her new spouse—but the original withdrawal period, established when the IRA owner first attained the age of 70½, *cannot* be extended! If the IRA owner were to establish a revocable Married IRA–QTIP Trust as the beneficiary of

the IRA and name the new spouse as the beneficiary of the Married IRA–QTIP Trust, the original time period for IRA withdrawals (established when the IRA owner attained the age of 70½) would still apply, even to the new spouse.

In contrast, however, if the IRA owner were to convert a traditional IRA to a Roth IRA, the new spouse could be named as the Roth IRA beneficiary, and the required withdrawal period would "disappear," since a Roth IRA has no lifetime-required withdrawal period. (The many advantages of the Roth IRA are discussed in the next chapter.)

The "Problem" with Revocable Living Trusts

As silly as this may sound, a standard revocable Living Trust is an invalid recipient (i.e., beneficiary) of an IRA if the Trust allocates the federal estate tax exemption (otherwise known as the "credit shelter amount") by the *pecuniary* method. The pecuniary method allocates an amount equal to the federal estate tax exemption to the decedent's B sub-trust. The IRS considers this to be an exact mathematical allocation—a pecuniary allocation.

If you designate a revocable Living Trust as the beneficiary of your IRA, you must use the *fractional* method of allocation. The fractional method can most easily be visualized as a mathematical fraction:

$$\frac{\text{Credit Shelter Amount}}{\text{Death Benefit}}$$

The credit shelter amount is the tax credit amount ($192,800) associated with the federal estate tax exemption ($600,000). The death benefit is the amount of the IRA to be distributed as of the decedent's date of death.

The easiest way to determine the amount passing outside the credit shelter is to use another simple formula, presented by Natalie B. Choate in her book *Life and Death Planning for Retirement Benefits*:

$$1 - \left(\frac{\text{Credit Shelter Amount}}{\text{Death Benefit}} \right) \times \text{Death Benefit}$$

If you use this formula, you end up with the identical amount that is allocated by the pecuniary method.

You need to be very aware (and you will not find this in any congressional bill) that if a revocable Living Trust is the beneficiary of your IRA, and the Trust has failed to specify the use of the fractional method of allocating the federal estate tax exemption, then your IRA will be fully taxed as income by December 31 of the year following your death!

The IRS Changes Its Mind

It is a very rare occasion when the IRS reverses itself. However, on December 30, 1997, and without any forewarning, the IRS issued an Amendment to a Proposed Regulation (IRS Proposed Regulation Amendment 1.401(a)(9)-1, which can also be found in CCH 1998 *Standard Federal Tax Reports* at paragraph 17,724B), which now permits a *revocable* Living Trust to be the beneficiary of an IRA without triggering serious income tax consequences on the death of the IRA owner after age 70½, if the decedent's share of the Living Trust becomes irrevocable upon his or her death. Previously, if an IRA owner attained age 70½ and died thereafter, having named his or her revocable Living Trust as the beneficiary of the IRA, the IRA would be fully taxable by December 31 of the following year. Since many IRA owners had named their revocable Living Trusts as the IRA beneficiary, this rule was a trap for the unwary taxpayer (a standard ploy of the IRS).

I believe that the IRS succumbed to the current scrutiny by Congress, as well as the public outcry calling for a revision of the tax code or outright abolishment of the IRS. It was never the intent of Congress to penalize the Living Trust as an IRA beneficiary, but it *was* the intent of the IRS to catch the unsuspecting and unwary taxpayer. Now the IRS is trying to appease the American public in the hope of forestalling the public's wrath.

Remain wary, however, because numerous IRS traps are still lying in wait for you. If you name your revocable Living Trust as the beneficiary of an IRA, the following requirements *must* be met:

- The decedent's share of the Living Trust must be irrevocable upon the death of the owner. You may satisfy the new IRS regulations by providing the IRA plan administrator with specific information (in lieu of a copy of your Living Trust). However, since the IRS is more interested in detail than substance, I strongly recommend that you continue to provide your IRA trustee with a complete copy of your Living Trust documents.
- The beneficiaries of the Trust must be identifiable and must be individuals.
- The Trust must use the fractional method (rather than the pecuniary method) of allocating the federal estate tax exemption. This obscure and essentially unknown requirement is yet another "gotcha" for the IRS. I now see numerous articles written by supposedly knowledgeable advisors, who advise the public that they can specify a revocable Living Trust as an IRA beneficiary—without the authors recognizing (or pointing out to the unsuspecting reader) that this very important negative feature still exists. Few, if any, revocable Living Trusts use the fractional method of allocation, nor do they incorporate all of the required legal language that is so important to the IRS.
- The Trust must be valid under state law (an obvious requirement).

Any attempt to try to explain how to utilize a revocable Living Trust as an IRA beneficiary is far too complicated and would destroy the readability of this book for most readers.

Cautionary Note About IRA Beneficiary Designations

As a result of the recent IRS Amendment to a Proposed Regulation, the legal experts at The Estate Plan have attempted to rewrite our Living Trusts to accommodate being the beneficiary of an IRA. After much fruitless effort, however, our experts decided that it was far more appropriate to utilize a Trust specifically designed for an IRA, instead of using a standard revocable Living Trust. The required IRS language for an IRA is so burdensome that the Living Trust becomes overly complicated for use with all of the other estate assets. The IRS seems to work much like the committee that tried to design a horse and instead came up with a camel.

Our legal experts concluded that the Living Trust should be retained, as it currently exists, for use with all assets *except retirement assets*. Our experts recommend that entirely separate vehicles should be created for retirement benefits—specifically, the Married IRA–QTIP Trust for an IRA and the Roth Legacy Trust℠ for a Roth IRA. (The Roth IRA is discussed in the next chapter, and the Roth Legacy Trust℠ [a licensed service mark of The Estate Plan] is discussed in Chapter 22, which presents advanced estate settlement options.)

The IRS recently ruled that if a revocable Living Trust specifies or even implies that the estate taxes are to be paid by the Living Trust, then that Living Trust is unacceptable as a beneficiary of an IRA and the IRA will become due and taxable by December 15 of the year following the date of death. This is just one more IRS "gotcha" and one more valid reason why you don't want to name your Living Trust as a beneficiary of your IRA.

If you feel that the restrictions described above are an unnecessary and complicated burden, I urge you to write to your congressperson and express your dissatisfaction. Maybe then the IRS will eventually become consumer friendly—but I don't think such a miracle will happen during my lifetime.

Some practitioners will design a Living Trust to accommodate the IRA and other assets, but the document becomes overly cumbersome with IRS-required legal language. Although such a Living Trust can be created, I do not recommend that course of action.

A Word of Caution: Use caution and be fully informed of the consequences before *you name your Living Trust as the beneficiary of your IRA.*

Making a Withdrawal Election Is Vitally Important

As I pointed out earlier in this chapter, most people are totally unaware that they must make specific IRA withdrawal elections, as well as name beneficiaries for their IRAs, before they reach the age of 70½. If you fail to make such an election before you reach the age of 70½, the IRS dictates onerous tax consequences for the remaining funds in your traditional IRA.

Previous sections of this chapter discussed several different IRA withdrawal options and beneficiary designations that are available to you. I cannot stress strongly enough that you *must* make these elections prior to reaching the age of 70½. If you fail to make any elections, the IRS will decimate the value of a substantial IRA, leaving the surviving spouse or children with little benefit from your well-intentioned and hard-earned savings. Regardless of whether you are a single person with a traditional IRA or a married person with a traditional IRA, I implore you not to fall victim to the sin of omission—not electing an IRA withdrawal method or designating a beneficiary for your IRA before you reach the age of 70½.

To be forewarned is to be forearmed. Don't let the error of omission cause such a monetary catastrophe to your IRA funds.

Warning: If you have a traditional IRA and fail to make a formal withdrawal election and designate a beneficiary before you reach the age of 70½, all of the remaining funds in the IRA must be withdrawn (and the income tax liability paid) prior to December 31 of the year following the death of the IRA owner.

IRA Beneficiary Designations

When designating a beneficiary(s) for an IRA (for distribution of the remaining IRA funds if the owner dies before depleting the IRA), the owner of an IRA has several options. The primary choices of beneficiary for an IRA fall into three categories:

- Named beneficiaries (such as a spouse, children, or grandchildren)
- Standard revocable Living Trust (the standard Living Trust)

- Revocable Single IRA Trust or Married IRA–QTIP Trust (discussed in Chapter 22)

The tax consequences differ, depending on the beneficiary designations made for an IRA and whether the owner of the IRA is single or married.

The intent of this section is to show you how IRA beneficiary designations have very different tax implications for the beneficiaries.

Single Person with an IRA

Each single person with an IRA has a number of beneficiary options. These options may be changed up until the IRA owner attains the age of 70½, at which time they are locked in. Upon the death of the IRA owner, different tax consequences are associated with each of the various beneficiary options.

Named Beneficiaries (Not a Trust)

If there are named beneficiaries for the deceased person's IRA, the named beneficiaries (e.g., children or grandchildren) may elect to take withdrawals from the IRA spread over the life expectancy of the *oldest beneficiary*. Alternatively, if the original owner of the IRA had divided the IRA into separate IRAs for each beneficiary, each named beneficiary of such a separate IRA could take the IRA withdrawals spread over his or her own life expectancy (usually a much longer time span), thereby requiring smaller withdrawals and, thus, smaller tax payments spread over a longer period of time.

Standard Revocable Living Trust as Beneficiary

If a *standard* revocable Living Trust (i.e., a revocable Living Trust that has not been specifically designed to satisfy the special IRS requirements pertaining to IRAs) is the named beneficiary of the IRA, the Trust beneficiaries must recognize the full amount of the IRA as taxable income by December 31 of the year following the death of the IRA owner. Although a revocable Living Trust may now be designated as the recipient of an IRA *if* the Living Trust properly allocates the federal estate tax exemption by the fractional method, our expe-

rience has shown that the additional requirements needed in order to accommodate the IRA require a specialized Trust that has been specifically designed for the IRA.

Revocable Single IRA Trust as Beneficiary

If a revocable Single IRA Trust—a Trust designed specifically to be the recipient of a single individual IRA—is named as the beneficiary of the IRA, then upon the death of the IRA owner, the named beneficiaries of the Single IRA Trust may spread their withdrawals from the IRA over the life expectancy of the *oldest beneficiary* of the IRA Trust. (The Single IRA Trust and the Married IRA–QTIP Trust are discussed in more detail in Chapter 22, which presents advanced estate settlement options.) Alternatively, if the IRA was split into separate IRAs for each beneficiary, then each beneficiary may spread his or her withdrawals from the IRA over his or her own life expectancy.

Married Couple with an IRA

Every married couple with an IRA has a number of beneficiary options, which may be changed up until the IRA owner attains the age of 70½, at which time the options are locked in. Different tax consequences are associated with each of these beneficiary options.

A married couple with an IRA has some obvious advantages over a single person. The owner of the IRA may withdraw funds from the IRA based on either the recalculation method (described earlier in this chapter) or the individual's life expectancy. Alternatively, the owner may withdraw funds based on the life expectancy of both spouses. However, as I mentioned previously, the most appropriate IRA withdrawal option for a married couple is the hybrid method (described earlier in this chapter), where the husband (the IRA owner) elects the recalculation method and the wife (the beneficiary) elects the life expectancy method. However, for you to select the different withdrawal methods, your IRA agreement must authorize such options. The withdrawal option is selected on a Beneficiary Statement, a lengthy form that is much more than a simple listing of beneficiaries.

Surviving Spouse as Beneficiary

If the surviving spouse is named as the primary beneficiary of the IRA, the surviving spouse may continue to receive funds from the IRA based upon the original life expectancy of the deceased spouse (the original beneficiary). If the surviving spouse elects to continue IRA withdrawals using the deceased spouse's original life expectancy, when the surviving spouse dies, the surviving children must also continue to withdraw the IRA funds over that same remaining life expectancy of the *original beneficiary* (the IRA owner)—often referred to as "ghost" life expectancy.

A more logical option, however, is for the surviving spouse, as the primary beneficiary, to roll over the deceased spouse's IRA into his or her *own* IRA and then elect to withdraw the IRA funds spread over the surviving spouse's own life expectancy. Then, upon the death of the surviving spouse, the children (as beneficiaries of the surviving spouse's IRA) could take the IRA withdrawals spread over the life expectancy of the oldest beneficiary.

Another option for the surviving spouse is to roll over the deceased spouse's IRA into his or her own IRA and then to divide the IRA into separate IRAs for each child (or grandchild, if so desired). Upon the death of the second spouse, each child or grandchild (as beneficiary of a separate IRA) may take the IRA withdrawals spread over his or her own individual life expectancy.

If the surviving spouse elects to roll over the deceased spouse's IRA into the surviving spouse's IRA or elects to change the method of fund withdrawal, he or she should make the election within six months if possible. At the latest, the surviving spouse should elect these changes no later than one year from the date of death of the first spouse.

Remember, if the surviving spouse dies before adding the children as beneficiaries, the beneficiary designations are locked in and cannot subsequently be changed to the children.

Children as Direct Beneficiaries

If the children are named as the direct beneficiaries of the deceased spouse's IRA, each child may take withdrawals from the IRA, but the withdrawal period is spread over the life expectancy of the *oldest child*. Alternatively, if the deceased spouse's IRA has been divided into separate IRAs for each child, then each child—as beneficiary of a separate IRA—may take the IRA withdrawals spread over his or her own individual life expectancy.

Standard Revocable Living Trust as Beneficiary

If a *standard* revocable Living Trust (a revocable Living Trust that has not been specifically designed to satisfy the special IRS requirements pertaining to IRAs) is the named beneficiary of the IRA, the Trust beneficiaries *must* recognize the full amount of the IRA distributions as taxable income by December 31 of the year following the death of the IRA owner. Although a revocable Living Trust may be designated as the recipient of an IRA if the Living Trust properly allocates the federal estate tax exemption by the fractional method, our experience has shown that the additional requirements needed in order to accommodate the IRA require a specialized Trust that has been specifically designed for the IRA.

Revocable Married IRA–QTIP Trust as Beneficiary

If the beneficiary of the IRA is a revocable Married IRA–QTIP Trust (a Trust specifically designed to be the recipient of a married couple's IRA), the named beneficiaries of the Married IRA–QTIP Trust may (upon the death of the IRA owner) spread their withdrawals from the IRA over the life expectancy of the *oldest beneficiary* of the Married IRA–QTIP Trust. (The Single IRA Trust and the Married IRA–QTIP Trust are discussed in greater detail in Chapter 22, which presents advanced estate settlement options.)

Upon the death of the surviving spouse, the children, as remainder beneficiaries of the surviving spouse, may continue to take withdrawals from the IRA based on the remaining "ghost" life expectancy of the second spouse. For example, assume a wife is age 65 when her husband dies, and as beneficiary of her husband's IRA, she elects to take withdrawals over her then-existing life expectancy of twenty years. However, the woman dies only five years later, leaving a balance of fifteen years of ghost life expectancy (unused life expectancy). The trustee representing the remainder beneficiaries is allowed to withdraw the remaining IRA funds based on the remaining ghost life expectancy of fifteen years.

A Word of Caution: If the named beneficiary of the IRA is a revocable Married IRA–QTIP Trust, the withdrawal period for the Trust beneficiaries may not *be changed once the IRA owner attains the age of 70½. The surviving beneficiary(s) of the revocable Married IRA–QTIP Trust must take the IRA withdrawals over the remaining "ghost" life expectancy of the* original *beneficiary.*

Most Advantageous IRA Allocations

Depending on whether an individual is single or married, certain IRA distribution options can be more advantageous, either to the person's estate or to the beneficiaries of his or her IRA(s).

Single Person

For a single person, the best solution is for the IRA owner—prior to attaining the age of 70½—to split his or her IRA into separate IRAs for each desired beneficiary, naming each person as the beneficiary of a separate IRA. Then, when the IRA owner reaches the age of 70½, he or she may elect to use either the recalculation method or the life expectancy method for withdrawing the IRA funds. Upon the death of the IRA owner, each beneficiary may then withdraw funds based on his or her own life expectancy.

If the IRA owner fails to split the IRA, the beneficial options are severely limited. If the IRA owner selects the recalculation method (preferred over the life expectancy method) for determining the amount of the yearly IRA withdrawals, and the individual also included one or more children as named beneficiaries of the IRA (to maximize the life expectancy used to compute withdrawals), the age of the children

must be assumed to be only *ten years younger* than that of the IRA owner! However, upon the death of the IRA owner, the children, as named IRA beneficiaries, may withdraw the remaining IRA funds based on the life expectancy of the oldest child.

Another alternative is for the IRA owner to elect to roll over his or her traditional (taxable) IRA into a Roth IRA. After the owner pays any income taxes due on the rollover amount (since it is considered to be a taxable distribution), the funds in the Roth IRA will grow tax free and can be later withdrawn by the children. The many beneficial uses of the new Roth IRA—one of the most powerful estate-planning concepts available for passing asset growth to your children or grandchildren—is discussed in more detail in the next chapter.

Married Couple

For a married couple, it is preferable to use the hybrid method for calculating the amount of yearly IRA withdrawals. (As detailed earlier, the hybrid method is simply using the recalculation method for the IRA owner and using the life expectancy method for the beneficiary.) Upon the death of the first spouse, the surviving spouse may roll over the remaining funds in the deceased spouse's IRA into the surviving spouse's IRA and may also name the children as beneficiaries of the surviving spouse's IRA. The surviving spouse may then elect the life expectancy method for determining the amount of the yearly IRA withdrawals and may also include one or more children as named beneficiaries of the IRA (to maximize the life expectancy used to compute withdrawals). Remember, that the children must be assumed to be only ten years younger than the surviving spouse when the life expectancy calculations are made. However, upon the death of the IRA owner, the children, as named IRA beneficiaries, may withdraw the remaining IRA funds based on the life expectancy of the oldest child.

An even better approach would be for the surviving spouse to divide the rollover IRA into separate IRAs, with each child named as the primary beneficiary of a separate IRA. Then, upon the death of the surviving spouse, each child may take the remaining IRA funds as withdrawals based on his or her own individual life expectancy. Splitting the rollover IRA into separate IRAs and naming each child as the primary beneficiary of an IRA provides the longest payout period for traditional IRA withdrawals, with the lowest required withdrawal amounts.

Another alternative is for either spouse to roll over his or her traditional (taxable) IRA into a Roth IRA. After the couple pays any taxes due on the rollover amount (since it is considered to be a taxable distribution), the funds in the Roth IRA will grow tax free. Ultimately, the children can withdraw those funds *without paying any income taxes whatsoever!* (The Roth IRA is discussed in greater detail in the next chapter.)

Do Not Name a Standard Living Trust as Your IRA Beneficiary

I strongly advise you not to name your standard Living Trust as the beneficiary of your IRA. It is much preferable to specify the surviving spouse or the children as the named beneficiaries.

HANDICAPPED BENEFICIARY

A handicapped individual creates a very special problem if he or she is receiving supplemental government benefits and is also named as a beneficiary of any significant assets. If the handicapped individual is named as a beneficiary of any asset, when the Trust owner(s) dies, the handicapped individual's government benefits would be seriously jeopardized. The government can even step in and seize any beneficial assets of the handicapped individual, as remuneration for government expenses incurred by the handicapped individual! A perfect example of the solution to this dilemma is the story of Alma Johnsen.

Alma Johnsen has two daughters, one of whom is handicapped. Alma has a home worth $200,000 and a traditional IRA worth $500,000, and she would like to use at least part of the funds in her IRA to provide for her handicapped daughter. In most situations, the logical approach would be to name Alma's Living Trust as the beneficiary of her IRA, because her Living Trust already incorporates the appropriate language for handicapped beneficiaries: It deletes her handicapped daughter as a beneficiary but directs the successor trustee to provide for the needs of the handicapped daughter "at the sole discretion of the trustee." Thus, the beneficial interest of the handicapped individual is only indirect and relies solely on the discretion of the successor trustee—and the government may not seize the asset.

However, as you are now aware, the problem with naming a standard Living Trust (a Trust that has *not* been tailored to meet the IRS requirements for an IRA) as the recipient of a traditional IRA is that, when the original owner of the traditional IRA (Alma Johnsen) dies, all remaining funds in the IRA must be withdrawn (and all income taxes paid) by December 31 of the year following Alma's death. A revocable Single IRA Trust or Married IRA–QTIP Trust would not qualify as a legitimate beneficiary of the traditional IRA because the beneficiaries of a traditional IRA must be specifically named. Remember, it would be inappropriate to name a handicapped person as beneficiary.

An appropriate solution in such a situation would be to roll over the traditional IRA into a Roth IRA, pay the income taxes due on the traditional IRA, and then designate a Roth Legacy Trust(SM) as the recipient of the Roth IRA. Placing a Roth IRA in a Roth Legacy Trust(SM) to support a handicapped individual would be perfectly legitimate. Appropriate Trust language would exclude the handicapped person as a beneficiary, and the successor trustee would be directed to provide for the needs of the handicapped individual "at the sole discretion of the successor trustee."

In such a situation, you must select your successor trustee carefully, since for the Trust to be valid from an IRS standpoint, you may not *require* that the successor trustee provide care for the handicapped individual! Upon the death of the handicapped individual, any remaining funds in the Roth IRA would then be distributed to other designated beneficiaries (usually other children in the family).

COMPLEXITY OF THE IRA

As I mentioned at the beginning of this chapter, the IRA is extremely complex—and Congress also continually changes its mind. The rules of the game for an IRA are in constant flux. If you have an IRA that exceeds a value of $100,000, I strongly urge you to seek experienced financial counsel on how best to protect your IRA from the federal income taxes and federal estate taxes that will likely ravage it upon your death. Remember that a traditional IRA was designed for *your* retirement only. The government assumes that you consumed your IRA until it was empty and then died. In reality, however, our lives seldom proceed that way, and therefore you need to do whatever you can to protect what you worked so hard for many years to build. With the advent of the new Roth IRA and the unique provisions that accompany it, you also now have the very special opportunity of passing on your hard-earned IRA to your children. (The next chapter will discuss the Roth IRA in more detail.)

I am firmly convinced that anyone with a substantial IRA (one valued at $100,000 or more) must seek competent financial-planning advice. Many financial advisors, certified public accountants (CPAs), and tax attorneys have a reasonable understanding of the enormously complicated subject of handling IRAs as part of an estate settlement. If you don't already know of a good financial advisor, you might consider contacting the Institute of Certified Financial Planners (3801 E. Florida Avenue, Suite 708, Denver, Colorado 80201-2544; telephone 800-282-7526).

If the value of your IRA exceeds $1 million, you may need the services of an expert with detailed knowledge of the financial nuances of large IRAs and the many tax consequences. Unfortunately, there are only ten to fifteen truly knowledgeable IRA experts in the United States today. If you need expert advice, I recommend Robert S. Keebler, CPA, MST, of Schumaker, Romenesko & Associates, S.C. (located in Green Bay, Wisconsin; telephone 1-920-498-9500).

It is essential that we each establish our own retirement program. We enjoy a longer life expectancy than ever before, but we are also confronted with a social security program that has a questionable future of solvency. Congress has given the American public the IRA. However, in its not uncommon bungling manner, and ably "assisted" by the IRS, Congress has created a highly complicated maze to traverse. It is unfortunate that a program so important to every American's future can be so incredibly complex. Few people understand the fundamentals of the IRA, and even experienced financial experts often make a misstep that has disastrous effects on a person's estate.

The subject of proper estate planning, including the shielding of large IRAs from onerous income taxes and estate taxes, is further complicated by different impacts on each type of beneficiary (whether a spouse, one or more children, or specifically named beneficiaries), as well as the varying scenarios involving a standard revocable Living Trust, a revocable Single IRA Trust, or a Married IRA–QTIP Trust. The complexities and variety of other advanced estate settlement options are discussed in Chapter 22.

ADVANCED ESTATE SETTLEMENT OPTIONS

This chapter has discussed the estate settlement options that apply to most people's estates. However, if you are one of those fortunate people who has accumulated great wealth and/or who has an IRA of significant value in comparison to the rest of your estate, then you are urged to read Part II, where you will find additional discussion of the following subjects relating to IRAs:

- Single IRA Trust
- Married IRA–QTIP Trust
- Handling very large IRAs in separate property states and community property states
- A large IRA as separate property in a second marriage
- Charitable Remainder Trust
- Aggregate Community Property Agreement
- Disclaiming an interest in an IRA

THE IRA—AN EXCELLENT RETIREMENT VEHICLE

The IRA is becoming more and more important in the financial plans of an ever-increasing number of people as a way to maintain an acceptable standard of living after their retirement.

For most people, social security benefits will not be adequate to provide an acceptable standard of living, and thus the IRA becomes an important source of retirement income.

As you have learned in this chapter, having an IRA to rely on during retirement is only one part of sound financial planning. It is vitally important to also know when and how (as well as whom) you name your IRA beneficiaries. The wrong decisions can cost your estate dearly in the form of unnecessary taxes, whereas the proper decisions can pass your remaining IRA funds to your beneficiaries in a manner that allows them to withdraw those funds over the longest period of time.

Even though the settlement of an estate involving an IRA raises several issues, I cannot stress enough the importance of all Americans supplementing their own future retirement by investing in an IRA during their working years. However, as you will see in Chapter 13, the Roth IRA provides you with a much more financially attractive vehicle for supplementing income in your retirement years.

The IRA is becoming more and more important in the financial plans of an ever-increasing number of people as a way to maintain an acceptable standard of living after retirement.

13

The Roth (or Dream) IRA

By now, almost everyone has heard about the Roth IRA, also commonly referred to as the "dream IRA." The Roth IRA provides a double advantage: It allows all of your contributions to grow and compound on a tax-free basis, and then all contributions and earnings can be eventually withdrawn totally income tax free! What a wonderful way for young people to save and ensure their own future retirement. The only disadvantage of the Roth IRA is that the contributions themselves are not tax deductible. Senator William V. Roth, Jr., Republican from Delaware, proposed an entirely new phenomenal concept in IRAs—which has now been rightly dubbed the dream IRA, because it truly is a prudent way for all Americans to save, whether for their own retirement or to jumpstart the savings plans for their children's or grandchildren's college education.

The key difference between a Roth IRA and a traditional IRA is that with a traditional IRA, all growth is tax deferred, but you must eventually pay income taxes on all distributions. Also, distributions must begin when the traditional IRA owner attains the age of 70½—and are typically consumed over a fifteen- to twenty-year period.

After spending several months analyzing the Roth IRA and comparing it with the traditional IRA, I am convinced that the Roth IRA can be a good *partial* solution to the ever-worsening social security dilemma. The federal government estimates that the social security surplus will disappear by 2029, leaving social security payments to be made solely from annual social security tax revenues, which, at the current tax rate, will provide only about 70 percent of the amount that will be due to the newly retired baby boomers. It is my firm belief that, if the government would simply increase the allowable annual contribution for a Roth IRA to more than the current maximum of $2,000 per year, the Roth IRA could very well turn out to be the long-sought-after solution to our social security dilemma. Americans of all ages would readily pour their own funds into a retirement plan that they control and that would provide a greatly enhanced retirement income in their later years.

ROTH IRA BASICS

Two significant parts of the Roth IRA legislation are often confused in the minds of people who are only vaguely acquainted with it. These areas of confusion involve the rules governing conversion of a traditional IRA to a Roth IRA and contributions to a Roth IRA.

Conversion of a Traditional IRA to a Roth IRA

An existing traditional IRA may be converted to a Roth IRA. The IRA owner must pay income taxes on the full amount of the conversion (taxed as ordinary income). If the Roth IRA conversion occurred during 1998, the income tax bite could have been spread over a four-year period (using four-year income averaging). For a Roth IRA conversion occurring after 1998, the income tax bite must be taken all at once in the year of the conversion. Income taxes generated as a result of the IRA conversion may be paid, if necessary, from funds in the Roth IRA—but *only* if the owner is over the age of 59½.

Contributions to and Withdrawals from a Roth IRA

Individuals may make a yearly contribution to a Roth IRA. These contributions are *not* tax deductible. The combined yearly contributions to an IRA (whether a traditional IRA, a Roth IRA, or a combination of the two) may not exceed $2,000 per year.

All growth and future distributions are tax free. To qualify for tax-free withdrawals, funds must be held in the Roth IRA for a minimum of five years (regardless of your age at withdrawal). However, you may withdraw your original investment at any time during the first five years without penalty.

A Dream Come True

The Roth IRA is truly a dream come true. As I continue to discover the potential of the Roth IRA, I am amazed that Congress actually granted such a benefit to the American people. How did a liberal president and a dysfunctional Congress ever agree enough to pass such a bill? The answer is really quite obvious. Congress saw the immediate benefit of generating increased tax dollars in 1998 from the conversions of traditional IRAs to Roth IRAs. This window of opportunity to convert to the Roth IRA would allow individuals to spread the realized income tax liability over a four-year period

(but only if the conversion was accomplished during 1998) and would result in a substantial increase in income taxes to the U.S. Treasury over four years. Congress realized that this tax windfall also meant a reduction in future income taxes (from those traditional IRAs that would be converted to Roth IRAs), but any such reduction would occur in the future (i.e., in someone else's term of office)! My perception is that very few people have looked closely at the long term and recognized the significant economic benefit to the American public of the Roth (or dream) IRA. As you will soon see in this chapter, all of us have good reason to be most thankful for the forward thinking of Senator Roth.

To appreciate the Roth IRA, you need to remember that the traditional IRA was designed to be consumed during our retirement years—*not* to be passed on to our children or grandchildren.

Be Aware: *If you fail to consume your traditional IRA (i.e., don't spend it all while you are alive), as much as 75 percent of it can be consumed by income taxes and estate taxes!*

The Roth IRA provides numerous advantages over the traditional IRA, particularly for people who have large IRAs. Regardless of the size of your IRA, however, if your financial advisor, accountant, or estate planner did not review your IRA and compare the economic value of converting versus not converting to a Roth IRA, your advisor is at fault for omission—for having failed to give you the opportunity to exercise your right to convert to a Roth IRA during 1998.

If you elect to invest in the Roth IRA, it is of utmost importance that you be aware of one very rigid requirement: You must wait five years before making withdrawals of the compounded growth, even if you are older than 59½. If you withdraw any compounded growth during the first five years, you will incur substantial penalties.

You must clearly understand that this five-year rule is cardinal—the rule is absolutely *inflexible*. You may, however, withdraw your principal (i.e., your contributions) at any time, even within the first five years.

KEY ADVANTAGES OF THE ROTH IRA

The Roth IRA has several substantial advantages over the traditional IRA that makes it a "must have" for every person's future financial enhancement. These advantages are summarized in Table 13-1 on page 150.

Roth IRA Requirement: You may not withdraw any compounded growth for the first five years without incurring penalties—even after the age of 59½.

Tax-Free Growth and Distributions

The Roth IRA allows you to make a *non-tax-deductible* contribution to your IRA; thereafter, all distributions (both principal and growth) can later be withdrawn absolutely *tax free*. The advantage of tax-free withdrawals far outweighs all the other advantages of the Roth IRA. The sheer beauty of the Roth IRA is that, although the contributions are with after-tax dollars, *all growth is tax free*—and this advantage is where the magic of compound interest can truly be seen.

To qualify for tax-free withdrawals, funds in your Roth IRA must have been in the IRA for at least five years, and you must be at least age 59½, disabled, or deceased. The key words are *tax-free withdrawals*—which apply to you, your spouse, your children, and your grandchildren. What a remarkable change from the traditional deductible IRA; now you can pass a nice tax-free growing asset on to your children, who may also later withdraw those same funds absolutely tax free (if the requisite withdrawal requirements are met). Remember that you may always withdraw your principal (i.e., your contributions) without penalty. However, if your Roth IRA is the result of a traditional IRA conversion, any withdrawal of funds other than your contributions *prior to the age of 59½* will be penalized.

No Required Distributions Beginning at Age 70½

With a traditional IRA, you must begin withdrawals from your IRA when you reach the age of 70½, but a Roth IRA has no such age limitation, and you may delay withdrawals for as long as you desire. (However, be aware that, with the potential growth of the Roth IRA, you could eventually end up with an estate that is subject to federal estate taxation and possibly even generation-skipping transfer taxes if you are passing your Roth IRA to your grandchildren.)

The "required withdrawals" (after the age of 70½) from a traditional IRA can much too easily decimate the value of an IRA. If it is your intention to consume your IRA during your lifetime, this provision has no effect on you; however, if you have a large traditional IRA and would like to pass some or all of it on to your children or grandchildren, then the required withdrawals commencing at age 70½ will almost always prevent you from doing so. Remember, however, that the answer to your dilemma is to convert your traditional IRA to a Roth IRA—and then you no longer need to commence required withdrawals when you reach the age of 70½.

It is important to understand that, although there are no required distributions from a Roth IRA *for the IRA owner or the surviving spouse*, the same is not true for the beneficiaries of the IRA. For example, when both parents have died, the children and/or grandchildren must begin to take distributions from the Roth IRA.

Another feature of a Roth IRA is that you can continue to make contributions to the IRA *after* you reach the age of 70½. (With a traditional IRA, you are precluded from making further contributions once you reach the age of 70½.) Being able to continue your Roth IRA contributions provides an outstanding opportunity to let your Roth IRA grow for the benefit of your children and/or grandchildren.

You may make your children or grandchildren the beneficiaries of your Roth IRA. This feature gives you the opportunity to provide an incredible legacy to your heirs because of the magic of tax-free compound interest. I know of no better way of adding to your inheritance, other than investing in insurance to cover the payment of estate taxes. (Chapter 18 discusses the subject of using life insurance, placed in an Insurance Preservation Trust, to pay estate

TABLE 13-1
ADVANTAGES OF THE ROTH IRA

TAX-FREE GROWTH AND DISTRIBUTIONS

- Contributions are after tax, but all growth is tax free.
- Asset growth is compounded, to increase the value of your IRA.
- Distributions—whether to you, your spouse, your children, or other named beneficiaries—are tax free. (The funds must be held for five years in order to qualify as tax free.)

NO REQUIRED WITHDRAWALS/DISTRIBUTIONS BEGINNING AT AGE 70½

- No withdrawals are required, making it a wonderful inheritance vehicle for your children.
- The balance of your Roth IRA can pass to your children or grandchildren.

YOU MAY ELECT THE ROTH IRA AFTER AGE 70½

- You may convert a traditional IRA to a Roth IRA even after age 70½.
- After you pay taxes on the conversion amount, you may withdraw all future growth tax free (after five years).

MORE FAVORABLE BENEFICIARY NAMING

- You retain the right to change the beneficiary, even after age 70½.
- The consequences of whom you name as beneficiaries are far more favorable than for the traditional IRA.
- You can change beneficiaries after age 70½ without any adverse consequences. (This feature is particularly important if your spouse dies and you subsequently remarry.)

EARLY WITHDRAWALS FOR FIRST-TIME HOME BUYERS

- You may withdraw up to $10,000 tax free to purchase your first home. (Funds must be used toward the purchase of a first-time home. Funds must be in your Roth IRA for five years in order to qualify as tax free.)
- You may withdraw your principal (i.e., contributions) at any time without penalty.

FREEDOM FROM IRS RESTRICTIONS

- A Roth IRA is not encumbered with many of the massive restrictions that apply to traditional IRAs.

ABILITY TO GIVE SPOUSE A COMMUNITY PROPERTY INTEREST

- In a community property state, you may split a Roth IRA and assign the community property interest to your spouse. (This ability enables you to fully utilize both federal estate tax exemptions.)

CONVERTING A TRADITIONAL IRA TO A ROTH IRA

- Four-year income averaging was allowed in 1998 to spread the income tax bite over a period of four years.
- You pay taxes now, and all future growth is tax free.
- There is an initial reduction in the value of your estate, when calculating estate taxes (assuming that conversion taxes were paid from other estate assets).
- A greater percentage of your estate passes to your children—they receive a larger inheritance.

GREATER ABILITY TO PROVIDE FOR HANDICAPPED BENEFICIARIES

- With a Roth IRA you can provide for handicapped beneficiaries without jeopardizing their government benefits.

$2,000 ANNUAL CONTRIBUTION

- Contributions may continue after you reach age 70½.
- Higher-income individuals are eligible for Roth IRAs. Eligibility is gradually phased out from $95,000 (full eligibility) to $110,000 (no eligibility) if single, and from $150,000 (full eligibility) to $160,000 (no eligibility) if married.

taxes, rather than forcing your heirs to sell off estate assets.)

You May Elect the Roth IRA After Age 70½

Another important aspect of the Roth IRA is that if you have passed the age of 70½ and have a traditional deductible IRA, you may still convert your traditional IRA to a Roth IRA. Since a Roth IRA has no withdrawal requirement, you may then revise your withdrawal method or cease IRA withdrawals altogether. To qualify to convert your traditional IRA to a Roth IRA, your adjusted gross income (AGI) must be less than $100,000. Contributions to a Roth IRA may be made by those with an adjusted gross income less than $150,000.

More Favorable Beneficiary Naming

With the Roth IRA, the consequences of whom you name as beneficiaries of your IRA are far more favorable than with a traditional IRA. With a Roth IRA, the owner can change the beneficiary(s) of the IRA even after the owner attains the age of 70½.

If you have a traditional IRA and have named your spouse as the beneficiary (before you attained age 70½) and your spouse then predeceases you, your beneficiary designation is locked in—since the beneficiary of a traditional IRA cannot be changed once the IRA owner reaches the age of 70½! If you were to remarry, however, you are allowed to name your new spouse as the beneficiary of your traditional IRA—but the new spouse *must retain the life expectancy of the now-deceased spouse* (which could be a significant detriment if the new spouse is several years younger than the deceased spouse). The answer to this dilemma is, of course, to convert your traditional IRA to a Roth IRA and then to name your new spouse as the beneficiary of the Roth IRA. Remember that you may convert a traditional IRA to a Roth IRA even after you have passed the age of 70½.

Surviving Spouse as Beneficiary

If the surviving spouse is the beneficiary of a traditional IRA, the surviving spouse can roll over the traditional IRA into the surviving spouse's own IRA and then convert the IRA to a Roth IRA (paying any income taxes due). Once the funds are in the Roth IRA, all growth thereafter will be tax free. If the surviving spouse dies without having named the children as IRA beneficiaries, then each child must take distributions based on the remaining ghost life expectancy of the now-deceased parent.

The surviving spouse could leave the Roth IRA to the children (i.e., name each child as a beneficiary of the Roth IRA), and they would be able to take tax-free withdrawals based on the life expectancy of the oldest child. Alternatively, the surviving spouse could split the Roth IRA into separate Roth IRAs for each child; then, upon the death of the surviving spouse, each child could take tax-free Roth IRA distributions based on his or her own individual life expectancy. Typically, the most prudent financial choice for a married couple is to name the surviving spouse as beneficiary of the Roth IRA.

Children as Direct Beneficiaries

If the children are named as direct beneficiaries of the deceased person's Roth IRA, each child may take tax-free withdrawals from the Roth IRA, but the withdrawal period for each child is spread over the life expectancy of the *oldest* child. However, if the deceased person's Roth IRA has been divided into separate Roth IRAs for each child, then each child—as beneficiary of a separate Roth IRA—may take the tax-free Roth IRA withdrawals spread over his or her own individual life expectancy.

Standard Revocable Living Trust as Beneficiary

If a standard revocable Living Trust is named as the beneficiary of a Roth IRA and the Trust was the recipient of the Roth IRA after the original IRA owner attained the age of 70½, the conservative position is that the entire IRA must be withdrawn by December 31 following the year of death. This withdrawal would, of course, be free of any income tax. An alternative position is that, because there is no required beginning date for Roth IRA distributions, as long as the Trust becomes irrevocable upon the death of the donor, all Trust beneficiaries may take distributions over the life expectancy of the oldest Trust beneficiary.

Revocable Single IRA Trust or Married IRA–QTIP Trust as Beneficiary

Although the Roth Legacy Trust℠ is the ideal vehicle to be named as the beneficiary of a Roth IRA, you may also use a revocable Single IRA Trust or a Married IRA–QTIP Trust. However, such use has unnecessary, and possibly undesirable, consequences. (The Roth Legacy Trust℠ is discussed in Chapter 22, which presents advanced estate settlement options.)

If you name a revocable Single IRA Trust or a Married IRA–QTIP Trust as the beneficiary of a Roth IRA, the named beneficiaries of the Single IRA Trust or Married IRA–QTIP Trust may spread their tax-free withdrawals over the life expectancy of the oldest beneficiary of the IRA Trust. (The Single IRA Trust and the Married IRA–QTIP Trust are discussed in Chapter 22.) Upon the death of the surviving spouse, the children, as beneficiaries of the surviving spouse, may continue to take withdrawals from the IRA based on the remaining ghost life expectancy of the second spouse. For example, assume a wife is age 65 when her husband dies, and as beneficiary of her husband's IRA, she elects to take withdrawals over her then-existing life expectancy of twenty years, but she dies only five years later. The woman leaves a balance of fifteen years of ghost life expectancy. The children, as beneficiaries, are allowed to withdraw the remaining IRA funds based on the remaining ghost life expectancy of fifteen years.

A Word of Caution: If you name a revocable Single IRA Trust or a Married IRA–QTIP Trust as beneficiary of the IRA, the surviving beneficiary(s) of the IRA Trust must take the IRA withdrawals over the remaining ghost life expectancy of the oldest named beneficiary.

Early Withdrawals for First-Time Home Buyers

The Roth IRA provides an additional opportunity to first-time home buyers by allowing them to withdraw, tax free, up to $10,000 from their Roth IRA for the down payment on a new home—without meeting any minimum age requirement. However, you must be aware that any such withdrawal *must* pass the five-year holding test to qualify as a tax-free withdrawal (the funds must be held in the Roth IRA for at least the first five years). If the funds are withdrawn before the five-year holding period has been satisfied, the IRS will assess premature withdrawal penalties.

When I talk about withdrawing the IRA funds "tax free," I am really only talking about the compounded growth of your invested funds—which can be a very substantial part of the total IRA value when the funds have been left undisturbed to grow for at least five years. Since you made your original Roth IRA contribution on an after-tax basis (i.e., you did not receive a tax deduction for the amount of the IRA contribution), you may *always* withdraw your basis (your initial IRA investment) without incurring any tax liability and without any penalty.

The Roth IRA Is Unencumbered with IRS Restrictions

The previous chapter took months to research and write, a process that left me appalled at the entangled mess the IRS has created for the traditional IRA. The IRS has created an incredible maze filled with traps for the unwary owner of a traditional IRA. Surprisingly, the Roth IRA presents a fresh approach—and one that is unencumbered by onerous IRS restrictions.

You May Split a Roth IRA and Assign Part to Your Spouse

You can, in effect, "split" a Roth IRA with your spouse. However, it is very important to understand the significant differences in what may (or may not) be done in separate property states versus community property states.

You may not split a traditional IRA, regardless of whether you live in a separate property state or in a community property state. This limitation can create a costly dilemma for those people with a traditional IRA that is large in relation to the overall estate. Remember, upon the death of the IRA owner, the IRA passes outside the Living Trust and ends up in the estate of the surviving spouse. Such a situation precludes using the decedent's federal estate tax exemption to offset the value of the IRA—which ultimately could be very costly to the estate when the surviving spouse dies.

In a separate property state, you may not even split a Roth IRA! However, in a community property state, you may split a Roth IRA and then assign the community property interest in the IRA (i.e., his or her half) to the other spouse. In a community property state, you may convert a traditional IRA to a Roth IRA and then assign half of the community property interest in the Roth IRA to the other spouse, thereby putting half of the IRA in each spouse's estate. Each spouse can be the beneficiary of the other spouse's Roth IRA, thus fully utilizing the federal estate tax exemptions of both spouses.

Converting Traditional IRAs to Roth IRAs
When Congress approved the Roth IRA, it gave most of us a special bonus—the right to convert our existing IRAs into Roth (or dream) IRAs. However, be very aware of a significant "gotcha" if you have a sizable IRA. When you make the IRA conversion, you must recognize the conversion distributions from your traditional IRA as "income" and pay the resultant income tax liability. However, once the traditional IRA has been converted into a Roth IRA (and any taxes paid), thereafter, *all* qualified withdrawals from your Roth IRA—by you, your spouse, or your beneficiaries—are tax free!

As an incentive to get people to convert their existing IRAs (and for Uncle Sam to collect a windfall in income taxes), the government provided a special one-time window of opportunity—but only during 1998. If you converted your traditional IRA to a Roth IRA during 1998, Congress allowed you to spread your additional income tax liability (from the conversion of your traditional IRA) over a four-year period, instead of requiring you to pay the entire income tax hit all in one year. By spreading the additional taxable income over four years, you actually realize a small overall tax savings. You need to be aware, however, that

this four-year income-averaging opportunity ceased after December 31, 1998. You may still convert your traditional IRA to a Roth IRA, but you must realize the additional income tax liability, on the entire amount of the IRA converted, in the tax year during which the conversion is made.

Be aware, however, that Congress, in its benevolent wisdom, has also placed restrictions on just who is allowed to convert a traditional IRA to a Roth IRA. To qualify to convert your traditional IRA, you must have a modified adjusted gross income (AGI)—including the amount of the traditional IRA–required withdrawal if you are over the age of 70½—of no more than $100,000. For most retired people, the income limitation is not a real stumbling block, particularly with some appropriate financial planning. However, this income limitation qualification can be most difficult if you are currently employed and earning more than $100,000 annually. If your income is above the $100,000 AGI limitation in 1998 but under $100,000 in a subsequent year, you may then convert your traditional IRA to a Roth IRA, but you must bite the bullet and recognize the IRA conversion income in one single year (the year in which you make the conversion). The rules change slightly in the year 2005, when you are allowed to exclude your traditional IRA-required withdrawals from your AGI in order to qualify to convert a traditional IRA to a Roth IRA. The tax bite on the conversion must be taken all in one year, since the four-year tax spread only applied to conversions made during 1998. Depending on the size of your IRA, your current modified AGI, and the number of years that you intend to let your IRA grow before withdrawing any funds, converting a traditional IRA to a Roth IRA may not make good financial sense due to the heavy taxation involved.

On the positive side, however, you need to be aware of some important reasons to consider converting a traditional IRA into a Roth IRA, even though a significant amount of tax may be due. By paying the income taxes on your traditional IRA when you convert it to a Roth IRA, you reduce the size of your estate accordingly (assuming that you used other estate assets to pay the income taxes) and, thus, also initially reduce any estate taxes due. The result is that you end up with a lower estate tax and also pass assets (in the form of a Roth IRA) to your children—assets that ultimately will be income tax free.

Size of Your Estate Is Reduced for Estate Taxes and Generation-Skipping Transfer Taxes

When you convert your traditional IRA to a Roth IRA, you must pay income taxes due on the value of your traditional IRA. Presumably, you do so by using other available funds, so that the full value of the IRA continues to grow and compound for your future benefit.

If you have a $500,000 traditional IRA and convert it to a Roth IRA, approximately 35 to 40 percent of the value of the IRA becomes an income tax liability, reducing the value of your estate by almost $175,000 to $200,000. If you were to pass away tomorrow, the value of the estate (for federal estate tax purposes) would be reduced by $200,000. Similarly, if you were passing your estate to your grandchildren, the estate value (for purposes of the generation-skipping tax) would also be reduced by $200,000.

Table 13-2 compares the taxation differences between a traditional IRA and a Roth IRA when passed to your heirs upon your death. This illustration assumes a $1 million IRA, along with other assets, yielding an estate that exceeds the federal estate tax exemption.

TABLE 13-2
TAXATION OF AN IRA AT DEATH

	Traditional IRA	Roth IRA
IRA	$1,000,000	$1,000,000
Less: Income tax at 40% (due to conversion)		($ 400,000)
IRA balance	$1,000,000	$ 600,000
Less: Estate tax	($ 550,000)	($ 330,000)
Less: Income tax	($ 212,000)	$ 0
Net to family	$ 238,000	$ 270,000

Source: Illustration courtesy of Robert S. Keebler, CPA, MST, of Schumaker, Romenesko & Associates, S.C.

Try to Pay the Income Tax from Sources Other Than Your IRA

For obvious reasons, you should pay the income taxes due from the traditional IRA conversion from sources other than the IRA itself. You have been saving money and earning tax-free compound growth on your contributions for many years, and your financial security is enhanced if the entire amount of the IRA can continue working for you.

When Congress initially passed the Roth IRA bill, it contained a requirement that income taxes due from converting a traditional IRA to a Roth IRA had to be paid from sources other than the IRA itself! However, such an onerous restriction inhibited many people from even thinking about converting their traditional IRAs, so Congress passed a "Technical Corrections" bill that allowed income taxes to be paid from the Roth IRA itself—if there were no other sources of funds to pay such taxes. Not everyone has the financial resources to be able to pay the income tax liability from available funds. In such a case, the technical corrections bill provides you with another option, as you will learn later, in the section "If You Must Pay the Taxes from Your IRA Funds." Having to pay the taxes from your Roth IRA funds leaves you with less money working for you, but all of it will be available to you—*absolutely tax free*—when you ultimately withdraw the funds after age 59½.

A Word of Advice: You will be well ahead financially if you use outside funds to pay any IRA conversion taxes, thus preserving your tax-free capital for continued compound growth.

Individuals with Handicapped Beneficiaries Can Better Provide for Them

If you wish to use an IRA to provide for a handicapped child, I strongly advise against naming the handicapped individual as a beneficiary of the IRA. If a handicapped child is named as a beneficiary, you may seriously jeopardize the government benefits that the handicapped child may be receiving. The government may reach in and "take" the IRA as repayment for the benefits the government has already extended to the child! If you named a Roth Legacy Trust℠ as the beneficiary of a traditional IRA, the Trust would not qualify as a legitimate beneficiary, because the beneficiaries of a traditional IRA must be specifically named individuals.

To properly use an IRA to care for a handicapped individual, the appropriate solution would be to convert a traditional IRA into a Roth IRA, pay the taxes due on the conversion, and then designate a Roth Legacy Trust℠ as the recipient of the Roth IRA. (The Roth Legacy Trust℠ is discussed in greater detail in Chapter 22.) The appropriate Trust language would exclude the handicapped person as a beneficiary, and the successor trustee would be directed to provide for the needs of the handicapped individual "at the sole discretion of the successor trustee." If you elect such an arrangement, select your successor trustee carefully, since for the Trust to be valid from an IRS standpoint, the Trust *must not require* the successor trustee to provide care for the handicapped individual. Proper Trust language prevents the handicapped person from becoming a direct beneficiary of the Trust, but his or her needs are adequately met by the trustee. Since the benefits to the handicapped person are at the sole discretion of the trustee, the government has no claim against the Trust, because the benefits are purely discretionary and not mandatory. (However, you know that the trustee is going to make certain that the handicapped individual receives proper care and treatment.)

Upon the death of the handicapped individual, any remaining funds in the IRA would then be distributed to the remainder beneficiaries (presumably, one or more children of the same family).

$2,000 Annual Contribution

Those who could not (or did not wish to) take advantage of the special tax considerations of converting a traditional IRA to a Roth IRA in 1998 should be aware that you may make annual contributions to a Roth IRA. Remember that contributions to a Roth IRA are not tax deductible, but the ability to later withdraw all principal and growth absolutely tax free provides a substantial benefit in your later years.

The annual contribution limit for a Roth IRA is the same as for the traditional IRA: $2,000 annually per person. You may elect to annually contribute $2,000 to a traditional IRA, or to a Roth IRA, or part to each IRA—but the total annual contribution to all IRAs must not exceed $2,000 per person. However, with a Roth IRA (unlike a traditional IRA), you may continue to make contributions to your Roth IRA after you reach the age of 70½. The maximum contribution that can be made to a Roth IRA is phased out as adjusted gross income (AGI) increases. For single taxpayers, eligibility ranges from full eligibility for those with AGIs at or below $95,000 to no eligibility when AGI exceeds $110,000. For a couple filing jointly, eligibility is phased out between $150,000 (full eligibility) and $160,000 (no eligibility).

CONVERSION TO A ROTH IRA IS NOT FOR EVERYONE

There are two situations in which you may wish *not* to convert a traditional IRA to a Roth IRA:

- You intend to consume all of your traditional IRA.
- To convert, you must pay the income taxes from funds in your traditional IRA.

If You Intend to Consume Your Traditional IRA

If you intend to fully consume your traditional IRA, it is probably appropriate to retain your traditional IRA, rather than convert it. On the other hand, you never know when you are going to die. If you pass away prematurely, you may want to pass the residual (i.e., the remaining value) of your IRA to your children or your grandchildren. Therefore, you may still want to consider the option of converting to a Roth IRA.

If You Must Pay the Taxes from Your IRA Funds

It is preferable to use funds other than the IRA itself to pay the additional income taxes resulting from converting to a Roth IRA. If you must use your IRA funds to pay the tax liability, you may decide against converting to a Roth IRA.

The most recent Technical Corrections Bill now provides a glimmer of hope to people who are financially unable to pay the income tax liability from non-IRA funds. If necessary, you may now legally pay these additional income taxes (due to converting your traditional IRA to a Roth IRA) from funds in your new Roth IRA. Think for a moment about the financial impact of this opportunity. The key opportunity here is that you do not have to convert taxable dollars in order to pay the additional income taxes. You are allowed to first make the conversion from your traditional IRA to a Roth IRA and then to withdraw *tax-free funds* from your new Roth IRA to pay the additional income taxes!

WHICH IRA IS RIGHT FOR YOU?

Because a much larger amount of money is involved in IRA conversions, most emphasis has been on converting a traditional IRA to a Roth IRA to realize the significant tax savings when the tax-free withdrawals are eventually made during retirement years. However, what about the individual who hasn't yet begun investing in an IRA or the individual who began investing only in the past few years? The more opportunity I have to review the Roth IRA, the more I am amazed at the many significant benefits of this new investment tool for people of all economic means.

I have been an investment advisor for many years, and my experience has shown that most investors are motivated to invest $2,000 (or $4,000 for an eligible married couple) because of the desire to create a future retirement fund, rather than because of any potential tax deduction that many (but not all) investors receive when they contribute to a traditional IRA. There is a substantial clamor today to analyze large traditional IRAs as candidates for potential conversion to a Roth IRA, but a question still remains: What about the beginning investor? Should he or she choose a traditional IRA or a Roth IRA?

Let me show you a comparison between a traditional IRA and a Roth IRA—first for a large IRA conversion, and then three examples of making yearly contributions for different periods of time.

Traditional IRA vs. Roth IRA (Large Conversion)

Let me show you a most startling comparison between a traditional IRA and a Roth IRA and the dramatic difference between the two IRA types for an elderly retired couple. The importance of converting a traditional IRA of substantial worth to a Roth IRA takes on an entirely new viewpoint when you can see the results, which the next several pages will reveal to you.

Traditional IRA

Let's assume a traditional IRA with a value of $500,000. (It makes no difference whether your own traditional IRA is worth $100,000 or $1 million—the results are simply proportionate to this example.) To simplify this illustration, let's also assume that the husband and wife are both 70 years old—the age at which withdrawals *must* be made from a traditional IRA. Let's further assume that the husband, the IRA owner, lives another fifteen years and dies at age 85. The wife, as beneficiary of her husband's IRA, then converts her husband's IRA into her own IRA and then names her son (who is twenty years younger) as the beneficiary of her IRA. This scenario presents the most conservative approach and provides the longest withdrawal period for the traditional IRA.

Roth IRA

To show you a surprising comparison, let's now assume that the same husband and wife decided to convert their $500,000 traditional IRA to a Roth IRA in 1998 and assume that they are in the 39.6 percent income tax bracket. (The highest income tax bracket of 39.6 percent is used due to the substantially increased taxable income that is created by converting the traditional IRA to a Roth IRA.) When the husband and wife converted their traditional IRA into a Roth IRA, they had to pay an additional income tax bite (spread over four years) on the IRA funds:

Year	Additional Income Tax
1998	$49,500
1999	$49,500
2000	$49,500
2001	$49,500

Let's further assume that the couple paid these additional income taxes from "outside funds" (i.e., funds not taken from the IRA itself), thus enabling the entire $500,000 to pass to the Roth IRA. The government benefits quite nicely from the additional income tax of $198,000, but as you will see, it will lose substantially more income tax revenue in the future, since all Roth IRA distributions will be tax free.

The Dramatic Difference

The dramatic difference between a traditional IRA and a Roth IRA can be shown most effectively if you look at three different comparisons:

- Comparison of required withdrawals
- Comparison of after-tax annual distributions
- Comparison of after-tax cumulative distributions (total amount of distributions made over the withdrawal period)

The following discussion includes a graph of each of these comparisons and uses the following assumptions:

- The investments grow at an annual rate of 10 percent.
- Withdrawals from the traditional IRA are taxed at 28 percent (a conservative rate for a retired individual).

Comparison of Required Withdrawals Let's first compare the required withdrawals from the traditional IRA versus the Roth IRA. Remember that traditional IRA withdrawals must begin when the IRA owner attains the age of 70½ (assumed to be in 1998 in the examples). Roth IRA distributions, however, may be delayed until the second spouse dies.

For this illustration, we will assume that both spouses died within the same year (2013), when their son reached the age of 65. The son must now take the IRA withdrawals over *his* life expectancy.

The graph in Figure 13-1 on page 158 dramatically shows the magic of delayed distribution and interest compounding over time. (The slight change in the Roth IRA curve in the year 2013 is due to the son beginning his withdrawals from the Roth IRA at age 65.)

Note how the required distributions from the traditional IRA absolutely devastate the value of the IRA, leaving less and less for growth, whereas, by comparison, the continued compound growth of the Roth IRA appears phenomenal. The required withdrawals from the traditional IRA totally consume the IRA. In contrast, the Roth IRA is permitted to grow for another fifteen years, annually compounding at 10 percent interest. When the son attains the age of 65 (in the year 2013), he begins his required withdrawals and continues until the Roth IRA is fully depleted when the son attains the age of 87 in the year 2035.

Comparison of After-Tax Annual Distributions Now let's compare the after-tax annual distributions from a traditional IRA versus a Roth IRA for the same $500,000. Figure 13-2 on page 158 reveals the dramatic difference, due to the magic of compound interest and delayed distribution, as well as the significant effect of taxable distributions versus nontaxable distributions. The parents would be required to withdraw funds from their traditional IRA, beginning at a high of $19,000 annually and eventually decreasing to only $356 in the final year of withdrawal. In contrast, however, with a Roth IRA and the son as the beneficiary, the first withdrawals are delayed until the year 2013 (when both parents die and the son attains the age of 65). Due to the magic of compound interest, the first withdrawal amount is $104,000 and rises to $637,000 in the year 2032, when the son is 84! Because of the required distributions, the last distribution is made in the year 2033, when the son is 85, and the final distribution amount is

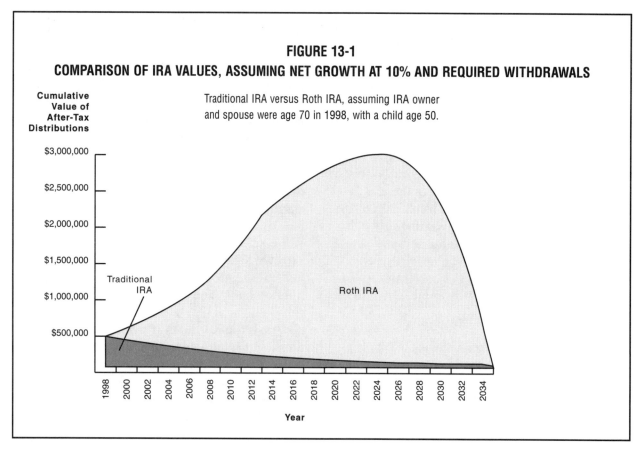

FIGURE 13-1

COMPARISON OF IRA VALUES, ASSUMING NET GROWTH AT 10% AND REQUIRED WITHDRAWALS

Cumulative Value of After-Tax Distributions

Traditional IRA versus Roth IRA, assuming IRA owner and spouse were age 70 in 1998, with a child age 50.

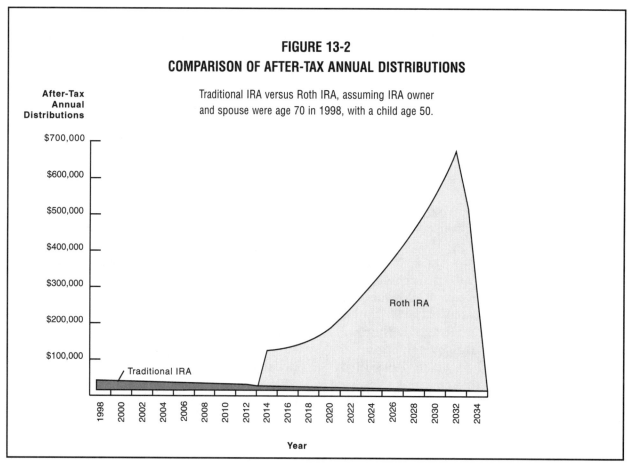

FIGURE 13-2

COMPARISON OF AFTER-TAX ANNUAL DISTRIBUTIONS

After-Tax Annual Distributions

Traditional IRA versus Roth IRA, assuming IRA owner and spouse were age 70 in 1998, with a child age 50.

$462,000. What a significant difference the compounding of money over time can make!

The taxation of the distributions from the traditional IRA appears to leave very little "spendable" return. By comparison, the tax-free distributions from the Roth IRA appear to be gigantic.

Comparison of After-Tax Cumulative Distributions Finally, let's compare the net after-tax cumulative distributions of the traditional IRA versus the Roth IRA for the same $500,000 investment. This comparison looks at the total of all distributions (made over the years) from the traditional IRA as compared to the total distributions made from the Roth IRA. Figure 13-3 presents yet another dramatic difference and indicates the extent to which the Roth IRA provides significantly more "spendable" money, largely because none of the Roth IRA distributions are diluted by income taxes. The total net after-tax distributions from the traditional IRA amount to $360,000, whereas the total net after-tax distributions from the Roth IRA

amount to over $6.5 million—a staggering difference!

Note the astounding difference between the two kinds of distributions. The traditional IRA, over time, provides only a small cumulative return because taxes must be paid on all distributions. The Roth IRA, in contrast, shows a phenomenal cumulative return—particularly because the funds have more years to grow before the required withdrawals begin, but also partly due to the *total lack of taxation* on any withdrawals, no matter how large those withdrawals are.

The Roth IRA Is the Clear Winner

From the previous illustrations, it should now be obvious to you that conversion from a traditional IRA to a Roth IRA has tremendous merit for many people. If you have not yet had your IRA alternatives analyzed (by either a professional or yourself), you need to do so at the earliest opportunity. Even after 1998, when the four-year income averaging benefit no longer applies, conversion still appears to be most

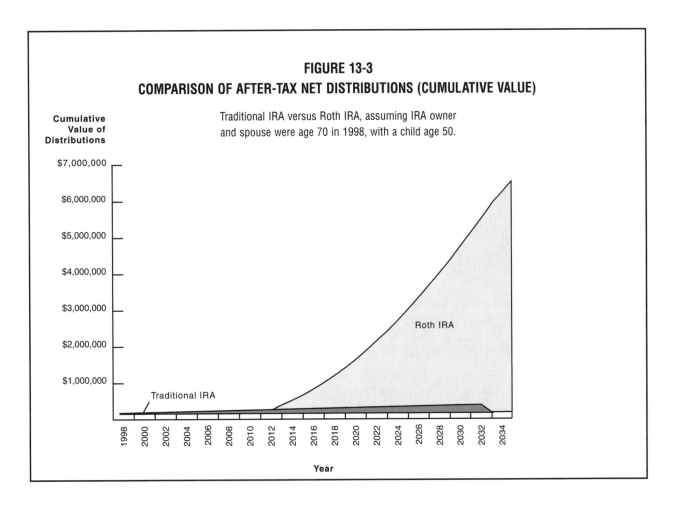

FIGURE 13-3

COMPARISON OF AFTER-TAX NET DISTRIBUTIONS (CUMULATIVE VALUE)

Traditional IRA versus Roth IRA, assuming IRA owner and spouse were age 70 in 1998, with a child age 50.

appealing if you are at all concerned about your "spendable" retirement income.

Good News: If you have attained the age of 70½ and have begun your IRS-required withdrawals from your traditional IRA, you may still convert to a Roth IRA!

Traditional IRA vs. Roth IRA (Yearly Contributions)

You have just learned about the dramatic difference that a Roth IRA can make for a retired couple, but what about younger people without a large IRA conversion, who are able to contribute $2,000 per year toward their retirement? How does the traditional IRA compare with the Roth IRA?

Let me illustrate the difference to you by using three different examples:

- A 35-year-old investor beginning an annual IRA investment
- A 45-year-old investor beginning an annual IRA investment
- A 55-year-old investor beginning an annual IRA investment

The dramatic differences between investing in a traditional IRA versus a Roth IRA can best be illustrated by using graphical comparisons. The examples assume a $2,000 annual investment, starting the investment at ages 35, 45, and 55. The examples assume a growth rate of 10 percent annually. For simplicity, the examples assume a single person who contributes $2,000 annually to a traditional IRA until the individual reaches the age of 70, at which time he or she retires and is required to take the traditional IRA withdrawals. In contrast, with a Roth IRA, the same individual invests the same amount of funds but forgoes any withdrawals—and passes the Roth IRA to a child who is twenty years younger. The child then begins required withdrawals from the Roth IRA when he or she reaches the age of 65, following the death of the IRA owner at age 85. (Even though these examples assume that the original investor takes no distributions from the Roth

IRA, please remember that the Roth IRA owner may withdraw any or all of the funds that may be needed for retirement.)

Thirty-Five-Year-Old Investor

Let's start with the 35-year-old investor. Since the investor will be contributing $2,000 annually for thirty-six years, there will be tremendous growth in the Roth IRA. Therefore, when the IRA owner dies at age 85, to be conservative, let's assume that federal estate taxes will consume 55 percent of the Roth IRA value. (The 55 percent federal estate tax rate is used, since it is prudent to assume that the individual has other assets in addition to the IRA.) Even with such an enormous tax bite, however, the growth of the Roth IRA is still awesome. Remember that estate taxes are due nine months following the date of death, as illustrated by the steep decline of the Roth IRA in the following year (when the individual would have been age 86).

As shown in Figure 13-4, the *required* distributions from the traditional IRA leave nothing when the individual dies at the age of 85. On the other hand, the Roth IRA still maintains a sizable value, even after the large federal estate tax hit, thus leaving a very substantial inheritance.

Even more impressive than the actual growth of the IRA, however, is the magic of compound interest. Assuming that $2,000 is invested each year, from age 35 to age 70, the total investment adds up to only $72,000. The compounding of tax-free interest over time builds the investment for this thirty-six-year period of time to $658,000. For the Roth IRA, this sum will be distributed totally free of any income tax. Figure 13-5 shows the dramatic impact (for the *same* investment dollars) of compound interest growth at 10 percent over a thirty-six-year period.

Forty-Five-Year-Old Investor

Now let's look at the 45-year-old investor. Since the investor will be contributing $2,000 annually for twenty-six years, there will be quite a large growth in the Roth IRA. Therefore, when the IRA owner dies at age 85, to be conservative, let's assume that federal estate taxes will

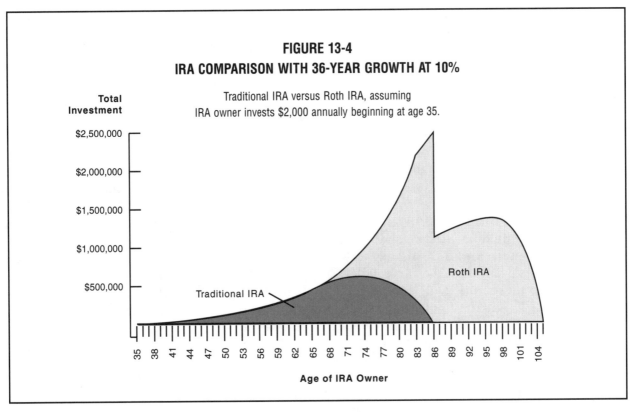

FIGURE 13-4

IRA COMPARISON WITH 36-YEAR GROWTH AT 10%

Traditional IRA versus Roth IRA, assuming
IRA owner invests $2,000 annually beginning at age 35.

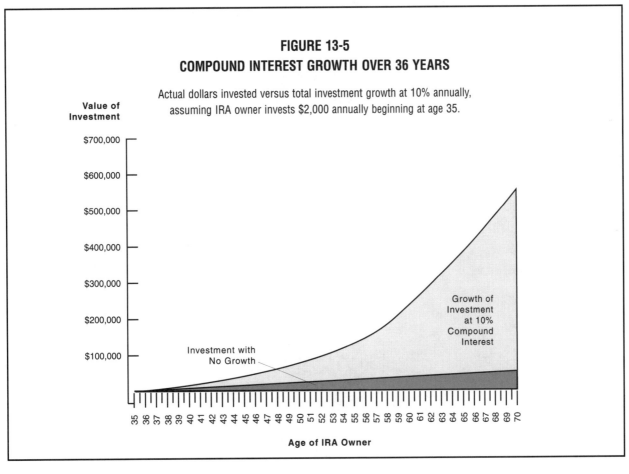

FIGURE 13-5

COMPOUND INTEREST GROWTH OVER 36 YEARS

Actual dollars invested versus total investment growth at 10% annually,
assuming IRA owner invests $2,000 annually beginning at age 35.

consume 40 percent of the Roth IRA value. (The 40 percent federal estate tax rate is used, since it is prudent to assume that the individual has other assets in addition to the IRA.) Even with this hefty tax bite, however, the growth of the Roth IRA is still very astounding. (Remember that the estate taxes are due nine months following the date of death, as illustrated by the sharp decline of the Roth IRA in the following year, when the individual would have been age 86.)

As shown in Figure 13-6, the required distributions from the traditional IRA leave nothing when the individual dies at age 85. In contrast, however, the Roth IRA still maintains a sizable value, even after the large federal estate tax bite, thus still leaving quite a large inheritance.

Even more impressive than the actual growth of the IRA, however, is the magic of compound interest. Assuming $2,000 is invested each year from age 45 to age 70, the total investment is only $52,000. The compounding of tax-free interest over time builds

the investment for this twenty-six-year period to $240,000. For the Roth IRA, this sum will be distributed totally free of any income tax. Figure 13-7 shows the impact (for the same investment dollars) of compound interest growth at 10 percent over a twenty-six-year period.

Fifty-Five-Year-Old Investor

Finally, let's look at the 55-year-old investor. Since the investor will be contributing $2,000 annually for only sixteen years, there will be much less growth in the IRA and therefore no need to consider the impact of any federal estate taxes consuming part of the IRA. When the IRA owner dies at age 85, however, the growth of the Roth IRA still provides a very impressive retirement investment, even with a much shorter period in which to grow.

As shown in Figure 13-8, the required distributions from the traditional IRA leave nothing when the individual dies at age 85. On the other hand, the Roth IRA still maintains a sizable value, thus leaving a very nice inheritance.

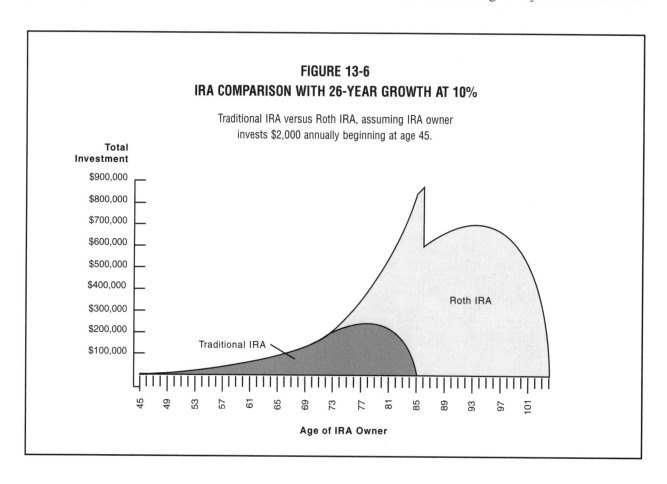

FIGURE 13-6
IRA COMPARISON WITH 26-YEAR GROWTH AT 10%

Traditional IRA versus Roth IRA, assuming IRA owner
invests $2,000 annually beginning at age 45.

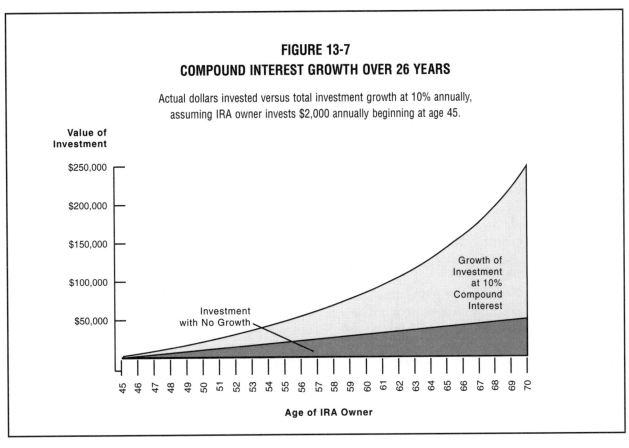

FIGURE 13-7
COMPOUND INTEREST GROWTH OVER 26 YEARS

Actual dollars invested versus total investment growth at 10% annually,
assuming IRA owner invests $2,000 annually beginning at age 45.

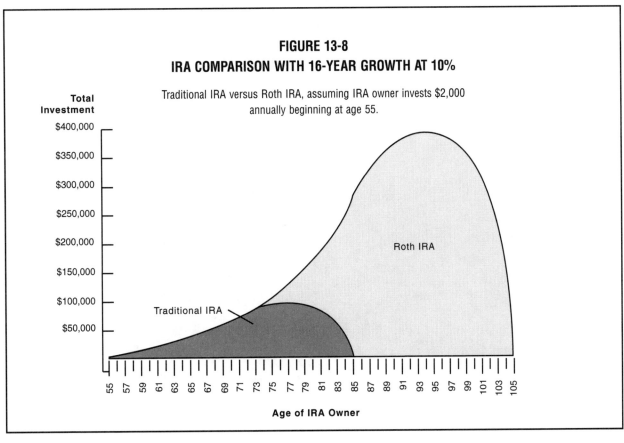

FIGURE 13-8
IRA COMPARISON WITH 16-YEAR GROWTH AT 10%

Traditional IRA versus Roth IRA, assuming IRA owner invests $2,000
annually beginning at age 55.

The slight change in the Roth IRA curve at age 85 is due to the start of the Roth required IRA withdrawals *by the children* since both spouses are now deceased.

Let's again look at the impressive magic of compound interest. Assuming $2,000 is invested each year from age 55 to age 70, the total investment is only $32,000. The compounding of interest over time builds the investment for this sixteen-year period to $79,000. Remember that all of this investment growth will be distributed totally free of any income tax. Figure 13-9 shows the still-sizable growth (for the same investment dollars) of compound interest over a sixteen-year period.

The Roth IRA—Best at Any Age

The preceding examples show a remarkably similar pattern: that the Roth IRA is clearly a wiser choice for investing retirement funds, regardless of the age of the investor. The wise individual should willingly give up an almost insignificant tax deduction (for a traditional IRA) in order to gain a financial windfall at retirement (tax-free distributions from a Roth IRA).

Senator Roth has given us all a great boon—an opportunity too good to overlook and one that all Americans should pursue.

The Roth IRA is clearly the retirement and wealth transfer investment vehicle of the future.

Recent Tax Changes

Numerous beneficial changes have resulted from the IRS Restructuring and Reform Act of 1998 and the various Technical Correction Bills. Two of these changes are significant to the analyses shown in this chapter.

If a traditional IRA is converted to a Roth IRA and the market value of the IRA drops appreciably, the Roth IRA may be converted back to a traditional IRA and then reconverted

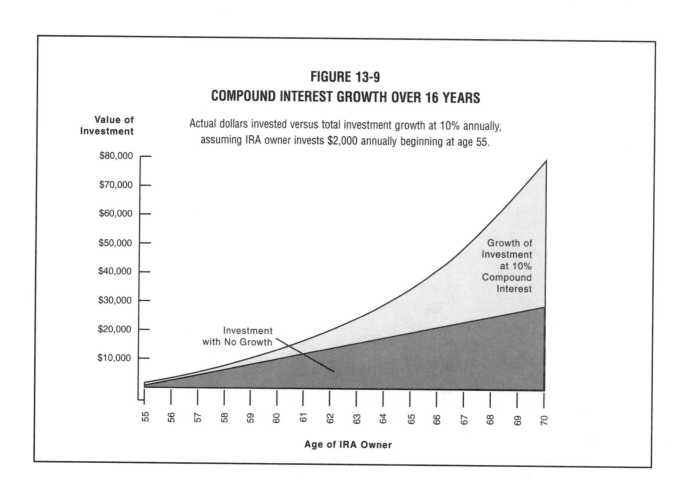

FIGURE 13-9
COMPOUND INTEREST GROWTH OVER 16 YEARS

Value of Investment

Actual dollars invested versus total investment growth at 10% annually, assuming IRA owner invests $2,000 annually beginning at age 55.

$80,000

$70,000

$60,000

$50,000

$40,000   Growth of Investment at 10% Compound Interest

$30,000

$20,000

Investment with No Growth

$10,000

55 56 57 58 59 60 61 62 63 64 65 66 67 68 69 70

Age of IRA Owner

back to a Roth IRA in order to value the conversion at the depreciated rate—resulting in lower taxation.

If a traditional IRA was converted to a Roth IRA in 1998, if the IRA owner elects to pay the conversion taxes over the four-year income-averaging period, and if the owner dies during this time, the surviving spouse may elect to continue to pay the taxes due over the remaining part of the four-year period—*if* the surviving spouse is the sole beneficiary of the Roth IRA.

ADVANCED ESTATE SETTLEMENT OPTIONS

This chapter has discussed the significant benefits that a Roth IRA can provide in your retirement years. If you have accumulated a large traditional IRA and choose to convert it to a Roth IRA so that the funds remaining after your death can be passed to your children or grandchildren, I urge you to read about the Roth Legacy Trust℠ in Chapter 22.

A WONDERFUL OPPORTUNITY

The Roth IRA has finally given Americans the financial savings incentive to more easily save for their retirement, to help ensure an improved quality of life in their well-deserved retirement years, and to provide a better inheritance for their children or grandchildren. The loss of IRA tax deductions granted to most people for traditional IRAs but not allowed for Roth IRA contributions is but a very small price to pay compared to the very large benefits that the Roth IRA bestows—providing tax-free distributions of all of the principal and compounded growth over the years! The importance of tax-free distributions on the compounded growth of a Roth IRA is especially important (and a wonderful boon to the prudent saver), since almost all of the increase in account value is due to the contributions growing at a tax-free compounded rate for many years.

Realize, for a moment, that, if you invested $2,000 per year beginning at age 25 and continuing to age 65 (a total investment of $80,000), your Roth IRA would grow and compound absolutely income-tax free. This compound growth would amount to $726,000 when you reach age 65! These figures assume a conservative 10 percent compounded annual growth rate. Now, *that*, my friends, is a nice retirement cushion!

I urge *all* Americans, both young and old, to start now—and help yourself build or enhance your retirement nest egg by taking advantage of the tax-free Roth IRA.

14

Allocation and Valuation of Assets upon the Death of the First Spouse
Married A-B and Married A-B-C Trusts

Many people have become acquainted with the advantages of a good Living Trust for protecting their estates from unnecessary estate taxes, passing on their hard-earned nest egg to their children, and protecting their individual privacy when a death ultimately overtakes one or both of the trustees. However, when the inevitable finally happens, the grief-stricken survivors seldom know what to do regarding the assets in their estates—and too often fall prey to unscrupulous attorneys and/or CPAs and financial planners who have little or no knowledge of how to settle an estate in a Living Trust.

For most people with a Married A-B Living Trust or a Married A-B-C Living Trust, the actions that must be taken when the first spouse dies are much simpler and less onerous than those that must be taken upon the death of the surviving spouse. The intent of the next several chapters is to cover the two separate situations in detail and to clearly spell out the differences that you face, depending on whether you live in a separate property state or a community property state.

- This chapter addresses the allocation and valuation of assets when the first spouse dies. In two separate parts, it addresses the allocation in separate property states and community property states.
- Chapter 15 addresses special considerations for the surviving spouse upon the death of the first spouse—the many options that need to be considered to ensure that the proper decisions are made for handling the estate assets.
- Chapters 16, 16A, and 16B address the valuation of the estate and the estate tax implications when the surviving spouse dies. The chapters also illustrate the allocation differences between separate property states and community property states.

My greatest challenge is to take the many methods of settling an estate and present them

167

in a simple manner that is understandable to all. Since there are different results, depending upon whether you are in a separate property state or a community property state, I will first summarize general principles, then address the specifics for each type of state. The second part of this chapter is therefore separated into two parts:

- Chapter 14A for separate property states
- Chapter 14B for community property states

Thus, when you need to settle an estate with a Married A-B or A-B-C Trust, refer to the part that is appropriate for your primary state of residence.

The examples in this chapter involve estate asset allocations to the various A, B, and C subtrusts. (Chapter 4 acquainted you with the survivor's A sub-trust and the decedent's B subtrust and C sub-trust.)

A LIVING TRUST—TWO EXTREMES

I have repeatedly emphasized the importance of having a Living Trust for couples who are involved in second marriages, especially where each spouse has children from his or her previous marriage. Usually, the allocation and distribution sections of the Living Trust, along with Separate Property Agreements, ensure that each of the spouse's children equitably receive their parent's assets.

Occasionally, however, the specific language of a Living Trust does not meet the desires (and sometimes a "hidden agenda") of one of the spouses. Let me share with you two contrasting stories about Living Trusts in second marriages.

Several years ago, George and Patricia Hawley came into my office to establish a Living Trust. George had been married before and had four children from his former marriage. This union was Patricia's first marriage. Together, George and Patricia now had one young son. After reviewing their personal situation, I recommended that they should create a Married A-B Trust, and they both concurred.

George specified that his assets, upon his death, were to remain in trust to provide for his surviving spouse and the young son; upon the death of his surviving spouse, his assets would flow equally to his five children (the four children from his previous marriage and his son from his current marriage). Patricia specified that her part of the estate was to go to her only son.

Time passed, and the two never formally executed (signed) their new Trust—failing to keep one appointment after another. Finally, I called George and expressed my concern that he and his wife had not completed their Trust. George told me that Patricia did not understand the Living Trust, and that I should invite her back to give her further information.

I did as George suggested and had a long discussion with his wife. At the end of two hours of extensive explanation of how the Married A-B Trust worked, I realized that Patricia really did understand the A-B Trust (almost as well as I did), but she had her own agenda. Patricia was a number of years younger than George, and she realized that most probably she would be the surviving spouse. Patricia did not like the idea that half of the estate would ultimately go to George's five children, four of whom were not hers. Patricia, sadly, wanted the entire estate to go to her only son.

Patricia realized that, if she and George executed their Living Trust and George died, his half of the estate eventually would be divided among all five of his children. Patricia, therefore, chose to forgo executing the Living Trust; she never explained the reason to George, but her intent was obvious to me. With joint Wills (which I refer to as "Loving Wills"), upon George's death all of his assets would flow to Patricia. In her Will, Patricia could then leave all of George's assets, as well as her own share of the assets, to their only child.

By her failure to complete the Trust process, Patricia was able to thwart her husband's desires for distributing his share of their estate to his own children.

Fortunately, seldom do I see cases similar to George and Patricia's. In second marriages, both spouses usually wish to equitably share the estate assets with children from their first marriages. This next story provides an interesting, and much more equitable, contrast.

Jerry Hempstead created a Living Trust with his new wife. This union was Jerry's second marriage, and the children of his former marriage were almost the same age as Jerry's current wife. Jerry and his current wife had a young son, age 7.

Jerry desired to retain his assets in trust to provide for his surviving spouse and young son in the event of his demise. Jerry further specified that upon his present wife's death, his assets should be divided equally among all of his children, including his 7-year-old son of this second marriage.

However, Jerry was also troubled by a logical concern. With the children of his first marriage being almost the same age as his present wife, Jerry feared that his older children would not outlive his present wife—and therefore would never receive any of his estate. Jerry therefore decided to leave his $50,000 retirement fund to the children of his first marriage when he died. I knew such a distribution would irritate his current wife, and I therefore recommended that Jerry take out an insurance policy on his life in the amount of $50,000 payable to his wife. By taking such action, Jerry equitably provided a benefit to both his older children and his young wife. His children were provided for, and his wife would continue to benefit from his total estate. Jerry agreed to my suggestion, and the new Trust was executed.

DO YOU RESIDE IN A SEPARATE PROPERTY STATE OR A COMMUNITY PROPERTY STATE?

When you value and allocate estate assets upon the death of the first spouse, begin by determining whether you reside in a separate property state or a community property state. Most states are separate property states. There are only nine community property states:

- Arizona
- California
- Idaho
- Louisiana
- Nevada
- New Mexico
- Texas
- Washington
- Wisconsin

If you reside in a separate property state, read Chapter 14A; if you reside in a community property state, read Chapter 14B. If you own property in more than one state, your primary state of residence will prevail. For instance, if you live in a community property state and also own property in a separate property state, your state of residence (the community property state) establishes the status of *all* of your marital assets as community property.

Although I use the term *reside*, the technical definition is where you intend to die. Howard Hughes is an excellent example of someone who attempted to fulfill this desire. In his last hours of life, Howard Hughes was flown from Mexico City to Houston, en route to Las Vegas, Nevada—a state that has no inheritance tax. Howard Hughes died en route to Houston, but his death didn't stop the states of Texas and California from both declaring that Howard Hughes really "intended to die" in their states.

Those living as "snowbirds"—in the scenic North during the summer and then in the warmer South during the winter—may choose their state of residence. Typically, there is little change in the consequences because most snowbirds are moving back and forth from one separate property state to another separate property state.

ITEMIZATION AND VALUATION METHODS IN MARRIED A-B AND MARRIED A-B-C TRUSTS

The method of allocating estate assets varies, depending on whether you live in a separate property state or a community property state:

- The itemization method is used in separate property states.
- The valuation method is used in community property states.

Itemization Method

The typical method of allocating assets in separate property states is the itemization method. The marital assets are divided right down the middle, with one-half of the assets going to the decedent's half of the ledger and one-half of the assets going to the survivor's side of the ledger. The separate property of the decedent flows directly to the decedent's side of the ledger, and the separate property of the survivor flows directly to the survivor's side of the ledger. All assets on the decedent's side of the ledger receive full stepped-up valuation to current market value, whereas the assets on the survivor's side of the ledger retain their original cost basis. Typically, any IRAs flow outside the Trust to the surviving beneficiary.

Valuation Method

The most common method of allocating assets in community property states is the aggregate, or valuation, method. The marital assets are allocated to the decedent's side of the ledger and to the survivor's side based on aggregate *value*, rather than by single whole items. Although the correct technical term for this allocation method is the *aggregate* method, for simplicity I will use the more descriptive term *valuation* method or "allocate by value." When allocating by value, half of the *value* of the marital assets is allocated to the decedent's side of the ledger, and the other half of the *value* of the marital assets is allocated to the survivor's side of the ledger. The most important feature of allocating by the valuation method is that you are able to include the IRA (if it is a marital asset) in the overall allocation split, even though the IRA passes to the surviving spouse outside the Living Trust. The separate property of the decedent passes directly to the decedent's side of the ledger, and the survivor's separate property passes directly to the survivor's side of the ledger.

Obviously, the valuation method offers greater flexibility of allocating marital assets than the itemization method typically used in separate property states. With the valuation method, *all* marital assets, regardless of the side of the ledger on which they appear, receive full stepped-up valuation upon the death of the first spouse. Only the survivor's separate property does not receive stepped-up valuation upon the death of the first spouse.

Other Methods

Although the itemization method and the valuation method are the most common methods of allocating assets, there are other less common methods used to accomplish special purposes. Other allocation methods are used when an estate has a large IRA and/or the size of the estate requires IRA protection, asset protection, or aggressive tax reduction.

Recommendation: If you live in a separate property state, use the itemization method. If you live in a community property state, use the valuation method.

WHEN A SPOUSE DIES

Until a spouse dies, there is nothing for you to do except ensure that all of your assets are placed in your Living Trust. Following the death of a spouse, you need to allocate assets to the sub-trusts.

When the First Spouse Dies

The most important part of settling an estate in a good Living Trust for a married couple is properly allocating the estate assets between the decedent's B sub-trust and/or C sub-trust and the survivor's A sub-trust. Chapters 14A and 14B are devoted to explaining the options available to you.

When the Second Spouse Dies

When the surviving spouse dies, different considerations come into play in settling the estate. The goal is to either eliminate or at least minimize any potential estate taxes, thus passing as much of the estate as possible to the heirs. These considerations are described in greater detail in Chapter 16.

ASSET ALLOCATION USING THE LEDGER METHOD

The ledger method is a simple way to allocate estate assets between the A sub-trust, B sub-trust, and C sub-trust upon the death of the first spouse, without the unnecessary step of formally retitling ownership of the assets.

Chapter 8 briefly discussed the ledger method of asset allocation. It is important for you to remember the following rules:

- Before allocating assets to the sub-trusts, the assets must be properly valued (as previously described in Chapter 7).
- Use the *net value* of the asset (i.e., the current market value of the asset minus any outstanding liabilities against that asset, such as a mortgage).
- The ledger method of asset allocation only applies after the death of the *first spouse* and only in allocating assets to the decedent's B sub-trust and/or C sub-trust and to the survivor's A sub-trust.
- In separate property states, assets must be allocated *by item* rather than by value (i.e., the entire asset must be allocated to the A, B, or C sub-trust and may not be split between sub-trusts).
- In community property states, assets may be allocated *by value* rather than by item (i.e., a portion of the asset may be allocated to the A, B, or C sub-trusts), which more easily allows both federal estate tax exemptions to be fully utilized.
- Substantiate your asset valuations with written documents, and retain those documents for future reference.
- Identify the full asset description on your ledger worksheets, including the net asset value (current value less any liabilities), the date of asset valuation, and the source of the valuation (e.g., account statement, list of comparable values, appraisal, and so on).
- Allocate an asset by a percentage of its total market value to the appropriate sub-trust, where appropriate.
- Each ledger sheet must be signed and dated by the trustee(s).

For you to better understand the asset allocations used in the examples in Chapters 14A and 14B, let me show you a typical example of using the ledger method to allocate estate assets between sub-trusts. Assume that an estate consists of the assets with current market values as shown in Table 14-1.

TABLE 14-1
ESTATE ASSET VALUES FOR LEDGER ILLUSTRATIONS

Estate Assets	Market Value	Cost Basis
Home	$ 400,000	$ 200,000
Other Real Estate	$ 800,000	$ 400,000
Decedent's Separate Property	$ 100,000	$ 50,000
Survivor's Separate Property	$ 100,000	$ 50,000
IRA*	$1,000,000	

*The cost basis of an IRA is zero.

Ledger Worksheets

Ledger worksheets have been developed to help you understand how to allocate estate assets to the appropriate sub-trusts—retaining the appropriate current market value (for the decedent's assets) and the original cost basis (for the survivor's assets). Figure 14-1 for separate property states on page 172 and Figure 14-2 for community property states on page 173 show you appropriate allocations between the sub-trusts for the estate assets shown in Table 14-2 on page 174. The shaded areas on the worksheets denote the assets that retain their cost basis (do not receive stepped-up valuation).

Using Ledger Sheets

When allocating assets to the ledger accounts in separate property states, remember that the current market value (as of the decedent's date of death) should be used for the decedent's share of marital assets and for the decedent's separate property. The original cost basis must be used for the survivor's share of marital assets and for the survivor's separate property. Although the asset allocations differ for community property states, the principle of allocating assets on the ledger sheets for the A sub-trust, B sub-trust, and C sub-trust remains the same.

Let's now assume that the estate assets have been allocated to the sub-trusts as shown in Table 14-2 for an estate in a separate property

FIGURE 14-1
SAMPLE LEDGER WORKSHEET FOR A SEPARATE PROPERTY STATE

Description of Property	SEPARATE PROPERTY		MARITAL SHARE OF ASSETS		TRUSTS		
	Deceased Net Stepped-Up Valuation	Survivor Net Cost Basis	Deceased Net Stepped-Up Valuation	Survivor Net Cost Basis	C Net Stepped-Up Valuation	B Net Stepped-Up Valuation	A Net Cost Basis
Checking	$	$	$	$	$	$	$
Money Market							
CD							
Bonds							
Home			$200,000	$ 100,000		$200,000	$ 100,000
Other Real Estate			$400,000	$ 200,000	$100,000	$300,000	$ 200,000
Personal Effects							
IRA				$1,000,000		$100,000	$1,000,000
Separate Property of Decedent Spouse	$100,000						
Separate Property of Surviving Spouse		$50,000					$ 50,000

The shaded areas denote that survivor's share of marital assets and survivor's separate property do not receive stepped-up valuation (and therefore must be shown at cost basis).

FIGURE 14-2

SAMPLE LEDGER WORKSHEET FOR A COMMUNITY PROPERTY STATE

Description of Property	SEPARATE PROPERTY		MARITAL SHARE OF ASSETS		TRUSTS		
	Deceased	Survivor	Deceased	Survivor	C	B	A
	Net Stepped-Up Valuation	Net Cost Basis	Net Stepped-Up Valuation	Net Stepped-Up Valuation	Net Stepped-Up Valuation	Net Stepped-Up Valuation	Net Stepped-Up Valuation
Checking	$	$	$	$	$	$	$
Money Market							
CD							
Bonds			$200,000	$ 200,000			
Home			$400,000	$ 400,000		$400,000	
Other Real Estate					$600,000	$100,000	
Personal Effects				$1,000,000			$1,000,000
IRA							
Separate Property of Decedent Spouse	$100,000					$100,000	
Separate Property of Surviving Spouse		$50,000					$ 50,000

The shaded areas denote that survivor's separate property does not receive stepped-up valuation (and therefore must be shown at cost basis).

TABLE 14-2
ESTATE ASSETS ALLOCATED TO SUB-TRUSTS

	Market Value	C Trust	B Trust	A Trust
Home	$ 400,000		$200,000	$ 100,000*
Other Real Estate	$ 800,000	$100,000	$300,000	$ 200,000*
Decedent's Separate Property	$ 100,000		$100,000	
Survivor's Separate Property	$ 100,000			$ 50,000*
IRA	$1,000,000			$1,000,000**
Total Value in Decedent's Estate			$700,000	
Total Value in Survivor's Estate				$1,350,000

*Surviving spouse's share entered at original cost basis.

**The IRA passes outside the Trust to the surviving spouse and thus is shown in the A sub-trust. The cost basis of an IRA is zero.

state. Figures 14-3, 14-4, and 14-5 on pages 175–176 show you how the assets would be allocated to the decedent's B sub-trust ledger, the decedent's C sub-trust ledger, and the survivor's A sub-trust ledger.

Transferring Assets Between Sub-Trusts
It is important for you to understand that assets can be transferred from one sub-trust ledger to another, since appropriate repositioning of estate assets can often have a significant impact on the amount of federal estate taxes that may eventually be due. However, you need to be very aware that any "transfer" of an asset between sub-trust ledgers *must be done on a dollar-for-dollar basis* (at current market values). When making any such transfer, you must account for any potential capital gains tax liability (i.e., determine the amount of capital gains and pay any tax liability that is due).

The illustration shown in Figure 14-6 on page 177 shows how assets can be transferred from one sub-trust ledger to another.

INCLUSION OF ADVANCED SETTLEMENT OPTIONS
Most estates are not large or complex enough to require the use of sophisticated estate preservation vehicles, such as the Married IRA–QTIP Trust, Debt Payment Power of Appointment (DPPA), or General Power of Appointment (GPOA). I include a very brief description of these options only to familiarize the more inquisitive readers with the many potential opportunities available to them. If you have an average estate (like most of the populace), you need not be concerned with these specialized estate-planning tools. If you have a large estate or complex settlement issues, read Part II, where you will find additional discussion of these subjects.

Married IRA–QTIP Trust
The Married IRA–QTIP Trust is required only for estates with a very large IRA. The Married IRA–QTIP Trust is a *revocable* Trust designed specifically to be the beneficiary of an IRA and to meet all of the IRS tests—in order to avoid the IRA being subject to immediate withdrawal of funds and the consequent burden of onerous income taxes when the IRA owner dies.

Inclusion of the Married IRA–QTIP Trust with either an A Trust, an A-B Trust, or an A-B-C Trust offers full utilization of the decedent's federal estate tax exemption for estates that include an IRA that is large in proportion to the other marital assets. The Married IRA–QTIP Trust is also effectively used in second marriages where the IRA is the separate property of one spouse, who desires to use it to provide for the surviving spouse but, upon the death of the surviving spouse, desires the IRA to ultimately pass to the heirs of the owner of the IRA. (The Married IRA–QTIP Trust is discussed in more detail in Chapter 22.)

Debt Payment Power of Appointment and General Power of Appointment

The Debt Payment Power of Appointment (DPPA) document or the General Power of Appointment (GPOA) document is used to attain full stepped-up valuation of *all* of the estate's assets and to protect the assets against creditors and frivolous lawsuits.

Use Advanced Options with Care

Combining the A, B, and/or C sub-trusts with the Married IRA–QTIP Trust, the DPPA, or the GPOA provides the opportunity to accomplish one or more of the objectives just described. Although the majority of Trusts need to use only the basic itemization method or valuation method of allocation when a spouse dies, a small percentage of estates can effectively use these other vehicles. I have mentioned these very sophisticated estate-planning tools because they are being used more frequently for large estates. However, be very cautious and diligent before including these highly specialized vehicles in your Living Trust. All too often, these tools are incorporated into a Trust without the trustors fully understanding that including these documents can also bring *negative* consequences to their estate.

Caution: Before implementing any of the advanced settlement options as part of your estate planning, you should seek very competent legal counsel and tax-planning expertise.

FIGURE 14-3
ASSET DISTRIBUTION BY TRUST

TRUST B

Asset Description	Valuation		
	Amount	Date	Source
50% of home located at 1538 Spruce	$200,000	2/16/81	Comparables
Drive, Canoga Park, CA			
37.5% of apartment building located at	$300,000	2/27/81	Comparables
3842 Pine St., North Hollywood, CA			
E. F. Hutton account #5648321	$100,000	2/12/81	Statement
(Decedent's Separate Property)			

Date: 2/27/81   Signature of Trustee: _____ *Mary R. Jones* _____
Mary B. Jones

FIGURE 14-4
ASSET DISTRIBUTION BY TRUST
TRUST C

Asset Description	Valuation		
	Amount	Date	Source
12.5% of apartment building located at	$100,000	2/27/81	Comparables
3842 Pine St., North Hollywood, CA			

Date: 2/27/81   Signature of Trustee: _Mary R. Jones_
                                     Mary R. Jones

FIGURE 14-5
ASSET DISTRIBUTION BY TRUST
TRUST A

Asset Description	Valuation		
	Amount	Date	Source
50% of home located at 1538 Spruce Drive,	$ 100,000	2/16/81	Comparables
Canoga Park, CA			
50% of apartment building located at	$ 200,000	2/27/81	Comparables
3842 Pine St., North Hollywood, CA			
IRA	$1,000,000	2/14/81	Statement
E. F. Hutton account #5648482	$ 50,000	2/12/81	Statement
(Survivor's Separate Property)			

Date: 2/27/81   Signature of Trustee: _Mary R. Jones_
                                     Mary R. Jones

FIGURE 14-6
ASSET TRANSFER FROM TRUST TO TRUST

| Asset Description | Valuation | | | Transfer | | Trustee Signature | Date |
	Amount	Date	Source*	From Trust	To Trust		
50% of home located at 1538 Spruce Drive, Canoga Park, CA	$ 200,000	2/16/81	Comparables	B	A	*Mary R. Jones*	2/27/81
25% of apartment building located at 3842 Pine St., North Hollywood, CA	$ 200,000	2/27/81	Comparables	A	B	*Mary R. Jones*	2/27/81

*Source of valuation

14A

Separate Property States
When the First Spouse Dies

There are a variety of methods for allocating estate assets to the A, B, and/or C sub-trusts. A combination of seven different allocation methods apply to separate property states:

- Itemization method with a Married A-B Trust
- Itemization method with a Married A-B-C Trust
- An A Trust with a Married IRA–QTIP Trust
- Itemization method with a Married A-B Trust or Married A-B-C Trust and a Married IRA–QTIP Trust
- Married A-B-C Trust with Debt Payment Power of Appointment
- Married A-B-C Trust with Debt Payment Power of Appointment and a Married IRA–QTIP Trust
- Married A-B Trust with Debt Payment Power of Appointment

Each of these allocation methods has a different effect on the estate, both in allocation and in valuation, based on the rules for separate property states.

The first two allocation methods apply to the estates of almost all people, regardless of the size of the estate. The primary purpose of this chapter is to present a thorough discussion of both methods. The last five allocation methods are used for highly valued and more complex estates, and each of them is discussed in more detail in Chapter 23. However, this chapter also provides you with a brief overview of all seven methods, in order to acquaint you with their existence and application in settling estates.

Although this chapter provides detailed explanations and illustrations for a Married A-B Trust and a Married A-B-C Trust, I urge you to take the simple approach. First read the following overview of the seven allocation methods in the next section, then read *only* the appropriate section that applies to your particular Living Trust (i.e., Married A-B Trust or Married A-B-C Trust). Finally, skip to the end of the chapter and read the section entitled "Tax Treatment for Separate Property States." The tax treatment section discusses the impact on your estate of both capital gains taxes and federal estate taxes, as well as asset transfers between the A, B, and/or C sub-trusts.

OVERVIEW OF THE SEVEN ALLOCATION METHODS

Before delving into the details of the two most common allocation methods, let me first acquaint you with all seven methods by presenting a brief synopsis of each, as well as citing their advantages and disadvantages. I suggest that you read each of these summaries, in order to see which alternatives might be appropriate for your particular estate-planning needs. Then, carefully study the allocation method that best fits the needs of your estate. As a general rule, the reader with an average-sized estate (which includes almost all of us) needs only to read either the first or second method and may ignore the rest.

Itemization Method with a Married A-B Trust

Using the itemization method of allocation in conjunction with a Married A-B Trust applies to most estates whose assets do not exceed two individual federal estate tax exemptions ($1.25 million in 1998, rising to $2 million in 2006). The itemization method is universal for all separate property states. Each marital asset is divided equally between the decedent spouse and the surviving spouse. Any IRA, which is outside the Living Trust, flows to the surviving spouse as the IRA beneficiary. Any separate property of either spouse is allocated to the estate of the appropriate spouse.

Itemization Method with a Married A-B-C Trust

Using the itemization method of allocation in conjunction with a Married A-B-C Trust applies to estates with assets, including any IRAs, that exceed two individual federal estate tax exemptions. The itemization method is most common for most larger estates in separate property states. Each marital asset is divided equally between the decedent's B sub-trust and/or C sub-trust and the surviving spouse's A sub-trust. Any IRA flows to the surviving spouse as the IRA beneficiary. Any separate property of either spouse is allocated to the estate of the appropriate spouse.

An A Trust with a Married IRA–QTIP Trust

An A Trust with a Married IRA–QTIP Trust is primarily designed for someone who has entered into a second marriage, brings into the marriage a large IRA accumulated prior to the second marriage, and does not create a joint Living Trust with his or her spouse for their new marital assets. The Married IRA–QTIP Trust is structured for a spouse who desires, upon his or her death, that the IRA remain in trust (for the benefit of the surviving spouse) but that upon the death of the surviving spouse, the remaining IRA funds pass to the heirs of the spouse who owned the IRA. The separate property of this individual, other than the IRA, is allocated to the A Trust. The Married IRA–QTIP Trust can use all or part of the decedent's federal estate tax exemption.

Itemization Method with a Married A-B Trust or A-B-C Trust and a Married IRA–QTIP Trust

Using the itemization method of allocation in conjunction with a Married A-B Trust or a Married A-B-C Trust and a Married IRA–QTIP Trust is a vital estate-planning tool for a married couple who has a joint Trust for their marital assets (a Married A-B Trust or a Married A-B-C Trust) and who also has a large IRA. Two basic situations call for the addition of the Married IRA–QTIP Trust:

- The individual has a large IRA as separate property, has entered into a second marriage, and desires that the surviving spouse have the right to the IRA funds while living but, after the surviving spouse dies, that the remaining IRA funds pass to the heirs of the first spouse (the owner of the IRA).
- A married couple has an IRA that is large in proportion to the marital assets. An example would be a 401(k) plan that was rolled over into an IRA and then grows to a substantial size, disproportionate to the marital assets (i.e., much larger than the rest of the combined assets)—say, an IRA worth $1 million and a home worth $400,000. Since the IRA

passes to the surviving spouse, the couple needs a way to fully utilize the decedent's federal estate tax exemption without triggering the potential income tax consequences. The addition of the Married IRA–QTIP Trust can be an excellent solution.

Married A-B-C Trust with Debt Payment Power of Appointment

The combination of a Married A-B-C Trust and a Debt Payment Power of Appointment (DPPA; similar to the General Power of Appointment [GPOA]) is used to pass *all* of the Living Trust marital assets to the decedent's estate. Typically, this approach is used to achieve full stepped-up valuation (i.e., the cost basis becomes the current market value) on *all* of the Living Trust assets, as well as to protect these assets from creditors and frivolous lawsuits.

However, you must be very aware that any such Power of Appointment also passes *all of the survivor's separate property* to the decedent's estate (unless the Power of Appointment expressly provides otherwise). If the spouses are in a second marriage, such a total shift of the survivor's assets could cause severe conflict with any children from the previous marriages. Any IRAs, like all retirement assets, are outside the Living Trust and flow directly to the surviving spouse as the IRA beneficiary.

The main disadvantage of using this allocation method is that you lose the survivor's federal estate tax exemption. However, any value of the remaining IRA funds at the survivor's death can be offset by the survivor's federal estate tax exemption.

Married A-B-C Trust with Debt Payment Power of Appointment and a Married IRA–QTIP Trust

The combination of a Married A-B-C Trust with a Debt Payment Power of Appointment (DPPA; similar to the General Power of Appointment [GPOA]), in conjunction with a Married IRA–QTIP Trust, is used to pass all of the Living Trust assets to the decedent's estate. This approach is typically used to achieve full stepped-up valuation on *all* of the Living Trust assets, including the survivor's separate property. However, you need to be keenly aware that any such Power of Appointment passes *all* of the survivor's separate property to the decedent's estate (unless the Power of Appointment expressly provides otherwise). If the spouses are in a second marriage and have children from a previous marriage as beneficiaries, such a shift of the survivor's assets could cause a great deal of conflict and resentment.

The Married IRA–QTIP Trust passes any IRAs to the decedent's estate as well, leaving the surviving spouse's estate without any assets whatsoever! Such a lopsided and seemingly unfair approach can be an excellent means of protecting your estate against creditors and frivolous lawsuits, thus preserving the assets for use by the surviving spouse (and/or providing an eventual inheritance to the heirs).

The main disadvantage of using this allocation method is that you lose the survivor's federal estate tax exemption.

An alternative approach is to split the IRA, with one part going to a Married IRA–QTIP Trust and the other part going to the surviving spouse. Using this approach allows the survivor's federal estate tax exemption to be used to offset the remaining value of the "spouse's" IRA.

Married A-B Trust with Debt Payment Power of Appointment

Combining a Married A-B Trust with a Debt Payment Power of Appointment (DPPA; similar to the General Power of Appointment [GPOA]) can be a potent estate-planning tool for certain estates. The DPPA passes all of the Trust assets to the decedent's estate, so *all* Trust assets receive full stepped-up valuation. Since the decedent lacks a C sub-trust (QTIP Trust) and the decedent's estate is limited to one federal estate tax exemption, the balance of the assets that exceeds the decedent's federal estate tax exemption flows back to the surviving spouse and into the survivor's A sub-trust. Any IRAs pass directly to the surviving spouse as the IRA beneficiary. The primary advantage of this estate-planning vehicle is to attain full stepped-up valuation on *all* Trust assets.

ALLOCATION METHODS FOR SEPARATE PROPERTY STATES

To make the two most common allocation methods (and the differences between them) fairly simple and, therefore, understandable, I will illustrate both allocation methods by using the same few basic Trust assets. The examples use the asset values shown in Table 14A-1. "Other real estate" is included in only some illustrations, where appropriate.

All of the examples use an IRA value of $1 million—not because this high value is common for most people's IRAs, but rather to illustrate the problem (and the possible solutions) for estates that have IRAs with a very large value in relation to the total value of the estate. Don't be distracted by the use of such a large IRA—the purpose is only to emphasize what happens to the IRA. (The actual dollar values for the assets are not intended to have any relationship to your own personal estate but are intended to clearly establish the basic principles that relate to applying an allocation method to your estate.)

Each illustration of the allocation methods uses a federal estate tax exemption of $600,000, even though this exemption was $625,000 in 1998 and increases to $1 million by the year 2006. (Remember that Congress has not given us any real boon, since the increase in the

exemption doesn't even keep pace with inflation.) If you want to clearly see the impact on your own estate in future years, simply change the values in the illustration to match those in your estate and the year in which you are making the calculations. Regardless of the actual numbers, the concepts remain the same.

The primary challenge in settling an estate is to determine how to allocate and value the estate assets upon the death of the *first* spouse. Both examples portray the asset allocation when the first spouse dies, for it is this allocation that can have the most serious estate-tax consequences if not done properly for the particular estate. (The assets of each estate will vary as to allocation and to value, but the same principles will apply.)

Upon the death of the second spouse, valuation and allocation of estate assets are fairly easy. This process is treated separately in Chapter 16.

Itemization Method with a Married A-B Trust

The universal method of allocation for separate property states is the itemization method. With this method, the marital assets are divided equally; one-half of each asset is allocated to each spouse. The separate property of each spouse remains with that particular spouse and is allocated to the appropriate sub-trusts. Retirement assets (represented here by an IRA), including annuities and life insurance

TABLE 14A-1

ASSET VALUES USED IN ILLUSTRATIONS FOR SEPARATE PROPERTY STATES

Basic Estate Assets	Cost Basis	Market Value
Home	$ 200,000	$ 400,000
Other real estate	$ 400,000	$ 800,000
Decedent's separate property	$ 50,000	$ 100,000
Survivor's separate property	$ 50,000	$ 100,000
Large IRA		$1,000,000*

*The cost basis of an IRA is zero.

policies not already placed in an Insurance Preservation Trust (discussed in Chapter 18), are the exception. Retirement assets pass outside the Living Trust (since these assets are not in the Living Trust per se) and flow directly to the named beneficiary, usually the surviving spouse. Thereafter, the retirement assets are considered to be a part of the surviving spouse's estate.

A Married A-B Trust is only appropriate for a married couple when the value of the estate, including the value of any IRAs and any life insurance, is less than two individual federal estate tax exemptions.

Allocation of Market Value and Cost Basis

The most complicated problem in allocating assets to the various sub-trusts is to determine which sub-trust (really the assets therein) receives full stepped-up valuation (i.e., where the cost basis becomes the current market value) and which sub-trust (the assets therein) retains the original cost basis of the assets. In a separate property state, only the decedent's share of the marital assets receives full stepped-up valuation to the current market value as of the decedent's date of death. The decedent's separate property also receives full stepped-up valuation to the current market value. However, the survivor's separate property retains its original cost basis.

Estate Before Demise of the First Spouse

While both spouses are living, the market value and cost basis of the estate assets are as shown in Table 14A-2.

Remember: There is no stepped-up valuation for an IRA. The cost basis of an IRA is zero.

Estate After Demise of the First Spouse

Upon the death of the first spouse, the separate property of each spouse, the joint marital property, and then any IRAs must be allocated to the appropriate sub-trust.

Allocation of Separate Property (at Market Value and Cost Basis) The separate property of the decedent spouse receives full stepped-up valuation to current market value as of the decedent's date of death and is allocated to the decedent's B sub-trust. The separate property of the surviving spouse does *not* receive stepped-up valuation and is allocated to the survivor's A sub-trust at the original cost basis. The top of Table 14A-3 on page 184 shows the separate property of both spouses. The bottom part of the table shows how the separate property is allocated to each of the sub-trusts after the death of the first spouse.

TABLE 14A-2
ESTATE ASSETS BEFORE DEATH OF FIRST SPOUSE
(MARRIED A-B TRUST IN A SEPARATE PROPERTY STATE)

Basic Estate Assets	MARKET VALUE		COST BASIS	
	First Spouse	Second Spouse	First Spouse	Second Spouse
Home	$200,000	$ 200,000	$100,000	$ 100,000
Decedent's separate property	$100,000		$ 50,000	
Survivor's separate property		$ 100,000		$ 50,000
IRA		$1,000,000		$1,000,000*

*The cost basis of an IRA is zero.

TABLE 14A-3
SEPARATE PROPERTY AFTER DEATH OF FIRST SPOUSE
(MARRIED A-B TRUST IN A SEPARATE PROPERTY STATE)

Separate Property	MARKET VALUE		COST BASIS	
	First Spouse	Second Spouse	First Spouse	Second Spouse
Decedent's separate property	$100,000			
Survivor's separate property				$50,000

SEPARATE PROPERTY ALLOCATION TO SUB-TRUSTS

	B Sub-Trust	A Sub-Trust
Decedent's separate property	$100,000	
Survivor's separate property		$50,000
Value in decedent's estate	$100,000	
Value in survivor's estate		$50,000

TABLE 14A-4
ESTATE ASSETS AFTER DEATH OF FIRST SPOUSE
(MARRIED A-B TRUST IN A SEPARATE PROPERTY STATE)

Estate Assets	MARKET VALUE		COST BASIS	
	First Spouse	Second Spouse	First Spouse	Second Spouse
Home	$200,000			$ 100,000
IRA				$1,000,000*
Decedent's separate property	$100,000			
Survivor's separate property				$ 50,000
Total	$300,000			$1,150,000

ALLOCATION OF ESTATE ASSETS TO SUB-TRUSTS

	B Sub-Trust	A Sub-Trust
Decedent's separate property	$100,000	
Survivor's separate property		$ 50,000
Home	$200,000	$ 100,000
IRA		$1,000,000
Total value in decedent's estate	$300,000	
Total value in survivor's estate		$1,150,000

*The cost basis of an IRA is zero.

Allocation of Marital Assets (at Market Value and Cost Basis) With the itemization method of allocation, the marital property is divided equally by *asset* rather than by value. One-half of each marital asset goes to the decedent's side of the ledger, and the other half of each marital asset goes to the survivor's side of the ledger. As explained earlier, only the decedent's share of the marital assets qualifies for stepped-up valuation to the current market value; therefore, the survivor's share retains the original cost basis. The retirement assets (illustrated in this example as an IRA, where the surviving spouse is the IRA beneficiary) pass outside the Living Trust to the surviving spouse as beneficiary. The retirement assets are shown in the survivor's A sub-trust. (Remember that placing an IRA in the decedent's B sub-trust can have significant adverse income tax consequences.) Table 14A-4 shows the estate asset valuation after the death of the first spouse. The top portion of the table shows the effect of stepped-up valuation on the decedent's share of the marital assets and the decedent's separate property, and the bottom part shows the allocation of all the assets to the appropriate sub-trusts.

The ledger worksheet is intended to help you allocate your estate assets to the sub-trusts. For this example, an appropriate allocation of estate assets to the A and B sub-trusts would be as shown in Figure 14A-1 on page 186. The shaded areas in the figure denote that the survivor's assets retain their original cost basis (i.e., do not receive stepped-up valuation to current market value).

To satisfy the IRS and follow the rules of the game, you must fill out the ledger sheets for both the decedent's B sub-trust and the survivor's A sub-trust, as shown in Figures 14A-2 and 14A-3 on page 187.

Please be aware that this allocation of assets is *not* arbitrary. The allocation of assets into the decedent's B sub-trust should not exceed the decedent's federal estate tax exemption; otherwise, federal estate taxes will be imposed on the excess value. However, if excess assets initially are allocated to the decedent's B sub-trust (and there is no C, or QTIP, sub-trust), taxes can be reduced by having the excess assets flow back to the survivor's A sub-trust. (This situation is discussed in Chapter 23,

which presents advanced settlement options.) It is important to understand that a decedent may pass any amount of assets to the surviving spouse without any tax impact. However, the reverse is not true—a surviving spouse may *not* gift assets to a decedent spouse. (My clients often ask me about this gifting, so it is important to understand the difference.)

Summary

In the allocation method just illustrated, the decedent's separate property flows into the decedent's B sub-trust and receives full stepped-up valuation to the current market value ($100,000) as of the decedent's date of death. The survivor's separate property flows into the survivor's A sub-trust at its original cost basis ($50,000). Half of the home flows equally into each sub-trust, with the decedent's share receiving full stepped-up valuation to current market value ($200,000), while the survivor's share retains its original cost basis ($100,000). The IRA is outside the Trust and flows to the surviving spouse as the IRA beneficiary; it is, therefore, shown in the survivor's A sub-trust. Remember, for an IRA, the cost basis is zero.

Itemization Method with a Married A-B-C Trust

The universal method of allocation for separate property states is the itemization method. With this method, the marital assets are divided equally; one-half of each asset is allocated to each spouse. The separate property of each spouse remains with that particular spouse and is allocated to the appropriate sub-trusts. Retirement assets (represented here by an IRA), including annuities and life insurance policies not already placed in an Insurance Preservation Trust (discussed in Chapter 18), are the exception. Retirement assets pass outside the Living Trust (since these assets are not in the Living Trust per se) and flow directly to the named beneficiary, usually the surviving spouse. Thereafter, the retirement assets are considered to be part of the surviving spouse's estate.

A Married A-B-C Trust is the appropriate choice for a married couple whose estate value, including the value of any IRAs and any life insurance, exceeds two individual federal estate tax exemptions.

FIGURE 14A-1

ALLOCATION OF ASSETS TO THE A AND B SUB-TRUSTS AFTER THE FIRST SPOUSE DIES (SEPARATE PROPERTY STATE)

Description of Property	SEPARATE PROPERTY		MARITAL SHARE OF ASSETS		SUB-TRUSTS		
	Deceased Net Stepped-Up Valuation	Survivor Net Cost Basis	Deceased Net Stepped-Up Valuation	Survivor Net Cost Basis	C Net Stepped-Up Valuation	B Net Stepped-Up Valuation	A Net Cost Basis
Checking	$	$	$	$	$	$	$
Money Market							
CD							
Bonds							
Home			$200,000	$ 100,000		$200,000	$ 100,000
Other Real Estate							
Personal Effects							
IRA			$1,000,000	$1,000,000		$100,000	$1,000,000
Separate Property of Decedent Spouse	$100,000						
Separate Property of Surviving Spouse		$50,000					$ 50,000

The shaded areas denote that the survivor's assets retain their original cost basis (i.e., do not receive stepped-up valuation to current market value).

FIGURE 14A-2
ASSET DISTRIBUTION BY TRUST

TRUST B

Asset Description	Valuation		
	Amount	Date	Source*
50% of home located at 1538 Spruce	$200,000	2/16/81	Comparables
Drive, Canoga Park, CA			
E. F. Hutton account #5648321	$100,000	2/12/81	Statement
(Decedent's Separate Property)			

Date: 2/27/81   Signature of Trustee: *Mary R. Jones*
Mary R. Jones

*Source of valuation

FIGURE 14A-3
ASSET DISTRIBUTION BY TRUST

TRUST A

Asset Description	Valuation		
	Amount	Date	Source*
50% of home located at 1538 Spruce	$ 100,000	2/16/81	Comparables
Drive, Canoga Park, CA			
E. F. Hutton account #5648482	$ 50,000	2/12/81	Statement
(Survivor's Separate Property)			
IRA	$1,000,000	2/14/81	Statement

Date: 2/27/81   Signature of Trustee: *Mary R. Jones*
Mary R. Jones

*Source of valuation

Allocation of Market Value and Cost Basis

The most complicated problem in allocating the assets to the various sub-trusts is to determine which sub-trusts (really the assets therein) receive full stepped-up valuation (where the cost basis becomes the current market value) and which sub-trusts retain the original cost basis of the assets. In a separate property state, only the decedent's share of the marital assets receives full stepped-up valuation to the current market value as of the decedent's date of death. The decedent's separate property also receives full stepped-up valuation to the current market value. However, the survivor's separate property retains its original cost basis. For an IRA, the cost basis is zero.

Estate Before Demise of the First Spouse

While both spouses are living, the market value and cost basis of the estate assets are as shown in Table 14A-5. (This example adds other real estate to the couple's estate in order to make it large enough to require an A-B-C Trust.)

Estate After Demise of the First Spouse

Upon the death of the first spouse, assets must be allocated to the sub-trusts. These assets include the separate property of each spouse, the joint marital property, and then any IRAs.

Allocation of Separate Property (at Market Value and Cost Basis) The separate property of the decedent spouse receives full stepped-up valuation to the current market value as of the decedent's date of death and is allocated to the decedent's B sub-trust. The separate property of the surviving spouse does *not* receive stepped-up valuation and is allocated to the survivor's A sub-trust at the original cost basis. The top of Table 14A-6 shows the separate property of both spouses. The bottom part of the table shows how the separate property is allocated in each of the sub-trusts after the death of the first spouse.

Allocation of Marital Assets (at Market Value and Cost Basis) With the itemization method of allocation, the marital property is divided equally by asset rather than by value. One-half of each marital asset goes to the decedent's side of the ledger, and the other half of each marital asset goes to the survivor's side of the ledger. As explained earlier, only the decedent's share of the marital assets qualifies for stepped-up valuation to the current market value; therefore, the survivor's share retains the original cost basis. The retirement assets (illustrated in this example as an IRA, where the surviving spouse is the IRA beneficiary) pass outside the Living Trust to the surviving spouse as beneficiary. The retirement assets are shown in the survivor's A sub-trust.

Table 14A-7 shows the estate asset valuation after the death of the first spouse. The top por-

---

TABLE 14A-5
ESTATE ASSETS BEFORE DEATH OF FIRST SPOUSE
(MARRIED A-B-C TRUST IN A SEPARATE PROPERTY STATE)

Basic Estate Assets	MARKET VALUE		COST BASIS	
	First Spouse	Second Spouse	First Spouse	Second Spouse
Home	$200,000	$ 200,000	$100,000	$ 100,000
Other real estate	$400,000	$ 400,000	$200,000	$ 200,000
Decedent's separate property	$100,000		$ 50,000	
Survivor's separate property		$ 100,000		$ 50,000
IRA		$1,000,000		$1,000,000*

*The cost basis of an IRA is zero.

TABLE 14A-6
SEPARATE PROPERTY AFTER DEATH OF FIRST SPOUSE
(MARRIED A-B-C TRUST IN A SEPARATE PROPERTY STATE)

Separate Property	MARKET VALUE		COST BASIS	
	First Spouse	Second Spouse	First Spouse	Second Spouse
Decedent's separate property	$100,000			
Survivor's separate property				$50,000

ALLOCATION OF SEPARATE PROPERTY TO SUB-TRUSTS

	C Sub-Trust	B Sub-Trust	A Sub-Trust
Decedent's separate property		$100,000	
Survivor's separate property			$50,000
Value in decedent's estate		$100,000	
Value in survivor's estate			$50,000

TABLE 14A-7
ESTATE ASSETS AFTER DEATH OF FIRST SPOUSE
(MARRIED A-B-C TRUST IN A SEPARATE PROPERTY STATE)

Estate Assets	MARKET VALUE		COST BASIS	
	First Spouse	Second Spouse	First Spouse	Second Spouse
Home	$200,000			$ 100,000
Other real estate	$400,000			$ 200,000
IRA				$1,000,000*
Decedent's separate property		$100,000		
Survivor's separate property				$ 50,000
Total		$700,000		$1,350,000

ALLOCATION OF ESTATE ASSETS TO SUB-TRUSTS

	C Sub-Trust	B Sub-Trust	A Sub-Trust
Decedent's separate property		$100,000	
Survivor's separate property			$ 50,000
Home		$200,000	$ 100,000
Other real estate	$100,000	$300,000	$ 200,000
IRA			$1,000,000
Value in decedent's estate	$700,000		
Value in survivor's estate			$1,350,000

*The cost basis of an IRA is zero.

FIGURE 14A-4

ALLOCATION OF ASSETS TO THE A, B, AND C SUB-TRUSTS AFTER THE FIRST SPOUSE DIES (SEPARATE PROPERTY STATE)

Description of Property	SEPARATE PROPERTY		MARITAL SHARE OF ASSETS		SUB-TRUSTS		
	Deceased Net Stepped-Up Valuation	Survivor Net Cost Basis	Deceased Net Stepped-Up Valuation	Survivor Net Cost Basis	C Net Stepped-Up Valuation	B Net Stepped-Up Valuation	A Net Cost Basis
Checking	$	$	$	$	$	$	$
Money Market							
CD							
Bonds							
Home			$200,000	$ 100,000		$200,000	$ 100,000
Other Real Estate			$400,000	$ 200,000	$100,000	$300,000	$ 200,000
Personal Effects							
IRA				$1,000,000		$100,000	$1,000,000
Separate Property of Decedent Spouse	$100,000						
Separate Property of Surviving Spouse		$50,000					$ 50,000

The shaded areas denote that the survivor's assets retain their original cost basis (i.e., do not receive stepped-up valuation to current market value).

FIGURE 14A-5
ASSET DISTRIBUTION BY TRUST
TRUST A

Asset Description	Valuation		
	Amount	Date	Source*
50% of home located at 1538 Spruce	$ 100,000	2/16/81	Comparables
Drive, Canoga Park, CA			
50% of apartment building located at	$ 200,000	2/27/81	Comparables
3842 Pine St., North Hollywood, CA			
IRA	$1,000,000	2/14/81	Statement
E. F. Hutton account #5648482	$ 50,000	2/12/81	Statement
(Survivor's Separate Property)			

Date: 2/27/81   Signature of Trustee: _Mary R. Jones_
Mary R. Jones

*Source of Valuation

tion of the table shows the effect of stepped-up valuation on the decedent's share of the marital assets and the decedent's separate property, and the bottom part shows the allocation of all the estate assets to the appropriate sub-trusts.

The ledger worksheet is to help you allocate your estate assets to the sub-trusts. For this example, an appropriate allocation of estate assets to the A, B, and C sub-trusts would be as shown in Figure 14A-4. The shaded areas in the figure denote that the survivor's assets retain their original cost basis (i.e., do not receive stepped-up valuation to current market value).

To play the game by the rules and also satisfy IRS requirements, you must fill out the ledger sheets for the decedent's B and C sub-trusts and the survivor's A sub-trust, as shown in Figures 14A-5 above and Figures 14A-6 and 14A-7 on page 192.

Please note that this allocation of assets is arbitrary only for assets placed in the B sub-trust or C sub-trust. Otherwise, there is no arbitrary allocation, since, in a separate property state, marital assets are allocated by itemization, with one-half of each marital asset allocated to each spouse. Remember that you do not want to exceed the decedent's federal estate tax exemption for the value of the assets placed in the decedent's B sub-trust—unless you want to pay federal estate taxes on the excess. To avoid estate taxes, any excess value in the decedent's B sub-trust is moved to the decedent's C sub-trust (QTIP Trust).

Summary
In the allocation method just illustrated, the decedent's separate property receives full stepped-up valuation to the current market value as of the decedent's date of death ($100,000) and flows into the decedent's B sub-

FIGURE 14A-6
ASSET DISTRIBUTION BY TRUST
TRUST B

Asset Description	Valuation		
	Amount	Date	Source*
50% of home located at 1538 Spruce Drive, Canoga Park, CA	$ 200,000	2/16/81	Comparables
37.5% of apartment building located at 3842 Pine St., North Hollywood, CA	$ 300,000	2/27/81	Comparables
E. F. Hutton account #5648321 (Decedent's Separate Property)	$ 100,000	2/12/81	Statement

Date: 2/27/81   Signature of Trustee: _Mary R. Jones_
Mary R. Jones

*Source of Valuation

FIGURE 14A-7
ASSET DISTRIBUTION BY TRUST
TRUST C

Asset Description	Valuation		
	Amount	Date	Source*
12.5% of apartment building located at 3842 Pine St., North Hollywood, CA	$100,000	2/27/81	Comparables

Date: 2/27/81   Signature of Trustee: _Mary R. Jones_
Mary R. Jones

*Source of Valuation

trust. The survivor's separate property retains its original cost basis ($50,000) and flows into the survivor's A sub-trust. The home is divided equally between the decedent and the survivor. The decedent's share of the home is placed in the decedent's B sub-trust and receives full stepped-up valuation to current market value ($200,000); the survivor's share is placed in the survivor's A sub-trust and retains its original cost basis ($100,000). The decedent's share of the other real estate is divided between the B sub-trust and C sub-trust and receives full stepped-up valuation to current market value ($400,000), with $300,000 of the total value going into the B sub-trust and $100,000 of the value going into the C sub-trust. The survivor's share of the other real estate retains its original cost basis ($200,000) and flows into the survivor's A sub-trust.

If all of the other real estate had been placed in the B sub-trust, the total value of assets in the couple's Married A-B-C Trust would have exceeded the decedent's federal estate tax exemption, and estate taxes would have had to be paid on the excess. By dividing the value of the other real estate—placing only the amount needed in the B sub-trust to fully utilize the decedent's federal estate tax exemption, but no more—and by placing the remaining value of the other real estate into the C sub-trust, the estate defers any federal estate taxation until the death of the second spouse.

The IRA is outside the Living Trust and flows to the surviving spouse as the IRA beneficiary. It is, therefore, shown in the survivor's A sub-trust. Remember, for an IRA, the cost basis is zero.

TAX TREATMENT FOR SEPARATE PROPERTY STATES

Understanding how to settle an estate in a good Living Trust involves more than just allocating assets to the sub-trusts and knowing how to value those assets. You also need to be aware of the impact of capital gains tax on future sales and transfers of estate assets, as well as be knowledgeable about federal estate tax consequences and the state inheritance tax differences among the states.

Capital Gains Treatment

To compute the amount of capital gains, you must remember that, upon the death of the first spouse, the assets in the survivor's A sub-trust retain their original cost basis but that the assets in the decedent's B sub-trust and/or C sub-trust receive full stepped-up valuation to the current market value. Let's see how this principle applies to various assets.

Sale of Home

For purposes of illustrating the tax consequences of selling your home, assume that a couple originally purchased a house for $200,000 (its cost basis); when the first spouse dies, the home has increased in value to $400,000 (its market value). Upon the death of the first spouse, the home therefore has a market value of $400,000. The value of the share of the home in the decedent's B sub-trust and/or C sub-trust would be $200,000 (half of the current market value) for both the cost basis and the market value, since the decedent's share of the home receives full stepped-up valuation. However, because the share of the home in the survivor's A sub-trust does not receive stepped-up valuation, it retains its original cost basis of $100,000. If the surviving spouse decided to sell the home, the capital gain realized would be $100,000 ($400,000 minus each spouse's cost basis). Table 14A-8 on page 194 shows each spouse's share of the value of the home (including stepped-up valuation for the decedent's share), as well as the capital gain that would be realized if the home were sold.

To offset the $100,000 capital gain generated if the surviving spouse were to sell the home, the surviving spouse could utilize his or her $250,000 homeowner's exemption for that part of the home in the survivor's A sub-trust (the part that did not receive stepped-up valuation to current market value). However, in order to use that exemption, the surviving spouse must satisfy the requirement of having lived in the home for two of the past five years. The IRS time clock starts on the date the spouses purchased the home.

If the surviving spouse decided to stay in the home for several years and were to sell it years later, the $250,000 homeowner's exemption would still apply, but only to the share of the home in the survivor's A sub-trust—regardless of how much the home's value had appreciated. In the following example, let's assume that the home increased in value from $400,000 to $600,000. Table 14A-9 shows how the increased value of the home (its current market value) and its cost basis are allocated to the decedent's B sub-trust and to the survivor's A sub-trust.

Remember that the homeowner's exemption applies *only to an individual* and not to an irrevocable Trust (i.e., the decedent's B sub-trust). When the home is sold, the share of the home in the decedent's B sub-trust will realize a $100,000 capital gain, which is taxable at the capital gains tax rate. For determining this rate, which depends on how long an asset has been held, assets in the decedent's B sub-trust retain the holding period established when the assets were originally purchased. The capital gains tax rate would be 28 percent if the home

has been held (from date of purchase) for less than 12 months, 20 percent if the home has been held for more than 12 months, or 18 percent if the home has been held for more than five years. (The 18 percent capital gains tax rate becomes effective in the year 2001.)

Remember, to satisfy the IRS requirement for the $250,000 homeowner's exemption, the spouse must have lived in the home for two of the past five years, including the time both spouses were living in the home. The IRS time clock starts on the date that the spouses purchased the home.

Sale of Other Real Estate

The sale of other real estate is handled in almost the same manner as the sale of the home, except the homeowner's exemption does not apply. For illustration purposes, let's assume that the other real estate had an original cost basis of $400,000. Upon the death of the first spouse, the other real estate has a

---

TABLE 14A-8
VALUE OF HOME WHEN FIRST SPOUSE DIES (SEPARATE PROPERTY STATE)

Home Allocation	Market Value	Cost Basis	Capital Gain
Decedent spouse (B sub-trust)	$200,000	$200,000	$ 0
Surviving spouse (A sub-trust)	$200,000	$100,000	$100,000
Total	$400,000	$300,000	$100,000

TABLE 14A-9
VALUE OF HOME WHEN EVENTUALLY SOLD (SEPARATE PROPERTY STATE)

Home Allocation	Market Value	Cost Basis	Capital Gain	Exemption
Decedent spouse (B sub-trust)	$300,000	$200,000	$100,000	$ 0
Surviving spouse (A sub-trust)	$300,000	$100,000	$200,000*	$250,000
Total	$600,000	$300,000	$100,000	

*Capital gain is offset by homeowner's exemption.

market value of $800,000. The value of the share of the other real estate in the decedent's B sub-trust would be $400,000 (the current market value). In the B sub-trust, this amount is both the cost basis and the market value, since the decedent's share of the other real estate receives full stepped-up valuation. The share of the other real estate in the survivor's A sub-trust does not receive stepped-up valuation and therefore retains its original cost basis of $200,000. If the surviving spouse decided to sell the other real estate, a capital gain of $200,000 would be realized upon the sale (or transfer) of the asset. Table 14A-10 shows each spouse's share of the value of the other real estate (including stepped-up valuation for the decedent's share), as well as the capital gain that would be realized if the other real estate were sold.

If the surviving spouse were to sell (or transfer) the other real estate, he or she would have to recognize a capital gain of $200,000 on the appreciation of that part of the other real estate held in the survivor's A sub-trust that did not receive stepped-up valuation to current mar-

ket value. Remember that the capital gains tax rate would be either 28 percent (if the asset were sold within the first 12 months after purchase), 20 percent (if the asset were sold after being held at least 12 months but less than five years) or—beginning in 2001—18 percent (if the asset were sold after being held at least five years). For determining the tax rate, the IRS time clock started when both spouses acquired the other real estate (including the share of the asset in the decedent's B sub-trust).

If the surviving spouse decided to keep the other real estate for several years and were to sell it years later, after it had appreciated in the A and B sub-trusts, the capital gains tax rate would be the same for each of the sub-trusts, since they have the same holding period. Let's assume the other real estate increased in value from $800,000 to $1 million. Table 14A-11 shows how the increased value of the other real estate (its current market value) and the cost basis are allocated to the decedent's B sub-trust and to the survivor's A sub-trust. If the other real estate were sold, the share of the other real estate in the decedent's B sub-trust would real-

---

TABLE 14A-10
VALUE OF OTHER REAL ESTATE WHEN FIRST SPOUSE DIES (SEPARATE PROPERTY STATE)

Other Real Estate	Market Value	Cost Basis	Capital Gain
Decedent spouse (B sub-trust)	$400,000	$400,000	$ 0
Surviving spouse (A sub-trust)	$400,000	$200,000	$200,000
Total	$800,000	$600,000	$200,000

TABLE 14A-11
VALUE OF OTHER REAL ESTATE WHEN EVENTUALLY SOLD (SEPARATE PROPERTY STATE)

Other Real Estate	Market Value	Cost Basis	Capital Gain
Decedent spouse (B sub-trust)	$500,000	$400,000	$100,000
Surviving spouse (A sub-trust)	$500,000	$200,000	$300,000
Total	$1,000,000	$600,000	$400,000

ize a $100,000 taxable capital gain on the appreciation of the asset, and the share of the other real estate in the survivor's A sub-trust would realize a $300,000 taxable capital gain on the appreciation for that share of the asset. The decedent's irrevocable B sub-trust and the survivor's revocable A sub-trust would be subject to the same tax rate, which would depend on how long the asset had been held since the couple purchased it.

Sale of Other Assets

The sale of other assets, such as stocks, mutual funds, partnerships, and the like, is handled in exactly the same manner as just described for other real estate. The decedent's share of the assets receives full stepped-up valuation to current market value, whereas the surviving spouse's share retains its original cost basis. Any capital gain realized on the sale of the asset is taxed at the appropriate rate, depending on how long the asset has been held.

Sale of Separate Property

The sale of each spouse's separate property follows the same basic guidelines as for the other assets that have already been described:

- The decedent's separate property receives full stepped-up valuation to the current market value (as of the date of the decedent's death). If the separate property is sold before it appreciates further, no capital gain will be realized on the sale, regardless of the asset's initial cost basis.
- The surviving spouse's separate property does not receive stepped-up valuation and, therefore, retains its original cost basis. When the separate property is sold, a taxable capital gain must be realized on the difference between the original cost basis and the current market value. The capital gains tax rate will depend on how long the asset was held before it was sold.

Transfer of Assets Between Sub-Trusts

You may transfer one or more assets from the survivor's revocable A sub-trust to the decedent's irrevocable B sub-trust and/or C sub-

trust. However, before doing so, you must understand some basic principles about the sub-trusts. Upon the death of the first spouse, the decedent's B sub-trust and C sub-trust become *irrevocable*; the allocation and distribution options specified by the decedent for passing on his or her assets to the named heirs become cast in concrete—unchangeable by the surviving spouse. The surviving spouse's A sub-trust remains *revocable*, meaning that the surviving spouse is able to change any part of the A sub-trust (as long as the surviving spouse is alive and competent). Because the surviving spouse's A sub-trust is revocable, the IRS considers those assets to be transparent. In other words, the IRS treats the assets as the individual assets of the surviving spouse, even though they are held in the name of the Trust. Therefore, when transferring assets, you are dealing with two separate entities: the decedent's B and/or C irrevocable sub-trusts and the surviving spouse (as an individual).

Since the asset transfers are, in effect, taking place between separate entities (and not two parts of the same entity), any such transfer is considered to be a sale and purchase, and any capital gain that is generated must be recognized at the time of transfer. In other words, assets must be transferred *at their current market value* and not at their original cost basis. A taxable capital gain must be realized, even on a *transfer*, whenever the current market value of the asset being transferred is greater than its cost basis as held in the particular sub-trust.

The Traditional IRA

No stepped-up valuation or capital gain is associated with a traditional IRA. When the IRA funds are withdrawn, the entire amount is treated as ordinary income and is taxed at the individual income tax rate of the person receiving the funds. (The traditional IRA was addressed in detail in Chapter 12.)

Federal Estate Tax Treatment

Any federal estate taxes due on the estate valuation when the first spouse dies may be deferred until the death of the second spouse. At that time, any federal estate taxes due on the valuation of the entire estate must be determined and paid within nine months after the death of the second spouse. Upon the death of the first spouse, if your estate value exceeds the then-current amount of two individual federal estate tax exemptions and your Living Trust incorporates a C (or QTIP) sub-trust, then you need to file Form 706, Schedule R, to make the QTIP election.

State Inheritance Tax

To the best of my knowledge, Delaware is the only separate property state to impose a state inheritance tax at the time of death of the first spouse if the surviving spouse is the beneficiary of the decedent's assets.

ASSET ALLOCATION IS CRUCIAL

When the first spouse dies, making the proper asset allocation is crucial to minimizing any potential federal estate tax bite—especially in separate property states, where the surviving spouse's assets do not receive stepped-up valuation to the current market value. If you have been fortunate enough to have accumulated a sizable estate, I recommend that you also read about the advanced settlement options for separate property states, which are discussed in Chapter 23.

No one wants to see his or her hard-earned estate unnecessarily consumed by federal estate taxes. You must be knowledgeable of both the consequences and the proper steps to take in order to avoid having Uncle Sam be one of your "best-paid" beneficiaries.

14B

Community Property States
When the First Spouse Dies

There are several methods for allocating estate assets to the A, B, and/or C sub-trusts. A combination of seven different allocation methods apply to community property states:

- Valuation method with a Married A-B Trust
- Valuation method with a Married A-B-C Trust
- An A Trust with a Married IRA–QTIP Trust
- Valuation method with a Married A-B Trust or Married A-B-C Trust and a Married IRA–QTIP Trust
- Married A-B-C Trust with Debt Payment Power of Appointment
- Married A-B-C Trust with Debt Payment Power of Appointment and a Married IRA–QTIP Trust
- Married A-B Trust with Debt Payment Power of Appointment

Each of these allocation methods has a different effect on the estate, both in allocation and in valuation, based on the rules for community property states.

The first two allocation methods apply to the estates of almost all people, regardless of the size of the estate. The primary purpose of this chapter is to present a thorough discussion of both methods. The last five allocation methods are used for highly valued and more complex estates, and each of them is discussed in more detail in Chapter 24. However, this chapter also provides you with a brief overview of all seven methods, in order to acquaint you with their existence and application in settling estates.

Although this chapter provides detailed explanations and illustrations for a Married A-B Trust and a Married A-B-C Trust, I urge you to take the simple approach. First read the following overview of the seven allocation methods in the next section, then read *only* the appropriate section that applies to your particular Living Trust (i.e., Married A-B Trust or Married A-B-C Trust). Finally, skip to the end of the chapter and read the section entitled "Tax Treatment for Community Property States." The tax treatment section discusses the impact on your estate of both capital gains taxes and federal estate taxes, as well as asset transfers between the A, B, and/or C sub-trusts.

OVERVIEW OF THE SEVEN ALLOCATION METHODS

Before delving into the details of the two most common allocation methods, let me first acquaint you with all seven methods by presenting a brief synopsis of each, as well as citing their unique advantages and disadvantages. I suggest that you read each of these summaries in order to see which alternatives, if any, might be appropriate for your particular estate-planning needs. Then, carefully study the allocation method that best fits the needs of your estate. As a general rule, the reader with an average-sized estate (which includes almost all of us) needs only to read either the first or second method and may ignore the rest.

The valuation method of asset allocation is peculiar to community property states. It allows the community property assets to be divided equally between both spouses by *value* rather than by asset.

Valuation Method with a Married A-B Trust

Although this method is technically referred to as the *aggregate method* of allocation, I will use the more descriptive common term *valuation method*. Using the valuation method of allocation in conjunction with a Married A-B Trust applies to most estates whose assets, including any IRAs, do not exceed two individual federal estate tax exemptions ($1.25 million in 1998, rising to $2 million in 2006). Any IRA, which is outside the Living Trust, flows to the surviving spouse as the IRA beneficiary. The remaining marital assets are divided so as to achieve an equal distribution of value. The advantage of the valuation method is that it enables the IRA, as a marital asset, to be included in this value allocation. Any separate property of each spouse is allocated to the estate of the appropriate spouse.

Valuation Method with a Married A-B-C Trust

Using the valuation method of allocation in conjunction with a Married A-B-C Trust applies to most estates with assets, including any IRAs, that exceed two individual federal estate tax exemptions. The valuation method

of allocation is ideal for community property states, since it allows the community property assets to be divided equally between both spouses by value rather than by asset. Any IRA, which is outside the Living Trust, flows to the surviving spouse as beneficiary, but with the valuation method the IRA, as community property, is included in the value allocation. Any separate property of either spouse is allocated to the estate of the appropriate spouse.

An A Trust with a Married IRA–QTIP Trust

An A Trust with a Married IRA–QTIP Trust is primarily designed for someone who has entered into a second marriage, brings into the marriage a large IRA accumulated prior to the second marriage, and does not create a joint Living Trust with his or her spouse for their new marital assets. The Married IRA–QTIP Trust is structured for a spouse who desires, upon his or her death, that the IRA remain in trust (for the benefit of the surviving spouse) but that upon the death of the surviving spouse, the remaining IRA funds pass to the heirs of the spouse who owned the IRA. The separate property of this individual, other than the IRA, is allocated to the A Trust. The Married IRA–QTIP Trust can use all or part of the decedent's federal estate tax exemption.

Valuation Method with a Married A-B Trust or A-B-C Trust and a Married IRA–QTIP Trust

Using the valuation method of allocation in conjunction with a Married A-B Trust or a Married A-B-C Trust and with a Married IRA–QTIP Trust is a vital estate-planning tool for a married couple who has a joint Trust for the marital assets (an A-B Trust or A-B-C Trust) and who also has a large IRA. Two basic situations call for the addition of the Married IRA–QTIP Trust:

• An individual has a large IRA as separate property, has entered into a second marriage, and desires that the surviving spouse have the right to the IRA funds while living but, after the surviving spouse dies, that the remaining IRA funds pass to the heirs of the first spouse (the owner of the IRA).

• A married couple has an IRA that is large in proportion to the marital assets. An example would be a 401(k) plan that was rolled over into an IRA and then grows to a substantial size, disproportionate to the marital assets (i.e., much larger than the rest of the combined assets)—say, an IRA worth $1 million and a home worth $400,000. Since the IRA passes to the surviving spouse, the couple needs a way to fully utilize the decedent's federal estate tax exemption without triggering the potential income tax consequences. The addition of the Married IRA–QTIP Trust can be an excellent solution.

Married A-B-C Trust with Debt Payment Power of Appointment

The combination of a Married A-B-C Trust with a Debt Payment Power of Appointment (DPPA; similar to the General Power of Appointment [GPOA]) is used to pass *all* of the Living Trust assets to the decedent's estate. Since all community property attains full stepped-up valuation (i.e., the cost basis becomes the current market value) upon the death of the first spouse, this approach only affects the survivor's separate property. The DPPA causes the survivor's separate property to flow into the decedent's estate, thereby receiving full stepped-up valuation to current market value. This approach also protects the survivor's assets from creditors and frivolous lawsuits

However, before selecting this allocation method, you must be very aware that *all of the survivor's separate property* passes to the decedent's estate (unless the Power of Appointment expressly provides otherwise)! If the spouses are in a second marriage, such a total shift of the survivor's assets could cause severe conflict with any children from the previous marriages. Any IRAs, like all retirement assets, are outside the Living Trust and flow directly to the surviving spouse as the IRA beneficiary, thus leaving the IRA still exposed to outsider claims.

The disadvantage of using this method is that the survivor's federal estate tax exemption is lost. However, any value of the remaining IRA funds at the survivor's death can be offset by the survivor's federal estate tax exemption.

Married A-B-C Trust with Debt Payment Power of Appointment and a Married IRA–QTIP Trust

The Debt Payment Power of Appointment (DPPA; similar to the General Power of Appointment [GPOA]) is used to pass *all* of the Living Trust assets to the decedent's estate. Thus, all of the survivor's separate property flows to the decedent's estate and thereby receives full stepped-up valuation to the current market value (unless the Power of Appointment expressly exempts the separate property). If the spouses are in a second marriage and have children from a previous marriage as beneficiaries, such a total shift of the survivor's assets could cause a great deal of conflict and resentment.

The Married IRA–QTIP Trust passes any IRAs to the decedent's estate as well, leaving the surviving spouse's estate without any assets whatsoever! Such a seemingly unfair allocation can be an excellent means of protecting your estate against creditors and frivolous lawsuits, thus preserving the assets for use by the surviving spouse.

The main disadvantage of using this allocation method is that the survivor's federal estate tax exemption is lost.

An alternative approach is to split the IRA, with one part going to the Married IRA–QTIP Trust and the other part going to the surviving spouse. With this approach, the survivor's federal estate tax exemption can be used to offset the remaining value of the "spouse's" IRA.

Married A-B Trust with Debt Payment Power of Appointment

Combining a Married A-B Trust with a Debt Payment Power of Appointment (DPPA; similar to the General Power of Appointment [GPOA]) can be a potent estate-planning tool for certain estates. The DPPA passes all of the Trust assets to the decedent's estate; thus, *all* Trust assets receive full stepped-up valuation. Since the decedent does not have a C sub-trust (or QTIP Trust) and the decedent's estate is limited to one federal estate tax exemption, the balance of the assets that exceeds the decedent's federal estate tax exemption flows back to the surviving spouse and into the survivor's

A sub-trust. Any IRAs pass directly to the surviving spouse as the IRA beneficiary. The primary advantage of this estate-planning vehicle is to attain full stepped-up valuation on *all* Trust assets, including the survivor's separate property.

ALLOCATION METHODS FOR COMMUNITY PROPERTY STATES

To make the two most common allocation methods (and the differences between them) fairly simple and therefore understandable, I will illustrate both allocation methods by using the same few basic Trust assets. The examples use the asset values shown in Table 14B-1. "Other real estate" is included in only some examples, where appropriate.

All of the examples use an IRA value of $1 million—not because this high value is common for most people's IRAs, but rather to illustrate the problem (and the possible solutions) for estates that have IRAs with a very large value in relation to the total value of the estate. Don't be distracted by the use of such a large IRA; the purpose is only to emphasize what happens to the IRA. (The actual dollar values for the assets are not intended to have any relationship to your own personal estate but are intended to clearly establish the basic principles that relate to applying the valuation method to allocate your estate assets.)

Each illustration of the allocation methods uses a federal estate tax exemption of $600,000, even though this exemption was $625,000 in

1998 and increases to $1 million by the year 2006. (Remember that Congress has not given us any real boon, since the increase in the exemption doesn't even keep pace with inflation.) If you want to clearly see the impact on your own estate in future years, simply change the values in the illustration to match those in your estate and the year in which you are making the calculations. Regardless of the actual number, the concepts remain the same.

The primary challenge in settling an estate is to determine how to value and allocate estate assets upon the death of the *first* spouse. Both examples portray the asset allocation when the first spouse dies, for it is this allocation that can have the most serious estate tax consequences if not done properly for the particular estate. (The assets of each estate will vary as to allocation and to value, but the same principles will apply.)

Upon the death of the second spouse, allocation and valuation of estate assets are fairly easy. This process is treated separately in Chapter 16.

Valuation Method with a Married A-B Trust

The ideal method of allocation for community property states is the valuation method, since it allows you to divide community property assets equally between both spouses by value rather than by asset. Equal division of assets by value between both spouses also applies to retirement assets (represented here by an IRA),

---

TABLE 14B-1
ASSET VALUES USED IN ILLUSTRATIONS FOR COMMUNITY PROPERTY STATES

Basic Estate Assets	Cost Basis	Market Value
Home	$ 200,000	$ 400,000
Other real estate	$ 400,000	$ 800,000
Decedent's separate property	$ 50,000	$ 100,000
Survivor's separate property	$ 50,000	$ 100,000
Large IRA		$1,000,000*

*The cost basis of an IRA is zero.

including annuities and any life insurance not already placed in an Insurance Preservation Trust (discussed in Chapter 18). Retirement assets pass outside the Living Trust (since these assets are not in the Living Trust per se) and flow directly to the named beneficiary, usually the surviving spouse. Thereafter, the retirement assets are considered to be a part of the surviving spouse's estate, but they may be included in the overall valuation.

Usually, an A-B Trust is used when the estate value, including the value of any IRAs, is less than two individual federal estate tax exemptions.

Allocation of Market Value and Cost Basis

In a community property state, upon the death of the first spouse, all marital assets (i.e., all community property) attain full stepped-up valuation to the current market value, as does the decedent's separate property. However, the survivor's separate property retains its original cost basis. For an IRA, the cost basis is zero.

Estate Before Demise of the First Spouse

While both spouses are living, the market value and cost basis of the estate assets are as shown in Table 14B-2.

Estate After Demise of the First Spouse

Upon the death of the first spouse, the separate property of each spouse, the joint community property, and then any IRAs must be allocated to the appropriate sub-trusts.

Allocation of Separate Property (at Market Value and Cost Basis)

The separate property of the decedent spouse receives full stepped-up valuation to the current market value as of the decedent's date of death and is allocated to the decedent's B sub-trust. The separate property of the surviving spouse *does not* receive stepped-up valuation and is allocated to the survivor's A sub-trust at the original cost basis. The top of Table 14B-3 on page 204 shows the separate property of both spouses. The bottom part of the table shows how the separate property is allocated in each of the sub-trusts after the death of the first spouse.

Allocation of Community Property Assets (at Market Value)

With the valuation method of allocation, the community property is divided equally by value rather than by asset. One of the primary advantages of using the valuation method of allocation is that any retirement assets (illustrated in this example as an IRA, where the surviving spouse is the IRA beneficiary), any annuities, and any insurance that were accumulated as community property may be included in the allocation by value. Although these particular assets are not in the Living Trust, because they pass to the surviving spouse (as beneficiary) outside the Living

---

TABLE 14B-2
ESTATE ASSETS BEFORE DEATH OF FIRST SPOUSE
(MARRIED A-B TRUST IN A COMMUNITY PROPERTY STATE)

Basic Estate Assets	MARKET VALUE		COST BASIS	
	First Spouse	Second Spouse	First Spouse	Second Spouse
Home	$200,000	$200,000	$100,000	$100,000
Decedent's separate property	$100,000		$ 50,000	
Survivor's separate property		$100,000		$ 50,000
IRA	$500,000	$500,000	$500,000*	$500,000*

*The cost basis of an IRA is zero.

TABLE 14B-3
SEPARATE PROPERTY AFTER DEATH OF FIRST SPOUSE
(MARRIED A-B TRUST IN A COMMUNITY PROPERTY STATE)

Separate Property	MARKET VALUE		COST BASIS	
	First Spouse	Second Spouse	First Spouse	Second Spouse
Decedent's separate property	$100,000			
Survivor's separate property				$50,000

SEPARATE PROPERTY ALLOCATION TO SUB-TRUSTS

	B Sub-Trust	A Sub-Trust
Decedent's separate property	$100,000	
Survivor's separate property		$50,000
Value in decedent's estate	$100,000	
Value in survivor's estate		$50,000

Trust, they may be included in the total value allocation.

Since the first spouse already has separate property of $100,000 (having received stepped-up valuation to current market value), only an additional $500,000 in asset value is needed to fully utilize the decedent's federal estate tax exemption. Any asset value going into the decedent's B sub-trust that exceeds the amount of the decedent's federal estate tax exemption would be subject to federal estate taxation. It is advantageous to place an appreciating asset, such as a home, in the decedent's B sub-trust, rather than a depreciating asset. A traditional IRA is a depreciating asset due to the eventual *required* withdrawals from the IRA. Remember, placing an IRA in the decedent's B sub-trust can have significant adverse income tax consequences; however, such placement is illustrated here to demonstrate the principle of allocation by value.

Table 14B-4 shows the estate asset valuation after the death of the first spouse. The top portion of the table shows the effect of stepped-up valuation on the marital assets and the dece-dent's separate property, and the bottom part shows the allocation of the assets to the appropriate sub-trusts.

The ledger worksheet is intended to help you allocate your estate assets to the sub-trusts. For this example, an appropriate allocation of estate assets to the A and B sub-trusts would be as shown in Figure 14B-1 on page 206. The shaded areas in the figure denote that the survivor's separate property retains its original cost basis (i.e., does not receive stepped-up valuation to current market value).

To satisfy the IRS and follow the rules of the game, you must fill out the ledger sheets for both the decedent's B sub-trust and the survivor's A sub-trust, as shown in Figures 14B-2 and 14B-3 on page 207.

Please be aware that the above allocation of assets is arbitrary. The assets may be allocated in any form desired, as long as the total *value* is equal for each spouse's share of the estate; (each asset does not have to be equally divided, as long as each spouse ends up with half of the community property value). The allocation of assets in the decedent's B sub-trust should not

TABLE 14B-4
ESTATE ASSETS AFTER DEATH OF FIRST SPOUSE
(MARRIED A-B TRUST IN A COMMUNITY PROPERTY STATE)

Estate Assets	MARKET VALUE		COST BASIS	
	First Spouse	Second Spouse	First Spouse	Second Spouse
Home	$400,000			
IRA	$100,000			$900,000
Decedent's separate property	$100,000			$ 50,000
Survivor's separate property				
Total	$600,000			$950,000

ALLOCATION OF ESTATE ASSETS TO SUB-TRUSTS

	B Sub-Trust	A Sub-Trust
Decedent's separate property	$100,000	
Survivor's separate property		$ 50,000
Home	$400,000	
IRA	$100,000	$900,000
Total value in decedent's estate	$600,000	
Total value in survivor's estate		$950,000

exceed the decedent's federal estate tax exemption; otherwise federal estate taxes will be imposed on the excess value. It is important to understand that a decedent may pass any amount of assets to the surviving spouse—without any tax impact. However, a surviving spouse may *not* gift assets to a decedent spouse. (My clients often ask me about this gifting, so it is important to understand the difference.)

Summary

In the allocation method just illustrated, the decedent's separate property flows into the decedent's B sub-trust and receives full stepped-up valuation to the current market value ($100,000) as of the decedent's date of death. The survivor's separate property flows into the survivor's A sub-trust at its original cost basis ($50,000), since it is not community property. The home, as community property, receives full stepped-up valuation to the current market value ($400,000). As an appreciating asset, the home is placed in the decedent's B sub-trust. Since the B sub-trust is insulated from further estate taxation, any future growth of the home's value will be exempt from further federal estate taxation.

The IRA, whose market value ($1 million in this example) retains its cost basis of zero, can be included as part of the community property assets and also allocated by value. Thus, $100,000 of IRA value is placed in the decedent's B sub-trust and the remaining $900,000 of the IRA is placed in the survivor's A sub-trust. Allocating the IRA value in this manner prevents the value of the B sub-trust from exceeding the amount of the decedent's federal estate tax exemption, and therefore no estate taxes are due. However, before placing any part

FIGURE 14B-1

ALLOCATION OF ASSETS TO THE A AND B SUB-TRUSTS AFTER THE FIRST SPOUSE DIES (COMMUNITY PROPERTY STATE)

Description of Property	SEPARATE PROPERTY		MARITAL SHARE OF ASSETS		SUB-TRUSTS		
	Deceased	Survivor	Deceased	Survivor	C	B	A
	Net Stepped-Up Valuation	Net Cost Basis	Net Stepped-Up Valuation	Net Cost Basis	Net Stepped-Up Valuation	Net Stepped-Up Valuation	Net Stepped-Up Valuation*
Checking	$	$	$	$	$	$	$
Money Market							
CD							
Bonds							
Home			$200,000	$ 200,000		$400,000	
Other Real Estate							
Personal Effects						$100,000	
IRA				$1,000,000		$100,000	$ 900,000
Separate Property of Decedent Spouse	$100,000						
Separate Property of Surviving Spouse		$50,000					$ 50,000

*The shaded areas in the figure denote that the survivor's separate property retains its original cost basis (i.e., does not receive stepped-up valuation to current market value).

FIGURE 14B-2
ASSET DISTRIBUTION BY TRUST

TRUST B

Asset Description	Valuation		
	Amount	Date	Source*
Home located at 1538 Spruce Drive,	$400,000	2/16/81	Comparables
Canoga Park, CA			
10% of IRA	$100,000	2/14/81	Statement
E. F. Hutton account #5648321	$100,000	2/12/81	Statement
(Decedent's Separate Property)			

Date: 2/27/81   Signature of Trustee: *Mary R. Jones*
Mary R. Jones

*Source of Valuation

FIGURE 14B-3
ASSET DISTRIBUTION BY TRUST

TRUST A

Asset Description	Valuation		
	Amount	Date	Source*
90% of IRA	$900,000	2/14/81	Statement
E. F. Hutton account #5648482	$ 50,000	2/12/81	Statement
(Survivor's Separate Property)			

Date: 2/27/81   Signature of Trustee: *Mary R. Jones*
Mary R. Jones

*Source of Valuation

TABLE 14B-5
ESTATE ASSETS BEFORE DEATH OF FIRST SPOUSE
(MARRIED A-B-C TRUST IN A COMMUNITY PROPERTY STATE)

Basic Estate Assets	MARKET VALUE		COST BASIS	
	First Spouse	Second Spouse	First Spouse	Second Spouse
Home	$200,000	$ 200,000	$100,000	$ 100,000
Other real estate	$400,000	$ 400,000	$200,000	$ 200,000
Decedent's separate property	$100,000		$ 50,000	
Survivor's separate property		$ 100,000		$ 50,000
IRA		$1,000,000		$1,000,000*

*The cost basis of an IRA is zero.

TABLE 14B-6
SEPARATE PROPERTY AFTER DEATH OF FIRST SPOUSE
(MARRIED A-B-C TRUST IN A COMMUNITY PROPERTY STATE)

Separate Property	MARKET VALUE		COST BASIS	
	First Spouse	Second Spouse	First Spouse	Second Spouse
Decedent's separate property	$100,000			
Survivor's separate property				$50,000

ALLOCATION OF SEPARATE PROPERTY TO SUB-TRUSTS

	C Sub-Trust	B Sub-Trust	A Sub-Trust
Decedent's separate property		$100,000	
Survivor's separate property			$50,000
Value in decedent's estate		$100,000	
Value in survivor's estate			$50,000

of the IRA in the decedent's B sub-trust, you should become familiar with the income tax consequences.

The asset allocations used in this example are arbitrary and may be altered to suit the estates of each unique couple. The important feature to remember, however, is the flexibility that is available to you when you allocate by value.

Valuation Method with a Married A-B-C Trust

The ideal method of allocation for community property states is the valuation method, since it allows you to divide the community property assets equally between both spouses by value rather than by asset. Equal division of assets between both spouses also applies to retirement assets such as IRAs and annuities and to any life insurance not already placed in an Insurance Preservation Trust (discussed in Chapter 18). Retirement assets pass outside the Living Trust (since they are not in the Living Trust per se) and flow directly to the named beneficiary, usually the surviving spouse. Thereafter, the retirement assets are considered to be part of the surviving spouse's estate, although they may be included in the overall valuation of estate assets for federal estate tax purposes.

A Married A-B-C Trust is the appropriate choice for a married couple whose estate value, including the value of any IRAs and any life insurance, exceeds two federal estate tax exemptions.

Estate Before Demise of the First Spouse

While both spouses are living, the market value and cost basis of the estate assets are as shown in Table 14B-5. This example adds other real estate to the couple's estate to make it large enough to require a Married A-B-C Trust.

Estate After Demise of the First Spouse

Upon the death of the first spouse, assets must be allocated to the sub-trusts. These assets include the separate property of each spouse, the community property, and then any IRAs.

Allocation of Separate Property (at Market Value and Cost Basis) The separate property of the decedent spouse receives full stepped-up valuation to the current market value as of the decedent's date of death and is allocated to the decedent's B sub-trust. The separate property of the surviving spouse does not receive stepped-up valuation and is allocated to the survivor's A sub-trust at the original cost basis. The top of Table 14B-6 shows the separate property of both spouses. The bottom part of the table shows how the separate property is allocated in each of the sub-trusts after the death of the first spouse.

Allocation of Community Property Assets (at Market Value) With the valuation method of allocation, the community property is divided equally by value rather than by asset. One of the primary advantages of using the valuation method of allocation is that the retirement assets (illustrated in this example as an IRA, where the surviving spouse is the IRA beneficiary), including annuities and insurance that were accumulated as community property, may be included in the allocation by value. Remember, these particular assets are not in the Living Trust; they pass to the surviving spouse (as beneficiary) outside the Living Trust, but they may be included in the total value allocation.

Since the first spouse already has separate property of $100,000 (having received stepped-up valuation to current market value), only an additional $500,000 of asset value is needed to fully utilize the decedent's federal estate tax exemption. Any asset value going into the decedent's B sub-trust that exceeds the amount of the decedent's federal estate tax exemption would be subject to federal estate taxation. It is advantageous to place an appreciating asset, such as a home and a portion of the other real estate ($100,000 in this example), in the decedent's B sub-trust, rather than a depreciating asset. An IRA is considered to be a depreciating asset because of the eventual required withdrawals from the IRA. Remember that placing an IRA in the decedent's B sub-trust can have significant adverse income tax consequences. The balance of the other real estate ($700,000) is placed in the decedent's C sub-trust ($600,000) and in the survivor's A sub-trust ($100,000).

Table 14B-7 on page 210 shows the estate asset valuation after the death of the first spouse. The top portion of the table shows the effect of stepped-up valuation on the marital assets and the decedent's separate property, and the bottom part shows the allocation of all the assets to the appropriate sub-trusts.

The ledger worksheet is intended to help you allocate your estate assets to the sub-trusts. For this example, an appropriate allocation of estate assets to the A, B, and C sub-trusts would

TABLE 14B-7
ESTATE ASSETS AFTER DEATH OF FIRST SPOUSE
(MARRIED A-B-C TRUST IN A COMMUNITY PROPERTY STATE)

Basic Estate Assets	MARKET VALUE First Spouse	MARKET VALUE Second Spouse	COST BASIS First Spouse	COST BASIS Second Spouse
Home	$ 400,000			
Other real estate	$ 700,000			$ 100,000
Decedent's separate property	$ 100,000			
Survivor's separate property				$ 50,000
IRA				$1,000,000*
Total	$1,200,000			$1,150,000

ALLOCATION OF ESTATE ASSETS TO SUB-TRUSTS

	C Sub-Trust	B Sub-Trust	A Sub-Trust
Home		$400,000	
Other real estate	$ 600,000	$100,000	$ 100,000
Decedent's separate property		$100,000	
Survivor's separate property			$ 50,000
IRA			$1,000,000
Total value in decedent's estate		$1,200,000	
Total value in survivor's estate			$1,150,000

*The cost basis of an IRA is zero.

be as shown in Figure 14B-4. The shaded area in the figure denotes that the survivor's separate property retains its original cost basis (i.e., does not receive stepped-up valuation to current market value).

To play the game by the rules and also satisfy the IRS requirements, you must fill out the ledger sheets for the decedent's B and C sub-trusts and the survivor's A sub-trust, as shown in Figures 14B-5, 14B-6, and 14B-7 on pages 212–213.

Please be aware that this allocation of assets is arbitrary; the assets may be allocated in any form desired, as long as the total value of the community property is equal for each spouse. In this example, the home ($400,000) and a major share of the other real estate ($700,000) were placed in the decedent's estate (the B and C sub-trusts). This placement of

asset value allowed the entire IRA ($1 million) plus a minor share of the other real estate ($100,000) to be placed in the survivor's estate (the A sub-trust). With this allocation, the value in the decedent's B sub-trust did not exceed the federal estate tax exemption, so no estate tax liability was incurred when the first spouse died.

Summary
In the allocation method just illustrated, the decedent's separate property flows into the decedent's B sub-trust and receives full stepped-up valuation to the current market value ($100,000) as of the decedent's date of death. The survivor's separate property flows into the survivor's A sub-trust at cost basis ($50,000), since it is not community property. The home, as community property, receives full

FIGURE 14B-4
ALLOCATION OF ASSETS TO THE A, B, AND C SUB-TRUSTS AFTER THE FIRST SPOUSE DIES (COMMUNITY PROPERTY STATE)

Description of Property	SEPARATE PROPERTY		MARITAL SHARE OF ASSETS		SUB-TRUSTS		
	Deceased	Survivor	Deceased	Survivor	C	B	A
	Net Stepped-Up Valuation	Net Cost Basis	Net Stepped-Up Valuation	Net Stepped-Up Valuation	Net Stepped-Up Valuation	Net Stepped-Up Valuation	Net Stepped-Up Valuation*
Checking	$	$	$	$	$	$	$
Money Market							
CD							
Bonds							
Home			$200,000	$ 200,000	$600,000	$400,000	
Other Real Estate			$400,000	$ 400,000		$100,000	$ 100,000
Personal Effects							
IRA				$1,000,000		$100,000	$1,000,000
Separate Property of Decedent Spouse	$100,000						
Separate Property of Surviving Spouse		$50,000					$ 50,000

*The shaded areas in the figure denote that the survivor's separate property retains its original cost basis (i.e., does not receive stepped-up valuation to current market value).

FIGURE 14B-5
ASSET DISTRIBUTION BY TRUST
TRUST B

Asset Description	Valuation		
	Amount	Date	Source*
Home located at 1538 Spruce	$400,000	2/16/81	Comparables
Drive, Canoga Park, CA			
12.5% of apartment building located at	$100,000	2/27/81	Comparables
3842 Pine St., North Hollywood, CA			
E. F. Hutton account #5648321	$100,000	2/12/81	Statement
(Decedent's Separate Property)			

Date: 2/27/81   Signature of Trustee: _Mary R. Jones_
Mary R. Jones

*Source of Valuation

FIGURE 14B-6
ASSET DISTRIBUTION BY TRUST
TRUST C

Asset Description	Valuation		
	Amount	Date	Source*
75% of apartment building located at	$600,000	2/27/81	Comparables
3842 Pine St., North Hollywood, CA			

Date: 2/27/81   Signature of Trustee: _Mary R. Jones_
Mary R. Jones

*Source of Valuation

FIGURE 14B-7
ASSET DISTRIBUTION BY TRUST
TRUST A

Asset Description	Valuation		
	Amount	Date	Source*
12.5% of apartment building located at	$100,000	2/27/81	Comparables
3842 Pine St., North Hollywood, CA			
IRA	$1,000,000	2/14/81	Statement
E. F. Hutton account #5648482	$50,000	2/12/81	Statement
(Survivor's Separate Property)			

Date: 2/27/81   Signature of Trustee: _____ *Mary R. Jones* _____
Mary R. Jones

*Source of Valuation

stepped-up valuation to the current market value ($400,000). Because the home is an appreciating asset, it is placed in the decedent's B sub-trust. Since the B sub-trust is insulated from further estate taxation, any future growth of the home's value will be exempt from further federal estate taxation.

The major share of the other real estate ($700,000) is placed in the decedent's B and C sub-trusts, with $600,000 in the C sub-trust and $100,000 in the B sub-trust to insulate it from further estate taxes and also to fully utilize the decedent's federal estate tax exemption. A minor share of the other real estate ($100,000) is placed in the survivor's A sub-trust. (With such an allocation, the asset value in the C sub-trust will be included in the estate of the second spouse upon his or her death for federal estate tax purposes.) The IRA, whose market value ($1 million in this example) retains its cost basis of zero, can be included as a part of the community property assets and also allocated by value. The entire IRA ($1 million) is placed in the survivor's A sub-trust, along with a minor share of the other real estate ($100,000), to equate the value in allocating the community property. (Before placing any part of an IRA in the decedent's B sub-trust and/or C sub-trust, you should become familiar with the serious adverse income tax consequences that can occur, as will be explained in Chapter 12.)

Remember that the asset allocations used in this example are arbitrary and may be altered to suit the estates of each unique couple. The important feature to remember, however, is the flexibility that is available to you when allocating by value.

TAX TREATMENT FOR COMMUNITY PROPERTY STATES

Understanding how to settle an estate in a good Living Trust involves more than just allocating assets to the sub-trusts and knowing how to value those assets. You also need to be aware of the impact of the capital gains tax on future sales and transfers of estate assets, as well as be knowledgeable about federal estate tax con-

TABLE 14B-8
VALUE OF HOME WHEN FIRST SPOUSE DIES (COMMUNITY PROPERTY STATE)

Home Allocation	Market Value	New Cost Basis	Capital Gain
Decedent spouse (B sub-trust)	$200,000	$200,000	$0
Surviving spouse (A sub-trust)	$200,000	$200,000	$0
Total	$400,000	$400,000	$0

TABLE 14B-9
VALUE OF HOME WHEN EVENTUALLY SOLD (COMMUNITY PROPERTY STATE)

Home Allocation	Market Value	Cost Basis	Capital Gain	Exemption
Decedent spouse (B sub-trust)	$300,000	$200,000	$100,000	$ 0
Surviving spouse (A sub-trust)	$300,000	$200,000	$100,000*	$250,000
Total	$600,000	$400,000	$100,000	

*Capital gain is offset by homeowner's exemption.

sequences and the state inheritance tax differences among the states.

Capital Gains Treatment

To compute the amount of capital gain, you must remember that, upon the death of the first spouse in a community property state, all community property assets in the survivor's A sub-trust and the decedent's B sub-trust and C sub-trust attain full stepped-up valuation to the current market value. The exception to this rule is the IRA, which retains its cost basis of zero. Let's see how this principle applies to various assets.

Sale of Home

For purposes of illustrating the tax consequences of selling your home, assume that a couple originally purchased a house for $200,000 (its cost basis); when the first spouse dies, the home has increased in value to $400,000 (its market value). Upon the death of

the first spouse, the home therefore has a market value of $400,000. The surviving spouse receives the benefit of full stepped-up valuation to the current market value for the entire house, whether the home is included in the survivor's A sub-trust or in the decedent's B sub-trust or C sub-trust. If the surviving spouse decided to sell the home, no capital gain would be realized on the sale. Table 14B-8 shows each spouse's share of the value of the house (including stepped-up valuation for both spouses' shares) and shows that no capital gain is realized on the sale, since the new cost basis is the same as the current market value.

If the surviving spouse decided to stay in the home for several years and were to sell it years later, the $250,000 homeowner's exemption would still apply, but only to the share of the home in the survivor's A sub-trust—regardless of how much the home's value had appreciated. In the following example, let's assume that the home increased in value from $400,000 to

$600,000. Table 14B-9 shows how the increased value of the home (its current market value) and the cost basis are allocated to the decedent's B sub-trust and the survivor's A sub-trust.

Remember that the homeowner's exemption applies *only to an individual* and not to an irrevocable Trust (i.e., the decedent's B sub-trust). When the home is sold, the share of the home in the decedent's B sub-trust will realize a $100,000 capital gain, which is taxable at the capital gains tax rate. For determining this rate, which depends upon how long an asset has been held, assets in the decedent's B sub-trust retain the holding period established when the assets were originally purchased. The capital gains tax rate would be 18 percent if the home has been held (from date of purchase) for at least five years; 20 percent if the home has been held for at least 12 months; or 28 percent if the home has been held for less than 12 months. (The 18 percent capital gains tax rate becomes effective in the year 2001.)

Remember, to satisfy the IRS requirement for the $250,000 homeowner's exemption, the spouse must have lived in the home for two of the past five years, including the time both spouses were living in the home. The IRS time clock starts on the date that the spouses purchased the home.

Sale of Other Real Estate

The sale of other real estate is handled in almost the same manner as the sale of the home, except the homeowner's exemption does not apply. For illustration purposes, let's assume that the other real estate had an original cost basis of $400,000. When the first spouse dies, this other real estate has a current market value of $800,000. Upon the death of the first spouse, the other real estate, as community property, would receive full stepped-up valuation to the current market value of $800,000. If the surviving spouse decides to sell the other real estate, no capital gain would be realized on the sale; thus, there would be no capital gains taxes to pay. Table 14B-10 on page 216 shows each spouse's share of the value of the other real estate (including stepped-up valuation for both

spouses' shares) and shows that no capital gain is realized on the sale since the new cost basis is the same as the current market value.

If the surviving spouse decided to keep the other real estate for several years and were to sell it years later, after it had appreciated in the A sub-trust and B sub-trust, the capital gains tax rate would be the same for each of the sub-trusts holding that real estate (since the holding period for the asset is obviously the same). In the following example, let's assume that the other real estate increased in value from $800,000 to $1 million. Table 14B-11 on page 216 shows how the increased value of the other real estate (its current market value) and the cost basis are allocated to the decedent's B sub-trust and to the survivor's A sub-trust.

If the other real estate were sold, the share of the other real estate in the decedent's B sub-trust would realize a taxable capital gain on the appreciation ($100,000). Assets in the decedent's B (and/or C) sub-trust retain the same holding period as the decedent—for purposes of the capital gains tax, where the tax rate depends on how long an asset has been held. The share of the other real estate in the survivor's A sub-trust would also realize a taxable capital gain on the appreciation ($100,000). Both the irrevocable Trust (the B sub-trust) and the survivor's A sub-trust would be subject to the same capital gains tax rate: 18 percent (beginning in 2001) if the real estate has been held for at least five years from the date of purchase; 20 percent if the real estate has been held for at least 12 months; or 28 percent if the real estate has been held for less than 12 months.

Sale of Other Assets

The sale of other assets, such as stocks, mutual funds, partnerships, and the like, is handled in exactly the same manner as just described for other real estate. All of the community property assets receive full stepped-up valuation to current market value upon the death of the first spouse. Any capital gain realized when an asset is eventually sold is taxed at the appropriate rate, depending on how long the asset has been held.

TABLE 14B-10
VALUE OF OTHER REAL ESTATE WHEN FIRST SPOUSE DIES (COMMUNITY PROPERTY STATE)

Other Real Estate	Market Value	New Cost Basis	Capital Gain
Decedent spouse (B sub-trust)	$400,000	$400,000	$0
Surviving spouse (A sub-trust)	$400,000	$400,000	$0
Total	$800,000	$800,000	$0

TABLE 14B-11
VALUE OF OTHER REAL ESTATE WHEN EVENTUALLY SOLD (COMMUNITY PROPERTY STATE)

Other Real Estate	Market Value	New Cost Basis	Capital Gain
Decedent spouse (B sub-trust)	$ 500,000	$400,000	$100,000
Surviving spouse (A sub-trust)	$ 500,000	$400,000	$100,000
Total	$1,000,000	$800,000	$200,000

Sale of Separate Property

The sale of each spouse's separate property follows the same basic guidelines as for the other assets that have already been described:

- The decedent's separate property receives full stepped-up valuation to current market value (as of the date of the decedent's death). If the separate property is sold before it appreciates further, no capital gain will be realized on the sale, regardless of the asset's initial cost basis.
- The surviving spouse's separate property does not receive stepped-up valuation and, therefore, retains its original cost basis. When the separate property is sold, a taxable capital gain must be realized on the difference between the original cost basis and the current market value. The capital gains tax rate will depend on how long the asset was held before it was sold.

Transfer of Assets Between Sub-Trusts

You may transfer one or more assets from the survivor's revocable A sub-trust to the decedent's irrevocable B sub-trust and/or C sub-trust. However, before doing so, you must understand some basic principles about the sub-trusts. Upon the death of the first spouse, the decedent's B sub-trust and C sub-trust become *irrevocable*; the allocation and distribution options specified by the decedent for passing on his or her assets to the named heirs become cast in concrete—unchangeable by the surviving spouse. The surviving spouse's A sub-trust remains *revocable*, meaning that the surviving spouse is able to change any part of the A sub-trust (as long as the surviving spouse is alive and competent). Because the surviving spouse's A sub-trust is revocable, the IRS considers those assets to be transparent. In other words, the IRS treats the assets as the individual assets of the surviving spouse, even though they are held in the name of the Trust. Therefore, when transferring assets, you are dealing with two separate entities: the decedent's B and/or C irrevocable sub-trusts and the surviving spouse (as an individual).

Since the asset transfers are, in effect, taking place between separate entities (and not two parts of the same entity), any such transfer is considered to be a sale and purchase, and any capital gain that is generated must be recognized at the time of transfer. In other words, assets must be transferred *at their current market value* and not at their original cost basis. A taxable capital gain must be realized, even on a *transfer*, whenever the current market value of the asset being transferred is greater than its cost basis as held in the particular sub-trust.

The Traditional IRA

No stepped-up valuation or capital gain is associated with a traditional IRA. When the IRA funds are withdrawn, the entire amount is treated as ordinary income and is taxed at the individual income tax rate of the person receiving the funds. (The traditional IRA was addressed in detail in Chapter 12.)

Federal Estate Tax Treatment

Any federal estate taxes due on the estate valuation when the first spouse dies may be deferred until the death of the second spouse. At that time, any federal estate taxes due on the valuation of the entire estate must be determined and paid within nine months after the date of death of the second spouse. Upon the death of the first spouse, if your estate value exceeds the then-current amount of two individual federal estate tax exemptions and your Living Trust incorporates a C (or QTIP) sub-trust, you need to file Form 706, Schedule R, to make the QTIP election.

State Inheritance Tax

To the best of my knowledge, Louisiana is the only community property state to impose a state inheritance tax at the time of death of the first spouse if the surviving spouse is the beneficiary of the decedent's assets.

ASSET ALLOCATION IS CRUCIAL

When the first spouse dies, making the proper asset allocation is crucial to minimizing any potential federal estate tax bite. If you have been fortunate enough to have accumulated a sizable estate, I recommend that you also read about the advanced settlement options for community property states, which are discussed in Chapter 24.

No one wants to see his or her hard-earned estate unnecessarily consumed by federal estate taxes, but you must be knowledgeable of both the consequences and the proper steps to take in order to avoid having Uncle Sam be one of your "best-paid" beneficiaries.

15

Special Considerations upon the Death of the First Spouse
Married A-B and Married A-B-C Trusts

In Chapter 14, you learned how to value assets and place them into the appropriate sub-trusts, depending on whether you reside in a separate property state or a community property state. A good Living Trust provides the surviving spouse with great flexibility. After the death of the first spouse and the subsequent valuation of estate assets and the allocation of those assets to the sub-trusts, the surviving spouse still needs to consider many options to ensure that the proper decisions are made for handling the assets of the estate. The intent of this chapter is to explore the many options available. These options point out the flexibility that a *well-written* Living Trust gives the surviving spouse.

LOSS OF A SPOUSE

The loss of a spouse is one of the most traumatic events in a person's life. Often, the death of a spouse is the end of a long relationship where each spouse has relied upon the other for companionship, as well as guidance in mak-

ing many decisions—the very important ones, as well as the menial ones—throughout a lifetime together. The death of a spouse brings not only the loss of an inseparable companion, but often deep concern about "Where do I go from here?" The surviving spouse needs time to grieve but then must begin the important task of reconstructing his or her life.

Losing a spouse creates fear—the fear of uncertainty and, therefore, of the unknown. Most of us have become so accustomed to intrusive big government that we anticipate the worst. What happens next in our lives?

For many people, losing a spouse often means having to take over duties and responsibilities previously handled by the now-deceased spouse. During this time of emotional trauma, few people think about the often unpleasant task that lies ahead—settling the estate of the deceased. There are very dramatically different outcomes to this onerous task, depending on whether or not the deceased individual had a Living Trust.

If You Don't Have a Living Trust

If you are one of the unfortunate many who do not have a Living Trust, your worst fears are about to be realized! You must go through the agony of probate, suffering unnecessary expenses, enduring long delays in settling the estate, and possibly suffering from unpleasant public exposure of your private estate matters. Yes, you will see big government and attorneys in their worst possible light.

If You Do Have a Living Trust

If you are one of the increasingly numerous people who have wisely sought out and created a good Living Trust, you avoid the numerous problems of probate. You quickly and privately settle the affairs of your estate (often with little or no expense involved), and you retain peace of mind, knowing that you and the heirs will reap the many benefits of having a Living Trust.

Settling a Living Trust is really quite easy, especially for most of us who have modest estates. A well-written Living Trust provides the surviving spouse and/or heirs great flexibility in allocating and distributing Trust assets.

I recently received a letter that, in part, said, "My father passed away earlier this year, and my wife and I learned firsthand how valuable the Living Trust can be in avoiding the probate process. And, most important, it enabled my mother to immediately begin reconstructing her life. We would now like to set up our own Living Trust."

This letter is typical of the myriad letters written to us regularly by people from all over the United States. A Living Trust avoids the intrusive legal process—called probate—that holds an estate, and its survivors, in limbo for a seemingly endless period.

DECISIONS THAT MUST BE MADE

After the death of the first spouse, the surviving spouse has many flexible options to consider—if his or her estate is in a *good* Living Trust. Each estate is different, and the desires and needs of each surviving spouse are unique. However, in almost every estate, there are decisions that must be made regarding the principal estate assets. These decisions involve the following:

- The valuation of assets upon the death of a spouse
- The allocation and distribution of assets
- Handling the separate property of the decedent spouse
- Filling the decedent's B sub-trust
- Disclaiming an interest in assets
- The family home—keeping it, selling it, or refinancing it
- Retirement assets
- Motor vehicles
- Life insurance policies

Valuation of Assets upon Death of a Spouse

The subject of valuing assets upon the death of a spouse is often confusing, and many people misunderstand it. In some situations, it is best to seek the highest valuation, but there are also situations where it is better to seek a lower valuation. If the assets ultimately could be subject to federal estate taxation, a "low" valuation is preferable (within reason, of course), allowing you to place the greatest value of assets in the decedent's B sub-trust. Assets placed in the decedent's B sub-trust are insulated from any future estate tax on the appreciation (increase in value) of those assets.

If you are not concerned about the estate value triggering federal estate taxes, then it is preferable to have the assets valued at their highest (but realistic) valuation, in order to attain the highest stepped-up valuation to their market value. Let's use the valuation of your home as an example. You can ask two or more real estate agents to give you a valuation of your home "on the high side," although selling your home with such a valuation may take considerable time before you find a willing buyer. On the other hand, you can ask the agents to value your home "on the low side," a price at which you will usually find a willing buyer much more quickly. Either valuation is legal and appropriate, as long as it is within reason (comparable to other homes sold in the same area).

When considering valuation of an asset, you also need to be cognizant of whether a capital gain is involved. The Taxpayer Relief Act of 1997 gave you several capital gains tax options. If the asset is a home, the surviving spouse may also use the homeowner's $250,000 exemption to reduce any capital gain exposure. If other types of assets are involved, the capital gains tax rate varies, depending on how long the asset has been held:

- A 28 percent capital gains tax rate is imposed on appreciation (the increase in value of the asset since it was originally purchased), if the asset has been held for less than twelve months.
- A 20 percent tax rate is imposed on appreciation if the asset has been held at least twelve months.
- Beginning in 2001, an 18 percent tax rate is imposed on appreciation if the asset has been held at least five years.

In community property states where the surviving spouse receives full stepped-up valuation to the current market value on all assets in the decedent's estate and on the marital assets in the survivor's estate, the capital gains liability can be significantly reduced (or totally eliminated).

Remember that the capital gains tax rate of 18 percent to 28 percent is always preferable to the burdensome federal estate tax rate, which ranges from 37 percent to 55 percent!

Allocation and Distribution of Assets

One of the areas of greatest misunderstanding regarding a Living Trust is knowing how to *allocate* assets and when to *distribute* the assets. Both terms are often mistakenly (and interchangeably) used to refer to giving assets to heirs, but they have very different meanings.

The term *allocation* all by itself also can be confusing, since the word refers to two different types of allocation:

- Following the death of a trustor, estate assets can be allocated to (assigned to or placed within) the various sub-trusts, such as the decedent's B sub-trust and the survivor's A sub-trust.

- In creating or modifying Trust documents, assets can be allocated to individuals (the heirs), or designated to be given to specified individuals when one or both spouses has passed away.

When talking about allocation and distribution of assets, I am referring to the latter situation. *Allocation* of assets occurs when the heirs are named to receive certain assets (or a portion thereof) at some point in time. The *distribution* of an asset to the named heir occurs when the heir is actually given the asset—usually when the heir attains a specified age or upon the death of one or more of the spouses.

Asset Distribution

When the first spouse dies, the surviving spouse is typically also the surviving trustee of the Trust, and he or she needs to determine whether any assets are to be distributed upon the death of the first spouse. The surviving spouse, as the surviving trustee, should look at the "Special Bequests" section in the Living Trust to see if the decedent spouse specified any such distributions. The special bequests are typically small bequests, specified either in a dollar amount or as a percentage of the estate, or they may be a named asset (such as a car, boat, family Bible, and so on) specifically designated to be given to particular individuals who are not otherwise named as primary beneficiaries of the Trust. These distributions should be made first, before any other estate assets are allocated and distributed.

Next, the surviving spouse, as the surviving trustee, should review the "Allocation and Distribution" section of the Trust to determine what asset or assets must be allocated and/or distributed to the beneficiaries after the death of the first spouse. In most Living Trusts, the assets are typically retained in trust for the benefit of the surviving spouse. Therefore, there is seldom any allocation or distribution of assets when the first spouse dies.

However, in second marriages, it is not unusual for a decedent spouse to leave part (or all) of the decedent's separate property to his or her children from a prior marriage. Such distributions should be made, as much as possible, from the decedent's B sub-trust, to avoid federal estate taxation. If such distributions are made from the decedent's C sub-trust (QTIP Trust), the assets are immediately subject to federal estate taxes. Also remember that for an asset to qualify for the decedent's C sub-trust (QTIP Trust), the surviving spouse must have an undisputed right to the income from that asset for his or her lifetime.

Timing of Distribution

A *good* Living Trust specifies when the assets are to be distributed to each named beneficiary. Remember, if the assets are to be distributed outright, such an instruction means *now* —not after a Form 706 has been initially filed, and not two years or three years from now after a Form 706 has been filed and the IRS has reviewed it and approved it!

However, if you are filing a Notice to Creditors, in order to cut off creditor claims in the first four months after the decedent's death, then any outright distribution should be delayed until the four-month period has elapsed. This Notice to Creditors comes under the Uniform Creditor Claims Act, which is a uniform code that has been adopted by a number of states and is rapidly being adopted by many others. During that four-month period, you should pay all debts of the decedent that are outstanding and due and payable. Once you have paid the debts and the four-month Notice to Creditors waiting period has elapsed, distribute to the named beneficiaries all assets specified to be "distributed outright."

Generally, no federal estate tax needs to be paid upon the death of the first spouse; however, a state inheritance tax may be due (depending on the decedent's state of residence). Set aside any such amount (i.e., leave it in a bank account) to pay the tax within nine months following the decedent's date of death. After you have paid the debts and set aside the amount needed to pay inheritance taxes, there is no excuse to withhold the distribution of assets that have been designated to be distributed outright. If an asset has been specified to be distributed to a beneficiary at a certain age, any such asset should be distributed to the beneficiary once he or she has attained that age (or immediately if he or she has already passed that age).

Handling the Separate Property of the Deceased Spouse

Upon the death of the first spouse, the separate property of the decedent spouse flows into the decedent's B sub-trust and/or C sub-trust. Remember that separate property is defined as any property received or generated prior to the current marriage or property received by gift or by inheritance. The husband and wife should have distinguished separate property as such by including Separate Property Agreements as part of their Living Trust.

An excellent example of handling inherited separate property is the story of Tom and Janet Parsons.

Tom and Janet had been married for some forty-five years before they first came into my office to create a Living Trust. Several years earlier, Janet had inherited $80,000 from her mother, with the charge from her mother that Janet was never to allow Tom to have access to any of the $80,000. Apparently, when Tom and Janet were a newly married couple, Tom frivolously spent their joint checking account, and Janet's mother had never forgotten this act of imprudence.

Janet adhered to her mother's wishes and placed a $10,000 CD in each of eight different banks. This money was Janet's toy; as the CDs would mature, she would determine the best interest rate at the various banks in her town and move the maturing $10,000 CD to the bank currently offering the best interest rate.

After the new Trust was executed, Janet called me and was very upset because her bank had told her that because of the new Living Trust, Janet now had to put all of the CD accounts in the name of both Tom and Janet, and such an arrangement was not her mother's desire. I calmed Janet down and told her that there was a very simple solution to her dilemma: we simply needed to change the transfer letters for the CD accounts. The standard transfer letter uses the full name of the Trust, which included Tom and Janet as both the trustors and trustees. It was very easy to develop a new transfer letter in which the transferor and the transferee were only Janet.

Using this new transfer letter, Janet transferred all of the CD accounts in each of the eight different banks into Tom and Janet's Living Trust, with Janet being the sole signatory on the account, thereby preventing Tom from withdrawing any of the funds. After forty-five years of marriage, Janet certainly wasn't concerned about Tom (and what he might do if he had access to her mother's funds), but she felt compelled to follow her mother's final instructions.

This situation points out one of the clear advantages of having a well-written Living Trust. Even though the accounts were set up with Janet as the sole signatory, upon Janet's death (if she were to die first), Tom (as the surviving trustor and trustee) would be able to go into each of the banks and—with the Trust and a certified copy of Janet's death certificate—have immediate access to those accounts.

Filling the Decedent's B Sub-Trust

I am often asked if the surviving spouse can increase the asset value in the decedent's B sub-trust (e.g., by adding some of the surviving spouse's assets to the decedent's sub-trust) in order to fully utilize the decedent's federal estate tax exemption. The quick answer is no, but let me explain an exception to this pat answer.

For example, let's assume an estate of $800,000. Let's further assume that the assets are all marital assets (i.e., community property); one-half of the assets ($400,000) would flow into the survivor's A sub-trust and the other half of the assets (the other $400,000) would flow into the decedent's B sub-trust. Table 15-1 shows this allocation.

TABLE 15-1		
ALLOCATION OF ESTATE ASSETS		
Estate Assets	B Sub-Trust	A Sub-Trust
$800,000	$400,000	$400,000

As you can see, the normal allocation (half of the assets going into each sub-trust) does not fully utilize the decedent's federal estate tax exemption of $600,000. Unfortunately, a sur-

viving spouse may not *gift* assets to a decedent spouse. However, the surviving spouse may *disclaim* a part of the survivor's estate, as described in the next section. In this manner, and in this manner only, the surviving spouse could transfer assets from the survivor's A sub-trust to the decedent's B sub-trust. Remember, however, that this arrangement is best suited for couples who are not involved in a second marriage.

Disclaiming an Interest in Assets

Upon the death of the first spouse, the surviving spouse may disclaim an interest in part of his or her assets and pass the disclaimed assets to the decedent's B sub-trust and/or C sub-trust. The disclaimer must be made within nine months from the date of death of the first spouse, and it must be made *before* the disclaimant receives any income whatsoever from the asset to be disclaimed. The surviving spouse, as the trustee and beneficiary of the decedent's B sub-trust, retains full rights to use or sell his or her disclaimed assets.

If you must disclaim assets, it is preferable that the disclaimed assets be non-income-producing assets. If you disclaim income-producing assets, you create a gift of income that is computed over the surviving spouse's life expectancy. Be particularly careful in states that require the payment of inheritance taxes on the death of the first spouse (Ohio and Louisiana).

If you wish to disclaim an interest in some of the assets, you should do so within thirty days from the date of death of the first spouse, in order to avoid the possibility of disqualification due to income distribution to the surviving spouse. If you, as the surviving spouse, receive income from an asset that is to be disclaimed, you are henceforth disqualified from ever disclaiming that asset. Therefore, the sooner you disclaim an interest in an asset, the less likely that the Internal Revenue Service will construe that you have received benefits from a disclaimed asset.

Disclaiming an interest in assets and placing them in an irrevocable Trust must be done by a written disclaimer and delivered to the trustee within nine months from the date of death of the first spouse. If the asset was inadvertently left outside the Trust, then a written disclaimer must be delivered to the executor within nine months from the date of death of the first spouse. Remember that assets left outside a Living Trust must go through probate before they can be placed inside the Living Trust.

The Home

Often, the family home is the single most important asset in an estate. Typically, the surviving spouse has full right to the home—to live in it or to sell it.

Allocation in a Separate Property State

If you live in a separate property state, the most common asset allocation method is the itemization method, where half the home is placed in the decedent's B sub-trust and the other half in the survivor's A sub-trust. The surviving spouse, as trustee and beneficiary of the decedent's B sub-trust, therefore has full rights to the home. Florida may be the exception to this rule.

Caution: *If you live in Florida, I urge you to engage very competent legal counsel for allocation advice, in order to preserve your homestead protection. Such counsel is advisable until the Florida state legislature gets around to clarifying its homestead laws.*

Allocation in a Community Property State

If you live in a community property state, the most common method of asset allocation is the valuation method, where you have the option of allocating by value. Thus, you have the option of placing all (or part) of the home in the decedent's B sub-trust (and/or C sub-trust) or in the survivor's A sub-trust. Regardless of which sub-trust contains the home, the surviving spouse (as trustee and beneficiary) has full rights to the home.

The controlling factor in allocating the home to a particular sub-trust usually is which assets are expected to attain the greatest appreciation over the ensuing years. Appreciating assets (those that are increasing in value) should be

placed in the decedent's B sub-trust, in order to avoid future estate taxes on the subsequent appreciation.

The Home in a Second Marriage

Second marriages are becoming more common today, and one spouse often owns the home in which the couple resides. In this situation, the home is usually identified (and it certainly should be) as the separate property of the spouse who owns the home. When the owner of the home dies, a *good* Living Trust contains explicit wording that the surviving spouse may continue to live in the home until his or her death.

However, a word of warning is appropriate here. If a Married A-B-C Trust places a restriction upon the surviving spouse, such as "The surviving spouse may continue to live in the home *unless the surviving spouse remarries,*" such a restriction violates the QTIP requirement of the decedent's C sub-trust that the surviving spouse must have the right to income for life. (Residence in a home is considered to be income.) In this situation, you should either remove any such restriction from the Trust language or place the home in the decedent's B sub-trust, which has no restrictions as long as the total value in the B sub-trust does not exceed the amount of one federal estate tax exemption.

If the home is the separate property of the surviving spouse, then there are obviously no restrictions. The home is simply placed in the survivor's A sub-trust.

Sale of Home

If the surviving spouse intends to sell the home and it is the separate property of the decedent spouse, the portion of the home in the decedent's B sub-trust and/or C sub-trust attains full stepped-up valuation to the current market value. Remember, in a separate property state, the portion of the home in the survivor's A sub-trust retains its original cost basis. Usually, the surviving spouse qualifies for the $250,000 homeowner's exemption, which can be used to offset capital gains on the sale of the home. In contrast, in a community property state, all marital assets (community property), including those assets in the survivor's A sub-trust, attain full stepped-up valuation to the current market value, and thus no capital gain is realized on the sale of the home. If the home were, instead, the survivor's separate property (and, therefore, did not receive stepped-up valuation), the surviving spouse could use his or her $250,000 homeowner's exemption (if the qualification requirements are met) to offset capital gains on the sale of the home.

Refinancing of Home

If the surviving spouse decides to refinance the home, you need to be aware of some important considerations, so that you do not run into problems with the financial institution. As I have mentioned before, I strongly urge you to use the ledger method for allocating assets to the sub-trusts. Do *not* change your deed from the standard Trust name upon the death of a spouse. If you do record the deed in the name of the decedent's irrevocable B sub-trust and/or C sub-trust, it may be difficult (and, in many cases, often impossible) to refinance the home. However, if you simply record the home in the ledger using the ledger method, you should have no difficulty in refinancing the home, since the original deed has not been changed.

If, despite my advice, you prefer to re-record the deed to the home upon the death of the first spouse, rather than using the ledger method only, I urge you to file a Preliminary Change of Ownership form to forgo being taxed on the transfer. This form is accepted in many states and is rapidly being adopted by others.

If you don't re-record the deed for the share of the home being placed in the decedent's B sub-trust and/or C sub-trust, then you forgo any property tax problem and can easily transfer the entire property (or a share of the property) from the decedent's B sub-trust to the survivor's A sub-trust or from the decedent's C sub-trust to the survivor's A sub-trust using the Ledger Transfer Form described in Chapter 14.

Retirement Assets

Retirement assets include tax-deferred savings plans such as IRAs, Keogh plans, simplified employee pension plans (SEPs), other pension plans, profit-sharing plans, employee stock ownership plans (ESOPs), and deferred-compensation plans. It is preferable to place these assets in the survivor's A sub-trust, since these assets presumably will be consumed, or at least reduced in value, over the remaining lifetime of the surviving spouse. However, if these retirement assets are held as separate property and the owner of the assets desires that, upon his or her death, the assets remain in trust for the benefit of the surviving spouse (and then pass on to his or her children of a former marriage), then these retirement assets should be placed in the decedent's C sub-trust (QTIP Trust). A Roth IRA should be placed in a Roth Legacy Trust[SM]. Remember that if the IRA is in a standard Living Trust, taxes *on the full amount of the IRA* are due and payable by December 31 of the year following the IRA owner's death. If the IRA is in a Married IRA–QTIP Trust, no taxes are due upon the death of the IRA owner.

The one exception to this allocation would be for an estate with a very large IRA. In such a case, it may be more beneficial to place the IRA in a separate Married IRA–QTIP Trust. (The traditional IRA and the Roth IRA were discussed in detail in Chapters 12 and 13.)

Motor Vehicles

You should keep your motor vehicles (such as automobiles, pickup trucks, and motor homes) in the survivor's A sub-trust. Such advice is particularly relevant to ex–military officers who have their vehicles insured by United Services Automobile Association (USAA) in San Antonio, Texas. To qualify for USAA insurance coverage, an individual must be a service member, former service member, or a spouse or child of a former member. Following the death of the first spouse, the decedent's B sub-trust and C sub-trust become irrevocable, and USAA does not deem the survivors to be "military personnel"; thus, any vehicles placed in those sub-trusts would no longer qualify for USAA coverage.

Life Insurance Policies

If the surviving spouse is named as the primary beneficiary of a life insurance policy, he or she may disclaim all or part interest in the policy—if an Insurance Preservation Trust has not been named as the owner or beneficiary of the insurance policy. You need to be aware that the surviving spouse can disclaim the decedent's interest but *not* the surviving spouse's interest.

If the Living Trust has been named as the contingent beneficiary of the insurance policy and the surviving spouse is named as the primary beneficiary, the surviving spouse may disclaim all or part interest in the insurance policy. In this case, the insurance policy would pass to the decedent's B sub-trust and/or C sub-trust:

- In separate property states, all of the insurance can be passed to the decedent's B sub-trust and/or C sub-trust.
- In a community property state, however, the surviving spouse may *not* disclaim his or her half-ownership interest in an insurance policy. Thus, half of the insurance policy may be disclaimed to the decedent's B sub-trust and/or C sub-trust, but the surviving spouse's half must be placed in the survivor's A sub-trust.

If the Living Trust has not been named as the contingent beneficiary of the insurance policy, the surviving spouse (as the primary beneficiary) may disclaim all or part interest in the insurance policy, and the policy would pass as just described. When the Living Trust is not named as the contingent beneficiary of the insurance policy, the surviving spouse is required to take this part of the estate through a simple probate process in order to disclaim an interest in the policy.

Therefore, the appropriate course of action is to name the surviving spouse as the primary beneficiary and the Living Trust as the contingent beneficiary of any life insurance policies that are intended to be passed to a Living Trust.

SUBSEQUENT REMARRIAGE OF SURVIVING SPOUSE

If the surviving spouse decides to remarry (as is often the case today), it is appropriate to leave the surviving spouse's assets in the original survivor's A sub-trust. This approach avoids commingling the surviving spouse's assets with the assets of the new spouse. Another alternative, of course, is for the surviving spouse, on entering into his or her second marriage, to create a Married A-B Trust with the new spouse, then to transfer the assets from the surviving spouse's original A sub-trust into the newly created Married A-B Trust. However, the assets of the surviving spouse should be transferred into the new Married A-B Trust as the specifically designated separate property of the surviving spouse. The original decedent spouse's irrevocable B sub-trust and/or C sub-trust would remain in place as initially established.

RIGHTS OF THE SURVIVING SPOUSE

Chapter 9 explained that a good Living Trust provides some important rights to the surviving spouse regarding the use of a decedent spouse's assets in the decedent's B and/or C sub-trust. Here is a review of these important rights.

Income Right of the Surviving Spouse as Beneficiary

Typically, the surviving spouse has the right to all of the *income* from the decedent's B sub-trust. The surviving spouse *must* also have the right to all of the income from the decedent's C sub-trust (QTIP Trust) in order for the QTIP Trust to qualify for deferral of federal estate taxes on the decedent's assets.

Right to Maintain Standard of Living

As a general rule, the surviving spouse has the right to use assets from the decedent's B sub-trust to maintain his or her same standard of living. (This same rule generally applies to the decedent's C sub-trust, or QTIP Trust, although it is not a requirement of the C Trust.) Standard of living is defined as the right to health, education, maintenance, and support (HEMS). The surviving spouse may therefore use the decedent's funds without restriction to maintain the surviving spouse's health, to improve the surviving spouse's education, and to maintain and support a standard of living that is essentially the same as that enjoyed when both spouses were still alive.

This standard of living is known as an "ascertainable standard," but it also has limitations. For example, if part (or all) of the home is in the decedent's B sub-trust, the surviving spouse has the right to live in the house, without restriction, as long as the surviving spouse lives. However, the surviving spouse does *not* have the right to pay the creditors of the surviving spouse from funds in the decedent's B sub-trust, since such an action does not qualify as a "need."

Frivolous Right

Most Living Trusts give the surviving spouse the "frivolous right" to annually use $5,000 or 5 percent of the assets in the decedent's B sub-trust, whichever amount is larger. The same right is usually extended to the assets in the decedent's C sub-trust. The surviving spouse may use $5,000 from *each* of these two sub-trusts (or 5 percent of the total assets in each of these two sub-trusts) once a year for any reason he or she chooses, regardless of how frivolous the use. For example, the surviving spouse could buy an expensive automobile or take a trip to Europe.

The one restriction on this frivolous right is that it must be used each year, rather than accumulated. If the right is not exercised this year, the "unused" amount cannot be added to next year's frivolous right.

Surviving Spouse as Trustee

Remember that the surviving spouse, as trustee, continues to have all the powers that were present when both spouses were living: the right to buy, sell, and transfer any of the assets in the decedent's B sub-trust and/or C sub-trust (or in the survivor's A sub-trust). The only exception to these powers would be if the surviving spouse were *not* named as the sole trustee of the decedent's sub-trust(s).

The three rights of the surviving spouse—all of the income, all of the principal as necessary to maintain the same standard of living, and the "frivolous right" of 5 percent or $5,000 (whichever is greater)—are considered to be *restricted* rights, so they allow the surviving spouse to serve as trustee of the Trust. Such reasoning and carefully worded Trust language are just one more reason that you want to make sure you have a *good* Living Trust. You must understand that if the surviving spouse is given *unrestricted* access to the assets in the decedent's B sub-trust and/or C sub-trust, then someone other than the surviving spouse must serve as trustee.

Caution: *You must understand that if the surviving spouse is given* unrestricted *access to the assets in the decedent's B sub-trust and/or C sub-trust, then someone other than the surviving spouse must serve as trustee.*

Excluded Gifts

The surviving spouse retains his or her right to make "excluded gifts" to one or more individuals each year. These gifts, if no greater than $10,000 in value, need not be reported to the IRS by either the person giving the gift or by the person receiving the gift. However, these "excluded gifts" *must* be made from the survivor's A sub-trust.

All too often, I see articles in professional journals stating that the $10,000 "excluded gift" may not be made from the decedent's B sub-trust and/or C sub-trust because they are irrevocable Trusts—and gifts may be made only by individuals. Such a statement is accurate, and I concur, but it leaves much to be said. It is a simple matter to pass income from the decedent's B sub-trust and/or C sub-trust to the surviving spouse. Thereafter, the surviving spouse can make the $10,000 gifts as he or she deems appropriate.

A LIVING TRUST IS NOT ALWAYS THE SOLUTION

A well-written Living Trust can solve most problems, but it is not the answer to every problem. The following story is the perfect example of trying to use a Living Trust as the imperfect solution to a personal dispute.

(Although the case received widespread coverage in the newspapers, and nothing presented here is new, I have taken the liberty of changing the names to avoid sensationalism.) It is the dilemma manifested in this example that is important for you to understand.

During the Depression, Martha Dowd created a line of cosmetics that she marketed through an unusual retail concept. As time passed, her cosmetics line expanded. Martha raised her nephew, George, who helped her mix the cosmetics in the bathtub.

As more time passed and the business expanded, Martha's husband, Harold, joined the enterprise as the financial manager, and Martha's nephew, George, took on the responsibility of producing the cosmetics. The business continued to grow.

Eventually, there were two separate businesses housed in two separate buildings: the retail cosmetics business, with Martha as president and her husband, Harold, as financial manager; and the production process, owned and managed by George. The two separate buildings were physically joined together but divided by an invisible line. More time passed, and the business continued to grow. George married and had two sons, who eventually joined him in the business.

Then trouble erupted for the thriving enterprise. Following scandalous news reports of infidelity, a bitter divorce battle ensued between Martha and Harold. In fact, the divorce became so disruptive that security forces had to be stationed in the offices to maintain some form of decorum, so that the business relationship could continue.

Unfortunately, George, as the nephew, was forced to take sides—and chose to support his aunt. Of course, George's siding with his aunt infuriated his Uncle Harold. Following the divorce, Martha had an office in one end of the building and handled the marketing, while Harold maintained an office in the other end of the building to manage the finances.

Harold never forgave his nephew, George, for siding against him. Harold had his attorney, Herman Franks, draw up a Trust speci-fying that George would never receive any of Harold's interest in the retail cosmetics business. Instead, Harold specified that when Harold died, his attorney, Herman Franks, was to become the trustee of the Trust until George's death, when Harold's 50 percent interest in the business would pass to George's two sons.

Harold died, and Herman Franks, as the attorney and trustee, unexpectedly decided to appoint himself as the company financial officer, replacing his client. At the same time, Martha decided to go into semiretirement and delegated her 50 percent interest in the business to her nephew, George, who now assumed the marketing responsibilities.

Herman Franks came in regularly and went to the office at the far end of the retail cosmetics building to manage the finances, and George remained in the production building, where his office was located. These two men came to hate each other because they pursued diametrically opposite goals.

Once a year, Herman and George met in the marketing office in an all-day, closed-door session—each with his own agenda. Herman wanted all of the profits (which are substantial in the cosmetics industry) to go into the Trust. Herman received a nice percentage of the funds going into the Trust, and he then distributed the funds to charity and once again received a nice percentage on the funds that were distributed. In fact, Herman became known in the local area as "Mr. Charity." In that part of town, there are now wings of a hospital dedicated to Herman Franks for the contributions he gave to the hospital from Harold's Trust funds! George, of course, had an opposite agenda. George wanted to invest the profits of the business in additional advertising in order to build the business for his two sons. At the end of the day, both individuals would emerge—exhausted but having reached a compromise. This process went on for years, but the inevitable result was becoming obvious—the eventual ruin of the entire business.

After doing some investigating, George discovered that Herman, although a knowledgeable attorney, knew very little about financial management. In fact, the company had $250,000 in undocumented and, therefore, unrecoverable receivables. Armed with this information, George demanded arbitration, and a solution to the dilemma had to be found. After days of haggling, Herman agreed to be bought out and resigned as trustee of the Trust (and also resigned as the company financial officer). George assumed the role of trustee, and the company was finally back on track. Under George's leadership, the company recovered and is still going strong today.

The purpose of this story is to point out that not all problems can be solved by a Living Trust. In fact, this particular problem almost caused the demise of a business. I caution you to think twice before you draw up a Trust in anger; think carefully about the ensuing potential consequences.

16

Valuation of Assets upon the Death of the Second Spouse
Married A-B and Married A-B-C Trusts

Settling an estate in a good Living Trust upon the death of the second spouse is very similar to settling an estate when the first spouse dies. However, you must be aware of some differences:

- The survivor's A sub-trust can no longer be changed (becomes irrevocable).
- The assets in the survivor's A sub-trust attain stepped-up valuation.
- Estate taxes may now be due and payable.
- Separate property of the first decedent must be allocated and/or distributed to the specified beneficiaries.

Upon the death of the surviving spouse, the survivor's A sub-trust becomes irrevocable. The allocation and distribution instructions in the A sub-trust are now cast in concrete and may not be changed by the successor trustees.

Valuation of estate assets upon the death of the second spouse is really quite simple. All assets of the second spouse, identified in the survivor's A sub-trust, receive full stepped-up valuation to the current market value. The assets in the decedent's B sub-trust retain their "new" cost basis that was established upon the death of the first spouse. If there is a decedent's C sub-trust (QTIP Trust), its assets also retain their "new" cost basis established upon the death of the first spouse.

Unfortunately, now it is also time to face the music and finally pay any federal estate taxes and state inheritance taxes that may be due. Estate taxes are due if the assets in the survivor's A sub-trust exceed the value of one federal estate tax exemption. Any assets in the decedent's C sub-trust, if one exists, are "added" to the assets in the survivor's A sub-trust, and the entire combined amount in the A sub-trust and C sub-trust is subject to federal estate taxes (and state inheritance taxes, if imposed by that particular state).

Remember, if the total asset current market value (in the A sub-trust and the C sub-trust) exceeds the value of one federal estate tax

231

exemption, federal estate tax is due on the amount exceeding the current value of the exemption. The assets in the decedent's B subtrust are insulated from any further federal estate taxes and state inheritance taxes, regardless of the value the assets may have attained when the second spouse died.

The following story is, sadly, one that I hear much too often. It tells of the lack of knowledge most people have about settling a Living Trust and of the unnecessary delays and unwarranted expenses that deprive the heirs of their full inheritance.

Three frustrating and costly years had passed since the death of their parents, and Charles (now age 30) and Barbara (now age 28) were still waiting for the distribution from their parents' Living Trust. Their mother and father had created the Trust fifteen years ago, but since the children were minors at that time, the parents had named the father's brother, Harry, as successor trustee.

The father died ten years ago, and the mother died three years ago. The parents had always intended to amend their Trust when both children reached the age of 18 and to name their children as successor trustees. Unfortunately, the couple had never gotten around to it.

The estate was not very large, having a value of about $800,000, which was fully "covered" by the parents' Married A-B Living Trust, so no federal estate taxes or state inheritance taxes needed to be paid. However, Uncle Harry was unfamiliar with the Living Trust, so he took the cautious approach and engaged the attorney who originally drew up the Living Trust to settle it. Even though the Trust specified that the estate was to be *distributed outright* to the two children, neither beneficiary (now both adults) had yet received any distribution. As is so often the case in such situations, attorney fees had consumed $8,500 of the children's inheritance, and accounting fees had consumed another $3,700. The unnecessary costs continued to mount, and the estate assets remained tied up in the unnecessary and frustrating administration process.

Such a situation is precisely what the parents wanted to *avoid* when they created their Living Trust. Such occurrences happen all too often and are absolutely unnecessary in settling a Living Trust.

The following story provides an interesting twist. In this case, being forced to wait for the distribution of estate assets turned out to be a boon to the beneficiaries—but this case is definitely an exception.

Gregory and Patricia Stint had two sons and owned an oil company. Patricia died in November 1977, five years after the death of her husband. The Stints had created a very good Living Trust, written by a highly respected attorney. The couple left almost all of their company's corporate stock to six charities, with only 3 percent of the stock going to each of the two sons. In 1977 the stock donation was valued at $2 million for each of the six charities, and about $340,000 for each of the two sons.

The sons were upset that they were receiving such a small portion of their parents' sizable estate. However, they were also very aware there was a clause in their parents' Living Trust explicitly stating that if a beneficiary challenged the Living Trust, that beneficiary would cease to be a beneficiary (i.e., would be disinherited). Therefore, the sons had the ex-wife of one of the sons sue the Trust on the basis that she "remembered" when she was living with her ex-husband in his parents' home that Gregory Stint had clearly said he wanted all of the estate to go to his two sons.

Due to the pending suit, the funds from the estate could not be distributed. Two years passed, and the attorneys for the six charities gave the suit little thought. Then the preliminary hearing was finally held, and with all attorneys present, the judge said he would hear the case. However, he then looked directly at the attorney for the sons (suing through the ex-wife) and said, "You don't have a prayer in hell." Thereafter, the two sons quickly dropped the suit.

Two years had now passed since the suit was initiated, and the price of oil had skyrocketed. Each son's share of stock was now worth $1 million, so neither was disappointed. The shares of stock designated for each charity (worth $2 million in 1977) were now worth $6 million!

Charities must be extremely conservative financially, and none of these charities could have held on to the donated oil company stock. If the stock had been distributed in 1977, the charities would have had to convert the $2 million of stock into more conservative CDs. Instead, since the stock was forcibly held in trust for two years, each charity now received $6 million in stock, which they quickly converted to CDs. Interestingly, the market then began to go down. In the end, what was once a challenge to the right to receive funds turned out to be a magnificent blessing—for all parties concerned.

VALUATION OF THE ESTATE

Valuation of an estate in a Married A-B Living Trust or a Married A-B-C Living Trust, upon the death of the second spouse, is really quite simple. Upon the death of the second spouse, the second spouse's share of any marital assets and all of the second spouse's separate property receive full stepped-up valuation to the current market value, regardless of whether the second spouse lived in a separate property state or a community property state. In essence, upon the death of the survivor, all assets in the survivor's A sub-trust receive full stepped-up valuation to current market value. Remember that the assets of the first spouse to die (the assets in the decedent's B sub-trust and/or C sub-trust) retain their "new" cost basis, having benefited from stepped-up valuation when the first spouse died. (Valuation of assets upon the death of the first spouse was discussed in detail in Chapter 14.)

Stepped-Up Valuation

Stepped-up valuation applies only to the assets held by an individual. Thus, all of the assets in the survivor's A sub-trust receive full stepped-up valuation. The assets in the decedent's B sub-trust and/or C sub-trust (whether a QTIP Trust or QDOT Trust) do not receive stepped-up valuation again, since they received

stepped-up valuation upon the death of the first spouse, at which time the decedent's B sub-trust and/or C sub-trust became irrevocable.

ILLUSTRATION OF SETTLEMENT OPTIONS

Even though valuation and allocation of estate assets, upon the death of the first spouse, are different for separate property states and for community property states, the valuation of estate assets upon the death of the second spouse is the same for both kinds of states. However, so that you can continue to follow the examples started in Chapters 14A and 14B, this chapter splits into two parts: Chapter 16A for separate property states and Chapter 16B for community property states. Each of these parts illustrates the settlement of a Married A-B Trust and then the settlement of a Married A-B-C Trust. If you live in a separate property state, read Chapter 16A; if you live in a community property state, skip ahead to Chapter 16B.

The most important action that you can take is properly allocating estate assets *when the first spouse dies* (discussed in Chapter 14). Due to the differences between separate property states and community property states, the proper allocation of estate assets can be crucial to minimizing any potential tax bite (incomes taxes, capital gains taxes, or federal estate taxes). When the surviving spouse dies, there is much less freedom in what can be done with the estate assets, since both the decedent's sub-trusts and the (newly deceased) survivor's sub-trust are now irrevocable.

Asset Valuation

Each of the estate settlement illustrations presents the same basic asset valuation principles:

- Upon the death of the first spouse, the decedent's assets received full stepped-up valuation to the then-current market value (as of the date of the first decedent's death) and are shown in the first column.
- Upon the death of the second spouse, the second spouse's assets receive full stepped-up valuation to the current market value (as of the date of death of the second decedent) and

are shown in the second column. For illustration purposes, the death of the second spouse is assumed to be several years after the death of the first spouse, and the second spouse's assets are shown at a substantially appreciated market value. The time span between the death of the first spouse and the death of the second spouse is purely academic; whether it is five years or fifteen years makes no difference. The intent of the increased market value, established upon the death of the second spouse, is to illustrate the various settlement principles that are discussed in Chapters 16A and 16B.

To make the following estate settlement examples fairly simple and, therefore, understandable, I will use the same basic Trust assets in each example. Table 16-1 shows the market value of these assets at the time of the first decedent's death (called "death of first spouse") and at the time of the surviving spouse's death (called "death of second spouse"). "Other real estate" is included in only some examples.

TABLE 16-1
ASSET VALUES USED IN ILLUSTRATIONS

Basic Estate Assets	Market Value upon Death of First Spouse	Market Value upon Death of Second Spouse
Home	$ 400,000	$ 800,000
Other real estate	$ 800,000	$1,200,000
Decedent's separate property	$ 100,000	$ 300,000
Survivor's separate property	$ 100,000	$ 300,000
IRA	$1,000,000	$1,000,000

The examples use an IRA of $1 million, not because this high value is common for most people's IRAs, but rather to illustrate the problem (and the possible solutions) for estates that have IRAs with a very large value in relation to the total value of the estate. As in Chapters 14A and 14B, the purpose of using such a large

IRA is only to emphasize what happens to the IRA. The actual dollar values for the assets are not intended to have any relationship to your own personal estate but are merely meant to show the basic principles that apply to settling an estate when the second spouse dies.

All of the illustrations use a federal estate tax exemption of $600,000, even though this exemption is $625,000 in 1998 and increases to $1 million by the year 2006. Remember that Congress has not given us any real boon, since the increase in the exemption does not even keep pace with inflation. If you want to clearly see the impact on your own estate in future years, simply change the values in the illustration to match those in your own personal estate and plug in the appropriate federal estate tax exemption amount for the year in which you are making the calculations. Regardless of the actual numbers, the concepts remain the same.

Do You Reside in a Separate Property State or a Community Property State?

As was the case in Chapter 14, you need only read the applicable section:

- If you live in a separate property state, you need to read Chapter 16A.
- If you live in a community property state, you need to read Chapter 16B.

Additionally, you need to read only that part of the chapter that pertains to your Living Trust type: a Married A-B Trust or a Married A-B-C Trust.

Remember, the following nine states are the only community property states:

- Arizona
- California
- Idaho
- Louisiana
- Nevada
- New Mexico
- Texas
- Washington
- Wisconsin

16A

Separate Property States
When the Second Spouse Dies

In a separate property state, the most common method of allocating assets is the itemization method. It is most commonly used with a Married A-B Trust or a Married A-B-C Trust. Therefore, for purposes of simplicity, I will address only the two most common types of estates:

• Estates with a Married A-B Living Trust
• Estates with a Married A-B-C Living Trust

Even though Chapter 14A briefly addressed the seven different allocation methods and described two of them in detail, the allocation method used when the second spouse dies is essentially the same for all types of estates, with slight differences depending on whether you have a Married A-B Trust or a Married A-B-C Trust. Remember that the asset allocations to the various sub-trusts were critically important when the first spouse died. You must use those *same allocations* for settling the estate upon the death of the second spouse.

To simplify the wording of the examples since there are now two decedents (i.e., both spouses have died), let me change the terminology slightly. I will refer to the "first spouse" to mean the original decedent whose assets

were placed in the decedent's B sub-trust and/or C sub-trust. The "second spouse" is the original surviving spouse, who has now died and whose assets were placed in the survivor's A sub-trust upon the death of the first spouse.

ITEMIZATION METHOD WITH A MARRIED A-B TRUST

Before proceeding with this example, let's briefly review how the estate assets were allocated upon the death of the first spouse. Then I will show the changes that occur with the death of the second spouse.

Allocation of Assets upon Death of First Spouse

In a separate property state, the itemization method is used; thus the marital property (i.e., the home) was divided equally by asset rather than by value. One-half of the home was placed in the original decedent's (the first spouse's) side of the ledger and, thus, in the decedent's B sub-trust; the other half of the home was placed in the survivor's (the second spouse's) side of the ledger and, thus, in the survivor's A sub-trust. The separate property of the first spouse was allocated to the decedent's B sub-trust, and the separate property of the second spouse was allocated to the survivor's A sub-trust.

The retirement assets (illustrated as an IRA) passed outside the Living Trust to the surviving spouse as the beneficiary and were shown in the survivor's A sub-trust. Remember that the IRA was intentionally not placed in the decedent's B sub-trust in order to avoid significant adverse income tax consequences.

When the estate assets were allocated to the appropriate sub-trusts—with the decedent's assets receiving full stepped-up valuation to market value—these assets would appear as shown in Table 16A-1.

Market Value of Assets upon Death of Second Spouse

Now that the second spouse has died, the rules change again. The assets of the second spouse finally receive stepped-up valuation to the current market value. The original cost basis is no longer of concern.

Assume that it is years later, and the estate assets, except for the IRA, have substantially appreciated in value. Upon the death of the second spouse, the home has doubled in market value to $800,000; each spouse's separate property has tripled in value from $100,000 to $300,000; and the value of the IRA has remained at $1 million. Thus, when the second

spouse dies, the market value of the estate assets would be as shown in the top portion of Table 16A-2. The bottom of the table shows the current value of the estate assets that were initially allocated to the sub-trusts *when the first spouse died*. Now that the second spouse has died, the same asset allocation must be used when determining any potential federal estate tax liability.

In the table, the shading of the assets in the B sub-trust (also known as the "Credit Shelter Trust") signifies that these assets are insulated from further estate taxes. Because of this insulation from taxation, the value of assets in the first spouse's B sub-trust is of no concern when valuing the assets for estate tax purposes. However, *all* assets in the second spouse's A sub-trust are subject to federal estate taxes at their current market value. The subject of estate taxes is explored in more detail later in this chapter.

Stepped-Up Valuation upon Death of Surviving Spouse

Upon the death of the second spouse, the assets in the survivor's A sub-trust receive full stepped-up valuation to the current market value. Since the assets of the first spouse attained full stepped-up valuation to the then-current market value when the first spouse died

---

TABLE 16A-1

ESTATE ASSETS ALLOCATED TO A AND B SUB-TRUSTS UPON DEATH OF FIRST SPOUSE (SEPARATE PROPERTY STATE)

Estate Assets	Market Value upon Death of First Spouse	(First Spouse) B Sub-Trust	(Second Spouse) A Sub-Trust
Home	$ 400,000	$200,000	$ 100,000*
First spouse's separate property	$ 100,000	$100,000	
Second spouse's separate property	$ 100,000		$ 50,000
IRA	$1,000,000		$1,000,000
Total value in first spouse's estate		$300,000	
Total value in second spouse's estate			$1,150,000

*Surviving spouse's share of marital assets does not receive stepped-up valuation.

TABLE 16A-2

VALUE OF ESTATE ASSETS WHEN SECOND SPOUSE DIES
(MARRIED A-B TRUST IN A SEPARATE PROPERTY STATE)

Basic Estate Assets	MARKET VALUE UPON DEATH OF FIRST SPOUSE		MARKET VALUE UPON DEATH OF SECOND SPOUSE	
	First Spouse	Second Spouse	First Spouse	Second Spouse
Home	$200,000	$ 200,000	$400,000	$ 400,000
First spouse's separate property	$100,000		$300,000	
Second spouse's separate property		$ 100,000		$ 300,000
IRA		$1,000,000		$1,000,000

CURRENT MARKET VALUE OF ASSETS IN SUB-TRUSTS

Estate Assets	B Sub-Trust	A Sub-Trust
Home	$400,000	$ 400,000
First spouse's separate property	$300,000	
Second spouse's separate property		$ 300,000
IRA		$1,000,000
Total value in first spouse's estate	$700,000*	
Total value in second spouse's estate		$1,700,000

*Assets in B sub-trust are insulated from further federal estate taxation

(and the assets were placed in the decedent's irrevocable B sub-trust), the first spouse's assets in the B sub-trust do not again receive stepped-up valuation upon the death of the second spouse.

Cost Basis of All Assets After Death of Second Spouse

One of the many advantages of a Married A-B Living Trust is that the assets of each spouse receive the benefit of stepped-up valuation to current market value upon that spouse's death. However, once assets have received stepped-up valuation to current market value and are placed in an irrevocable Trust (e.g., the decedent's B sub-trust when the first spouse dies), the asset values become the new cost basis and are frozen at that level; no further stepped-up valuation is allowed. Congress was very specific about granting the boon of stepped-up valuation to assets held by individuals, but *not* to

assets held in an irrevocable Trust. Therefore, the assets of the first spouse (allocated to the B sub-trust) retain as their cost basis the stepped-up valuation to market value that was determined when the first spouse died. The assets of the second spouse (allocated to the A sub-trust) receive full stepped-up valuation to the current market value as of the date of death of the second spouse.

The retained cost basis (for the decedent's assets) and "new" stepped-up basis (for the second spouse's assets) are itemized in Table 16A-3 on page 238. The numbers in bold type are the current cost basis of the assets established upon the death of each spouse.

TAX TREATMENT OF A MARRIED A-B TRUST

When the second spouse dies and the estate must be settled, you must be aware of several potential tax impacts:

TABLE 16A-3

**MARKET VALUE VS. COST BASIS OF ESTATE ASSETS
(MARRIED A-B TRUST IN A SEPARATE PROPERTY STATE)**

Basic Estate Assets	MARKET VALUE UPON DEATH OF FIRST SPOUSE		MARKET VALUE UPON DEATH OF SECOND SPOUSE	
	First Spouse	Second Spouse	First Spouse	Second Spouse
Home	**$200,000**	$ 200,000	$400,000	$ 400,000
First spouse's separate property	**$100,000**		$300,000	
Second spouse's separate property		$ 100,000		$ 300,000
IRA		$1,000,000*		$1,000,000*

*The cost basis of an IRA is zero.
Note: Numbers in **boldface** represent asset cost basis upon death of each spouse.

- When the heirs eventually sell estate assets, any capital gain is subject to capital gains taxation.
- Depending on the size of the estate when the second spouse dies, federal estate taxes may be due.
- If you are unlucky enough to reside in one of the states that imposes an inheritance tax, such a tax may be due when the second spouse dies.

You also need to be aware of the impact of capital gains tax on future sales and transfers.

Capital Gains Treatment

Receiving stepped-up valuation for the assets can have a significant impact (a pleasant one, for a change) on any potential capital gains taxes that may be due when the assets are sold in the future. After the death of the second spouse, you need to be aware of a few basic principles regarding the treatment of capital gains:

- Upon the death of the second spouse, no capital gain is realized if the assets in the A subtrust are sold soon after the spouse's death, since the cost basis of the assets and the market value are now the same.
- Assets that are distributed to the beneficiaries do not incur any capital gains tax liability until the first spouse's assets are actually *sold*.
- The time period (i.e., the holding period) that determines the capital gains tax rate for assets in the first spouse's irrevocable B subtrust extends to the beneficiaries—the heirs who eventually receive the assets. In other words, the time period for determining which capital gains tax rate must be used upon the sale of the asset extends back to the date of purchase by the first spouse.
- The time period for assets in the second spouse's now-irrevocable A sub-trust is the same as that just described for the assets in the B sub-trust (i.e., when the assets were first purchased by the husband and/or wife).

Of these principles, the most important is that, since the assets in the survivor's A subtrust receive full stepped-up valuation to the current market value as of the second spouse's date of death, no immediate capital gain is realized if the assets of the second spouse are sold soon after the date of death.

The Home

Upon the death of the second spouse, only the second spouse's share of the home receives stepped-up valuation to the current market value, because the assets of the first spouse (in the B sub-trust) retain the "new" cost basis established upon the death of the first spouse. Given our assumption that, upon the death of the second spouse, the home has a market value of $800,000, the second spouse's share of the home (in the A sub-trust) receives full stepped-up valuation to the current market value ($400,000). The first spouse's share of the home retains its cost basis of $200,000, established upon that spouse's death. If the beneficiaries decided to sell the home, they would realize a capital gain of $200,000 (and would owe capital gains taxes), as shown in Table 16A-4.

Remember that the transfer of the home to the beneficiaries does not create a capital gain event. However, if the beneficiaries decide to sell the home, they have two options:

- The beneficiaries can live in the home for two of five years and, thus, qualify for the $250,000 homeowner's exemption (for *each* beneficiary living therein).
- The beneficiaries can sell the home and recognize a capital gain based upon the time at which the home was first purchased by the individual(s) or the Trust. If the home

was held for less than twelve months, the capital gains tax rate would be 28 percent; if the home was held for more than twelve months, the tax rate would be 20 percent; if the home was held for more than five years, the tax rate would be 18 percent (beginning in 2001). These tax rates apply on the sale, whether the home is sold inside the Trust or outside the Trust.

Any other marital asset held in either the first spouse's B sub-trust or the second spouse's A sub-trust would be treated in the same way as just described for the home.

Separate Property

The separate property of the second spouse receives full stepped-up valuation to the current market value ($300,000) as of the date of death of the second spouse. If the beneficiaries sold the separate property soon after receiving it, there would be no capital gain on the resultant sale of this asset, as shown in Table 16A-5.

Remember, however, that the separate prop-

TABLE 16A-4

CAPITAL GAIN ON SALE OF HOME
(MARRIED A-B TRUST IN A SEPARATE PROPERTY STATE)

Home	Market Value	New Cost Basis	Capital Gain
Second spouse (A sub-trust)	$400,000	$400,000	$ 0
First spouse (B sub-trust)	$400,000	$200,000	$200,000
Total	$800,000	$600,000	$200,000

TABLE 16A-5

CAPITAL GAIN ON SALE OF SECOND SPOUSE'S SEPARATE PROPERTY
(MARRIED A-B TRUST IN A SEPARATE PROPERTY STATE)

Separate Property	Current Market Value	New Cost Basis	Capital Gain
Second spouse (A sub-trust)	$300,000	$300,000	$0

erty of the first spouse received full stepped-up valuation (to $100,000) upon the death of the first spouse, and this value became the "new" cost basis. Therefore, the beneficiaries of the Trust receive the first spouse's separate property with a cost basis of $100,000 but with a current market value of $300,000. No capital gain is realized upon the transfer of this separate property to the beneficiaries, but the beneficiaries would realize a capital gain of $200,000 (and would have to pay capital gains taxes) upon the *sale* of this separate property, as shown in Table 16A-6.

The time period used for establishing the applicable capital gains tax rate for the first spouse's separate property (in the B sub-trust) is the same as previously specified for the home. Remember that the IRS time clock began when the asset was *originally* purchased, and this time period passes on to the beneficiaries, along with the asset.

IRAs

No stepped-up valuation is associated with IRAs passing to the beneficiaries. Remember that the IRA cost basis is zero, as you learned in Chapter 12.

Federal Estate Tax Treatment

Upon the death of the second spouse, no additional federal estate taxes are due on the assets in the first spouse's B sub-trust. Remember that when the assets were first placed in the B sub-trust, no federal estate taxes were due because the value of the assets did not exceed the estate tax exemption in effect at that time. Now these

---

TABLE 16A-6
CAPITAL GAINS DUE ON SALE OF FIRST SPOUSE'S SEPARATE PROPERTY
(MARRIED A-B TRUST IN A SEPARATE PROPERTY STATE)

Separate Property	Current Market Value	New Cost Basis	Capital Gain
First spouse (B sub-trust)	$300,000	$100,000	$200,000

TABLE 16A-7
ALLOCATION OF CURRENT MARKET VALUE TO SUB-TRUSTS
(MARRIED A-B TRUST IN A SEPARATE PROPERTY STATE)

Estate Assets	Current Market Value	B Sub-Trust	A Sub-Trust
Home	$ 800,000	$400,000	$ 400,000
First spouse's separate property	$ 300,000	$300,000	
Second spouse's separate property	$ 300,000		$ 300,000
IRA	$1,000,000		$1,000,000
Total market value in first spouse's estate		$700,000	
Total market value in second spouse's estate			$1,700,000

Note: Assets in B sub-trust are insulated from further federal estate taxation.

assets are insulated from any further estate tax liability; their current market value, as shown in the shaded portion of Table 16A-7, is now $700,000.

Upon the death of the second spouse, all of the assets in the second spouse's A sub-trust are subject to federal estate taxes. However, the value of the assets can be offset by the second spouse's federal estate tax exemption (the amount that is applicable in the year of the second spouse's demise). The current market value of the estate assets in the second spouse's A sub-trust is $1.7 million (see Table 16A-7).

The individual federal estate tax exemption rises to $1 million by the year 2006 (an increase that does not even keep up with a 3 percent inflation rate). For the sake of simplicity, however, we will compute the federal estate taxes on the second spouse's assets in the A sub-trust using the old estate tax exemption of $600,000. Table 16A-8 shows the computation of the estate tax.

After the federal estate taxes are paid, the value of estate assets in the first spouse's B sub-trust and the second spouse's A sub-trust can be passed on to the named beneficiaries, as shown in Table 16A-9 on page 242.

Capital Gains Tax vs. Federal Estate Tax

Because federal estate tax rates are significantly higher than capital gains tax rates, it is far better for your assets to be subject to capital gains tax rates, which range from 18 percent (beginning in 2001) to 28 percent, rather than to federal estate tax rates ranging from 37 percent to 55 percent.

TABLE 16A-8

ESTATE TAX COMPUTATION UPON DEATH OF SECOND SPOUSE (MARRIED A-B TRUST IN A SEPARATE PROPERTY STATE)

MARKET VALUE	SECOND SPOUSE'S A SUB-TRUST
Home	$ 400,000
Second spouse's separate property	$ 300,000
IRA	$1,000,000
Total assets in second spouse's A sub-trust	$1,700,000
Less: Second spouse's federal estate tax exemption	($ 600,000)
Taxable estate	$1,100,000
Federal estate tax (from IRS Estate Tax Table)*	$ 450,000

NET VALUE (AFTER ESTATE TAXES) OF THE A SUB-TRUST

Total value in A sub-trust	$1,700,000	
Less: Federal estate tax	($ 450,000)	
Balance of second spouse's A sub-trust	$1,250,000	
Net amount distributed to beneficiaries of A sub-trust		$1,250,000

*Tax rate is based on an escalating estate tax scale.

Note: The author uses the tax computation approach shown above in an effort to not detract from the basic principle being presented. In actuality, the federal estate tax would be computed on the total taxable estate of $1,700,000. The estate tax would amount to $645,800, minus the tax credit of $192,800 (for the $600,000 federal estate tax exemption). The net result leaves an actual federal estate tax of $453,000.

TABLE 16A-9
ESTATE VALUE PASSED TO BENEFICIARIES
(MARRIED A-B TRUST IN A SEPARATE PROPERTY STATE)

NET VALUE (AFTER ESTATE TAXES) OF SECOND SPOUSE'S A SUB-TRUST

Total of A sub-trust	$ 1,700,000	
Less: Federal estate tax	($ 450,000)	
Net value of second spouse's A sub-trust	$ 1,250,000	
Value of second spouse's estate		$1,250,000

VALUE OF FIRST SPOUSE'S B SUB-TRUST

Value of first spouse's B sub-trust*	$ 700,000	
Value of first spouse's estate		$ 700,000
Total estate passed to beneficiaries		$1,950,000

*Appreciated value insulated from further taxation.

- Although the assets in the second spouse's A sub-trust receive full stepped-up valuation to the current market value (upon the death of the second spouse) and, thus, avoid any tax on capital gains if sold before they appreciate further, the assets in the A sub-trust are subject to the higher and more consumptive federal estate tax rates.
- Any increase in the value of the assets in the first spouse's B sub-trust is subject to *capital gains taxation*, but those assets are excluded from further *federal estate tax* liability.

State Inheritance Tax

If you reside in a state that imposes an inheritance tax, any such taxes are in addition to the federal estate tax—and, thus, further erode the value of the estate that is ultimately passed on to the beneficiaries. Appendix E contains a list of the states that still pursue the antiquated system of imposing inheritance taxes.

ITEMIZATION METHOD WITH A MARRIED A-B-C TRUST

The primary difference between a Married A-B Trust and a Married A-B-C Trust is that, upon the death of the second spouse, the assets in the C sub-trust (whether a QTIP Trust, a Mar-

ried IRA–QTIP Trust, or a QDOT Trust) are subject to estate taxation. The assets in the C sub-trust are added to the assets in the A sub-trust, and the estate tax computation is based on the total asset value of these sub-trusts. If the value of assets in the A sub-trust is less than one federal estate tax exemption, the overall estate taxation can be reduced, since any "left-over" exemption (the amount of exemption remaining after the exemption has been applied to the A sub-trust) can be applied to the asset value in the C sub-trust.

Any federal estate tax liability (and any state inheritance tax liability) should be apportioned between the A sub-trust and the C sub-trust, based on the proportionate asset value in each sub-trust. Such apportioning of taxes to the sub-trusts (based on the asset value within each sub-trust) is particularly relevant if there are different beneficiaries for each of the sub-trusts, since each sub-trust "shares" an equitable amount of estate tax liability.

Allocation of Assets upon Death of First Spouse

Before proceeding with the settlement of an estate in a Married A-B-C Trust, let's briefly review how the estate assets were allocated

TABLE 16A-10
ESTATE ASSETS ALLOCATED TO A, B, AND C SUB-TRUSTS
UPON DEATH OF FIRST SPOUSE (SEPARATE PROPERTY STATE)

Estate Assets	Market Value upon Death of First Spouse	C Sub-Trust	(First Spouse) B Sub-Trust	(Second Spouse) A Sub-Trust
Home	$ 400,000		$200,000	$ 100,000*
Other real estate	$ 800,000	$100,000	$300,000	$ 200,000*
First spouse's separate property	$ 100,000		$100,000	
Second spouse's separate property	$ 100,000			$ 50,000
IRA	$1,000,000			$1,000,000
Total value in first spouse's estate			$700,000	
Total value in second spouse's estate				$1,350,000

*Surviving spouse's share of marital assets does not receive stepped-up valuation.

upon the death of the first spouse. In a separate property state, the itemization method is used, wherein the marital property (the home and other real estate) was divided equally by asset rather than by value. One-half of the home and other real estate were placed in the original decedent's (first spouse's) side of the ledger and, thus, placed in the decedent's B sub-trust and C sub-trust. The other half of the home and other real estate were placed in the survivor's (the second spouse's) side of the ledger and, thus, placed in the survivor's A sub-trust. The separate property of the first spouse was allocated to the decedent's B sub-trust, and the separate property of the second spouse was allocated to the survivor's A sub-trust.

The retirement assets (illustrated as an IRA) passed outside the Living Trust to the surviving spouse as the beneficiary and were shown in the survivor's A sub-trust. Remember that the IRA was intentionally not placed in the decedent's B sub-trust and/or C sub-trust in order to avoid significant adverse income tax consequences. I would seriously recommend consideration of a Married IRA–QTIP Trust (see Chapter 22).

When the estate assets were allocated to the appropriate sub-trusts—with the decedent's assets receiving full stepped-up valuation to market value—these assets would appear as shown in Table 16A-10.

Market Value of Assets upon Death of Second Spouse

When the second spouse dies, the rules change again. The assets of the second spouse finally receive stepped-up valuation to the current market value, so the original cost basis no longer need be of concern.

Assume that it is years later, and the estate assets, except for the IRA, have substantially appreciated in value. Upon the death of the second spouse, the home has doubled in market value to $800,000; the other real estate has increased in value from $800,000 (when the first spouse died) to $1.2 million; and, similarly, the value of each spouse's separate property has tripled from $100,000 to $300,000. Let's assume that the value of the IRA has remained at $1 million. Thus, when the second spouse dies, the market value of the estate assets would be as shown in Table 16A-11 on page 244. The bottom of the table shows the current value of the estate assets that were initially allocated to the sub-trusts *when the first spouse died*. Now that the second spouse has died,

TABLE 16A-11
MARKET VALUE OF ESTATE ASSETS WHEN SECOND SPOUSE DIES
(MARRIED A-B-C TRUST IN A SEPARATE PROPERTY STATE)

Basic Estate Assets	MARKET VALUE UPON DEATH OF FIRST SPOUSE		MARKET VALUE UPON DEATH OF SECOND SPOUSE	
	First Spouse	Second Spouse	First Spouse	Second Spouse
Home	$200,000	$ 200,000	$400,000	$ 400,000
Other real estate	$400,000	$ 400,000	$600,000	$ 600,000
First spouse's separate property	$100,000		$300,000	
Second spouse's separate property		$ 100,000		$ 300,000
IRA		$1,000,000		$1,000,000

CURRENT MARKET VALUE OF ASSETS IN SUB-TRUSTS

Estate Assets	(First Spouse) C Sub-Trust	(First Spouse) B Sub-Trust	(Second Spouse) A Sub-Trust
Home		$400,000	$ 400,000
Other real estate	$150,000	$450,000	$ 600,000
First spouse's separate property		$300,000	
Second spouse's separate property			$ 300,000
IRA			$1,000,000
Total value in first spouse's estate		$1,300,000	
Total value in second spouse's estate			$2,300,000

Note: Value of first spouse's assets in the C sub-trust (at current market value) are *not* exempt from federal estate taxation.

the same asset allocation must be used when determining any potential federal estate tax liability.

In the table, the shading of the assets in the B sub-trust (also known as the "Credit Shelter Trust") signifies that these assets are insulated from further estate taxes. Because of this insulation, the value of assets in the first spouse's B sub-trust is of no concern when valuing the assets for estate tax purposes. However, *all* assets in the A and C sub-trusts are subject to federal estate taxes at their current market value. The subject of estate taxes is explored in more detail later in this chapter.

Stepped-Up Valuation upon Death of Surviving Spouse

Upon the death of the second spouse, the assets in the survivor's A sub-trust receive full stepped-up valuation to the current market value. Since the assets of the first spouse attained full stepped-up valuation to the then-current market value when the first spouse died (and these assets were placed in the decedent's irrevocable B and C sub-trusts), the first spouse's assets do not again receive stepped-up valuation upon the death of the second spouse.

Cost Basis of All Assets upon Death of Second Spouse

Once assets have received stepped-up valuation to current market value and are then placed in an irrevocable Trust (i.e., the decedent's B sub-trust and/or C sub-trust) when the first spouse dies, the asset values become the new cost basis and are frozen at that level; no further stepped-up valuation is allowed. Remember, Congress specifically granted stepped-up valu-

TABLE 16A-12
MARKET VALUE VS. COST BASIS OF ESTATE ASSETS
(MARRIED A-B-C TRUST IN A SEPARATE PROPERTY STATE)

Estate Assets	MARKET VALUE UPON DEATH OF FIRST SPOUSE		MARKET VALUE UPON DEATH OF SECOND SPOUSE	
	First Spouse	Second Spouse	First Spouse	Second Spouse
Home	**$200,000**	$ 200,000	$400,000	$ 400,000
Other real estate	**$400,000**	$ 400,000	$600,000	$ 600,000
First spouse's separate property	**$100,000**		$300,000	
Second spouse's separate property		$ 100,000		$ 300,000
IRA		$1,000,000*		$1,000,000*

*The cost basis of an IRA is zero.

Note: Numbers in **boldface** represent asset cost basis upon death of each spouse.

ation to assets held by individuals, not to assets held in an irrevocable Trust. Therefore, the assets of the first spouse (allocated to the B sub-trust and C sub-trust) retain as their cost basis the stepped-up valuation to market value that was determined when the first spouse died. The assets of the second spouse (allocated to the A sub-trust) receive full stepped-up valuation to the current market value as of the date of death of the second spouse.

The retained cost basis (for the decedent's assets) and the "new" stepped up basis (for the second spouse's assets) are itemized in Table 16A-12. The numbers in bold type are the current cost basis of the assets upon the death of each spouse.

TAX TREATMENT OF A MARRIED A-B-C TRUST

When the second spouse dies and the estate must be settled, you must be aware of several potential tax impacts:

- When the heirs eventually sell estate assets, they may realize a capital gain and, thus, be subject to capital gains taxation.
- Depending on the size of the estate when the second spouse dies, federal estate taxes may be due.
- If you reside in one of the states that imposes

an inheritance tax, such a tax may be due when the second spouse dies.

You also need to be aware of the impact of capital gains taxes on future sales and transfers.

Capital Gains Treatment

Receiving stepped-up valuation for the assets can have a significant impact (a pleasant one, for a change) on any potential capital gains that may be due when the assets are sold in the future. After the death of the second spouse, you need to be aware of a few basic principles regarding the treatment of capital gains:

- Upon the death of the second spouse, no capital gain is realized if the assets in the A sub-trust are sold soon after the spouse's death, since the cost basis and market value of the assets are now the same.
- Assets that are distributed to the beneficiaries do not incur any capital gains tax liability until the assets are actually *sold*.
- The time period (i.e., the holding period) that determines the capital gains tax rate for assets in the first spouse's irrevocable B sub-trust and C sub-trust extends to the beneficiaries—the heirs who eventually receive the assets. In other words, the time period for determining which capital gains tax rate

must be used upon the sale of the asset extends back to the date of purchase by the first spouse.

- The time period for assets in the second spouse's now-irrevocable A sub-trust is the same as that just described for the assets in the B sub-trust and C sub-trust (i.e., when the assets were first purchased by the husband and/or wife).

Of these principles, the most important is that, since the assets in the survivor's A sub-trust receive full stepped-up valuation to the current market value as of the second spouse's date of death, no immediate capital gain is realized if the assets of the second spouse are sold soon after the date of death.

The Home

Upon the death of the second spouse, only the second spouse's share of the home receives stepped-up valuation to the current market value, because the assets of the first spouse (in the B sub-trust and C sub-trust) previously received stepped-up valuation, and these assets retain the "new" cost basis established upon the death of the first spouse. Given our assumption that, upon the death of the second spouse, the home has a market value of $800,000, the second spouse's share of the home (in the survivor's A sub-trust) receives full stepped-up valuation to the current market value ($400,000). The first spouse's share of the home retains its cost basis of $200,000 established upon that spouse's death. If the beneficiaries decided to sell the home, they would realize a capital gain

of $200,000 (and would owe capital gains taxes), as shown in Table 16A-13.

Remember that the transfer of the home to the beneficiaries does not create a capital gain event. However, if the beneficiaries decide to sell the home, they have two options:

- The beneficiaries can live in the home for two of five years and, thus, qualify for the $250,000 homeowner's exemption (for *each* beneficiary living therein).
- The beneficiaries can sell the home and recognize a capital gain based upon the time at which the home was first purchased by the individual(s) or the Trust. If the home was held for less than twelve months, the capital gains tax rate would be 28 percent; if the home was held for more than twelve months, the tax rate would be 20 percent; if the home was held for more than five years, the tax rate would be 18 percent (beginning in 2001). These rates apply on the sale, whether the home is sold inside the Trust or outside the Trust.

Other Real Estate

Upon the death of the second spouse, only the second spouse's share of the other real estate receives stepped-up valuation to the current market value. The assets of the first spouse (in the B sub-trust and C sub-trust) previously received stepped-up valuation and retain the "new" cost basis established when the first spouse died. Let's assume that, upon the death of the second spouse, the other real estate has a market value of $1.2 million. The share of the

---

TABLE 16A-13

CAPITAL GAIN ON SALE OF HOME
(MARRIED A-B-C TRUST IN A SEPARATE PROPERTY STATE)

Home	Market Value	New Cost Basis	Capital Gain
Second spouse (A sub-trust)	$400,000	$400,000	$ 0
First spouse (B sub-trust)	$400,000	$200,000	$200,000
Total	$800,000	$600,000	$200,000

other real estate included in the survivor's A sub-trust receives full stepped-up valuation to the current market value ($600,000), whereas the first spouse's share of the other real estate retains the "new" cost basis that was established upon the death of the first spouse ($400,000). If the beneficiaries decided to sell the real estate, they would realize a capital gain of $200,000 (and would owe capital gains taxes) when the real estate was sold, as shown in Table 16A-14.

Remember that the transfer of the other real estate to the beneficiaries does not create a capital gain event. However, when the beneficiaries sell the other real estate, they must recognize a capital gain. As with the sale of the home, the capital gains tax rate for the sale is based on the time period starting from the time the real estate was first purchased by the individual(s) or the Trust: 28 percent if the real estate was held for less than twelve months, 20 percent if it was held for more than twelve months, and (effective in 2001) 18 percent if it was held for more than five years. These tax rates apply on the sale regardless of whether the real estate is sold inside the Trust or outside the Trust.

Any other marital asset held in the first spouse's B sub-trust or C sub-trust and/or the second spouse's A sub-trust would be treated in the same manner as just described for other real estate.

Separate Property

The separate property of the second spouse receives full stepped-up valuation to the current market value ($300,000) as of the date of death of the second spouse. If the beneficiaries sold the separate property soon after receiving it, there would be no capital gain on the sale, as shown in Table 16A-15.

Remember, however, that the separate property of the first spouse received full stepped-up valuation (to $100,000) upon the death of the first spouse, and this value then became the "new" cost basis. Therefore, the beneficiaries of the Trust receive the first spouse's separate property with a cost basis of

---

TABLE 16A-14

CAPITAL GAIN ON SALE OF OTHER REAL ESTATE
(MARRIED A-B-C TRUST IN A SEPARATE PROPERTY STATE)

Other Real Estate	Market Value	New Cost Basis	Capital Gain
Second spouse (A sub-trust)	$ 600,000	$ 600,000	$ 0
First spouse (B and C sub-trusts)	$ 600,000	$ 400,000	$200,000
Total	$1,200,000	$1,000,000	$200,000

TABLE 16A-15

CAPITAL GAIN ON SALE OF SECOND SPOUSE'S SEPARATE PROPERTY
(MARRIED A-B-C TRUST IN A SEPARATE PROPERTY STATE)

Separate Property	Market Value	New Cost Basis	Capital Gain
Second spouse (A sub-trust)	$300,000	$300,000	$ 0

$100,000 and a current market value of $300,000. No capital gain is realized upon the *transfer* of this separate property to the beneficiaries, but the beneficiaries would realize a capital gain of $200,000 upon the *sale* of this separate property, as is illustrated below in Table 16A-16.

The time period used for establishing the applicable capital gains tax rate for the first spouse's separate property (in the B sub-trust) is the same as previously specified for the home and the other real estate. Remember that the IRS time clock began when the asset was *originally* purchased, and this time period passes on to the beneficiaries, along with the asset.

IRAs

No stepped-up valuation is associated with IRAs passing to the beneficiaries. Remember that the IRA cost basis is zero, as you learned in Chapter 12.

Federal Estate Tax Treatment

Upon the death of the second spouse, no additional federal estate taxes are due on the assets in the first spouse's B sub-trust. Remember that when the assets were first placed in the B sub-trust, no federal estate taxes were due because the value of the assets did not exceed the estate tax exemption in effect at that time. Now these assets are insulated from any further estate

---

TABLE 16A-16
CAPITAL GAIN ON SALE OF FIRST SPOUSE'S SEPARATE PROPERTY
(MARRIED A-B-C TRUST IN A SEPARATE PROPERTY STATE)

Separate Property	Market Value	New Cost Basis	Capital Gain
First spouse (B sub-trust)	$300,000	$100,000	$200,000

TABLE 16A-17
ALLOCATION OF CURRENT MARKET VALUE TO SUB-TRUSTS
(MARRIED A-B-C TRUST IN A SEPARATE PROPERTY STATE)

Estate Assets	Current Market Value	C Sub-Trust	B Sub-Trust	A Sub-Trust
Home	$ 800,000		$ 400,000	$ 400,000
Other real estate	$1,200,000	$150,000	$ 450,000	$ 600,000
First spouse's separate property	$ 300,000		$ 300,000	
Second spouse's separate property	$ 300,000			$ 300,000
IRA	$1,000,000			$1,000,000
Insulated value of first spouse's estate			$1,150,000	
Taxable value of first spouse's estate		$150,000		
Total value of second spouse's estate				$2,300,000
Total taxable estate		$2,450,000		

Note: Assets in B sub-trust are insulated from further federal estate taxation.

tax liability. Their current market value, as shown in the shaded portion of Table 16A-17, is $1,150,000.

The assets in the second spouse's A sub-trust are subject to federal estate taxation. However, the value of the assets can be offset by the second spouse's federal estate tax exemption (the amount that is applicable in the year of the second spouse's demise). The total current market value of the estate assets in the second spouse's A sub-trust is $2.3 million. In calculating the estate tax, the current market value of the assets in the first spouse's C sub-trust ($150,000) must also be included. Thus, upon the death of the second spouse, federal estate taxes must be calculated on a total estate value of $2.45 million (see Table 16A-17).

The individual federal estate tax exemption rises to $1 million by the year 2006 (an increase that does not even keep up with a 3 percent inflation rate). For the sake of simplicity, however, we will compute the federal estate taxes on the second spouse's assets in the A sub-trust and the remaining assets in the first spouse's C sub-trust using the old federal estate tax exemption of $600,000. Table 16A-18 shows the computation of the estate tax.

The federal estate taxes should be deducted proportionately from the second spouse's A sub-trust and from the first spouse's C sub-trust. For example, if the value of the A sub-trust is 92 percent of the total taxable estate, then 92 percent of the federal estate taxes should be paid from asset value in the A sub-trust. Determining the proportion of federal estate taxes to be paid from the second spouse's A sub-trust and the first spouse's C sub-trust is really not difficult and amounts to little more

---

TABLE 16A-18

ESTATE TAX COMPUTATION UPON DEATH OF SECOND SPOUSE (MARRIED A-B-C TRUST IN A SEPARATE PROPERTY STATE)

MARKET VALUE	FIRST SPOUSE'S C SUB-TRUST	SECOND SPOUSE'S A SUB-TRUST
Home		$ 400,000
Other real estate	$150,000	$ 600,000
Second spouse's separate property		$ 300,000
IRA		$1,000,000
Total asset value in first spouse's C sub-trust	$150,000	
Total asset value in second spouse's A sub-trust		$2,300,000
TAXABLE ESTATE		
Total asset value in first spouse's C sub-trust	$ 150,000	
Total asset value in second spouse's A sub-trust	$2,300,000	
Total taxable estate (before exemption)	$2,450,000	
Less: Second spouse's federal estate tax exemption	($ 600,000)	
Total taxable estate	$1,850,000	
Federal Estate Tax (from IRS Estate Tax Table)*	$ 800,000*	

*Tax rate is based on an escalating estate tax scale.

Note: The author uses the tax computation approach shown above in an effort to not detract from the basic principle being presented. In actuality, the federal estate tax would be computed on the total taxable estate of $2,450,000. The estate tax would amount to $1,001,300, minus the tax credit of $192,800 (for the $600,000 federal estate tax exemption). The net result leaves an actual federal estate tax of $808,500.

TABLE 16A-19

APPORTIONMENT OF ESTATE TAXES BETWEEN SUB-TRUSTS
(MARRIED A-B-C TRUST IN A SEPARATE PROPERTY STATE)

	Calculation Values	Result
CALCULATE TOTAL TAXABLE ESTATE		
Value of second spouse's A sub-trust	$2,300,000	
Less: Second spouse's federal estate tax exemption	($ 600,000)	
Taxable value of A sub-trust	$1,700,000	
Plus: Value of first spouse's C sub-trust	$ 150,000	
Total taxable estate		$1,850,000
CALCULATE PORTION OF ESTATE IN THE A SUB-TRUST		
Taxable amount of second spouse's A sub-trust	$1,700,000	
Divide by: Total taxable estate	$1,850,000	
A sub-trust estate tax proportion		0.92 (92%)
CALCULATE PORTION OF ESTATE IN THE C SUB-TRUST		
Value of first spouse's C sub-trust	$ 150,000	
Divide by: Total taxable estate	$1,850,000	
C sub-trust estate tax proportion		0.08 (8%)
(Double-check: 0.92 + 0.08 = 1.00—estate proportions are OK.)		
DETERMINE FEDERAL ESTATE TAXES DUE		
Total taxable estate	$1,850,000	
Federal estate tax (from IRS Estate Tax Table)*	$ 800,000	
CALCULATE SECOND SPOUSE'S PORTION OF TAXES		
Total federal estate tax due	$800,000	
Multiply by: A sub-trust estate tax proportion	0.92	
Federal estate tax due from A sub-trust		$736,000
CALCULATE FIRST SPOUSE'S PORTION OF TAXES		
Total federal estate tax due	$800,000	
Multiply by: C sub-trust estate tax proportion	0.08	
Federal estate tax due from C sub-trust		$64,000
(Double-check: $736,000 + $64,000 = $800,000—estate tax proportions are OK.)		

---

*Tax rate is based on an escalating estate tax scale.

Note: The author uses the tax computation approach shown above in an effort to not detract from the basic principle being presented. In actuality, the federal estate tax would be computed on the total taxable estate of $2,450,000. The estate tax would amount to $1,001,300, minus the tax credit of $192,800 (for the $600,000 federal estate tax exemption). The net result leaves an actual federal estate tax of $808,500.

TABLE 16A-20
ESTATE VALUE PASSED TO BENEFICIARIES
(MARRIED A-B-C TRUST IN A SEPARATE PROPERTY STATE)

NET VALUE (AFTER ESTATE TAXES) OF SECOND SPOUSE'S ESTATE (A SUB-TRUST)

Total of A sub-trust	$2,300,000	
Less: Federal estate tax	($ 736,000)	
Net value of second spouse's A sub-trust	$1,564,000	
Value of second spouse's estate		$1,564,000

NET VALUE (AFTER ESTATE TAXES) OF FIRST SPOUSE'S ESTATE (B AND C SUB-TRUSTS)

Total of C sub-trust	$ 150,000	
Less: Federal estate tax	($ 64,000)	
Net value of first spouse's C sub-trust	$ 86,000	
Value of first spouse's B sub-trust*	$1,150,000	
Value of first spouse's estate		$1,236,000

TOTAL ESTATE DISTRIBUTED TO BENEFICIARIES

Value of second spouse's estate	$1,564,000	
Value of first spouse's estate	$1,236,000	
	$2,800,000	
Total estate distributed to beneficiaries		$2,800,000

*Appreciated value insulated from further taxation.

than simple math. The steps involved in determining the apportionment of federal estate taxes are as follows and also illustrated in Table 16A-19.

- *Calculate the total taxable estate*: First, subtract the second spouse's federal estate tax exemption from the value of the A sub-trust. Then add this difference to the value in the C sub-trust. The result is the total taxable estate amount.
- *Calculate the proportion of the estate in the second spouse's A sub-trust*: Divide the taxable value of the A sub-trust by the total taxable estate amount. The result is the A sub-trust estate tax proportion.
- *Calculate the proportion of the estate in the first spouse's C sub-trust*: Divide the value of the C sub-trust by the total taxable estate

amount. The result is the C sub-trust estate tax proportion.
- *Calculate the federal estate tax liability on the total taxable estate*: Use the federal estate tax table to determine the total federal estate tax due.
- *Calculate the second spouse's portion of estate taxes*: Multiply the total federal estate tax due by the A sub-trust estate tax proportion. The result is the federal estate tax due from the A sub-trust.
- *Calculate the first spouse's portion of estate taxes*: Multiply the total federal estate tax due by the C sub-trust estate tax proportion. The result is the federal estate tax due from the C sub-trust.

Although the two "double-check" calculations of the C sub-trust portion in the third and the last steps may seem redundant to those who are mathematically inclined, such calculations serve as an excellent way to double-check that your calculations are correct. The proportionate shares for the A sub-trust and the C sub-trust should add up to a total of 1, and the total tax liability of the A sub-trust and the C sub-trust should add up to the total amount of federal estate taxes due.

Once the federal estate tax liability has been determined for the second spouse's A sub-trust and the first spouse's C sub-trust, the net value of the estate assets (the value remaining after estate taxes are paid) is then available for distribution to the heirs, as shown in Table 16A-20 on page 251. Remember that the assets in the first spouse's B sub-trust are insulated from further federal estate taxation. Thus, although the assets in the B sub-trust grew in value over the years from $600,000 to $1.15 million, this $550,000 growth incurs no additional federal estate tax liability. The net total estate passed to the beneficiaries would be $2.8 million (see Table 16A-20 on page 251).

Capital Gains Tax vs. Federal Estate Tax
Because federal estate tax rates are significantly higher than capital gains tax rates, it is far better for your assets to be subject to cap-ital gains tax rates, which range from 18 percent (beginning in 2001) to 28 percent, rather than to federal estate tax rates ranging from 37 percent to 55 percent.

- The assets in the second spouse's A sub-trust receive full stepped-up valuation to the current market value (upon the death of the second spouse) and, thus, avoid any tax on capital gains if sold before they appreciate further. The assets in the A sub-trust are subject to the higher and more consumptive federal estate tax.
- The assets in the first spouse's B sub-trust are subject to capital gains tax, but those assets are excluded from further federal estate tax liability.
- The assets in the first spouse's C sub-trust are subject to federal estate taxation and will also be subject to capital gains tax upon sale.

State Inheritance Tax
If you reside in a state that imposes an inheritance tax, any such taxes are in addition to the federal estate tax—and, thus, further erode the value of the estate that is ultimately passed on to the beneficiaries. Appendix E contains a list of the states that still pursue the antiquated system of imposing inheritance taxes.

16B

Community Property States
When the Second Spouse Dies

In a community property state, the most common method of allocating assets is the valuation method. It is most commonly used with a Married A-B Trust or a Married A-B-C Trust. Therefore, for purposes of simplicity, I will address only the two most common types of estates:

- Estates with a Married A-B Living Trust
- Estates with a Married A-B-C Living Trust

Even though Chapter 14B addressed seven different allocation methods and described two of them in detail, the allocation method used when the second spouse dies is essentially the same for all types of estates, with slight differences depending on whether you have a Married A-B Trust or a Married A-B-C Trust. Remember that the asset allocations to the various sub-trusts were critically important when the first spouse died. You must use those *same* allocations for settling the estate upon the death of the second spouse.

To simplify the wording of the examples now that there are two decedents (i.e., both spouses have died), let me change the terminology slightly. I will refer to the "first spouse" to mean the original decedent whose assets were placed in the decedent's B sub-trust and/or C sub-trust. The "second spouse" is the original surviving spouse, who has now died and whose assets were placed in the survivor's A sub-trust upon the death of the first spouse.

VALUATION METHOD WITH A MARRIED A-B TRUST

Before proceeding with this example, let's review how the estate assets were allocated upon the death of the first spouse. Then I will show the changes that occur with the death of the second spouse.

Allocation of Assets upon Death of First Spouse

In a community property state, the valuation method is used; thus, the community property (i.e., the home and the IRA) was divided equally by value rather than by asset. The separate property of the first spouse (the original decedent) was allocated to the decedent's B sub-trust, and the separate property of the second spouse (the original surviving spouse) was allocated to the survivor's A sub-trust.

TABLE 16B-1

**ESTATE ASSETS ALLOCATED TO A AND B SUB-TRUSTS UPON
DEATH OF FIRST SPOUSE (COMMUNITY PROPERTY STATE)**

Estate Assets	Market Value upon Death of First Spouse	(First Spouse) B Sub-Trust	(Second Spouse) A Sub-Trust
Home	$ 400,000	$400,000	
First spouse's separate property	$ 100,000	$100,000	
Second spouse's separate property	$ 100,000		$ 50,000
IRA	$1,000,000	$100,000	$900,000
Total value in first spouse's estate		$600,000	
Total value in second spouse's estate			$950,000

One of the primary advantages of the valuation method of asset allocation is that the retirement assets (illustrated in this example as an IRA) are generated as community property; therefore, they may be considered in the value allocation. If we assume that the first spouse's B sub-trust holds $100,000 of separate property, only $500,000 in additional value is needed to fully utilize the first spouse's federal estate tax exemption. (All of the examples in this chapter use $600,000 for the value of the individual federal estate tax exemption, even though the value in 1998 is $625,000.) Remember that it is advantageous to place an appreciating asset, such as a home, in the decedent's B sub-trust. The home was valued at $400,000, leaving $100,000 of the IRA to be placed in the B sub-trust. Part of the IRA was intentionally placed in the decedent's B sub-trust in order to avoid federal estate taxation, but this allocation may produce significant adverse income tax consequences. I would seriously recommend consideration of a Married IRA–QTIP Trust (see Chapter 22).

When the estate assets were allocated to the appropriate sub-trusts—with both the decedent's and survivor's marital assets receiving full stepped-up valuation to market value—these assets would appear as shown in Table 16B-1.

Market Value of Assets upon Death of Second Spouse

When the second spouse dies, the separate property assets of the second spouse in the A sub-trust receive stepped-up valuation to the current market value; thus, the original cost basis of the assets is no longer of concern.

Assume that it is now years later, and the estate assets, except for the IRA, have substantially appreciated in value. Upon the death of the second spouse, the home has doubled in market value to $800,000; the value of each spouse's separate property has tripled from $100,000 to $300,000; and the value of the IRA has remained at $1 million. Thus, when the second spouse dies, the market value of the estate assets would be as shown in the top portion of Table 16B-2. The bottom portion of the table shows the current value of the estate assets that were initially allocated to the sub-trusts *when the first* spouse died. Now that the second spouse has died, the same asset allocation must be used when determining any potential federal estate tax liability.

In the table, the shading of the assets in the B sub-trust (also known as the "Credit Shelter Trust") signifies that these assets are insulated from further estate taxes. Because of this insulation from taxation, the value of assets in the

TABLE 16B-2

VALUE OF ESTATE ASSETS WHEN SECOND SPOUSE DIES
(MARRIED A-B TRUST IN A COMMUNITY PROPERTY STATE)

Basic Estate Assets	MARKET VALUE UPON DEATH OF FIRST SPOUSE		MARKET VALUE UPON DEATH OF SECOND SPOUSE	
	First Spouse	Second Spouse	First Spouse	Second Spouse
Home	$400,000		$800,000	
First spouse's separate property	$100,000		$300,000	
Second spouse's separate property		$100,000		$300,000
IRA	$100,000	$900,000	$100,000	$900,000

CURRENT MARKET VALUE OF ASSETS IN SUB-TRUSTS

Estate Assets	B Sub-Trust	A Sub-Trust
Home	$800,000	
First spouse's separate property	$300,000	
Second spouse's separate property		$300,000
IRA	$100,000	$900,000
Total value in first spouse's estate	$1,200,000*	
Total value in second spouse's estate		$1,200,000

*Assets in B sub-trust are insulated from further federal estate taxation.

first spouse's B sub-trust need not be of concern when valuing the assets for estate tax purposes. However, *all* assets in the second spouse's A sub-trust are subject to federal estate taxes at their current market value. The subject of estate taxes is explored in more detail later in this chapter.

Stepped-Up Valuation upon Death of Surviving Spouse

Upon the death of the second spouse, the assets in the survivor's A sub-trust receive full stepped-up valuation to the current market value. Since the assets of the first spouse attained full stepped-up valuation to the then-current market value when the first spouse died (and the assets were placed in the irrevocable decedent's B sub-trust), the decedent's assets do not again receive stepped-up valuation upon the death of the second spouse.

Cost Basis of All Assets upon Death of Second Spouse

One of the many advantages of a Married A-B Living Trust is that the assets of each spouse receive the benefits of stepped-up valuation to current market value upon his or her death. However, once assets have received stepped-up valuation to current market value and are placed in an irrevocable Trust (e.g., the decedent's B sub-trust when the first spouse dies), the asset values become the new cost basis and are frozen at that level; no further stepped-up valuation is allowed. Congress was explicit about granting the boon of stepped-up valuation to assets held by individuals, but *not* to assets held in an irrevocable Trust. Therefore, the assets of the first spouse (allocated to the B sub-trust) retain as their cost basis the stepped-up valuation to market value that was determined when the first spouse died. The

TABLE 16B-3
MARKET VALUE VS. COST BASIS OF ESTATE ASSETS
(MARRIED A-B TRUST IN A COMMUNITY PROPERTY STATE)

Basic Estate Assets	MARKET VALUE UPON DEATH OF FIRST SPOUSE		MARKET VALUE UPON DEATH OF SECOND SPOUSE	
	First Spouse	Second Spouse	First Spouse	Second Spouse
Home	**$400,000**		$800,000	
First spouse's separate property	**$100,000**		$300,000	
Second spouse's separate property		$100,000		**$300,000**
IRA	**$100,000***	$900,000*	$100,000*	**$900,000***

*The cost basis of an IRA is zero.

Note: Numbers in **boldface** represent asset cost basis upon death of each spouse.

assets of the second spouse (allocated to the A sub-trust) receive full stepped-up valuation to the current market value as of the date of death of the second spouse.

The retained cost basis (for the decedent's assets) and the "new" stepped-up basis (for the second spouse's assets) are itemized in Table 16B-3. The numbers in bold type are the cost basis of the assets, established upon the death of each spouse.

TAX TREATMENT OF A MARRIED A-B TRUST

When the second spouse dies and the estate must be settled, you must be aware of several potential tax impacts:

- When the heirs sell estate assets, any capital gain is subject to capital gains taxation.
- Depending on the size of the estate when the second spouse dies, federal estate taxes may be due.
- If you are unlucky enough to reside in one of the states that imposes an inheritance tax, such a tax may be due when the second spouse dies.

You also need to be aware of the impact of capital gains tax on future sales and transfers.

Capital Gains Treatment

Receiving stepped-up valuation for the assets can have a significant impact (a pleasant one, for a change) on any potential capital gains that may be due if and when the assets are sold in the future. After the death of the second spouse, you need to be aware of a few basic principles regarding the treatment of capital gains:

- Upon the death of the second spouse, no capital gain is realized if the assets in the A sub-trust are sold soon after the spouse's death, since the cost basis and the market value of the assets are now the same.
- Assets that are distributed to the beneficiaries do not incur any capital gains tax liability until the assets are actually *sold*.
- The time period (i.e., the holding period) that determines the capital gains tax rate for assets in the first spouse's irrevocable B sub-trust extends to the beneficiaries—the heirs who eventually receive the assets. In other words, the time period for determining which capital gains tax rate must be used upon the sale of the asset extends back to the date of purchase by the first spouse.
- The time period for assets in the second spouse's now-irrevocable A sub-trust is the

same as that just described for the assets in the B sub-trust (i.e., when the assets were first purchased by the husband and/or wife).

Of these principles, the most important is that, since the assets in the survivor's A sub-trust receive full stepped-up valuation to the current market value as of the second spouse's date of death, no immediate capital gain is realized if the assets of the second spouse are sold soon after the date of death.

The Home

Upon the death of the second spouse, in this example, only the second spouse's separate property receives stepped-up valuation to the current market value. Since the home was allocated entirely to the first spouse's B sub-trust, the cost basis does not change upon the death of the second spouse. The assets of the first spouse (in the B sub-trust) retain the "new" cost basis established upon the death of the first spouse. Upon the death of the second spouse, the "new" cost basis for the first spouse's share (100 percent) of the home remains at $400,000. Given our assumption that the home's market value has grown to $800,000, if the beneficiaries decided to sell the home, they would realize a capital gain of $400,000 (and would owe capital gains taxes) when the home was sold, as shown in Table 16B-4.

Remember that the transfer of the home to the beneficiaries does not create a capital gain event. However, if the beneficiaries decide to sell the home, they have two options:

- The beneficiaries can live in the home for two of five years and, thus, qualify for the $250,000 homeowner's exemption (for each beneficiary living therein).
- The beneficiaries can sell the home and recognize a capital gain based upon the time at which the home was first purchased by the individual(s) or the Trust. If the home was held for less than twelve months, the capital gains tax rate would be 28 percent; if the home was held for more than twelve months, the tax rate would be 20 percent; if the home was held for more than five years, the capital gains tax rate would be 18 percent (beginning in 2001). These rates apply on the sale, whether the home is sold inside the Trust or outside the Trust.

Any other community property asset held in either the first spouse's B sub-trust or the second spouse's A sub-trust would be treated in the same way as just described for the home.

Separate Property

The separate property of the second spouse receives full stepped-up valuation to the current market value ($300,000) as of the date of death of the second spouse. If the beneficiaries sold the separate property soon after receiving it, there would be no capital gain on the resultant sale of this asset, as shown in Table 16B-5 on page 258.

Remember, however, that the separate property of the first spouse received full stepped-up valuation (to $100,000) upon the death of the first spouse, and this value then became the

---

TABLE 16B-4

CAPITAL GAIN ON SALE OF HOME
(MARRIED A-B TRUST IN A COMMUNITY PROPERTY STATE)

Home	Market Value	New Cost Basis	Capital Gain
First spouse (B sub-trust)	$800,000	$400,000	$400,000

"new" cost basis. Therefore, the beneficiaries of the Trust receive the first spouse's separate property with a cost basis of $100,000 but with a current market value of $300,000. No capital gain is realized upon the transfer of this separate property to the beneficiaries, but the beneficiaries would realize a capital gain of $200,000 (and would have to pay capital gains taxes) upon the sale of this separate property, as shown in Table 16B-6.

The time period used for establishing the applicable capital gains tax rate for the first spouse's separate property (in the B sub-trust) is the same as previously specified for the home. Remember that the IRS time clock began when the asset was *originally* purchased, and this time period passes on to the beneficiaries, along with the asset.

IRAs

No stepped-up valuation is associated with IRAs passing to the beneficiaries. Remember that the IRA cost basis is zero, as you learned in Chapter 12.

Federal Estate Tax Treatment

Upon the death of the second spouse, no additional federal estate taxes are due on the assets in the first spouse's B sub-trust. Remember that when the assets were first placed in the B sub-trust, no federal estate taxes were due because the value of the assets did not exceed the estate tax exemption in effect at that time. Now these assets are insulated from any further estate tax liability, even though their current market value, as shown in the shaded portion of Table 16B-7, is now $1.2 million.

Upon the death of the second spouse, all of the assets in the second spouse's A sub-trust are subject to federal estate taxes. However, the value of the assets can be offset by the second spouse's federal estate tax exemption (the amount that is applicable in the year of the second spouse's demise). The current market value of the estate assets in the second spouse's A sub-trust is $1.2 million (see Table 16B-7).

The federal estate tax exemption rises to $1 million by the year 2006 (an increase that does not even keep up with a 3 percent inflation

---

TABLE 16B-5
CAPITAL GAIN ON SALE OF SECOND SPOUSE'S SEPARATE PROPERTY
(MARRIED A-B TRUST IN A COMMUNITY PROPERTY STATE)

Separate Property	Current Market Value	New Cost Basis	Capital Gain
Second spouse (A sub-trust)	$300,000	$300,000	$0

TABLE 16B-6
CAPITAL GAINS DUE ON SALE OF FIRST SPOUSE'S SEPARATE PROPERTY
(MARRIED A-B TRUST IN A COMMUNITY PROPERTY STATE)

Separate Property	Current Market Value	New Cost Basis	Capital Gain
First spouse (B sub-trust)	$300,000	$100,000	$200,000

TABLE 16B-7
ALLOCATION OF CURRENT MARKET VALUE TO SUB-TRUSTS
(MARRIED A-B TRUST IN A COMMUNITY PROPERTY STATE)

Estate Assets	Current Market Value	B Sub-Trust	A Sub-Trust
Home	$ 800,000	$ 800,000	
First spouse's separate property	$ 300,000	$ 300,000	
Second spouse's separate property	$ 300,000		$ 300,000
IRA	$1,000,000	$ 100,000	$ 900,000
Total market value in first spouse's estate		$1,200,000	
Total market value in second spouse's estate			$1,200,000

Note: Assets in B sub-trust are insulated from further federal estate taxation.

rate). For the sake of simplicity, we will compute the federal estate taxes on the second spouse's assets in the A sub-trust using the old estate tax exemption of $600,000. Table 16B-8 on page 260 shows the computation of the estate tax.

After the federal estate taxes are paid, the value of assets in the first spouse's B sub-trust and the second spouse's A sub-trust can be passed on to the named beneficiaries, as shown in Table 16B-9 on page 260.

Capital Gains Tax vs. Federal Estate Tax
Because federal estate tax rates are significantly higher than capital gains tax rates, it is far better for your assets to be subject to capital gains tax rates, which range from 18 percent (effective in 2001) to 28 percent, rather than to federal estate tax rates ranging from 37 percent to 55 percent.

- Although the assets in the second spouse's A sub-trust receive full stepped-up valuation to the current market value (upon the death of the second spouse) and, thus, avoid any tax on capital gains if sold before they appreciate further, the assets in the A sub-trust are subject to the higher and more consumptive federal estate tax rates.
- Any increase in the value of the assets in the first spouse's B sub-trust is subject to *capital gains tax*, but those assets are excluded from further *federal estate tax* liability.

State Inheritance Tax
If you reside in a state that imposes an inheritance tax, any such taxes are in addition to the federal estate tax—and, thus, further erode the value of the estate that is ultimately passed on to the beneficiaries. Appendix E contains a list of the states that still pursue the antiquated system of imposing inheritance taxes.

VALUATION METHOD WITH A MARRIED A-B-C TRUST
The primary difference between a Married A-B Trust and a Married A-B-C Trust is that, upon the death of the second spouse, the assets in the C sub-trust (whether a QTIP Trust, a Married IRA–QTIP Trust, or a QDOT Trust) are subject to estate taxation. The assets in the C sub-trust are added to the assets in the A sub-trust, and the estate tax computation is based on the total asset value of these sub-trusts. If

TABLE 16B-8
ESTATE TAX COMPUTATION UPON DEATH OF SECOND SPOUSE
(MARRIED A-B TRUST IN A COMMUNITY PROPERTY STATE)

MARKET VALUE		SECOND SPOUSE'S A SUB-TRUST
Home		$ 0
Second spouse's separate property		$ 300,000
IRA		$ 900,000
Total assets in second spouse's A sub-trust		$1,200,000
Less: Second spouse's federal estate tax exemption		($ 600,000)
Taxable estate		$ 600,000
Federal estate tax (from IRS Estate Tax Table)*		$ 340,000

NET VALUE (AFTER ESTATE TAXES) OF THE A SUB-TRUST

Total value in A sub-trust	$1,200,000	
Less: Federal estate tax	($ 340,000)	
Balance of second spouse's A sub-trust	$ 860,000	
Net amount distributed to beneficiaries of A sub-trust		$ 860,000

*Tax rate is based on an escalating estate tax scale.

Note: The author uses the tax computation approach shown above in an effort to not detract from the basic principle being presented. In actuality, the federal estate tax would be computed on the total taxable estate of $1,200,000. The estate tax would amount to $534,000, minus the tax credit of $192,800 (for the $600,000 federal estate tax exemption). The net result leaves an actual federal estate tax of $341,200.

TABLE 16B-9
ESTATE VALUE PASSED TO BENEFICIARIES
(MARRIED A-B TRUST IN A COMMUNITY PROPERTY STATE)

NET VALUE (AFTER ESTATE TAXES) OF SECOND SPOUSE'S A SUB-TRUST

Total of A sub-trust	$1,200,000	
Less: Federal estate tax	($ 340,000)	
Net value of second spouse's A sub-trust	$ 860,000	
Value of second spouse's estate		$ 860,000

VALUE OF FIRST SPOUSE'S B SUB-TRUST

Value of first spouse's B sub-trust*	$1,200,000	
Value of first spouse's estate		$1,200,000
Total estate passed to beneficiaries		$2,060,000

*Appreciated value insulated from further taxation.

the value of assets in the A sub-trust is less than one federal estate tax exemption, the overall estate taxation can be reduced, since any "leftover" exemption (the amount of exemption remaining after the exemption has been applied to the A sub-trust) can be applied to the asset value in the C sub-trust.

Any federal estate tax liability (and any state inheritance tax liability) should be apportioned between the A sub-trust and the C sub-trust, based on the proportionate asset value in each sub-trust. Such apportioning of taxes to the sub-trusts (based on the asset value within each sub-trust) is particularly relevant if the sub-trusts have different beneficiaries, since each sub-trust "shares" an equitable amount of the estate tax liability.

Allocation of Assets upon Death of First Spouse

Before proceeding with the settlement of an estate in a Married A-B-C Trust, let's briefly review how the assets were allocated upon the death of the first spouse. In a community property state, the valuation method is used, wherein the community property (the home, other real estate, and the IRA) are divided equally by value rather than by asset. One of the primary advantages of the valuation method of asset allocation is that retirement assets (illustrated as an IRA) are generated as community property and, therefore, may be considered in the value allocation.

The separate property of the first spouse was allocated to the first spouse's B sub-trust, and the separate property of the second spouse was allocated to the second spouse's A sub-trust. In this example, the first spouse's B sub-trust held $100,000 of separate property; thus, only $500,000 in additional value was needed to fully utilize the first spouse's federal estate tax exemption. Remember that it was advantageous to place an appreciating asset (such as the home) in the decedent's B sub-trust. With the home valued at $400,000, this left $100,000 of the other real estate to be placed in the B sub-trust, with the balance of the other real estate being allocated between the first spouse's C sub-trust ($600,000) and the second spouse's A sub-trust ($100,000).

Remember, placing part of the IRA in the decedent's B sub-trust would avoid federal estate taxation but could create significant adverse income tax consequences. I would seriously recommend consideration of a Married IRA–QTIP Trust (see Chapter 22).

When the estate assets were allocated to the appropriate sub-trusts—with all community property assets and the decedent's separate property receiving full stepped-up valuation to market value, these assets would appear as shown in Table 16B-10.

TABLE 16B-10

**ESTATE ASSETS ALLOCATED TO A, B, AND C SUB-TRUSTS
UPON DEATH OF FIRST SPOUSE (COMMUNITY PROPERTY STATE)**

Estate Assets	Market Value upon Death of First Spouse	(First Spouse) C Sub-Trust	(First Spouse) B Sub-Trust	(Second Spouse) A Sub-Trust
Home	$ 400,000		$400,000	
Other real estate	$ 800,000	$ 575,000	$100,000	$ 125,000
First spouse's separate property	$ 100,000		$100,000	
Second spouse's separate property	$ 100,000			$ 50,000
IRA	$1,000,000			$1,000,000
Total value in first spouse's estate		$1,175,000		
Total value in second spouse's estate				$1,175,000

Market Value of Assets upon Death of Second Spouse

When the second spouse dies, the rules change again. The separate property assets of the second spouse receive stepped-up valuation to the current market value; thus, the original cost basis is no longer of concern.

Assume that it is years later, and the estate assets, except for the IRA, have substantially appreciated in value. Upon the death of the second spouse, the home has doubled in market value to $800,000; the other real estate has increased in value from $800,000 (when the first spouse died) to $1.2 million; and, similarly, the value of each spouse's separate property has tripled from $100,000 to $300,000. Let's assume that the value of the IRA has remained at $1

million. When the second spouse dies, the market value of the estate assets would be as shown in the top portion of Table 16B-11. The bottom portion of the table shows the current value of the estate assets that were initially allocated to the sub-trusts *when the first spouse died.* Now that the second spouse has died, the same asset allocation must be used when determining any potential federal estate tax liability.

In the table, the shading of the assets in the B sub-trust (also known as the "Credit Shelter Trust") signifies that these assets are insulated from further estate taxes. Because of this insulation, the value of assets in the first spouse's B sub-trust is of no concern when valuing the assets for estate tax purposes. However, *all* assets in the A sub-trust and C sub-trust are

TABLE 16B-11
MARKET VALUE OF ESTATE ASSETS WHEN SECOND SPOUSE DIES
(MARRIED A-B-C TRUST IN A COMMUNITY PROPERTY STATE)

Basic Estate Assets	MARKET VALUE UPON DEATH OF FIRST SPOUSE		MARKET VALUE UPON DEATH OF SECOND SPOUSE	
	First Spouse	Second Spouse	First Spouse	Second Spouse
Home	$400,000		$ 800,000	
Other real estate	$700,000	$ 100,000	$1,050,000	$ 150,000
First spouse's separate property	$100,000		$ 300,000	
Second spouse's separate property		$ 100,000		$ 300,000
IRA		$1,000,000		$1,000,000

CURRENT MARKET VALUE OF ASSETS IN SUB-TRUSTS

Estate Assets	(First Spouse) C Sub-Trust	(First Spouse) B Sub-Trust	(Second Spouse) A Sub-Trust
Home	$ 900,000	$800,000	$ 150,000
Other real estate		$150,000	
First spouse's separate property		$300,000	
Second spouse's separate property			$ 300,000
IRA			$1,000,000
Total value in first spouse's estate	$2,150,000		
Total value in second spouse's estate			$1,450,000

Note: Value of first spouse's assets in the C sub-trust (at current market value) are *not* exempt from federal estate taxation.

subject to federal estate taxes at their current market value. The subject of estate taxes is explored in more detail later in this chapter.

Stepped-Up Valuation upon
Death of Surviving Spouse

Upon the death of the second spouse, the assets in the survivor's A sub-trust receive full stepped-up valuation to the current market value. Since the assets of the first spouse attained full stepped-up valuation to the then-current market value when the first spouse died (and the assets were placed in the decedent's irrevocable B sub-trust and C sub-trust), those assets do not again receive stepped-up valuation upon the death of the second spouse.

Cost Basis of All Assets upon
Death of Second Spouse

One of the many advantages of a Married A-B-C Living Trust is that the assets of each spouse receive the benefits of stepped-up valuation to current market value upon that spouse's death. However, once assets have received stepped-up valuation to current market value and then placed in an irrevocable Trust (e.g., the decedent's B sub-trust when the first spouse dies), the asset values become the new cost basis and are frozen at that level; no further stepped-up valuation is allowed. Remember, Congress specifically granted stepped-up valuation to assets held by individuals, not to assets held in an irrevocable Trust. Therefore, the assets of the first spouse (allocated to the B sub-trust and C sub-trust) retain as their cost basis the stepped-up valuation to market value that was determined when the first spouse died. The assets of the second spouse (allocated to the A sub-trust) receive full stepped-up valuation to current market value as of the date of death of the second spouse.

The retained cost basis (for the decedent's assets) and the "new" stepped-up basis (for the second spouse's assets) are itemized in Table 16B-12. The numbers in bold type are the current cost basis of the assets upon the death of each spouse.

TAX TREATMENT OF A
MARRIED A-B-C TRUST

When the second spouse dies and the estate must be settled, you must be aware of several potential tax impacts:

TABLE 16B-12
MARKET VALUE VS. COST BASIS OF ESTATE ASSETS
(MARRIED A-B-C TRUST IN A COMMUNITY PROPERTY STATE)

Estate Assets	MARKET VALUE UPON DEATH OF FIRST SPOUSE		MARKET VALUE UPON DEATH OF SECOND SPOUSE	
	First Spouse	Second Spouse	First Spouse	Second Spouse
Home	$ 400,000		$ 800,000	
Other real estate	$ 700,000	$ 100,000	$1,050,000	$ 150,000
First spouse's separate property	$ 100,000		$ 300,000	
Second spouse's separate property		$ 100,000		$ 300,000
IRA		$1,000,000*		$1,000,000*

*The cost basis of an IRA is zero.

Note: Numbers in **boldface** represent asset cost basis upon death of each spouse.

- When the heirs eventually sell estate assets, they may realize a capital gain and, thus, be subject to capital gains taxation.
- Depending on the size of the estate when the second spouse dies, federal estate taxes may be due.
- If you are unlucky enough to reside in one of the states that imposes an inheritance tax, such a tax may be due when the second spouse dies.

You also need to be aware of the impact of capital gains tax on future sales and transfers.

Capital Gains Treatment

Receiving stepped-up valuation for the assets can have a significant impact (a pleasant one, for a change) on any potential capital gains taxes that may be due if and when the assets are sold in the future. After the death of the second spouse, you need to be aware of a few basic principles regarding the treatment of capital gains:

- Upon the death of the second spouse, no capital gain is realized if the assets in the A sub-trust are sold soon after the spouse's death, since the cost basis and the market value of the assets are now the same.
- Assets that are distributed to the beneficiaries do not incur any capital gains tax liability until the assets are actually *sold*.
- The time period (i.e., the holding period) that determines the capital gains tax rate for assets in the first spouse's irrevocable B sub-trust and C sub-trust extends to the beneficiaries—the heirs who eventually receive the assets. In other words, the time period for

determining which capital gains tax rate must be used upon the sale of the asset extends back to the date of purchase by the first spouse.

- The time period for assets in the second spouse's now-irrevocable A sub-trust is the same as that just described for the assets in the B sub-trust and C sub-trust.

Of these principles, the most important is that, since the assets in the survivor's A sub-trust receive full stepped-up valuation to the current market value as of the second spouse's date of death, no immediate capital gain is realized if the assets of the second spouse are sold soon after the date of death.

The Home

Upon the death of the second spouse in this example, only the second spouse's separate property receives stepped-up valuation to the current market value. Since the home was allocated entirely to the decedent's B sub-trust, the home receives no stepped-up valuation to the current market value. The assets of the first spouse (in the B sub-trust and C sub-trust) previously received stepped-up valuation, and these assets retain the "new" cost basis established upon the death of the first spouse. Upon the death of the second spouse, the home has a market value of $800,000, but the "new" cost basis for the first spouse's share of the home (established when the first spouse died) remains at $400,000. If the beneficiaries decided to sell the home, they would realize a capital gain of $400,000 (and would owe capital gains taxes), as shown in Table 16B-13.

Remember that the transfer of the home to

TABLE 16B-13
CAPITAL GAIN ON SALE OF HOME
(MARRIED A-B-C TRUST IN A COMMUNITY PROPERTY STATE)

Home	Market Value	New Cost Basis	Capital Gain
First spouse (B sub-trust)	$800,000	$400,000	$400,000

the beneficiaries does not create a capital gain event. However, if the beneficiaries decide to sell the home, they have two options:

- The beneficiaries can live in the home for two of five years and, thus, qualify for the $250,000 homeowner's exemption (for each beneficiary living therein).
- The beneficiaries can sell the home and recognize a capital gain based upon the time the home was first purchased by the individual(s) or the Trust. If the home was held for less than twelve months, the capital gains tax rate would be 28 percent; if the home was held for more than twelve months, the tax rate would be 20 percent; if the home was held for more than five years, the tax rate would be 18 percent (effective in 2001). These rates apply whether the home is sold inside the Trust or outside the Trust.

Other Real Estate

Let's assume that, upon the death of the second spouse, the other real estate has increased in value to $1.2 million. The second spouse's share (in the A sub-trust) receives full stepped-up valuation to the current market value ($150,000), but the first spouse's share of other real estate (in the B sub-trust and C sub-trust) retains the original stepped-up valuation ($700,000) that was established upon the death of the first spouse. If the beneficiaries decided to sell the real estate, they would realize a capital gain of $350,000 (and would owe capital gains taxes) when the real estate was sold, as shown in Table 16B-14.

The transfer of the other real estate to the beneficiaries does not create a capital gain event. However, when the beneficiaries sell the other real estate, they must then recognize a capital gain liability. As with the sale of the home, the capital gains tax rate is based on the length of time the real estate has been held since it was first purchased by the individual(s) or the Trust: 28 percent if the real estate was held for less than twelve months, 20 percent if it was held for more than twelve months, and 18 percent if it was held for more than five years (effective in 2001). These tax rates apply on the sale whether the real estate is sold inside the Trust or outside the Trust.

Any other community property asset held in the first spouse's B sub-trust or C sub-trust and/or the second spouse's A sub-trust would be treated in the same manner as just described for other real estate.

Separate Property

The separate property of the second spouse receives full stepped-up valuation to the current market value ($300,000) upon the death of the second spouse. If the beneficiaries sold the separate property soon after receiving it, there would be no capital gain on the sale, as shown in Table 16B-15 on page 266.

Remember, however, that the separate property of the first spouse received full stepped-up valuation (to $100,000) upon the death of the first spouse, and this value then became the "new" cost basis. Therefore, the beneficiaries of the Trust receive the first spouse's separate property with a cost basis of $100,000 and a

---

TABLE 16B-14

CAPITAL GAIN ON SALE OF OTHER REAL ESTATE
(MARRIED A-B-C TRUST IN A COMMUNITY PROPERTY STATE)

Other Real Estate	Market Value	New Cost Basis	Capital Gain
Second spouse (A sub-trust)	$ 150,000	$150,000	$ 0
First spouse (B and C sub-trusts)	$1,050,000	$700,000	$350,000
Total	$1,200,000	$850,000	$350,000

current market value of $300,000. No capital gain is realized upon the transfer of this separate property to the beneficiaries, but the beneficiaries would realize a capital gain of $200,000 (and would owe capital gains taxes) upon the sale of this separate property, as shown in Table 16B-16.

The time period used for establishing the applicable capital gains tax rate for the first spouse's separate property (in the B sub-trust) is the same as previously specified for the home and the other real estate. Remember that the IRS time clock began when the asset was *originally* purchased, and this time period passes on to the beneficiaries, along with the asset.

IRAs

No stepped-up valuation is associated with IRAs passing to the beneficiaries. Remember that the IRA cost basis is zero, as you learned in Chapter 12.

Federal Estate Tax Treatment

Upon the death of the second spouse, no additional federal estate taxes are due on the assets in the first spouse's B sub-trust. Remember that when the assets were first placed in the B sub-trust, no federal estate taxes were due because the value of the assets did not exceed the estate tax exemption in effect at that time. Now these assets are insulated from any further estate tax liability. Their current market value, as shown in the shaded portion of Table 16B-17, is now $1.25 million.

Upon the death of the second spouse, all of the assets in the second spouse's A sub-trust and all of the assets in the first spouse's C sub-trust are subject to federal estate taxes. However, the value of the assets in the A sub-trust can be offset by the second spouse's federal estate tax exemption (the amount that is applicable in the year of the second spouse's demise). The total market value of the assets in the second spouse's A sub-trust is $1.45 million. In calculating the estate tax, the current market value of the assets in the first spouse's C sub-trust ($900,000) must also be included. Thus, upon the death of the second spouse, federal estate taxes must be calculated on a total estate value of $2.35 million (see Table 16B-17).

The federal estate tax exemption rises to $1 million by the year 2006 (an increase that does

---

TABLE 16B-15

CAPITAL GAIN ON SALE OF SECOND SPOUSE'S SEPARATE PROPERTY (MARRIED A-B-C TRUST IN A COMMUNITY PROPERTY STATE)

Separate Property	Market Value	New Cost Basis	Capital Gain
Second spouse (A sub-trust)	$300,000	$300,000	$0

TABLE 16B-16

CAPITAL GAIN ON SALE OF FIRST SPOUSE'S SEPARATE PROPERTY (MARRIED A-B-C TRUST IN A COMMUNITY PROPERTY STATE)

Separate Property	Market Value	New Cost Basis	Capital Gain
First spouse (B sub-trust)	$300,000	$100,000	$200,000

TABLE 16B-17

ALLOCATION OF CURRENT MARKET VALUE TO SUB-TRUSTS
(MARRIED A-B-C TRUST IN A COMMUNITY PROPERTY STATE)

Estate Assets	Current Market Value	C Sub-Trust	B Sub-Trust	A Sub-Trust
Home	$ 800,000		$ 800,000	$ 150,000
Other real estate	$1,200,000	$900,000	$ 150,000	
First spouse's separate property	$ 300,000		$ 300,000	
Second spouse's separate property	$ 300,000			$ 300,000
IRA	$1,000,000			$1,000,000
Insulated value of first spouse's estate			$1,250,000	
Taxable value of first spouse's estate		$900,000		
Total value of second spouse's estate				$1,450,000
Total taxable estate			$2,350,000	

Note: Assets in the B sub-trust are insulated from further federal estate taxation.

not even keep up with a 3 percent inflation rate). For the sake of simplicity, however, we will compute the federal estate taxes on the second spouse's assets in the A sub-trust ($1.45 million) and the remaining assets in the first spouse's C sub-trust ($900,000) using the old federal estate tax exemption of $600,000. Table 16B-18 on page 268 shows the computation of the estate tax.

The federal estate taxes should be deducted proportionately from the second spouse's A sub-trust and from the first spouse's C sub-trust. For example, if the value of the A sub-trust is 49 percent of the total estate, then 49 percent of the federal estate taxes should be paid from asset value in the A sub-trust. Determining the proportion of federal estate taxes to be paid from the second spouse's A sub-trust and the first spouse's C sub-trust is really not difficult and amounts to little more than simple math. The steps involved in determining the apportionment of federal estate taxes are listed below and also illustrated in Table 16B-19 on page 269.

- *Calculate the total taxable estate*: First, subtract the second spouse's federal estate tax exemption from the value of the A sub-trust. Then, add this difference to the value in the C sub-trust. The result is the total taxable estate.
- *Calculate the proportion of the estate in the second spouse's A sub-trust*: Divide the taxable value of the A sub-trust by the total taxable estate amount. The result is the A sub-trust estate tax proportion.
- *Calculate the proportion of the estate in the first spouse's C sub-trust*: Divide the value of the C sub-trust by the total taxable estate amount. The result is the C sub-trust estate tax proportion.
- *Calculate the federal estate tax liability on the total taxable estate*: Use the federal estate tax table to determine the total federal estate tax.
- *Calculate the second spouse's portion of estate taxes*: Multiply the total federal estate tax due by the A sub-trust estate tax proportion. The result is the federal estate tax due from the A sub-trust.
- *Calculate the first spouse's portion of estate taxes*: Multiply the total federal estate tax by the C sub-trust estate tax proportion. The result is the federal estate tax due from the C sub-trust.

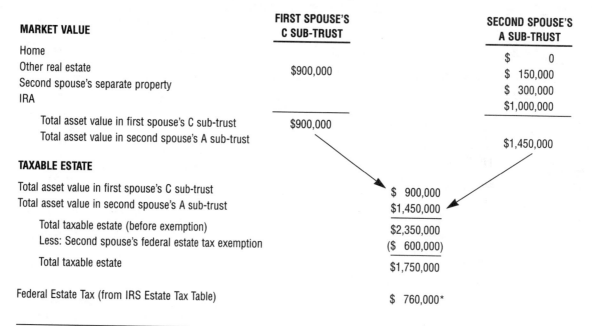

TABLE 16B-18

ESTATE TAX COMPUTATION UPON DEATH OF SECOND SPOUSE
(MARRIED A-B-C TRUST IN A COMMUNITY PROPERTY STATE)

MARKET VALUE	FIRST SPOUSE'S C SUB-TRUST	SECOND SPOUSE'S A SUB-TRUST
Home		$ 0
Other real estate	$900,000	$ 150,000
Second spouse's separate property		$ 300,000
IRA		$1,000,000
Total asset value in first spouse's C sub-trust	$900,000	
Total asset value in second spouse's A sub-trust		$1,450,000
TAXABLE ESTATE		
Total asset value in first spouse's C sub-trust		$ 900,000
Total asset value in second spouse's A sub-trust		$1,450,000
Total taxable estate (before exemption)		$2,350,000
Less: Second spouse's federal estate tax exemption		($ 600,000)
Total taxable estate		$1,750,000
Federal Estate Tax (from IRS Estate Tax Table)		$ 760,000*

*Tax rate is based on an escalating estate tax scale.

Note: The author uses the tax computation approach shown above in an effort to not detract from the basic principle being presented. In actuality, the federal estate tax would be computed on the total taxable estate of $2,350,000. The estate tax would amount to $952,300, minus the tax credit of $192,800 (for the $600,000 federal estate tax exemption). The net result leaves an actual federal estate tax of $759,500.

Although the two "double-check" calculations of the C sub-trust portion in the third and the last steps may seem redundant to those who are mathematically inclined, such calculations serve as an excellent way to double-check that your calculations are correct. The proportionate shares for the A sub-trust and the C sub-trust should add up to a total of 1, and the tax liability of the A sub-trust and the C sub-trust should add up to the total amount of federal estate taxes due.

Once the federal estate tax liability has been determined for the second spouse's A sub-trust

and the first spouse's C sub-trust, the net value of the estate assets (the value remaining after estate taxes are paid) is then available for distribution to the heirs, as shown on page 270 in Table 16B-20. Remember that the assets in the first spouse's B sub-trust are insulated from further federal estate taxation. Thus, although the assets in the B sub-trust grew in value over the years from $600,000 to $1.25 million, this $650,000 growth incurs no additional federal estate tax liability. The net estate passed to the beneficiaries would be over $2.8 million (see Table 16B-20).

TABLE 16B-19
APPORTIONMENT OF ESTATE TAXES BETWEEN SUB-TRUSTS
(MARRIED A-B-C TRUST IN A COMMUNITY PROPERTY STATE)

	Calculation Values	Result
CALCULATE TOTAL TAXABLE ESTATE		
Value of second spouse's A sub-trust	$1,450,000	
Less: Second spouse's federal estate tax exemption	($ 600,000)	
Taxable value of A sub-trust	$ 850,000	
Plus: Value of first spouse's C sub-trust	$ 900,000	
Total taxable estate		$1,750,000
CALCULATE PORTION OF ESTATE IN THE A SUB-TRUST		
Taxable amount of second spouse's A sub-trust	$ 850,000	
Divide by: Total taxable estate	$1,750,000	
A sub-trust estate tax proportion		0.49 (49%)
CALCULATE PORTION OF ESTATE IN THE C SUB-TRUST		
Value of first spouse's C sub-trust	$ 900,000	
Divide by: Total taxable estate	$1,750,000	
C sub-trust estate tax proportion		0.51 (51%)
(Double-check: 0.49 + 0.51 = 1.00—estate proportions are OK.)		
DETERMINE FEDERAL ESTATE TAXES DUE		
Total taxable estate	$1,750,000	
Federal estate tax (from IRS Estate Tax Table)	$ 760,000	
CALCULATE SECOND SPOUSE'S PORTION OF TAXES		
Total federal estate tax due	$ 760,000	
Multiply by: A sub-trust estate tax proportion	0.49	
Federal estate tax due from A sub-trust		$372,000
CALCULATE FIRST SPOUSE'S PORTION OF TAXES		
Total federal estate tax due	$ 760,000	
Multiply by: C sub-trust estate tax proportion	0.51	
Federal estate tax due from C sub-trust		$388,000
(Double-check: $372,000 + $388,000 = $760,000—		
estate tax proportions are OK.)		

*Tax rate is based on an escalating estate tax scale.

Note: The author uses the tax computation approach shown above in an effort to not detract from the basic principle being presented. In actuality, the federal estate tax would be computed on the total taxable estate of $2,350,000. The estate tax would amount to $952,300, minus the tax credit of $192,800 (for the $600,000 federal estate tax exemption). The net result leaves an actual federal estate tax of $759,500.

TABLE 16B-20
ESTATE VALUE PASSED TO BENEFICIARIES
(MARRIED A-B-C TRUST IN A COMMUNITY PROPERTY STATE)

NET VALUE (AFTER ESTATE TAXES) OF SECOND SPOUSE'S ESTATE (A SUB-TRUST)

Total of A sub-trust	$1,450,000	
Less: Federal estate tax	($ 372,000)	
Net value of second spouse's A sub-trust	$1,078,000	
Value of second spouse's estate		$1,078,000

NET VALUE (AFTER ESTATE TAXES) OF FIRST SPOUSE'S ESTATE (B AND C SUB-TRUSTS)

Total of C sub-trust	$ 900,000	
Less: Federal estate tax	($ 388,000)	
Net value of first spouse's C sub-trust	$ 512,000	
Value of first spouse's B sub-trust*	$1,250,000	
Value of first spouse's estate		$1,762,000

TOTAL ESTATE DISTRIBUTED TO BENEFICIARIES

Value of second spouse's estate	$1,078,000	
Value of first spouse's estate	$1,762,000	
	$2,840,000	
Total estate distributed to beneficiaries		$2,840,000

*Appreciated value insulated from further taxation.

Capital Gains Tax vs. Federal Estate Tax

Because federal estate tax rates are significantly higher than capital gains tax rates, it is far better for your assets to be subject to capital gains tax rates, which range from 18 percent (beginning in 2001) to 28 percent, rather than to federal estate tax rates ranging from 37 percent to 55 percent.

- The assets in the second spouse's A sub-trust attain full stepped-up valuation to the current market value (upon the death of the second spouse) and, thus, avoid any tax on capital gains if sold before they appreciate further. The assets in the A sub-trust are subject to the higher and more consumptive federal estate tax rates.

- The assets in the first spouse's B sub-trust are subject to capital gains tax, but those assets are excluded from further federal estate tax liability.

- The assets in the first spouse's C sub-trust are subject to federal estate taxation and will also be subject to capital gains taxation upon sale.

State Inheritance Tax

If you reside in a state that imposes an inheritance tax, any such taxes are in addition to the federal estate tax—and, thus, further erode the value of the estate that is ultimately passed on to the beneficiaries. Appendix E contains a list of the states that still pursue the antiquated system of imposing inheritance taxes.

17

Allocation and Distribution of Assets upon the Death of the Second Spouse

Married A-B Trusts and Married A-B-C Trusts

The procedures for settling an estate following the death of the second spouse are quite similar to the procedures used upon the death of the first spouse. Table 17-1 on page 272 provides a brief overview of the procedures required to settle an estate.

The Living Trust, accompanied by several important ancillary documents, can be a godsend to those who have lost a beloved family member. It enables the estate to be settled easily, quickly, and privately.

Paul Sanders lived for another ten years following the death of his wife, Frances. However, following his wife's death, Paul's health steadily declined. Many years before, Paul and Frances had created a Living Trust, but it was only with the decline in Paul's health that their sons, Michael and Daniel, learned to appreciate the importance of these documents. Following Frances's death, the estate had been settled quickly and easily—but Paul had handled the settlement process, so the sons did not really see or experience the effect of having a good Living Trust.

When Paul's health began to worsen, the sons had to step in and help manage the estate. Eventually, because of Paul's deteriorating health, the sons had to place him in a convalescent home that provided meals and cleaning service. The sons had to sell the family home and manage Paul's investments. Later, they had to use these investments to pay for Paul's ongoing care. Paul's Living Trust facilitated such tasks with ease.

Both sons stepped in as co-trustees of the Trust to lighten the load on their ailing father. The sons made sure that their father was given the finest care up to the day that he died—a day that came as a great shock, since the sons dearly loved their father.

Following the death of their father, the sons soon realized, with great surprise, the foresight of their parents in creating a Living

271

TABLE 17-1
PROCEDURES FOR SETTLING AN ESTATE

Chapter 5

Locate copy of Living Trust
Review personal data sheet
Check safe-deposit box
Locate veteran's papers
Determine desired disposition of deceased
Order death certificates
Notify Social Security Administration and other
    institutions and agencies
Notify ex-employer
Notify insurance companies
Cancel credit cards

Chapter 6

Determine need for probate
Settle financial matters
Take inventory of assets
File a Notice to Creditors
Determine whether inheritance taxes are due

Chapter 7

Value assets (includes stepped-up valuation)
Value any business interests
Settle business interests (if any)
Value personal effects

Chapter 8

File Form 706 U.S. Estate (and Generation-Skipping Transfer)
    Tax Return, if federal estate taxes are owed
File Form 1041 U.S. Income Tax Return for Estates and Trusts
Complete any remaining tasks on list of responsibilities
    to assign

Trust. The value of Paul and Frances's estate was slightly less than $1 million. The sons discovered that there was no federal estate tax to pay, no state inheritance tax to pay, and no lengthy or expensive probate process to endure. As the sole and joint beneficiaries of their parents' Trust, the two sons simply divided the estate and distributed it to themselves. And that was the end—the estate was settled, and the assets were distributed. The two sons and their wives were so astonished at the ease of settling the estate that they immediately had Living Trusts established for their own families.

This story—with a happy ending due to a good Living Trust—is repeated almost daily now. However, such is not always the case, as illustrated in the next story.

Jonathan, Terry, and Chris were the sole survivors of their parents' estate. Their father, Thomas Sullivan, had died some fifteen years

before, and their mother, Christine, had passed away three years ago. The parents had created a Living Trust many years ago and had named their three sons as successor trustees and equal beneficiaries.

When their mother died, the sons had no experience with a Living Trust and didn't know what to do. Therefore, they took what they thought was the logical course of action and went to the attorney who initially drew up their parents' Trust. The sons were at least astute enough to inquire about the attorney's experience in settling Living Trusts, and, of course, he assured the sons that he was an "expert" in Living Trusts.

The sons then proceeded, with Mr. Harmon, Esq., handling the estate settlement. The value of the estate exceeded $1.5 million, and, therefore, there were federal estate taxes to be paid—and the estate was held in limbo until the taxes were paid. Following the payment of estate taxes, Mr. Harmon then informed the sons that they must wait until the IRS reviewed and approved their Form 706 U.S. Estate (and Generation-Skipping Transfer) Tax Return before any funds could be distributed from the estate. After almost three years, not a penny of the estate had yet been distributed—except for Mr. Harmon's fee, which had grown to $17,000!

Finally, the IRS approved the Form 706 tax return, and the sons were ready to distribute the estate to themselves. However, the accountant retained by the attorney now had to have his say and told the sons (erroneously), "You can't distribute the funds, because the Trust must pay capital gains taxes first, and we won't know what the capital gains taxes will be for another three months." So the sons waited some more, as the legal and accounting fees continued to mount—and they fumed.

Sadly, but all too commonly, neither the delay nor the fees paid to the attorney or the accountant were necessary. Any capital gains taxes need only be paid by the sons, as beneficiaries, after filing the final Form 1041 U.S. Income Tax Return for Estates and Trusts along with the associated Schedule K-1 that proportionately allocates the capital gain to each of the beneficiaries. (The scenario related in this story would result only if the Living Trust had been very poorly drawn.)

SPECIAL BEQUESTS

Upon the death of the second spouse, you should ensure that any special bequests of the deceased spouse are carried out and that the specified gifts or personal effects are distributed to the named organizations and individuals. Review the Living Trust document to see whether any special bequests are to be made to charities, relatives, and friends. Any special bequests to charity should be made first, since charitable distributions are deductible from the taxable estate, thus reducing any federal estate taxes due.

Once you have valued the estate assets and made any charitable bequests, determine whether any federal estate taxes and state inheritance taxes are due. Set aside the total amount due for all federal and state taxes in a separate account (such as a money market account) for the payment of such taxes, since these funds are due and payable within nine months from the date of death of the second spouse. Finally, distribute the special bequests to family and friends.

To reduce the size of the taxable estate, you should always make charitable bequests first. When the first spouse dies, make charitable bequests before allocating any assets to the sub-trusts. If you make the bequests *after* allocating the decedent's assets to the B sub-trust and/or C sub-trust, you may have to make the bequests equally from both the B sub-trust and the C sub-trust, thus leaving a lesser asset value in the B sub-trust.

When you specify charitable bequests, you should make the bequests in the form of a *percentage* of your estate rather than a fixed dollar amount. Years ago, a California probate judge wrote a heart-rending plea to all people writing Wills to make their charitable bequests as a percentage of the estate rather than as a fixed dollar amount. According to this judge, it was all too often his experience that the estate value had deteriorated after a couple had created their Wills, and the judge often had to intervene in order to leave an adequate estate for the surviving widow. For example, a couple could have a $1 million estate and decide to leave $400,000 to charity upon the death of the first spouse. However, by the time the first spouse dies, the investments could have faltered and the estate be worth only $500,000. To grant the $400,000 bequest to charity would leave the surviving spouse only $100,000 on which to live. Such an approach is certainly not prudent estate planning. This caution applies to all types of special bequests, whether they be destined to be distributed upon the death of the first spouse or upon the death of the second spouse.

Recommendation: Charitable bequests should be made in the form of a percentage of the estate asset value, rather than in the form of a fixed dollar amount.

DISTRIBUTION OF ASSETS

Before distributing estate assets, make sure that the Notice to Creditors has been published and its four-month waiting period has elapsed, so that the estate is protected from creditors. If your state has not yet approved the Notice to Creditors for a Living Trust, it is still prudent to wait the four months for the appearance of any unknown creditors. Also, make sure to pay any outstanding (unpaid) debts before making any distribution of estate assets.

Disclaimers

The beneficiaries have the right to disclaim an interest in part (or all) of the assets bequeathed to them. However, remember that any such disclaimer must be made within nine months from the date of death. Also, the beneficiary may not receive income from an asset before it is disclaimed. If the beneficiary has received *any* income from the asset to be disclaimed, the beneficiary no longer qualifies to disclaim the asset. In addition, the beneficiary who disclaims an asset has no future right to receive any income from or "enjoyment" of that asset.

Typically, a grown child who has already established his or her estate may elect to disclaim an interest in the estate assets in order to prevent those assets from being included in his or her own estate. In the typical scenario, the disclaimed assets usually flow to the children of the disclaiming adult child. However, such a disclaimer could trigger the imposition of a generation-skipping tax.

Distribute Assets "in Kind"

The beneficiaries generally receive the greatest value if you distribute the assets "in kind"—meaning that the beneficiaries accept the assets "as is" (i.e., a house, stocks, bonds, mutual fund shares, and the like) and then, after receiving the assets, they decide whether they want to keep the assets or sell them. For example, if the trustee were to sell the stock in the Trust, a stockbroker would receive a commission to make that sale, thus, reducing the value received by the beneficiary. Upon receipt of this money distributed from the Trust to the beneficiary, the beneficiary would likely reinvest these funds and pay another commission. A much more efficient and less costly approach would be to simply transfer the stock (or any other securities or mutual fund shares) directly to the named beneficiary.

This distribution approach also applies to real estate. For instance, if the assets include a home and there are four children as beneficiaries, the children should be asked whether they desire to keep the home. If the children agree to retain the home, each of the four children would then receive an *undivided one-fourth interest* in the home. The deed to the home would be redrawn, showing each of the four children holding a one-fourth interest.

If two of the beneficiaries decide that they want the home, although the other two beneficiaries do not, the solution is also quite simple. The two children who want the home could simply borrow against the value of the home and place a share of money (comparable to the other two beneficiaries' interest in the home) in the Trust. The home would then be distributed to the two beneficiaries, with each beneficiary having an *undivided one-half interest*; the money obtained from the new mortgage on the home would be distributed to the other two beneficiaries.

If none of the beneficiaries wanted the home, then the home could be sold. Proceeds from the home sale would be distributed equally to each of the beneficiaries. The real estate broker's fee for selling the home is deductible from any federal estate taxes. However, any capital loss on the home (if it is sold for *less* than its cost basis) cannot be deducted by the Trust. If the home is sold inside the Trust, such a loss is "wasted" and cannot be used to offset other Trust income. However, if the home is first distributed to the beneficiaries, who then sell it, the beneficiaries, as individuals, can declare the loss on their personal income tax returns.

When distributing assets in kind, I recommend that the trustee get the beneficiaries to agree, in writing, to such distribution. If the beneficiaries cannot all agree to such a distribution, then the next prudent course of action is to sell the assets and distribute the proceeds of the sale to the beneficiaries.

Outright Distribution

Outright distribution of assets means *right now*—not two years from now, not after the Form 706 Federal Estate Tax Return is filed, and not after the IRS has audited and approved the Form 706 tax return. However, remember that before you distribute *any* Trust assets, you need to determine whether any federal estate taxes (and any state inheritance taxes) are due and then set that money aside in a separate bank account, to be paid nine months following the date of death of the second spouse. Also, as mentioned earlier, you should pay all of the creditors of the estate and wait for the four-month Notice to Creditors time period to elapse before distributing any estate assets.

Once you have completed these steps, distribute the assets outright (if so stated in the Trust). Thus, outright distribution of assets ideally should be done four months following the date of death. The time period before the assets are distributed to the beneficiaries can be extremely important when the assets are expected to appreciate in value and the beneficiaries anticipate selling the assets. The longer the assets are held in trust, the longer the beneficiaries are denied the right to manage their own destinies. (They also may end up owing capital gains tax if the assets have appreciated in value.)

Once the beneficiaries receive the assets, if they decide to sell the assets, any capital gains tax is predicated on the length of time the assets have been held from the time they were first bought (whether by one or both decedent spouses or by the trustee—typically, the surviving spouse—of the decedent's B sub-trust and/or C sub-trust). Remember that the rates are 28 percent if the asset has been held for less than twelve months, 20 percent if the asset has been held for at least twelve months, or, effective in 2001, 18 percent if the asset has been held for more than five years. If the asset is held in trust and then sold while still in the Trust, any resultant capital gain should be distributed to the beneficiaries. To distribute any capital gain among the beneficiaries, the trustee need only file a Form 1041 Trust Income Tax Return and the associated Schedule K-1s.

Deferred Distribution

One of the greatest areas of confusion in settling an estate in a Living Trust—yet one with a very simple solution—is the allocation and then eventual distribution of assets to a number of beneficiaries at different points in time. Most Living Trusts stipulate the age of a beneficiary at which time part (or all) of the assets are to be distributed. For example, let's assume that you have four children who are to receive the assets equally, but only when each beneficiary has attained a certain age: one-third of the distribution at age 25, one-third of the distribution at age 30, and the final one-third of the distribution at age 35. Since the value of estate assets held in trust can fluctuate, the accounting of such value could be a horrendous nightmare. However, there is a very simple solution to this potential problem.

If the assets to be distributed are securities, the easiest solution is to invest them equally in four separate mutual funds—all in the name of the Trust, but identified as fund A, fund B, fund C, and fund D. With such an arrangement, the brokerage firm is now doing the accounting for you, and you will receive a monthly statement showing the value in each separate fund. If the brokerage firm resists your request for such a breakdown, then simply offer to take your business elsewhere. You will be amazed at how quickly most firms will comply with your request.

Let's assume that fund A is for the oldest child, fund B is for the second-oldest child, fund C is for the third-oldest child, and fund D is for the youngest child. When the oldest child reaches age 25, one-third of fund A is distributed to that child in kind—the child receives a certificate for the appropriate number of shares of stock, not the cash from the sale of any shares. Five years later, when that child attains age 30, one-half of the *remaining balance* of fund A is distributed in kind to that child. Making the distribution in this way automatically takes into account any appreciation in the value of the fund. Then when the child attains age 35, the entire remaining balance of fund A is distributed to that child in kind, again automatically taking into account any appreciation in the fund. Similarly, as each of the other children attains the specified age for distribution, each receives his or her share of the fund.

Let me illustrate the distribution process in a somewhat lengthy example. Assume that an estate of $1.2 million is allocated equally to four children and is to be distributed to each beneficiary at ages 25, 30, and 35. Thus, each child is to receive $300,000 as his or her share of the estate. Let's further assume that each child's original investment of $300,000 increases 10 percent annually. Table 17-2 shows how the distribution would be made to each child when he or she attains the specified age for distribution. (For the sake of simplicity, the example shows only the pattern for the first ten years and therefore does not show all distributions to all of the children.) Distributions will result in a one-third interest in the share being distributed at age 25, one-half of the balance of the share distributed at age 30, and the residual of the share distributed at age 35.

The distribution to the beneficiaries would continue as shown in the table until each of the four beneficiaries had received his or her entire share of the inheritance. Even though the process may seem complicated, you vastly simplify it by dividing the initial asset value into separate accounts—and letting the financial institution do the accounting for you.

If the asset were something other than securities or mutual funds (e.g., a home, other real estate, or a business), it would be a simple process to distribute a one-third undivided interest in one-fourth of a home or other real estate—which would be simply a *one-twelfth undivided interest* for each beneficiary when he or she attained the appropriate age for distribution. The deed would simply be rewritten to show the undivided interest owned by each beneficiary. Rewriting the deed in such a manner would automatically account for any appreciation in the value of the house.

The same would be true for a private business. If the business were a corporation, you would simply distribute the appropriate percentage of stock to each beneficiary when he

or she attained the specified age for distribution. If the business were a partnership, the appropriate percentage of the partnership interest could be issued to the beneficiary when he or she attained the specified age for distribution. If the business were a sole proprietorship, the appropriate percentage could be distributed to each beneficiary through a Bill of Sale/Letter of Agreement. (See my first book, *The Living Trust*, for an example of a Bill of Sale/Letter of Agreement.)

Distribution of Income

Usually, assets that are retained in the Trust will generate income. This income should be distributed each year to the beneficiaries—and, thus, will be taxed at the beneficiaries' tax rate. It is unwise to retain income inside the Trust, because the Trust tax rate is the highest of any individual income tax rate (i.e., 39.6 percent). Likewise, any capital gain generated from Trust assets should also be distributed to the beneficiaries. The trustee would satisfy the IRS tax reporting requirements by filing a Form 1041 Trust Income Tax Return and the associated Schedule K-1, which shows the Trust income and capital gain distributed to each beneficiary. The beneficiaries are then responsible for reporting these Trust distributions on their own Form 1040 Individual Income Tax Returns.

If the beneficiary is designated to receive *only income* from the Trust, the same IRS tax reporting rules apply.

Beneficial Interest

If all of the beneficiaries act together as trustees, there should never be a challenge to the Trust administration, since any challenge would only be to themselves. Thus, it is preferable to have all of the beneficiaries act as co-trustees. I believe there is security in numbers—the more involved the beneficiaries are in the Trust, the more certain the spouses can be that their wishes for the allocation and distribution of their estate assets will ultimately be fulfilled in the manner that they originally intended for the heirs.

The successor trustees of the Trust should openly communicate with the beneficiaries

TABLE 17-2
SAMPLE DISTRIBUTION OF A $1.2 MILLION ESTATE AT ATTAINED AGES

AMOUNT REMAINING IN ESTATE

Year	Child A	Child B	Child C	Child D	Comments
1	$300,000	$300,000	$300,000	$300,000	
2	$330,000 less: **($110,000)** $220,000	$330,000	$330,000	$330,000	Child A turns 25 and receives ⅓ of her share.
3	$242,000	$363,000 less: **($121,000)** $242,000	$363,000	$ 363,000	Child B turns 25 and receives ⅓ of his share.
4	$266,000	$266,000	$399,000 less: **($133,000)** $266,000	$399,000	Child C turns 25 and receives ⅓ of his share.
5	$293,000	$293,000	$293,000	$439,000	
6	$322,000	$322,000	$322,000	$483,000	
7	$354,000 less: **($177,000)** $177,000	$354,000	$354,000	$531,000	Child A turns 30 and receives ½ of amount left in her share.
8	$195,000	$390,000 less: **($195,000)** $195,000	$389,000	$584,000	Child B turns 30 and receives ½ of amount left in his share.
9	$215,000	$215,000	$428,000 less: **($214,000)** $214,000	$642,000	Child C turns 30 and receives ½ of amount left in his share.
10	$237,000	$237,000	$235,000	$706,000 less: **($235,000)** $471,000	Child D turns 25 and receives ⅓ of her share.

Note: Account balances are rounded off to simplify this illustration. This example assumes that each investment grows 10% annually and that distributions are made at ages 25, 30, and 35.

(who often are not the trustees). Time and again, it has been shown that the more information provided to the beneficiaries, the more comfortable they feel about the Trust administration and that their interests are not being slighted. Thus, I recommend that the succes-sor trustees consciously strive to provide the beneficiaries with as much information as possible.

To avoid future problems, let me make one final recommendation. When it comes time to make the final distribution to each beneficiary, the trustee(s) should ask each beneficiary to formally sign off on the receipt of their final distribution and state that the beneficiary is satisfied that he or she has received their specified share of the Trust.

Final Distribution If Outright upon Death of Second Spouse

Upon the death of the surviving spouse, the entire Trust is irrevocable; all of the sub-trusts—the A, B, and/or C sub-trusts—are now cast in concrete. Since a Trust identification number was previously obtained for the decedent's B sub-trust and/or the C sub-trust, that same identification number can be used for the second spouse's A sub-trust. Once the four-month Notice to Creditors period has elapsed, all of the remaining estate assets can be distributed to the beneficiaries.

If all of the assets are being distributed outright, you do not need to file a Form 1041 Trust Income Tax Return or the associated Schedule K-1 for the assets in the survivor's A sub-trust. The Trust income and any capital gains earned will be reported on a final Form 1040 Individual Income Tax Return filed for the second spouse. However, if you retain any income in the Trust, you must file a Form 1041 Trust Income Tax Return and a Schedule K-1 to show any income, capital gains, and any distributions for the assets in the B sub-trust and/or C sub-trust for that part of the year prior to the second spouse's death. Once the estate assets have been distributed to the beneficiaries, the beneficiaries will report any income and capital gains on their Form 1040 Individual Income Tax Returns.

If estate assets must be retained in the Trust for distribution at a later date, you can use the same Trust identification number for the second spouse's A sub-trust as you used for the first spouse's B sub-trust and/or C sub-trust. Upon the death of the second spouse, the original Trust identification number now applies to the entire Trust. I continually hear of instances where an attorney or an accountant requests a Trust identification number for each sub-trust. Such action is entirely unnecessary and complicates Trust administration. When there are three separate Trust identification numbers, you must file three separate Form 1041 Trust Income Tax Returns and associated Schedule K-1s. Technically and legally, there is nothing wrong with such an approach—it is just overkill!

SIMULTANEOUS DEATH

The simultaneous death of husband and wife creates a unique situation. Legally, a simultaneous death occurs either when both spouses die at the same time (e.g., in an automobile accident) or, more technically speaking, when one spouse dies within nine months of the other. If the estate assets are designated to be distributed outright to the beneficiaries, then such assets may be distributed almost immediately to the named beneficiaries (following the four-month Notice to Creditors time period). The final Form 1040 Individual Income Tax Return filed for the decedents would report any Trust income for the part of the year before the simultaneous death. Any Trust income received after the death of the spouses would be passed on to the beneficiaries and recognized on their Form 1040 Individual Income Tax Returns.

In the case of simultaneous death, it is not usually necessary to file a Form 1041 Trust Income Tax Return and associated Schedule K-1, unless assets must be retained in the Trust. You would also not have to allocate the Trust assets to the ledger accounts for the A, B, and/or C sub-trusts, since all of the sub-trusts are now irrevocable.

The simultaneous death of a husband and wife poses an interesting estate tax problem. If the value of the estate of both husband and wife exceeds the current value of one federal estate tax exemption, it is essential that the heirs play the game by the rules—*exactly.* You must take the following steps in order to preserve the federal estate tax exemption for each spouse. If the successor trustees (usually the heirs) fail to take the following actions, the IRS can deny the use of one of the spouse's federal estate tax exemptions!

- Submit Form SS-4 to request a tax identification number for the Trust, if this was not done when the Trust was created.

- File a Form 1041 Trust Income Tax Return, along with the associated Schedule K-l.
- Obtain a valuation of all of the estate assets.
- Allocate the assets to the ledger accounts for the A sub-trust and the B sub-trust to establish the portion exempt from federal estate taxes for each spouse. (Since both spouses died at the same time, the C sub-trust is of no use.)

If the successor trustees fail to complete these steps when both spouses die simultaneously, the end result can be very costly. Failure to follow these steps can drastically reduce the value of the estate passed to the beneficiaries.

If the value of the estate exceeds two federal estate tax exemptions, then estate taxes are due. You must file a Form 706 Federal Estate Tax Return and pay the estate taxes owed within nine months following the date of the death of the second spouse. (Similar inheritance tax filings may be necessary if the deceased spouse's state of residence requires the payment of state inheritance taxes.) You may not elect the C sub-trust (QTIP Trust) if both spouses die within nine months of each other.

DISSOLUTION OF THE TRUST

Once all of the estate assets have been distributed from the Trust (i.e., nothing is left in the Trust), the Trust dissolves automatically. There is nothing further that the successor trustees need to do legally to dissolve (or terminate) the Trust. Since the Trust has done its job, it can be thrown in the wastebasket or put up on a shelf. However, I heartily recommend that you retain (for five years) the entire Trust document and all its ancillary documents, along with all of the records of the actions that the trustees have taken, in order to protect the trustees (and the heirs' inheritance) in case the IRS or a beneficiary has questions in the future. Keeping these documents is not only fiscally wise, but also common sense. A prudent person would retain the Trust and its accompanying documents for ten years.

You do not have to notify the IRS when the Trust is terminated. However, you need to be aware that the following year you will probably receive a letter from the IRS stating that a Form 1041 Trust Income Tax Return was not filed for the current tax year. Don't be alarmed; the IRS takes this action all the time. If you receive such a letter, simply write across the face of the "Failure to File 1041" notification "The Trust has been terminated and all assets distributed," and return the notice to the IRS. When successor trustees file the last Form 1041 tax return (when no further assets remain in the Trust and the Trust has been dissolved), they often write "FINAL RETURN" at the top of the Form 1041 to alert the IRS that no further returns will be submitted. However, such action does not guarantee that the IRS will not send out the "Failure to File 1041" notification the following year.

18

Use the Right Strategy
Insurance Preservation Trust

When you play a game, the idea is to win—to outwit or outplay your opponent—and the same can be said of your estate. If you plan ahead and use the right strategy, you can win the game, thus preserving your hard-earned estate from the ravages of federal estate taxes. However, having the proper strategy does little good if it is not carried out correctly.

Half of the battle in estate planning is to be prepared—to anticipate what can and will happen to your estate upon your demise and what you can do to preserve your hard-earned estate for your family or friends. If you are unprepared, all of the assets that you have worked to attain throughout your lifetime are placed in jeopardy.

In the mid-1970s, a magnificent racehorse won two of the Triple Crown races. The horse suddenly became very valuable, and the owners (a husband and wife) received enormous press coverage. About three months later, both the husband and wife were killed in a terrible accident. Following the untimely deaths, the press focused on the surviving daughter, who was an only child.

In spite of the daughter's grief over losing her parents, there was a silver lining. The young lady had inherited the valuable racehorse and was now the sole owner.

Some eight months following the death of her parents, the daughter was told what the estate taxation would be on her parents' estate—and she was absolutely stunned! There was almost no liquidity in the parents' estate, and the daughter was forced to sell "most" of the horse to a group of thirty-four investors in order to pay the estate taxes (which she had not anticipated). Instead of a sizable inheritance, the daughter ended up with only a minuscule one thirty-fifth interest in the magnificent racehorse.

This sad story has long influenced my life and my efforts to guide people through the estate-planning maze, helping people to preserve their estates from being almost obliterated just to pay estate taxes.

Even if people develop a good strategy for handling their estates, it is often left to the surviving children to carry out the game plan laid out for them by their parents. Unfortunately, the survivors much too often do not follow the game plan, which results in disastrous consequences for the estate.

Charles and Emily Thornton had built up an estate of about $3 million. The husband and wife recognized their mortality, and they planned and took steps to preserve their estate for their son and daughter, James and Martha. Charles and Emily anticipated that federal estate taxes (and state inheritance taxes) would consume about one-third of their estate—approximately $1 million. Therefore, as part of the planning process, the Thorntons took out a $1 million life insurance policy on their lives with the children named as the beneficiaries of the policy. The Thorntons' insurance agent arranged that the children would purchase the insurance policy with annual gifts made to each child by the parents—a procedure that satisfied all IRS requirements. When the parents died, the children would receive sufficient funds from the insurance policy to pay the estate taxes on their parents' estate.

Years passed, and eventually Charles, and then Emily, died. Following Emily's death, the insurance company paid off the $1 million insurance policy to the children—$500,000 to James and $500,000 to Martha. However, by the time the parents died, both children were married and had their own families. The sudden influx of such large sums of money came as a great boon to the young families; it was an unexpected windfall. The two married children were aware that they would eventually have to pay estate taxes on their parents' estate, but neither child believed that the estate taxes would be anything close to $1 million!

Several months passed, and the two young families had almost completely spent the insurance funds on their own needs and desires. Then the inevitable happened. The parents' attorney advised the children that the estate taxes were due—"next month"—in the amount of $1 million! The children were shocked and dismayed. The estate of their parents lacked liquidity (i.e., did not contain

assets, such as stocks, bonds, or mutual funds, that could be quickly and easily sold). The children faced a massive tax bill and had only thirty days in which to raise almost the entire sum of money! You can imagine the unfortunate consequences. The estate was liquidated to pay the estate taxes. With so little time in which to sell, the assets were sacrificed for only a small part of their true worth.

What a sad ending to a well-thought-out estate plan. The children ruined the inheritance that their parents had tried to leave them. Unfortunately, similar stories are all too common. Few people can really imagine just how devastating estate taxes can be to the value of an estate. If the parents were smart enough to plan ahead and to provide adequate liquidity for the estate taxes (which is a fairly rare occurrence), the children are utterly stunned when they eventually learn of the estate tax consequences.

Developing a sound estate preservation strategy means knowing how the game is to be played—and then leave nothing to chance, especially if the surviving children don't use the strategy or game plan set up for them by the parents. Concerned parents can take additional steps to ensure that their hard-earned estate is not decimated to almost oblivion by federal estate taxes, regardless of the actions (or inactions) taken by the surviving children.

Edward and Barbara Houston also did some estate planning. The Houstons had spent their lives building an estate of $3.5 million, and they desired to preserve their estate for their three children, Mary, Susan, and Jonathan. The Houstons also took out a life insurance policy on their lives in the amount of $1.5 million to be used for paying federal estate taxes. However, the Houstons took an important additional step: They established an Insurance Preservation Trust and named this Trust as the beneficiary of the insurance policy. Each child was named as a trustee of the Insurance Preservation Trust, as well as an equal beneficiary of the Trust. In addition, the Houstons also made sure that they jumped through all of the appropriate legal hoops to satisfy the IRS requirements for an Insurance Preservation Trust.

The Insurance Preservation Trust specified that the insurance funds must be held in trust for ten months following the death of the second spouse. Even though the three children were the trustees of the Insurance Preservation Trust, they could not use those funds for personal purposes for ten crucial months. The Trust specified that nine months following the death of the second spouse, the children, as trustees of the Insurance Preservation Trust, were authorized to use the insurance funds to buy assets worth $1.5 million from their parent's Living Trust and then use those funds to pay the estate taxes.

At the end of the ten-month period, the estate assets in the Insurance Preservation Trust would be distributed equally to the three children.

There is a right way to plan to preserve your estate, and there is a wrong way. You should always take the wise and safe steps to preserve your hard-earned estate for your loved ones.

DEATH (AND TAXES) ARE INEVITABLE

Death is undeniably inevitable—life is but a temporary condition. However, taxes have a slightly different fate.

- Estates can be ruined by the payment of unnecessary estate taxes.
- Proper estate planning can minimize estate taxes.
- Proper estate planning can ensure that any estate taxes are paid without depleting the estate.
- Insurance is the cheapest way to pay for estate taxes.
- The value of insurance usually increases the value of your estate.

If the value of your estate exceeds the current value of allowable federal estate tax exemption(s), federal estate taxes will eventually be due. Federal estate taxes are confiscatory and can all too easily decimate an estate.

Many times, I have heard someone say, "My estate is large enough to pay the estate taxes and still leave sufficient assets for my heirs." However, this somewhat cavalier approach assumes that there is sufficient *liquidity* in the estate assets so that the estate taxes can be paid when due. In truth, most estates are built by investing most, if not all, of the assets in hard assets (such as a house, a business, or other real estate). When a trustee must sell such assets to satisfy estate taxes, the sale is often forced and hurried—and usually results in liquidation with the estate having to settle for pennies on the dollar.

You must recognize that Uncle Sam is in business with you. When you die and step out of the picture, Uncle Sam wants his share—and he wants it now! Far too frequently, the consequence is that estates must liquidate assets for pennies on the dollar in order to pay the estate taxes. Although there are sophisticated solutions (such as using a Family Limited Partnership, a Charitable Remainder Trust, or various irrevocable Trusts), most people don't want to stress their imaginations by getting involved in sophisticated techniques for protecting their estates from onerous federal estate taxes. For most people facing the eventual confiscation of their estate by estate taxes, the easiest tactic is to pay estate taxes with life insurance proceeds.

PAY ESTATE TAXES WITH INSURANCE

Life insurance is an inexpensive solution to paying federal estate taxes while at the same time preserving what you have spent a lifetime building for your heirs. By using the proceeds from a life insurance policy to pay federal estate taxes, you are effectively only paying "pennies on the dollar" for the estate taxes. When the heirs use life insurance to pay the estate taxes, they receive the *full benefit* of the estate assets passed on to them—rather than receiving only about 50 percent of the estate value.

The type of insurance most often used to pay estate taxes is called whole life insurance. If you have built your estate so well that you are facing the eventual need to pay federal estate taxes, then you need permanent insurance to meet a permanent need. Purchasing the proper type of whole life insurance results in the lowest overall cost of the insurance, because the premium does not increase as your age advances.

If an individual is single, the insurance is written on the life of the single individual. When the person dies, the insurance proceeds are used to pay the federal estate taxes, allowing the heirs to receive the full value of estate assets. Typically, such insurance should cost only about ten to fifteen cents on the dollar, assuming that the individual is in fair health and is not extremely elderly. Insurance companies have come a long way in the past two decades in evaluating the life expectancy of individuals who are on a course of medication or are following an appropriate exercise routine.

A husband and wife will typically purchase joint and survivor life insurance or "second to die" life insurance. This type of life insurance is payable only upon the death of the *second* spouse. Using this type of life insurance to pay federal estate taxes should cost only about five to ten cents on the dollar. By using "second to die" insurance, one spouse can be in poor health and still obtain life insurance at a reasonable rate, since the insurance company is really looking at the health of the marital partner who has the longest life expectancy.

I continue to run across individuals who say, "I'm going to spend it all before I die, so I won't have any estate taxes to pay." My response is the same as that of many financial planners: "If you know when you are going to die, I can tell you how much money to spend each year." None of us knows when we are going to die— and the older we get, the more conservative we become in wanting to preserve our estate for our own use, in the event that we live to a ripe old age. Unfortunately, none of us has a crystal ball that can foretell an untimely accident or the sudden onset of an unexpected terminal illness. Therefore, the best defense is to be prepared for any eventuality.

Exclude Life Insurance from Your Estate

You need to be acutely aware, however, that the face amount of any life insurance owned by the husband or wife must be included in the value of the estate when computing federal estate taxes! Thus, if you already have a sizable estate and purchase life insurance to eventually pay your estate taxes, you have also increased the size of your estate—so Uncle Sam wants a bigger bite from the estate for taxes.

If you are single, you are looking at a federal estate taxation rate of 37 percent to 55 percent, not only on your estate assets, but also on the value of any life insurance. If you are married, you are looking at a federal estate taxation rate of 40 percent to 55 percent on your estate assets, including any life insurance. For example, if you are married and have an estate worth $2 million, estate taxes will be imposed at the rate of 40 percent. In addition, if you held insurance in the amount of $500,000, 50 percent ($250,000) would go to Uncle Sam— and that is certainly not the reason why you purchased your life insurance.

Many people believe that they can exclude life insurance from their estates by making their children the owners and beneficiaries of the parents' life insurance. The insured (the parents) pay to the children each year an amount equal to the insurance premiums. The children then pay the insurance premiums, and eventually the children receive the death benefit from the life insurance (with which to supposedly pay the estate taxes). Yes, such an approach can work to exclude life insurance from the parents' estate—but *only* if both the parents and the children take certain steps. (You will learn more about these steps later on in this chapter.)

Many parents are shocked by the potential federal estate tax bill that will be due when the second spouse dies. Unfortunately, all too often, the children (even though grown adults) cannot begin to even imagine the huge amount of their parents' estate that can be eaten away by the pernicious federal estate tax. Sadly, most children think that most of the insurance money is really theirs to spend—and they are usually stunned when they finally learn (usually during the seventh or eighth month after their last parent has died) the staggering amount of federal estate taxes that is due within only a month or two.

In the interim, the children have been the recipients of a vast sum of money that too often proves to be a tempting remedy to solve their own immediate family financial needs. The children often spend the insurance funds on their own families, since they cannot comprehend the extent to which Uncle Sam makes claim to their parents' estate. Sadly, when it finally comes time to pay those enormous estate taxes, much of the insurance funds have already been spent, and the estate must now be partially or fully liquidated (i.e., assets sold off at pennies on the dollar) in order to raise the necessary estate tax money. What a shame!

However, don't give up hope. There *is* a way to keep the life insurance value from being included in the value of your estate—a way that is better, safer, and much simpler. The solution is to properly utilize an irrevocable Insurance Preservation Trust, which is specifically designed to exclude the insurance from being included in the value of your estate, thus preserving your estate.

Insurance Preservation Trust

The Insurance Preservation Trust, funded with life insurance, is the most common and least sophisticated vehicle used to pay estate taxes without depleting estate assets. When you purchase insurance to pay your federal and state taxes, you are essentially paying only pennies on the dollar, since the life insurance proceeds are the funds used to pay the estate taxes. When the life insurance is placed in the Insurance Preservation Trust—which is an irrevocable Trust—it is excluded from being subject to federal estate taxes (and possible state inheritance taxes as well). The use of an Insurance Preservation Trust is explained in great detail in my first book, *The Living Trust*.

Let me share with you some key observa-

tions that I hope can help you to prevent disastrous consequences. Obviously, the IRS would like to defeat the Insurance Preservation Trust, since the IRS would generate substantially more money in federal estate taxes. If you have an Insurance Preservation Trust or are considering one as part of your estate planning, you need to avoid any potential weaknesses that would enable your Trust to be attacked by the IRS.

- You (as an individual) or you and your spouse (as a married couple) should not be the trustees of the Insurance Preservation Trust. If you are the trustees, the IRS will challenge your Trust on the basis that you are not at "arm's length." A logical choice would be to name the beneficiaries of the Insurance Preservation Trust (usually your heirs) as trustees.

- Do not name your Living Trust as a beneficiary or contingent beneficiary of your Insurance Preservation Trust. If you do, the IRS will challenge your Insurance Preservation Trust, citing that you have too much freedom to change the ultimate beneficiaries of your Trust. Typically, your children are named as the beneficiaries of the Insurance Preservation Trust, and therefore, it is logical for you to also name your children as trustees.

- If you are paying the premiums for the insurance policy, as is usually the case, you must *carefully* follow the directions for utilizing the Crummey provision, which ensures that the IRS will deem that the money used for paying the insurance premiums is truly a *gift* to the children (and that it is the children who are ultimately paying the premium with these gifts). The Crummey provision is explained in greater detail in the latest revision of my first book, *The Living Trust*.

Ten-Month Waiting Period

Typically, an Insurance Preservation Trust names your children as the trustees and as the beneficiaries. If the Trust is properly drawn, it should specify that the children shall not receive any Trust funds for their personal use until ten months following the date of death of an individual (if single) or the date of death of the second spouse (if married).

You may be wondering why the waiting period is ten months, given that taxes are due within nine months and the life insurance proceeds are paid out almost immediately after the death of the insured. The reason is that a well-written Insurance Preservation Trust specifies that the life insurance proceeds be retained in the Trust until the funds are needed to pay for the estate tax liability. No Trust funds are available to the beneficiaries for their personal use until *after* the estate taxes have been paid. This requirement prevents the situation where the children use the insurance proceeds for their own immediate benefits, instead of using them to pay the federal estate taxes (as the parents had originally intended). Federal estate taxes are due within nine months following the date of death. Just before the time that the federal estate taxes are due, the trustees simply transfer an appropriate value of assets from the deceased person(s) Living Trust to the Insurance Preservation Trust in exchange for the dollars in the Insurance Preservation Trust. The Insurance Preservation Trust thus purchases the estate assets at their actual value, rather than at a highly discounted liquidated value. The trustee(s) of the Living Trust then use these dollars to pay the federal estate tax liability. When the ten-month period has elapsed and the estate taxes have been paid, the estate assets transferred into the Insurance Preservation Trust flow, unencumbered, to the beneficiaries.

Using an Existing Insurance Policy

If you are considering putting an existing insurance policy in the Insurance Preservation Trust (instead of buying a new insurance policy), you should be very aware of the consequences. If you put an existing insurance policy into your Insurance Preservation Trust, you are effectively gifting that policy (from your estate to the Insurance Preservation Trust). If you die within three years of making such a gift, the IRS deems that you made the gift "in antici-

pation of death" and will immediately add the face value of the insurance policy back into your estate for estate tax purposes!

A Word of Caution: If you use an existing insurance policy to fund the Insurance Preservation Trust, you must make any such transfer three years prior to the death of the insured in order to satisfy the IRS rule regarding "gifts in anticipation of death."

Simplicity of Using an Insurance Preservation Trust

The proper use of an Insurance Preservation Trust also simplifies payment of the insurance premiums. Instead of having to make out separate checks to each beneficiary annually and then relying on the beneficiaries to pay the insurance premium in a timely manner, you need only open one checking account for the insurance policy premiums and then annually deposit one check sufficient to pay for the insurance premium into this special checking account. Then you utilize the Crummey provision (regarding gifts) to effectively pass the gifted insurance premium funds to your children, who then pay the insurance company.

After you have deposited the gifts for insurance premium funds in the bank account, the children are authorized to withdraw those funds from the account if they so desire. This authority satisfies the Crummey provision requirement for the IRS. If the children do not withdraw the funds, the funds are then used to pay the insurance company for the insurance premium—and the children, technically, have thus paid the insurance premium. This approach takes advantage of the $10,000 gift exclusion from income taxes, but you avoid having to pay the funds to each child separately.

The Insurance Preservation Trust is a win-win solution, and everyone gets his or her share. The federal government receives any federal estate taxes due (and, where appropriate, the state government receives any state inheritance taxes due), and the estate is preserved for the beneficiaries.

19

Summary

Settling an Estate

It is one thing to have a Living Trust, but it is quite another to have your Living Trust function properly for you. Many people have adopted the Living Trust as the vehicle to protect their estates and themselves if they were to become incompetent, to protect their estates upon their deaths for their beloved spouses, and, ultimately, to protect their estates for their children and/or grandchildren. However, far too many people have been abandoned after having created their Living Trusts. The people received a Living Trust but no guidance in what to do with it—especially when it came time to settle their estates. In effect, many people are left pondering a dilemma: "I have a Living Trust, but what do I do now?"

In writing this book, I have tried to provide you with those answers. Unfortunately, when taken as a whole, the process can seem quite complicated. In actual practice, however, it is not difficult to settle an estate in a Living Trust. Let me summarize for you the steps your surviving trustee or your successor trustee(s) need to take in the event of your incompetency or death. Remember, you don't need an attorney; the trustee simply needs to follow some basic steps.

WITHOUT A LIVING TRUST

Let me share with you several stories of estates that did not have Living Trusts—and the costly results of such an omission.

The Check for $193,000

Years ago a woman came up to me just before the start of a seminar and handed me a photocopy of a check for $193,000 written to the IRS. Below the copy of the check were the handwritten words "Warning: This is what happens with no estate planning."

As we talked, I learned that her mother had died ten months before, and her father had died the previous year. Since the woman's parents lacked a Trust, all of the assets flowed to the mother upon the father's death, thus throwing away his federal estate tax exemption. Then, when the mother died, she had only one federal estate tax exemption (her own) with which to offset the value of the estate. As a result of losing the father's federal estate tax exemption, the daughter had to pay $193,000 to the IRS—money taken from the estate (and the daughter's inheritance). Had the woman's parents had a Living Trust, both federal estate tax exemptions (for the husband

287

and the wife) would have been preserved, and no estate taxes would have been due.

This story should serve as a reminder of a very costly lesson, one that so many children learn after it is too late. Every person should be able to use the rights that the government has determined are rightfully available. It is important to remember, however, that each of us has the right to preserve our share of our estate by utilizing our federal estate tax exemption, but if we don't elect to use it (by utilizing a Married A-B Trust), then we lose it.

Estate of William Harrah

William Harrah was well known for his large casino hotels in Reno, South Lake Tahoe, and Las Vegas. He was also known for his restoration of hundreds of antique cars.

Mr. Harrah died, leaving an estate of approximately $120 million in a Testamentary Trust for the benefit of his children. However, with the Testamentary Trust there was the problem of paying federal estate taxes and settling the estate (since the assets first had to go through probate before being placed in the Trust). Naturally, the government received a substantial share of the estate, as did the attorneys who worked so hard to settle it. In the end, the children received only about $20 million!

Although $20 million is still a lot of money, the children were denied a large part of their inheritance. Ending up with about $100 million less than what the estate started with following Mr. Harrah's death is a devastating price to pay for ignorance or lack of action.

Estate of Jacqueline Kennedy Onassis

Jacqueline Kennedy Onassis was probably one of the most private individuals in the public spotlight during our time. She could afford the best attorneys—and engaged them. I'm sure she stressed her desire for continued privacy to these attorneys. In response, however, her attorneys wrote only a Testamentary Trust—wherein all assets must go through probate before being placed in the Trust and thus are open to public scrutiny.

What a shame that Mrs. Onassis's desires were not carried out. Today, as I mentioned in Chapter 2, anyone may view her most private desires by looking up her Testamentary Trust on the Internet. You can even go to the county court office in the New York City borough and look up the actual financial data on her estate.

This lack of privacy was absolutely unnecessary. A Living Trust would have given Mrs. Onassis all of the privacy that she desired.

The Milkman

George Henley delivered milk daily for thirty years in the California cities of Riverside and Anaheim. Between those two cities lay many small farms that were eventually gobbled up by the expanding urban population. Over time, as George traveled his route and saved his money, he bought those small farms one by one. Thirty years later, when George retired, he had sold most of his farms for redevelopment and had an estate worth $6 million.

George started his Living Trust but died suddenly of a massive heart attack ten days later—before he had signed and notarized his Living Trust, steps that were necessary to have made it a legal document.

George's intention of getting a Living Trust was correct but, unfortunately, did him no good. The probate courts are littered with well-meaning intentions, and George was one of those cases.

The Waiter's Story

Roger Harrison recently waited on our table. He was very friendly and inquired about my line of work. I briefly told him, and he responded, "I know all about the Living Trust—and I would never want one." At this response, I perked up my ears, curious to hear more. He told me that his grandparents had built a very successful restaurant in Reno and later opened up two more restaurants in Las Vegas. The grandparents eventually sold these very profitable restaurants and retired. Roger's grandparents had passed away some twenty years ago, leaving $8 million in a Living Trust—with one of the nation's largest banks as trustee.

Roger said that each year he would receive financial statements from the bank advising him that the estate had lost around $250,000. This scenario had continued each year until the present time. Roger said only a small amount was left, and he was disappointed—not for himself, but for his parents, who could really use the money. I asked Roger what he meant by "a small amount," and Roger replied "$50,000." I had to agree with him that it was a small amount indeed to remain from an estate once worth $8 million!

The problem was *not* the Living Trust but the financial institution that was managing it (or *not* managing it). What a terrible waste—and yet another example of why I urge you to consider a financial institution as trustee only as a last resort!

EVERYONE NEEDS A *GOOD* LIVING TRUST

With a well-written Living Trust, you can avoid the agony of probate and pass on most or all of your estate assets to your heirs in complete privacy.

You Need a Good Living Trust with Your Assets Placed Therein

You need a good Living Trust in order to preserve the federal estate tax exemption for both spouses; to avoid the time, cost, and agony of probate; and to provide privacy for your estate. Throughout the chapters of this book, I have often referred to the need for a *good* Living Trust that incorporates all of the necessary contingency provisions. Certainly, no one will use all of the contingency provisions, but everyone will eventually find a need—expected or unexpected—for some of them. Having a good Living Trust prepares you for meeting almost any unexpected event.

However, even the best Living Trust is useless unless you have placed *all* of your assets inside the Trust. Even an inadvertent slip of omitting just one asset from your Trust can force the expensive and undesirable conse-

quences of probate. Therefore, I again urge you to make certain that all of your assets are placed in your Living Trust by transferring the title of each asset into the name of your Living Trust.

Organize Your Estate and Advise Your Successor Trustees Where Your Trust Is Kept

Organize your estate. The Estate Plan Binder, as described in my first book, *The Living Trust*, is a perfect example of how to accomplish this task simply and easily.

Equally important, however, is for you to tell your successor trustees where you keep your Living Trust. Your successor trustees don't need to read or know the contents of your Living Trust while you are maintaining it. You may desire to change your Trust in time, and you don't need to consult with your successor trustees or beneficiaries. However, you do need to keep your successor trustees advised of where you keep your Trust so that they can find it in time of need.

Avoid "Living Probate"

There is nothing worse than becoming incompetent and having to rely upon the courts to see to your needs—a process called "Living Probate." You can avoid this humiliating and degrading process by having a good Living Trust. However, you must also have, in effect and current, all of the appropriate ancillary documents such as the Durable Power of Attorney for Health Care, the Durable Power of Attorney for General Assets, the Competency Clause, the Nomination of Conservator/ Guardian provision, and the Living Will (the Right-to-Die Clause). These ancillary documents identify whom you want to provide for your personal needs and to see that your assets are used, as you would so desire, to provide for your future financial needs.

You Must Have a Good Trustee

To assure the proper administration of your Living Trust, you need to have good trustees— one or more persons whom you trust. The obvious first choice is your spouse. However, if your spouse is neither living nor competent, you need someone else whom you trust. I recommend that you choose one or more of your adult children, close family members, or close friends.

Remember, also, that there is security in numbers. You should therefore consider naming more than one successor trustee, all of whom must "act in concert" (agree) when dealing with matters pertaining to your Trust.

Incompetency or Inability to Serve as Trustee

If you feel it appropriate to surrender your responsibility as trustee, you may do so. Preferably, you could ask in writing for the surviving trustee or the successor trustee(s) to act with you. In this manner, you could rely on someone to do the work, and you could then co-sign the results.

Remember, if you resign as trustee, the successor trustee(s) must obtain a Trust identification number as if the Trust were irrevocable. Also, the surviving trustee or successor trustee(s) must also annually file a Form 1041 Trust Income Tax Return, along with the appropriate Schedule K-1.

Guardianship Documents and Separate Property Agreements

Guardianship documents can provide for your minor or handicapped children. Separate Property Agreements ensure that your assets will be used as you so desire.

UPON THE DEATH OF THE FIRST SPOUSE

Typically, the surviving spouse has the right to all income, the right to the principal as necessary to maintain the same standard of living, and the annual frivolous right of $5,000 or 5 percent of the estate value. Unless restrictions have been placed on the decedent's share of the assets, the surviving spouse essentially has the right to use the assets in the decedent's B sub-trust and/or C sub-trust without any restriction.

Upon the death of the first spouse, you need to take the necessary steps to preserve both federal estate tax exemptions. Failure to accomplish these steps will seriously affect the future imposition of estate taxes:

- Open a separate bank account, to be used exclusively for all Trust transactions of the decedent's B sub-trust and/or C sub-trust.
- File a Notice to Creditors to effectively forestall any unexpected claims against the estate. You should file this form with the appropriate county clerk within six weeks following the date of death. Each state has its own form. Even where such a form is not authorized, I still recommend that you publish it as a preventive measure.
- File a Form SS-4 to obtain a Trust identification number for the decedent's irrevocable B sub-trust and/or C sub-trust.
- Do not file a Form 56.
- File a Form 1040 Individual Income Tax Return for the deceased individual.
- Preferably, income should be distributed to the beneficiary, so that it is taxed at the beneficiary's tax rate (and not at the often higher Trust tax rate).
- File a Form 1041 Trust Income Tax Return, along with the accompanying Schedule K-1s (showing the individuals to whom the Trust income was distributed).
- Obtain written valuation of the real assets (the home, other real estate, stocks, bonds, mutual funds, and so on) as soon as possible after the date of death.
- Allocate the assets to the A, B, and/or C sub-trusts utilizing the ledger method.
- Do not change title of the real assets. For securities that are placed in the decedent's B sub-trust and/or C sub-trust, ask the brokerage firm to simply identify them as assets being placed in a separate account called Account B and to use the surviving spouse's social security number on the new account.
- Determine whether your state imposes an inheritance tax. If it does, pay any such taxes within nine months of the date of death.
- Determine whether there are any bequests or distributions to be made upon the death of the first spouse. After four months, distribute the appropriate assets, preferably in kind, to the beneficiaries.
- Search for a Memorandum to determine whether there are specific personal effects to be distributed to designated individuals.
- Consider using a financial investment manager to assist in managing the estate assets.

- Provide the appropriate information, particularly an annual financial statement, to the remainder beneficiaries. (This requirement can be satisfied by giving each beneficiary a copy of the Form 1041 Trust Income Tax Return and the associated Schedule K-1.)
- Determine whether the decedent's share of assets exceeds one federal estate tax exemption. If so, within nine months of the date of death, file a Form 706, Schedule R, Estate Tax Return to elect the QTIP Trust and also to elect the generation-skipping tax exemption for the decedent.

UPON THE DEATH OF A SINGLE INDIVIDUAL OR THE SECOND SPOUSE (IF MARRIED)

Upon the death of a single person or the second spouse (if married), the estate will be concluded per se. Either the Trust assets will be distributed outright, or they will be retained in trust for the benefit of the beneficiaries.

Assets Distributed Outright

If the assets are to be distributed outright, you do not need to file a Form 1041 Trust Income Tax Return nor the accompanying Schedule K-1. Also, you do not need to file Form SS-4 to request a Trust identification number. Remember to take the following actions:

- Open a separate bank account, to be used exclusively for all Trust transactions.
- File a Notice to Creditors to effectively forestall any unexpected claims against the estate. You should file this form with the appropriate county clerk within six weeks following the date of death. Each state has its own form. Even where such a form is not authorized, I still recommend that you publish it as a preventive measure.
- File a Form 1040 Individual Income Tax Return for the deceased individual.
- Obtain written valuation of the real assets (i.e., the home, other real estate, stocks, bonds, mutual funds, and so on) as soon as possible after the date of death.
- Do not file a Form 56.
- If the value of the estate exceeds the allowed federal estate tax exemption, file a Form 706

Estate Tax Return and pay the appropriate estate taxes within nine months of the date of death.
- Determine whether your state imposes an inheritance tax. If it does, pay any such tax within nine months of the date of death.
- Provide an accounting to the beneficiaries and receive Receipt and Release.
- After four months (when the Notice to Creditors period has elapsed), distribute the assets, preferably in kind, to the beneficiaries.
- Search for a Memorandum to determine whether specific personal effects are to be distributed to designated individuals.
- Preferably, income should be distributed to the beneficiaries, so that it is taxed at the beneficiaries' tax rate (and not at the often higher Trust tax rate).
- The beneficiaries should report any income from the Trust on their own Form 1040 Individual Income Tax Returns.

Assets Retained in Trust

If assets are to be retained in trust, you must take the following additional steps:

- File a Form SS-4 to obtain a Trust identification number for the decedent's irrevocable Trust. (If you already have a Trust identification number for the B and/or C sub-trusts, use that same number for the entire Trust.)
- File a Form 1041 Trust Income Tax Return, along with the accompanying Schedule K-1s, showing the individuals to whom the Trust income was distributed.
- Do not file a Form 56.
- Consider using a financial investment manager to assist in managing the estate assets.
- Provide the appropriate information, particularly an annual financial statement, to the remainder beneficiaries.

UPON THE SIMULTANEOUS DEATH OF BOTH SPOUSES

If both spouses die simultaneously or both die within a nine-month period, and if the estate exceeds one federal estate tax exemption and the assets are to be distributed outright, the following steps must be taken to preserve both federal estate tax exemptions:

- File a Form SS-4 to obtain a Trust identification number for the decedents' irrevocable Trust.
- File a Form 1041 Trust Income Tax Return and the accompanying Schedule K-1.
- Do not file a Form 56.

UPON AN INDIVIDUAL'S DEATH

Upon the loss of a loved one, people tend to become mentally paralyzed. However, several important steps must be taken:

- Review personal data sheet.
- Attempt to determine the desire of the deceased individual regarding cremation or burial.
- Order at least a dozen death certificates.
- Check the safe-deposit box for documents and assets.
- Locate the Living Trust.
- Create an Affidavit of Death of Trustee to accompany the death certificate and the Living Trust—to be used when dealing with financial institutions.
- Create a Trust Certification form to accompany the Living Trust documents.
- Assign responsibilities, as detailed in Chapter 8.
- Locate any veteran's papers. If the deceased was a veteran, file the required paperwork to request the cemetery allowance, a burial flag, and a grave marker.
- Keep accurate records of the costs associated with the deceased person's last illness and funeral. These costs may be applied to offset income on either the deceased person's Form 1040 Individual Income Tax Return or the Form 706 Estate Tax Return.
- Identify which credit cards should be canceled and which ones, if any, should be retained.
- If the individual was receiving social security benefits, notify the Social Security Administration. Be sure to retain in the checking account any funds from future social security checks received (which eventually must be returned to the Social Secu-

rity Administration). If the surviving spouse is eligible for social security benefits, he or she should apply for them. The application requires a copy of the marriage certificate and death certificate of the deceased spouse. The Social Security Administration also provides a small burial benefit for the deceased.

- If the individual was receiving Medicaid, notify Medicaid that the individual has passed away.
- If the individual was employed, notify the employer's human resources department and find out what employee benefits are available.
- Notify the insurance companies that issued any annuities and insurance policies to the deceased person.
- Make sure that you remember to continue to pay the fire and theft insurance fees on the home and personal effects.
- Inventory and obtain a valuation of all estate assets—the real assets and the retirement assets but not the personal effects. Include bank and credit union accounts, securities, insurance, annuities, and real estate.
- Determine whether the deceased had any ownership in a business and, especially, if there is a Buy/Sell Agreement and whether the agreement is funded with life insurance.
- Allocate the assets to the ledger accounts for the A and B sub-trusts to establish the portion exempt from federal estate taxes for each spouse.

UPON THE DEATH OF A GAY OR LESBIAN PARTNER

Upon the death of a gay or lesbian partner, take the following steps:

- If there are separate Trusts for each individual, follow the steps previously specified in the section "Upon the Death of a Single Individual or the Second Spouse (If Married)" (page 291).
- If there is a joint A-B Trust for both partners, follow the steps itemized for death of the first spouse. If the decedent's assets exceed one federal estate tax exemption, file a Form 706

Federal Estate Tax Return and pay the federal estate taxes due. Form 706 will *not* be filed to elect the QTIP Trust.

CONCLUSION

If I can impart any message with this book, it is that settling an estate in a Living Trust is simple. Just follow the steps itemized in this chapter, which were explained more thoroughly in the previous chapters. In so doing, you will avoid the time, cost, and agony that so many Living Trust owners are now being unnecessarily subjected to by the Will and Probate attorneys who are attempting to settle existing Living Trusts. Life can be simple—if you know the rules of the game and the proper strategy. Like a good mariner, set your course and then follow it.

Remember: Settling an estate in a Living Trust is really quite simple. Family members can do it themselves at little or no cost—and with complete privacy.

—20—

Your Story
A Treasured Gift

When thinking about estate planning, we tend to think about the material and monetary aspects—how much of our estate is left to whom and how to minimize any potential tax consequences. Few people think about leaving a different kind of legacy to their children and grandchildren: the legacy of the written, spoken, or visual images that represent a lifetime of experiences, trials and tribulations, and love.

Please, give your heirs a treasured gift—a gift that only requires your time and little or no expense: the gift of your life's perspective, as only you know it. I strongly urge you to write, or at the very least record, your life story. Your children would like to know of your experiences—the good and the bad, the happy and the sad—and how you handled difficulties. As the years pass by and your children are confronted with similar situations, they can seek solace in knowing how you handled the good and the bad. What did you do? How did you handle various situations? What would you have done differently? Your grandchildren would like to know as well.

PERSONAL REFLECTIONS

Although my greatest joy is my wife and my children and my grandchildren, one of my great pleasures has been to race and sail all over the world. Knowing this tiny bit of information, you can imagine how I felt when I read a two-page summary written by my maternal grandfather about his life.

My Maternal Grandfather

In one paragraph of my grandfather's story, he wrote, "I left New York at the age of sixteen on a four-masted rigger, sailing around the Horn to San Francisco." Sadly, that's all he had written about the voyage!

My grandfather died when I was only four years old. How I would have loved to have had him elaborate upon his experiences at age 16, sailing on a four-masted schooner, and his experience sailing around Cape Horn, the southernmost tip of South America (long before the Panama Canal was dug). I would have read and reread that story. Obviously, I will never have such an opportunity.

My Paternal Grandparents

My aunt, who has long since passed away, did a wonderful job of writing about her mother and father, my paternal grandparents. From her writings, I learned that my grandparents were incredibly fine people, who, in the face of great adversity, chose honor over wealth. Their story has been a great influence on my life, and I have tried to model what I do after the way they handled their adversities.

My Father

I loved my father. He was a proud man but, unfortunately, not one taken to showing affection. My father died suddenly of a stroke when I was in my midthirties. I remember going to the funeral home, seeing my father lying in his casket, and wishing that I could have heard some last words from him. I later discovered writings of my father where it was very apparent how much he loved me as his son, but it just wasn't his nature to say that to me in real life. How I wish he had! How I wish he had left some audible message to me—a remembrance that I could return to again and again.

LEAVE AN EVERLASTING MESSAGE

You can give your children and grandchildren marvelous thrills and marvelous support by taking the time to write down, or otherwise record for posterity, your life history—not only about what you've done, but how you've dealt with the obstacles that you've encountered. Your children and grandchildren are likely to meet similar challenges as they grow and prosper. Your help and guidance on how to overcome life's real difficulties can be a wonderful benefit in smoothing out life's occasional bumpy times.

The Importance of the Spoken Word

I beseech you to leave at least a tape-recorded message to your children and grandchildren. Today, for many people, a videotape is the medium of choice, for you can be seen as well as heard. For many busy people, picking up an audiotape recorder and simply "talking" your life story and recollections is the easiest and least time-consuming option for leaving your legacy. However, whether your choice is videotape or audiotape is immaterial—it is the spoken word that can be so incredibly powerful. I know many surviving children who have listened, over and over, to a simple audiotape left to them by their parent or parents. It is the reassuring voice of a departed loved one that children most want to hear.

I know that most of us wish that we could go on living forever. However, neither you nor I have found the secret to immortality, and someday our time on this earth will end. I urge you to make time and take the opportunity to sit down and, at the very least, use a tape recorder to dictate a message of love, pride, and support to your children and grandchildren. Do this now, while you are still able, so that the day you step from this life (whether it be tomorrow, unexpectedly by accident, or thirty years from now when you are older, wizened, and wrinkled), you will have left your loved ones with a prized personal message that they can turn to from time to time—for comfort and solace or to bring back memories of happier times as a youth.

Leaving your family with such a legacy of written, spoken, or visual images is one of the greatest gifts that you can bestow. If you are married, I also urge you to leave a very special message to your loving spouse.

Part II

Advanced Estate Settlement Options Professionals Need to Know to Settle Your Living Trust

Financial and accounting professionals working in conjunction with surviving family members can settle highly valued and/or complex estates with minimal loss of the estate to income taxes and federal estate taxes. The following chapters describe the techniques that are appropriate for each particular estate.

—21—

Advanced Settlement Options
Know and Follow the Rules

Chapter 8 acquainted you with the basic concepts of settling an estate in a Living Trust but concentrated on the "average" estate with a value of less than $1.5 million. However, for more and more of the populace, the value of their estates is becoming far greater than people could imagine even only twenty years ago. With the ever-increasing value of real estate and the surprising growth in the value of IRAs and 401(k) plans due to the phenomenal growth of the stock market, many people find themselves in the awkward situation of having a highly valued estate but little or no idea of how to minimize the eventual federal estate tax liability that could so easily wipe out much of their children's inheritance.

This chapter will acquaint you with the following concepts that may apply to your estate if its value exceeds $2 million:

- QDOT Trust (where one spouse is not a citizen)
- Generation skip
- Generation-skipping exemption
- Reverse QTIP Provision
- Generation-Skipping Trust

MARRIED COUPLE WITH AN A-B-C TRUST

If a married couple has a Married A-B-C Trust, the first spouse dies, and the net estate value approaches or exceeds two federal estate tax exemptions (currently $1.25 million but rising to $2 million in the year 2006), the surviving spouse should file a Form 706 U.S. Estate (and Generation-Skipping Transfer) Tax Return, even though no federal estate taxes should be due upon the death of the first spouse. Form 706 should be filed in order to elect the QTIP or QDOT Trust and also to preserve the decedent's generation-skipping exemption. The QTIP and QDOT Trusts, as well as a discussion about generation-skipping exemptions and Generation-Skipping Trusts, are covered more fully later on in this chapter. Figure 21-1 (on page 300) provides an example of a Form 706 Federal Estate Tax Return (Schedule R), showing the QTIP election and the generation-skipping exemption.

Upon the death of the *surviving* spouse, if the net value of the estate in the survivor's A sub-trust and the first decedent's C sub-trust exceeds one federal estate tax exemption

299

FIGURE 21-1

FORM 706 FEDERAL ESTATE TAX RETURN WITH QTIP TRUST ELECTION AND GENERATION-SKIPPING TRANSFER TAX EXEMPTION (SCHEDULE R)

Form **706** (Rev. April 1997) Department of the Treasury Internal Revenue Service	**United States Estate (and Generation-Skipping Transfer) Tax Return** Estate of a citizen or resident of the United States (see separate instructions). To be filed for decedents dying after October 8, 1990. For Paperwork Reduction Act Notice, see page 1 of the separate instructions.	OMB No. 1545-0015

Part 1 — Decedent and Executor

1a Decedent's first name and middle initial (and maiden name, if any) JOHN H.	**1b** Decedent's last name JONES	**2** Decedent's social security no. 123-45-6789

3a Legal residence (domicile) at time of death (county/state, or foreign country) LOS ANGELES, CALIFORNIA	**3b** Year domicile established	**4** Date of birth	**5** Date of death 02/04/1981

6a Name of executor (see page 2 of the instructions) MARY R. JONES	**6b** Executor's address (number and street including apartment or suite no. or rural route; city, town, or post office; state; and ZIP code)
6c Executor's social security number (see page 2 of the instructions) 012-34-5678	LOS ANGELES, CALIFORNIA

7a Name and location of court where will was probated or estate administered	**7b** Case number

8 If decedent died testate, check here ▶ ☐ and attach a certified copy of the will.   **9** If Form 4768 is attached, check here ▶ ☐

10 If Schedule R-1 is attached, check here ▶ ☐

Part 2 — Tax Computation

1	Total gross estate (from Part 5, Recapitulation, page 3, item 10)	1	1,000,000
2	Total allowable deductions (from Part 5, Recapitulation, page 3, item 20)	2	400,000
3	Taxable estate (subtract line 2 from line 1)	3	600,000
4	Adjusted taxable gifts (total taxable gifts (within the meaning of section 2503) made by the decedent after December 31, 1976, other than gifts that are includible in decedent's gross estate (section 2001(b))	4	0
5	Add lines 3 and 4	5	600,000
6	Tentative tax on the amount on line 5 from Table A on page 10 of the instructions	6	192,800
7a	If line 5 exceeds $10,000,000, enter the lesser of line 5 or $21,040,000. If line 5 is $10,000,000 or less, skip lines 7a and 7b and enter -0- on line 7c. **7a**		
b	Subtract $10,000,000 from line 7a **7b**		
c	Enter 5% (.05) of line 7b	7c	0
8	Total tentative tax (add lines 6 and 7c)	8	192,800
9	Total gift tax payable with respect to gifts made by the decedent after December 31, 1976. Include gift taxes by the decedent's spouse for such spouse's share of split gifts (section 2513) only if the decedent was the donor of these gifts and they are includible in the decedent's gross estate (see instructions)	9	0
10	Gross estate tax (subtract line 9 from line 8)	10	192,800
11	Maximum unified credit against estate tax **11** 192,800		
12	Adjustment to unified credit. (This adjustment may not exceed $6,000. See page 7 of the instructions.) **12** 0		
13	Allowable unified credit (subtract line 12 from line 11)	13	192,800
14	Subtract line 13 from line 10 (but do not enter less than zero)	14	0
15	Credit for state death taxes. Do not enter more than line 14. Figure the credit by using the amount on line 3 less $60,000. See Table B in the instructions and **attach credit evidence** (see instructions)	15	0
16	Subtract line 15 from line 14	16	0
17	Credit for Federal gift taxes on pre-1977 gifts (sec. 2012)(attach computation) **17**		
18	Credit for foreign death taxes (from Schedule(s) P). (Attach Form(s) 706CE) **18**		
19	Credit for tax on prior transfers (from Schedule Q) **19**		
20	Total (add lines 17, 18, and 19)	20	0
21	Net estate tax (subtract line 20 from line 16)	21	0
22	Generation-skipping transfer taxes (from Schedule R, Part 2, line 10)	22	0
23	Section 4980A increased estate tax (from Schedule S, Part I, line 17)(see page 20 of the instructions)	23	0
24	Total transfer taxes (add lines 21, 22, and 23)	24	0
25	Prior payments. Explain in an attached statement **25**		
26	United States Treasury bonds redeemed in payment of estate tax **26**		
27	Total (add lines 25 and 26)	27	0
28	Balance due (or overpayment) (subtract line 27 from line 24)	28	0

Under penalties of perjury, I declare that I have examined this return, including accompanying schedules and statements, and to the best of my knowledge and belief, it is true, correct, and complete. Declaration of preparer other than the executor is based on all information of which preparer has any knowledge.

Signature(s) of executor(s) _____   Date _____

P.O. BOX 1060
CARSON CITY   NV 89702

Signature of preparer other than executor _____   Address (and ZIP code)   Date _____

Cat. No. 20548R

($625,000 in 1998, rising to $1 million in 2006), Form 706 must be filed and the appropriate federal estate taxes paid within nine months of the date of death of the second spouse. Remember, if no federal estate taxes are due, do *not* file Form 706.

QDOT TRUST

In 1988, Congress established the QDOT Trust to be used by resident non-citizens in lieu of the QTIP Trust. QDOT stands for Qualified Domestic Trust, and this Trust is identical to the QTIP Trust, with one significant exception: The QDOT Trust mandates that a trustee or co-trustee (if the non-citizen surviving spouse desires to also serve as co-trustee of the QDOT Trust) must be a citizen of the United States. The citizen has the specific responsibility of ensuring that the appropriate federal estate taxes will be paid to the IRS upon the death of the surviving resident non-citizen spouse.

Why the QDOT Trust?

Congress has placed a reasonable restriction on resident non-citizens by requiring them to use the QDOT Trust instead of the QTIP Trust, since the federal estate tax laws were often being circumvented by resident non-citizens. Prior to 1988, a spouse could die, leaving his or her assets in a Married A-B-C Trust for the benefit of his or her resident non-citizen spouse. For example, let's assume that a resident non-citizen husband and wife had an estate valued at $2 million, owned equally by both spouses. Upon the death of the first spouse, $1 million would flow into the survivor's A sub-trust, and $1 million would flow into the decedent's B sub-trust and C sub-trust ($600,000 into the decedent's B sub-trust and

$400,000 into the decedent's C sub-trust), as illustrated below.

By electing the C sub-trust (the QTIP Trust), the surviving spouse deferred the payment of estate taxes amounting to $160,000. The $2 million value of the estate fell in the 40 percent federal estate tax bracket, and 40 percent of $400,000 (placed in the C sub-trust or QTIP Trust) would amount to $160,000 in taxes that would normally be due the IRS, if it were not for the privilege of being able to elect the QTIP Trust. As the original scenario was designed to operate, the IRS would eventually collect those taxes upon the death of the second spouse. However, all too often, the IRS was "denied" the collection of these taxes, because the surviving spouse, being a non-citizen, would often return to his or her family roots in another country. When this repatriated spouse died, the IRS was obviously totally unaware of it and, therefore, unable to collect the taxes due. The IRS was denied the $160,000 in federal estate taxes, plus any additional taxes on the growth of those assets. You can see why the IRS mandated the QDOT Trust for resident non-citizens.

Citizen Trustee of QDOT Trust

When my clients and I discuss the QDOT Trust, I counsel them that, presumably, they have many years before the citizen trustee requirement would come into effect. The first spouse must die (but hopefully not for twenty or more years hence). Much can happen in the intervening years—the non-citizen spouse could become a citizen, the couple could have children (who would automatically be citizens and thus qualify as co-trustees), or the couple could establish close trusted friends who are citizens

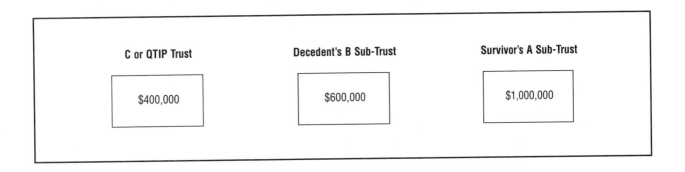

C or QTIP Trust	Decedent's B Sub-Trust	Survivor's A Sub-Trust
$400,000	$600,000	$1,000,000

(and thus also qualify as co-trustees). Alternatively, upon the death of the first spouse, the resident non-citizen surviving spouse could elect to pay the federal estate tax on the assets that could have been placed in the QDOT Trust. The requirement of a citizen trustee applies only to the QDOT Trust and not to the decedent's B sub-trust nor to the survivor's A sub-trust.

The citizen trustee of a QDOT Trust must file a Form 706-QDT whenever *any part of the principal* is paid out to the non-citizen surviving spouse. This requirement does not apply to income, however, which is rightfully payable at all times to the surviving spouse. Otherwise, only the annual Form 1041 Trust Tax Return and any accompanying Schedule K-1s need to be filed for the decedent's B sub-trust and C sub-trust.

A Word of Caution: If the value of the QDOT Trust exceeds $2 million, Congress now requires that the trustee be a bank or a financial institution!

Congress also denies a spouse the right to pass his or her estate to a resident non-citizen surviving spouse by using the Unlimited Marital Deduction. For example, let's use the same figures as the previous example: a $2 million estate owned equally by a husband and wife. In the past, by Will, the Unlimited Marital Deduction enabled the decedent spouse to pass his or her share ($1 million) to the surviving resident non-citizen spouse without paying any estate taxes. However, Congress soon learned that it faced the same problem as in the previous example. The surviving spouse would often return to his or her country and eventually die—and the IRS would not collect any federal estate taxes.

Spousal Gift

Initially, eliminating the right to the Unlimited Marital Deduction appeared to be an appropriate solution. However, this change created yet another problem—and a solution. For example, let's assume that an individual with an estate valued at $2 million marries a resident non-citizen with few, if any, assets. Together, the couple create a Married A-B Trust and also desire to make use of both federal estate tax exemptions. How do they do it?

The answer is really quite simple. Congress allows a spouse to gift $100,000 *annually* to a non-citizen spouse. Thus, each year for six years the spouse transfers $100,000 of the estate to the non-citizen spouse and ensures that the transfer is formalized with a Spousal Gift form, as shown in Figure 21-2.

I hope this discussion of the tax treatment involving resident non-citizens has helped, at least a bit, to lift the shroud of confusion that so frequently clouds this subject.

Rights of Non-Citizens

There has been much misinformation, both written and spoken, about the rights of non-citizens, especially when it comes to tax matters. This subject is of particular concern to those many fine people who have immigrated legally to the United States but have not yet become citizens, as well as those wonderful immigrant non-citizens who have married U.S. citizens. Let me attempt to set the record straight and relate how non-citizens are treated differently in some tax situations. For purposes of the following discussion, note that a non-citizen is a legal alien who holds a "green card."

Resident Non-Citizen vs. Non-Resident Citizen

A non-citizen is considered to be a resident of the United States if he or she lives in any of the fifty states or the District of Columbia. In contrast, a resident of Guam, Puerto Rico, or the U.S. Virgin Islands is considered to be a non-resident citizen. The designation of non-resident citizen also applies to a U.S. citizen who has legally established his or her domicile outside the United States.

A resident non-citizen of the United States is eligible for the same standard individual federal estate tax exemption as a resident citizen ($625,000 in 1998, rising to $1 million by 2006). It is important to note (but has always been a difficult issue to convey) that anyone who legally moves to the United States as a res-

FIGURE 21-2
SPOUSAL GIFT FORM

SPOUSAL GIFT

In consideration of our mutual love and affection, I, John H. Jones, give to my spouse, Mary R. Jones, the following described property as her sole and separate property:

My interest in the E. F. Hutton Account Number 5648482.

Signature _John H. Jones_   Date: _October 9, 1980_
John H. Jones

Note: Notary Certificate of Acknowledgment omitted from illustration.

ident non-citizen will have all of his or her assets subject to federal estate taxation upon his or her death, regardless of where those assets may be located!

In the mid-1980s, I had many fine Armenian clients who had emigrated from Iran during the latter years of the Shah and the Peacock Empire. These people had retained substantial business interests in Iran, and they were appalled to learn that their business interests in Iran would be included in the value of their U.S. estates when they died. Many of them just could not believe what I was saying. Eventually, I gave up trying to convince them, and instead I simply gave them a copy of Internal Revenue Code 2033 to read for themselves.

The primary point I am trying to make is that the IRS treats resident non-citizens with the same degree of estate tax fairness as it does resident citizens. The resident non-citizen receives the same federal estate tax exemption. Unfortunately, the same cannot be said for individuals living in Guam, Puerto Rico, or the Virgin Islands (considered to be non-resident citizens), who are only eligible for a federal estate tax exemption of $60,000 (comparable to a $13,000 tax credit) for their assets held in those U.S. territories. This unfairly low estate tax exemption is exactly the same exemption

that applies to assets in the United States that are held by foreigners. However, these same non-resident citizens receive the standard ($625,000) federal estate tax exemption for assets held outside the territory or in the fifty states and the District of Columbia.

GENERATION SKIP

Congress has decreed that a "generation skip" takes place when estate assets pass to anyone, other than the trustor's spouse or children, who is more than 37½ years younger than the trustors. Theoretically, if assets are left to someone more than 37½ years younger (other than spouse or children), such an action circumvents the federal estate tax. Thus, if you leave your assets to your grandchildren, instead of your children, you thereby bypass any federal estate tax on those assets—estate tax that would otherwise be imposed on those same assets if they were left to your children. Therefore, Congress has imposed the maximum estate tax rate of 55 percent on such a generation skip.

Inadvertent Generation Skip

It is significant to note that even if you leave all of your assets to your children, you could inadvertently still be subject to a generation skip (in terms of the law). For example, let's assume that, God forbid, one of your children were to die before your assets were distributed from your Trust. Presumably, it would be your desire that those assets pass to that child's issue (his or her children), your grandchildren. However, this fairness in sharing your assets would be considered an inadvertent generation skip.

My wife and I have specified in our Living Trust that, upon our deaths, our assets are to pass to our four children equally—one-third at age 25, one-third at age 30, and one-third at age 35. If we were to die and then one of our children were to follow us in death before his or her final distribution, that child's share would pass to that child's issue, our grandchildren.

That distribution of assets is correct, but such a distribution would also create, under current tax law, an inadvertent generation skip—and be subject to the consumptive 55 percent generation-skipping tax rate!

Generation-Skipping Exemption

When Congress established the generation-skipping tax, it granted each of us a $1 million generation-skipping exemption. And, as with

the federal estate tax exemption, if you don't take the appropriate and wise estate-planning steps, you can lose all of it or at least part of it. If you have a Will and you die, typically all of your assets flow to your surviving spouse—thus, effectively throwing away the decedent's $1 million generation-skipping exemption. Similarly, with only a Married A-B Trust, you effectively throw away $400,000 of your exemption.

For example, if you have an estate of $2 million and have only a Married A-B Trust, $600,000 would go into the decedent's B sub-trust, and the balance of $1.4 million would flow into the survivor's A sub-trust. Then, upon the death of the surviving spouse, the surviving spouse's $1 million generation-skipping exemption would offset the $1.4 million in the A sub-trust, which still leaves a balance of $400,000 subject to the consumptive generation-skipping tax.

Now, let's assume that you could circumvent the generation-skipping tax problem with a Married A-B-C Trust—but the assumption is only partly true. The generation-skipping exemption doesn't apply automatically, even if you have a decedent's C sub-trust (QTIP Trust). Here is what would happen, using the previ-

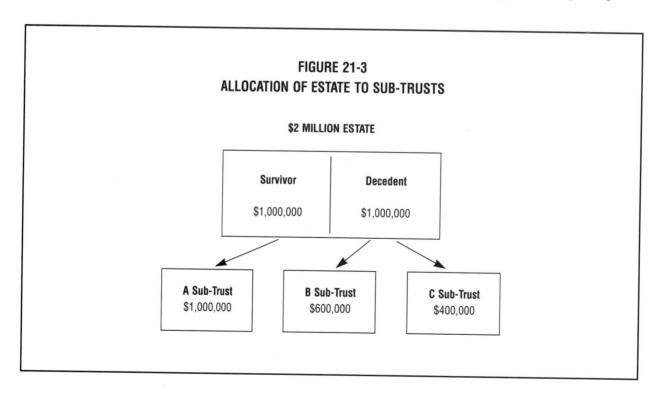

FIGURE 21-3
ALLOCATION OF ESTATE TO SUB-TRUSTS

$2 MILLION ESTATE

Survivor	Decedent
$1,000,000	$1,000,000

A Sub-Trust $1,000,000

B Sub-Trust $600,000

C Sub-Trust $400,000

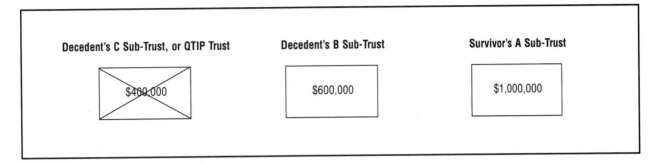

| Decedent's C Sub-Trust, or QTIP Trust | Decedent's B Sub-Trust | Survivor's A Sub-Trust |
| $400,000 | $600,000 | $1,000,000 |

ous figures. Of the decedent's $1 million share of the estate, $600,000 would flow into the decedent's B sub-trust, and $400,000 would flow into the decedent's C sub-trust (QTIP Trust), as illustrated in Figure 21-3.

The solution sounds logical, but beware—the QTIP portion of the decedent's estate will fail to qualify for the generation-skipping exemption if there is no QTIP election. Specifically, the $400,000 placed in the QTIP Trust would be "recaptured" in the surviving spouse's estate for application of the generation skipping tax. Thus, the decedent spouse would only qualify for a $600,000 generation-skipping exemption for the assets placed in the decedent's B sub-trust (see diagram above).

Once again, here is an excellent example of "not all Trusts are created equal." You must ensure that you have a well-written Trust—one that is detailed and lengthy, and includes all of the necessary provisions that may (or may not) be required during your lifetime. Since you seldom know ahead of time what provisions your Trust might require, you are best served by starting out with a comprehensive Trust that has been designed to meet every contingency.

Beware: An improperly worded Trust will cause the decedent's assets in the QTIP Trust (C sub-trust) to fail to qualify for the genera-tion-skipping exemption.

Reverse QTIP Provision

In contrast, a QTIP Trust that includes a Reverse QTIP Provision will protect the dece-dent's full generation-skipping exemption. The Reverse QTIP Provision reverses the flow of the decedent's generation-skipping exemption to the surviving spouse and retains the right to the full exemption in the decedent's B sub-trust and C sub-trust. This vital provision could pre-vent very costly tax consequences.

However, I strongly recommend that the Reverse QTIP Provision in the QTIP Trust be accompanied by a complete Generation-Skip-ping Trust—and I caution you to consider this approach very carefully. Even though, at the present moment, your estate may not be large enough to be subject to this consumptive tax-ation, it may well increase in value over the next ten or twenty years, because of inflation and the appreciation of your real estate.

GENERATION-SKIPPING TRUST

A Generation-Skipping Trust protects the $1 million generation-skipping exemption for an individual, if single, and for each spouse in the case of a married couple. A Generation-Skipping Trust also permits the children of a trustor to disclaim their interest in their par-ents' estate in favor of their own children and yet retain their right to any Trust income for life.

For example, let's assume a $2 million estate of a mother and father who pass away and leave their estate to their only child. Let's further assume that the son is married, has two children, and has already accumulated his own estate of $2 million. The son's estate is already subject to a 40 percent tax rate on the value that exceeds two federal estate tax exemptions ($1.25 million in 1998, rising to $2 million in 2006). The tax rate increases to 55 percent for an estate of $3.5 million.

If the son were to "accept" his parents' estate, this addition to his own estate of $2 million would be subject to a tax rate ranging from 40 percent to 55 percent. However, by disclaiming his interest in the principal of his parents' estate, the son can have the best of both worlds. The son would retain the right to use the income from his parents' $2 million estate for his entire lifetime, and upon the son's death, his parents' estate would pass to his children (his parents' grandchildren) free of any federal estate tax. However, the portion of the estate that "skips" the children and passes to the grandchildren would be considered to be a generation skip.

The Generation-Skipping Trust performs another important service: It enables you to specify which assets are exempt (i.e., which assets are included in the generation-skipping exemption) and which assets are not exempt. Each individual has a $1 million generation-skipping exemption that may be claimed. All future growth of exempt assets continues to be free of any further estate tax liability, whereas the value of nonexempt assets is included in the surviving spouse's estate when determining federal estate tax liability for the second spouse to die.

To illustrate, let's assume that the same trustors had an estate of $3 million and a Generation-Skipping Trust. Let's further assume that the estate assets were to remain in trust for a specified period—until the death of the son—and then be distributed to the grandchildren.

The Generation-Skipping Trust permits you to identify which specific assets are exempt (i.e., fall within the $1 million exemption allowed for each of the trustors). The generation-skipping tax is theoretically imposed when the assets are distributed to the grandchildren; if the assets appreciate over time, then the generation-skipping tax increases proportionately. However, by designating which of the assets are to be exempt, you can directly affect the ultimate amount of taxation.

For example, let's assume that the estate consists of $2 million of real estate that has a good chance of appreciating over the years, as well as $1 million in certificates of deposit (CDs) that only produce income but whose

value never appreciates, as illustrated in Figure 21-4. Simple logic tells us that it is the real estate, worth $2 million, that should be declared exempt.

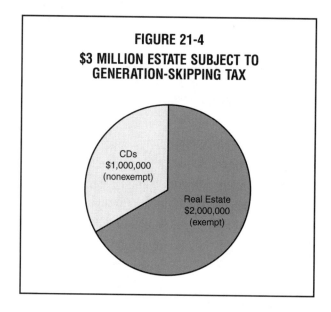

FIGURE 21-4
$3 MILLION ESTATE SUBJECT TO GENERATION-SKIPPING TAX

CDs $1,000,000 (nonexempt)

Real Estate $2,000,000 (exempt)

Years later, when the estate is to be distributed to the grandchildren, the real estate has appreciated to $4 million, but the value of the CDs has remained at $1 million. Since the real estate was initially declared exempt, the generation-skipping tax would be imposed only on the $1 million in CDs, which now represents a smaller portion of the total estate value, as illustrated in Figure 21-5.

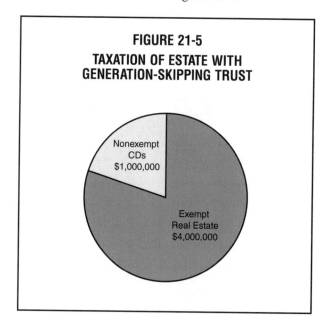

FIGURE 21-5
TAXATION OF ESTATE WITH GENERATION-SKIPPING TRUST

Nonexempt CDs $1,000,000

Exempt Real Estate $4,000,000

Remember, however, that without a Generation-Skipping Trust, no specific assets would be considered exempt. Therefore, the total estate—which has now appreciated to $5 million—would be included for allocating the generation-skipping tax. Thus, the $5 million estate would be prorated using the ratio (as of the date of death) of the originally exempt portion of the estate ($2 million, which represents two-thirds of the estate) to the nonexempt portion ($1 million, one-third of the original estate). Thus, if the appreciated estate value of $5 million were subjected to the consumptive generation-skipping tax, two-thirds of the appreciated value of the estate ($3.3 million) would be exempt from the generation-skipping tax, and one-third of the appreciated estate ($1.65 million) would be nonexempt (i.e., subject to the generation-skipping tax).

In summary, without the Generation-Skipping Trust, which allows you to allocate specific assets instead of a percentage of the estate, you would be faced with a generation-skipping tax on $1.65 million of the appreciated estate value, instead of on only $1 million, as shown in Figure 21-6.

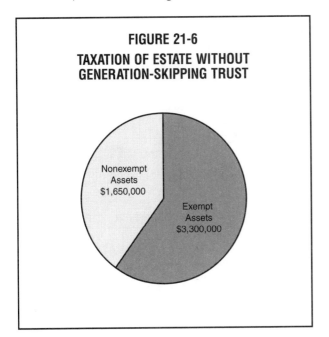

FIGURE 21-6
TAXATION OF ESTATE WITHOUT GENERATION-SKIPPING TRUST

Nonexempt Assets $1,650,000

Exempt Assets $3,300,000

Even though the generation-skipping tax is theoretically computed when the assets are distributed to the grandchildren, in practice, the tax is computed (and must be paid) following the death of the trustors, regardless of when the grandchildren actually receive the funds.

Remember: The generation-skipping exemption must be filed for both *spouses, necessitating that a Form 706 and Schedule R be filed upon the death of each spouse.*

Upon the death of the first spouse, you should file Form 706 and its associated Schedule R (Generation-Skipping Transfer Tax Exemption) for the decedent spouse's estate, in order to preserve the decedent's right to the full exemption. Even though the decedent's estate may be worth much less than $1 million, it is prudent to file the Schedule R for the full exemption of $1 million. The filing of Form 706 for the QTIP election and the generation-skipping exemption (Schedule R) must be done within nine months after the date of death.

Upon the death of the surviving spouse (or a single person), you should file Parts 2 and 3 of Form 706, along with Schedule R (Generation-Skipping Transfer Tax Exemption) within nine months of the date of death to establish the generation-skipping exemption and to pay any generation-skipping taxes due. Figure 21-7 on page 308 shows an example of a Form 706 (Schedule R) for a $3 million estate being "generation-skipped" to two grandchildren.

ADVANCED SETTLEMENT OPTIONS ARE COMPLEX

If you are one of the fortunate few who have amassed a sizable estate and if you are interested in preserving as much of it as possible for your children or grandchildren, I must caution you that implementing any of the advanced settlement options in Part II is definitely *not* a do-it-yourself project!

Caution: Before implementing any of the advanced settlement options as part of your estate planning, seek out and use the services of very knowledgeable estate preservation specialists and legal counsel with a master's in taxation.

FIGURE 21-7

FORM 706 (SCHEDULE R) FOR A $3 MILLION ESTATE
"GENERATION-SKIPPED" TO TWO GRANDCHILDREN

Form **706** (Rev. April 1997) Department of the Treasury Internal Revenue Service	United States Estate (and Generation-Skipping Transfer) Tax Return Estate of a citizen or resident of the United States (see separate instructions). To be filed for decedents dying after October 8, 1990. For Paperwork Reduction Act Notice, see page 1 of the separate instructions.	OMB No. 1545-0015

Part 1 **Decedent and Executor**

1a Decedent's first name and middle initial (and maiden name, if any) MARY R.	**1b** Decedent's last name JONES	**2** Decedent's social security no.
3a Legal residence (domicile) at time of death (county/state, or foreign country) LOS ANGELES, CALIFORNIA	**3b** Year domicile established **4** Date of birth	**5** Date of death 10/25/1993

6a Name of executor (see page 2 of the instructions) | **6b** Executor's address (number and street including apartment or suite no. or rural route; city, town, or post office; state; and ZIP code)

6c Executor's social security number (see page 2 of the instructions)

7a Name and location of court where will was probated or estate administered | **7b** Case number

8 If decedent died testate, check here ▶ ☐ and attach a certified copy of the will.   **9** If Form 4768 is attached, check here ▶ ☐

10 If Schedule R-1 is attached, check here ▶ ☐

Part 2 Tax Computation

1	Total gross estate (from Part 5, Recapitulation, page 3, item 10)	**1**	3,000,000
2	Total allowable deductions (from Part 5, Recapitulation, page 3, item 20)	**2**	0
3	Taxable estate (subtract line 2 from line 1)	**3**	3,000,000
4	Adjusted taxable gifts (total taxable gifts (within the meaning of section 2503) made by the decedent after December 31, 1976, other than gifts that are includible in decedent's gross estate (section 2001(b)) . . .	**4**	0
5	Add lines 3 and 4	**5**	3,000,000
6	Tentative tax on the amount on line 5 from Table A on page 10 of the instructions	**6**	1,290,800
7a	If line 5 exceeds $10,000,000, enter the lesser of line 5 or $21,040,000. If line 5 is $10,000,000 or less, skip lines 7a and 7b and enter -0- on line 7c. **7a**		
b	Subtract $10,000,000 from line 7a **7b**		
c	Enter 5% (.05) of line 7b	**7c**	0
8	Total tentative tax (add lines 6 and 7c)	**8**	1,290,800
9	Total gift tax payable with respect to gifts made by the decedent after December 31, 1976. Include gift taxes by the decedent's spouse for such spouse's share of split gifts (section 2513) only if the decedent was the donor of these gifts and they are includible in the decedent's gross estate (see instructions) . .	**9**	0
10	Gross estate tax (subtract line 9 from line 8)	**10**	1,290,800
11	Maximum unified credit against estate tax **11** 192,800		
12	Adjustment to unified credit. (This adjustment may not exceed $6,000. See page 7 of the instructions.) **12** 0		
13	Allowable unified credit (subtract line 12 from line 11)	**13**	192,800
14	Subtract line 13 from line 10 (but do not enter less than zero)	**14**	1,098,000
15	Credit for state death taxes. Do not enter more than line 14. Figure the credit by using the amount on line 3 less $60,000. See Table B in the instructions and **attach credit evidence** (see instructions) . .	**15**	182,000
16	Subtract line 15 from line 14	**16**	916,000
17	Credit for Federal gift taxes on pre-1977 gifts (sec. 2012)(attach computation) **17**		
18	Credit for foreign death taxes (from Schedule(s) P). (Attach Form(s) 706CE) **18**		
19	Credit for tax on prior transfers (from Schedule Q) **19**		
20	Total (add lines 17, 18, and 19)	**20**	0
21	Net estate tax (subtract line 20 from line 16)	**21**	916,000
22	Generation-skipping transfer taxes (from Schedule R, Part 2, line 10)	**22**	0
23	Section 4980A increased estate tax (from Schedule S, Part I, line 17)(see page 20 of the instructions)	**23**	0
24	Total transfer taxes (add lines 21, 22, and 23)	**24**	916,000
25	Prior payments. Explain in an attached statement **25**		
26	United States Treasury bonds redeemed in payment of estate tax **26**		
27	Total (add lines 25 and 26)	**27**	0
28	Balance due (or overpayment) (subtract line 27 from line 24)	**28**	916,000

Under penalties of perjury, I declare that I have examined this return, including accompanying schedules and statements, and to the best of my knowledge and belief, it is true, correct, and complete. Declaration of preparer other than the executor is based on all information of which preparer has any knowledge.

Signature(s) of executor(s) _____   Date _____

P.O. BOX 1060
CARSON CITY   NV 89702

Signature of preparer other than executor _____   Address (and ZIP code)   Date _____

Cat. No. 20548R

22

Advanced Settlement Options for the Mysterious IRA
(Including the Roth IRA)

If you have accumulated a large IRA, you face severe adverse tax consequences if you die before you have fully consumed (i.e., used up or spent) *all* of the funds in your IRA. This chapter is devoted to presenting several advanced estate settlement concepts that help to preserve your estate for your heirs by minimizing onerous taxation that would occur if you were to die with a substantial amount of funds in your IRA(s). The chapter discusses the following estate preservation concepts related to IRAs:

- Single IRA Trust
- Married IRA–QTIP Trust
- Handling very large IRAs in a separate property state and in a community property state
- A large IRA as separate property in a second marriage
- Charitable Remainder Trust
- Aggregate Community Property Agreement
- Disclaiming an interest in an IRA
- Roth Legacy Trust℠

Although the first part of this chapter explains what you should do if you have a large IRA, I urge you to consider the simplest solution for creating potential wealth to pass on to your heirs—the Roth Legacy Trust℠ discussed later in this chapter.

SINGLE IRA TRUST

The Single IRA Trust is specifically designed to be the beneficiary of a traditional IRA for a single person or a surviving spouse. It is simply a Married IRA–QTIP Trust designed to meet the needs of a single person, although still satisfying all of the cumbersome IRS tax code requirements. For example, a single individual will use the Single IRA Trust as the beneficiary of a traditional IRA when minor children are designated as the end beneficiaries, because you do not want to leave assets directly to minor or handicapped children. (I encourage you to read my advice on this subject in my previous book, *The Living Trust*.)

The Single IRA Trust incorporates the fractional method of allocating the federal estate tax exemption, as well as all of the appropriate legal language required by the IRS to accommodate an IRA. The Single IRA Trust is the ideal vehicle to become the recipient of an IRA where minor children are scheduled to be the beneficiaries upon the death of the IRA owner. Upon the death of the IRA owner, the IRA would be distributed over the life expectancy of the oldest child. If the IRA owner separated the IRA into different accounts, each with one child as a beneficiary, then upon the death of the IRA owner, the IRA would be distributed over the life expectancy of each named beneficiary (each child). However, an even better approach would be to consider converting the traditional IRA to a Roth IRA. (The benefits of this approach were detailed in Chapter 13.)

Even if you are single, you should still read the following section on the Married IRA–QTIP Trust, since the Single IRA Trust contains all of the benefits of a Married IRA–QTIP Trust.

MARRIED IRA–QTIP TRUST

The Married IRA–QTIP Trust is a dynamic vehicle with a special function; it is a unique Trust designed to provide a surviving spouse with income from the IRA for his or her remaining lifetime. However, upon the death of the surviving spouse, the residual IRA funds flow to the beneficiaries specified by the first spouse to die. Proper use of the Married IRA–QTIP Trust can be extremely important in enabling you to fully utilize the federal estate tax exemptions of both spouses.

Need for a Married IRA–QTIP Trust

The Married IRA–QTIP Trust plays a most important role in three primary financial situations:

- For a couple in a separate property state with a large IRA whose value is disproportionate to the size of their estate
- For a couple in a community property state with a large IRA whose value is disproportionate to the size of their estate
- For an individual who has been previously married, has children from the first mar-

riage, comes into a second marriage with a large IRA that is his or her separate property, and wants to use the IRA income to provide for his or her spouse (if the IRA owner dies first) but, upon the death of the surviving spouse, wants the residual of the IRA to pass to his or her children from the first marriage

The Married IRA–QTIP Trust is specifically designed to provide the surviving spouse with the income and/or principal from the IRA, whichever is greater, in order to satisfy the highly complex marital deduction and required IRA distribution rules. The Married IRA–QTIP Trust is a special Trust designed for a married couple and is specifically structured so that the Trust can be named as a "traditional IRA beneficiary" without triggering the onerous income tax consequences normally triggered by this action. The Married IRA–QTIP Trust can be replaced by a Roth Legacy Trust℠ if the traditional IRA is converted to a Roth IRA (to permit the spread of tax-free withdrawals based on the life expectancy of the oldest beneficiary).

Full Utilization of Decedent's Federal Estate Tax Exemption

The Married IRA–QTIP Trust and the Roth Legacy Trust℠ are structured to include the right to fully utilize the decedent spouse's federal estate tax exemption. Therefore, you can use these Trusts in conjunction with an A Trust, an A-B Trust, or an A-B-C Trust. However, for the Married IRA–QTIP Trust and the Roth Legacy Trust℠ to be fully effective, the surviving spouse must be the income beneficiary with the right to take the income and principal as required, according to the IRA withdrawal requirements. If the IRA owner desires to name his or her children as beneficiaries, in lieu of the spouse, the Single IRA Trust (discussed previously) would be a more appropriate vehicle.

IRS Requirements

For the IRS to recognize the Married IRA–QTIP Trust as legitimate for tax purposes, the Trust must meet the following requirements:

- All of the Trust income must be paid to the surviving spouse.
- Only the surviving spouse can receive Trust distributions.
- The Trust must eliminate any General Power of Appointment for the surviving spouse.
- The Trust must have defined (i.e., specifically named) beneficiaries.
- Allocation of the federal estate tax exemption must be fractional (rather than pecuniary).
- The Trust should restrict the standard frivolous right (the right to $5,000 or 5 percent of the assets, whichever is greater) to the last month of the year.
- The Trust must be valid by state law.

None of the IRS requirements affects or impinges on the right of the surviving spouse to act as the surviving trustee of the IRA–QTIP Trust.

Estate Taxes Allocated upon Death of Second Spouse

Upon the death of the second spouse, if estate taxes are due on any part of the Married IRA–QTIP Trust, the IRS tax code specifies that a proportionate share of the taxes must be paid from funds in the QTIP Trust. If there is no QTIP Trust, then the proportionate share of federal estate taxes must be paid from the Married IRA–QTIP Trust.

If the IRA in the Married IRA–QTIP Trust is a traditional IRA, all or part of the traditional IRA must be withdrawn to pay estate taxes, and these funds are immediately subject to income taxes—usually with disastrous financial consequences. If the IRA in the Married IRA–QTIP Trust is a Roth IRA, the funds from the IRA that are withdrawn to pay estate taxes will be free of any income tax, but the beneficiaries have just been deprived of a tax-free growth asset that could have been extremely valuable to them in the years to come.

The solution is to have other liquid assets (besides an IRA) in a QTIP Trust, or even in a Married IRA–QTIP Trust, since a Married IRA–QTIP Trust can hold other assets in addition to an IRA. However, the best solution by far is to have sufficient insurance to pay all of the estate taxes, both federal and state, with an irrevocable Insurance Preservation Trust named as the beneficiary of the insurance. With this solution, you can pay all estate taxes without reducing the size of the estate that is passed on to the heirs.

Right to Take Withdrawals over Beneficiary's Life Expectancy

The beneficiary of a Married IRA–QTIP Trust has the right to take withdrawals from the IRA based on the IRS guidelines of the beneficiary's life expectancy.

Surviving Spouse as Beneficiary

If the surviving spouse is the beneficiary of the Married IRA–QTIP Trust, the surviving spouse has the right to take withdrawals based on his or her life expectancy. When the second spouse dies, the children, as contingent beneficiaries, have the right to have the IRA funds distributed to them in kind, rather than receive the money from the liquidation of the IRA. Then the children could take IRA withdrawals based on the remaining life expectancy of the deceased second spouse (the "ghost" life expectancy). If the IRA in the Married IRA–QTIP Trust is a traditional IRA, then any such withdrawals will be subject to income tax when the funds are withdrawn. However, if the IRA in the Trust is a Roth IRA, then any withdrawals will be tax free.

Children as Remainder Beneficiaries

If the children are the remainder beneficiaries of a spousal rollover IRA following the death of the surviving spouse, the children have the right to IRA withdrawals based on the remaining "ghost" life expectancy of the decedent spouse who was the beneficiary of the Married IRA–QTIP Trust. The children have the right to have the IRA funds distributed to them in kind. If the IRA in the Married IRA–QTIP Trust is a traditional IRA, any such withdrawals will be subject to income tax when the funds are withdrawn. However, if the IRA in the Trust is a Roth IRA, then any withdrawals will be tax free.

TAX PLANNING FOR VERY LARGE IRAs

If you are among those fortunate few people who have accumulated very large IRAs (more

TABLE 22-1

**ASSET ALLOCATION WHEN HUSBAND DIES WITHOUT MARRIED IRA-QTIP TRUST
(SEPARATE PROPERTY STATE)**

ALLOCATION OF ASSETS TO SUB-TRUSTS

Assets	Market Value	Decedent's B Sub-Trust	Survivor's A Sub-Trust
Home	$ 200,000	$100,000	$ 100,000
IRA	$1,000,000		$1,000,000

than $1 million), how you handle the allocation of the IRA can have a significant impact on your estate—either positive or negative. From the viewpoint of good estate planning (i.e., minimizing your estate taxes and maximizing your children's inheritance), the manner in which you should handle a large IRA differs according to whether you live in a separate property state or a community property state. (To maintain simplicity, the following illustrations will use $600,000 as the value of the federal estate tax exemption.)

Large IRA in a Separate Property State

In a separate property state, the marital assets in the Trust are typically divided by the itemization method, and the IRA passes to the surviving spouse outside the Trust.

As I illustrate different methods of handling a large IRA in an estate, along with the tax consequences of each method, you will see that how you handle a large IRA can make a significant difference, both in taxes paid to Uncle Sam as well as to the size of your estate left as an inheritance to your children.

Patrick Ashley is a retired Delta Air Lines pilot living in Atlanta. When Patrick retired, he rolled over his 401(k) retirement plan into his IRA, which is now worth $1 million. Besides the IRA, Patrick and his wife, Laurel, own their own home, which is worth $200,000.

Since Patrick resides in a separate property state, when he dies, the asset allocation of his estate would be as shown in Table 22-1. The surviving spouse's interest in the IRA is shown in the surviving spouse's A sub-trust (for illustration purposes), even though the surviving spouse remains the beneficiary of the IRA.

This allocation of assets substantially underfunded the decedent's B sub-trust; it did not make full use of the decedent's $600,000 federal estate tax exemption. Unfortunately, when the surviving spouse dies, her heirs will be faced with federal estate taxes on a $500,000 estate (after deducting her $600,000 federal estate tax exemption) at a tax rate of 40 percent, yielding an unnecessary estate tax bite of about $200,000—a very high price to pay (see Table 22-2).

TABLE 22-2

**ESTATE TAX COMPUTATIONS
WHEN SURVIVING SPOUSE DIES**

IRA	$1,000,000
Home (one-half share)	$ 100,000
Total estate	$1,100,000
Less: Federal estate tax exemption	($ 600,000)
Taxable estate:	$ 500,000
Federal estate tax (40%)	$ 200,000

Another allocation approach would be for Patrick to "split" his IRA. As detailed in Table 22-3, half of his IRA could be allocated to his spouse and the other half to his standard Living Trust. Although this allocation of assets would fully utilize Patrick's $600,000 federal estate tax exemption, the allocation creates a new problem, since the decedent's B sub-trust is now the beneficiary of half of his substantial IRA. All of the traditional IRA funds that have been passed to the decedent's B sub-trust are fully taxed as income (and become subject to federal income taxation at the highest rate— presumably, 39.6 percent) by December 31 of the year following Patrick's death, resulting in almost the same onerous tax situation as before.

For Patrick and Laurel's estate allocation dilemma, the Married IRA–QTIP Trust provides an excellent solution. Patrick could split his IRA into two separate IRAs, naming his spouse as beneficiary of one IRA and specifying the Married IRA–QTIP Trust as the beneficiary of the second IRA. Since the spouse is always the income beneficiary of the Married IRA–QTIP Trust, Laurel would continue to receive the full benefit of both IRAs. Upon Laurel's death, the children, as the next beneficiaries of the Married IRA–QTIP Trust, could continue to withdraw funds from the IRA based on their mother's "ghost" life expectancy.

An alternative would be for Patrick to name the Married IRA–QTIP Trust as the contingent beneficiary of his IRA and to name Laurel as the primary beneficiary. Upon Patrick's death, Laurel could disclaim part of her interest in the IRA in an amount that is sufficient to fully utilize Patrick's federal estate tax exemption.

Since the spouse is always the income beneficiary of the Married IRA–QTIP Trust, Laurel would continue to receive the full benefit of both IRAs. Upon Laurel's death, the children, as the next beneficiaries of the Married IRA–QTIP Trust, could continue to withdraw funds from the IRA based on their mother's previously determined life expectancy (the mother's ghost life expectancy). If Patrick were to die under these circumstances, the asset allocation of his estate would be as shown in Table 22-4 on page 314.

A married couple with an A-B-C Trust and a Married IRA–QTIP Trust would have almost the same sub-trust allocation (and it would be redundant to show it here). The A, B, and C sub-trusts would contain the marital and separate property assets, and the Married IRA–QTIP Trust would contain part or all of the IRA, providing the same advantages for protecting the IRA as described previously.

However, what would happen if Laurel were the first to die? This situation would pose an interesting dilemma, since the husband cannot gift a traditional IRA to a spouse. Unfortunately, although Patrick could roll over his IRA into a Roth IRA (and suffer the income tax consequences of a large IRA distribution), he would still face the same dilemma. In a separate property state, he cannot split a Roth IRA either! Thus, most of Laurel's individual federal estate tax exemption would go unused, and much of Patrick's IRA would be consumed by federal estate taxes.

Large IRA in a Community Property State
In a community property state, the valuation method (also referred to as the aggregate

---

TABLE 22-3
ALLOCATION OF ASSETS TO SUB-TRUSTS (IF SPLITTING THE IRA)

Assets	Market Value	Decedent's B Sub-Trust	Survivor's A Sub-Trust
Home	$ 200,000	$100,000	$100,000
IRA	$1,000,000	$500,000	$500,000

TABLE 22-4

ASSET ALLOCATION WHEN HUSBAND DIES WITH MARRIED IRA-QTIP TRUST
(SEPARATE PROPERTY STATE)

Assets	Market Value	Married IRA–QTIP Trust	Decedent's B Sub-Trust	Survivor's A Sub-Trust
Home	$ 200,000		$100,000	$100,000
IRA	$1,000,000	$500,000		$500,000

method) of allocation can be better used to take full advantage of the decedent's federal estate tax exemption and, thus, minimize estate taxes. With the valuation method of allocation, the total value of the marital assets—including the IRA—can be divided equally by value, even though the IRA passes to the surviving spouse or heirs outside the couple's Living Trust.

Harold and Shirley Partridge, who live in San Rafael, California, created their Living Trust twelve years ago. Harold and Shirley had a home worth $100,000 and an IRA valued at $200,000. Today, Harold is retired from his job as a plant manager and has a home worth $200,000, and his IRA has grown to a value of $1 million. The sizable growth in Harold's IRA is typical of many people today and is not all that unusual—but it is obvious that Harold wisely chose an investment vehicle other than the typical low-interest-rate CD.

Since Harold and Shirley live in a community property state, when Harold dies, the assets may be allocated by value, as shown in Table 22-5, where the IRA is allocated (40 percent to the decedent's B sub-trust and 60 percent to the survivor's A sub-trust) to fully utilize Harold's federal estate tax exemption. The $200,000 home can be placed in the decedent's B sub-trust, and the IRA can then be allocated, by value, between the decedent's B sub-trust and the survivor's A sub-trust, thus equating the value of estate assets in both sub-

trusts. The surviving spouse's interest in the IRA is shown in the surviving spouse's A sub-trust (for illustration purposes), even though the surviving spouse remains the beneficiary of the IRA.

Using the valuation method of allocation fully utilizes each spouse's federal estate tax exemption, thus (in this case) eliminating any estate taxes. However, with this option, the allocation creates a serious problem: The decedent's B sub-trust is now the beneficiary of $400,000 of the IRA. All of the traditional IRA funds that have passed to the decedent's B sub-trust must be withdrawn from the IRA (and subject to federal income taxation at the highest rate—presumably, 39.6 percent) by December 31 of the year following Harold's death, resulting in almost the same onerous tax situation as before.

For Harold and Shirley's estate allocation problem, the Married IRA–QTIP Trust once again provides an excellent solution. Harold could name his spouse as the primary beneficiary of his IRA and name the Married IRA–QTIP Trust as the contingent beneficiary. Upon Harold's death, Shirley could disclaim part of her interest in the IRA (in an amount that is sufficient to fully utilize Harold's federal estate tax exemption). Since the spouse is always the income beneficiary of the Married IRA–QTIP Trust, Shirley would continue to receive the full benefit of both IRAs. Upon Shirley's death, the children, as the next beneficiaries of the Married IRA–QTIP Trust, could continue to withdraw funds from the IRA

TABLE 22-5

**ASSET ALLOCATION WHEN HUSBAND DIES WITHOUT MARRIED IRA–QTIP TRUST
(COMMUNITY PROPERTY STATE)**

Assets	Market Value		Decedent's B Sub-Trust	Survivor's A Sub-Trust
Home	$ 200,000		$200,000	
IRA	$1,000,000		$400,000	$600,000

based on their mother's "ghost" life expectancy. If Harold were to die under these circumstances, the asset allocation of the estate would be as shown in Table 22-6.

A married couple with an A-B-C Trust and a Married IRA–QTIP Trust would have almost the same sub-trust allocation (and it would be redundant to show it here). The A, B, and C sub-trusts would contain the community and separate property assets, and the Married IRA–QTIP Trust would contain part or all of the IRA, providing the same advantages for protecting the IRA as described previously.

LARGE IRA AS SEPARATE PROPERTY IN A SECOND MARRIAGE

When allocating the separate property of individuals rather than marital assets, it makes no difference whether you reside in a separate property state or a community property state.

Jeremy Harrison, as a young naval officer, was married in 1952 and had two daughters. Jeremy's wife Jenny passed away six years ago. Last year, Jeremy married a wonderful lady, Maryanne, who has two grown sons, both doctors, from her previous marriage.

Jeremy brought to this second marriage his IRA, valued at $1 million (his separate property). Jeremy would like to use the IRA funds to provide for Maryanne in the event of his demise; however, after Maryanne's death, Jeremy would like the remaining proceeds of his IRA to go to his two daughters from his first marriage. (If Jeremy is over the age of 70½, although he can change the primary

TABLE 22-6

**ASSET ALLOCATION WHEN HUSBAND DIES WITH MARRIED IRA–QTIP TRUST
(COMMUNITY PROPERTY STATE)**

Assets	Market Value	Married IRA–QTIP Trust	Decedent's B Sub-Trust	Survivor's A Sub-Trust
Home	$ 200,000		$100,000	$100,000
IRA	$1,000,000	$500,000		$500,000

beneficiary from his deceased wife to his new wife, the withdrawal requirements established at age 70½ must continue, regardless of Maryanne's age. However, Jeremy can circumvent this restriction by converting the traditional IRA to a Roth IRA.)

Maryanne brought her home, worth $400,000, into the marriage (her separate property).

Due to the size of the estate, the couple wisely chose to get a Married A-B-C Trust to protect their estate from unnecessary taxation.

If Jeremy were to die, the asset allocation of the estate would be as shown in Table 22-7.

By making the decedent's B sub-trust and C sub-trust the beneficiary of Jeremy's large IRA, the unsuspecting couple have created a horrendous income tax problem! All of the traditional IRA funds that passed to the decedent's B sub-trust and C sub-trust would be fully taxed as income (and subject to federal income taxation at the highest rate—presumably, 39.6 percent) by December 31 of the year following Jeremy's death, resulting in almost the same onerous tax situation as before. This scenario assumes that neither the B nor C sub-trusts have been altered to satisfy the many legal tax requirements established by the IRS.

The Married IRA–QTIP Trust turns out to be an excellent solution for Jeremy and Maryanne's estate. Jeremy would name the Married IRA–QTIP Trust as the primary bene-ficiary of his IRA. (Since both Jeremy and Maryanne brought significant separate property into their marriage, each of them should have executed Separate Property Agreements and included these documents in their Living Trust binder, to clearly identify their separate property assets.) Since the spouse is always the income beneficiary of the Married IRA–QTIP Trust, Maryanne would continue to receive the full benefit of the IRA. Upon Maryanne's death, Jeremy's children, as the next beneficiaries of the Married IRA–QTIP Trust, could continue to withdraw funds from the IRA based on Maryanne's "ghost" life expectancy.

An alternative approach would be for Jeremy to name his spouse as the primary beneficiary of his IRA and to name the Married IRA–QTIP Trust as the contingent beneficiary. Upon Jeremy's death, Maryanne could disclaim her interest in the IRA in an amount that is sufficient to fully utilize Jeremy's federal estate tax exemption. Since the spouse is always the income beneficiary of the Married IRA–QTIP Trust, Maryanne would continue to receive the full benefit of both IRAs. Upon Maryanne's death, Jeremy's children, as the next beneficiaries of the Married IRA–QTIP Trust, could continue to withdraw funds from the IRAs based on Maryanne's previously determined life expectancy (her ghost life expectancy).

If Jeremy were to die under these circumstances, the asset allocation of the estate would be as shown in Table 22-8.

TABLE 22-7

ASSET ALLOCATION WHEN HUSBAND DIES WITHOUT MARRIED IRA–QTIP TRUST (SECOND MARRIAGE)

Assets	Market Value	Decedent's C Sub-Trust	Decedent's B Sub-Trust	Survivor's A Sub-Trust
Home	$ 400,000			$400,000
IRA	$1,000,000	$400,000	$600,000	

If the Spousal Beneficiary Predeceases the IRA Owner

Under current law, nothing can be done to split an IRA and then allocate a portion of the IRA to the other spouse. However, an alternative would be to convert the traditional IRA to a Roth IRA and to then assign the community property interest in the IRA to the other spouse. In this manner, if the spousal beneficiary of the IRA were to die before the IRA owner, the community property interest would be included in the spousal beneficiary's estate—and, thus, both federal estate tax exemptions would eventually be utilized.

CHARITABLE REMAINDER TRUST

Those of you who have substantial wealth in an IRA are potentially facing a disastrous 75 percent loss in the value of that IRA through federal and state income and estate taxes! (I consider a traditional IRA with a value of $2 million or more to be in the "substantial wealth" category.) If you are one of the fortunate few to have this "problem," you should consider the potential benefits of using a Charitable Remainder Trust. The Charitable Remainder Trust is described in great detail in my first book, *The Living Trust.*

This unique area of estate planning requires great expertise, and very few individuals in the United States have such knowledge. If you would like expert advice on the Charitable Remainder Trust, I would recommend, without hesitation, Robert S. Keebler of Schu-maker, Romenesko & Associates, S.C. The firm is located in Green Bay, Wisconsin, and can be reached by calling 920-498-9500. When you are faced with the potential of losing more than 75 percent of your IRA to income and estate taxes, a long-distance telephone call can be a very wise investment.

AGGREGATE COMMUNITY PROPERTY AGREEMENT

If you reside in a community property state and have substantial value in one or more IRAs, I strongly recommend that you implement an Aggregate Community Property Agreement. Such an agreement enables the surviving spouse to allocate assets—and thus, "split" IRA ownership between the decedent's estate and the survivor's estate—and then allocate the assets by value. This empowerment would, in most cases, allow the surviving spouse to allocate real assets to the decedent's B sub-trust and/or C sub-trust and to allocate the IRA to the survivor's A sub-trust. Without an Aggregate Community Property Agreement, a surviving spouse cannot "allocate" assets in a community property state, since the surviving spouse owns half of the assets.

DISCLAIMING AN INTEREST IN AN IRA

A spouse may disclaim part or full interest in an IRA but must do so within nine months from the date of death of the first spouse. Likewise, a child named as an IRA beneficiary may disclaim part or full interest in an IRA

TABLE 22-8

ASSET ALLOCATION WHEN HUSBAND DIES WITH MARRIED IRA–QTIP TRUST (SECOND MARRIAGE)

Assets	Market Value	Married IRA–QTIP Trust	Decedent's B Sub-Trust	Survivor's A Sub-Trust
Home	$ 400,000			$400,000
IRAs	$1,000,000	$1,000,000		

within nine months from the date of death of the surviving spouse. The main reason for disclaiming an interest in an asset is to remove the disclaimed portion from your estate, thus allowing the disclaimed portion to be placed in the decedent's estate—usually to fully utilize the decedent's federal estate tax exemption.

As with any disclaimed asset, if you disclaim an interest in the IRA, you must do so before receiving any income. Once you have received *any* income from an asset (such as an IRA), you are disqualified from disclaiming any interest in that asset. Since beneficiaries have the ability to disclaim an interest in an IRA, it is appropriate for you to name not only beneficiaries, but also contingent beneficiaries for the IRA. If your spouse were to disclaim an interest in your IRA, that interest would flow directly to the contingent beneficiaries (presumably your children). If your children had named contingent beneficiaries and were to later disclaim their interest in the IRA, the interest would pass to their contingent beneficiaries—presumably their children (i.e., your grandchildren).

If you disclaim an interest in an IRA, and if a Trust (whether revocable or irrevocable) is the contingent beneficiary of that IRA, the Trust should restrict to the last calendar month the "frivolous right" provision, which allows the surviving spouse to use $5,000 or 5 percent of the assets, whichever is greater, for his or her own use. The Trust must also not contain any limited power of appointment for the surviving spouse. Remember, however, that these restrictions do not affect the right of the surviving spouse to act as the surviving trustee of the Trust.

It would also be most appropriate to name a Married IRA–QTIP Trust as contingent beneficiary of a large IRA, allowing your spouse the opportunity to disclaim an interest in the IRA. The surviving spouse could disclaim a specified fractional amount of the IRA that would pass to the Married IRA–QTIP Trust and would fully utilize the first spouse's entire federal estate tax exemption.

HANDLING LARGE IRAS

Properly handling a large IRA is *not* a do-it-yourself program. To successfully utilize a large IRA and preserve any unused value for your heirs, you must obtain good, sound, and experienced financial advice. Unfortunately, far too few professionals are truly knowledgeable about the subject of IRAs. My primary purpose in writing this book is to explain to the general public how to settle a Living Trust, and the intent of this chapter has been to help guide you through some typical IRA scenarios and to acquaint you with the many entanglements that may eventually ensnare your hard-earned IRA. My intent was not to provide you with a particular solution to your own unique IRA situation. If you have a large IRA, you will need far greater expertise than I can provide in this text.

ROTH LEGACY TRUSTˢᴹ

The Roth Legacy Trustˢᴹ (a licensed service mark of The Estate Plan) is one of the greatest vehicles for transferring wealth to your children and grandchildren. Whether you created your Roth IRA as a conversion from a traditional IRA or started your Roth IRA as an investment from scratch (by contributing $2,000 per year), the Roth Legacy Trustˢᴹ permits you to pass on to your heirs all of your unused Roth IRA retirement funds, with the funds continuing to grow over the ensuing years and with the magic of compound interest helping to grow your legacy even more. When your children withdraw those IRA funds from the Roth Legacy Trustˢᴹ, only the growth within that Trust is subject to taxation.

Potential Legacy of the Roth IRA

Let me show you the great potential of the Roth IRA in building a wonderful legacy for your children. For illustration purposes, let's assume that George and Martha Hamilton have converted their traditional IRA to a Roth IRA that is now worth $500,000. George is the Roth IRA owner, and Martha is the named beneficiary of the IRA. As the owner, George may withdraw any funds from the Roth IRA without penalty and totally tax free, assuming that he is at least age 59½ and that at least five years have passed since the IRA conversion. When George dies, his wife, as the Roth IRA beneficiary, can then roll George's Roth IRA over into her own Roth IRA and also name the children as beneficiaries. Thus, during the remainder of Martha's life, she may withdraw any of the IRA funds without penalty and totally tax free. When Martha passes away, the Roth IRA will pass to the children, who will be required to make subsequent IRA withdrawals based on the life expectancy of the oldest child.

Alternatively, Martha could have split her Roth IRA into separate Roth IRAs, naming each child as the beneficiary of an IRA. During Martha's lifetime, she would still have full access to all of the Roth IRA funds. On her demise, each child named as beneficiary could take withdrawals from his or her Roth IRA based on his or her own life expectancy.

In contrast to a traditional IRA, for which the tax code requires the owner to take withdrawals upon reaching the age of 70½, the tax code for the Roth IRA does not require the owner to take any withdrawals, regardless of his or her age. Required Roth IRA withdrawals are imposed only upon the *beneficiaries* of the Roth IRA. Thus, during the lifetime of the Roth IRA owner, the magic of tax-free compound growth can be used to increase the value of the Roth investment. Later, when the original IRA owner has passed away, the Roth IRA growth can be further magnified (for eventual withdrawals by the beneficiaries), since any required withdrawals are based upon the life expectancy of the beneficiaries, substantially extending the time period that the Roth IRA funds can enjoy continued tax-free compound growth!

Use of the Roth Legacy Trust℠

As awesome as the magic of compounding interest can be in a Roth IRA, the real beauty of building wealth for the future of our children is in the Roth Legacy Trust℠. To show you the advantage of using a Roth Legacy Trust℠, I will use the same example as before.

George and Martha Hamilton have a $500,000 Roth IRA. Their two married daughters, Cathy and Barbara, each have two sons (the four grandchildren of George and Martha). George and Martha decide to create a Roth Legacy Trust℠, naming Cathy and Barbara as the beneficiaries of the Trust and giving them the right to pass on their shares of the Roth IRA to their own children (George and Martha's grandsons).

If George and Martha grant their two daughters a Limited Power of Appointment over the daughters' share of the Roth IRA (withdrawals that pass from the Roth IRA to the Roth Legacy Trust℠), the daughters have the opportunity to take those funds or may forgo their withdrawals and, thus, ultimately pass their share of the Roth IRA withdrawals to their own children (George and Martha's grandsons). The disadvantage to this approach, however, is that the Roth IRA funds will be included in the daughters' estates for estate tax purposes.

The Roth IRA and the Roth Legacy Trust℠—Working Together

To better understand the function of the Roth Legacy Trust℠, you need to realize that the total amount of funds in the Roth IRA does not pass into the Roth Legacy Trust℠. Only the *required distributions* to the beneficiaries pass into the Trust. Thus, during George's lifetime, the funds in the Roth IRA continue to grow tax free, although George could utilize the Roth IRA funds, at any time he wanted, for his retirement pleasure.

Upon George's death, the funds in the Roth IRA pass to Martha, who is the named beneficiary of the Roth IRA. Let's now assume that Martha rolls George's Roth IRA over into her own Roth IRA and then names the Roth Legacy Trust℠ as the beneficiary of her new Roth IRA. During Martha's lifetime, she has the right to withdraw any or all of her Roth IRA funds for whatever reason she desires. However, if we assume that Martha allows her Roth IRA to continue to grow, the magic of compound interest just keeps multiplying—and the value of her Roth IRA increases dramatically. Upon

Martha's demise, the Roth Legacy Trust^{SM} becomes the beneficiary of Martha's Roth IRA. Even after Martha's death, the value of the Roth IRA continues to grow substantially, since only the *required distributions* of the Roth IRA to the beneficiaries of the Roth IRA pass into the Roth Legacy Trust^{SM}.

As an alternative, George could have selected a more cautious approach and named the Roth Legacy Trust^{SM} as the beneficiary of his Roth IRA. With this approach, upon George's death, Martha would have no further right to any of the Roth IRA funds. This scenario necessarily assumes that George left Martha with sufficient other assets to provide for her lifetime needs.

Revocability of the Roth Legacy Trust^{SM}

The Roth Legacy Trust^{SM} remains revocable during the lifetime of the trustors (George and Martha, in our example), thus permitting the trustors to change the trustees, beneficiaries, and allocations and distributions. However, upon the death of the last trustor (in our example, when Martha dies), the Roth Legacy Trust^{SM} becomes *irrevocable*; no further changes can be made to the already established trustees, beneficiaries, allocations, and distributions.

However, if a Limited Power of Appointment is used with adult children, even though the Roth Legacy Trust^{SM} is irrevocable, the adult children may forgo their specified distributions from the Roth Legacy Trust^{SM} and pass their share of the Trust funds to their own children (in our example, George and Martha's grandsons). Be aware, however, that by enabling the adult children to have access to the Roth IRA funds, these funds then must be included in the adult children's estates for estate tax purposes. In this scenario, the adult children would be a logical choice to be the trustees of the Roth Legacy Trust^{SM}.

Distributions from the Roth IRA to the Roth Legacy Trust^{SM}

Distribution of funds from the Roth IRA to the Roth Legacy Trust^{SM} are based upon the life expectancy of the oldest child, unless the Roth IRA has been previously divided into separate Roth IRAs for each child. Each child may withdraw the distributions from the Roth IRA to the Roth Legacy Trust^{SM} at a specified age or (if they have a Limited Power of Appointment) forgo such distributions and pass them on to his or her own children.

Advantages of the Roth Legacy Trust^{SM}

The Roth Legacy Trust^{SM}, when funded by distributions from a Roth IRA, provides a number of advantages to increase the amount of your legacy:

- Income-tax-free growth
- Great potential wealth transfer
- Great potential for growth of wealth (after estate taxes and generation-skipping transfer tax)
- Provision for withdrawal of necessary funds for health, education, maintenance, and support of children and grandchildren
- Financial discipline for your beneficiaries
- Financially sophisticated investment planning
- Protection from creditors (especially important in states that do not protect the Roth IRA from creditor claims)
- Protection from future claims by the child's or grandchild's spouse

Income-Tax-Free Growth

One of the most powerful features of the Roth IRA is that all growth is exempt from income taxation. This exemption permits compound growth that is unfettered by consumptive income taxes.

Great Potential Wealth Transfer

Free from the required withdrawals of a traditional IRA (starting when you reach the age of 70½), the Roth IRA is able to grow over your entire lifetime. Using the earlier case of George and Martha Hamilton, assume that George converts his traditional IRA to a Roth IRA when he reaches the age of seventy. After conversion, the Roth IRA is worth $500,000. George lives another ten years (and dies at age eighty), while Martha lives five additional years following George's death. Therefore, the $500,000 Roth IRA grows tax free at an annual rate of 10 percent for fifteen years—to a remarkable $1,296,000 in ten years and an amazing $2,089,000 in fifteen years. Figure 22-1 graphs this phenomenal growth.

Great Potential for Wealth Growth

Following the death of Martha (the second spouse to die), the entire estate, including the Roth IRA, becomes subject to federal estate taxation. Let's assume that George and Martha had followed sound financial planning principles and set up an Insurance Preservation Trust, funded with the appropriate amount of life insurance, to pay the federal estate tax liability and also any generation-skipping taxes, without having to disturb any of the Roth IRA funds. If George and Martha have included the right of their grandchildren to share as beneficiaries of the Roth Legacy Trust[SM], then the estate valuation must include the value of the Roth IRA when calculating any generation-

skipping transfer tax liability. (The subject of generation-skipping transfer taxes was discussed in the previous chapter.) I strongly encourage you to understand the importance of recognizing *and paying* any required generation-skipping tax liability when the second spouse dies, thus allowing the Roth IRA to continue to grow in the future (ultimately to enormous proportions) for the benefit of the grandchildren with no further generation-skipping tax liability.

A Word of Advice: Pay any required generation-skipping tax liability when the second spouse dies, thus allowing the Roth IRA to continue to grow in the future (ultimately to enormous proportions) for the benefit of the grandchildren with no further generation-skipping tax liability.

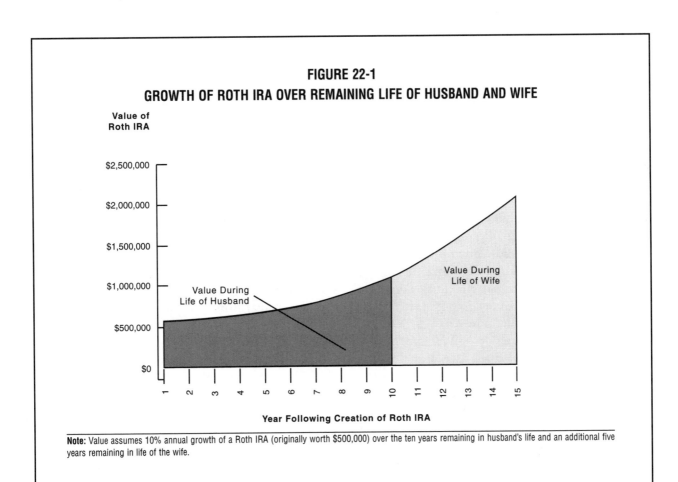

FIGURE 22-1

GROWTH OF ROTH IRA OVER REMAINING LIFE OF HUSBAND AND WIFE

Note: Value assumes 10% annual growth of a Roth IRA (originally worth $500,000) over the ten years remaining in husband's life and an additional five years remaining in life of the wife.

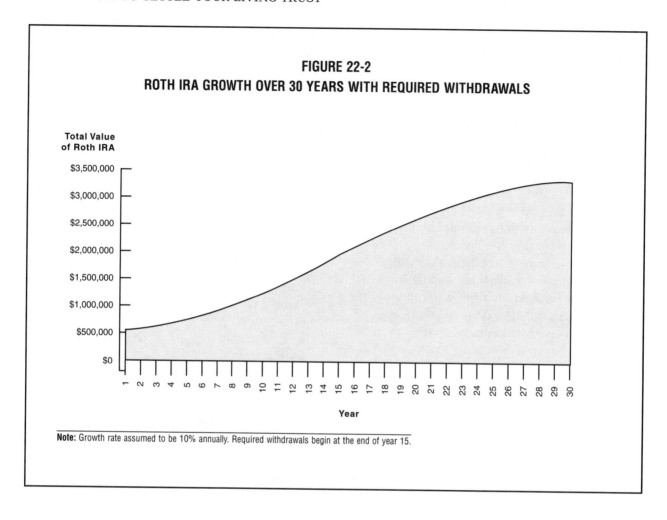

FIGURE 22-2
ROTH IRA GROWTH OVER 30 YEARS WITH REQUIRED WITHDRAWALS

Total Value of Roth IRA

Year

Note: Growth rate assumed to be 10% annually. Required withdrawals begin at the end of year 15.

The combination of a Roth IRA and a Roth Legacy Trust℠ provides an excellent opportunity for growth, even after paying estate taxes and generation-skipping taxes. In addition, I also urge you to consider the approach of dividing the Roth IRA into separate IRAs for each child or grandchild, thus minimizing the IRA distribution while maximizing the magic of compound interest growth. Let's continue with our example of George and Martha and assume that Martha has now died.

Continued Growth of Roth IRA For illustration purposes, let's assume that there is only one Roth IRA and that George and Martha's two daughters are the named beneficiaries of the Roth Legacy Trust℠. Let's further assume that the daughters are ages 45 and 50 when their mother dies. Under this scenario, the Roth IRA must now be paid out over the life expectancy of the older child (who is 50 years

old). Let's further assume that the Roth IRA continues to grow income tax free at a conservative growth rate of 10 percent. The required Roth IRA distributions to the beneficiaries (Martha's daughters), based on the life expectancy of the older child, flow into the Roth Legacy Trust℠, where those funds can continue to grow at the conservative rate of 10 percent annually.

Be aware, however, that growth in a Roth Legacy Trust℠ is subject to income tax at the Trust tax rate of 39.6 percent. If the Roth Legacy Trust℠ assets were invested in growth vehicles, the capital gain would be taxed only when the investment is liquidated. At that time, the growth would be taxable at capital gains tax rates of 28, 20, or, effective in 2001, 18 percent, depending on how long the investments had been held. In contrast, growth in the form of income would be taxable annually at the Trust income tax rate. To be conservative, we will assume that all growth in our example is income and is taxed at the highest income tax rate of 39.6 percent.

Be Aware: Although all growth and distributions from a Roth IRA are tax free, all growth and distributions from a Roth Legacy Trust^{SM} are fully taxed.

Continuing with our example, assume that when Martha dies, the grandchildren are ages 20, 18, 16, and 15, and the Roth Legacy Trust^{SM} has been designed to make outright distributions when each grandchild attains the age of 35. In the interim, all of the funds in trust are available for the grandchildren's health, education, maintenance, and support. For simplicity of this example, however, assume that no withdrawals are made from the Roth Legacy Trust^{SM} for at least the next fifteen years.

As illustrated in Figure 22-2, the value of the Roth IRA has grown from $2,089,000 in the fifteenth year to $3,433,000 by the thirtieth year—including the required withdrawals beginning at the end of the fifteenth year (when the oldest child reaches the age of 35).

Growth of Roth Legacy Trust^{SM} The required withdrawals for the grandchildren flow into the Roth Legacy Trust^{SM}, where the funds continue to grow at a conservative rate of 10 percent. We also assume the highest tax rate (39.6 percent) on the growth. As shown in Figure 22-3 on page 324, due to the growth in the Roth Legacy Trust^{SM}, specified distributions to the grandchildren from the Roth Legacy Trust^{SM} increase from an initial amount of $90,027 at the end of the fifteenth year to the phenomenal amount of more than $4.8 million at the end of the thirtieth year!

Combined Growth of Roth IRA and Roth Legacy Trust^{SM} The combined growth of the Roth IRA (adjusted for the required withdrawals) and the Roth Legacy Trust^{SM} presents a financial windfall that is almost astronomical! The Roth IRA begins with a value of $500,000 and grows to an awesome $8.3 mil-

lion in thirty years. Distributions from the Roth IRA are placed in the Roth Legacy Trust^{SM} where the growth continues. The combined growth of the Roth IRA ($8.3 million) and the Roth Legacy Trust^{SM} ($4.7 million) provide phenomenal growth (see Figure 22-4 on page 325).

The required withdrawals from the Roth IRA are based on the life expectancy of the oldest child. If the grandchildren rather than the children had been named as beneficiaries, the required Roth IRA withdrawals would be based upon the life expectancy of the oldest grandchild. Since the required withdrawals would be much smaller (due to the lesser age of the grandchildren), the growth rate of the Roth IRA would be even more astounding.

What is important for you to visualize is the magic of compound growth when you use these two vehicles, the Roth IRA and the Roth Legacy Trust^{SM}, together. An investment that began with "only" $500,000 was multiplied sixteen times over the thirty-year period! Whether you start with a Roth IRA value of $100,000, $500,000, or $1 million is almost immaterial; the end result for your heirs is a wonderful legacy of consideration and caring. If you desire to provide a legacy for your heirs, the Roth IRA, in combination with the Roth Legacy Trust^{SM}, will surpass your greatest dreams.

Provision for Withdrawal of Necessary Funds for Children and Grandchildren

The Roth Legacy Trust^{SM} authorizes the trustee of the Trust to distribute any funds necessary to provide for the health, education, maintenance, and support of the beneficiaries of the Trust. If necessary, the trustee of the Roth Legacy Trust^{SM} may even invade the value of the Roth IRA (beyond its current required withdrawals) in order to meet the specific needs of a beneficiary.

Financial Discipline for Your Beneficiaries

Another important feature of the Roth Legacy Trust^{SM} is that it provides financial discipline for the beneficiaries, whether they be your children or grandchildren. (Only 3 percent of our nation's population are considered to be disci-

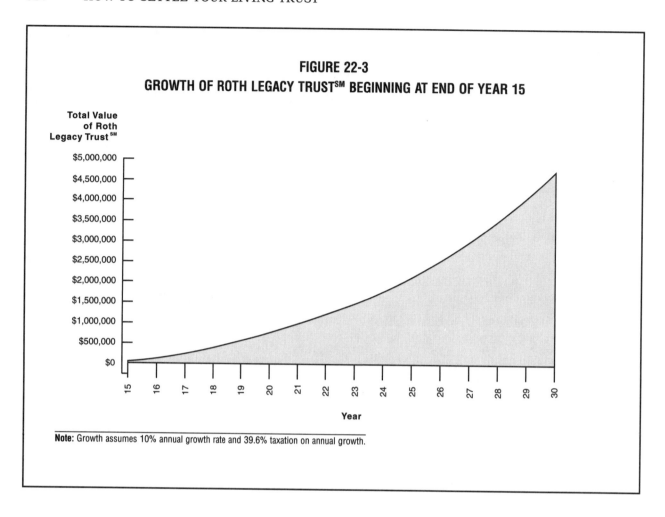

FIGURE 22-3
GROWTH OF ROTH LEGACY TRUST℠ BEGINNING AT END OF YEAR 15

Note: Growth assumes 10% annual growth rate and 39.6% taxation on annual growth.

plined investment builders.) The Roth IRA funds eventually pass to the Roth Legacy Trust℠, where fund growth is maximized, but these funds are available for access if the need arises. When the beneficiaries are ready to retire, they have a nice nest egg already set aside—and they don't have to worry about the questionable future of social security benefits.

Financially Sophisticated Investment Planning

Your children or grandchildren may not be sophisticated investors, but the Roth Legacy Trust℠ provides the vehicle to ensure that your children or grandchildren properly manage investments for their future. For years, I worked as an investment advisor with presidents of small to middle-sized corporations. To my great surprise, I learned that although these individuals were extremely knowledgeable in

their particular field of endeavor, they had little or no understanding of how to successfully invest or manage financial investments. And so it may be with your children.

Remember that all IRAs, whether traditional IRAs or Roth IRAs, *must be managed by a trustee.* Typically, the trustee of the Roth IRA is a trustee similar to that of a traditional IRA. The trustors, and eventually the trustees, of the Roth Legacy Trust℠ have the right to direct the Roth IRA trustee to make the appropriate growth investments. This power should be included in the Beneficiary Designation Form. The trustees of the Roth Legacy Trust℠ presumably will be your children, close family, or close friends, who, through your initial direction, will select an astute and experienced investment firm to guide them in their investment planning for both the Roth IRA and the Roth Legacy Trust℠.

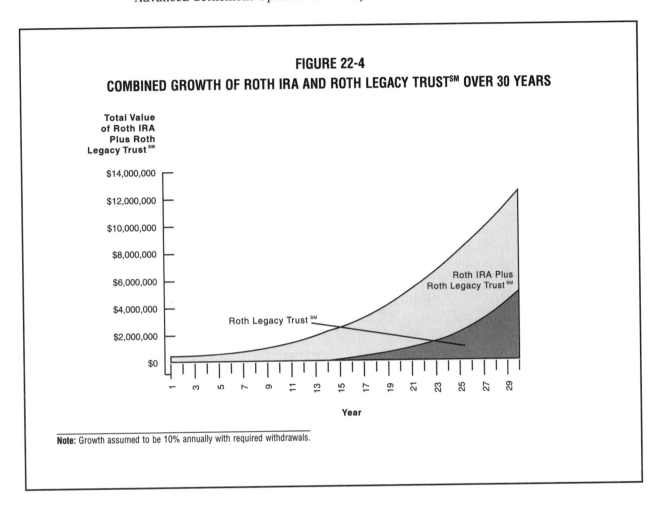

FIGURE 22-4

COMBINED GROWTH OF ROTH IRA AND ROTH LEGACY TRUST^{SM} OVER 30 YEARS

Note: Growth assumed to be 10% annually with required withdrawals.

Protection from Creditors

A number of states do not protect Roth IRA funds from creditors. A list of these states would serve no purpose here, since few of us can predict where our children or grandchildren will eventually take up residence. We cannot foresee whether these states will eventually adopt creditor protection statutes. However, the Roth Legacy Trust^{SM} can act as a barrier against creditors for all of the Roth IRA funds, except funds that have been distributed to a beneficiary. Thus, Roth IRA funds are protected from creditors as well as from lawsuits, where judgments could decimate a child's or grandchild's inheritance.

Protection from Future Claims by the Child's or Grandchild's Spouse

Since the Roth Legacy Trust^{SM} is the beneficiary of the Roth IRA and the child or grand-child is the beneficiary of the Roth Legacy Trust^{SM}, a beneficiary's spouse has no legal claim to the funds within either the Roth IRA or the Roth Legacy Trust^{SM}. Only the funds eventually *distributed* to the beneficiary are exposed to any potential claims by the beneficiary's spouse.

A Most Welcome Legacy

Realize, for a moment, that, if you invested $2,000 a year beginning at age 25 and continued to age 65 (a total investment of $80,000), your Roth IRA would compound its growth absolutely free of income tax. Assuming a conservative 10 percent compounded annual growth rate, this growth would amount to $726,000 when you reach the age of 65. Now, that, my friends, is a nice retirement cushion!

The Roth Legacy Trust^{SM} is an ideal way to create a legacy of wealth for your children and/or your grandchildren. By properly combining a Roth IRA and a Roth Legacy Trust℠, you ensure that the future of your children can be secure—regardless of their investment acumen.

PROPER ESTATE PLANNING IS A MUST

The subject of proper estate planning, including the shielding of large IRAs from onerous income taxes and estate taxes, is complicated by different impacts on each type of beneficiary, whether a spouse, one or more children, or specifically named beneficiaries, as well as by the varying scenarios involving a revocable Living Trust or a revocable Married IRA–QTIP Trust. Table 22-9 summarizes the income tax consequences for the beneficiaries of traditional IRAs and Roth IRAs, which you must consider in order to ensure that you minimize unnecessary taxation and that your heirs receive as much of your estate as possible. (In this table, Standard Revocable Living Trust

TABLE 22-9
CONSEQUENCES FOR BENEFICIARIES OF IRAs

| Beneficiaries | STANDARD TAX DEDUCTIBLE IRA | | ROTH IRA |
	Individual	Married Couple	Single or Married
Spouse		Ghost life expectancy of decedent; or roll over into Spousal IRA with ghost life expectancy of oldest child; or roll over and split into separate IRAs for each child.	Ghost life expectancy of decedent; or roll over into Spousal IRA with ghost life expectancy of oldest child; or roll over and split into separate IRAs for each child.
Children or Named Beneficiaries	Life expectancy of oldest beneficiary; or split IRA for life expectancy of each beneficiary.	Life expectancy of oldest beneficiary; or split IRA for life expectancy of each beneficiary.	Life expectancy of oldest beneficiary; or split IRA for life expectancy of each beneficiary.
Standard Revocable Living Trust**	Must recognize IRA income by December 31 of year following death of IRA owner.	Must recognize IRA income by December 31 of year following death of IRA owner, if recalculating.*	Life expectancy of oldest beneficiary.
Single IRA Trust or Married IRA–QTIP Trust	Life expectancy of oldest beneficiary; or split IRA for life expectancy of each beneficiary.	Life expectancy of spouse and ghost life expectancy of spouse.	Life expectancy of spouse and ghost life expectancy of spouse.

*If using life expectancy, can ghost remaining life expectancy.

**Caution: Prudent position is to use a revocable Trust designed for a Roth IRA, a Roth Legacy Trust℠.

©1998, Henry W. Abts III, The Estate Plan, 800-292-0223

refers to a typical Living Trust that has *not* specifically been designed to meet the rigid legal requirements of the IRS for handling IRAs.)

Tax Planning for IRAs

As you have learned in Chapters 12 and 13 and this chapter, proper tax planning for IRAs is of utmost importance to the health of your estate and to retain the legacy that you have built for your children or grandchildren. Tax planning for IRAs is a complex subject itself, but the subject is not the primary focus of this book. If you would like to learn more about tax planning for IRAs, I recommend that you read *Life and Death Planning for Retirement Benefits*, written for professionals by Natalie B. Choate. (You can order by calling 1-800-247-6553.)

Advanced Settlement Options Require Professional Guidance

When properly used, IRAs can provide you with an excellent source of retirement income.

However, if you die with a large IRA but without proper estate planning, as much as 75 percent of your remaining IRA funds can be gobbled up by Uncle Sam. Advanced settlement options for IRAs provide you with several vehicles to consider as part of your estate planning strategy. However, do not be lulled into a false sense of security, and do not implement these strategies without the advice of legal and tax-planning professionals.

Caution: I urge you to seek *very knowledgeable estate preservation specialists* before *you implement any of the advanced settlement options for your IRA(s).*

23

Advanced Settlement Options in Separate Property States
When the First Spouse Dies

There are several advanced settlement options for allocating estate assets to the A, B, and/or C sub-trusts. Each of these options has a different effect on the estate, both in allocation and in valuation, depending upon the rules for separate property states. Five different advanced settlement allocation options apply to separate property states:

- An A Trust with a Married IRA–QTIP Trust
- Itemization method with a Married A-B or A-B-C Trust and a Married IRA–QTIP Trust
- Married A-B-C Trust with Debt Payment Power of Appointment
- Married A-B-C Trust with Debt Payment Power of Appointment and a Married IRA–QTIP Trust
- Married A-B Trust with Debt Payment Power of Appointment

This chapter first provides you with a brief overview of the five advanced settlement allocation options applicable to separate property states. Then each option is discussed in more detail. All of these options can be used for highly valued and complex estates.

I urge you to take the simple approach: First read the following overview of the five advanced settlement allocation options. Then read only the section that applies to your particular Living Trust.

OVERVIEW OF THE FIVE ADVANCED SETTLEMENT OPTIONS

Before delving into the details of each option, let me first acquaint you with the five different advanced settlement options that are pertinent to settling highly valued and/or complex estates. I will present a brief synopsis of each one, as well as cite their unique advantages and disadvantages. Read each of these summaries in order to see which (if any) alternatives might be appropriate for your particular estate-planning needs. Then, carefully study the allocation option that best fits the needs of your estate.

An A Trust with a Married IRA–QTIP Trust
An A Trust with a Married IRA–QTIP Trust is primarily designed for someone who has entered into a second marriage, brings into the marriage a large IRA accumulated prior to the second marriage, and does not create a joint Living Trust with his or her spouse for their new marital assets. The Married IRA–QTIP Trust is structured for the spouse who desires, upon his or her death, that the IRA remain in the Trust for the benefit of the surviving spouse and that, upon the death of the surviving spouse, the remaining IRA funds pass to the heirs of the spouse who owned the IRA. The separate property of this individual, other than the IRA, is allocated to the A Trust. The Married IRA–QTIP Trust also incorporates the decedent's federal estate tax exemption.

Itemization Method with a Married A-B Trust or Married A-B-C Trust and a Married IRA–QTIP Trust
Using the itemization method of allocation in conjunction with a Married A-B Trust or a Married A-B-C Trust and with a Married IRA–QTIP Trust is a vital estate-planning tool for a married couple who has a joint Trust for its marital assets (an A-B Trust or an A-B-C Trust) and who also has a large IRA. Two basic situations call for the addition of the Married IRA–QTIP Trust:

• An individual has a large IRA as separate property, has entered into a second marriage, and desires that the surviving spouse have the right to the IRA funds while living and that, after the surviving spouse dies, the remaining IRA funds pass to the heirs of the first spouse (the owner of the IRA).
• A married couple has an IRA that is large in proportion to the marital assets. An example would be a 401(k) plan that was rolled over into an IRA and that has grown to a substantial size which is disproportionate to the marital assets (i.e., whose value is much greater than that of the rest of the combined assets)—say, an IRA worth $1 million and a home worth $400,000. Since the IRA passes to the surviving spouse, the couple needs a way to fully utilize the decedent's federal

estate tax exemption without triggering potential income tax consequences. The addition of the Married IRA–QTIP Trust can be an excellent solution.

Married A-B-C Trust with Debt Payment Power of Appointment
When a Married A-B-C Trust is combined with a Debt Payment Power of Appointment (DPPA; similar to the General Power of Appointment [GPOA]), *all* of the Living Trust's marital assets pass to the decedent's estate. Typically, this approach is used to achieve full stepped-up valuation (i.e., the cost basis becomes the current market value) on all of the Living Trust assets, as well as to protect these assets from creditors and frivolous lawsuits.

If you select this option, you must be very aware that any such Power of Appointment passes all of the survivor's separate property to the decedent's estate (unless the Power of Appointment expressly provides otherwise). If the spouses are in a second marriage, such a total shift of the survivor's assets could cause severe conflict among children from the previous marriages. Any IRAs, like all retirement assets, are outside the Living Trust and flow directly to the surviving spouse as the IRA beneficiary.

The main disadvantage of using this allocation option is that the survivor's federal estate tax exemption is lost. However, any value of the remaining IRA funds at the survivor's death can be offset by the survivor's federal estate tax exemption.

Married A-B-C Trust with Debt Payment Power of Appointment and a Married IRA–QTIP Trust
If a Married A-B-C Trust is combined with a Debt Payment Power of Appointment (DPPA; similar to the General Power of Appointment [GPOA]) and used in conjunction with a Married IRA–QTIP Trust, all of the Living Trust assets pass to the decedent's estate. This approach is typically used to achieve full stepped-up valuation on all of the Living Trust assets—including the survivor's separate property.

In considering this approach, however, you need to be keenly aware that the Power of

Appointment passes all of the survivor's separate property to the decedent's estate (unless the Power of Appointment expressly provides otherwise). If the spouses are in a second marriage and have, as beneficiaries, children from a previous marriage, such a shift of the survivor's assets could cause a great deal of conflict and resentment.

The Married IRA–QTIP Trust passes any IRAs to the decedent's estate as well, leaving the surviving spouse's estate without any assets whatsoever! Such a lopsided and seemingly unfair approach can be an excellent means of protecting your estate against creditors and frivolous lawsuits, thus preserving the assets for use by the surviving spouse (and/or providing an eventual inheritance to the heirs).

The main disadvantage of using this allocation option is that the survivor's federal estate tax exemption is lost.

An alternative approach is to split the IRA, with one part going to a Married IRA–QTIP Trust and the other part going to the surviving spouse. With this approach, the survivor's federal estate tax exemption can be used to offset the remaining value of the surviving "spouse's" IRA.

Married A-B Trust with Debt Payment Power of Appointment

Combining a Married A-B Trust with a Debt Payment Power of Appointment (DPPA; similar to the General Power of Appointment [GPOA]) can be a potent estate-planning tool for certain estates. The DPPA passes all of the Trust assets to the decedent's estate, so that all Trust assets receive full stepped-up valuation. With this option, since the decedent lacks a C sub-trust (QTIP Trust) and the decedent's estate is limited to one federal estate tax exemption, the balance of the asset value exceeding the decedent's federal estate tax exemption flows back to the surviving spouse and into the survivor's A sub-trust. Any IRAs pass directly to the surviving spouse as the IRA beneficiary.

The primary advantage of this estate-planning vehicle is the attainment of full stepped-up valuation on all Trust assets—including the survivor's separate property.

ALLOCATION OPTIONS FOR SEPARATE PROPERTY STATES

To make each of the allocation options (and the differences among them) fairly simple and, therefore, understandable, I will illustrate each option by using the same few basic Trust assets. The examples use the values shown in Table 23-1. In some of the cases, where appropriate, the assets include "other real estate."

All but one of the examples use an IRA value of $1 million, not because this high value is common for most people's IRAs, but rather to illustrate the problem (and the possible solutions) for estates that have IRAs with a very

TABLE 23-1

ASSET VALUES USED IN EXAMPLES FOR ADVANCED SETTLEMENT OPTIONS IN SEPARATE PROPERTY STATES

Basic Estate Assets	Cost Basis	Market Value with Large IRA	Market Value with Smaller IRA
Home	$ 200,000	$ 400,000	$400,000
Other real estate	$ 400,000	$ 800,000	$800,000
Decedent's separate property	$ 50,000	$ 100,000	$100,000
Survivor's separate property	$ 50,000	$ 100,000	$100,000
Large IRA	$1,000,000*	$1,000,000	
Smaller IRA	$ 100,000*		$100,000

*The cost basis of an IRA is zero.

TABLE 23-2

VALUE OF ESTATE ASSETS BEFORE DEATH OF FIRST SPOUSE
(AN A TRUST AND MARRIED IRA–QTIP TRUST IN A SEPARATE PROPERTY STATE)

Basic Estate Assets	MARKET VALUE		COST BASIS	
	First Spouse	Second Spouse	First Spouse	Second Spouse
First spouse's separate property	$ 100,000		$ 50,000	
IRA (separate property)	$1,000,000		$1,000,000*	

*The cost basis of an IRA is zero.

large value in relation to the total value of the estate. Don't be distracted by the use of such a large IRA; the purpose is only to emphasize what happens to the IRA. One example uses a $100,000 IRA to minimize the effect of the IRA. (The actual dollar values for the assets are not intended to have any relationship to your own personal estate but are intended to clearly establish the basic principles that relate to applying an allocation option to your estate.)

Each illustration of the allocation options uses a federal estate tax exemption of $600,000, even though this exemption is $625,000 in 1998 and increases to $1 million by the year 2006. (Remember that Congress has not given us any real boon, since the increase in the exemption doesn't even keep pace with inflation.) If you want to clearly see the impact on your own estate in future years, simply change the values in the illustration to match those in your estate and the year in which you are making the calculations. Regardless of the actual numbers, the concepts remain the same.

In settling an estate, the primary challenge is to determine how to allocate and value the estate assets upon the death of the *first* spouse. All of the illustrations portray the asset allocation when the first spouse dies, because this allocation can have the most serious estate tax consequences if not done properly for the particular estate. (The assets of each estate will vary as to allocation and to value, but the same principles still apply.) Upon the death of the

second spouse, valuation and allocation of estate assets are fairly easy to accomplish, as discussed in Chapter 16A.

AN A TRUST WITH A MARRIED IRA–QTIP TRUST

The A Trust, used in conjunction with a Married IRA–QTIP Trust, is primarily designed for someone who has entered into a second marriage, brings into the marriage a large IRA accumulated prior to the second marriage, and does not create a joint Living Trust with his or her spouse for their marital assets. The Married IRA–QTIP Trust is structured for the spouse who desires, upon his or her death, that the IRA remain in trust for the benefit of the surviving spouse and that, upon the death of the surviving spouse, the remaining IRA funds pass to the heirs of the spouse who owned the IRA. Therefore, in this scenario, only two Trusts come into play: the individual's A Trust (revocable until he or she dies) and the revocable Married IRA–QTIP Trust. The Married IRA–QTIP Trust has the ability to utilize any remaining portion of the decedent's federal estate tax exemption. Therefore, between the A Trust and the Married IRA–QTIP Trust, the individual's entire federal estate tax exemption can be fully utilized.

As you learned in Chapters 13 and 22, there is a significant advantage in converting your traditional IRA to a Roth IRA and then using a Roth Legacy Trust℠ to hold your new Roth

TABLE 23-3

ESTATE ASSETS AFTER DEATH OF FIRST SPOUSE
(AN A TRUST AND MARRIED IRA–QTIP TRUST IN A SEPARATE PROPERTY STATE)

Separate Property	Market Value	Decedent's Share
Decedent's separate property	$ 100,000	$ 100,000
IRA (separate property)	$1,000,000	$1,000,000
Total	$1,100,000	$1,100,000

ESTATE ASSET ALLOCATION TO TRUSTS

Estate Assets	Married IRA–QTIP Trust	A Trust
Decedent's separate property		$100,000
IRA (separate property)	$1,000,000	
Total value in decedent's estate	$1,100,000	

IRA. If you elect to make such a conversion, the Roth Legacy Trust℠ will simply replace the Married IRA–QTIP Trust. For estate valuation, the end result will typically be the same for a Roth Legacy Trust℠ and for a Married IRA–QTIP Trust.

Estate Before Demise of the First Spouse

While both spouses are still living, the market value and cost basis of the first spouse's separate property have the values shown in Table 23-2. For simplicity, this example omits marital property from the assets. (If any marital property existed in the estate, the decedent's share would be included in the A sub-trust.)

Estate After Demise of the First Spouse

Upon the death of the first spouse, the allocation of estate assets can best be illustrated in one step—the allocation of the decedent's other separate property and the allocation of the IRA as the decedent's separate property. Table 23-3 shows the other separate property and the IRA of the decedent and how these assets are allocated to both of the Trusts after the death of the first spouse. Please note that this allocation of assets is *not* arbitrary.

The decedent's other separate property is allocated to the A Trust and receives full stepped-up valuation to the current market value (as of the decedent's date of death). As beneficiary of the IRA, the Married IRA–QTIP Trust is the recipient of the entire IRA (or the Roth Legacy Trust℠ is the recipient of a Roth IRA). However, in such a case, the IRA must be the separate property of the decedent spouse; otherwise, the surviving spouse would be considered to have gifted his or her share to the decedent spouse.

If the IRA is not properly identified as separate property, the surviving spouse could "take against the Trust," which means that the intent of the decedent spouse could be nullified in court—and the surviving spouse could be given his or her share of the IRA as marital property. Remember that for an IRA, there is no stepped-up valuation. The cost basis for an IRA is zero.

Summary

In the allocation option just illustrated, the decedent's separate property receives full stepped-up valuation to the current market value ($100,000) and flows into the A Trust.

Since the IRA is the decedent's separate property and the Married IRA–QTIP Trust is named as beneficiary of the IRA, the IRA flows directly into the Married IRA–QTIP Trust. The surviving spouse has the right to all of the benefits of the IRA funds, but upon the death of the surviving spouse, any remaining IRA funds pass to the heirs of the first spouse, the owner of the IRA. The decedent's separate property of $100,000 plus half ($500,000) of the value of the IRA in the Married IRA–QTIP Trust fully utilizes the decedent's federal estate tax exemption (because the Married IRA–QTIP Trust also can make use of the decedent's federal estate tax exemption).

ITEMIZATION METHOD WITH A MARRIED A-B TRUST OR MARRIED A-B-C TRUST AND A MARRIED IRA–QTIP TRUST

The itemization method of allocation, in conjunction with a Married A-B Trust or Married A-B-C Trust and a Married IRA–QTIP Trust, has two distinct uses, depending on the particulars of an estate:

- This allocation option is well suited for an IRA that is separate property and used in conjunction with a joint marital Trust (a Married A-B or A-B-C Trust).
- This option can also be used for an IRA that is disproportionately large relative to the overall value of the marital estate.

Large IRA as Separate Property

The Married IRA–QTIP Trust is appropriate for someone who has entered into a second marriage, has a large IRA generated prior to this marriage, and has created a joint Trust with his or her spouse to hold the marital assets and other separate property. The spouse desires, upon his or her death, that the IRA remain in trust for the benefit of the surviving spouse and that, upon the death of the surviving spouse, the IRA go to the heirs of the spouse who owned the IRA. In such a scenario, there are either two or three sub-trusts (Married A-B Trust or a Married A-B-C Trust) and the Married IRA–QTIP Trust. The Married IRA–QTIP Trust can utilize any remaining portion of the decedent's unused federal estate tax exemption (if the exemption has not been fully used to offset the value of assets in the decedent's B sub-trust). Thus, the decedent's federal estate tax exemption can be fully utilized between the decedent's B sub-trust and the Married IRA–QTIP Trust.

Chapters 13 and 22 pointed out the significant advantage of converting your traditional IRA to a Roth IRA and then using a Roth Legacy Trust℠ to hold your new Roth IRA. If you elect to make such a conversion, the Roth Legacy Trust℠ will simply replace the Married IRA–QTIP Trust. For estate valuation, the end result typically will be the same for either a Roth Legacy Trust℠ or a Married IRA–QTIP Trust.

TABLE 23-4

**VALUE OF ESTATE ASSETS BEFORE DEATH OF FIRST SPOUSE
(MARRIED A-B OR A-B-C TRUST AND MARRIED IRA–QTIP TRUST IN A SEPARATE PROPERTY STATE)**

Basic Estate Assets	MARKET VALUE		COST BASIS	
	First Spouse	Second Spouse	First Spouse	Second Spouse
Home	$ 200,000	$200,000	$ 100,000	$100,000
First spouse's separate property	$ 100,000		$ 50,000	
Second spouse's separate property		$100,000		$ 50,000
IRA (separate property)	$1,000,000		$1,000,000*	

*The cost basis of an IRA is zero.

Estate Before Demise of the First Spouse

While both spouses are living, the market value and cost basis of the estate assets have the values shown in Table 23-4.

Estate After Demise of the First Spouse

Upon the death of the first spouse, the estate assets must be allocated to the appropriate sub-trusts. When there is a large IRA as separate property of one spouse, asset allocation involves three steps:

- Allocation of the decedent's and the survivor's separate property
- Allocation of the joint marital property
- Allocation of the IRA as the decedent's separate property

Allocation of Separate Property (at Market Value and Cost Basis) The separate property of the decedent spouse receives full stepped-up valuation to the current market value (as of the decedent's date of death) and is allocated to the decedent's B sub-trust and/or C sub-trust. The separate property of the surviving spouse does

not receive stepped-up valuation and is allocated to the survivor's A sub-trust at the original cost basis. Table 23-5 shows the asset valuation for both spouses' separate property after the death of the first spouse (including the effect of stepped-up valuation for the decedent's separate property). The bottom portion of the table shows how the separate property of both spouses is allocated to the appropriate sub-trusts.

Note that the decedent's separate property placed in the B sub-trust does not fully utilize the decedent's federal estate tax exemption.

Allocation of Marital Assets (at Market Value and Cost Basis) With the itemization method (which is required in a separate property state), one-half of each marital asset goes equally to each spouse. The decedent's share of each asset receives full stepped-up valuation to the current market value, whereas the survivor's share of each asset retains its original cost basis. In this example, the only marital asset is the home. One-half of the home is placed in the decedent's B sub-trust and

---

TABLE 23-5

SEPARATE PROPERTY OF BOTH SPOUSES AFTER DEATH OF FIRST SPOUSE
(MARRIED A-B TRUST AND MARRIED IRA–QTIP TRUST IN A SEPARATE PROPERTY STATE)

Separate Property	MARKET VALUE		COST BASIS	
	First Spouse	Second Spouse	First Spouse	Second Spouse
Decedent's separate property	$100,000			
Survivor's separate property				$50,000

SEPARATE PROPERTY ALLOCATION TO SUB-TRUSTS

Separate Property	Married IRA–QTIP Trust	B Sub-Trust	A Sub-Trust
Decedent's separate property		$100,000	
Survivor's separate property			$50,000
Value in decedent's estate	$100,000		
Value in survivor's estate			$50,000

TABLE 23-6

MARITAL ASSETS AFTER DEATH OF FIRST SPOUSE
(MARRIED A-B TRUST AND MARRIED IRA–QTIP TRUST IN A SEPARATE PROPERTY STATE)

Marital Property	MARKET VALUE		COST BASIS	
	First Spouse	Second Spouse	First Spouse	Second Spouse
Home	$200,000			$100,000

ALLOCATION OF MARITAL ASSETS TO SUB-TRUSTS

Assets	Married IRA–QTIP Trust	B Sub-Trust	A Sub-Trust
Home		$200,000	$100,000
Value in decedent's estate	$200,000		
Value in survivor's estate			$100,000

TABLE 23-7

SEPARATE AND MARITAL PROPERTY ALLOCATED TO SUB-TRUSTS
(MARRIED A-B TRUST AND MARRIED IRA–QTIP TRUST IN A SEPARATE PROPERTY STATE)

Separate and Marital Property	Married IRA–QTIP Trust	B Sub-Trust	A Sub-Trust
Decedent's separate property		$100,000	
Survivor's separate property			$ 50,000
Home		$200,000	$100,000
Value in decedent's estate	$300,000		
Value in survivor's estate			$150,000

receives stepped-up valuation to current market value ($200,000), and the other half is placed in the survivor's A sub-trust at its original cost basis ($100,000). Table 23-6 shows the marital asset valuation after the death of the first spouse (including the effect of stepped-up valuation on the decedent's share of the assets), as well as the allocation of the assets to the appropriate sub-trusts.

When the spouses' separate property and the joint marital property are both allocated to the appropriate sub-trusts, the distribution is as shown in Table 23-7.

Allocation of the IRA

Since the IRA is the decedent's separate property, the Married IRA–QTIP Trust (rather than the spouse) is the named beneficiary of the

IRA. Once the IRA passes to the Married IRA–QTIP Trust (or the Roth Legacy Trust[SM] for a Roth IRA) after the death of the IRA owner, the surviving spouse has the right to all of the IRA benefits while living. However, following the death of the surviving spouse, the remainder of the IRA flows to the IRA owner's (the first spouse's) heirs.

When the owner of the IRA dies, the value of the IRA becomes its current market value, and the IRA is allocated to the Married IRA–QTIP Trust, as shown in Table 23-8. Remember, for an IRA, there is no stepped-up valuation. The cost basis of an IRA is zero.

When all of the estate's assets—each spouse's separate property, the joint marital property, and the IRA (as separate property of the decedent spouse)—have been allocated, the final estate asset allocations to the various sub-trusts are as shown in Table 23-9 on page 338. Because of the large value of the IRA (as separate property), this allocation of assets to the sub-trusts is not arbitrary.

Summary

In the allocation option just illustrated, the decedent's separate property receives full stepped-up valuation to the current market value ($100,000) and is placed in the decedent's

B sub-trust. The survivor's separate property retains its original cost basis ($50,000) and flows into the survivor's A sub-trust. The home, as a marital asset, is allocated by the itemization method—one-half to the decedent's estate and one-half to the survivor's estate. The home receives full stepped-up valuation to current market value ($200,000) for the decedent's share but retains its cost basis ($100,000) for the survivor's share. The entire IRA, as the decedent's separate property ($1 million), flows into the Married IRA–QTIP Trust. Since the Married IRA–QTIP Trust can also make use of the decedent's federal estate tax exemption, the decedent's maximum federal estate tax exemption is fully utilized (between the decedent's B sub-trust and the Married IRA–QTIP Trust).

The surviving spouse has the right to all of the benefits of the IRA in the Married IRA–QTIP Trust. Upon the death of the surviving spouse, the remaining balance of the IRA funds passes to the heirs specified by the first spouse (the owner of the IRA).

Large IRA as a Disproportionate Part of the Estate

If a husband and wife have an IRA as part of their marital assets and the value of the IRA is quite large in proportion to the rest of their

---

TABLE 23-8

ALLOCATION OF IRA UPON DEATH OF OWNER
(MARRIED A-B TRUST AND MARRIED IRA–QTIP TRUST IN A SEPARATE PROPERTY STATE)

IRA (as Separate Property)	Market Value	Decedent's Share	Survivor's Share
IRA	$1,000,000	$1,000,000	$0

ALLOCATION OF IRA TO SUB-TRUSTS

Asset	Married IRA–QTIP Trust	B Sub-Trust	A Sub-Trust
IRA	$1,000,000		
Value in decedent's estate		$1,000,000	
Value in survivor's estate			$0

TABLE 23-9

**FINAL ALLOCATION OF ESTATE TO SUB-TRUSTS
(MARRIED A-B TRUST AND MARRIED IRA–QTIP TRUST IN A SEPARATE PROPERTY STATE)**

Estate Assets	Married IRA–QTIP Trust	B Sub-Trust	A Sub-Trust
Decedent's separate property		$100,000	
Survivor's separate property			$ 50,000
Home		$200,000	$100,000
IRA (as decedent's separate property)	$1,000,000		
Value in decedent's estate	$1,300,000		
Value in survivor's estate			$150,000

TABLE 23-10

**VALUE OF ESTATE ASSETS BEFORE DEATH OF FIRST SPOUSE
(ESTATE WITH LARGE IRA IN A SEPARATE PROPERTY STATE)**

Basic Estate Assets	MARKET VALUE		COST BASIS	
	First Spouse	Second Spouse	First Spouse	Second Spouse
Home	$ 200,000	$200,000	$ 100,000	$100,000
First spouse's separate property	$ 100,000		$ 50,000	
Second spouse's separate property		$100,000		$ 50,000
IRA	$1,000,000		$1,000,000*	

*The cost basis of an IRA is zero.

estate, they can use the Married IRA–QTIP Trust in conjunction with a Married A-B Trust or a Married A-B-C Trust to fully utilize the decedent's federal estate tax exemption. Since the Married IRA–QTIP Trust can utilize the decedent's federal estate tax exemption, the couple can combine this Trust with the decedent's B sub-trust (which also makes use of the decedent's federal estate tax exemption) to reduce estate taxes. The most common tech-

nique is to name the surviving spouse as the primary beneficiary of the IRA and the Married IRA–QTIP Trust as the contingent beneficiary of the IRA, thus allowing the surviving spouse to later disclaim any part of the IRA that is needed to fully utilize the decedent's federal estate tax exemption. To disclaim an asset is to renounce an interest in the named asset, but disclaiming an interest does not renounce an individual's right to the income from that asset.

TABLE 23-11
SEPARATE PROPERTY OF BOTH SPOUSES AFTER DEATH OF FIRST SPOUSE
(ESTATE WITH LARGE IRA IN A SEPARATE PROPERTY STATE)

Separate Property	MARKET VALUE		COST BASIS	
	First Spouse	Second Spouse	First Spouse	Second Spouse
Decedent's separate property	$100,000			
Survivor's separate property				$50,000

ALLOCATION OF SEPARATE PROPERTY TO SUB-TRUSTS

Separate Property	Married IRA–QTIP Trust	B Sub-Trust	A Sub-Trust
Decedent's separate property		$100,000	
Survivor's separate property			$50,000
Value in decedent's estate	$100,000		
Value in survivor's estate			$50,000

Estate Before Demise of the First Spouse

While both spouses are living, the market value and cost basis of the estate assets have the values shown in Table 23-10.

Estate After Demise of the First Spouse

When there is a large IRA as marital property of both spouses, asset allocation takes place in three steps:

- Allocation of the decedent's and survivor's separate property
- Allocation of the marital assets other than the IRA
- Allocation of the IRA as a marital asset

Allocation of Separate Property (at Market Value and Cost Basis) The separate property of the decedent spouse receives full stepped-up valuation to the current market value (as of the decedent's date of death) and is allocated to the decedent's B sub-trust and/or C sub-trust. The separate property of the surviving spouse does not receive stepped-up valuation and is allocated to the survivor's A sub-trust at the original cost basis. The top section of Table 23-11 shows the asset valuation for both spouses' separate property after the death of the first spouse (including the effect of stepped-up valuation for the decedent's separate property). The bottom portion of the table shows the allocation of the separate property to the appropriate sub-trusts.

Note that the decedent's separate property placed in the B sub-trust does not fully utilize the decedent's federal estate tax exemption.

Allocation of the Marital Assets (at Market Value and Cost Basis) In a separate property state, marital assets are allocated by the itemization method, with one-half of each marital asset being attributed to each spouse. In this illustration, the home is divided equally between each spouse. The decedent's share of the home receives full stepped-up valuation to the current market value and is placed in the

TABLE 23-12
MARITAL ASSETS AFTER DEATH OF FIRST SPOUSE
(ESTATE WITH LARGE IRA IN A SEPARATE PROPERTY STATE)

Marital Property	MARKET VALUE		COST BASIS	
	First Spouse	Second Spouse	First Spouse	Second Spouse
Home	$200,000			$100,000

ALLOCATION OF MARITAL ASSETS TO SUB-TRUSTS

Asset	Married IRA–QTIP Trust	B Sub-Trust	A Sub-Trust
Home		$200,000	$100,000
Value in decedent's estate		$200,000	
Value in survivor's estate			$100,000

TABLE 23-13
SEPARATE AND MARITAL PROPERTY (EXCEPT IRA) ALLOCATED TO SUB-TRUSTS
(ESTATE WITH LARGE IRA IN A SEPARATE PROPERTY STATE)

Separate and Marital Property	Married IRA–QTIP Trust	B Sub-Trust	A Sub-Trust
Decedent's separate property		$100,000	
Survivor's separate property			$ 50,000
Home		$200,000	$100,000
Value in decedent's estate		$300,000	
Value in survivor's estate			$150,000

decedent's B sub-trust. The survivor's share of the home retains its original cost basis and is placed in the survivor's A sub-trust. Table 23-12 shows the marital asset valuation after the death of the first spouse (including the effect of stepped-up valuation on the decedent's share of the assets), as well as the allocation of the assets to the appropriate sub-trusts.

When each spouse's separate property and their joint marital property (excluding the IRA for the moment) are both allocated to the appropriate sub-trusts, the distribution is as shown in Table 23-13.

Allocation of the Marital IRA Since the decedent's federal estate tax exemption is still

TABLE 23-14

VALUE OF IRA AFTER PART DISCLAIMED BY SURVIVING SPOUSE
(ESTATE WITH LARGE IRA IN A SEPARATE PROPERTY STATE)

IRA (as Marital Asset)	Market Value	Decedent's Share	Survivor's Share
IRA	$1,000,000	$300,000	$700,000

ALLOCATION OF IRA TO SUB-TRUSTS

Asset	Married IRA–QTIP Trust	B Sub-Trust	A Sub-Trust
IRA	$300,000		$700,000
Value in decedent's estate	$300,000		
Value in survivor's estate			$700,000

not fully utilized, let's now bring in the use of the Married IRA–QTIP Trust to utilize fully the decedent's federal estate tax exemption. Realize, also, that an IRA is a consumable asset and does not belong in the decedent's *insulated* B sub-trust, to say nothing about the potential income tax consequences.

In a separate property state, the IRA passes outside the Living Trust to the beneficiary, usually the surviving spouse. The marital IRA could be allocated in two ways, each with different tax consequences.

- You could split the IRA, naming the decedent's B sub-trust as the beneficiary of one part of the IRA and the spouse as the beneficiary of the other part. This approach fully utilizes the decedent's federal estate tax exemption, but placing *any* of the IRA in either the decedent's B sub-trust or C sub-trust could have serious adverse income tax consequences. The solution is to have a Married IRA–QTIP Trust that circumvents these potentially disastrous tax consequences.
- You could name the surviving spouse as the beneficiary of the entire IRA and name the Married IRA–QTIP Trust as the contingent

beneficiary of the IRA. With this more sophisticated approach, the surviving spouse could simply disclaim any portion of the IRA that is needed inside the Married IRA–QTIP Trust in order to fully utilize the decedent's federal estate tax exemption. The disclaimed interest would flow to the contingent beneficiary, the Married IRA–QTIP Trust.

In this example, the surviving spouse must disclaim 30 percent ($300,000) of the IRA value in order to fully utilize the decedent's federal estate tax exemption. If the first spouse were to die in later years, when the federal estate tax exemption has increased, the surviving spouse would simply disclaim a larger amount of the IRA to fully use the federal estate tax exemption available at that time.

Table 23-14 shows the decedent's share of the IRA that has been disclaimed by the surviving spouse, as well as the allocation of the two parts of the IRA to the appropriate sub-trusts. Remember that, for the IRA, there is no stepped-up valuation. The cost basis of an IRA is zero.

When all of the assets—both separate property and marital property—have been allocated among the various sub-trusts, the final estate

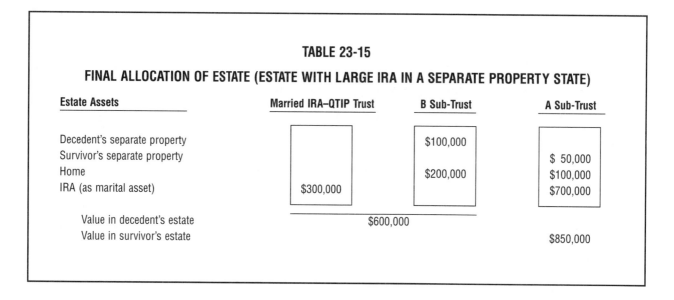

TABLE 23-15

FINAL ALLOCATION OF ESTATE (ESTATE WITH LARGE IRA IN A SEPARATE PROPERTY STATE)

Estate Assets	Married IRA–QTIP Trust	B Sub-Trust	A Sub-Trust
Decedent's separate property		$100,000	
Survivor's separate property			$ 50,000
Home		$200,000	$100,000
IRA (as marital asset)	$300,000		$700,000
Value in decedent's estate		$600,000	
Value in survivor's estate			$850,000

asset allocations will be as shown above in Table 23-15.

If the Other Spouse Dies First The previous example assumed that the IRA owner was the decedent (died first). However, what happens if the other spouse (the IRA beneficiary but not the owner of the IRA) dies first? Since you can't gift an IRA in a separate property state, there is little else that can be done to fully utilize the other spouse's exemption.

Summary

In the allocation option just illustrated, the decedent's separate property receives full stepped-up valuation to the current market value ($100,000) and flows into the decedent's B sub-trust. The survivor's separate property retains its original cost basis ($50,000), since it is not a marital asset, and flows into the survivor's A sub-trust. The home, as a marital asset, receives full stepped-up valuation to current market value only for the decedent's share ($200,000), which is placed in the decedent's B sub-trust. The survivor's share of the home retains its original cost basis ($100,000) and is placed in the survivor's A sub-trust. The portion of the IRA that was disclaimed ($300,000) passes to the Married IRA–QTIP Trust (named as contingent beneficiary of the IRA). The balance of the IRA passes to the surviving spouse.

Allocating the IRA as shown in this example fully utilizes the decedent's federal estate tax exemption. The surviving spouse has the right to all of the benefits of the IRA in the Married IRA–QTIP Trust. However, upon the death of the surviving spouse, the balance of the remaining IRA funds passes to the couple's heirs.

MARRIED A-B-C TRUST WITH DEBT PAYMENT POWER OF APPOINTMENT

The Debt Payment Power of Appointment (DPPA), similar to the General Power of Appointment (GPOA), is used to pass all of the Living Trust assets to the decedent's estate. Because the survivor's share of marital assets and all of the survivor's separate property flows to the decedent's estate, it receives full stepped-up valuation to the current market value. This allocation method is typically used to achieve full stepped-up valuation to current market value for all assets in the Living Trust.

However, you must remember that this Power of Appointment passes all of the survivor's separate property to the decedent's estate (unless the Power of Appointment expressly exempts the separate property). If this is a second marriage, with children from a previous marriage as named beneficiaries, the loss of the surviving spouse's separate property to the decedent's estate could cause severe conflict!

TABLE 23-16

VALUE OF ESTATE ASSETS BEFORE DEATH OF FIRST SPOUSE
(MARRIED A-B-C TRUST WITH DEBT PAYMENT POWER OF APPOINTMENT
IN A SEPARATE PROPERTY STATE)

Basic Estate Assets	MARKET VALUE		COST BASIS	
	First Spouse	Second Spouse	First Spouse	Second Spouse
Home	$ 200,000	$200,000	$ 100,000	$100,000
Other real estate	$ 400,000	$400,000	$ 200,000	$200,000
First spouse's separate property	$ 100,000		$ 50,000	
Second spouse's separate property		$100,000		$ 50,000
IRA	$1,000,000		$1,000,000*	

*The cost basis of an IRA is zero.

The Debt Payment Power of Appointment protects the survivor's assets from creditors and frivolous lawsuits, but the IRA is still exposed to such claims. The IRA, like all retirement assets, is outside the Living Trust and, when the first spouse dies, it flows to the surviving spouse, as the beneficiary.

Estate Before Demise of the First Spouse

Table 23-16 shows the valuation of the estate assets at market value and cost basis before the death of the first spouse. Please note that I have included other real estate as marital property to demonstrate the valuation method of allocation. In this instance, you can use the valuation method of allocation in a separate property state, because the DPPA passes all Trust assets to the decedent's B sub-trust and C sub-trust. All assets receive stepped-up valuation to the current market value, and thus, the valuation method of allocation can be used.

Estate After Demise of the First Spouse

Upon the death of the first spouse, the estate assets must be allocated to the appropriate sub-trusts. Since all of the Trust assets flow to the decedent spouse's estate, all estate assets receive full stepped-up valuation to the current market value (as of the decedent's date of death). The IRA is outside the Trust, so it flows to the surviving spouse (the IRA beneficiary) and is valued at the current market value.

The top portion of Table 23-17 on page 344 shows the asset valuation of all estate assets after the death of the first spouse (including the effect of stepped-up valuation for all estate assets). The bottom part of the table shows how the estate assets are allocated to the appropriate sub-trusts. Please note that this asset allocation is arbitrary for the decedent's B sub-trust and C sub-trust.

Summary

In this example of asset allocation, all of the Trust assets flow to the decedent's estate, receive full stepped-up valuation to the current market value, and are allocated between the decedent's B sub-trust and C sub-trust. Therefore, even the survivor's separate property flows to the decedent's estate and receives full stepped-up valuation (unless the Power of Appointment specifically exempts the separate property). Since the IRA is outside the Living Trust, it flows to the surviving spouse (as the IRA beneficiary) and is placed in the survivor's A sub-trust. Remember that there is no stepped-up valuation for an IRA. The cost basis of an IRA is zero.

Properly utilized, the Debt Payment Power of Appointment can protect the survivor's

TABLE 23-17

ESTATE ASSETS AFTER DEATH OF FIRST SPOUSE
(MARRIED A-B-C TRUST WITH DEBT PAYMENT POWER OF APPOINTMENT
IN A SEPARATE PROPERTY STATE)

Basic Estate Assets	MARKET VALUE		COST BASIS	
	First Spouse	Second Spouse	First Spouse	Second Spouse
Home	$400,000			
Other real estate	$800,000			
Decedent's separate property	$100,000			
Survivor's separate property	$100,000			
IRA				$1,000,000*

ALLOCATION OF ESTATE ASSETS TO SUB-TRUSTS

Estate Assets	C Sub-Trust	B Sub-Trust	A Sub-Trust
Home		$400,000	
Other real estate	$600,000	$200,000	
Decedent's separate property	$100,000		
Survivor's separate property	$100,000		
IRA			$1,000,000
Value in decedent's estate	$1,400,000		
Value in survivor's estate			$1,000,000

*The cost basis of an IRA is zero.

assets from creditors and frivolous lawsuits; however, the IRA is still exposed to such potential hazards. The allocation option illustrated in the next section shows you how to protect the IRA as well.

MARRIED A-B-C TRUST WITH DEBT PAYMENT POWER OF APPOINTMENT AND A MARRIED IRA–QTIP TRUST

The Debt Payment Power of Appointment (DPPA), similar to the General Power of Appointment (GPOA), is used to pass all of the Living Trust assets to the decedent's estate. This allocation method is typically used to achieve full stepped-up valuation to the current market value for all of the assets in the Living Trust. However, you must be very aware that a DPPA passes all of the survivor's separate property to the decedent's estate (unless the Power of Appointment expressly exempts the separate property). If the couple is in a second marriage, with children from a previous marriage named as beneficiaries, the loss of the surviving spouse's assets to the decedent's estate could cause grave conflicts among the heirs!

Caution: Using a Debt Payment Power of Appointment can cause unwanted estate tax consequences, since all of the assets flow to the decedent's side, leaving no assets in the survivor's A sub-trust.

Use of the Married IRA–QTIP Trust passes the entire IRA to the decedent's estate as well, thus leaving the surviving spouse's estate totally bare. Though this seemingly unfair allocation may appear to be ill advised, it can be an excellent means of protecting your estate against creditors and frivolous lawsuits. However, the Trust needs to balance the distributions for the surviving spouse's heirs in order to yield an equitable distribution of estate assets to all heirs.

Estate Before Demise of the First Spouse
Table 23-18 below shows the valuation of the estate assets before the death of the first spouse. Please note that, for this illustration, I have included the other real estate as marital property.

Estate After Demise of the First Spouse
Upon the death of the first spouse, the estate assets must be allocated to the appropriate sub-trusts. Since a Debt Payment Power of Appointment is used, all of the Trust assets flow to the decedent spouse's estate and receive full stepped-up valuation to the current market value. An IRA is always valued at its current market value.

The top portion of Table 23-19 on page 346 shows the asset valuation for all estate assets after the death of the first spouse (including the effect of stepped-up valuation for all estate

assets). The bottom part of the table shows the allocation of the estate assets to the appropriate sub-trusts. Please note that this asset allocation is arbitrary for the assets placed in the decedent's B sub-trust and C sub-trust.

Summary
In this example of asset allocation, all of the Trust assets flow to the decedent's estate, receive full stepped-up valuation to the current market value, and are allocated between the decedent's B sub-trust and C sub-trust. Thus, the survivor's separate property flows to the decedent's estate and receives full stepped-up valuation. Since the Married IRA–QTIP Trust is the beneficiary of the IRA, the IRA flows into the Married IRA–QTIP Trust, and the surviving spouse receives full benefits from it while alive. Upon the death of the surviving spouse, the balance of the remaining IRA funds passes to the heirs specified by the first spouse (the owner of the IRA). The IRA is valued at market value.

Combining the Debt Payment Power of Appointment (to protect the estate assets) and the Married IRA–QTIP Trust (to protect the IRA) can be an excellent way to insulate all of the estate assets—including the IRA—from creditors and frivolous lawsuits.

TABLE 23-18

VALUE OF ESTATE ASSETS BEFORE DEATH OF FIRST SPOUSE
(MARRIED A-B-C TRUST WITH DEBT PAYMENT POWER OF APPOINTMENT AND
MARRIED IRA–QTIP TRUST IN A SEPARATE PROPERTY STATE)

Basic Estate Assets	MARKET VALUE		COST BASIS	
	First Spouse	Second Spouse	First Spouse	Second Spouse
Home	$ 200,000	$200,000	$ 100,000	$100,000
Other real estate	$ 400,000	$400,000	$ 200,000	$200,000
First spouse's separate property	$ 100,000		$ 50,000	
Second spouse's separate property		$100,000		$ 50,000
IRA	$1,000,000		$1,000,000*	

*The cost basis of an IRA is zero.

TABLE 23-19

ESTATE ASSETS AFTER DEATH OF FIRST SPOUSE
(MARRIED A-B-C TRUST WITH DEBT PAYMENT POWER OF APPOINTMENT AND
MARRIED IRA–QTIP TRUST IN A SEPARATE PROPERTY STATE)

Basic Estate Assets	MARKET VALUE		COST BASIS	
	First Spouse	Second Spouse	First Spouse	Second Spouse
Home	$ 400,000			
Other real estate	$ 800,000			
Decedent's separate property	$ 100,000			
Survivor's separate property	$ 100,000			
IRA	$1,000,000			

ALLOCATION OF ESTATE ASSETS TO SUB-TRUSTS AND MARRIED IRA–QTIP TRUST

Estate Assets	Married IRA–QTIP Trust	C Sub-Trust	B Sub-Trust	A Sub-Trust
Home			$400,000	
Other real estate		$ 600,000	$200,000	
Decedent's separate property		$ 100,000		
Survivor's separate property		$ 100,000		
IRA	$1,000,000			
Value in decedent's estate		$2,400,000		
Value in survivor's estate				$0

MARRIED A-B TRUST WITH DEBT PAYMENT POWER OF APPOINTMENT

Combining a Married A-B Trust with a Debt Payment Power of Appointment (DPPA) can be a potent estate-planning tool for certain estates. The principal advantage of this estate-planning vehicle is the attainment of full stepped-up valuation to the current market value for all Trust assets. The DPPA passes all of the Trust assets—including any of the surviving spouse's separate property—to the decedent's estate, where all Trust assets receive full stepped-up valuation to the current market value.

However, this method can cause unwanted estate tax consequences. The "overflow" or balance of the assets that exceeds the decedent's exemption flows back to the surviving spouse and is placed in the survivor's A sub-trust. The assets flowing back to the survivor's A sub-trust may be insufficient to utilize the survivor's federal estate tax exemption. Since the IRA is outside the Trust, it passes to the surviving spouse as the beneficiary and is placed in the survivor's A sub-trust.

Estate Before Demise of the First Spouse
Table 23-20 shows the valuation of the estate assets before the death of the first spouse. For this illustration, the value of the IRA has been reduced to $100,000 to minimize the effect of the IRA.

Estate After Demise of the First Spouse
Upon the death of the first spouse, the estate assets must be allocated to the appropriate sub-trusts. The asset allocation option used in this example is best illustrated in two steps:

TABLE 23-20

VALUE OF ESTATE ASSETS BEFORE DEATH OF FIRST SPOUSE
(MARRIED A-B TRUST AND DEBT PAYMENT POWER OF APPOINTMENT
IN A SEPARATE PROPERTY STATE)

Basic Estate Assets	MARKET VALUE		COST BASIS	
	First Spouse	Second Spouse	First Spouse	Second Spouse
Home	$200,000	$200,000	$100,000	$100,000
Other real estate	$400,000	$400,000	$200,000	$200,000
First spouse's separate property	$100,000		$ 50,000	
Second spouse's separate property		$100,000		$ 50,000
IRA	$100,000		$100,000*	

*The cost basis of an IRA is zero.

- All assets are allocated to the decedent's estate.
- Assets that exceed the decedent's federal estate tax exemption flow back to the surviving spouse's estate.

Allocation of All Assets to Decedent's Estate

The Debt Payment Power of Appointment, similar to the General Power of Appointment (GPOA), is used to pass all of the Trust assets—except the retirement assets (the IRA)—to the decedent's estate. Thus, all of the Trust assets, including the survivor's separate property, receive full stepped-up valuation to the current market value. Since the IRA is outside the Trust, it flows to the surviving spouse, as the beneficiary, at the current market value. The top portion of Table 23-21 on page 348 shows the asset valuation for the estate assets after the death of the first spouse (including the effect of stepped-up valuation on all estate assets). The bottom part of the table shows the initial allocation of the assets to the appropriate sub-trusts.

Allocation of Assets Exceeding Decedent's Federal Estate Tax Exemption

Since there is no C (QTIP Trust) sub-trust and the decedent's B sub-trust can hold only one federal estate tax exemption, there is an "overflow." The excess amount (above the amount of the exemption) flows back to the surviving spouse and into the surviving spouse's A sub-trust. The "overflow" assets flow back to the survivor's A sub-trust by valuation rather than by itemization. The IRA remains in the surviving spouse's A sub-trust at the current market value.

Table 23-22 on page 348 shows the reallocation of estate assets to the appropriate sub-trusts in a way that places in the B sub-trust only an asset value that equals the decedent's federal estate tax exemption. This reallocation avoids the unnecessary payment of estate taxes upon the death of the first spouse. Please note that this reallocation of assets from the decedent's B sub-trust back to the survivor's A sub-trust is arbitrary.

Summary

In this example of asset allocation, all of the Trust assets—including the survivor's separate property—flow to the decedent's estate, where all assets receive full stepped-up valuation to the current market value. Since the IRA is outside the Trust, it flows to the surviving spouse (as the IRA beneficiary) and is placed in the survivor's A sub-trust. (Remember that there is no stepped-up valuation for an IRA.)

Since the decedent's B sub-trust can hold the equivalent of only one federal estate tax exemption without triggering federal estate taxes, the balance of the assets that exceed the amount of the decedent's exemption flow back to the

TABLE 23-21

ESTATE ASSETS AFTER DEATH OF FIRST SPOUSE
(MARRIED A-B TRUST AND DEBT PAYMENT POWER OF APPOINTMENT
IN A SEPARATE PROPERTY STATE)

Basic Estate Assets	MARKET VALUE		COST BASIS	
	First Spouse	Second Spouse	First Spouse	Second Spouse
Home	$400,000			
Other real estate	$800,000			
Decedent's separate property	$100,000			
Survivor's separate property	$100,000			
IRA		$100,000		

INITIAL ALLOCATION OF ESTATE ASSETS TO SUB-TRUSTS

Estate Assets	B Sub-Trust	A Sub-Trust
Home	$ 400,000	
Other real estate	$ 800,000	
Decedent's separate property	$ 100,000	
Survivor's separate property	$ 100,000	
IRA		$100,000
Total value in decedent's estate	$1,400,000	
Total value in survivor's estate		$100,000

TABLE 23-22

REALLOCATION OF DECEDENT'S "OVERFLOW" ASSETS
(SEPARATE PROPERTY STATE)

Estate Assets	B Sub-Trust	A Sub-Trust
Home	$400,000	
Other real estate	$100,000	$700,000
Decedent's separate property	$100,000	
Survivor's separate property		$100,000
IRA		$100,000
Total value in decedent's estate	$600,000	
Total value in survivor's estate		$900,000

survivor's A sub-trust at full stepped-up valuation. These "overflow" assets flow back to the survivor's A sub-trust by valuation (i.e., by dollar value) rather than by itemization.

ADVANCED SETTLEMENT OPTIONS— NOT FOR THE FAINT OF HEART

The use of one or more of the advanced settlement options can significantly affect your estate, especially in separate property states. If you use the vehicles described in this chapter in the wrong circumstances, the consequences can be disastrous. Each estate is a unique case and must be thoroughly analyzed by professionals before you implement any of the strategies. Especially in separate property states, deciding which advanced settlement option, if any, is appropriate for your estate is *not* a do-it-yourself project!

Caution: Before implementing any of the advanced settlement options, be extremely cautious and seek out very competent *estate preservation specialists and legal counsel with a master's degree in taxation. Making the wrong choice could be devastating to your estate!*

24

Advanced Settlement Options in Community Property States
When the First Spouse Dies

There are several advanced settlement options for allocating estate assets to the A, B, and/or C sub-trusts. Each of these options has a different effect on the estate, both in allocation and in valuation, depending upon the rules for community property states. Five different advanced settlement allocation options apply to community property states:

- An A Trust with a Married IRA–QTIP Trust
- Valuation method with a Married A-B Trust or Married A-B-C Trust and a Married IRA–QTIP Trust
- Married A-B-C Trust with Debt Payment Power of Appointment
- Married A-B-C Trust with Debt Payment Power of Appointment and a Married IRA–QTIP Trust
- Married A-B Trust with Debt Payment Power of Appointment

All five options use the aggregate (or valuation) method of asset allocation, which is peculiar to community property states. This method allows the community property assets to be divided equally between both spouses by value rather than by asset. Although the allocation method used in community property states is technically known as the *aggregate method*, I will use the more descriptive common term *valuation method*.

This chapter first provides you with a brief overview of the five advanced settlement allocation options applicable to community property states. Then each option is discussed in more detail. All of these options can be used for highly valued and complex estates.

I urge you to take the simple approach: First read the following overview of the five advanced settlement allocation options. Then read only the section that applies to your particular Living Trust.

OVERVIEW OF THE FIVE ADVANCED SETTLEMENT ALLOCATION OPTIONS
Before delving into the details of each option, let me first acquaint you with the five different advanced settlement allocation options that are

pertinent to settling highly valued and/or complex estates. I will present a brief synopsis of each one, as well as cite their unique advantages and disadvantages. Read each of these summaries in order to see which (if any) alternatives might be appropriate for your particular estate-planning needs. Then, carefully study the allocation option that best fits the needs of your estate.

An A Trust with a Married IRA–QTIP Trust

An A Trust with a Married IRA–QTIP Trust is primarily designed for someone who has entered into a second marriage, brings into the marriage a large IRA that was accumulated prior to the second marriage, and does not create a joint Living Trust with his or her spouse for their new marital assets. The Married IRA–QTIP Trust is structured for the spouse who desires, upon his or her death, that the IRA remain in the Trust for the benefit of the surviving spouse and that, upon the death of the surviving spouse, the remaining IRA funds pass to the heirs of the spouse who owned the IRA. The separate property of this individual, other than the IRA, is allocated to the A Trust. The Married IRA–QTIP Trust also incorporates the decedent's federal estate tax exemption.

Valuation Method with a Married A-B Trust or Married A-B-C Trust and a Married IRA–QTIP Trust

Using the valuation method of allocation in conjunction with a Married A-B Trust or a Married A-B-C Trust and with a Married IRA–QTIP Trust is a vital estate-planning tool for a married couple who has a joint Trust for their marital assets (an A-B Trust or A-B-C Trust) and who also has a large IRA. Two basic situations call for the addition of the Married IRA–QTIP Trust:

- An individual has a large IRA as separate property, has entered into a second marriage, and desires that the surviving spouse have the right to the IRA funds while living and that, after the surviving spouse dies, the remaining IRA funds pass to the heirs of the first spouse (the owner of the IRA).

- A married couple has an IRA that is large in proportion to their marital assets. An example would be a 401(k) plan that was rolled over into an IRA and that has grown to a substantial size that is disproportionate to the marital assets (i.e., whose value is much greater than that of the rest of the combined assets)—say, an IRA worth $1 million and a home worth $400,000. Since the IRA passes to the surviving spouse, the couple needs a way to fully utilize the decedent's federal estate tax exemption without triggering potential income tax consequences. The addition of the Married IRA–QTIP Trust can be an excellent solution.

Married A-B-C Trust with Debt Payment Power of Appointment

When a Married A-B-C Trust is combined with a Debt Payment Power of Appointment (DPPA; similar to the General Power of Appointment [GPOA]), *all* of the Living Trust's assets pass to the decedent's estate. Since all community property attains full stepped-up valuation (i.e., the cost basis becomes the current market value) upon the death of the first spouse, this approach affects only the survivor's separate property. The DPPA causes the survivor's separate property to flow into the decedent's estate, thereby receiving full stepped-up valuation to current market value. This approach also protects the survivor's assets from creditors and frivolous lawsuits.

If you select this allocation option, you must be very aware that all of the survivor's separate property passes to the decedent's estate (unless the Power of Appointment expressly provides otherwise). If the spouses are in a second marriage, such a total shift of the survivor's assets could cause severe conflict among children from the previous marriages. Any IRAs, like all retirement assets, are outside the Living Trust and flow directly to the surviving spouse as the IRA beneficiary, which leaves the IRA exposed to outsider claims.

The disadvantage of using this option is that the survivor's federal estate tax exemption is lost. However, any value of the remaining IRA funds at the survivor's death can be offset by the survivor's federal estate tax exemption.

Married A-B-C Trust with Debt Payment Power of Appointment and a Married IRA–QTIP Trust

If a Married A-B-C Trust is combined with a Debt Payment Power of Appointment (DPPA; similar to the General Power of Appointment [GPOA]) and used in conjunction with a Married IRA–QTIP Trust, *all* of the Living Trust assets pass to the decedent's estate. With this approach, all of the survivor's separate property flows to the decedent's estate and thereby receives full stepped-up valuation to the current market value. Before selecting this allocation option, however, you must be very aware that all of the survivor's separate property passes to the decedent's estate (unless the Power of Appointment expressly provides otherwise). If the spouses are in a second marriage and have, as beneficiaries, children from each spouse's previous marriage, this total shift of the survivor's assets could cause a great deal of conflict and resentment.

The Married IRA–QTIP Trust passes any IRAs to the decedent's estate as well, leaving the surviving spouse's estate without any assets whatsoever! Such a seemingly unfair allocation can be an excellent means of protecting your estate against creditors and frivolous lawsuits, thus preserving the assets for use by the surviving spouse (and/or providing an eventual inheritance to the heirs).

The main disadvantage of using this allocation option is that the survivor's federal estate tax exemption is lost.

An alternative approach is to split the IRA, with one part going to the Married IRA–QTIP Trust and the other part going to the surviving spouse. With this approach, the survivor's federal estate tax exemption can be used to offset the remaining value of the surviving spouse's IRA.

Married A-B Trust with Debt Payment Power of Appointment

Combining a Married A-B Trust with a Debt Payment Power of Appointment (DPPA; similar to the General Power of Appointment [GPOA]) can be a potent estate-planning tool for certain estates. The DPPA passes all of the Trust assets to the decedent's estate, so that all

Trust assets receive full stepped-up valuation. With this option, since the decedent lacks a C sub-trust (QTIP Trust) and the decedent's estate is limited to one federal estate tax exemption, the balance of the asset value exceeding the decedent's federal estate tax exemption flows back to the surviving spouse and into the survivor's A sub-trust. Any IRAs pass directly to the surviving spouse as the IRA beneficiary.

The primary advantage of this estate-planning vehicle is the attainment of full stepped-up valuation on all Trust assets—including the survivor's separate property.

ALLOCATION OPTIONS FOR COMMUNITY PROPERTY STATES

To make each of the different allocation options (and the differences among them) fairly simple and, therefore, understandable, I will illustrate each option by using the same few basic Trust assets. The examples use the values shown in Table 24-1 on page 354. In some of the cases, where appropriate, the assets include "other real estate."

All but one of the examples use an IRA value of $1 million, not because this high value is common for most people's IRAs, but rather to illustrate the problem (and the possible solutions) for estates that have IRAs with a very large value in relation to the total value of the estate. Don't be distracted by the use of such a large IRA; the purpose is only to emphasize what happens to the IRA. One example uses a $100,000 IRA to minimize the effect of the IRA on an estate. (The actual dollar values for the assets are not intended to have any relationship to your own personal estate but are intended to clearly establish the basic principles that relate to applying an allocation option to your estate.)

Each illustration of the allocation options uses a federal estate tax exemption of $600,000, even though this exemption is $625,000 in 1998 and increases to $1 million by 2006. (Remember that Congress has not given us any real boon, since the increase in the exemption does not even keep pace with inflation.) If you want to clearly see the impact on your own estate in future years, simply change the values in the illustration to match those in your estate and

TABLE 24-1

ASSET VALUES USED IN EXAMPLES FOR
ADVANCED SETTLEMENT OPTIONS IN COMMUNITY PROPERTY STATES

Basic Estate Assets	Cost Basis	Market Value with Large IRA	Market Value with Smaller IRA
Home	$ 200,000	$ 400,000	$400,000
Other real estate	$ 400,000	$ 800,000	$800,000
Decedent's separate property	$ 50,000	$ 100,000	$100,000
Survivor's separate property	$ 50,000	$ 100,000	$100,000
Large IRA	$1,000,000*	$1,000,000	
Smaller IRA	$ 100,000*		$100,000

*The cost basis of an IRA is zero.

the year in which you are making the calculations. Regardless of the actual numbers, the concepts remain the same.

In settling an estate, the primary challenge is to determine how to allocate and value the estate assets upon the death of the *first* spouse. All of the illustrations portray the asset allocation when the first spouse dies because this allocation can have the most serious estate tax consequences if not done properly for the particular estate. (The assets of each estate will vary as to allocation and to value, but the same principles still apply.) Upon the death of the second spouse, valuation and allocation of estates are fairly easy to accomplish, as discussed in Chapter 16B.

AN A TRUST WITH A MARRIED IRA–QTIP TRUST

The A Trust, used in conjunction with a Married IRA–QTIP Trust, is primarily designed for someone who has entered into a second marriage, brings into the marriage a large IRA that was accumulated prior to the second marriage, and does not create a joint Living Trust with his or her spouse for their marital assets. The Married IRA–QTIP Trust is structured for the spouse who desires, upon his or her death, that the IRA remain in trust for the benefit of the surviving spouse and that, upon the death of the surviving spouse, the remaining IRA funds

pass to the heirs of the spouse who owned the IRA. Therefore, in this scenario, only two Trusts come into play: the individual's A Trust (revocable until he or she dies) and the revocable Married IRA–QTIP Trust. The Married IRA–QTIP Trust has the ability to utilize any remaining portion of the decedent's federal estate tax exemption. Therefore, between the A Trust and the Married IRA–QTIP Trust, the individual's entire federal estate tax exemption can be fully utilized.

As you learned in Chapters 13 and 22, there is a significant advantage in converting your traditional IRA to a Roth IRA and then using a Roth Legacy Trust^{SM} to hold your new Roth IRA. If you elect to make such a conversion, the Roth Legacy Trust^{SM} will simply replace the Married IRA–QTIP Trust. For estate valuation, the end result will typically be the same—for a Roth Legacy Trust^{SM} and for a Married IRA–QTIP Trust.

Estate Before Demise of the First Spouse

While both spouses are still living, the market value and cost basis of the first spouse's separate property have the values shown in Table 24-2. For simplicity, this example omits community property from the estate assets. (If any community property existed in the estate, the decedent's share would be included in the A sub-trust.)

TABLE 24-2

VALUE OF ESTATE ASSETS BEFORE DEATH OF FIRST SPOUSE
(AN A TRUST AND MARRIED IRA–QTIP TRUST IN A COMMUNITY PROPERTY STATE)

Basic Estate Assets	MARKET VALUE		COST BASIS	
	First Spouse	Second Spouse	First Spouse	Second Spouse
First spouse's separate property	$ 100,000		$ 50,000	
IRA (separate property)	$1,000,000		$1,000,000*	

*The cost basis of an IRA is zero.

TABLE 24-3

ESTATE ASSETS AFTER DEATH OF FIRST SPOUSE
(AN A TRUST AND MARRIED IRA–QTIP TRUST IN A COMMUNITY PROPERTY STATE)

Separate Property	Market Value	Decedent's Share
Decedent's separate property	$ 100,000	$ 100,000
IRA (separate property)	$1,000,000	$1,000,000
Total	$1,100,000	$1,100,000

ESTATE ASSET ALLOCATION TO TRUSTS

Estate Assets	Married IRA–QTIP Trust	A Trust
Decedent's separate property		$100,000
IRA (separate property)	$1,000,000	
Total value in decedent's estate	$1,100,000	

Estate After Demise of the First Spouse

Upon the death of the first spouse, the allocation of estate assets can best be illustrated in one step—the allocation of the decedent's other separate property and the allocation of the IRA as the decedent's separate property. Table 24-3 shows the other separate property of the decedent and how the other separate property and IRA are allocated in both of the Trusts after the death of the first spouse. Please note that this allocation is *not* arbitrary.

The decedent's other separate property is allocated to the A Trust and receives stepped-up valuation to the current market value (as of the decedent's date of death). As beneficiary of the IRA, the Married IRA–QTIP Trust is the recipient of the entire IRA (or the Roth Legacy Trust℠ is the recipient of a Roth IRA). However, in such a case, the IRA must be the separate property of the decedent spouse; otherwise, the surviving spouse would be considered to have gifted his or her share to the decedent spouse.

If the IRA is not properly identified as separate property, the surviving spouse could "take against the Trust," which means that the intent of the decedent spouse could be nullified in court—and the surviving spouse could be given his or her share of the IRA as community property. Remember that for an IRA, there is no stepped-up valuation. The cost basis of an IRA is zero.

Summary
In the allocation option just illustrated, the decedent's separate property receives full stepped-up valuation to the current market value ($100,000) and flows into the A Trust. Since the IRA is the decedent's separate property and the Married IRA–QTIP Trust is named as beneficiary of the IRA, the IRA flows directly into the Married IRA–QTIP Trust. The surviving spouse has the right to all of the benefits of the IRA funds, but upon the death of the surviving spouse, any remaining IRA funds pass to the heirs of the first spouse, the owner of the IRA. The decedent's separate property of $100,000 plus half ($500,000) the value of the IRA in the Married IRA–QTIP Trust fully utilizes the decedent's federal estate tax exemption (because the Married IRA–QTIP Trust also can make use of the decedent's federal estate tax exemption).

VALUATION METHOD WITH A MARRIED A-B TRUST OR MARRIED A-B-C TRUST AND A MARRIED IRA–QTIP TRUST
The valuation method of allocation, in conjunction with a Married A-B Trust or Married A-B-C Trust and a Married IRA–QTIP Trust, has two distinct uses, depending on the particulars of an estate:

- For an IRA that is separate property and used in conjunction with a joint marital Trust (a Married A-B or A-B-C Trust)
- For an IRA that is disproportionately large relative to the overall value of the marital estate

Large IRA as Separate Property
The Married IRA–QTIP Trust is appropriate for someone who has entered into a second marriage, has a large IRA generated prior to this marriage, and has created a joint Trust with his or her spouse to hold the marital assets and other separate property. The spouse desires, upon his or her death, that the IRA remain in trust for the benefit of the surviving spouse and that, upon the death of the surviving spouse, the IRA go to the heirs of the spouse who owned the IRA. In such a scenario, there are either two or three sub-trusts (a Married A-B Trust or a Married A-B-C Trust) and a Married IRA–QTIP Trust. The Married IRA–QTIP Trust can utilize any remaining portion of the decedent's unused federal estate tax exemption (if the exemption has not been fully used to offset the value of assets in the decedent's B sub-trust). Thus, the decedent's federal estate tax exemption can be fully utilized between the decedent's B sub-trust and the Married IRA–QTIP Trust.

As you already learned in Chapters 13 and 22, there is quite a significant advantage to converting your traditional IRA to a Roth IRA and then using a Roth Legacy Trust℠ to hold your new Roth IRA. If you should elect to make such a conversion, the Roth Legacy Trust℠ will simply replace the Married IRA–QTIP Trust. For the purpose of estate valuation, the end result typically will be the same whether for a Roth Legacy Trust℠ or for a Married IRA–QTIP Trust.

Estate Before Demise of the First Spouse
While both spouses are living, the market value and cost basis of the estate assets have the values shown in Table 24-4.

Estate After Demise of the First Spouse
Upon the death of the first spouse, the estate assets must be allocated to the appropriate sub-trusts. When there is a large IRA as separate property of one spouse, asset allocation involves three steps:

- Allocation of the decedent's and the survivor's separate property
- Allocation of the community property

TABLE 24-4
VALUE OF ESTATE ASSETS BEFORE DEATH OF FIRST SPOUSE
(MARRIED A-B OR A-B-C TRUST AND MARRIED IRA–QTIP TRUST
IN A COMMUNITY PROPERTY STATE)

Basic Estate Assets	MARKET VALUE		COST BASIS	
	First Spouse	Second Spouse	First Spouse	Second Spouse
Home	$ 200,000	$200,000	$ 100,000	$100,000
First spouse's separate property	$ 100,000		$ 50,000	
Second spouse's separate property		$100,000		$ 50,000
IRA (separate property)	$1,000,000		$1,000,000*	

*The cost basis of an IRA is zero.

TABLE 24-5
SEPARATE PROPERTY OF BOTH SPOUSES AFTER DEATH OF FIRST SPOUSE
(MARRIED A-B TRUST AND MARRIED IRA–QTIP TRUST IN A COMMUNITY PROPERTY STATE)

Separate Property	MARKET VALUE		COST BASIS	
	First Spouse	Second Spouse	First Spouse	Second Spouse
Decedent's separate property	$100,000			
Survivor's separate property				$50,000

SEPARATE PROPERTY ALLOCATION TO SUB-TRUSTS

Separate Property	Married IRA–QTIP Trust	B Sub-Trust	A Sub-Trust
Decedent's separate property		$100,000	
Survivor's separate property			$50,000
Value in decedent's estate	$100,000		
Value in survivor's estate			$50,000

- Allocation of the IRA as the decedent's separate property

Allocation of Separate Property (at Market Value and Cost Basis) The separate property of the decedent spouse receives full stepped-up valuation to the current market value (as of the decedent's date of death) and is allocated to the decedent's B sub-trust and/or C sub-trust. The separate property of the surviving spouse does not receive stepped-up valuation and is allocated to the survivor's A sub-trust at the original cost basis. Table 24-5 shows the asset valuation for both spouses' separate property after the death of the first spouse (including the effect of stepped-up valuation for the decedent's separate property). The bottom portion of the table shows how the separate property of both spouses is allocated to the appropriate sub-trusts.

Note that the decedent's separate property placed in the B sub-trust does not fully utilize the decedent's federal estate tax exemption.

Allocation of Community Property Assets (at Market Value) With the valuation method of allocation (used in a community property state), all community property assets receive full stepped-up valuation to the current market value when the first spouse dies and are allocated by value rather than by asset. Thus, the total value of all marital assets is added together and then divided equally. Half the value is placed in the decedent's B sub-trust and half in the survivor's A sub-trust. In this example, the only community property is the home, which is divided equally by value; one-half is placed in the decedent's B sub-trust, and

---

TABLE 24-6

COMMUNITY PROPERTY AFTER DEATH OF FIRST SPOUSE
(MARRIED A-B TRUST AND MARRIED IRA–QTIP TRUST IN A COMMUNITY PROPERTY STATE)

Community Property	Market Value	Decedent's Share	Survivor's Share
Home	$400,000	$200,000	$200,000

ALLOCATION OF COMMUNITY PROPERTY TO SUB-TRUSTS

Community Property	Married IRA–QTIP Trust	B Sub-Trust	A Sub-Trust
Home		$200,000	$200,000
Value in decedent's estate	$200,000		
Value in survivor's estate			$200,000

TABLE 24-7

SEPARATE AND COMMUNITY PROPERTY ALLOCATED TO SUB-TRUSTS
(MARRIED A-B TRUST AND MARRIED IRA–QTIP TRUST IN A COMMUNITY PROPERTY STATE)

Separate and Community Property	Married IRA–QTIP Trust	B Sub-Trust	A Sub-Trust
Decedent's separate property		$100,000	
Survivor's separate property			$ 50,000
Home		$200,000	$200,000
Value in decedent's estate	$300,000		
Value in survivor's estate			$250,000

one-half is placed in the survivor's A sub-trust. Table 24-6 shows the community property asset valuation after the death of the first spouse (including the effect of stepped-up valuation on the community property), as well as the allocation of the asset to the appropriate sub-trusts.

When the spouses' separate property and the community property are both allocated to the appropriate sub-trusts, the distribution is as shown in Table 24-7.

Allocation of the IRA Since the IRA is the decedent's separate property, the Married IRA–QTIP Trust is the named beneficiary of the IRA (rather than the spouse). Once the IRA passes to the Married IRA–QTIP Trust (or the Roth Legacy Trust℠ for a Roth IRA) after the death of the IRA owner, the surviving spouse has the right to all of the IRA benefits while living. However, following the death of the surviving spouse, the remainder of the IRA flows to the IRA owner's (the first spouse's) heirs.

When the owner of the IRA dies, the value of the IRA becomes its current market value, and the IRA is allocated to the Married IRA–QTIP Trust, as shown in Table 24-8. (Remember, for an IRA, there is no stepped-up valuation. The cost basis of an IRA is zero.)

When all of the estate's assets—each spouse's separate property, the community property, and the IRA (as separate property of the decedent spouse)—have been allocated, the final estate asset allocations to the various sub-trusts are as shown in Table 24-9 on page 360. Because of the large value of the IRA (as separate property), this allocation of assets to the sub-trusts is not arbitrary.

Summary

In the allocation option just illustrated, the decedent's separate property receives full stepped-up valuation to the current market value ($100,000) and is placed in the decedent's B sub-trust. The survivor's separate property retains its original cost basis ($50,000), since it is not a community property asset, and flows into the survivor's A sub-trust. The home, as community property, receives full stepped-up valuation to current market value ($400,000) and is allocated by the valuation method—one-half to the decedent's estate and one-half to the survivor's estate. The entire IRA, as the decedent's separate property ($1 million), flows to the Married IRA–QTIP Trust. Since the Married IRA–QTIP Trust can also make use of the decedent's federal estate tax exemption, the decedent's maximum federal estate tax exemp-

---

TABLE 24-8

**ALLOCATION OF IRA UPON DEATH OF OWNER
(MARRIED A-B TRUST AND MARRIED IRA–QTIP TRUST IN A COMMUNITY PROPERTY STATE)**

IRA (as Separate Property)	Market Value	Decedent's Share	Survivor's Share
IRA	$1,000,000	$1,000,000	$0

ALLOCATION OF IRA TO SUB-TRUSTS

Asset	Married IRA–QTIP Trust	B Sub-Trust	A Sub-Trust
IRA	$1,000,000		
Value in decedent's estate	$1,000,000		
Value in survivor's estate			$0

TABLE 24-9
FINAL ALLOCATION OF ESTATE TO SUB-TRUSTS
(MARRIED A-B TRUST AND MARRIED IRA–QTIP TRUST IN A COMMUNITY PROPERTY STATE)

Estate Assets	Married IRA–QTIP Trust	B Sub-Trust	A Sub-Trust
Decedent's separate property		$100,000	
Survivor's separate property			$ 50,000
Home		$200,000	$200,000
IRA (community property)	$1,000,000		
Total value in decedent's estate		$1,300,000	
Total value in survivor's estate			$250,000

tion is fully utilized (between the decedent's B sub-trust and the Married IRA–QTIP Trust).

The surviving spouse has the right to all of the benefits of the IRA in the Married IRA–QTIP Trust. Upon the death of the surviving spouse, the remaining balance of the IRA funds passes to the heirs specified by the first spouse (the owner of the IRA).

Large IRA as a Disproportionate Part of the Estate

If a husband and wife have an IRA as part of their community property assets and the value of the IRA is quite large in proportion to the rest of their estate, they can use the Married IRA–QTIP Trust in conjunction with a Married A-B Trust or a Married A-B-C Trust to fully utilize the decedent's federal estate tax exemption. Since the Married IRA–QTIP Trust can utilize the decedent's federal estate tax exemption, the couple can combine it with the decedent's B sub-trust (which also uses the decedent's federal estate tax exemption) to reduce estate taxes. The most common technique is to name the surviving spouse as the primary beneficiary of the IRA and the Married IRA–QTIP Trust as the contingent beneficiary of the IRA, thus allowing the surviving spouse to later disclaim any part of the IRA that is needed to fully uti-

lize the decedent's federal estate tax exemption. To disclaim an asset is to renounce an interest in the named asset, but disclaiming an interest does *not* renounce an individual's right to the income from that asset.

Estate Before Demise of the First Spouse
While both spouses are living, the market value and cost basis of the estate assets have the values shown in Table 24-10.

Estate After Demise of the First Spouse
When there is a large IRA as community property of both spouses, asset allocation takes place in three steps:

- Allocation of the decedent's and the survivor's separate property
- Allocation of the community property other than the IRA
- Allocation of the IRA as community property

Allocation of Separate Property (at Market Value and Cost Basis) The separate property of the decedent spouse receives full stepped-up valuation to the current market value (as of the decedent's date of death) and is allocated to the decedent's B sub-trust and/or C sub-trust. The separate property of the surviving spouse does

TABLE 24-10
VALUE OF ESTATE ASSETS BEFORE DEATH OF FIRST SPOUSE
(ESTATE WITH LARGE IRA IN A COMMUNITY PROPERTY STATE)

Basic Estate Assets	MARKET VALUE		COST BASIS	
	First Spouse	Second Spouse	First Spouse	Second Spouse
Home	$200,000	$200,000	$100,000	$100,000
First spouse's separate property	$100,000		$ 50,000	
Second spouse's separate property		$100,000		$ 50,000
IRA	$500,000	$500,000	$500,000*	$500,000*

*The cost basis of an IRA is zero.

TABLE 24-11
SEPARATE PROPERTY OF BOTH SPOUSES AFTER DEATH OF FIRST SPOUSE
(ESTATE WITH LARGE IRA IN A COMMUNITY PROPERTY STATE)

Separate Property	MARKET VALUE		COST BASIS	
	First Spouse	Second Spouse	First Spouse	Second Spouse
Decedent's separate property	$100,000			
Survivor's separate property				$50,000

ALLOCATION OF SEPARATE PROPERTY TO SUB-TRUSTS

Separate Property	Married IRA–QTIP Trust	B Sub-Trust	A Sub-Trust
Decedent's separate property		$100,000	
Survivor's separate property			$50,000
Value in decedent's estate	$100,000		
Value in survivor's estate			$50,000

not receive stepped-up valuation and is allocated to the survivor's A sub-trust at the original cost basis. The top section of Table 24-11 shows the asset valuation for both spouses' separate property after the death of the first spouse (including the effect of stepped-up valuation for the decedent's separate property). The bottom part of the table shows the allocation of the separate property to the appropriate sub-trusts.

Note that the decedent's separate property placed in the B sub-trust does not fully utilize the decedent's federal estate tax exemption.

Allocation of Community Property Assets (at Market Value) In a community property state, all community property assets receive full stepped-up valuation to the current market value upon the death of the first spouse. When using the valuation method of allocation, community property assets may be allocated by value rather than by asset. The IRA also may be allocated by value.

All of the community property assets (the home worth $400,000 and the IRA worth $1 million) could be added together (yielding a value of $1.4 million) then divided equally by value, with one-half of the community property ($700,000) placed in the survivor's A sub-trust and the other half in the decedent's B sub-trust. In the example, a logical division of community property assets would place the home ($400,000) in the decedent's B sub-trust, along with $300,000 of the IRA. For the surviving spouse to have an equal value of community property, $700,000 of the IRA would then be placed in the surviving spouse's A sub-trust. Although this allocation of assets is *possible* in a community property state, it would be inadvisable, since placing any of the IRA in the decedent's B sub-trust could have serious adverse income tax consequences.

For the moment, let's concentrate on allocating only the home, since the IRA will be handled separately in a subsequent section. In this illustration, the home is allocated entirely to the decedent's B sub-trust. This allocation is preferred since the home is an appreciating asset. Placing the home in the decedent's B sub-trust insulates all future appreciation from estate taxation. In contrast, the IRA is a depreciating asset (because of required withdrawals) and, therefore, is best placed in the survivor's A sub-trust and the Married IRA–QTIP Trust. The top portion of Table 24-12 shows the asset valuation of the community property (excluding the IRA) after the death of the first spouse, including the effect of stepped-up valuation on the community property assets. The bottom part of the table shows the allocation of the assets to the appropriate sub-trusts.

When each spouse's separate property and their community property (excluding the IRA for the moment) are both allocated to the appropriate sub-trusts, the distribution is as shown in Table 24-13.

Allocation of the Marital IRA Since the decedent's federal estate tax exemption is still not fully utilized, let's now bring in the use of the Married IRA–QTIP Trust to utilize fully the decedent's federal estate tax exemption. Note that the home has been arbitrarily placed in the decedent's estate as an appreciating asset.

TABLE 24-12

COMMUNITY PROPERTY ASSETS AFTER DEATH OF FIRST SPOUSE (ESTATE WITH LARGE IRA IN A COMMUNITY PROPERTY STATE)

Community Property	Market Value	Decedent's Share	Survivor's Share
Home	$400,000	$400,000	$0

ALLOCATION OF COMMUNITY PROPERTY ASSET TO SUB-TRUSTS

Asset	Married IRA–QTIP Trust	B Sub-Trust	A Sub-Trust
Home		$400,000	
Value in decedent's estate		$400,000	
Value in survivor's estate			$0

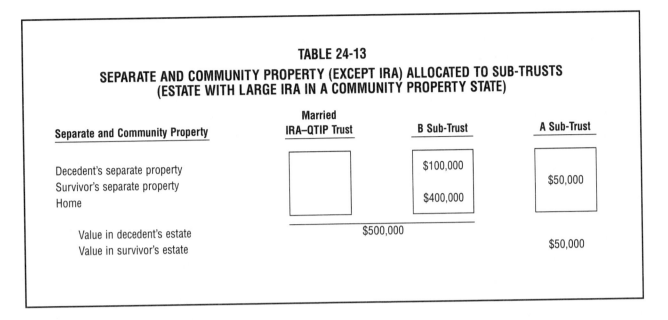

TABLE 24-13

SEPARATE AND COMMUNITY PROPERTY (EXCEPT IRA) ALLOCATED TO SUB-TRUSTS (ESTATE WITH LARGE IRA IN A COMMUNITY PROPERTY STATE)

Separate and Community Property	Married IRA–QTIP Trust	B Sub-Trust	A Sub-Trust
Decedent's separate property		$100,000	$50,000
Survivor's separate property			
Home		$400,000	
Value in decedent's estate	$500,000		
Value in survivor's estate			$50,000

Each case can be different, and this allocation is simply to illustrate the flexibility of the valuation method. (Realize, also, that an IRA is a consumable asset and does not belong in the decedent's *insulated* B sub-trust, to say nothing of the potential income tax consequences.)

To avoid the inadvisable asset allocation presented earlier, the solution is to have a Married IRA–QTIP Trust that circumvents these potentially disastrous tax consequences. The marital IRA could be allocated in two ways, each with different tax consequences.

- The spouse who owns the IRA could split it into two separate IRAs while both spouses are still living, naming the Married IRA–QTIP Trust as the beneficiary of one IRA and the surviving spouse as the beneficiary of the second IRA.
- The IRA's owner could name the surviving spouse as the beneficiary of the entire IRA and name the Married IRA–QTIP Trust as the contingent beneficiary. With this more sophisticated approach, the surviving spouse could simply disclaim any portion of the IRA that is needed inside the Married IRA–QTIP Trust in order to fully utilize the decedent's federal estate tax exemption. The disclaimed interest would flow to the contingent beneficiary, the Married IRA–QTIP Trust.

In this example, the surviving spouse must disclaim 10 percent ($100,000) of the IRA value in order to fully utilize the decedent's federal estate tax exemption. If the first spouse were to die in later years, when the federal estate tax exemption has increased, the surviving spouse would simply disclaim a larger amount of the IRA to fully use the federal estate tax exemption available at that time.

Table 24-14 on page 364 shows the decedent's share of the IRA that has been disclaimed by the surviving spouse, as well as the allocation of the two parts of the IRA to the appropriate sub-trusts. Remember that there is no stepped-up valuation for the IRA. The cost basis of an IRA is zero.

When all of the assets—separate property and community property—have been allocated to the various sub-trusts, the final estate asset allocations are as shown in Table 24-15 on page 364.

If the Other Spouse Dies First The previous examples assumed that the IRA owner was the decedent (died first). However, what happens if the other spouse (the person who was the IRA beneficiary but not the owner of the IRA) dies first? In a community property state, you can convert to a Roth IRA and then allocate half of the marital share of the Roth IRA to the other spouse. Thus, one solution is to split the Roth

TABLE 24-14
VALUE OF IRA AFTER PART DISCLAIMED BY SURVIVING SPOUSE
(ESTATE WITH LARGE IRA IN A COMMUNITY PROPERTY STATE)

IRA (as Community Property)	Market Value	Decedent's Share	Survivor's Share
IRA	$1,000,000	$100,000	$900,000

ALLOCATION OF IRA TO SUB-TRUSTS

Asset	Married IRA–QTIP Trust	B Sub-Trust	A Sub-Trust
IRA	$100,000		$900,000
Value in decedent's estate	$100,000		
Value in survivor's estate			$900,000

TABLE 24-15
FINAL ALLOCATION OF ESTATE
(ESTATE WITH LARGE IRA IN A COMMUNITY PROPERTY STATE)

Estate Assets	Married IRA–QTIP Trust	B Sub-Trust	A Sub-Trust
Decedent's separate property			
Survivor's separate property		$100,000	$ 50,000
Home		$400,000	
IRA (as community property)	$100,000		$900,000
Value in decedent's estate	$600,000		
Value in survivor's estate			$950,000

IRA and allocate one-half of the split Roth IRA *while both spouses are living* to the other spouse in order to fully utilize that person's federal estate tax exemption.

Summary

In the allocation option just illustrated, the decedent's separate property receives full stepped-up valuation to the current market value ($100,000) and flows into the decedent's B sub-trust. The survivor's separate property retains its original cost basis ($50,000), since it is not community property, and flows into the survivor's A sub-trust. The home, as community property, receives full stepped-up valuation to current market value ($400,000). The home is arbitrarily allocated to the decedent's estate and placed in the decedent's B sub-trust.

TABLE 24-16
VALUE OF ESTATE ASSETS BEFORE DEATH OF FIRST SPOUSE
(MARRIED A-B-C TRUST WITH DEBT PAYMENT POWER OF APPOINTMENT
IN A COMMUNITY PROPERTY STATE)

	MARKET VALUE		COST BASIS	
Basic Estate Assets	**First Spouse**	**Second Spouse**	**First Spouse**	**Second Spouse**
Home	$ 200,000	$200,000	$ 100,000	$100,000
Other real estate	$ 400,000	$400,000	$ 200,000	$200,000
First spouse's separate property	$ 100,000		$ 50,000	
Second spouse's separate property		$100,000		$ 50,000
IRA	$1,000,000		$1,000,000*	

*The cost basis of an IRA is zero.

The portion of the IRA that was disclaimed ($100,000) passes to the Married IRA–QTIP Trust named as contingent beneficiary of the IRA. The balance of the IRA passes to the surviving spouse.

Allocating the IRA as shown in this example fully utilizes the decedent's maximum federal estate tax exemption. The surviving spouse has the right to all of the benefits of the IRA in the Married IRA–QTIP Trust. However, upon the death of the surviving spouse, the balance of the remaining IRA funds passes to the couple's heirs.

MARRIED A-B-C TRUST WITH DEBT PAYMENT POWER OF APPOINTMENT

The Debt Payment Power of Appointment (DPPA), similar to the General Power of Appointment (GPOA), is used to pass all of the Living Trust assets to the decedent's estate. Because the survivor's separate property flows to the decedent's estate, it receives full stepped-up valuation to current market value. Typically, this allocation approach is used to achieve full stepped-up valuation to the current market value for all assets in a Living Trust.

However, anyone using this allocation approach must be fully aware that all of the survivor's separate property passes to the dece-

dent's estate. If this union is a second marriage, with children from each spouse's previous marriage as named beneficiaries, the loss of the surviving spouse's separate property to the decedent's estate could cause severe conflict!

The Debt Payment Power of Appointment protects the survivor's assets from creditors and frivolous lawsuits, but the IRA is still exposed to such claims. The IRA, like all retirement assets, is outside the Living Trust and flows to the surviving spouse, as the beneficiary.

Estate Before Demise of the First Spouse

Table 24-16 shows the valuation of the estate assets at market value and cost basis before the death of the first spouse. Please note that I have included other real estate as community property to demonstrate the flexibility in the valuation method of allocation. Also, the IRA is shown as the separate property of the first spouse.

Estate After Demise of the First Spouse

Upon the death of the first spouse, the estate assets must be allocated to the appropriate subtrusts. The DPPA causes all of the Trust assets to flow to the decedent spouse's estate, so all estate assets receive full stepped-up valuation

TABLE 24-17

ESTATE ASSETS AFTER DEATH OF FIRST SPOUSE
(MARRIED A-B-C TRUST WITH DEBT PAYMENT POWER OF APPOINTMENT
IN A COMMUNITY PROPERTY STATE)

Basic Estate Assets	MARKET VALUE		COST BASIS	
	First Spouse	Second Spouse	First Spouse	Second Spouse
Home	$400,000			
Other real estate	$800,000			
Decedent's separate property	$100,000			
Survivor's separate property	$100,000			
IRA				$1,000,000*

ALLOCATION OF ESTATE ASSETS TO SUB-TRUSTS

Estate Assets	C Sub-Trust	B Sub-Trust	A Sub-Trust
Home		$400,000	
Other real estate	$600,000	$200,000	
Decedent's separate property	$100,000		
Survivor's separate property	$100,000		
IRA			$1,000,000
Value in decedent's estate	$1,400,000		
Value in survivor's estate			$1,000,000

*The cost basis of an IRA is zero.

to the current market value (as of the decedent's date of death). The IRA is outside the Trust, so it flows to the surviving spouse (the IRA beneficiary) and is valued at the current market value.

The top portion of Table 24-17 shows the asset valuation of all estate assets after the death of the first spouse (including the effect of stepped-up valuation for all estate assets). The bottom part of the table shows how the estate assets are allocated to the appropriate sub-trusts. Please note that this asset allocation is arbitrary for the decedent's B sub-trust and C sub-trust.

Summary

In this example of asset allocation, all of the Trust assets flow to the decedent's estate, receive full stepped-up valuation to the current market value, and are allocated between the B sub-trust and C sub-trust. Therefore, even the survivor's separate property flows to the decedent's estate and receives full stepped-up valuation (unless the Power of Appointment specifically exempts the separate property). Since the IRA is outside the Living Trust, it flows to the surviving spouse (as the IRA beneficiary) and is placed in the survivor's A sub-trust. (Remember that there is no stepped-up valuation for an IRA. The cost basis of an IRA is zero.)

Properly utilized, the Debt Payment Power of Appointment can protect the survivor's assets from creditors and frivolous lawsuits. However, the IRA is still exposed to such hazards. The allocation option illustrated in the next section shows you how to protect the IRA as well.

MARRIED A-B-C TRUST WITH DEBT PAYMENT POWER OF APPOINTMENT AND A MARRIED IRA–QTIP TRUST

The Debt Payment Power of Appointment (DPPA), similar to the General Power of Appointment (GPOA), is used to pass all of the Living Trust assets to the decedent's estate. All of the survivor's separate property flows to the decedent's estate and thereby receives full stepped-up valuation. This allocation method is typically used to achieve full stepped-up valuation to the current market value for all of the assets in the Living Trust.

Anyone using this asset allocation method must be fully aware that a DPPA passes all of the survivor's separate property to the decedent's estate. If this is a second marriage, with children from each spouse's previous marriage named as beneficiaries, the loss of the surviving spouse's assets to the decedent's estate could cause grave conflicts among the heirs!

Caution: Using a Debt Payment Power of Appointment can cause unwanted estate tax consequences, since all of the assets flow to the decedent's side, leaving no assets in the survivor's A sub-trust.

Use of the Married IRA–QTIP Trust passes the entire IRA to the decedent's estate as well, thus leaving the surviving spouse's estate totally bare. Though this seemingly unfair allocation may appear to be ill advised, it can be an excellent means to protect your estate against creditors and frivolous lawsuits. However, the Trust needs to balance the distributions for the surviving spouse's heirs in order to yield an equitable distribution of estate assets to all heirs.

Estate Before Demise of the First Spouse

Table 24-18 shows the valuation of the estate assets before the death of the first spouse. Please note that, for this illustration, I have included other real estate as community property.

Estate After Demise of the First Spouse

Upon the death of the first spouse, the estate assets must be allocated to the appropriate sub-trusts. Since a Debt Payment Power of Appointment is used, all of the Trust assets flow to the decedent spouse's estate and receive full stepped-up valuation to the current market value—including all of the survivor's separate property. An IRA is always valued at its current market value.

TABLE 24-18

**VALUE OF ESTATE ASSETS BEFORE DEATH OF FIRST SPOUSE
(MARRIED A-B-C TRUST WITH DEBT PAYMENT POWER OF APPOINTMENT AND
MARRIED IRA–QTIP TRUST IN A COMMUNITY PROPERTY STATE)**

Basic Estate Assets	MARKET VALUE		COST BASIS	
	First Spouse	Second Spouse	First Spouse	Second Spouse
Home	$ 200,000	$200,000	$ 100,000	$100,000
Other real estate	$ 400,000	$400,000	$ 200,000	$200,000
First spouse's separate property	$ 100,000		$ 50,000	
Second spouse's separate property		$100,000		$ 50,000
IRA	$1,000,000		$1,000,000*	

*The cost basis of an IRA is zero.

TABLE 24-19

ESTATE ASSETS AFTER DEATH OF FIRST SPOUSE
(MARRIED A-B-C TRUST WITH DEBT PAYMENT POWER OF APPOINTMENT AND MARRIED IRA–QTIP TRUST IN A COMMUNITY PROPERTY STATE)

Basic Estate Assets	MARKET VALUE		COST BASIS	
	First Spouse	Second Spouse	First Spouse	Second Spouse
Home	$ 400,000			
Other real estate	$ 800,000			
Decedent's separate property	$ 100,000			
Survivor's separate property	$ 100,000			
IRA	$1,000,000			

ALLOCATION OF ESTATE ASSETS TO SUB-TRUSTS AND MARRIED IRA–QTIP TRUST

Estate Assets	Married IRA–QTIP Trust	C Sub-Trust	B Sub-Trust	A Sub-Trust
Home			$400,000	
Other real estate		$ 600,000	$200,000	
Decedent's separate property		$ 100,000		
Survivor's separate property		$ 100,000		
IRA	$1,000,000			
Value in decedent's estate		$2,400,000		
Value in survivor's estate				$0

The top portion of Table 24-19 shows the asset valuation for all estate assets after the death of the first spouse (including the effect of stepped-up valuation for all estate assets). The bottom part of the table shows the allocation of the estate assets to the appropriate sub-trusts. Please note that this asset allocation is arbitrary for the assets placed in the decedent's B sub-trust and C sub-trust.

Summary

In this example of asset allocation, all of the Trust assets flow to the decedent's estate, receive full stepped-up valuation to the current market value, and are allocated between the decedent's B sub-trust and C sub-trust. Thus, the survivor's separate property flows to the decedent's estate and receives full stepped-up valuation. Since the Married IRA–QTIP Trust is the beneficiary of the IRA, the IRA flows into the Married IRA–QTIP Trust.

Combining the Debt Payment Power of Appointment (to protect the estate assets) and the Married IRA–QTIP Trust (to protect the IRA) can be an excellent way to insulate all of the estate assets—including the IRA—from creditors and frivolous lawsuits.

MARRIED A-B TRUST WITH DEBT PAYMENT POWER OF APPOINTMENT

Combining a Married A-B Trust with a Debt Payment Power of Appointment (DPPA) can be a potent estate-planning tool for certain estates. The principal advantage of this estate-planning vehicle is the attainment of full stepped-up valuation to the current market value for all Trust assets. In a community property state, the DPPA affects only the survivor's

TABLE 24-20
VALUE OF ESTATE ASSETS BEFORE DEATH OF FIRST SPOUSE
(MARRIED A-B TRUST AND DEBT PAYMENT POWER OF APPOINTMENT IN A COMMUNITY PROPERTY STATE)

Basic Estate Assets	MARKET VALUE		COST BASIS	
	First Spouse	Second Spouse	First Spouse	Second Spouse
Home	$200,000	$200,000	$100,000	$100,000
Other real estate	$400,000	$400,000	$200,000	$200,000
First spouse's separate property	$100,000		$ 50,000	
Second spouse's separate property		$100,000		$ 50,000
IRA	$100,000		$100,000*	

*The cost basis of an IRA is zero.

separate property. Such Power of Appointment passes all of the Trust assets—including any of the surviving spouse's separate property—to the decedent's estate, where all Trust assets receive full stepped-up valuation to the current market value.

However, this method can cause unwanted estate tax consequences. The "overflow" or balance of the assets that exceeds the decedent's exemption flows back to the surviving spouse and is placed in the survivor's A sub-trust. The assets flowing back to the survivor's A sub-trust may be insufficient to utilize the full amount of the survivor's federal estate tax exemption. Since the IRA is outside the Trust, it passes to the surviving spouse as the beneficiary and is placed in the survivor's A sub-trust.

Estate Before Demise of the First Spouse
Table 24-20 shows the valuation of the estate assets before the death of the first spouse. For this illustration, I have used an IRA with a value of $100,000 to minimize the effect of the IRA.

Estate After Demise of the First Spouse
Upon the death of the first spouse, the estate assets must be allocated to the appropriate sub-trusts. The asset allocation option used in this example is best illustrated in two steps:

- All assets are allocated to the decedent's estate.
- Assets that exceed the decedent's federal estate tax exemption flow back to the surviving spouse's estate.

Remember, in a community property state, you have the advantage of being able to allocate the community property by value rather than by asset.

Allocation of All Assets to the Decedent's Estate
The Debt Payment Power of Appointment, similar to the General Power of Appointment (GPOA), is used to pass all of the Trust assets—except the retirement assets (the IRA)—to the decedent's estate. Thus, all of the Trust assets, including the survivor's separate property, receive full stepped-up valuation to the current market value. Since the IRA is outside the Trust, it flows to the surviving spouse, as the IRA beneficiary, at the current market value. The top portion of Table 24-21 on page 370 shows the asset valuation for the estate assets after the death of the first spouse (including the effect of stepped-up valuation on all estate assets). The bottom part of the table shows the initial allocation of the estate assets to the appropriate sub-trusts.

TABLE 24-21
ESTATE ASSETS AFTER DEATH OF FIRST SPOUSE
(MARRIED A-B TRUST AND DEBT PAYMENT POWER OF APPOINTMENT
IN A COMMUNITY PROPERTY STATE)

Basic Estate Assets	MARKET VALUE		COST BASIS	
	First Spouse	Second Spouse	First Spouse	Second Spouse
Home	$400,000			
Other real estate	$800,000			
Decedent's separate property	$100,000			
Survivor's separate property	$100,000			
IRA		$100,000		

INITIAL ALLOCATION OF ESTATE ASSETS TO SUB-TRUSTS

Estate Assets	B Sub-Trust	A Sub-Trust
Home	$ 400,000	
Other real estate	$ 800,000	
Decedent's separate property	$ 100,000	
Survivor's separate property	$ 100,000	
IRA		$100,000
Total value in decedent's estate	$1,400,000	
Total value in survivor's estate		$100,000

TABLE 24-22
REALLOCATION OF DECEDENT'S "OVERFLOW" ASSETS
(COMMUNITY PROPERTY STATE)

Estate Assets	B Sub-Trust	A Sub-Trust
Home	$400,000	
Other real estate	$100,000	$700,000
Decedent's separate property	$100,000	
Survivor's separate property		$100,000
IRA		$100,000
Total value in decedent's estate	$600,000	
Total value in survivor's estate		$900,000

Allocation of Assets Exceeding Decedent's Federal Estate Tax Exemption

Since there is no C sub-trust (QTIP Trust) and the decedent's B sub-trust can hold only one federal estate tax exemption, there is an "overflow." The excess amount (above the amount of the exemption) must flow back to the surviving spouse and into the surviving spouse's A sub-trust. The "overflow" assets flow back to the survivor's A sub-trust by valuation. The IRA remains in the surviving spouse's A sub-trust at the current market value.

Table 24-22 shows the reallocation of estate assets to the appropriate sub-trusts in a way that places in the B sub-trust only an asset value that equals the decedent's federal estate tax exemption. This reallocation avoids the unnecessary payment of estate taxes upon the death of the first spouse. Please note that this reallocation of assets from the decedent's B sub-trust back to the survivor's A sub-trust is arbitrary.

Summary

In this example of asset allocation, all of the Trust assets—including the survivor's separate property—flow to the decedent's estate, where all assets receive full stepped-up valuation to the current market value (as of the date of death of the first spouse). Since the IRA is outside the Trust, it flows to the surviving spouse (as the IRA beneficiary) and is placed in the survivor's A sub-trust. (Remember that there is no stepped-up valuation for an IRA. The cost basis is zero.)

Since the decedent's B sub-trust can hold the equivalent of only one federal estate tax exemption without triggering federal estate taxes, the balance of the assets that exceed the amount of the decedent's exemption flows back to the survivor's A sub-trust at full stepped-up valuation. These "overflow" assets flow back to the survivor's A sub-trust by value rather than by item, thus demonstrating the flexibility of allocation by value.

ADVANCED SETTLEMENT OPTIONS— SEEK PROFESSIONAL GUIDANCE

The use of one or more advanced settlement options can dramatically affect the preservation of your estate from onerous taxation. However, each estate must be analyzed as a unique entity; there are many different factors to prudently consider before making any decisions. The majority of estates may not even need these settlement options. I cannot emphasize enough that making the wrong decision can be devastating to your estate and your heirs.

Selecting an advanced settlement option is critically important. I urge you to seek out very knowledgeable estate preservation specialists and legal professionals with a master's degree in taxation and ensure that you understand the impacts (both positive and negative) on your particular estate. Be prudent—don't make an uninformed decision in haste or in ignorance.

Caution: Before implementing any of the advanced settlement options, be extremely careful. Seek professional guidance from very knowledgeable *estate preservation specialists and legal counsel before making any decisions.*

Appendix A

A Commentary on the Taxpayer Relief Act of 1997

As this book was being written, President Clinton signed into law the Taxpayer Relief Act of 1997. Although this new legislation was hailed by President Clinton, along with Democrats and Republicans alike, its substance is really little more than smoke and mirrors. Even though the President and congressional leaders claim to have given the taxpayer great relief, the provisions (except for the reduced capital gains tax rate) offer little relief—and that relief is spread out over many years yet to come. This law will *eventually* change some of the taxation limits that affect the settling of an estate. The primary features of this new tax legislation are as follows:

- A slow increase in the amount of the individual federal estate tax exemption from $625,000 in 1998 to $1 million in the year 2006.
- An enhanced $250,000 homeowner's exemption for selling your home, not limited to once in a lifetime (replacing the former one-time $185,000 exclusion).
- A much-needed Small Business and Farm Exclusion (which is of minimal benefit to

many and almost disappears in just a few short years).
- Reduction of the capital gains tax rate when you sell real estate (other than your primary residence) and when you sell stocks and mutual funds that you have held for more than twelve months.

The Taxpayer Relief Act of 1997 contains many new and, sometimes, very confusing and complex tax issues. In a nutshell, much of this new tax law is little more than a hoax perpetrated on the American taxpayer in the guise of tax relief. Each of the features just listed has many restrictions, limitations, and exclusions—much too detailed for discussion in this book. However, some features will affect people who are settling an estate; therefore this appendix includes a brief discussion of the salient points, as well as some of my thoughts about this new tax law.

FEDERAL ESTATE TAX EXEMPTION

There has been much hoopla about the increase in the individual federal estate tax exemption to $1 million over ten years. However, a closer look shows that the real increases don't materialize until the last three years. People must live for seven to ten more years to utilize this new "boon." As shown in Table A-1, the first significant increase in the exemption occurs in 2004. As I discussed and illustrated at length in Chapter 1, the increases in the individual tax exemption don't even keep pace with inflation.

TABLE A-1
INDIVIDUAL FEDERAL ESTATE TAX EXEMPTION

Year	Exemption Amount
1997	$ 600,000
1998	$ 625,000
1999	$ 650,000
2000	$ 675,000
2001	$ 675,000
2002	$ 700,000
2003	$ 700,000
2004	$ 850,000
2005	$ 950,000
2006	$1,000,000

HOMEOWNER'S EXEMPTION

When married homeowners sell their home, they immediately receive a $500,000 exemption from capital gains taxation; single homeowners receive a $250,000 exemption. The former $125,000 exemption (usable once in a lifetime) is no longer in effect. To qualify for the new exemption, you must have lived in your home for two of the last five years. If, for some reason, you are not able to live in the home for the entire two-year period, you are allowed to claim part of the exclusion based on the fraction of the two-year period that you have resided in the home. The IRS Restructuring and Reform Act of 1998 allows individuals to utilize the $250,000 homeowner's exclusion even if they have lived in the home less than two years and then move. The amount of exclusion allowed is based on the fraction of the two-year period that the home ownership and use requirement was met.

You are no longer allowed to roll the gain from the sale of one home to your next home.

Instead, when you sell your home, you must "settle" with the tax collector then and there. Interestingly, however, you are allowed to sell your home—and claim this enhanced homeowner's exemption—every two years.

For people whose equity exceeds the amount of the exemption, any capital gain realized on the sale of the home will be taxed at a rate of 20 percent. If you depreciated part of your home for business purposes (such as a home office), that fraction will be taxed at a 25 percent rate.

SMALL BUSINESS AND FARM EXCLUSION

The Small Business and Farm Exclusion allows you to exclude up to $1.3 million of the value of a small business or farm from estate taxes. However, the exclusion is too little, too late and *vanishes with time*. What is hailed as a $1.3 million protective gift to small business is really worth only $675,000—and declines to only $300,000 by 2006. But watch out! The exclusion is not all that it seems.

The reason that the Small Business and Farm Exclusion declines is that it includes your federal estate tax exemption. In 1998, the individual federal estate tax exemption of $625,000 would be applied first (deducted from the $1.3 million business exclusion). Thus, if you have utilized your individual federal estate tax exemption on assets other than your business, you only have $675,000 left to apply against your business. As the federal estate tax exemption increases, the Small Business and Farm Exclusion—which only became effective on January 1, 1998—decreases.

Your business also has to qualify for the Small Business and Farm Exclusion. To do so, your business must meet certain requirements:

- The business or farm must constitute more than 50 percent of your estate.
- You or a member of your family must have owned and materially participated in the business or farm for at least five of the last eight years preceding your death.
- Your heirs must maintain ownership and an active participation in the business or farm for the next ten years.

TAX SAVINGS ON REAL ESTATE OTHER THAN YOUR HOME

For gains on the sale of real estate *other than your primary residence*, the tax rate has been reduced to 20 percent, except for any portion of your real estate that was depreciated (where the tax rate will be 25 percent). To qualify for this revised tax rate on real estate, you must have held (owned) the real estate for at least twelve months. Effective in 2001, this tax legislation will allow the gain from the sale of real estate to be taxed at a rate of 18 percent if the asset has been held for at least five years. (Recapture depreciation will be taxed at 25 percent.)

STOCKS AND MUTUAL FUNDS

The 1997 tax law revises the tax rates for capital gains on stocks and mutual funds, based on how long those assets are held. Capital gains on stocks or mutual funds held for less than twelve months will be taxed as ordinary income. If the securities are held for more than twelve months but less than five years, any gain will be taxed at a 20 percent rate. Beginning in 2001, if any securities (i.e., stocks, bonds, and mutual funds) are held for at least five years, the gain on sale will be taxed at 18 percent.

This varying capital gains tax rate structure poses a challenge for the financial planner: whether to recommend investing in mutual funds that have an average turnover of thirteen months, investing in low-turnover funds or index funds, or buying and holding individual stocks. On balance, however, the *Wall Street Journal* reports that the mutual fund companies plan no changes, since the companies believe that their net return after taxes is still more favorable to the average investor. After the 1997 Taxpayer Relief Act was enacted, the Republican Congress was later able to reduce the time period for the 20 percent capital gains tax rate from eighteen to twelve months.

ANNUITIES

The capital gains tax rates implemented by the new Taxpayer Relief Act hit annuities the hardest. A fixed annuity is a special investment vehicle offered by insurance companies. Annuities enjoy favorable tax privileges that allow your investment dollars to accrue tax free until the funds are withdrawn—at which time all growth is taxed at the ordinary income tax rate. Because fixed annuities enjoy a favorable tax status on their growth, annuities are offered to the investor at lower interest rates (i.e., a slower growth rate). In contrast, mutual funds are taxed annually on their growth, but they often enjoy the more favorable 20 percent capital gains tax rate.

With the top capital gains rate at 28 percent, many financial advisors traditionally told investors they must hold on to variable annuities for ten to fifteen years before they could expect to break even (i.e., receive a return comparable to those of mutual funds). It typically took that long for annuities' compounding and tax deferral to begin to compare favorably with the return on other investments. With the capital gains tax rate dropping to 20 percent (for an asset held at least twelve months), breaking even will now take at least twenty years.

COLLEGE TUITION

Under the Taxpayer Relief Act, families receive a tax credit of up to $1,500 per year for the first two years of college (a 100 percent credit for the first $1,000 in tuition and a 50 percent credit for the second $1,000 of tuition), along with credits of up to $1,000 for every additional year of college or graduate school (equating to a 20 percent credit for up to $5,000 in tuition). Eligibility for this education credit phases out for married couples with incomes between $80,000 (full eligibility) and $100,000 (no eligibility) and phases out for individuals with incomes between $50,000 (full eligibility) and $60,000 (no eligibility).

In addition, for some middle-income families, interest on student loans up to $2,500 a year for five years is tax deductible.

CHILD TAX CREDIT

Beginning in 1998, parents of children under the age of 17 received a $400-per-child tax credit, and the credit increased to $500 in 1999. This tax credit is phased out for higher-income people: married taxpayers when their adjusted gross income (AGI) reaches $110,000 and individuals when their AGI reaches $75,000.

IRAs

As expected, the IRA changes introduced with the Taxpayer Relief Act are incredibly complex and the result of bureaucratic compromise. The maximum contribution for an IRA remains at $2,000 per year, but the eligibility restrictions, based on AGI, have been raised to $50,000 (for couples), rising to $80,000 by the year 2007, and to $30,000 (for individuals), rising to $50,000 by the year 2005. If an individual is covered by a retirement plan at work, that individual is ineligible to make a tax-deductible IRA contribution, but a nonworking spouse may now annually contribute a full $2,000 to an IRA.

Another new provision is that you may also make an annual, non-deductible $500-per-child contribution to an Education IRA for higher education. If the child does not use such funds, the education fund can be rolled over to another child. However, if the other child does not attend college, the Education IRA funds must be withdrawn, and the tax liability paid, when the child reaches the age of 30.

This tax package also repeals the 15 percent excise tax that formerly affected affluent investors who withdrew more than $165,000 per year from their IRAs and other retirement plans.

Roth (or Dream) IRA

The Taxpayer Relief Act of 1997 established a new IRA, called a Roth IRA, wherein your investment is not tax deductible, but all interest and capital gains accumulate tax free (i.e., *all* of your eventual withdrawals from the IRA will be totally tax free). Eligibility for the Roth IRA, based on AGI, begins to phase out at $150,000 for a married couple and $95,000 for an individual. You may not withdraw any growth from the IRA investment for a full five years. However, after five years, you may make early withdrawals (before age 59½)—without any penalty—for a first-time home purchase and for education costs. You are still limited to a maximum total annual IRA contribution of $2,000 per person.

The Roth IRA, already commonly referred to as the "dream IRA," is an opportunity that too easily can go unnoticed—but it is too good an opportunity to pass up. With a Roth IRA, you may make non-tax-deductible contributions to the Roth IRA, but then withdraw all of your original investment plus *all compounded growth* absolutely tax free after you reach the age of 59½.

You may now "salvage" your existing traditional IRA from the claws of the IRS—and at the same time build up a substantial estate for your children and grandchildren. Amazingly, the Taxpayer Relief Act allows you to convert your existing traditional IRA into a Roth IRA, but you must recognize all of the IRA proceeds as income and pay any tax liability at the time of the conversion. Once the traditional IRA funds are converted into a Roth IRA, there is no further tax whatsoever on any withdrawals, and you are not required to begin withdrawing funds at the age of 70½. The magic of tax-free growth can be awesome—and, thereafter, all withdrawals by your children or grandchildren will be tax free! During 1998, if you converted an existing traditional IRA into a Roth IRA, the IRS allowed you to spread the resultant income tax liability over a four-year period. This one-time income-averaging opportunity expired in December 1998; now you may still convert your traditional IRA to a Roth IRA, but you must pay the entire tax liability in the year of the conversion. However, for you to qualify for the conversion of your traditional IRA to a Roth IRA, your AGI cannot exceed $100,000.

A Ray of Hope: There is one bright ray of light in this otherwise seemingly dark cloud called the Taxpayer Relief Act of 1997—the Roth (or dream) IRA.

Whether or not you have a traditional IRA to roll over to a Roth IRA, you may make annual $2,000 non-tax-deductible contributions to a Roth IRA. The primary benefit of the Roth IRA is that all growth and ultimate withdrawals are absolutely tax free. However, to be eligible for this benefit, the funds must have been in the Roth IRA for a minimum of five years, regardless of your age at withdrawal. You may withdraw funds from your Roth IRA without penalty anytime after you reach the age of 59½. Alternatively, you may let the funds grow and then pass them to your children or grandchildren tax free, since a Roth IRA has no required withdrawals after 70½ or any other age. The Roth IRA can be an ideal retirement vehicle to protect you against the potential demise of social security.

Eligibility for Roth IRA contributions is phased out for taxpayers as AGI rises. If you are filing separately, eligibility ranges from full eligibility for incomes up to $95,000 to no eligibility at an income of $110,000 or more. For married couples filing jointly, eligibility is phased out between $150,000 (full eligibility for incomes up to that amount) and $160,000 (no eligibility).

Appendix B
IRS Life Expectancy Tables

IRS life expectancy tables are used to determine the life expectancy of an individual, a married couple, or two individuals. A life expectancy figure based on the appropriate table value must be used when calculating the amount of required withdrawals from a traditional IRA.

The IRS table for single life expectancy shown in Table B-1 is used to determine the life expectancy of an individual when calculating the required withdrawals.

The IRS table for joint life and last survivor expectancy shown in Table B-2 is used when calculating the joint life expectancy of two individuals (a husband and wife, a surviving spouse and the oldest child, a gay or lesbian couple, etc.).

IRS Publication 590 provides detailed information about how these tables are used to calculate the life expectancy on which the IRA withdrawals must be made.

TABLE B-1
IRS TABLE V: SINGLE LIFE EXPECTANCY

Age	Divisor	Age	Divisor	Age	Divisor	Age	Divisor
35	47.3	55	28.6	73	13.9	93	4.1
36	46.4	56	27.7	74	13.2	94	3.9
37	45.4	57	26.8	75	12.5	95	3.7
38	44.4	58	25.9	76	11.9	96	3.4
39	43.5	59	25.0	77	11.2	97	3.2
40	42.5	60	24.2	78	10.6	98	3.0
41	41.5	61	23.3	79	10.0	99	2.8
42	40.6	62	22.5	80	9.5	100	2.7
43	39.6	63	21.6	81	8.9	101	2.5
44	38.7	64	20.8	82	8.4	102	2.3
45	37.7	65	20.0	83	7.9	103	2.1
46	36.8	66	19.2	84	7.4	104	1.9
47	35.9	67	18.4	85	6.9	105	1.8
48	34.9	68	17.6	86	6.5	106	1.6
49	34.0	69	16.8	87	6.1	107	1.4
50	33.1	70	16.0	88	5.7	108	1.3
51	32.2	71	15.3	89	5.3	109	1.1
52	31.3	72	14.6	90	5.0	110	1.0
53	30.4			91	4.7		
54	29.5			92	4.4		

Source: IRS Publication 590.

TABLE B-2
IRS TABLE VI: JOINT LIFE AND LAST SURVIVOR EXPECTANCY

AGE OF BENEFICIARY	AGE OF PARTICIPANT		AGE OF BENEFICIARY	AGE OF PARTICIPANT	
	70	71		70	71
35	47.5	47.5	55	29.9	29.7
36	46.6	46.6	56	29.1	29.0
37	45.7	45.6	57	28.4	28.2
38	44.7	44.7	58	27.6	27.5
39	43.8	43.8	59	26.9	26.7
40	42.9	42.8	60	26.2	26.0
41	41.9	41.9	61	25.6	25.3
42	41.0	41.0	62	24.9	24.7
43	40.1	40.1	63	24.3	24.0
44	39.2	39.1	64	23.7	23.4
45	38.3	38.2	65	23.1	22.8
46	37.4	37.3	66	22.5	22.2
47	36.5	36.5	67	22.0	21.7
48	35.7	35.6	68	21.5	21.2
49	34.8	34.7	69	21.1	20.7
50	34.0	33.9	70	20.6	20.2
51	33.1	33.0	71	20.2	19.8
52	32.3	32.2	72	19.8	19.4
53	31.5	31.4	73	19.4	19.0
54	30.7	30.5	74	19.1	18.6

Source: IRS Publication 590.

Appendix C
Sample Separate Property Agreement

Separate Property Agreements are used to identify the separate property of individuals. Such agreements are particularly beneficial in second marriages when there are children from previous marriages. These agreements identify the separate property that each individual brought into the marriage (or received as a gift or inheritance) and, thus, is intended to be distributed to that parent's children upon the death of the parent. Separate exhibits are used for a husband and a wife to clearly describe the assets (and value thereof) of his or her separate property.

The sample Separate Property Agreement that follows shows how the separate property of each individual is specified in separate exhibits.

SEPARATE PROPERTY AGREEMENT
(ADDENDUM TO LIVING TRUST)

This Agreement is entered into by and between John H. Jones and Mary R. Jones who were married October 15, 1970, at Los Angeles, California, and who intend by this Agreement to acknowledge their respective rights in the property of the other, and to avoid such interests which, except for the operation of this Agreement, they might acquire in the property of the other as incidents of their marriage relationship.

Separate Property

The parties desire that all property acknowledged by them as their separate property, and any additional property which may come to either of them by gift or bequest, or by rights acquired prior to their marriage, shall be and remain their respective sole and separate property.

Consideration

This Agreement is entered into in consideration of marriage, the continuing and ongoing relationship of the parties, and the mutual covenants, conditions, releases, and rights herein granted and relinquished.

Mutual Release of Property

Mary R. Jones covenants and agrees that all of the separate property as of the date of this Agreement of John H. Jones of whatsoever nature and wheresoever located, and any property which he may hereafter acquire as his separate property, whether real, personal, or mixed, including any and all earnings and profits therefrom, shall be and remain his sole and separate property to use and dispose of as he sees fit and as if no marriage had been entered into.

John H. Jones covenants and agrees that all of the separate property as of the date of this Agreement of Mary R. Jones of whatsoever nature and wheresoever located, and any property which she may hereafter acquire as her separate property, whether real, personal, or mixed, including any and all earnings and profits therefrom, shall be and remain her sole and separate property to use and dispose of as she sees fit and as if no marriage had been entered into.

© Copyright The Estate Plan® 1998. All Rights Reserved.

Mutual Release of Rights

It is mutually agreed that each party waives, discharges, and releases any and all claims and rights, actual, inchoate, or contingent, in law and equity which he or she has acquired or may acquire in the separate property of the other by reason of such marriage, including but not limited to:

a. The right to a family allowance;

b. The right to probate a homestead;

c. The rights or claims of dower, curtesy, or any statutory substitutes therefore as provided by the statutes of the State in which the parties or either of them may die, be domiciled, or may own real property;

d. The right of election to take against the will of the other;

e. The right to a distributive share in the estate of the other should he or she die intestate;

f. The right to declare a homestead in the separate property of the other;

g. The right to act as administrator of the estate of the other.

Exhibits

The parties have attached Exhibits hereto, listing their separate property. The parties' rights in this listed property, together with all other property to which either party shall take title as his or her sole and separate property, shall be governed by this Agreement.

After Acquired Separate Property

This Agreement is not intended to prohibit other property acquired by a spouse as separate property of that spouse from remaining separate property of that spouse if not listed in this Agreement. Further, the parties agree that any property which is sold, traded, refinanced, or which otherwise changes its form, character, or nature, the new property resulting therefrom shall have the same separate property characterization as the original property so sold, traded, refinanced, or otherwise changed in form, character, or nature.

Living Trust

The parties are executing this Separate Property Agreement coincidentally with the execution of a revocable Living Trust, to which this Agreement is attached as an addendum. The parties intend that each and every provision of this Agreement shall be effective with respect to any and all designated property which is held in the said Trust.

Other Documents

Both parties covenant that they will willingly, at the request of the other, or their successors or assigns, execute, deliver, and properly acknowledge whatever additional instruments may be required to carry out the intention of this Agreement, and shall execute, deliver, and properly acknowledge any deeds or other documents in order that good and marketable title to any separate property can be conveyed by one party free from any claim of the other party.

Revocation

This Agreement is not intended to revoke a Pre-Marital Agreement executed by the parties hereto, if any. The parties do intend, however, that this Agreement shall modify any such Pre-Marital Agreement, or Agreements, if any, to the extent that they are in conflict with the provisions hereof.

Resolution of Conflict

The parties agree that should any dispute arise between them regarding properties which are subject to this Agreement, or a dispute as to whether or not a property or properties are subject to this Agreement, or a dispute about the construction of the terms or conditions of this Agreement, such dispute shall be resolved by a hearing of the conflict and dispute by a "Rent-A-Judge." The parties agree that the judge so selected shall be from the list of judges made available by the County Bar Association or the County Legal Bar Association of the County of residence of the parties or situs of the property. If the parties cannot agree on a particular "Rent-A-Judge," then the parties agree to submit that particular issue to arbitration under the rules and procedures of the American Arbitration Association.

Representations and Release

Each party represents that he or she has made a full and complete disclosure of all property that he or she wishes to be subject of this Agreement. Should either party, subsequent to the execution of this Agreement, gift, commingle, or transmute through their respective actions, the nature or character of the listed property, which may cause loss of their separate property rights, then such party releases his or her attorneys and advisors, the Estate Plan, and its agents and employees from all losses or damages or changes in position that may result or flow from such party's actions.

Governing Law

This Agreement shall be governed by the laws of the State of California.

Binding on Heirs

This Agreement is binding upon the heirs, beneficiaries, Trustees, Successor Trustees, Executors, Personal Representatives, Administrators, assigns and successors in interest to the parties hereto.

Modifications

This Agreement may be modified only by an Agreement in writing signed by the party or parties to be charged.

Execution

IN WITNESS WHEREOF, the parties have executed this Agreement this 17th day of September, 1979.

_____   _____
John H. Jones   Mary R. Jones

Note: Notary Certificate of Acknowledgment omitted from illustration.

EXHIBIT TO SEPARATE PROPERTY AGREEMENT

Separate Property of John H. Jones

Item	Source*	Net Value	Description	Both Spouses Initial**
1.	P	$100,000	E. F. Hutton, Account 5648482	*JHJ* *MRJ*
2.				
3.				
4.				
5.				
6.				
7.				
8.				
9.				
10.				
11.				
12.				
13.				
14.				
15.				

 * Source Code: **P** = Prior to Current Marriage; **G** = Gift; **I** = Inheritance.
** Initial new items **written** in.

© Copyright The Estate Plan® 1998. All Rights Reserved.

EXHIBIT TO SEPARATE PROPERTY AGREEMENT

Separate Property of Mary R. Jones

Item	Source*	Net Value	Description	Both Spouses Initial**
1.	P	$100,000	E. F. Hutton, Account 5648321	*JHJ* *MRJ*
2.				
3.				
4.				
5.				
6.				
7.				
8.				
9.				
10.				
11.				
12.				
13.				
14.				
15.				

* Source Code: **P** = Prior to Current Marriage; **G** = Gift; **I** = Inheritance.

** Initial new items **written** in.

© Copyright The Estate Plan® 1998. All Rights Reserved.

Appendix D

Sample Aggregate Community Property Agreement

An Aggregate Community Property Agreement allows marital assets to be divided by *dollar value* rather than item by item. A carefully drawn agreement can exempt each spouse's separate property from being included as joint assets. Without such an agreement, asset allocation must be done by item rather than by value, even in a community property state.

An example of a complete Aggregate Community Property Agreement follows.

THE JONES COMMUNITY PROPERTY AGREEMENT

THIS AGREEMENT entered into by and between John H. Jones ("Husband") and Mary R. Jones ("Wife") and shall be effective as of this 17 day of September, 1979.

RECITALS AND TERMS

JOINT TENANCY PROPERTY. The parties may have acquired certain real property, personal property, or both which is currently held as joint tenants or as commonly held property. The parties intend by this agreement to transmute any such joint tenancy or commonly owned property to community property.

SEPARATE PROPERTY. The parties may have acquired certain real property, personal property, or both, prior to marriage or by gift or inheritance which is currently held as their sole and separate property. The parties intend by this agreement to transmute any such separate property to community property.

FAMILY TRUST AGREEMENT. The parties have entered into a revocable inter vivos (living) trust agreement for estate planning purposes this date which is known as "The Jones Family Trust, dated September 17, 1979, John H. Jones and Mary R. Jones, Trustors and/or Trustees" (hereinafter, the "Trust").

COMMUNITY PROPERTY ESTATE. The term "Community Property Estate" refers to any and all property in which Husband and Wife have present and existing interests under state law. The term "Trust Community Property" shall refer to that portion of the Community Property Estate held by the trustee of the Trust.

RETIREMENT PROCEEDS. HUSBAND may own and participate in a qualified retirement plan known as (the "Plan"). Following his retirement, HUSBAND intends to roll over the proceeds from the Plan (except for employee contributions to that plan, if any) to an Individual Retirement Account. Such retirement benefits are hereinafter referred to as "Husband's Retirement Plan" regardless of whether they are represented by an interest in the Plan or by one or more Individual Retirement Accounts.

In addition, WIFE may own and participate in a qualified retirement plan known as (the "Plan"). Following her retirement, WIFE intends to roll over the proceeds from the Plan (except for employee contributions to that plan, if any) to an Individual Retirement Account. Such retirement benefits are hereinafter referred to as "Wife's Retirement Plan" regardless of whether they are represented by an interest in the Plan or by one or more Individual Retirement Accounts.

© Copyright The Estate Plan® 1998. All Rights Reserved.

ESTATE PLANNING OBJECTIVES. The parties desire to enter into an agreement which achieves the following estate planning objectives: (i) clarify the status of their various property interests; and (ii) provide for and facilitate the division of their Community Property Estate when the community terminates on the death of either of them in a manner which results in the allocation of all retirement proceeds to the surviving spouse, but which still results in a division of the Community Property Estate between the deceased spouse and the surviving spouse which is as equal as possible in the aggregate value of assets allocated to each.

AGREEMENT

In order to give effect to their intent, the parties agree as follows:

1. ALL PROPERTY IS COMMUNITY PROPERTY. HUSBAND and WIFE mutually agree that all property now owned or hereafter acquired by HUSBAND, WIFE or both shall be the community property of HUSBAND and WIFE, including property interests which up to the date of this Agreement may have constituted separate property or quasi-community property, and including property held in their names as tenants in common, joint tenants, or in any other manner. This Agreement is specifically intended to be an express declaration by each party to hold all such property as community property.

2. EXCEPTION FOR CERTAIN JOINT TENANCY ASSETS. Notwithstanding the provisions of Paragraph A above, the parties agree that the following assets held by them as joint tenants (whether now owned or hereafter acquired) shall be owned by them as true joint tenants and not as community property: (i) checking accounts at a bank or savings and loan association; (ii) automobiles, boats, trailers, and other motor vehicles; and (iii) U.S. savings bonds. The parties understand and agree, with respect to joint tenancy assets listed above, that: (i) each party owns an undivided one-half (½) interest in such assets as his or her separate property; and (ii) the deceased spouse's interest in such assets will pass by operation of law to the surviving joint tenant, notwithstanding anything to the contrary in the deceased's will or the Family Trust.

3. COMMUNITY PROPERTY AGREEMENT. The parties agree that each of them owns an undivided one-half (½) interest in the total aggregate value of their Community Property Estate (sometimes known as the "Aggregate Theory") rather than an undivided one-half (½) interest in each and every community property asset (sometimes known as the "Item Theory").

4. DIVISION OF COMMUNITY PROPERTY ESTATE. Following the death of the first to die, HUSBAND and WIFE intend to effect a division of their Community Property Estate in order to accomplish their certain estate planning objectives as set forth above. Accordingly, the parties agree that: (i) the surviving spouse will own, as a part of his or her share of the Community Prop-

erty Estate, all of the Plans held in either spouse's name; and (ii) the deceased spouse's share of the Community Property Estate shall consist of other community property assets as equal as possible in value to the value of such retirement proceeds. For purposes of this division, all assets shall be valued as of the date of death of the deceased spouse in the amount as finally determined for federal estate tax purposes. This division shall be accomplished by the following:

A. HUSBAND DIES FIRST. WIFE shall be designated as the primary death beneficiary of Husband's Retirement Plan so that if HUSBAND is the first spouse to die, WIFE shall become the sole owner of Husband's Retirement Plan. Further, WIFE shall continue as the sole owner of Wife's Retirement Plan by operation of HUSBAND's death beneficiary designation consent under appropriate law, which HUSBAND hereby agrees to provide. HUSBAND's interest in the Community Property Estate shall be: (i) that portion of the Community Property Estate, up to the whole thereof, which equals the value of Husband's Retirement Proceeds plus the value of Wife's Retirement Proceeds; and (ii) one-half of the Community Property Estate in excess of such portion, if any.

B. WIFE DIES FIRST. HUSBAND shall be designated as the primary death beneficiary of Wife's Retirement Plan so that if WIFE is the first spouse to die, HUSBAND shall become the sole owner of Wife's Retirement Plan. Further, HUSBAND shall continue as the sole owner of Husband's Retirement Plan by operation of WIFE's death beneficiary designation consent under appropriate law, which WIFE hereby agrees to provide. WIFE's interest in the Community Property Estate shall be: (i) that portion of the Community Property Estate, up to the whole thereof, which equals the value of Husband's Retirement Proceeds plus the value of Wife's Retirement Proceeds; and (ii) one-half of the Community Property Estate in excess of such portion, if any.

C. DISCRETION TO DIVIDE COMMUNITY PROPERTY ESTATE. The parties further agree that the division of the Community Property Estate as agreed by the parties and set forth in this agreement shall be accomplished through the discretion of: (i) the trustee(s) serving under the Trust who shall select those assets from the Trust Community Property which shall constitute the deceased spouse's interest in the Community Property Estate; and (ii) the deceased spouse's executor who shall select those assets, if any, not in the Trust Community Property which shall constitute the deceased spouse's interest in the Community Property Estate.

D. SURVIVING SPOUSE'S RIGHT TO CHANGE BENEFICIARY OF RETIREMENT PROCEEDS. The parties expressly agree that the surviving spouse shall have the unrestricted right to: (i) change the beneficiary designation of all or any part of the retirement proceeds; and (ii) elect a different benefit or payment option with respect to all or any part of the retirement proceeds. It is expressly provided for and agreed to herein that the surviving spouse shall have sole ownership, title and rights to both his or her own Plan as well as the deceased spouse's Plan.

3. BINDING AGREEMENT. This Agreement shall be binding on the administrators, executors, successors, and assigns of the parties hereto.

4. WRITTEN MODIFICATIONS. The parties acknowledge that this Agreement is the only Agreement between them. Any modifications or changes to this Agreement must be in writing, making specific reference to this Agreement and must be signed by each party before a Notary Public. If a party is unable to so execute a modification or change by reason of incapacity, such modification or change may be executed only by a court-appointed conservator of the incompetent spouse's estate or by an agent under such incompetent spouse's Durable Power of Attorney for Asset Management.

5. SEVERABILITY. If any provision, or part of a provision, of this Agreement shall be determined to be void or unenforceable by a court of competent jurisdiction, the remainder of the Agreement shall remain valid and enforceable.

6. APPLICABLE LAW. Except where otherwise provided for herein, all matters pertaining to the validity, construction, interpretation, and effect of this Agreement shall be governed by the laws of the State of California.

7. WAIVER OF NONMARITAL AND OTHER RIGHTS AND REPRESENTATION. Each party acknowledges that he or she has had the opportunity to discuss the rights that each party may have gained by reason of contracts between them, their nonmarital relationship, past conduct, and statements made orally to each other; and by this Agreement each of them waives and renounces all claims, interests, or rights that he or she might have acquired by reason of any such contracts, relationships, conduct, or statements.

IN WITNESS WHEREOF, the parties have executed this agreement as of September 17, 1979.

_____
John H. Jones, Husband

_____
Mary R. Jones, Wife

_____

Note: Notary Certificate of Acknowledgment omitted from illustration.

EXHIBIT TO SEPARATE PROPERTY AGREEMENT

Separate Property of John H. Jones

Item	Source*	Net Value	Description	Both Spouses Initial**
1.	P	$100,000	E. F. Hutton, Account 5648482	JHJ MRJ
2.				
3.				
4.				
5.				
6.				
7.				
8.				
9.				
10.				
11.				
12.				
13.				
14.				
15.				

  * Source Code: **P** = Prior to Current Marriage; **G** = Gift; **I** = Inheritance.
** Initial new items **written** in.

© Copyright The Estate Plan® 1998. All Rights Reserved.

EXHIBIT TO SEPARATE PROPERTY AGREEMENT

Separate Property of Mary R. Jones

Item	Source*	Net Value	Description	Both Spouses Initial**
1.	P	$100,000	E. F. Hutton, Account 5648321	JHJ MRJ
2.				
3.				
4.				
5.				
6.				
7.				
8.				
9.				
10.				
11.				
12.				
13.				
14.				
15.				

* Source Code: **P** = Prior to Current Marriage; **G** = Gift; **I** = Inheritance.

** Initial new items **written** in.

© Copyright The Estate Plan® 1998. All Rights Reserved.

Appendix E
States Imposing an Inheritance Tax

As of the time this book was written, the states listed in Table E imposed an inheritance tax on some or all beneficiaries. Note that the amount of the tax these states impose ranges from 0 to as much as 30 percent and may vary according to the survivor's relationship to the deceased.

TABLE E
STATES IMPOSING AN INHERITANCE TAX
Tax Rate for Beneficiaries

State	Surviving Spouse, Children, Parents	Brothers, Sisters, Grandparents	Aunts, Uncles	All Others
Connecticut	0%	3–6%	4–10%	8–14%
Delaware	2–4%	1–6%	5–10%	10–16%
Indiana	0%	1–10%	7–15%	10–20%
Iowa	0%	1–8%	5–10%	10–15%
Kansas	0%	1–5%	3–12½%	10–15%
Kentucky	0%	2–10%	4–16%	6–16%
Louisiana	2–3%	2–3%	5–7%	5–10%
Maryland	0%	1%	10%	10%
Mississippi	0%	1–16%	1–16%	1–16%
Montana	0%	0%	6–24%	8–32%
Nebraska	0%	1%	6–9%	6–9%
New Hampshire	0%	0%	18%	18%
New Jersey	0%	0%	11–16%	15–16%
North Carolina	0%	1–12%	4–16%	8–17%
Ohio	0%	2–7%	2–7%	2–7%
Oklahoma	0%	1–15%	1–15%	1–15%
Pennsylvania	0%	6%	15%	15%
South Dakota	0%	3¾–15%	4–25%	6–30%
Tennessee	0%	9½%	9½%	9½%

Appendix F
Instructions for Completing Form SS-4

Upon the death of a trustor, either the surviving trustee or the successor trustee(s) must file IRS Form SS-4 to obtain an Employer Identification Number (EIN) in order to establish the resulting Trusts or the Trust estate as a separate taxpayer. A sample of Form SS-4 is shown in Figure F, following the instructions.

MARRIED OR UNMARRIED DECEDENT WITH A JOINT TRUST

If the decedent was married or single with a joint Trust, the surviving trustee must file Form SS-4 upon the death of the first trustor to establish Trust B and, if applicable, Trust C as separate taxpayers.

SINGLE DECEDENT WITH SINGLE TRUST

If the decedent was single, the successor trustee must file Form SS-4 upon the death of the trustor to establish the decedent's Trust estate as a separate taxpayer for the period between the death and the distribution of the Trust assets.

GENERAL INSTRUCTIONS FOR COMPLETING FORM SS-4

Use the following instructions as a guide for completing Form SS-4 for the establishment of a Trust as a separate taxpayer.

Line 1—Enter the name of the Trust for which the application is being filed (e.g., The Doe Family Trust, dated June 7, 1979).

Line 2—You can skip this line as the information requested is the same as in Line 1.

Line 3—Enter the name of the surviving or successor trustee.

Lines 4 through 5—Enter mailing address of surviving or successor trustee.

Line 6—Enter county and state where Trust will be administered.

Line 7—Enter name and social security number of decedent trustor.

Line 8a—Check the box marked "Trust."

Line 8b—Skip (leave blank).

Line 9—Check the box marked "Created a Trust," and specify that it is "Irrevocable."

Line 10—Enter the decedent trustor's date of death.

Line 11—Enter "December 31" as the closing month of the accounting year.

Lines 12 and 13—Skip (leave blank).

Line 14—Enter "Trust Administration."

Line 15—Check the box marked "No."

Line 16—Check the box marked "N/A."

Lines 17a—Check the box marked "No."

Lines 17b and 17c—Skip (leave blank).

Signature Block—Print name of the surviving trustee or successor trustee and designate his or her title as "Trustee." The surviving or successor trustee must sign and date the form and include a telephone number where he or she can be contacted.

HOW TO APPLY
You can apply for an EIN using Form SS-4 by telephone or by mail. You can obtain an EIN immediately by calling the Tele-Tin phone number of the service center for your state. You may dial 1-800-829-1040 to verify the Tele-Tin number for your particular state. Alternatively, you may send the completed Form SS-4 directly to the IRS service center for your state to receive an EIN by mail. You should allow four to five weeks for processing if you apply by mail. You can obtain the address for the service center for your particular state by dialing 1-800-829-1040.

FIGURE F

SAMPLE FORM SS-4

Form **SS-4** (Rev. December 1995) Department of the Treasury Internal Revenue Service	**Application for Employer Identification Number** (For use by employers, corporations, partnerships, trusts, estates, churches, government agencies, certain individuals, and others. See instructions.) ▶ Keep a copy for your records.	EIN _____ OMB No. 1545-0003

Please type or print clearly.

1 Name of applicant (Legal name) (See instructions.)
The Jones Family Trust, dated September 17, 1979

2 Trade name of business (if different from name on line 1)

3 Executor, trustee, "care of" name
Mary R. Jones, Trustee

4a Mailing address (street address) (room, apt., or suite no.)
450 N. Rossmore Ave.

5a Business address (if different from address in lines 4a and 4b)

4b City, state, and ZIP code
Los Angeles, CA 90004

5b City, state, and ZIP code

6 County and state where principal business is located
Los Angeles, CA

7 Name of principal officer, general partner, grantor, owner, or trustor — SSN required (See instructions.) ▶ 545-32-3940
John Howard Jones

8a Type of entity (Check only one box.) (See instructions.)

☐ Sole proprietor (SSN) _____
☐ Partnership   ☐ Personal service corp.
☐ REMIC   ☐ Limited liability co.
☐ State/local government   ☐ National Guard
☐ Other nonprofit organization (specify) ▶ _____
☐ Other (specify) ▶

☐ Estate (SSN of decedent) _____
☐ Plan administrator - SSN _____
☐ Other corporation (specify) ▶ _____
☒ Trust   ☐ Farmers' cooperative
☐ Federal Government/military   ☐ Church or church-controlled organization
(enter GEN if applicable) _____

8b If a corporation, name the state or foreign country (if applicable) where incorporated

State	Foreign country

9 Reason for applying (Check only one box.)

☐ Started new business (specify) ▶ _____
☐ Hired employees
☐ Created a pension plan (specify type) ▶

☐ Banking purpose (specify) ▶ _____
☐ Changed type of organization (specify) ▶ _____
☐ Purchased going business
☒ Created a trust (specify) ▶ Irrevocable
☐ Other (specify) ▶

10 Date business started or acquired (Mo., day, year) (See instructions.)
February 4, 1981

11 Closing month of accounting year (See instructions.)
December 31

12 First date wages or annuities were paid or will be paid (Mo., day, year). Note: If applicant is a withholding agent, enter date income will first be paid to nonresident alien. (Mo., day, year) .... ▶

13 Highest number of employees expected in the next 12 months. Note: If the applicant does not expect to have any employees during the period, enter -0- (See instructions.) .... ▶

Nonagricultural	Agricultural	Household

14 Principal activity (See instructions.) ▶ Trust Administration

15 Is the principal business activity manufacturing? .... ☐ Yes   ☒ No
If "Yes," principal product and raw material used ▶

16 To whom are most of the products or services sold? Please check the appropriate box.   ☐ Business (wholesale)
☐ Public (retail)   ☐ Other (specify) ▶   ☒ N/A

17a Has the applicant ever applied for an identification number for this or any other business? .... ☐ Yes   ☒ No
Note: If "Yes," please complete lines 17b and 17c.

17b If you checked "Yes" on line 17a, give applicant's legal name and trade name shown on prior application, if different than name shown on line 1 or 2 above.
Legal name ▶   Trade name ▶

17c Approximate date when and city and state where the application was filed. Enter previous employer identification number if known.

Approximate date when filed (Mo., day, year)	City and state where filed	Previous EIN

Under penalties of perjury, I declare that I have examined this application, and to the best of my knowledge and belief, it is true, correct, and complete.

Business telephone number (include area code)
213-469-8732

Fax telephone number (include area code)

Name and title (Please type or print clearly.) ▶ Mary R. Jones, Trustee

Signature ▶ *Mary R. Jones*   Date ▶ February 12, 1981

Note: Do not write below this line. For official use only.

Please leave blank ▶	Geo.	Ind.	Class	Size	Reason for applying

For Paperwork Reduction Act Notice, see page 4.
ISA

Form **SS-4** (Rev. 12-95)

Appendix G
Passing Trust Income to Beneficiaries

This appendix illustrates how Trust income is passed to the beneficiaries so that no income remains in the Trust and, thus, subject to Trust income taxation.

FORM 1041

Figure G-1 (beginning on page 406) shows a filled-in Form 1041 U.S. Income Tax Return for Estates and Trusts. This form shows that $20,000 of Trust income was received, that all of the income was distributed to the beneficiary, and that no Trust income tax is due.

SCHEDULE K-1

Figure G-2 (beginning on page 410) shows a filled-in Schedule K-1, Beneficiary's Share of Income, Deductions, Credits, etc. This form shows that the $20,000 of Trust income was distributed to the surviving spouse. (The spouse must declare this income on his or her Form 1040 Individual Income Tax Return.)

FIGURE G-1

FILLED-IN FORM 1041

Form **1041**	Department of the Treasury-Internal Revenue Service **U.S. Income Tax Return for Estates and Trusts 1997**	

For the calendar year 1997 or fiscal year beginning _____ ,1997, and ending _____ ,19___   OMB No. 1545-0092

A Type of Entity

☐ Decedent's estate

☒ Simple trust

☐ Complex trust

☐ Grantor type trust

☐ Bankruptcy estate-Ch. 7

☐ Bankruptcy estate-Ch. 11

☐ Pooled income fund

JOHN H. JONES MARITAL TRUST
MARY R. JONES, TRUSTEE
LOS ANGELES, CA

C Employer identification number
95 – 2693713

D Date entity created
02/04/81

E Nonexempt charitable and split-interest trusts, check applicable boxes (see pg 10 of instructions):

☐ Described in section 4947(a)(1)

☐ Not a private foundation

☐ Described in section 4947(a)(2)

B No Schedules K-1 attached ▶ 1

F Check applicable boxes:
☐ Initial return   ☐ Final Return   ☐ Amended return
☐ Change in fiduciary's name   ☐ Change in fiduciary's address

G Pooled mortgage account (see page 10 of the instructions):
☐ Bought   ☐ Sold   Date: _____

Income

1	Interest income	1	20,000.
2	Dividends	2	
3	Business income or (loss) (attach Schedule C or C-EZ (Form 1040))	3	
4	Capital gain or (loss) (attach Schedule D (Form 1041))	4	
5	Rents, royalties, partnerships, other estates and trusts, etc. (attach Schedule E (Form 1040))	5	
6	Farm income or (loss) (attach Schedule F (Form 1040))	6	
7	Ordinary gain or (loss) (attach Form 4797)	7	
8	Other income. List type and amount _____	8	
9	**Total income.** Combine lines 1 through 8 ▶	9	20,000.

Deductions

10	Interest. Check if Form 4952 is attached ▶ ☐	10	
11	Taxes	11	
12	Fiduciary fees	12	
13	Charitable deduction (from Schedule A, line 7)	13	
14	Attorney, accountant, and return preparer fees	14	
15a	Other deductions NOT subject to the 2% floor (attach schedule)	15a	
b	Allowable miscellaneous itemized deductions subject to the 2% floor	15b	
16	**Total.** Add lines 10 through 15b	16	0.
17	Adjusted total income or (loss). Subtract line 16 from line 9. Enter here and on Schedule B, line 1 ▶	17	20,000.
18	Income distribution deduction (from Schedule B, line 15) (attach Schedules K-1 (Form 1041))	18	20,000.
19	Estate tax deduction (including certain generation-skipping taxes) (attach computation)	19	
20	Reserved	20	
21	Exemption	21	300.
22	**Total deductions.** Add lines 18, 19, and 21 ▶	22	20,300.
23	Taxable income. Subtract line 22 from line 17. If a loss, see page 14 of the instructions	23	-300.

Tax and Payments

24	**Total tax** (from Schedule G, line 8)	24	0.
25	Payments: **a** 1997 estimated tax payments and amount applied from 1996 return	25a	
	b Estimated tax payments allocated to beneficiaries (from Form 1041-T)	25b	
	c Subtract line 25b from line 25a	25c	
	d Tax paid with extension of time to file: ☐ Form 2758 ☐ Form 8736 ☐ Form 8800	25d	
	e Federal income tax withheld. If any is from Form(s) 1099, check ▶ ☐	25e	
	Other payments: **f** Form 2439 _____ ; **g** Form 4136 _____ ; Total ▶	25h	
26	**Total payments.** Add lines 25c through 25e, and 25h ▶	26	
27	Estimated tax penalty (see page 15 of the instructions)	27	
28	**Tax due.** If line 26 is smaller than the total of lines 24 and 27, enter amount owed	28	0.
29	**Overpayment.** If line 26 is larger than the total of lines 24 and 27, enter amount overpaid	29	0.
30	Amount of line 29 to be: **a** Credited to 1998 estimated tax ▶ ; **b** Refunded ▶	30	

Please Sign Here

Under penalties of perjury, I declare that I have examined this return, including accompanying schedules and statements, and to the best of my knowledge and belief, it is true, correct, and complete. Declaration of preparer (other than fiduciary) is based on all information of which preparer has any knowledge.

▶ _____ Signature of fiduciary or officer representing fiduciary   Date _____

▶ _____ EIN of fiduciary if a financial institution (see pg 5 of instr.)

Paid Preparer's Use Only

Preparer's signature ▶		Date	Check if self-employed ▶ ☐	Preparer's social security no. 530-34-5341

Firm's name (or yours if self-employed) and address ▶
NEWTON W. FREEMAN IV
FREEMAN & WILLIAMS, LLP
P.O. BOX 1060
CARSON CITY, NV

EIN ▶ 88-0141764

ZIP code ▶ 89702

DIA   **For Paperwork Reduction Act Notice, see the separate instructions.**   Form **1041** (1997)

Form 1041 (1997) JOHN H. JONES MARITAL TRUST   −   Page **2**

Schedule A   Charitable Deduction. Do not complete for a simple trust or a pooled income fund.

1	Amounts paid or permanently set aside for charitable purposes from gross income (see page 15)	**1**	
2	Tax-exempt income allocable to charitable contributions (see page 16 of the instructions)	**2**	
3	Subtract line 2 from line 1	**3**	
4	Capital gains for the tax year allocated to corpus and paid or permanently set aside for charitable purposes	**4**	
5	Add lines 3 and 4	**5**	
6	Section 1202 exclusion allocable to capital gains paid or permanently set aside for charitable purposes (see page 16 of the instructions)	**6**	
7	**Charitable deduction.** Subtract line 6 from 5. Enter here and on page 1, line 13	**7**	0.

Schedule B   Income Distribution Deduction

1	Adjusted total income (from page 1, line 17) (see page 16 of the instructions)	**1**	20,000.
2	Adjusted tax-exempt interest	**2**	
3	Total net gain from Schedule D (Form 1041), line 16, column (1) (see page 16 of the instructions)	**3**	
4	Enter amount from Schedule A, line 4 (reduced by any allocable section 1202 exclusion)	**4**	
5	Capital gains for the tax year included on Schedule A, line 1 (see page 16 of the instructions)	**5**	
6	Enter any gain from page 1, line 4 as a negative number. If page 1, line 4, is a loss, enter the loss as a positive number	**6**	
7	**Distributable net income (DNI).** Combine lines 1 through 6. If zero or less, enter -0-	**7**	20,000.
8	If a complex trust, enter accounting income for the tax year as determined under the governing instrument and applicable local law 8 0.		
9	Income required to be distributed currently	**9**	20,000.
10	Other amounts paid, credited, or otherwise required to be distributed	**10**	
11	Total distributions. Add lines 9 and 10. If greater than line 8, see page 17 of the instructions	**11**	20,000.
12	Enter the amount of tax-exempt income included on line 11	**12**	
13	Tentative income distribution deduction. Subtract line 12 from line 11	**13**	20,000.
14	Tentative income distribution deduction. Subtract line 2 from line 7. If zero or less, enter -0-	**14**	20,000.
15	**Income distribution deduction. Enter the smaller of line 13 or line 14 here and on page 1, line 18**	**15**	20,000.

Schedule G   Tax Computation (see page 17 of the instructions)

1	Tax: a ☒ Tax rate schedule or ☐ Schedule D (Form 1041) **1a**		
	b Other taxes **1b**		
	c Total. Add lines 1a and 1b ▶ **1c**		
2a	Foreign tax credit (attach Form 1116) **2a**		
b	Check: ☐ Nonconventional source fuel credit ☐ Form 8834 **2b**		
c	General business credit. Enter here and check which forms are attached: ☐ Form 3800 or ☐ Forms (specify) ▶ _____ **2c**		
d	Credit for prior year minimum tax (attach Form 8801) **2d**		
3	**Total credits.** Add lines 2a through 2d ▶	**3**	
4	Subtract line 3 from line 1c	**4**	
5	Recapture taxes. Check if from: ☐ Form 4255 ☐ Form 8611	**5**	
6	Alternative minimum tax (from Schedule I, line 42)	**6**	
7	Household employment taxes. Attach Schedule H (Form 1040)	**7**	
8	**Total tax.** Add lines 4 through 7. Enter here and on page 1, line 24 ▶	**8**	0.

Other Information

		Yes	No
1	Did the estate or trust receive tax-exempt income? If "Yes," attach a computation of the allocation of expenses. Enter the amount of tax-exempt interest income and exempt-interest dividends ▶ $_____		X
2	Did the estate or trust receive all or any part of the earnings (salary, wages, and other compensation) of any individual by reason of a contract assignment or similar arrangement?		
3	At any time during calendar year 1997, did the estate or trust have an interest in or a signature or other authority over a bank, securities, or other financial account in a foreign country? See page 19 of the instructions for exceptions and filing requirements for Form TD F 90-22.1. If "Yes," enter the name of the foreign country ▶ _____		
4	During the tax year, did the estate or trust receive a distribution from, or was it the grantor of, or transferor to, a foreign trust? If "Yes," the estate or trust may have to file Form 3520 or 926. See page 19 of the instructions		
5	Did the estate or trust receive, or pay, any seller-financed mortgage interest? If "Yes," see page 19 for required attachment		
6	If this is an estate or complex trust making the section 663(b) election, check here (see page 19) ▶ ☐		
7	To make a section 643(e)(3) election, attach Schedule D (Form 1041), and check here (see page 19) ▶ ☐		
8	If the decedent's estate has been open for more than 2 years, check here ▶ ☐		
9	Are any trust beneficiaries skip persons? See page 19 of the instructions.		

Form 1041 (1997)   JOHN H. JONES MARITAL TRUST   –   Page **3**

Schedule I   **Alternative Minimum Tax (see pages 19 through 24 of the instructions)**

Part I—Estate's or Trust's Share of Alternative Minimum Taxable Income

1	Adjusted total income or (loss) (from page 1, line 17)	**1**	20,000.
2	Net operating loss deduction. Enter as a positive amount	**2**	
3	Add lines 1 and 2	**3**	20,000.
4	**Adjustments and tax preference items:**		

a	Interest	4a	
b	Taxes	4b	
c	Miscellaneous itemized deductions (from page 1, line 15b)	4c	
d	Refund of taxes	4d	( )
e	Depreciation of property placed in service after 1986	4e	
f	Circulation and research and experimental expenditures	4f	
g	Mining exploration and development costs	4g	
h	Long-term contracts entered into after February 28, 1986	4h	
i	Amortization of pollution control facilities	4i	
j	Installment sales of certain property	4j	
k	Adjusted gain or loss (including incentive stock options)	4k	
l	Certain loss limitations	4l	
m	Tax shelter farm activities	4m	
n	Passive activities	4n	
o	Beneficiaries of other trusts or decedent's estates	4o	
p	Tax-exempt interest from specified private activity bonds	4p	
q	Depletion	4q	
r	Accelerated depreciation of real property placed in service before 1987	4r	
s	Accelerated depr of leased personal property placed in service before 1987	4s	
t	Intangible drilling costs	4t	
u	Other adjustments	4u	

5	Combine lines 4a through 4u	**5**	
6	Add lines 3 and 5	**6**	20,000.
7	Alternative tax net operating loss deduction (see page 23 of the instructions for limitations)	**7**	
8	Adjusted alternative minimum taxable income. Subtract line 7 from line 6. Enter here and on line 14	**8**	20,000.
	Note: Complete Part II below before going to line 9.		
9	Income distribution deduction from line 28 below	**9** 20,000.	
10	Estate tax deduction (from page 1, line 19)	**10**	
11	Reserved	**11**	
12	Add lines 9 and 10	**12**	20,000.
13	Estate's or trust's share of alternative minimum taxable income. Subtract line 12 from line 8	**13**	

If line 13 is:
● $22,500 or less, stop here and enter -0- on Schedule G, line 6. The estate or trust is not liable
for the alternative minimum tax.
● Over $22,500, but less than $165,000, go to line 29.
● $165,000 or more, enter the amount from line 13 on line 35 and go to line 36.

Part II—Income Distribution Deduction on a Minimum Tax Basis

14	Adjusted alternative minimum taxable income (from line 8)	**14**	20,000.
15	Adjusted tax-exempt interest (other than amounts included on line 4p)	**15**	
16	Total net gain from Schedule D (Form 1041), line 16, column (1). If a loss, enter -0-	**16**	
17	Cap. gains for tax yr allocated to corpus, paid or permanently set aside for charitable purposes (Sch.A, ln4)	**17**	
18	Capital gains paid, permanently set aside for charitable purposes from gross income (pg. 23 of the inst.)	**18**	
19	Capital gains computed on a minimum tax basis included on line 8	**19**	( )
20	Capital losses computed on a minimum tax basis included on line 8. Enter as a positive amount	**20**	
21	Distributable net alternative min. taxable income (DNAMTI). Combine ln. 14-20. If zero or less, enter -0-	**21**	20,000.
22	Income required to be distributed currently (from Schedule B, line 9)	**22**	20,000.
23	Other amounts paid, credited, or otherwise required to be distributed (from Schedule B, line 10)	**23**	
24	Total distributions. Add lines 22 and 23	**24**	20,000.
25	Tax-exempt income included on line 24 (other than amounts included on line 4p)	**25**	
26	Tentative income distribution deduction on a minimum tax basis. Subtract line 25 from line 24	**26**	20,000.
27	Tentative income distribution deduction on a minimum tax basis. Ln. 21 minus ln. 15. If zero or less, enter -0-	**27**	20,000.
28	**Income distribution deduction on a minimum tax basis.** Smaller of ln. 26 or ln. 27. Enter here and on ln. 9	**28**	20,000.

(continued on page 4)

Form 1041 (1997)   JOHN H. JONES MARITAL TRUST   –   Page **4**

Part III—Alternative Minimum Tax

29	Exemption amount	29	$22,500
30	Enter the amount from line 13	30	
31	Phase-out of exemption amount	31	$75,000
32	Subtract line 31 from line 30. If zero or less, enter -0-	32	0.
33	Multiply line 32 by 25% (.25)	33	
34	Subtract line 33 from line 29. If zero or less, enter -0-	34	22,500.
35	Subtract line 34 from line 30	35	

36 If the estate or trust completed Schedule D (Form 1041) and had an amount on line 24 or 27 (as refigured for the AMT, if necessary), go to Part IV to figure line 36. **All others:** If line 35 is-
- $175,000 or less, multiply line 35 by 26% (.26).
- Over $175,000, multiply line 35 by 28% (.28) and subtract $3,500 from the result ... 36

37	Alternative minimum foreign tax credit (see page 24 of instructions)	37	
38	Tentative minimum tax. Subtract line 37 from line 36	38	
39	Regular tax before credits (see page 24 of instructions)	39	
40	Section 644 tax included on Schedule G, line 1b	40	
41	Add lines 39 and 40	41	
42	**Alternative minimum tax.** Subtract line 41 from line 38. If zero or less, enter -0-. Enter here and on Schedule G, line 6	42	0.

Part IV—Line 36 Computation Using Maximum Capital Gains Rates

43	Enter the amount from line 35	43	
44	Enter the amount from Schedule D (Form 1041), line 27 (as refigured for AMT, if necessary)	44	
45	Enter the amount from Schedule D (Form 1041), line 24 (as refigured for AMT, if necessary)	45	
46	Add lines 44 and 45. If zero or less, enter -0-	46	
47	Enter the amount from Schedule D (Form 1041), line 21 (as refigured for AMT, if necessary)	47	
48	Enter the smaller of line 46 or line 47	48	
49	Subtract line 48 from line 43. If zero or less, enter -0-	49	
50	If line 49 is $175,000 or less, multiply line 49 by 26% (.26). Otherwise, multiply line 49 by 28% (.28) and subtract $3,500 from the result	50	
51	Enter the amount from Schedule D (Form 1041), line 36 (as figured for the regular tax)	51	
52	Enter the smallest of line 43, or line 44, or line 51	52	
53	Multiply line 52 by 10% (.10)	53	
54	Enter the smaller of line 43 or line 44	54	
55	Enter the amount from line 52	55	
56	Subtract line 55 from line 54. If zero or less, enter -0-	56	
57	Multiply line 56 by 20% (.20)	57	
58	Enter the amount from line 43	58	
59	Add lines 49, 52, and 56	59	
60	Subtract line 59 from line 58.	60	
61	Multiply line 60 by 25% (.25)	61	
62	Add lines 50, 53, 57, and 61	62	
63	If line 43 is $175,000 or less, multiply line 43 by 26% (.26). Otherwise, multiply line 43 by 28% (.28) and subtract $3,500 from the result	63	
64	Enter the smaller of line 62 or line 63 here and on line 36	64	

FIGURE G-2

FILLED-IN SCHEDULE K-1

SCHEDULE K-1 (Form 1041)	Beneficiary's Share of Income, Deductions, Credits, etc.	OMB No. 1545-0092
Department of the Treasury Internal Revenue Service	for the calendar year 1997, or fiscal year beginning _____, 1997, ending _____, 19 _____ ▶ Complete a separate Schedule K-1 for each beneficiary.	**1997**

Name of trust or decedent's estate   JOHN H. JONES MARITAL TRUST

☐ Amended K-1
☐ Final K-1

Beneficiary's identifying number ▶ 541-38-3210	Estate's or trust's EIN ▶ 95 – 2693713
Beneficiary's name, address, and ZIP code MARY R. JONES LOS ANGELES, CA	Fiduciary's name, address, and ZIP code MARY R. JONES, TRUSTEE LOS ANGELES, CA

	(a) Allocable share item		(b) Amount	(c) Calendar year 1997 Form 1040 filers enter the amounts in column (b) on:
1	Interest	1	20,000.	Schedule B, Part I, line 1
2	Dividends	2		Schedule B, Part II, line 5
3	Net short-term capital gain	3		Schedule D, line 5
4	Net long-term capital gain: a 28% rate gain	4a		Schedule D, line 12, column (g)
b	unrecaptured section 1250 gain	4b		See the instructions for Schedule D, line 25
c	Total for year	4c		Schedule D, line 12, column (f)
5a	Annuities, royalties, and other nonpassive income before directly apportioned deductions	5a		Schedule E, Part III, column (f)
b	Depreciation	5b		⎫
c	Depletion	5c		Include on the applicable line of the appropriate tax form
d	Amortization	5d		⎭
6a	Trade or business, rental real estate, and other rental income before directly apportioned deductions (see instructions)	6a		Schedule E, Part III
b	Depreciation	6b		⎫
c	Depletion	6c		Include on the applicable line of the appropriate tax form
d	Amortization	6d		⎭
7	Income for minimum tax purposes	7	20,000.	
8	Income for regular tax purposes (add lines 1, 2, 3, 4c, 5a, and 6a)	8	20,000.	
9	Adjustment for minimum tax purposes (subtract line 8 from line 7)	9		Form 6251, line 12
10	Estate tax deduction (including certain generation-skipping transfer taxes)	10		Schedule A, line 27
11	Foreign taxes	11		Form 1116 or Schedule A (Form 1040), line 8
12	Adjustments and tax preference items (itemize):			
a	Accelerated depreciation	12a		⎫
b	Depletion	12b		Include on the applicable line of Form 6251
c	Amortization	12c		⎭
d	Exclusion items	12d		1998 Form 8801
13	Deductions in the final year of trust or decedent's estate:			
a	Excess deductions on termination (see instructions) . .	13a		Schedule A, line 22
b	Short-term capital loss carryover	13b		Schedule D, line 5
c	Long-term capital loss carryover	13c		Schedule D, line 12, columns (f) and (g)
d	Net operating loss (NOL) carryover for regular tax purposes	13d		Form 1040, line 21
e	NOL carryover for minimum tax purposes	13e		See the instructions for Form 6251, line 20
f	_____	13f		⎤ Include on the applicable line
g	_____	13g		⎦ of the appropriate tax form
14	Other (itemize):			
a	Payments of estimated taxes credited to you	14a		Form 1040, line 55
b	Tax-exempt interest	14b		Form 1040, line 8b
c	_____	14c		⎤
d	_____	14d		⎟
e	_____	14e		Include on the applicable line
f	_____	14f		of the appropriate tax form
g	_____	14g		⎟
h	_____	14h		⎦

For Paperwork Reduction Act Notice, see the Instructions for Form 1041.

Schedule K-1 (Form 1041) 1997

─────────────Appendix H─────────────
Declaring Trust Income on Personal Tax Return

This appendix illustrates how income received from a Trust is declared on the beneficiary's personal income tax return.

Figure H shows a filled-in Form 1040 U.S. Individual Income Tax Return. This form shows that $20,000 of interest income was received from the John H. Jones Marital Trust and declared by the surviving spouse on her personal tax return.

FIGURE H

FILLED-IN FORM 1040

Form **1040**	Department of the Treasury-Internal Revenue Service **U.S. Individual Income Tax Return** 1997	(99)	IRS Use Only-Do not write or staple in this space.

For the year Jan. 1-Dec. 31, 1997, or other tax year beginning , 1997, ending , 19 | OMB No. 1545-0074

Label (See instructions on page 10.)	L A B E L	Your first name and initial MARY R.	Last name JONES	Your social security number 541-38-3210
		If a joint return, spouse's first name and initial	Last name	Spouse's social security number
Use the IRS label. Otherwise, please print or type.	H E R E	Home address (number and street). If you have a P.O. box, see page 10.	Apt. no.	**For help in finding line instructions, see pages 2 and 3 in the booklet.**
		City, town or post office, state, and ZIP code. If you have a foreign address, see page 10. LOS ANGELES CA		

Presidential Election Campaign (See page 10.) ▶ Do you want $3 to go to this fund? .... If a joint return, does your spouse want $3 to go to this fund? ....

Yes	No	**Note:** Checking "Yes" will not change your tax or reduce your refund.

Filing Status

Check only one box.

1 [X] Single
2 ☐ Married filing joint return (even if only one had income)
3 ☐ Married filing separate return. Enter spouse's social security no. above and full name here. ▶
4 ☐ Head of household (with qualifying person). (See page 10.) If the qualifying person is a child but not your dependent, enter this child's name here. ▶
5 ☐ Qualifying widow(er) with dependent child (year spouse died ▶ 19). (See page 10.)

Exemptions

6a [X] **Yourself.** If your parent (or someone else) can claim you as a dependent on his or her tax return, **do not** check box 6a .... ▶

b ☐ Spouse ....

c Dependents:

(1) First name Last name	(2) Dependent's social security number	(3) Dependent's relationship to you	(4) No. of months lived in your home in 1997
		.	

If more than six dependents, see page 10.

No. of boxes checked on 6a and 6b ▶ **1**

No. of your children on 6c who:
● lived with you
● did not live with you due to divorce or separation (see page 11)

Dependents on 6c not entered above

Add numbers entered on lines above ▶ **1**

d Total number of exemptions claimed ....

Income

Attach Copy B of your Forms W-2, W-2G, and 1099-R here.

If you did not get a W-2, see page 12.

Enclose, but do not attach any payment. Also, please use Form 1040-V.

7	Wages, salaries, tips, etc. Attach Form(s) W-2	7	
8a	**Taxable** interest. Attach Schedule B if required	8a	25,000
b	**Tax-exempt** interest. DO NOT include on line 8a 8b		
9	Dividends. Attach Schedule B if required	9	25,000
10	Taxable refunds, credits, or offsets of state and local income taxes (see page 12)	10	
11	Alimony received	11	
12	Business income or (loss). Attach Schedule C or C-EZ	12	
13	Capital gain or (loss). Attach Schedule D	13	
14	Other gains or (losses). Attach Form 4797	14	
15a	Total IRA distributions 15a	b Taxable amount (see page 13)	15b	
16a	Total pensions and annuities 16a	b Taxable amount (see page 13)	16b	
17	Rental real estate, royalties, partnerships, S corporations, trusts, etc. Attach Schedule E	17	0
18	Farm income or (loss). Attach Schedule F	18	
19	Unemployment compensation	19	
20a	Social security benefits 20a	b Taxable amount (see page 14)	20b	
21	Other income. List type & amount-see pg. 15	21	
22	Add the amounts in the far right column for lines 7 through 21. This is your **total income** ...... ▶	22	50,000

Adjusted Gross Income

If line 32 is under $29,290 (under $9,770 if a child did not live with you), see EIC inst. on page 21.

23	IRA deduction (see page 16) 23			
24	Medical savings account deduction. Attach Form 8853 24			
25	Moving expenses. Attach Form 3903 or 3903-F 25			
26	One-half of self-employment tax. Attach Schedule SE 26			
27	Self-employed health insurance deduction (see page 17) 27			
28	Keogh and self-employed SEP and SIMPLE plans 28			
29	Penalty on early withdrawal of savings 29			
30	a Alimony paid b Recipient's SSN ▶ 30a			
31	Add lines 23 through 30a		31	
32	Subtract line 31 from line 22. This is your **adjusted gross income** ...... ▶		32	50,000

For Privacy Act and Paperwork Reduction Act Notice, see page 38.

Form **1040** (1997)

Form 1040 (1997)   MARY R. JONES   Page **2**

Tax Compu- tation	33	Amount from line 32 (adjusted gross income)	33	50,000
	34a	Check if: ☐ **You** were 65 or older, ☐ Blind; ☐ **Spouse** was 65 or older, ☐ Blind.		
		Add the number of boxes checked above and enter the total here . . . . ▶ 34a		
	b	If you are married filing separately and your spouse itemizes deductions or		
		you were a dual-status alien, see page 18 and check here . . . . ▶ 34b ☐		
	35	Enter the **larger** of your: **Itemized deductions** from Schedule A, line 28, **OR Standard deduction** shown below for your filing status. **But** see page 18 if you checked any box on line 34a or 34b **OR** someone can claim you as a dependent. ●Single-$4,150 ●Married filing jointly or Qualifying widower(er)-$6,900 ●Head of household-$6,050 ●Married filing separately-$3,450	35	4,150
If you want the IRS to figure your tax, see page 18.	36	Subtract line 35 from line 33	36	45,850
	37	If line 33 is $90,900 or less, multiply $2,650 by the total number of exemptions claimed on line 6d. If line 33 is over $90,900, see the worksheet on page 19 for the amount to enter	37	2,650
	38	**Taxable income.** Subt. line 37 from line 36. If ln. 37 is more than ln. 36, enter -0-	38	43,200
	39	**Tax.** See page 19. Check if any tax from a ☐ Form(s) 8814 b ☐ Form 4972 . . . . ▶	39	8,899

Credits	40	Credit for child and dependent care expenses. Attach Form 2441	40		
	41	Credit for the elderly or the disabled. Attach Schedule R	41		
	42	Adoption credit. Attach Form 8839	42		
	43	Foreign tax credit. Attach Form 1116	43		
	44	Other. Check if from a ☐ Form 3800 b ☐ Form 8396 c ☐ Form 8801 d ☐ Form (specify) _____	44		
	45	Add lines 40 through 44		45	
	46	Subtract line 45 from line 39. If line 45 is more than line 39, enter -0- . . . . ▶		46	8,899

Other Taxes	47	Self-employment tax. Attach Schedule SE	47	
	48	Alternative minimum tax. Attach Form 6251	48	
	49	Social security and Medicare tax on tip income not reported to employer. Attach Form 4137	49	
	50	Tax on qualified retirement plans (including IRAs) & MSAs. Attach Form 5329 if required	50	
	51	Advance earned income credit payments from Form(s) W-2	51	
	52	Household employment taxes. Attach Schedule H	52	
	53	Add lines 46 - 52. This is your **total tax** . . . . ▶	53	8,899

Payments	54	Federal income tax withheld from Forms W-2 and 1099	54		
	55	1997 estimated tax payments & amount applied from 1996 return	55	9,000	
	56a	**Earned income credit.** Attach Sch. EIC if you have a qualifying child b Nontaxable earned inc.: amt ▶ _____ and type ▶ _____	56a		
Attach Forms W-2, W-2G, and 1099-R on the front.	57	Amount paid with Form 4868 (request for extension)	57		
	58	Excess social security and RRTA tax withheld (see page 27)	58		
	59	Other payments. Check if from a ☐ Form 2439 b ☐ Form 4136	59		
	60	Add ln. 54, 55, 56a, 57, 58, & 59. These are your **total payments** . . . . ▶		60	9,000

Refund	61	If line 60 is more than line 53, subtract line 53 from line 60. This is the amount you **OVERPAID**	61	101
Have it directly deposited! See page 27 and fill in 62b, 62c, and 62d.	62a	Amount of line 61 you want **REFUNDED TO YOU** . . . . ▶	62a	101
	b	Routing number _____ ▶ c Type: ☐ Checking ☐ Savings		
	d	Account number _____		
	63	Amount of line 61 you want **APPLIED TO YOUR 1998 EST. TAX** ▶	63	
Amount You Owe	64	If line 53 is more than line 60, subtract line 60 from line 53. This is the **AMOUNT YOU OWE** For details on how to pay, see page 27 . . . . ▶	64	
	65	Estimated tax penalty. Also include on line 64	65	

Sign Here Keep a copy of this return for your records.	Under penalties of perjury, I declare that I have examined this return and accompanying schedules and statements, and to the best of my knowledge and belief, they are true, correct, and complete. Declaration of preparer (other than taxpayer) is based on all information of which preparer has any knowledge.

▶	Your signature	Date	Your occupation
▶	Spouse's signature. If a joint return, BOTH must sign.	Date	Spouse's occupation

Paid Preparer's Use Only	Preparer's signature ▶	Date	Check if self-employed ☐		Preparer's social security no.
	Firm's name (or yours if self-employed) and address ▶	FREEMAN & WILLIAMS, LLP P.O. BOX 1060 CARSON CITY NV		EIN	88-0141764
				ZIP code	89702

DAA

Schedules A&B (Form 1040) 1997   OMB No. 1545-0074   **Page 2**

Name(s) shown on Form 1040. Do not enter name and social security number if shown on other side.

MARY R. JONES

Your social security number
541-38-3210

Schedule B-Interest and Dividend Income

Attachment
Sequence No. **08**

Part I

Interest Income

(See pages 12 and B-1.)

Note: If you had over $400 in taxable interest income, you must also complete Part III.

		Amount
1	List name of payer. If any interest is from a seller-financed mortgage and the buyer used the property as a personal residence, see page B-1 and list this interest first. Also, show that buyer's social security number and address ▶	
	CITY OF LOS ANGELES BANK	5,000
	INTEREST FROM SCHEDULE K-1S	20,000

Note: If you received a Form 1099-INT, Form 1099-OID, or substitute statement from a brokerage firm, list the firm's name as the payer and enter the total interest shown on that form.

2	Add the amounts on line 1	**2**	25,000
3	Excludable interest on series EE U.S. savings bonds issued after 1989 from Form 8815, line 14. You MUST attach Form 8815 to Form 1040	**3**	
4	Subtract line 3 from line 2. Enter the result here and on Form 1040, line 8a ▶	**4**	25,000

Part II

Dividend Income

(See pages 12 and B-1.)

Note: If you had over $400 in gross dividends and/or other distributions on stock, you must also complete Part III.

		Amount
5	List name of payer. Include gross dividends and/or other distributions on stock here. Any capital gain distributions and nontaxable distributions will be deducted on lines 7 and 8 ▶	
	AG EDWARDS	25,000

Note: If you received a Form 1099-DIV or substitute statement from a brokerage firm, list the firm's name as the payer and enter the total dividends shown on that form.

6	Add the amounts on line 5	**6**	25,000
7	Capital gain distributions. Enter here and on Schedule D **7**		
8	Nontaxable distributions. (See the instr. for Form 1040, line 9.) **8**		
9	Add lines 7 and 8	**9**	
10	Subtract line 9 from line 6. Enter the result here and on Form 1040, line 9 ▶	**10**	25,000

Part III

Foreign Accounts and Trusts

(See page B-2.)

You must complete this part if you **(a)** had over $400 of interest or dividends; **(b)** had a foreign account; or **(c)** received a distribution from, or were a grantor of, or a transferor to, a foreign trust.

		Yes	No
11a	At any time during 1997, did you have an interest in or a signature or other authority over a financial account in a foreign country, such as a bank account, securities account, or other financial account? See page B-2 for exceptions and filing requirements for Form TD F 90-22.1		X
b	If "Yes," enter the name of the foreign country ▶		
12	During 1997, did you receive a distribution from, or were you the grantor of, or transferor to, a foreign trust? If "Yes," you may have to file Form 3520 or 926. See page B-2		X

For Paperwork Reduction Act Notice, see Form 1040 instructions.   Schedule B (Form 1040) 1997

DAA

Schedule E (Form 1040) 1997   Attachment Sequence No. **13**   Page **2**

Name(s) shown on return. Do not enter name and social security number if shown on other side. | **Your social security number**

MARY R. JONES

Note: If you report amounts from farming or fishing on Schedule E, you must enter your gross income from those activities on line 41 below. Real estate professionals must complete line 42 below.

Part II   Income or Loss From Partnerships and S Corporations   **Note:** If you report a loss from an at-risk activity, you MUST check either col. **(e)** or **(f)** on ln. 27 to describe your investment in the activity. See page E-4. If you check col. **(f)**, you must attach **Form 6198**.

27	(a) Name	(b) Enter P for partnership; S for S corp.	(c) Check if foreign partnership	(d) Employer identification number	**Investment At Risk?**	
					(e) All is at risk	(f) Some is not at risk
A						
B						
C						
D						
E						

	Passive Income and Loss		**Nonpassive Income and Loss**		
	(g) Passive loss allowed (attach **Form 8582** if required)	(h) Passive income from **Schedule K-1**	(i) Nonpassive loss from **Schedule K-1**	(j) Section 179 expense deduction from **Form 4562**	(k) Nonpassive income from **Schedule K-1**
A					
B					
C					
D					
E					
28a Totals					
b Totals					

29	Add columns (h) and (k) of line 28a	29	
30	Add columns (g), (i), and (j) of line 28b	30	( )
31	Total partnership and S corporation income or (loss). Combine lines 29 and 30. Enter the result here and include in the total on line 40 below	31	

Part III   Income or Loss From Estates and Trusts

32	(a) Name	(b) Employer identification number
A	JOHN H. JONES MARITAL TRUST	95 – 2693713
B		

	Passive Income and Loss		**Nonpassive Income and Loss**	
	(c) Passive deduction or loss allowed (attach **Form 8582** if required)	(d) Passive income from **Schedule K-1**	(e) Deduction or loss from **Schedule K-1**	(f) Other income from **Schedule K-1**
A	0			
B				
33a Totals				
b Totals				

34	Add columns (d) and (f) of line 33a	34	0
35	Add columns (c) and (e) of line 33b	35	(0)
36	Total estate and trust income or (loss). Combine lines 34 and 35. Enter the result here and include in the total on line 40 below	36	0

Part IV   Income or Loss From Real Estate Mortgage Investment Conduits (REMICs)-Residual Holder

37	(a) Name	(b) Employer identification number	(c) Excess inclusion from **Schedules Q**, line 2c (see page E-5)	(d) Taxable income (net loss) from **Schedules Q**, line 1b	(e) Income from **Schedules Q**, line 3b

38	Combine columns (d) and (e) only. Enter the result here and include in the total on line 40 below	38	

Part V   Summary

39	Net farm rental income or (loss) from **Form 4835.** Also, complete line 41 below	39	
40	TOTAL income or (loss). Combine lines 26, 31, 36, 38, and 39. Enter the result here and on Form 1040, line 17 ▶	40	
41	**Reconciliation of Farming and Fishing Income.** Enter your **gross** farming and fishing income reported on Form 4835, line 7; Schedule K-1 (Form 1065), line 15b; Schedule K-1 (Form 1120S), line 23; and Schedule K-1 (Form 1041), line 14 (see page E-5)	41	
42	**Reconciliation for Real Estate Professionals.** If you were a real estate professional (see page E-4), enter the net income or (loss) you reported anywhere on Form 1040 from all rental real estate activities in which you materially participated under the passive activity loss rules	42	

DAA

Form **1040**	K-1 Reconciliation Worksheet	**1997**

Name
MARY R. JONES

Taxpayer Identification Number
541-38-3210

Activity   JOHN H. JONES MARITAL TRUST   **Form** K1T   **Unit** 1

Type   TRUST/ESTATE

	K1 & K1T input	At-Risk Adjustment	Suspended passive losses	Passive losses Disallowed	Tax Return
Schedule E pg 2					
Ordinary income (loss)					
Rental real estate income (loss)					
Other rental income (loss)					
Intangible drilling costs					
Depletion					
Investment interest exp (Sch E)					
Depreciation / Sec. 179					
Disallowed Sec. 179 expense					
Expenses other than auto					
Auto expenses					
Other income (loss), Sch E					
Total Schedule E pg 2					
Guaranteed payments					
Schedule E pg 1					
Royalties					
Production tax					
Depletion					
Total Schedule E pg 1					
Schedule B					
Interest income	20,000				20,000
Dividend income					
Tax-exempt interest income					
Schedule D					
Short-term capital gain (loss)					
Long-term capital gain (loss)					
Form 4797					
Part I gain (loss)					
Part II gain (loss)					
Section 179 recapture					
Schedule A					
Charitable contributions					
Deductions subj to 2% AGI					
Deductions not subj. to 2% AGI					
Form 4952					
Investment interest expense					
Investment income adjustment					
Credits & Payments					
Low income housing pre '90					
Low income housing post '89					
Rehabilitation credit					
Work opportunity credit					
Nonconv. source fuel credit					
Enhanced oil recovery credit					
Federal Income Tax payments					
Form 6251					
Post 86 depreciation adjustment					
Adjusted gain (loss)					
Depletion					
Pre 87 depreciation adjustment					
Intangible drilling costs					
Beneficiary's AMT adjustment					

─────Appendix I─────
Making the QTIP Election

This appendix illustrates how the QTIP election is made after the death of the first spouse when the value of the estate exceeds two federal estate tax exemptions.

Figure I shows a filled-in Form 706 United States Estate (and Generation-Skipping Transfer) Tax Return, including Schedule R for making the QTIP election. This form shows that $400,000 of the decedent's estate is included in the QTIP election.

FIGURE I

FILLED-IN FORM 706 INCLUDING SCHEDULE R FOR QTIP ELECTION

Form **706**	United States Estate (and Generation-Skipping Transfer)	
(Rev. April 1997)	**Tax Return**	OMB No. 1545-0015
Department of the Treasury Internal Revenue Service	Estate of a citizen or resident of the United States (see separate instructions). To be filed for decedents dying after October 8, 1990. For Paperwork Reduction Act Notice, see page 1 of the separate instructions.	

Part 1 Decedent and Executor

1a Decedent's first name and middle initial (and maiden name, if any) JOHN H.	**1b** Decedent's last name JONES	**2** Decedent's social security no. 123-45-6789

3a Legal residence (domicile) at time of death (county/state, or foreign country) LOS ANGELES, CALIFORNIA	**3b** Year domicile established	**4** Date of birth	**5** Date of death 02/04/1981

6a Name of executor (see page 2 of the instructions) MARY R. JONES	**6b** Executor's address (number and street including apartment or suite no. or rural route; city, town, or post office; state; and ZIP code)
6c Executor's social security number (see page 2 of the instructions) 012-34-5678	LOS ANGELES, CALIFORNIA

7a Name and location of court where will was probated or estate administered	**7b** Case number

8 If decedent died testate, check here ▶ ☐ and attach a certified copy of the will. **9** If Form 4768 is attached, check here ▶ ☐

10 If Schedule R-1 is attached, check here ▶ ☐

Part 2 Tax Computation

1	Total gross estate (from Part 5, Recapitulation, page 3, item 10) **1**	1,000,000
2	Total allowable deductions (from Part 5, Recapitulation, page 3, item 20) **2**	400,000
3	Taxable estate (subtract line 2 from line 1) **3**	600,000
4	Adjusted taxable gifts (total taxable gifts (within the meaning of section 2503) made by the decedent after December 31, 1976, other than gifts that are includible in decedent's gross estate (section 2001(b)) . . **4**	0
5	Add lines 3 and 4 . . . . **5**	600,000
6	Tentative tax on the amount on line 5 from Table A on page 10 of the instructions **6**	192,800
7a	If line 5 exceeds $10,000,000, enter the lesser of line 5 or $21,040,000 . If line 5 is $10,000,000 or less, skip lines 7a and 7b and enter -0- on line 7c. **7a**	
b	Subtract $10,000,000 from line 7a **7b**	
c	Enter 5% (.05) of line 7b **7c**	0
8	Total tentative tax (add lines 6 and 7c) **8**	192,800
9	Total gift tax payable with respect to gifts made by the decedent after December 31, 1976. Include gift taxes by the decedent's spouse for such spouse's share of split gifts (section 2513) only if the decedent was the donor of these gifts and they are includible in the decedent's gross estate (see instructions) . . **9**	0
10	Gross estate tax (subtract line 9 from line 8) **10**	192,800
11	Maximum unified credit against estate tax **11** 192,800	
12	Adjustment to unified credit. (This adjustment may not exceed $6,000. See page 7 of the instructions.) **12** 0	
13	Allowable unified credit (subtract line 12 from line 11) **13**	192,800
14	Subtract line 13 from line 10 (but do not enter less than zero) **14**	0
15	Credit for state death taxes. Do not enter more than line 14. Figure the credit by using the amount on line 3 less $60,000. See Table B in the instructions and **attach credit evidence** (see instructions) . . **15**	0
16	Subtract line 15 from line 14 . . . . **16**	0
17	Credit for Federal gift taxes on pre-1977 gifts (sec. 2012)(attach computation) **17**	
18	Credit for foreign death taxes (from Schedule(s) P). (Attach Form(s) 706CE) . **18**	
19	Credit for tax on prior transfers (from Schedule Q) **19**	
20	Total (add lines 17, 18, and 19) **20**	0
21	Net estate tax (subtract line 20 from line 16) **21**	0
22	Generation-skipping transfer taxes (from Schedule R, Part 2, line 10) **22**	0
23	Section 4980A increased estate tax (from Schedule S, Part I, line 17)(see page 20 of the instructions) **23**	0
24	Total transfer taxes (add lines 21, 22, and 23) **24**	0
25	Prior payments. Explain in an attached statement **25**	
26	United States Treasury bonds redeemed in payment of estate tax . **26**	
27	Total (add lines 25 and 26) **27**	0
28	Balance due (or overpayment) (subtract line 27 from line 24) **28**	0

Under penalties of perjury, I declare that I have examined this return, including accompanying schedules and statements, and to the best of my knowledge and belief, it is true, correct, and complete. Declaration of preparer other than the executor is based on all information of which preparer has any knowledge.

Signature(s) of executor(s) _____ Date _____

Signature of preparer other than executor _____

P.O. BOX 1060
CARSON CITY   NV 89702

Address (and ZIP code)   Date _____

Cat. No. 20548R

Form 706 (Rev. 4-97)

Estate of: JOHN H. JONES   123-45-6789

Part 3.—Elections by the Executor

Please check the ``Yes'' or ``No'' box for each question. (See instructions beginning on page 3.)	Yes	No
1 Do you elect alternate valuation?		X
2 Do you elect special use valuation?		X
If ``Yes,'' you must complete and attach Schedule A-1.		
3 Do you elect to pay the taxes in installments as described in section 6166?		X
If ``Yes,'' you must attach the additional information described on page 5 of the instructions.		
4 Do you elect to postpone the part of the taxes attributable to a reversionary or remainder interest as described in section 6163?		X

Part 4.—General Information (Note: Please attach the necessary supplemental documents. **You must attach the death certificate.**)
(See instructions beginning on page 6.)

Authorization to receive confidential tax information under Regulations section 601.504(b)(2)(i), to act as the estate's representative before the Internal Revenue Service, and to make written or oral presentations on behalf of the estate if return prepared by an attorney, accountant, or enrolled agent for the executor:

Name of representative (print or type)	State	Address (number, street, and room or suite no., city, state, and ZIP code)

I declare that I am the ☐ attorney/ ☐ certified public accountant/ ☐ enrolled agent (you must check the applicable box) for the executor and prepared this return for the executor. I am not under suspension or disbarment from practice before the Internal Revenue Service and am qualified to practice in the state shown above.

Signature	CAF number	Date	Telephone number

1   Death certificate number and issuing authority (attach a copy of the death certificate to this return).

2   Decedent's business or occupation. If retired, check here ▶ ☐ and state decedent's former business or occupation.

3   Marital status of the decedent at time of death:
☒ Married
☐ Widow or widower—Name, SSN and date of death of deceased spouse ▶ ----------------------------------

☐ Single
☐ Legally separated
☐ Divorced—Date divorce decree became final ▶

4a Surviving spouse's name MARY R. JONES	4b Social security number 012-34-5678	4c Amount received (see page 6 of the instructions) 400,000

5   Individuals (other than the surviving spouse), trusts, or other estates who receive benefits from the estate (do not include charitable beneficiaries shown in Schedule O)(see instructions). For Privacy Act Notice (applicable to individual beneficiaries only), see the instructions for Form 1040.

Name of individual, trust, or estate receiving $5,000 or more	Identifying number	Relationship to decedent	Amount (see instructions)
JOHN H. JONES EXEMPTION TRUST		TRUST	600,000
All unascertainable beneficiaries and those who receive less than $5,000 ▶			0
Total			600,000

(Continued on next page)   **Page 2**

Form 706 (Rev. 4-97)

Part 4.—General Information (continued)   JOHN H. JONES

Please check the "Yes" or "No" box for each question.

		Yes	No
6	Does the gross estate contain any section 2044 property (qualified terminable interest property (QTIP) from a prior gift or estate) (see page 6 of the instructions)?		X
7a	Have Federal gift tax returns ever been filed?		X
	If "Yes," please attach copies of the returns, if available, and furnish the following information:		

7b Period(s) covered	7c Internal Revenue office(s) where filed		

If you answer "Yes" to any of questions 8-16, you must attach additional information as described in the instructions.

		Yes	No
8a	Was there any insurance on the decedent's life that is not included on the return as part of the gross estate?		X
b	Did the decedent own any insurance on the life of another that is not included in the gross estate?		X
9	Did the decedent at the time of death own any property as a joint tenant with right of survivorship in which (a) one or more of the other joint tenants was someone other than the decedent's spouse, and (b) less than the full value of the property is included on the return as part of the gross estate? If "Yes," you must complete and attach Schedule E		X
10	Did the decedent, at the time of death, own any interest in a partnership or unincorporated business or any stock in an inactive or closely held corporation?		X
11	Did the decedent make any transfer described in section 2035, 2036, 2037, or 2038 (see the instructions for Schedule G beginning on page 11 of the separate instructions)? If "Yes," you must complete and attach Schedule G	X	
12	Were there in existence at the time of the decedent's death:		
a	Any trusts created by the decedent during his or her lifetime?	X	
b	Any trusts not created by the decedent under which the decedent possessed any power, beneficial interest, or trusteeship?		X
13	Did the decedent ever possess, exercise, or release any general power of appointment? If "Yes," you must complete and attach Schedule H		X
14	Was the marital deduction computed under the transitional rule of Public Law 97-34, section 403(e)(3) (Economic Recovery Tax Act of 1981)?		X
	If "Yes," attach a separate computation of the marital deduction, enter the amount on item 18 of the Recapitulation, and note on item 18 "computation attached."		
15	Was the decedent, immediately before death, receiving an annuity described in the "General" paragraph of the instructions for Schedule I? If "Yes," you must complete and attach Schedule I.		X
16	Did the decedent have a total "excess retirement accumulation" (as defined in section 4980A(d)) in qualified employer plans and individual retirement plans? If "Yes," you must complete and attach Schedule S		X

Part 5.—Recapitulation

Item number	Gross estate	Alternate value	Value at date of death
1	Schedule A-Real Estate		750,000
2	Schedule B-Stocks and Bonds		0
3	Schedule C-Mortgages, Notes, and Cash		250,000
4	Schedule D-Insurance on the Decedent's Life (attach Form(s) 712)		0
5	Schedule E-Jointly Owned Property (attach Form(s) 712 for life insurance)		0
6	Schedule F-Other Miscellaneous Property (attach Form(s) 712 for life insurance)		0
7	Schedule G-Transfers During Decedent's Life (attach Form(s) 712 for life insurance)		0
8	Schedule H-Powers of Appointment		0
9	Schedule I-Annuities		0
10	Total gross estate (add items 1 through 9). Enter here and on line 1 of the Tax Computation		1,000,000

Item number	Deductions	Amount
11	Schedule J-Funeral Expenses and Expenses Incurred in Administering Property Subject to Claims	0
12	Schedule K-Debts of the Decedent	0
13	Schedule K-Mortgages and Liens	0
14	Total of items 11 through 13	0
15	Allowable amount of deductions from item 14 (see the instructions for item 15 of the Recapitulation)	0
16	Schedule L-Net Losses During Administration	0
17	Schedule L-Expenses Incurred in Administering Property Not Subject to Claims	0
18	Schedule M-Bequests, etc., to Surviving Spouse	400,000
19	Schedule O-Charitable, Public, and Similar Gifts and Bequests	0
20	Total allowable deductions (add items 15 through 19). Enter here and on line 2 of the Tax Computation	400,000

Page 3

Form 706 (Rev. 4-97)

Estate of: JOHN H. JONES   123-45-6789

SCHEDULE A—Real Estate

- For jointly owned property that must be disclosed on Schedule E, see the instructions on the reverse side of Schedule E.
- Real estate that is part of a sole proprietorship should be shown on Schedule F.
- Real estate that is included in the gross estate under section 2035, 2036, 2037, or 2038 should be shown on Schedule G.
- Real estate that is included in the gross estate under section 2041 should be shown on Schedule H.
- If you elect section 2032A valuation, you must complete Schedule A and Schedule A-1.

Item number	Description	Alternate valuation date	Alternate value	Value at date of death
1	PERSONAL RESIDENCE			1,500,000
	Less 50% community interest of surviving spouse			-750,000
	Total from continuation schedules or additional sheets attached to this schedule			
	TOTAL. (Also enter on Part 5, Recapitulation, page 3, at item 1.)			750,000

(If more space is needed, attach the continuation schedule from the end of this package or additional sheets of the same size.)

(See the instructions on the reverse side.)

Schedule A—Page 4

Form 706 (Rev. 4-97)

Estate of: JOHN H. JONES   123-45-6789

SCHEDULE C—Mortgages, Notes, and Cash

(For jointly owned property that must be disclosed on Schedule E, see the instructions for Schedule E.)

Item number	Description	Alternate valuation date	Alternate value	Value at date of death
1	LOS ANGELES CITY BANK SAVINGS ACCOUNT			500,000
	Less 50% community interest of surviving spouse			-250,000
	Total from continuation schedules (or additional sheets) attached to this schedule			
	TOTAL. (Also enter on Part 5, Recapitulation, page 3, at item 3.)			250,000

(If more space is needed, attach the continuation schedule from the end of this package or additional sheets of the same size.)
(See the instructions on the reverse side.)

Schedule C—Page 13

Form 706 (Rev. 4-97)

Estate of: JOHN H. JONES   123-45-6789

SCHEDULE F—Other Miscellaneous Property Not Reportable Under Any Other Schedule

(For jointly owned property that must be disclosed on Schedule E, see the instructions for Schedule E.)

(If you elect section 2032A valuation, you must complete Schedule F and Schedule A-1.)

		Yes	No
1	Did the decedent at the time of death own any articles of artistic or collectible value in excess of $3,000 or any collections whose artistic or collectible value combined at date of death exceeded $10,000?		
	If ``Yes,'' submit full details on this schedule and attach appraisals.		
2	Has the decedent's estate, spouse, or any other person, received (or will receive) any bonus or award as a result of the decedent's employment or death?		
	If ``Yes,'' submit full details on this schedule.		
3	Did the decedent at the time of death have, or have access to, a safe deposit box?		

If ``Yes,'' state location, and if held in joint names of decedent and another, state name and relationship of joint depositor.

If any of the contents of the safe deposit box are omitted from the schedules in this return, explain fully why omitted.

Item number	Description For securities, give CUSIP number, if available.	Alternate valuation date	Alternate value	Value at date of death
	NONE			

Total from continuation schedules (or additional sheets) attached to this schedule . . . . .

TOTAL. (Also enter on Part 5, Recapitulation, page 3, at item 6.)   0

(If more space is needed, attach the continuation schedule from the end of this package or additional sheets of the same size.)

(See the instructions on the reverse side.)   **Schedule F—Page 19**

Form 706 (Rev. 4-97)

Estate of: JOHN H. JONES   123-45-6789

SCHEDULE G—Transfers During Decedent's Life

(If you elect section 2032A valuation, you must complete Schedule G and Schedule A-1.)

Item number	Description For securities, give CUSIP number, if available.	Alternate valuation date	Alternate value	Value at date of death
A.	Gift tax paid by the decedent or the estate for all gifts made by the decedent or his or her spouse within 3 years before the decedent's death (section 2035(c))	X X X X X		
B.	Transfers includible under section 2035(a), 2036, 2037, or 2038:			
1	The Jones Family Trust dated September 17, 1979. Copy of trust agreement is attached. Trust assets are reported on Schedules A and C of this return.			
	Total from continuation schedules (or additional sheets) attached to this schedule			
	TOTAL. (Also enter on Part 5, Recapitulation, page 3, at item 7.)			0

SCHEDULE H—Powers of Appointment

(Include ``5 and 5 lapsing'' powers (section 2041(b)(2)) held by the decedent.)
(If you elect section 2032A valuation, you must complete Schedule H and Schedule A-1.)

Item number	Description	Alternate valuation date	Alternate value	Value at date of death
	NONE			
	Total from continuation schedules (or additional sheets) attached to this schedule			
	TOTAL. (Also enter on Part 5, Recapitulation, page 3, at item 8.)			0

(If more space is needed, attach the continuation schedule from the end of this package or additional sheets of the same size.)
(The instructions to Schedules G and H are in the separate instructions.)

Schedules G and H—Page 21

Form 706 (Rev. 4-97)

Estate of: JOHN H. JONES   123-45-6789

SCHEDULE M—Bequests, etc., to Surviving Spouse

Election To Deduct Qualified Terminable Interest Property Under Section 2056(b)(7).—If a trust (or other property) meets the requirements of qualified terminable interest property under section 2056(b)(7), and

    a. the trust or other property is listed on Schedule M, and

    b. the value of the trust (or other property) is entered in whole or in part as a deduction on Schedule M,

then unless the executor specifically identifies the trust (all or a fractional portion or percentage) or other property to be excluded from the election, the executor shall be deemed to have made an election to have such trust (or other property) treated as qualified terminable interest property under section 2056(b)(7).

    If less than the entire value of the trust (or other property) that the executor has included in the gross estate is entered as a deduction on Schedule M, the executor shall be considered to have made an election only as to a fraction of the trust (or other property). The numerator of this fraction is equal to the amount of the trust (or other property) deducted on Schedule M. The denominator is equal to the total value of the trust (or other property).

Election To Deduct Qualified Domestic Trust Property Under Section 2056A.—If a trust meets the requirements of a qualified domestic trust under section 2056A(a) and this return is filed no later than 1 year after the time prescribed by law (including extensions) for filing the return, and

    a. The entire value of a trust or trust property is listed on Schedule M, and

    b. The entire value of the trust or trust property is entered as a deduction on Schedule M,

then unless the executor specifically identifies the trust to be excluded from the election, the executor shall be deemed to have made an election to have the entire trust treated as qualified domestic trust property.

		Yes	No
1	Did any property pass to the surviving spouse as a result of a qualified disclaimer?		X
	If "Yes," attach a copy of the written disclaimer required by section 2518(b).		
2a	In what country was the surviving spouse born? UNITED STATES		
b	What is the surviving spouse's date of birth? 01/01/1930		
c	Is the surviving spouse a U.S. citizen?	X	
d	If the surviving spouse is a naturalized citizen, when did the surviving spouse acquire citizenship?		
e	If the surviving spouse is not a U.S. citizen, of what country is the surviving spouse a citizen?		
3	**Election out of QTIP Treatment of Annuities.**—Do you elect under section 2056(b)(7)(C)(ii) **not** to treat as qualified terminable interest property any joint and survivor annuities that are included in the gross estate and would otherwise be treated as qualified terminable interest property under section 2056(b)(7)(C)? (see instructions)		X

Item number	Description of property interests passing to surviving spouse	Amount
1	Qualified Terminable Interest - 100% of marital trust	400,000

	Total from continuation schedules (or additional sheets) attached to this schedule		
4	**Total** amount of property interests listed on Schedule M	**4**	400,000
5a	Federal estate taxes (including section 4980A taxes) payable out of property interests listed on Schedule M	5a	
b	Other death taxes payable out of property interests listed on Schedule M	5b	
c	Federal and state GST taxes payable out of property interests listed on Schedule M	5c	
d	Add items a, b, and c	5d	0
6	Net amount of property interests listed on Schedule M (subtract 5d from 4). Also enter on Part 5, Recapitulation, page 3, at item 18	6	400,000

(If more space is needed, attach the continuation schedule from the end of this package or additional sheets of the same size.)

(See the instructions on the reverse side.)   **Schedule M—Page 27**

Form 706 (Rev. 7-98)

JOHN H. JONES **Schedule R—Generation-Skipping Transfer Tax**   123-45-6789

Note: To avoid application of the deemed allocation rules, Form 706 and Schedule R should be filed to allocate the GST exemption to trusts that may later have taxable terminations or distributions under section 2612 even if the form is not required to be filed to report estate or GST tax.

The GST tax is imposed on taxable transfers of interests in property located **outside the United States** as well as property located inside the United States.

See instructions beginning on page 17.

Part 1.—GST Exemption Reconciliation (Section 2631) and Section 2652(a)(3) (Special QTIP) Election

You no longer need to check a box to make a section 2652(a)(3) (special QTIP) election. If you list qualifying property in Part 1, line 9, below, you will be considered to have made this election. See page 19 of the separate instructions for details.

1 Maximum allowable GST exemption	1	$1,000,000
2 Total GST exemption allocated by the decedent against decedent's lifetime transfers	2	
3 Total GST exemption allocated by the executor, using Form 709, against decedent's lifetime transfers.	3	
4 GST exemption allocated on line 6 of Schedule R, Part 2	4	
5 GST exemption allocated on line 6 of Schedule R, Part 3	5	
6 Total GST exemption allocated on line 4 of Schedule(s) R-1	6	1,000,000
7 Total GST exemption allocated to intervivos transfers and direct skips (add lines 2-6)	7	1,000,000
8 GST exemption available to allocate to trusts and section 2032A interests (subtract line 7 from line 1).	8	

9 Allocation of GST exemption to trusts (as defined for GST tax purposes):

A Name of trust	B Trust's EIN (if any)	C GST exemption allocated on lines 2-6, above (see instructions)	D Additional GST exemption allocated (see instructions)	E Trust's inclusion ratio (optional-see instructions)
The Jones Family Trust, dated September 19, 1979 John Jones & Mary Jones, trustors and trustees	95-2693713			

9D **Total.** May not exceed line 8, above 9D		0
10 GST exemption available to allocate to section 2032A interests received by individual beneficiaries (subtract line 9D from line 8). You must attach special use allocation schedule (see instructions) 10		0

(The instructions to Schedule R are in the separate instructions.)   **Schedule R—Page 33**

Form 706 (Rev. 4-97)

Estate of: JOHN H. JONES 123-45-6789

Part 2.–Direct Skips Where the Property Interests Transferred Bear the GST Tax on the Direct Skips

Name of skip person	Description of property interest transferred	Estate tax value

1 Total estate tax values of all property interests listed above — **1**
2 Estate taxes, state death taxes, and other charges borne by the property interests listed above — **2**
3 GST taxes borne by the property interests listed above but imposed on direct skips other than those shown on this Part 2 (see instructions) — **3**
4 Total fixed taxes and other charges (add lines 2 and 3) — **4**
5 Total tentative maximum direct skips (subtract line 4 from line 1) — **5**
6 GST exemption allocated — **6**
7 Subtract line 6 from line 5 — **7**
8 GST tax due (divide line 7 by 2.818182) — **8**
9 Enter the amount from line 8 of Schedule R, Part 3 — **9**
10 **Total GST taxes payable by the estate** (add lines 8 and 9) Enter here and on line 22 of the Tax Computation on page 1 — **10** 0

Schedule R—Page 34

Form 706 (Rev. 4-97)

Estate of: JOHN H. JONES   123-45-6789

Part 3.—Direct Skips Where the Property Interests Transferred Do Not Bear the GST Tax on the Direct Skips

Name of skip person	Description of property interest transferred	Estate tax value

1 Total estate tax values of all property interests listed above	1	
2 Estate taxes, state death taxes, and other charges borne by the property interests listed above	2	
3 GST taxes borne by the property interests listed above but imposed on direct skips other than those shown on this Part 3 (see instructions)	3	
4 Total fixed taxes and other charges (add lines 2 and 3)	4	
5 Total tentative maximum direct skips (subtract line 4 from line 1)	5	
6 GST exemption allocated	6	
7 Subtract line 6 from line 5	7	
8 GST tax due (multiply line 7 by .55). Enter here and on Schedule R, Part 2, line 9	8	0

Schedule R—Page 35

SCHEDULE R-1 (Form 706) (Rev. April 1997) Department of the Treasury Internal Revenue Service	**Generation-Skipping Transfer Tax** Direct Skips From a Trust Payment Voucher	OMB No. 1545-0015

Executor: File one copy with Form 706 and send two copies to the fiduciary. Do not pay the tax shown. See the separate instructions.
Fiduciary: See instructions on the following page. Pay the tax shown on line 6.

Name of trust THE JONES FAMILY TRUST	Trust's EIN 88-0123456	
Name and title of fiduciary MARY R. JONES, TRUSTEE	Name of decedent JOHN H. JONES	
Address of fiduciary (number and street)	Decedent's SSN 123-45-6789	Service Center where Form 706 was filed
City, state, and ZIP code	Name of executor MARY R. JONES	
Address of executor (number and street)	City, state, and ZIP code LOS ANGELES, CALIFORNIA	
Date of decedent's death 02/04/1981	Filing due date of Schedule R, Form 706 (with extensions) 11/04/81	

Part 1.—Computation of the GST Tax on the Direct Skip

Description of property interests subject to the direct skip	Estate tax value
SCHEDULE A, ITEM 1	1,000,000

1 Total estate tax value of all property interests listed above	1	1,000,000
2 Estate taxes, state death taxes, and other charges borne by the property interests listed above	2	
3 Tentative maximum direct skip from trust (subtract line 2 from line 1)	3	1,000,000
4 GST exemption allocated	4	1,000,000
5 Subtract line 4 from line 3	5	
6 GST tax due from fiduciary (divide line 5 by 2.818182) **(See instructions if property will not bear the GST tax.)**	6	0

Under penalties of perjury, I declare that I have examined this return, including accompanying schedules and statements, and to the best of my knowledge and belief, it is true, correct, and complete.

Signature(s) of executor(s) _____   Date _____

_____   Date _____

Signature of fiduciary or officer representing fiduciary _____   Date _____

Schedule R-1 (Form 706)—Page 36

Appendix J

Using the Generation-Skipping Exemption

This appendix illustrates how the generation-skipping exemption is used to "generation-skip" Trust assets directly to the grandchildren (bypassing the children's parents).

Figure J shows a filled-in Form 706 United States Estate (and Generation-Skipping Transfer) Tax Return, including Schedule R for using the generation-skipping exemption. This form shows that a $3 million estate is generation-skipped to two grandchildren and shows how the decedent's $1 million lifetime GST exemption is used.

FIGURE J
FILLED-IN FORM 706 INCLUDING SCHEDULE R FOR GST EXEMPTION

Form **706** (Rev. April 1997) Department of the Treasury Internal Revenue Service	**United States Estate (and Generation-Skipping Transfer) Tax Return** Estate of a citizen or resident of the United States (see separate instructions). To be filed for decedents dying after October 8, 1990. For Paperwork Reduction Act Notice, see page 1 of the separate instructions.	OMB No. 1545-0015

Part 1 Decedent and Executor

1a Decedent's first name and middle initial (and maiden name, if any) MARY R.	**1b** Decedent's last name JONES	**2** Decedent's social security no. 012-34-5678
3a Legal residence (domicile) at time of death (county/state, or foreign country) LOS ANGELES, CALIFORNIA	**3b** Year domicile established	**4** Date of birth	**5** Date of death 10/25/1993

6a Name of executor (see page 2 of the instructions)	**6b** Executor's address (number and street including apartment or suite no. or rural route; city, town, or post office; state; and ZIP code)
6c Executor's social security number (see page 2 of the instructions)	

7a Name and location of court where will was probated or estate administered	**7b** Case number

8 If decedent died testate, check here ▶ ☐ and attach a certified copy of the will. **9** If Form 4768 is attached, check here ▶ ☐

10 If Schedule R-1 is attached, check here ▶ ☐

Part 2 Tax Computation

1	Total gross estate (from Part 5, Recapitulation, page 3, item 10)	1	3,000,000
2	Total allowable deductions (from Part 5, Recapitulation, page 3, item 20)	2	0
3	Taxable estate (subtract line 2 from line 1)	3	3,000,000
4	Adjusted taxable gifts (total taxable gifts (within the meaning of section 2503) made by the decedent after December 31, 1976, other than gifts that are includible in decedent's gross estate (section 2001(b))	4	0
5	Add lines 3 and 4	5	3,000,000
6	Tentative tax on the amount on line 5 from Table A on page 10 of the instructions	6	1,290,800
7a	If line 5 exceeds $10,000,000, enter the lesser of line 5 or $21,040,000. If line 5 is $10,000,000 or less, skip lines 7a and 7b and enter -0- on line 7c. **7a**		
b	Subtract $10,000,000 from line 7a **7b**		
c	Enter 5% (.05) of line 7b	7c	0
8	Total tentative tax (add lines 6 and 7c)	8	1,290,800
9	Total gift tax payable with respect to gifts made by the decedent after December 31, 1976. Include gift taxes by the decedent's spouse for such spouse's share of split gifts (section 2513) only if the decedent was the donor of these gifts and they are includible in the decedent's gross estate (see instructions)	9	0
10	Gross estate tax (subtract line 9 from line 8)	10	1,290,800
11	Maximum unified credit against estate tax **11** 192,800		
12	Adjustment to unified credit. (This adjustment may not exceed $6,000. See page 7 of the instructions.) **12** 0		
13	Allowable unified credit (subtract line 12 from line 11)	13	192,800
14	Subtract line 13 from line 10 (but do not enter less than zero)	14	1,098,000
15	Credit for state death taxes. Do not enter more than line 14. Figure the credit by using the amount on line 3 less $60,000. See Table B in the instructions and **attach credit evidence** (see instructions)	15	182,000
16	Subtract line 15 from line 14	16	916,000
17	Credit for Federal gift taxes on pre-1977 gifts (sec. 2012)(attach computation) **17**		
18	Credit for foreign death taxes (from Schedule(s) P. (Attach Form(s) 706CE) **18**		
19	Credit for tax on prior transfers (from Schedule Q) **19**		
20	Total (add lines 17, 18, and 19)	20	0
21	Net estate tax (subtract line 20 from line 16)	21	916,000
22	Generation-skipping transfer taxes (from Schedule R, Part 2, line 10)	22	0
23	Section 4980A increased estate tax (from Schedule S, Part I, line 17)(see page 20 of the instructions)	23	0
24	Total transfer taxes (add lines 21, 22, and 23)	24	916,000
25	Prior payments. Explain in an attached statement **25**		
26	United States Treasury bonds redeemed in payment of estate tax **26**		
27	Total (add lines 25 and 26)	27	0
28	Balance due (or overpayment) (subtract line 27 from line 24)	28	916,000

Under penalties of perjury, I declare that I have examined this return, including accompanying schedules and statements, and to the best of my knowledge and belief, it is true, correct, and complete. Declaration of preparer other than the executor is based on all information of which preparer has any knowledge.

Signature(s) of executor(s) _____ Date _____

P.O. BOX 1060
CARSON CITY   NV 89702

Signature of preparer other than executor _____ Address (and ZIP code) _____ Date _____

Cat. No. 20548R

Form 706 (Rev. 4-97)

Estate of: MARY R. JONES   012-34-5678

Part 3.—Elections by the Executor

Please check the "Yes" or "No" box for each question. (See instructions beginning on page 3.)	Yes	No
1 Do you elect alternate valuation?		X
2 Do you elect special use valuation?		X
If "Yes," you must complete and attach Schedule A-1.		
3 Do you elect to pay the taxes in installments as described in section 6166?		X
If "Yes," you must attach the additional information described on page 5 of the instructions.		
4 Do you elect to postpone the part of the taxes attributable to a reversionary or remainder interest as described in section 6163?		X

Part 4.—General Information (Note: Please attach the necessary supplemental documents. You must attach the death certificate.)
(See instructions beginning on page 6.)

Authorization to receive confidential tax information under Regulations section 601.504(b)(2)(i), to act as the estate's representative before the Internal Revenue Service, and to make written or oral presentations on behalf of the estate if return prepared by an attorney, accountant, or enrolled agent for the executor.

Name of representative (print or type)	State	Address (number, street, and room or suite no., city, state, and ZIP code)

I declare that I am the ☐ attorney/ ☐ certified public accountant/ ☐ enrolled agent (you must check the applicable box) for the executor and prepared this return for the executor. I am not under suspension or disbarment from practice before the Internal Revenue Service and am qualified to practice in the state shown above.

Signature	CAF number	Date	Telephone number

1   Death certificate number and issuing authority (attach a copy of the death certificate to this return).

2   Decedent's business or occupation. If retired, check here ▶ ☐ and state decedent's former business or occupation.

3   Marital status of the decedent at time of death:

☐ Married
☒ Widow or widower—Name, SSN and date of death of deceased spouse ▶ JOHN H. JONES _____ 123-45-6789
    D.O.D. 02/04/1981
☐ Single
☐ Legally separated
☐ Divorced—Date divorce decree became final ▶

4a Surviving spouse's name	4b Social security number	4c Amount received (see page 6 of the instructions)
NONE		

5   Individuals (other than the surviving spouse), trusts, or other estates who receive benefits from the estate (do not include charitable beneficiaries shown in Schedule O)(see instructions). For Privacy Act Notice (applicable to individual beneficiaries only), see the instructions for Form 1040.

Name of individual, trust, or estate receiving $5,000 or more	Identifying number	Relationship to decedent	Amount (see instructions)
ANDREW F. JONES		GRANDSON	951,000
SARAH B. FOSTER		GRANDDAUGHTER	951,000
All unascertainable beneficiaries and those who receive less than $5,000 ▶			0
Total			1,902,000

(Continued on next page)   **Page 2**

Form 706 (Rev. 4-97)

Part 4.—General Information (continued)

MARY R. JONES   012-34-5678

Please check the "Yes" or "No" box for each question.

		Yes	No
6	Does the gross estate contain any section 2044 property (qualified terminable interest property (QTIP) from a prior gift or estate) (see page 6 of the instructions)?		
7a	Have Federal gift tax returns ever been filed?		

If "Yes," please attach copies of the returns, if available, and furnish the following information:

7b Period(s) covered	7c Internal Revenue office(s) where filed

If you answer "Yes" to any of questions 8-16, you must attach additional information as described in the instructions.

		Yes	No
8a	Was there any insurance on the decedent's life that is not included on the return as part of the gross estate?		
b	Did the decedent own any insurance on the life of another that is not included in the gross estate?		
9	Did the decedent at the time of death own any property as a joint tenant with right of survivorship in which (a) one or more of the other joint tenants was someone other than the decedent's spouse, and (b) less than the full value of the property is included on the return as part of the gross estate? If "Yes," you must complete and attach Schedule E		
10	Did the decedent, at the time of death, own any interest in a partnership or unincorporated business or any stock in an inactive or closely held corporation?		
11	Did the decedent make any transfer described in section 2035, 2036, 2037, or 2038 (see the instructions for Schedule G beginning on page 11 of the separate instructions)? If "Yes," you must complete and attach Schedule G		
12	Were there in existence at the time of the decedent's death:		
a	Any trusts created by the decedent during his or her lifetime?		
b	Any trusts not created by the decedent under which the decedent possessed any power, beneficial interest, or trusteeship?		
13	Did the decedent ever possess, exercise, or release any general power of appointment? If "Yes," you must complete and attach Schedule H		
14	Was the marital deduction computed under the transitional rule of Public Law 97-34, section 403(e)(3) (Economic Recovery Tax Act of 1981)? If "Yes," attach a separate computation of the marital deduction, enter the amount on item 18 of the Recapitulation, and note on item 18 "computation attached."		
15	Was the decedent, immediately before death, receiving an annuity described in the "General" paragraph of the instructions for Schedule I? If "Yes," you must complete and attach Schedule I.		
16	Did the decedent have a total "excess retirement accumulation" (as defined in section 4980A(d)) in qualified employer plans and individual retirement plans? If "Yes," you must complete and attach Schedule S		

Part 5.—Recapitulation

Item number	Gross estate	Alternate value	Value at date of death
1	Schedule A-Real Estate		2,250,000
2	Schedule B-Stocks and Bonds		0
3	Schedule C-Mortgages, Notes, and Cash		750,000
4	Schedule D-Insurance on the Decedent's Life (attach Form(s) 712)		0
5	Schedule E-Jointly Owned Property (attach Form(s) 712 for life insurance)		0
6	Schedule F-Other Miscellaneous Property (attach Form(s) 712 for life insurance)		0
7	Schedule G-Transfers During Decedent's Life (attach Form(s) 712 for life insurance)		0
8	Schedule H-Powers of Appointment		0
9	Schedule I-Annuities		0
10	Total gross estate (add items 1 through 9). Enter here and on line 1 of the Tax Computation		3,000,000

Item number	Deductions	Amount
11	Schedule J-Funeral Expenses and Expenses Incurred in Administering Property Subject to Claims	0
12	Schedule K-Debts of the Decedent	0
13	Schedule K-Mortgages and Liens	0
14	Total of items 11 through 13	0
15	Allowable amount of deductions from item 14 (see the instructions for item 15 of the Recapitulation)	0
16	Schedule L-Net Losses During Administration	0
17	Schedule L-Expenses Incurred in Administering Property Not Subject to Claims	0
18	Schedule M-Bequests, etc., to Surviving Spouse	0
19	Schedule O-Charitable, Public, and Similar Gifts and Bequests	0
20	Total allowable deductions (add items 15 through 19). Enter here and on line 2 of the Tax Computation	0

Page 3

Form 706 (Rev. 4-97)

Estate of: MARY R. JONES   012-34-5678

SCHEDULE A—Real Estate

- For jointly owned property that must be disclosed on Schedule E, see the instructions on the reverse side of Schedule E.
- Real estate that is part of a sole proprietorship should be shown on Schedule F.
- Real estate that is included in the gross estate under section 2035, 2036, 2037, or 2038 should be shown on Schedule G.
- Real estate that is included in the gross estate under section 2041 should be shown on Schedule H.
- If you elect section 2032A valuation, you must complete Schedule A and Schedule A-1.

Item number	Description	Alternate valuation date	Alternate value	Value at date of death
1	50% INTEREST IN PERSONAL RESIDENCE			2,250,000
	Total from continuation schedules or additional sheets attached to this schedule			
	TOTAL. (Also enter on Part 5, Recapitulation, page 3, at item 1.)			2,250,000

(If more space is needed, attach the continuation schedule from the end of this package or additional sheets of the same size.)

(See the instructions on the reverse side.)

Schedule A—Page 4

Estate of: MARY R. JONES   012-34-5678

SCHEDULE C—Mortgages, Notes, and Cash

(For jointly owned property that must be disclosed on Schedule E, see the instructions for Schedule E.)

Item number	Description	Alternate valuation date	Alternate value	Value at date of death
1	LOS ANGELES CITY BANK SAVINGS ACCOUNT			750,000

Total from continuation schedules (or additional sheets) attached to this schedule . . . . . .

TOTAL. (Also enter on Part 5, Recapitulation, page 3, at item 3.) . . . . | | 750,000

(If more space is needed, attach the continuation schedule from the end of this package or additional sheets of the same size.)
(See the instructions on the reverse side.)

Schedule C—Page 13

Estate of: MARY R. JONES   012-34-5678

SCHEDULE F—Other Miscellaneous Property Not Reportable Under Any Other Schedule

(For jointly owned property that must be disclosed on Schedule E, see the instructions for Schedule E.)

(If you elect section 2032A valuation, you must complete Schedule F and Schedule A-1.)

		Yes	No
1	Did the decedent at the time of death own any articles of artistic or collectible value in excess of $3,000 or any collections whose artistic or collectible value combined at date of death exceeded $10,000?		X
	If ``Yes,'' submit full details on this schedule and attach appraisals.		
2	Has the decedent's estate, spouse, or any other person, received (or will receive) any bonus or award as a result of the decedent's employment or death?		X
	If ``Yes,'' submit full details on this schedule.		
3	Did the decedent at the time of death have, or have access to, a safe deposit box?		X

If ``Yes,'' state location, and if held in joint names of decedent and another, state name and relationship of joint depositor.

If any of the contents of the safe deposit box are omitted from the schedules in this return, explain fully why omitted.

Item number	Description For securities, give CUSIP number, if available.	Alternate valuation date	Alternate value	Value at date of death
	NONE			
	Total from continuation schedules (or additional sheets) attached to this schedule			
	TOTAL. (Also enter on Part 5, Recapitulation, page 3, at item 6.)			0

(If more space is needed, attach the continuation schedule from the end of this package or additional sheets of the same size.)

(See the instructions on the reverse side.)   **Schedule F—Page 19**

Form 706 (Rev. 7-98)

012-34-5678

MARY R. JONES **Schedule R—Generation-Skipping Transfer Tax**

Note: To avoid application of the deemed allocation rules, Form 706 and Schedule R should be filed to allocate the GST exemption to trusts that may later have taxable terminations or distributions under section 2612 even if the form is not required to be filed to report estate or GST tax.

The GST tax is imposed on taxable transfers of interests in property located **outside the United States** as well as property located inside the United States.

See instructions beginning on page 17.

Part 1.—GST Exemption Reconciliation (Section 2631) and Section 2652(a)(3) (Special QTIP) Election

You no longer need to check a box to make a section 2652(a)(3) (special QTIP) election. If you list qualifying property in Part 1, line 9, below, you will be considered to have made this election. See page 19 of the separate instructions for details.

1	Maximum allowable GST exemption	**1**	$1,000,000
2	Total GST exemption allocated by the decedent against decedent's lifetime transfers	**2**	1,000,000
3	Total GST exemption allocated by the executor, using Form 709, against decedent's lifetime transfers.	**3**	
4	GST exemption allocated on line 6 of Schedule R, Part 2	**4**	
5	GST exemption allocated on line 6 of Schedule R, Part 3	**5**	
6	Total GST exemption allocated on line 4 of Schedule(s) R-1	**6**	
7	Total GST exemption allocated to intervivos transfers and direct skips (add lines 2-6)	**7**	1,000,000
8	GST exemption available to allocate to trusts and section 2032A interests (subtract line 7 from line 1).	**8**	

9 Allocation of GST exemption to trusts (as defined for GST tax purposes):

A Name of trust	B Trust's EIN (if any)	C GST exemption allocated on lines 2-6, above (see instructions)	D Additional GST exemption allocated (see instructions)	E Trust's inclusion ratio (optional-see instructions)
The Jones Family Trust, dated September 19, 1979 John Jones & Mary Jones, trustors and trustees	95-2693713			

9D Total. May not exceed line 8, above **9D**	0	
10 GST exemption available to allocate to section 2032A interests received by individual beneficiaries (subtract line 9D from line 8). You must attach special use allocation schedule (see instructions)	**10**	0

(The instructions to Schedule R are in the separate instructions.)

Schedule R—Page 33

Estate of: MARY R. JONES

012-34-5678

Part 2.–Direct Skips Where the Property Interests Transferred Bear the GST Tax on the Direct Skips

Name of skip person	Description of property interest transferred	Estate tax value

1 Total estate tax values of all property interests listed above	**1**	
2 Estate taxes, state death taxes, and other charges borne by the property interests listed above	**2**	
3 GST taxes borne by the property interests listed above but imposed on direct skips other than those shown on this Part 2 (see instructions)	**3**	
4 Total fixed taxes and other charges (add lines 2 and 3)	**4**	
5 Total tentative maximum direct skips (subtract line 4 from line 1)	**5**	
6 GST exemption allocated	**6**	
7 Subtract line 6 from line 5	**7**	
8 GST tax due (divide line 7 by 2.818182)	**8**	
9 Enter the amount from line 8 of Schedule R, Part 3	**9**	
10 Total GST taxes payable by the estate (add lines 8 and 9) Enter here and on line 22 of the Tax Computation on page 1	**10**	0

Schedule R—Page 34

Estate of: MARY R. JONES   012-34-5678

Part 3.—Direct Skips Where the Property Interests Transferred Do Not Bear the GST Tax on the Direct Skips

Name of skip person	Description of property interest transferred	Estate tax value

1 Total estate tax values of all property interests listed above	1	
2 Estate taxes, state death taxes, and other charges borne by the property interests listed above	2	
3 GST taxes borne by the property interests listed above but imposed on direct skips other than those shown on this Part 3 (see instructions)	3	
4 Total fixed taxes and other charges (add lines 2 and 3)	4	
5 Total tentative maximum direct skips (subtract line 4 from line 1)	5	
6 GST exemption allocated	6	
7 Subtract line 6 from line 5	7	
8 GST tax due (multiply line 7 by .55). Enter here and on Schedule R, Part 2, line 9	8	0

Schedule R—Page 35

Index

441